William Henry Green

A grammar of the Hebrew language

William Henry Green

A grammar of the Hebrew language

ISBN/EAN: 9783337729257

Printed in Europe, USA, Canada, Australia, Japan

Cover: Foto ©Paul-Georg Meister /pixelio.de

More available books at **www.hansebooks.com**

A

GRAMMAR

OF THE

HEBREW LANGUAGE.

BY

WILLIAM HENRY GREEN,
PROFESSOR IN THE THEOLOGICAL SEMINARY AT PRINCETON, N. J.

THIRD EDITION,

NEW YORK:
JOHN WILEY.
1863.

PREFACE.

This work was begun at the instance of my friend, preceptor, and colleague, DR. J. ADDISON ALEXANDER. The aid of his counsels and suggestions was freely promised in the undertaking; and he was to give to it the sanction of his name before the public. It appears shorn of these advantages. A few consultations respecting the general plan of the book and the method to be observed in its preparation, were all that could be had before this greatest of American orientalists and scholars was taken from us. Deprived thus early of his invaluable assistance, I have yet found a melancholy satisfaction in the prosecution of a task begun under such auspices, and which seemed still to link me to one with whom I count it one of the greatest blessings of my life to have been associated.

The grammatical system of Gesenius has, from causes which can readily be explained, had a predominance in this country to which it is not justly entitled. The grammar of Prof. Stuart, for a long time the text-book in most common use, was substantially a reproduction of that of Gesenius. Nordheimer was an adherent of the same system in its essential features, though he illustrated it with wonderful clearness and philosophical tact. And finally, the smaller grammar of Gesenius became current in the excellent translation of Prof. Conant. Now, while Gesenius is unquestionably the prince of Hebrew lexicographers, Ewald is as certainly entitled to the precedence among grammarians; and the latter cannot be ignored by him who would appreciate correctly the existing state of oriental learning.

The present work is mainly based upon the three leading grammars of Gesenius, Ewald, and Nordheimer, and the attempt has been made to combine whatever is valuable in each. For the sake of a more complete survey of the history of opinion, the grammars of R. Chayug, R. Kimchi, Reuchlin, Buxtorf, Schultens, Simonis, Robertson, Lee, Stier, Hupfeld, Freytag, Nägelsbach, and Stuart, besides others of less consequence from Jewish or Christian sources, have also been consulted to a greater or less extent. The author has not, however, contented himself with an indolent compilation; but, while availing himself freely of the labours of his predecessors, he has sought to maintain an independent position by investigating the whole subject freshly and thoroughly for himself. His design in the following pages has been to reflect the phenomena of the language precisely as they are exhibited in the Hebrew Bible; and it is believed that this is more exactly accomplished than it has been in any preceding grammar. The rule was adopted at the outset, and rigorously adhered to, that no supposititious forms should be admitted, that no example should be alleged which is not found in actual use, that no statement should be made and no rule given the evidence of which had not personally been subjected to careful scrutiny. Thus, for example, before treating of any class of verbs, perfect or imperfect, every verb of that description in the language was separately traced through all its forms as shown by a concordance; the facts were thus absolutely ascertained in the first instance before a single paradigm was prepared or a word of explanation written.

Some may be disposed, at first, to look suspiciously upon the triple division of the Hebrew vowels, adopted from Ewald, as an innovation: further reflection, however, will show that it is the only division consistent with accuracy, and it is really more ancient than the one which commonly prevails.

The importance of the accent, especially to the proper understanding of the vowels of a word and the laws of vowel-changes, is such that the example of Ewald has been followed in constantly marking its position by an appropriate sign. He uses a Methegh for this purpose, which is objectionable on account of the liability to error and confusion when the same sign is used for distinct purposes. The use of any one of the many Hebrew accents would also be liable to objection, since they not only indicate the tone-syllable, but have besides a conjunctive or disjunctive force, which it would be out of place to suggest. Accordingly, a special symbol has been employed, analogous to that which is in use in our own and other languages, thus קָטַל֫ *kātal'*.

The remarks upon the consecution of poetic accents were in type before the appearance of the able discussion of that subject by Baer, in an appendix to the Commentary of Delitzsch upon the Psalms. The rules of Baer, however, depend for their justification upon the assumption of the accurate accentuation of his own recent edition of the Hebrew Psalter, which departs in numerous instances from the current editions as they do in fact from one another. Inasmuch as this is a question which can only be settled by manuscripts that are not accessible in this country, it seems best to wait until it has been tested and pronounced upon by those who are capable of doing so. What has here been written on that subject, has accordingly been suffered to remain, imperfect and unsatisfactory as it is.

The laws which regulate the formation of nouns have been derived from Ewald, with a few modifications chiefly tending to simplify them.

The declensions of nouns, as made out by Gesenius, are purely artificial. Cumbrous as they are, they are not exhaustive, and the student often finds no little difficulty in deciding to which declension certain nouns of frequent occurrence are to be referred. For these reasons they were abandoned by Nordheimer, who substituted a different system, which is itself, however, more perplexing than serviceable. The fact is, that there are no declensions, properly speaking, in Hebrew; and the attempt to foist upon the language what is alien to its nature, embarrasses the subject instead of relieving it. A few general rules respecting the vowel-changes, which are liable to occur in different kinds of syllables, solve the whole mystery, and are all that the case requires or even admits.

In the syntax the aim has been to develop not so much what is common to the Hebrew with other languages, as what is characteristic and distinctive of the former, those points being particularly dwelt upon which are of chief importance to the interpreter.

In the entire work special reference has been had to the wants of theological students. The author has endeavoured to make it at once elementary and thorough, so that it might both serve as a manual for beginners and yet possess all that completeness which is demanded by riper scholars. The parts of most immediate importance to those commencing the study of the language are distinguished by being printed in large type.

PRINCETON, *August* 22*d*, 1861.

CONTENTS.

PART I.—ORTHOGRAPHY.

Divisions of Grammar, § 1.

ORTHOGRAPHIC SYMBOLS.

THE LETTERS.—Alphabet, § 2; Sounds, § 3; Double forms, § 4; Names, § 5; Order, § 6; Classification, § 7; Words never divided, § 8; Abbreviations and Signs of Number, § 9.

THE VOWELS.—Masoretic Points, § 10; Vowel Letters, § 11; Signs for the Vowels, § 12; Mutual Relation of this twofold Notation, §§ 13, 14; Pure and Diphthongal Vowels, § 15.

Sh'va, silent and vocal, simple and compound, § 16.

Pattahh Furtive, § 17.

Syllables, § 18.

Ambiguous Signs.—Hhirik, Shurek, and Kibbuts, § 19. 1; Kamets and Kamets-Hhatuph, § 19. 2; Silent and Vocal Sh'va, § 20.

POINTS AFFECTING CONSONANTS:—Daghesh-lene, §§ 21, 22.

Daghesh-forte, § 23; different kinds, § 24; omission of, § 25.

Mappik, § 26.

Raphe, § 27.

POINTS ATTACHED TO WORDS.—Accents, their design, § 28; forms and classes, § 29; like forms distinguished, § 30; poetic accents, § 31; position as determined by the character of the syllables, § 32. 1; in uninflected words, § 32. 2. 3; with affixes, suffixes and prefixes, § 33; use in distinguishing words, § 34; shifted in special cases, § 35.

Consecution of the Accents in Prose.—Clauses and their subdivisions, § 36; tabular view, § 37; explanation of the table, § 38; adaptation of the trains of accents to sentences, § 39.

Poetic Consecution.—Clauses and their subdivisions, § 40; tabular view and explanation, § 41; adaptation of the trains of accents to sentences, § 42.

Makkeph, § 43.

Methegh, its form and position, § 44; special rules, § 45; K'ri and K'thibh, meaning of the terms, § 46; constant K'ris not noted in the margin, § 47; their design and value, § 48.

Accuracy of the points, § 49.

ORTHOGRAPHIC CHANGES.

Significant mutations belong to the domain of the lexicon, §§ 50, 51; euphonic mutations to the domain of grammar, § 52.

MUTATIONS OF CONSONANTS at the beginning of syllables, § 53; at the close of syllables, § 54; at the end of words, § 55; special rules, § 56.

CHANGES OF CONSONANTS TO VOWELS in reduplicated syllables and letters and in quiescents, § 57.

MUTATIONS OF VOWELS, significant and euphonic, § 58; due to syllabic changes, § 59; to contiguous gutturals, § 60; to concurrent consonants, § 61; concurring vowels, § 62; proximity of vowels, § 63; the accent, § 64; pause accents, § 65; shortening or lengthening of words, § 66.

PART II.—ETYMOLOGY.

ROOTS OF WORDS.—Design of Etymology, three stages in the growth of words, § 67; pronominal and verbal roots, § 68; formation and inflection of words by external and internal changes, § 69; parts of speech, § 70.

PRONOUNS personal, § 71; pronominal suffixes, § 72; demonstrative, § 73; relative, § 74; interrogative and indefinite, § 75.

VERBS, the species and their signification, §§ 76-80.

PERFECT VERBS, § 81; formation of the species, §§ 82, 83; their inflection, §§ 84, 85. 1; paradigm of קָטַל, § 85. 2.

   Remarks on the Perfect Verbs.—Kal preterite, § 86; Infinitive, § 87; Future, § 88; Imperative, § 89; Participles, § 90; Niphal, § 91; Piel, § 92; Pual, § 93; Hiphil, § 94; Hophal, § 95; Hithpael, § 96.

   Paragogic and Apocopated Future, § 97; and Imperative, § 98.

   Vav Conversive with the Future, § 99; with the Preterite, § 100.

   Verbs with suffixes, §§ 101, 102; paradigm, § 103; Remarks on the Perfect Verbs with suffixes, Preterite, § 104; Future, § 105; Infinitive and Imperative, § 106.

IMPERFECT VERBS, classified, § 107.

   Pe Guttural Verbs, their peculiarities, §§ 108, 109; paradigm, § 110; Remarks, §§ 111-115.

Ayin Guttural Verbs, their peculiarities, §116; paradigm, §117; Remarks, §§118-122.
Lamedh Guttural Verbs, their peculiarities, §123; paradigm, §124; Remarks, §§125-128.
Pe Nun Verbs, their peculiarities, §129; paradigm, §130; Remarks, §§131, 132.
Ayin Doubled Verbs, their peculiarities, §§133-137; paradigm, §138; Remarks, §§139-142.
Pe Yodh Verbs, their peculiarities, §§143-145; paradigm, §146; Remarks, §§147-151.
Ayin Vav and Ayin Yodh Verbs, their peculiarities, §§152-154; paradigm, §155; Remarks, §§156-161.
Lamedh Aleph Verbs, their peculiarities, §162; paradigm, §163; Remarks, §§164-167.
Lamedh He Verbs, their peculiarities, §§168, 169; paradigm, §170; shortened future and imperative, §171; Remarks, §§172-177.
Doubly Imperfect Verbs, §178.
Defective Verbs, §179.
Quadriliteral Verbs, §180.
NOUNS, their formation, §181; Class I. §§182-186; Class II. §§187, 188; Class III. §§189-192; Class IV. §§193, 194; Multiliterals, §195.
  Gender and Number.—Feminine endings, §196; anomalies in the use of, §197; employment in the formation of words, §198; plural endings, §199; anomalies, §200; nouns confined to one number, §201; Dual ending, §202; usage of the dual, §203; changes consequent upon affixing the endings for gender and number, §§206-211.
The Construct State, its meaning and formation, §§212-216.
Declension of Nouns, paradigm, §217.
Paragogic Vowels added to Nouns, §§218, 219.
Nouns with suffixes, §§220, 221; paradigm, §222.
NUMERALS.—Cardinal numbers, §§223-226; Ordinals, etc., §227.
PREFIXED PARTICLES, §228; the Article, §229: the Interrogative, §230; Inseparable prepositions, §§231-233; Vav Conjunctive, §234.
SEPARATE PARTICLES.—Adverbs, §235; with suffixes, §236; Prepositions, §237; with suffixes, §238; Conjunctions, §239; Interjections, §240.

PART III.—SYNTAX.

Office of Syntax, §241. 1; Elements of the sentence, §241. 2.
THE SUBJECT, a noun or pronoun, §242; when omitted, §243; its extension, §244.
The Article, when used, §245; nouns definite without it, §246; omitted in poetry, §247; indefinite nouns, §248.
Adjectives and Demonstratives qualifying a noun, §249.

CONTENTS.

Numerals.—Cardinal numbers, §§ 250, 251; Ordinals, etc., § 252.
Apposition, § 253.
The Construct state and Suffixes, §§ 254–256; resolved by the preposition לְ § 257.
THE PREDICATE, Copula, § 258; Nouns, adjectives, and demonstratives, § 259.
Comparison of adjectives, § 260.
Verbs.—Hebrew conception of time, § 261; the primary tenses: use of the preterite, § 262; the future, § 263; paragogic and apocopated future, § 264; the secondary tenses, § 265; participles, § 266; Infinitive, §§ 267–269.
Object of Verbs.—The direct object of transitive verbs, § 270; transitive construction of intransitive verbs, § 271; indirect object of verbs, § 272; verbs with more than one object, § 273.
Adverbs and adverbial expressions, § 274.
Neglect of agreement, § 275; compound subject, § 276; nouns in the construct, § 277; dual nouns, § 278; changes of person, § 279.
Repetition of nouns, § 280; pronouns, § 281; verbs, § 282.
INTERROGATIVE SENTENCES, §§ 283, 284.
COMPOUND SENTENCES.—Relative pronoun, § 285; poetic use of the demonstrative, § 286; conjunctions, § 287.

GRAMMATICAL ANALYSIS, . . . page 315
INDEX I. Subjects, ... " 323
INDEX II. Texts of Scripture, ... " 331
INDEX III. Hebrew Words, ... " 343
INDEX IV. Hebrew Grammatical Terms, . . . " 399

PART FIRST.

ORTHOGRAPHY.

§1. LANGUAGE is the communication of thought by means of spoken or written sounds. The utterance of a single thought constitutes a sentence. Each sentence is composed of words expressing individual conceptions or their relations. And words are made up of sounds produced by the organs of speech and represented by written signs. It is the province of grammar as the science of language to investigate these several elements. It hence consists of three parts. First, Orthography, which treats of the sounds employed and the mode of representing them. Second, Etymology, which treats of the different kinds of words, their formation, and the changes which they undergo. Third, Syntax, which treats of sentences, or the manner in which words are joined together to express ideas. The task of the Hebrew grammarian is to furnish a complete exhibition of the phenomena of this particular language, carefully digested and referred as far as practicable to their appropriate causes in the organs of speech and the operations of the mind.

THE LETTERS.

§2. The Hebrew being no longer a spoken tongue, is only known as the language of books, and particularly of the Old Testament, which is the most interesting and important as well as the only pure monument of it. The first step towards its investigation must accordingly be to ascertain the meaning of the symbols in which it is recorded. Then having learned its sounds, as they are thus represented, it will be possible to advance one step further, and inquire into the laws by which these are governed in their employment and mutations.

The symbols used in writing Hebrew are of two sorts, viz. letters (אוֹתִיּוֹת) and points (נְקֻדִּים). The number of the letters is twenty-two; these are written from right to left, and are exclusively consonants. The following alphabetical table exhibits their forms, English equivalents, names, and numerical values, together with the corresponding forms of the Rabbinical character employed to a considerable extent in the commentaries and other writings of the modern Jews.

Order.	Forms and Equivalents.		Names.		Rabbinical Alphabet.	Numerical values.
1	א	——	אָלֶף	Áleph	פ	1
2	ב	Bh, B	בֵּית	Bēth	ב	2
3	ג	Gh, G	גִּימֶל	Gī′-mel	ג	3
4	ד	Dh, D	דָּלֶת	Dā′-leth	ד	4
5	ה	H	הֵא	Hē	ס	5
6	ו	V	וָו	Vāv	ו	6
7	ז	Z	זַיִן	Záyin	ו	7
8	ח	Hh	חֵית	Hhēth	ח	8
9	ט	T	טֵית	Tēth	ט	9
10	י	Y	יוֹד	Yōdh	,	10
11	ך כ	Kh, K	כַּף	Kaph	כ ך	20
12	ל	L	לָמֶד	Lā′-medh	ל	30
13	ם מ	M	מֵם	Mēm	מ	40
14	ן נ	N	נוּן	Nūn	נ ן	50
15	ס	S	סָמֶךְ	Sā′-mekh	ס	60
16	ע	——	עַיִן	Áyin	ע	70
17	ף פ	Ph, P	פֵא	Pē	פ ף	80
18	ץ צ	Ts	צָדֵי	Tsā′-dhē	צ ץ	90
19	ק	K	קוֹף	Kōph	ק	100
20	ר	R	רֵישׁ	Rēsh	ר	200
21	שׁ	Sh, S	שִׁין	Shīn	ש	300
22	ת	Th, T	תָו	Tāv	ת	400

§3. There is always more or less difficulty in representing the sounds of one language by those of another. But this is in the case of the Hebrew greatly aggravated by its having been for ages a dead language, so that some of its sounds cannot now be accurately determined, and also by its belonging to a different family or group of tongues from our own, possessing sounds entirely foreign to the English, for which it consequently affords no equivalent, and which are in fact incapable of being pronounced by our organs. The equivalents of the foregoing table are not therefore to be regarded as in every instance exact representations of the proper powers of the letters. They are simply approximations sufficiently near the truth for every practical purpose, the best which can now be proposed, and sanctioned by tradition and the conventional usage of the best Hebraists.

1. It will be observed that a double pronunciation has been assigned to seven of the letters. A native Hebrew would readily decide without assistance which of these was to be adopted in any given case, just as we are sensible of no inconvenience from the various sounds of the English letters which are so embarrassing to foreigners learning our language. The ambiguity is in every case removed, however, by the addition of a dot or point indicating which sound they are to receive. Thus ב with a point in its bosom has the sound of *b*, ב unpointed that of the corresponding *v*, or as it is commonly represented for the sake of uniformity in notation, *bh*; ג is pronounced as *g*, ג unpointed had an aspirated sound which may accordingly be represented by *gh*, but as it is difficult to produce it, or even to determine with exactness what it was, and as there is no corresponding sound in English, the aspiration is mostly neglected, and the letter, whether pointed or not, sounded indifferently as *g*; ד is *d*, ד unpointed is the aspirate *dh*, equivalent to *th* in *the*; כ is *k*, כ unpointed its aspirate *kh*, perhaps resembling the German *ch* in *ich*, though its aspiration, like that of ג, is commonly neglected in modern reading; פ is *p*, פ unpointed is *ph* or *f*; ת is *t*, ת unpointed *th* in *thin*. The letter שׁ with a dot over its right arm is pronounced like *sh*, and called *Shīn*; שׂ with a dot over its left arm is called *Sīn*, and pronounced like *s*, no attempt being made in modern

usage to discriminate between its sound and that of ס Samekh. Although there may anciently have been a distinction between them, this can no longer be defined nor even positively asserted; it has therefore been thought unnecessary to preserve the individuality of these letters in the notation, and both of them will accordingly be represented by *s*.

a. The double sound of the first six of the letters just named is purely euphonic, and has no effect whatever upon the meaning of the words in which they stand. The case of שׁ is different. Its primary sound was that of *sh*, as is evident from the contrast in Judg. 12 : 6 of שִׁבֹּלֶת *shibboleth* with סִבֹּלֶת *sibboleth*. In certain words, however, and sometimes for the sake of creating a distinction between different words of like orthography, it received the sound of *s*, thus almost assuming the character of a distinct letter, e. g. שָׂבַר *to break*, שָׂבַר *to hope*. That Sin and Samekh were distinguishable to the ear, appears probable from the fact that there are words of separate significations which differ only in the use of one or the other of these letters, and in which they are never interchanged, e. g. שָׁכַל *to be bereaved*, שָׂכַל *to be wise*, סָכַל *to be foolish;* שָׁכַר *to be drunken,* שָׂכַר *to hire,* סָכַר *to shut up;* שׁוּר *to look,* שׂוּר *to rule,* סוּר *to turn back;* שָׂפָה *a lip,* סָפָה *to destroy.* The close affinity between the sounds which they represent is, however, shown by the fact that ס is in a few instances written for שׂ, e. g. נָסָה Ps. 4: 7 from נָשָׂא, שִׂכְלוּת Eccles. 1: 17 for סִכְלוּת. The original identity of שׁ and שׂ is apparent from the etymological connection between שְׂאֹר *leaven* and מִשְׁאֶרֶת *a vessel in which bread is leavened;* שָׂעַר *to shudder,* שְׂעָרָה *horrible, causing a shudder*. In Arabic the division of single letters into two distinguished by diacritical points is carried to a much greater length, the alphabet of that language being by this means enlarged from twenty-two to twenty-eight letters.

2. In their original power ט *t* differed from ת *t*, and כ *k* from ק *k*, for these letters are not confused nor liable to interchange, and the distinction is preserved to this day in the cognate Arabic; yet it is not easy to state intelligibly wherein the difference consisted. They are currently pronounced precisely alike.

3. The letter ח has a stronger sound than ה the simple *h*, and is accordingly represented by *hh;* ר is represented by *r*, although it had some peculiarity of sound which we cannot at this day attempt to reproduce, by which it was allied to the gutturals.

4. For two letters, א and ע, no equivalent has been given in the table, and they are commonly altogether neglected in pronunciation. א is the weakest of the letters, and was probably always inaudible. It stands for the slight and involuntary emission of breath necessary to the utterance of a vowel unattended by a more distinct consonant sound. It therefore merely serves to mark the beginning or the close of the syllable of which it is a part, while to the ear it is entirely lost in the accompanying or preceding vowel. Its power has been likened to that of the smooth breathing (') of the Greeks or the English silent *h* in *hour*. On the other hand ע had a deep guttural sound which was always heard, but like that of the corresponding letter among the Arabs is very difficult of utterance by occidental organs; consequently no attempt is made to reproduce it. In the Septuagint it is sometimes represented by γ, sometimes by the rough and sometimes by the smooth breathing; thus עֲמֹרָה $Γόμορρα$, עֵלִי '$Ηλί$, עֲמָלֵק '$Ἀμαλήκ$. Some of the modern Jews give it the sound of *ng* or of the French *gn* in *campagne*, either wherever it occurs or only at the end of words, e. g. שָׁמַע *Sh'mang*, עָמֹד *gnāmōdh*.

§4. The forms of the letters exhibited in the preceding table, though found without important variation in all existing manuscripts, are not the original ones. An older character is preserved upon the Jewish coins struck in the age of the Maccabees, which bears a considerable resemblance to the Samaritan and still more to the Phenician. Some of the steps in the transition from one to the other can still be traced upon extant monuments. There was first a cursive tendency, disposing to unite the different letters of the same word, which is the established practice in Syriac and Arabic. This was followed by a predominance of the calligraphic principle, which again separated the letters and reduced them to their present rectangular forms and nearly uniform size. The cursive stage has, however, left its traces upon the five letters which appear in the table with double forms ; צ פ נ מ כ when standing at the beginning or in the middle of words terminate in a bottom horizontal stroke, which is the remnant of the connecting link with the following letter; at the end of words no such link was needed, and the letter was continued vertically downward in a sort of terminal flourish thus, ץ ך ן ף, or closed up by joining its last with its initial stroke, thus ם.

a. The few instances in which final letters are found in the middle of words, as לְבַרְבֵּה Isa. 9: 6, or their ordinary forms at the end, as הֵמ Neh. 2: 13, בְּי Job 38 : 1, are probably due to the inadvertence of early transcribers which has been faithfully perpetuated since, or if intentional they may have had a connection now unknown with the enumeration of letters or the signification of words. The same may be said of letters larger than usual, as וְכָזָה Ps. 80: 16, or smaller, as בְּהִבָּרְאָם Gen. 2: 4, or above the line, as מִיַּעַר Ps. 80 : 14, or inverted, as בַּסֹּעַ Num. 10: 35, (in manuscripts and the older editions, e. g. that of Stephanus in 1541), or with extraordinary points, as וַיִּשָּׁקֵהוּ Gen. 33 : 4, לוּלֵא Ps. 27 : 13, in all which the Rabbins find concealed meanings of the most fanciful and absurd character. Thus in their opinion the suspended נ in מְנַשֶּׁה Judg. 18 : 30 suggests that the idolaters described were descended from Moses but had the character of Manasseh. In גָּחוֹן Lev. 11 :42 the Vav, which is of unusual size, is the middle letter of the Pentateuch; וּבְיִרְיוֹ Gen. 16: 5 with an extraordinary point over the second Yodh, is the only instance in which the word is written with that letter ; the large letters in Deut. 6: 4 emphasize the capital article of the Jewish faith. All such anomalous forms or marks, with the conceits of the Rabbins respecting them, are reviewed in detail in Buxtorf's Tiberias. pp. 152 etc.

§5. All the names of the letters were probably significant at first, although the meanings of some of them are now doubtful or obscure. It is commonly supposed that these describe the objects to which their forms originally bore a rude resemblance. If this be so, however, the mutations which they have since undergone are such, that the relation is no longer traceable, unless it be faintly in a few. The power of the letter is in every instance the initial sound of its name.

a. The opinion advocated by Schultens, Fundamenta Ling. Heb. p. 10, that the invention of the letters was long anterior to that of their names, and that the latter was a pedagogical expedient to facilitate the learning of the letters by associating their forms and sounds with familiar objects, has met with little favour and possesses little intrinsic probability. An interesting corroboration of the antiquity of these names is found in their preservation in the Greek alphabet, though destitute of meaning in that language, the Greeks having borrowed their letters at an early period from the Phenicians, and hence the appended *a* of "Αλφα, etc., which points to the Aramaeic form אַלְפָא.

b. The Semitic derivation of the names proves incontestably that the alphabet had its origin among a people speaking a language kindred to the Hebrew. Their most probable meanings, so far as they are still explicable, are as follows, viz: Aleph, *an ox;* Beth, *a house;* Gimel, *a camel;* Daleth, *a door;* He, doubtful, possibly *a window;* Vav, *a hook;* Zayin, *a weapon;* Hheth, probably *a fence;* Teth, probably *a snake;* Yodh, *a hand;* Kaph, *the palm of the hand;* Lamedh, *an ox-goad;* Mem, *water;* Nun, *a fish;* Samekh, *a prop;* Ayin, *an eye;* Pe, *a mouth;* Tsadhe, *a fish-hook* or *a hunter's dart;* Koph, perhaps *the back of the head;* Resh, *a head;* Shin, *a tooth;* Tav, *a cross mark.*

§6. The order of the letters appears to be entirely arbitrary, though it has been remarked that the three middle mutes ב ג ד succeed each other, as in like manner the three liquids ל מ נ. The juxtaposition of a few of the letters may perhaps be owing to the kindred signification of their names, e. g. Yodh and Kaph *the hand,* Mem *water* and Nun *a fish,* Resh *the head* and Shin *a tooth.* The antiquity of the existing arrangement of the alphabet is shown, 1. by psalms and other portions of the Old Testament in which successive clauses or verses begin with the letters disposed in regular order, viz: Ps. 25 (ק omitted), 34, 37 (alternate verses, ו omitted), 111 (every clause), 112 (every clause), 119 (each letter eight times), 145 (נ omitted), Prov. 31: 10–31, Lam. ch. 1, 2, 3 (each letter three times), 4. In the first chapter of Lamentations the order is exactly preserved, but in the remaining three chapters ע and פ are transposed. 2. By the correspondence of the Greek and Roman alphabets, which have sprung from the same origin with the Hebrew.

a. The most ingenious attempt to discover a regular structure in the Hebrew alphabet is that of Lepsius, in an essay upon this subject published in 1836. Omitting the sibilants and Resh, he finds the following triple correspondence of a breathing succeeded by the same three mutes carried through each of the three orders, the second rank being enlarged by the addition of the liquids.

	Breathings.	Mutes.		Liquids.
Middle	א	ד ג ב		
Smooth	ה	ט ח ו	(כי)	נ מ ל
Rough	ע	ת ק פ		

Curious as this result certainly is, it must be confessed that the alleged correspondence is in part imaginary, and the method by which it is reached is too arbitrary to warrant the conclusion that this scheme was really in the mind of the author of the alphabet, much less to sustain the further speculations built upon it, reducing the original number and modifying the powers of the letters.

b. It is curious to see how, in the adaptation of the alphabet to different languages, the sounds of the letters have been modified, needless ones dropped, and others found necessary added at the end, without disturbing the arrangement of the original stock. Thus the Greeks dropped ו and ק, only retaining them as numerical signs, while the Roman alphabet has F and Q; on the other hand the Romans found צ and ס superfluous, while the Greeks made of them ϑ and ξ; ג and ו, in Greek γ and ζ, become in Latin C and G, while ח, in Latin H, is in Greek converted like the rest of the gutturals into a vowel η.

§ 7. The letters may be variously divided:

1. First, with respect to the organs by which they are pronounced.

Gutturals	א	ה	ח	ע
Palatals	ג	י	כ	ק
Linguals	ד	ט	ל	נ	ת
Dentals	ז	ס	צ	ש
Labials	ב	ו	מ	פ

ר has been differently classed, but as its peculiarities are those of the gutturals, it is usually reckoned with them.

2. Secondly, according to their respective strength, into three classes, which may be denominated weak, medium, and strong. The strong consonants offer the greatest resistance to change, and are capable of entering into any combinations which the formation or inflection of words may require. The weak have not this capacity, but when analogy would bring them into combinations foreign to their nature, they are either

liable to mutation themselves or occasion changes in the rest of the word. Those of medium strength have neither the absolute stability of the former nor the feeble and fluctuating character of the latter.

Weak,	{ י ו ה א ע ח ה א	Vowel-Letters, Gutturals.
Medium,	{ ר נ מ ל ז ס צ שׁ	Liquids, Sibilants.
Strong,	{ פ ב ק כ ג ט ת ד	} Aspirates and Mutes.

The special characteristics of these several classes and the influence which they exert upon the constitution of words will be considered hereafter. It is sufficient to remark here that the vowel-letters are so called because they sometimes represent not consonant but vowel-sounds.

<small>*a*. It will be observed that while the *p*, *k*, and *t*-mutes agree in having smooth פ כ ת and middle forms ד ג ב, which may be either aspirated or unaspirated, the two last have each an additional representative ק צ which is lacking to the first. This, coupled with the fact that two of the alphabetic Psalms, Ps. 25, 34, repeat פ as the initial of the closing verse, has given rise to the conjecture that the missing *p* mute was supplied by this letter, having a double sound and a double place in the alphabet. In curious coincidence with this ingenious but unsustained hypothesis, the Ethiopic alphabet has an additional *p*, and the Greek and Roman alphabets agree one step and only one beyond the letter T, viz. in adding next a labial, which in Greek is divided into υ and φ, and in Latin into U and V. as י into I and J.</small>

3. Thirdly, The letters may be divided, with respect to their function in the formation of words, into radicals and serviles. The former, which comprise just one half of the alphabet, are never employed except in the roots or radical portions of words. The latter may also enter into the constitution of roots, but they are likewise put to the less independent use of the formation of derivatives and inflections, of prefixes and suffixes. The serviles are embraced in the

memorial words אֵיתָן מֹשֶׁה וְכָלֵב (Ethan Moses and Caleb); of these, besides other uses, איתן are prefixed to form the future of verbs, and the remainder are prefixed as particles to nouns. The letters הָאֱמָנְתִּיו are used in the formation of nouns from their roots. The only exception to the division now stated is the substitution of ש for servile ת in a certain class of cases, as explained § 54. 4.

a. Kimchi in his Mikhlol (מִכְלוֹל) fol. 46, gives several additional anagrams of the serviles made out by different grammarians as aids to the memory, e. g. שמלאבתו בינה *for his work is understanding;* אני שלמה כותב *I Solomon am writing;* שלומי אך תבנה *only build thou my peace;* משה כתב אלינו *like a branch of the father of multitude;* משה כתב אלינו *Moses has written to us.* To which Nordheimer has added שאל הון מכתבי *consult the riches of my book.*

§ 8. In Hebrew writing and printing, words are never divided. Hence various expedients are resorted to upon occasion, in manuscripts and old printed editions, to fill out the lines, such as giving a broad form to certain letters, ה א ה ם ל, occupying the vacant space with some letter, as ק, repeated as often as may be necessary, or with the first letters of the next word, which were not, however, accounted part of the text, as they were left without vowels, and the word was written in full at the beginning of the following line. The same end is accomplished more neatly in modern printing by judicious spacing.

§ 9. 1. The later Jews make frequent use of abbreviations. There are none, however, in the text of the Hebrew Bible; such as are found in the margin are explained in a special lexicon at the back of the editions in most common use, e. g. וגו for וְגוֹמֵר *et completio* = etc.

2. The numerical employment of the letters, common to the Hebrews with the Greeks, is indicated in the table of the alphabet. The hundreds from 500 to 900 are represented either by the five final letters or by the combination of ת with the letters immediately preceding; thus ך or תק 500, ם or תר 600, ן or תש 700, ף or תת 800, ץ or תתק 900. Thou-

sands are represented by units with two dots placed over them, thus א̈ 1000, etc. Compound numbers are formed by joining the appropriate units to the tens and hundreds, thus תכא 421. Fifteen is, however, made not by יה, which are the initial letters of the divine name Jehovah, יהוה, but by טו 9+6.

This use of the letters is found in the accessories of the Hebrew text, e. g. in the numeration of the chapters and verses, and in the Masoretic notes, but not in the text itself. Whether these or any other signs of number were ever employed by the original writers of Scripture, or by the scribes in copying it, may be a doubtful matter. It has been ingeniously conjectured, and with a show of plausibility, that some of the discrepancies of numbers in the Old Testament may be accounted for by assuming the existence of such a system of symbols, in which errors might more easily arise than in fully written words.

The Vowels.

§ 10. The letters now explained constitute the body of the Hebrew text. These are all that belonged to it in its original form, and so long as the language was a living one nothing more was necessary, for the reader could mentally supply the deficiencies of the notation from his familiarity with his native tongue. But when Hebrew ceased to be spoken the case was different; the knowledge of the true pronunciation could no longer be presumed, and difficulties would arise from the ambiguity of individual words and their doubtful relation to one another. It is the design of the Masoretic points (מָסוֹרָה *tradition*) to remedy or obviate these inconveniences by supplying what was lacking in this mode of writing. The authors of this system did not venture to make any change in the letters of the sacred text. The signs which they introduced were entirely supplementary, consisting of dots and marks about the text fixing its true pronunciation and auxiliary to its proper interpretation. This has been done with the utmost nicety and minuteness, and with such evident accuracy and care as to make them reliable and efficient if not indispensable helps. These points or signs are of three kinds, 1. those representing the vowels, 2. those affecting the consonants, 3. those attached to words.

a. As illustrations of the ambiguity both as to sound and sense of individual words, when written by the letters only, it may be stated that דבר is in Gen. 12: 4 דִּבֶּר *he spake*, in Ex. 6: 29 דַּבֵּר *speak* and דֹּבֵר *speaking*, in Prov. 25: 11 דָּבָר *spoken*, in Gen. 37: 14 דְּבַר *word*, in 1 Kin. 6: 16 דְּבִר *the oracle* or most holy place of the temple, in Ex. 9: 3 דֶּבֶר *pestilence*. So וישק is in Gen. 29: 10 וַיַּשְׁקְ *and he watered*, and in the next verse וַיִּשַּׁק *and he kissed;* ויבא occurs twice in Gen. 29: 23, the first time it is יָבֵא *and he brought*, the second יָבֹא *and he came;* והשבתים is in Jer. 32: 37 first וַהֲשִׁבֹתִים *and I will bring them again*, and then וְהֹשַׁבְתִּים *and I will cause them to dwell;* שמים is in Gen. 14: 19 שָׁמַיִם *heaven*, and in Isa. 5: 20 שָׂמִים *putting*. This ambiguity is, however, in most cases removed by the connection in which the words are found, so that there is little practical difficulty for one who is well acquainted with the language. Modern Hebrew is commonly written and read without the points: and the same is true of its kindred tongues the Syriac and Arabic, though each of these has a system of points additional to the letters.

§ 11. 1. The alphabet, as has been seen, consisted exclusively of consonants, since these were regarded as a sufficiently exact representation of the syllables into which in Hebrew they invariably enter. And the omission of the vowels occasioned less embarrassment, because in the Semitic family of languages generally, unlike the Indo-European, they form no part, properly speaking, of the radical structure of the word, and consequently do not aid in expressing its essential meaning, but only its nicer shades and modifications. Still some notation of vowels was always necessary, and this was furnished in a scanty measure by the vowel-letters, or, as they are also called, quiescents, or *matres lectionis* (guides in reading). The weakest of the palatals י was taken as the representative of the vowels $\bar{\imath}$ and $\bar{e}$ of the same organ to which in sound it bears a close affinity; the weakest of the labials ו was in like manner made to represent its cognates $\bar{u}$ and $\bar{o}$; and the two weak gutturals א and ה were written for the guttural vowel $\bar{a}$, as well as for the compound vowels $\bar{e}$ and $\bar{o}$ of which a is one of the elements. Letters were more rarely employed to represent short vowels; ה or י for $\breve{e}$ is the most frequent case; others are exceptional.

a. Medial $\bar{a}$ when written at all, as it very rarely is, is denoted by א, e. g. לאט lat Judg. 4: 21, דאג $d\bar{a}g$ Neh. 13: 16 K'thibh, קאם $k\bar{a}m$ Hos. 10: 14, כזאול $z\bar{a}z\bar{e}l$ Lev. 16: 8, ראש $r\bar{a}sh$ Prov. 10: 4 and in a few other passages, sometimes for $r\bar{a}moth$, ראמות, צואר $tsavvar$, אבאסאך Hos. 4: 6 if not an error in the text perhaps for $em\bar{a}sak$; final $\bar{a}$, which is much more frequently written, is denoted by ה, e. g. גלה $g\bar{a}l\bar{a}$, מלכה $malk\bar{a}$, אתה $att\bar{a}$, rarely and only as an Aramœism by א, e. g. הגא $hhogg\bar{a}$ Isa. 19: 17, קרחא $korhh\bar{a}$ Ezek. 27: 31 K'thibh, גבהא $gabh'h\bar{a}$ Ezek. 31: 5 K'thibh. The writing of $\bar{e}$ and $\bar{i}$, $\bar{o}$ and $\bar{u}$ is optional in the middle of words but necessary at the end, e. g. צויתם or צוויתם $tsivv\bar{i}th\bar{i}m$, צויתי $tsivv\bar{i}th\bar{i}$; שבו or שובו $sh\bar{u}bh\bar{u}$. In the former position י stands for the first pair of vowels, and ו for the second, e. g. מיניקות $m\bar{e}n\bar{i}koth$, נסוגתי $n'sugh\bar{o}th\bar{i}$; א for $\bar{e}$ and $\bar{o}$ so situated is rare and exceptional, e. g. ראש $r\bar{e}sh$ Prov. 6: 11, 30: 8, and perhaps יגאץ $yan\bar{e}ts$ Eccles. 12: 5; זאת $z\bar{o}th$, פראת $p\bar{o}roth$ Ezek. 31: 8, בצאתו $bitsts\bar{o}thav$ Ezek. 47: 11. At the end of words $\bar{e}$ is commonly expressed by י, and $\bar{o}$ by ו, though ה is frequently and א rarely employed for the same purpose, e. g. מלכי $malkh\bar{e}$, מלכו $malk\bar{o}$; היה $h'y\bar{e}$, פרעה $par\bar{o}$; לא $l\bar{o}$. Final $\bar{e}$ is represented by ה, medial $\bar{e}$ if written at all by י, e. g. יהיה $yih'ye$, תהיינה or תחינה $tih'yen\bar{a}$.

b. The employment of the vowel-letters in conformity with the scale just given, is further governed, (1.) By usage, which is in many words and forms almost or quite invariable; in others it fluctuates, thus $sobh\bar{e}bh$ is commonly סבב or סובב, only once סביב 2 Kin. 8: 21; $ya'kobh$ is יעקב except in Jer. 33: 26 where it is יעקוב; $th\bar{e}ase$ is תשה, but in Ex. 25: 31 תירשה; $\bar{e}tham$ according to the analogy of similar grammatical forms would be אהם, but in Ps. 19: 14 it is איתם; $h\bar{e}m\bar{i}r$ is in Jer. 2: 11 written in both the usual and an unusual way, חמיר and הימיר; $m'l\bar{a}kh\bar{i}m$ is מלכים except in 2 Sam. 11: 1, where it is מלאכים; $g'bhul\bar{o}th$ is in Deut. 32: 8 גבלת, in Isa. 10: 13 גבולת, in Ps. 74: 17 גבולות; $l\bar{o}$ meaning not is לא, meaning to him is לו, though these are occasionally interchanged; $z\bar{o}$ is written both זה and זו; and po פה, פו and פא. (2.) The indisposition to multiply the vowel-letters unduly in the same word, e. g. $'l\bar{o}'h$ אלוה, $'l\bar{o}h\bar{i}m$ אלהים; $n\bar{a}th\bar{u}n$ נתון, $n'th\bar{u}n\bar{i}m$ נתנים or נתונם. (3.) The increased tendency to their employment in the later books of the Bible, e. g. כוה $ko'hh$ Dan. 11: 6, always elsewhere כה; קודש $kodhesh$ Dan. 11: 30, for קדש; דויד $d\bar{a}v\bar{i}dh$ in the books of Chronicles, Ezra, Nehemiah and Zechariah, elsewhere commonly דוד. This must, however, be taken with considerable abatement, as is shown by such examples as $addir\bar{i}m$ אדירים Ex. 15: 10, אדרם Ezek. 32: 18.

It is to be observed that those cases in which א is used to record vowels must be carefully distinguished from those in which it properly belongs to the consonantal structure of the word, though from its weakness it may have lost its sound, as מצא *matsa*, ראשון *rīshōn*. § 57, 2.

2. When used to represent the Hebrew vowels, $\bar{a}$ is sounded as in *father*, $\breve{a}$ as in *fat*, $\bar{e}$ as in *there*, $\breve{e}$ as in *met*, $\bar{\imath}$ as in *machine*, $\breve{\imath}$ as in *pin*, $\bar{o}$ as in *note*, $\breve{o}$ as in *not*, $\bar{u}$ as in *rule*, and $\breve{u}$ as in *full*. The quantity will be marked when the vowels are long, but not when they are short.

§ 12. There are nine points or masoretic signs representing vowels (תְּנוּעוֹת *motions*, viz., by which consonants are moved or pronounced); of these three are long, three short, and three doubtful. They are shown in the following table, the horizontal stroke indicating their position with reference to the letters of the text.

Long Vowels.

קָמֵץ	Kā'-mets	$\bar{a}$	ָ
צֵרִי	Tsē'-rē	$\bar{e}$	ֵ
חוֹלֶם	Hhō'-lem	$\bar{o}$	ֹ

Short Vowels.

פַּתָּח	Pút-tahh	$\breve{a}$	ַ
סְגוֹל	Se'-ghōl	$\breve{e}$	ֶ
קָמֵץ חָטוּף	Kā'-mets Hhā-tūph'	$\breve{o}$	ָ

Doubtful Vowels.

חִירֶק	Hhī'-rik	ִ	$\bar{\imath}$ or $\breve{\imath}$
שׁוּרֶק	Shū'-rek	וּ	$\bar{u}$ or $\breve{u}$
קִבּוּץ	Kĭb'-buts	ֻ	

All these vowel-points are written under the letter after which they are pronounced except two, viz., Hholem and Shurek. Hholem is placed over the left edge of the letter to which it belongs, and is thus distinguished from the accent R'bhiᵃ, which is a dot over its centre. When followed by שׁ or preceded by שׂ it coincides with the diacritical point over the letter, e. g. מֹשֶׁה *mōshe*, שֹׂנֵא *sōnē;* when it follows שׁ or precedes שׂ it is written over its opposite arm,

e. g. שֹׁמֵר *shōmēr*, תִּרְפֹּשׂ *tirpōs*. Its presence in these cases must accordingly be determined by the circumstances. If preceded by a letter without a vowel-sign, שׁ will be *ōsh* and שׂ *ōs;* if it have itself no vowel-sign, שׂ will be *sō* and שׁ *shō*, except at the end of words. Shurek is a dot in the bosom of the letter Vav, thus וּ. It will be observed that there is a double notation of the vowel *u*. When there is a ו in the text this vowel, whether long or short, is indicated by a single dot within it, and called Shurek; in the absence of ו it is indicated by three dots placed obliquely beneath the letter to which it belongs, and called Kibbuts.

a. The division of the vowels given above differs from the common one into five long and five short, according to which Hhirik is counted as two, viz., Hhirik magnum וּ. = *î*, and Hhirik parvum ִ = *ĭ;* and Shurek is reckoned a distinct vowel from Kibbuts, the former being *û* and the latter *ŭ*. To this there are two objections. (1.) It confuses the masoretic signs with the letters of the text, as though they were coeval with them and formed part of the same primitive mode of writing, instead of being quite distinct in origin and character. The masoretic vowel-sign is not וּ. but ִ. The punctuators never introduced the letter י into the text; they found it already written precisely where it is at present, and all that they did was to add the point. And instead of using two signs for *i*, as they had done in the case of *a, e*, and *o*, they used but one, viz., a dot beneath the letter, whether *i* was long or short. The confusion of things thus separate in their nature was pardonable at a time when the points were supposed to be an original constituent of the sacred text, but not now when their more recent origin is universally admitted. (2.) It is inaccurate. The distinction between וּ. and ִ, וּ and ֻ, is not one of quantity, for *î* and *û* are expressed indifferently with or without Yodh and Vav.

Gesenius, in his Lehrgebäude, while he retains the division of the vowels into five long and five short, admits that it is erroneous and calculated to mislead; and it has been discarded by Rödiger in the latest editions of his smaller grammar. That which was proposed by Gesenius, however, as a substitute, is perplexed and obscure, and for this reason, if there were no others, is unfitted for the wants of pupils in the early stage of their progress. On the other hand, the triple arrangement here adopted after the example of Ewald, has the recommendation not only of clearness and correctness, but of being, instead of an innovation, a return to old opinions. The scheme of five long and five short vowels originated with Moses and David Kimchi, who were led to it by a comparison of the Latin and its derivatives. From them it was adopted by Reuchlin in his Rudimenta Hebraica, and thus became current among Christians. The Jewish grammarians, before the Kimchis, however, reckoned Kibbuts and Shurek as one vowel, Hhirik as one, and even Kamets and Kamets-

Hhatuph as one on account of the identity of the symbol employed to represent them. They thus made out seven vowels, the same number as in Greek, where the distinction into long, short and doubtful also prevails. That the literary impulses of the Orientals were chiefly received from the Greeks is well known; that the suggestion of a vowel-system came to the Syrians from this quarter is certain, both from direct testimony to this effect and from the shapes of their vowels, which still betray their origin. May not the Hebrews have learned something from the same school?

b. The names of the vowels, with the exception of Kamets-Hhatuph, contain the sounds of the vowels which they are intended to represent; Kibbuts in the last, the others in their first syllable. Their signification is indicative either of the figure of the vowel or the mode of pronouncing it. Kamets and Kibbuts, *contraction*, i. e. of the mouth; Pattahh, *opening*; T'sere, *bursting forth*; Seghol, *cluster of grapes*; Hhirik, *gnashing*; Hholem, *strength*; Kamets-Hhatuph, *hurried Kamets*; Shurek, *whistling*. It is a curious circumstance that notwithstanding the diversity of the vowel-systems in the Syriac, Arabic, and Hebrew, the name Pattahh is common to them all.

§13. This later and more complete method of noting the vowels does not displace but is superinduced upon the scanty one previously described. Hence it comes to pass that such vowels as were indicated by letters in the first instance are now doubly written, i. e. both by letters and points. By this combination each of the two methods serves to illustrate and explain the other. Thus the added signs determine whether the letters אהוי (which have been formed into the technical word אֲהֵוִי *Eh°vī*) are in any given case to be regarded as vowels or as consonants. If these letters are themselves followed by a vowel or a Sh'va, §16, or have a Daghesh forte, §23, they retain their consonant sound; for two vowels never come together in Hebrew, and Sh'va and Daghesh forte belong only to consonants: thus קֹלְיָה *kōvekā*, מִצְוֹת *mitsvōth* (where צ being provided with a separate point, the Hholem must belong after ו), וְהָיָה *v'hāyā* קִיָּם *kiyyam*. Otherwise they quiesce in a preceding or accompanying vowel-sign, provided it is homogeneous with themselves; that is to say, they have the sound indicated by it, the vowel-sign merely interpreting what was originally denoted by the

2

letter. *E* and *i* are homogeneous to י, *o* and *u* to ו, and these being the only vowels which they were ever employed to represent, they can quiesce in no others; thus מִי בִּי *bī*, מֵה *mē*, גֵּיא *gē*, בּוֹ *bō*, לוּ *lū*, but שָׂרַי *sāray*, גּוֹי *gōy*, גָּלוּי *gāluy*, תָּו *tāv*, שָׁלֵו *shālēv*, זִו *zīv*; the combination יו is pronounced *āv*, עָלָיו and עָנָו *ānāv*, סְתָיו and סְתָו *s'thāv*. *A*, *e*, and *o* are homogeneous to א and ה. These letters deviate so far from the rule just given that א from its extreme weakness not only quiesces when it is properly a vowel-letter, but may give up its consonant sound and character after any vowel whatever, e. g. מָאתֶא *tītē*, רִאשׁוֹן *rīshōn*, פֹּארָה *pūrā*; ה is never used as a vowel-letter except at the end of words, and there it always quiesces unless it receives a Mappik, §26.

a. As a letter was scarcely ever used to express *ŏ*, the quiescence of ו in Kamets-Hhatuph is very rare, and where it does occur the margin always substitutes a reading without the ו, e. g. יְכָנְיָה Jer. 27:20, הַיְבָנִים Ezek. 27:15, בְּיְגִיְדִי־בֹּוֹר Ps. 30:4, יְסֻגְּדִי־בֹּוֹ Isa. 44:17, לְבִיל Jer. 33:8, וּגְדוֹל־בֹּחַ Nah. 1:3. In אֲוִיּלֹה 2 Chron. 8:18, and צְמֻיתַי Deut. 32:13, ו represents or quiesces in the still briefer *ŏ* of Hhateph-Kamets, § 16. 3.

b. In a few proper names medial ה quiesces at the end of the first member of the compound, e. g. פְּדָהצוּר Num. 1:10, עֲשָׂהאֵל 2 Sam. 2:19, also written עֲשָׂה־אֵל 1 Chron. 2:16. In such words as נוֹשָׁבָה Jer. 22:6, שְׁפָבָה Deut. 21:7, ה does not quiesce in Kibbuts, for the points belong to the marginal readings נושבו, שפכו § 46.

§14. On the other hand the vowel-letters shed light upon the stability of the vowels and the quantity of the doubtful signs. 1. As $\check{\imath}$ was scarcely ever and $\check{u}$ seldom represented by a vowel-letter, Hhirik with Yodh (י.) is almost invariably long and Shurek (וּ) commonly so. 2. The occasional absence in individual cases of the vowel-letters, does not determine the quantity of the signs for *i* and *u*; but their uniform absence in any particular words or forms makes it almost certain that the vowel is short. 3. The occasional presence of ו and י to represent one of their homogeneous long vowels proves nothing as to its character; but if in any word or form these letters are regularly written, the vowel is, as a general rule, immutable. When ו and י stand for their long homogeneous vowels, these latter are said to be written fully, e. g. קוֹל *kōl*, נִיר *nīr*, מוּת *mūth;* without these quiescent letters they are said to be written defectively, e. g. הֲקִמֹתִי *h^akimōthī*, קָמֻס *kāmus*.

a. Hhirik with Yodh is short in וַהֲמִיתִיו *vah^amittīv* 1 Sam. 17:35, בִּיקְרוֹתֶיךָ *bikk'rōthekha* Ps. 45:10, לִיקְהַת *likk'hath* Prov. 30:17. In צִיקְלַג 1 Chron. 12:1, 20, *i* is probably long, although the word is always elsewhere written without the Yodh; as it sometimes has a secondary accent on the first syllable and sometimes not (see 1 Sam. 30:1), it may have had a twofold pronunciation *tsīk'lag*, and *tsiklag*. Shurek as *ŭ* is of much more frequent occurrence, e. g. חֻקֵּי *hhukkē*, לְאֻמִּים *l'ummīm*, חֻקָּה *hhukkā* Ps. 102:5, אֲלֻגִּים 2 Chron. 2:7, זוּת *zūth* Ezek. 16:34.

§15. The vowels may be further distinguished into pure, *a, i, u,* and diphthongal, *e, o ; e* being a combination of *a* and *i*, or intermediate between them, and *o* holding the same relation to *a* and *u*.

Sh'va.

§16. 1. The absence of a vowel is indicated by ְ Sh'vā (שְׁוָא *emptiness*, or as written by Chayug, the oldest of Jewish grammarians, שְׁבָא), which serves to assure the reader that one has not been inadvertently omitted. It is accordingly placed under all vowelless consonants except at the end of words, where it is regarded as unnecessary, the absence of a vowel being there a matter of course. If, however, the last letter of a word be ךְ, or if it be immediately preceded by another vowelless letter, or be doubled by the point called Daghesh-forte, § 23, Sh'va is written to preclude the doubt which is possible in these cases, e. g. מִשְׁמַרְכֶם, מַלְכֵּךְ, קָשְׁתְּ, אֲמָרְתְּ, אַתְּ, נָתַתְּ. Sh'va is not given to a quiescent letter, since it represents not a consonant but a vowel, e. g. הַיְצִיקָה, nor as a general rule to a final consonant preceded by a quiescent; thus מַשָּׂאת, וּבָאת Ruth 3 : 4; וְהָיִית Isa. 62 : 3, though in this case it is sometimes written, e. g. וּבָאתָ 2 Sam. 14 : 3; וְהָיִיתָ 2 Sam. 14 : 2; וְהָיִית Judg. 13 : 3; הוֹצֵאת 1 Kin. 11 : 13. א at the end of a word, preceded either by a vowelless letter or a quiescent, is termed otiant, and is left unpointed, e. g. הוּא רָבוֹא וַיִּרָא חֵטְא.

a. Final ך may receive Sh'va for the sake of distinction not only from ה, as already suggested, but also from ר with which it might be in danger of being confounded in manuscripts; Freytag conjectures that it is properly a part of the letter, like the stroke in the corresponding final ك in Arabic. In such forms as רַגְלָיו Sh'va is omitted with the closing letters because the י is not sounded.

2. Sh'va may be either silent (נָח *quiescens*), or vocal (נָע *mobile*). At the close of syllables it is silent. But at the beginning of a syllable the Hebrews always facilitated the pronunciation of concurrent consonants by the introduction of a hiatus or slight breathing between them; a Sh'va so situated is consequently said to be vocal, and has a sound approaching that of a hastily uttered *e*, as in *given*. This will be represented by an apostrophe, thus, בְּמִדְבָּר *b'midhbar*, פְּקַדְתֶּם *p'kadhtem*.

a. According to Kimchi (Mikhlol fol. 189) Sh'va was pronounced in three different ways, according to circumstances. (1.) Before a guttural it inclined to the sound of the following vowel, e. g. יַאֲבֵד *y^aabbēdh*, שְׂאֵת *s'ēth*, רְאִי *d^aa*, and if accompanied by Methegh, § 44, it had the full sound of that vowel, e. g. שָׂאוּ *sāa*, חֳרִי *tihhī*, לְעוֹלָם *loolam*. (2.) Before Yodh it inclined to *i*, c. g. בְּיַעֲקֹב *b'ya^akobh*, בְּיוֹם *k'yom*, and with Methegh was sounded as Hhirik, e. g. בְּיַד *biyadh*. (3.) Before any other letter it inclined to *a*, e. g. בְּרָכָה *b^erakha*, גְּלִילִים *g^elilim*, and with Methegh was pronounced as Pattahh בְּמַקְהֵלוֹת *bamakhēloth*.

3. Sh'va may, again, be simple or compound. Sometimes, particularly when the first consonant is a guttural, which from its weakness is in danger of not being distinctly heard, the hiatus becomes still more audible, and is assimilated in sound to the short guttural vowel *ă*, or the diphthongal *ĕ* or *ŏ*, into which it enters. This assimilation is rep-

resented by combining the sign for Sh'va with those for the short vowels, thus forming what are called the compound Sh'vas in distinction from the simple Sh'va previously explained.

These are,

Hhātĕph-Pattahh	ֲ ;	thus,	עֲמֹד	^{a}mŏdh.
Hhātĕph-Seghol	ֱ ;	thus,	אֱמֹר	^{e}mōr.
Hhātĕph-Kamets	ֳ ;	thus,	חֳלִי	hh^{o}lī.

a. Hhātĕph (חֲטֵף *snatching*) denotes the rapidity of utterance or the hurried character of the sounds represented by these symbols.

b. The compound Sh'vas, though for the most part restricted to the gutturals, are occasionally written under other consonants in place of simple Sh'va, to indicate more distinctly that it is vocal: thus, Hhateph-Pattahh וַיַּחַתְּ Gen. 2:12, הֶבְרָלָה Gen. 27:38; Hhateph-Kamets לְקָחָה Gen. 2:23, אֲכְתְּבֶנָּה Jer. 31:33; but never Hhateph-Seghol except צִלְצְלִים 2 Sam. 6:5 in some editions, e. g. that of Stephanus. This is done with so little uniformity that the same word is differently written in this respect, e. g. בְּסֵצְלָה 2 Kin. 2:1, בִּסְעָרָה ver. 11.

Pattahh Furtive.

§17. A similar hiatus or slight transition sound was used at the end of words in connection with the gutturals. When ע, ח, or the consonantal ה at the end of words is preceded by a long heterogeneous vowel (i. e. another than *a*), or is followed by another vowelless consonant, it receives a Pattahh furtive ֲ , which resembles in sound an extremely short *a*, and is pronounced before the letter under which it is written, e. g. רוּחַ rū^{a}hh, שָׁמֹעַ shāmō^a, מַגְבִּיהַּ maghbī^{a}h, שָׁמַעַתְּ shāma^{a}t, יִחַדְּ yi^{a}hhd.

a. Some grammarians deny that Pattahh furtive can be found under a penultimate guttural, contending that the vowel-sign is in such cases a proper Pattahh. and that שָׁמַעַתְּ should accordingly be read *shāmaat*, and יַחַדְּ *yihhad*. But both the Sh'va under the final letter, §16, and the Daghesh-lene in it, §21, show that the guttural is not followed by a vowel. The sign beneath it must consequently be Pattahh furtive, and represent an antecedent vowel-sound. In some manuscripts Pattahh furtive is written as Hhateph-Pattahh, or even as simple Sh'va; thus, רָקִיעַ or רָקִיעֲ for רָקִיעַ.

Syllables.

§18. 1. Syllables are formed by the combination of consonants and vowels. As two vowels never come together in the same word in Hebrew without an intervening consonant, there can never be more than one vowel in the same syllable; and with the single exception of ו occurring at the beginning of words, no syllable ever consists of a vowel alone. Every syllable, with the exception just stated, must begin with a consonant, and may begin with two, but never with more than two. Syllables ending with a vowel, whether represented by a quiescent letter or not, are called simple, e. g. לְךָ *l'khā*, עוֹלָה *ō-lā*. (The first syllable of this second example begins, it will be perceived, with the consonant ע, though this disappears in the notation given of its sound.) Syllables ending with a consonant, or, as is possible at the close of a word, with two consonants, are said to be mixed: thus קַמְתֶּם *kam-tem*, הָלַכְתְּ *hā-lakht*. As the vocal Sh'vas, whether simple or compound, are not vowels properly speaking, but simply involuntary transition sounds, they, with the consonants under which they stand, cannot form distinct syllables, but are attached to that of the following vowel. Pattahh furtive in like manner belongs to the syllable formed by the preceding vowel. Thus זְרוֹעַ *z'rō^a*, אֲנִי *°nī* are monosyllables.

2. Long vowels always stand in simple syllables, and short vowels in mixed syllables, unless they be accented. But accented syllables, whether simple or mixed, may contain indifferently a long or a short vowel.

a. The following may serve as a specimen of the division of Hebrew words into their proper syllables; thus,

אָדָם אֱלֹהִים בָּרָא בְּיוֹם אָדָם תּוֹלְדוֹת סֵפֶר זֶה
ā-dha'm 'lo-hī'm b'ro' b'yo'm ā-dha'm tō-l'dho'th sē'-pher zē'
Gen. 5:1. אֹתוֹ עָשָׂה אֱלֹהִים בְּרֹאשִׁית
ō-tho' ā-sā' 'lo-hī'm bidh-mū'th

b. The reason of the rule for the quantity of syllables appears to be this. In consequence of their brevity, the short vowels required the addition of a following consonant to make the utterance full and complete, unless the want of this was compensated by the greater energy of pronunciation due to the accent. The long vowels were sufficiently complete without any such addition, though they were capable of receiving it under the new energy imparted by the accent. This pervading regularity, which is so striking a feature of the Hebrew language, was the foundation of the *systema morarum* advocated by some of the older grammarians of Holland and Germany. The idea of this was, that each syllable was equal to three *morae*, that is, three rests, or a bar of three beats; a long vowel being equivalent to two *morae*, or two beats, a short vowel to one, and the initial or final consonant or consonants also to one: thus קָטְלָה $k(1) + a(2) = 3$, $t(1) + a(1) + lt(1) = 3$. An accented syllable might have one *mora* or beat either more or less than the normal quantity. This system was not only proposed by way of grammatical explanation, but also made the basis of a peculiar theory of Hebrew prosody. See Gesenius, Geschichte d. Heb. Sprache, p. 123.

c. The cases in which short vowels occur in unaccented simple syllables, are all due to the disturbing influence exerted by the weak letters upon the normal forms of words; thus, חָלַת *hă-ĕth* is for חָיְתָה, and הָחוּא *hă-hū'* for *hāh-hū'*: such words as לָשֵׁא, אֶרֶא, אֵפֶּה, הֱיֵה, קְצֵה are formed after the analogy of קְטֹל. A long vowel in an unaccented mixed syllable is found in but one word, and that of foreign origin, בֵּלְשַׁאצַּר *bēl-t'shăts-tsăr*; though here, as in the majority of instances falling under the previous remark, the syllable receives, if not the primary, yet the secondary accent, e. g. תָּצְמֹד, חֲתֻלִּים, חֲבִירוֹתַי. The same is the case when a long vowel is retained before Makkeph, e. g. שֵׁת־לִי. In the Arabic, which is exceedingly rich in vowels, there are comparatively few mixed syllables; nearly every consonant has its own vowel, and this more frequently short than long. The Chaldee, which is more sparing in its use of vowels than the Hebrew, observes in general the same rule with respect to the quantity of syllables, though not with the same inflexible consistency.

Ambiguous Signs.

§19. It will now be possible, by aid of the principles already recited, to determine the quantity of the doubtful vowels, and to remove the ambiguity which appears to exist in certain vowel-signs.

1. Hhirik, Shurek, and Kibbuts, in unaccented simple syllables, must be long, and in unaccented mixed syllables, short, e. g. יִירַשׁ or יִרַשׁ *yī-rash*, יִבְנוּ *yibh-nū*, גְּבוּלוֹ or גְּבֻלוֹ *g'bhū-lō*, יֻלַּד or יוּלַד *yul-ladh*, כֻּלָּם or כּוּלָם *kul-lām*, מְעִידִּי

or מָעֻזִּי *mäuzzī*. In accented syllables, whether simple or mixed, they are always long, e. g. שִׂיחִים or שִׂיחִים *sī-ḥīm*, לִי *lī*, גְּבוּל or גְּבוּל *g'bhūl*, דְּרָשׁוּהוּ or דְּרָשׁוּהוּ *d'rā-shū-hū*, the only exception being that Ḥhirik is short in the monosyllabic particles אִם, אִשׁ, עִם, מִן, and in some abbreviated verbal forms of the class called Lamedh-He, e. g. וַיִּז, רַיּשְׁבְּ, לְרָב.

The only cases of remaining doubt are those in which these vowels are followed by a letter with Sh'va, either simple or compound. If the former, it might be a question whether it was silent or vocal, and consequently whether the syllable was simple or mixed. If the latter, though the syllable is of course simple, the weak letter which follows may interfere with the operation of the law. Here the etymology must decide. The vowel is long or short as the grammatical form may require; thus in יִרְאֶה־לֹּו, תֶּחֱלַךְ, יִחֲלָה Gen. 22:8, which follow the analogy of יִקְטֹל, and in סַבְבֵי Isa. 10:34, קָמְצוּ the first vowel is short; in יִשְׁמָךְ, גְּבָלְכֶם the first vowel is long. In a few instances the grammatical form in which Ḥhirik is employed is itself doubtful; the distinction is then made by means of Methegh, §44, which is added to the vowel-sign if it is long, but not if it is short; thus, יִרְאוּ *yī-r'ū*, from יָרֵא *to fear*, and יִשְׁנוּ *yī-sh'nū* from יָשֵׁן *to sleep*; but יִרְאוּ *yir-ū* from רָאָה *to see*, and יִשְׁנוּ *yish-nū* from שָׁנָה *to do a second time*.

2. Kamets *ā* and Kamets-Ḥhatuph *ŏ* are both represented by the same sign (ָ), but may be distinguished by rules similar to those just given. In an unaccented simple syllable it is Kamets; in an unaccented mixed syllable it is Kamets-Ḥhatuph; in an accented syllable, whether simple or mixed it is Kamets, e. g. דָּבָר *dā-bhār*, חָפְשִׁי *ḥhoph-shī*, מָוֶת *mā-veth*, לָמָּה *lām-mā*, בָּתִּים *bot-tīm*. Before a letter with simple Sh'va, the distinction is mostly made by Methegh, §44; without Methegh it is always Kamets-Ḥhatuph, with it commonly Kamets, e. g. חָכְמָה *ḥhokh-mā*, חָכְמָה *ḥhā-kh'mā*. Before a guttural with Ḥhateph-Kamets or Kamets-Ḥhatuph

it is frequently ŏ, though standing in a simple syllable and accompanied by Methegh, e. g. בָּחֳרִי *bo-hkʰorī*, תָּעָבְדֵם *to-obhắdhēm*. The surest criterion, however, and in many cases the only decisive one, is found in the etymology. If the vowel be derived from Hholem, or the grammatical form requires an *o* or a short vowel, it is Kamets-Hhatuph; but if it be derived from Pattahh, or the form requires an *a* or a long vowel, it is Kamets: thus וַאֲנִיּוֹת with the prefixed conjunction *voʰniyyōth*, הָאֳנִיָּה with the article *hăʰniyyā*; יָעֳמָד in the Hophal *yoʰmadh*, יְתָאֳרֵהוּ Isa. 44:13 in the Piel *y'thăʰrēhū*. The first vowel is ŏ in צָהֳרַיִם from צֹהַר, קָדְשִׁים from קֹדֶשׁ, שָׁרָשִׁים from שֹׁרֶשׁ, עֲשָׂרָה־לִּי Isa. 38:14, קָבְחִי־לִי Num. 22:11, אָרְחִי־לִי Num. 23:7 and the like, and the first two vowels in such words as פָּעֳלָם from פֹּעַל, מָאָסְכָם Isa. 30:12 from מָאֹס, קָרְבָּם Deut. 20:2, קָבְדָּה Hos. 13:14, קָצְפִּי 2 Chron. 10:10, קָבָל־עָם 2 Kin. 15:10, because they are shortened from Hholem. On the other hand the first vowel is *ā* in שָׁהֲרִי Job 16:19 from שַׁהַר, חָרָשִׁים from חָרָשׁ, בָּמָתִי from בָּמָה, and in קָרְבִּי, מָאַסְתָּ and the like, because it is originally and properly Kamets. The word שָׁמְרָה is in Ps. 86:2 the imperative *shomrā*, in Job 10:12 the preterite *shām'rā*.

a. In a very few instances Kamets-Hhatuph is found in a syllable bearing a conjunctive accent, viz.: רָדְפִי Ps. 38:21, כָּל Ps. 35:10, also Prov. 19:7 (in some copies), and in the judgment of Ewald מְאֹד Judg. 19:5, comp. ver. 8 and עַם Ezek. 41:25; in Dan. 11:12 יָרִים the points belong to the marginal reading ורם, and the vowel is consequently Kamets. There are also a few cases in which Kamets remains in a mixed syllable, deprived of its accent by Makkeph, §43, without receiving Methegh, viz.: מִנְהָ Ps. 16:5, חָרָב Ps. 55:19, 22, סָכָךְ Ps. 74:5; and a final unaccented Kamets is not affected by the insertion of Daghesh-forte conjunctive, §24, in the initial letter of the following word, e. g. מָשַׁחְתָּ שָּׁם Gen. 31:13. When an accent takes the place of Methegh, it serves equally to distinguish *ā* from *ŏ*, e. g. וְנָגְפוּ Ex. 21:22 *v'nāgh'phu*, וּלְבָנָה Ex. 21:35 *āmākh'rū*. §45. 5.

b. Inasmuch as מָחֳרָת is derived from מָחָר *mahhar*, its first vowel might be suspected to be *ā*; but as it is so constantly written with Hhateph-Kamets, the preceding vowel is probably conformed to it. It is consequently regarded and pronounced as *ŏ*. Kimchi (Mikhlol, fol. 188) declares that the first vowel in דָּרְבָּן 1 Sam. 13:21, דָּרְבֹנוֹת Eccles. 12:11

and הִלְלִי Num. 24:7 was universally held to be Kamets, and that with the exception of Rabbi Jonah ben Gannach, who was of a contrary mind, the same unanimity prevailed in regard to the first vowel of קָרְנֹ֫ Ezek. 40:43. As, however, this last word is in every other place written without the Methegh, and there is no analogy for such words as those mentioned above having *a* in their initial syllable, the best authorities are now agreed that the vowel is *ŏ*, and the words are accordingly read *dorbhăn*, etc. In יָהֲשֵׁפֵה *jasper*, and בָּרְקַת *emerald*, Ezek. 28:13, which are mentioned by Kimchi in the same connection, the first vowel is Kamets.

c. In some manuscripts and a few of the older printed books, e. g. Stephanus' Hebrew Bible and Reuchlin's Rudimenta Hebraica, Kamets-Hhatuph is denoted by (ֳ). It then differs from Kamets, but is liable to be confounded with Hhateph-Kamets. It can, however, be distinguished from it by the circumstance that Kamets-Hhatuph is always followed either by simple Sh'va, Daghesh-forte, or Methegh; none of which ever immediately succeed Hhateph-Kamets. Such a form as קָרְבָּ֫ Ezek. 26:9 in the editions of Michaelis and Van der Hooght is an impossible one if (ֳ) have its ordinary meaning.

d. It is surprising that in so minute and careful a system of orthography as that of the Masorites, there should be no symbol for *ŏ* distinct from that for *ă*; and some have felt constrained in consequence to suppose that the signs for these two vowels were originally different, but became assimilated in the course of transcription. This seems unlikely, however. The probability is that *ă* and *ŏ*, whose resemblance even we can perceive, were so closely allied in the genuine Hebrew pronunciation, that one sign was thought sufficient to represent them, especially as the Masorites were intent simply on indicating sounds without concerning themselves with grammatical relations.

§ 20. 1. As simple Sh'va is vocal at the beginning of a syllable and silent at its close, there can be no doubt as to its character when it stands under initial or final letters. Preceding the first vowel of a word it must of course be vocal, and following the last vowel it must be silent, זְכַרְתָּם *z'khartām*, זָכַרְתְּ *zākhart*. In the middle of a word, the question whether it belongs to the syllable of the preceding or the following vowel must be determined by the circumstances. If a complete syllable precedes, that is, either an unaccented long vowel or a vowelless consonant serving as the complement of a previous short vowel, it is vocal. If it be preceded by a short vowel which cannot make a complete syllable without the aid of a following consonant, or by a long accented vowel, it is silent: זָכְרֵי zō-kh'rē, תִּזְכְּרוּ tiz-k'rū, זִכְרוּ zikh-rū, תִּקְטֹלְנָה liktōl-nā. Sh'va under a letter doubled by Daghesh-forte, § 23, is vocal, such a letter being equivalent to two, the first of which completes the previous syllable, and the second begins the syllable which follows: הַזְזְכָרִים = הַזְּכָרִים haz-z'khārīm.

2. In addition to this it is to be remarked that Sh'va is vocal after what may be called intermediate syllables; that is to say, when the consonant under which it stands performs, as it occasionally does, the double office of completing one syllable and beginning the next. Thus, when it follows a consonant from which Daghesh-forte has been omitted, וַיְבַקְשׁוּ vay'bhak'shū for vay-y'bhak-k'shū, or the first of two similar letters, in order that the reduplication may be made more distinct, הַלְלוּ hal'lū, קִלְלַת kil'lath, צִלְלוֹ tsil'lō, אַלְלַי al'lay, הִקְּכֵּי hhik'kē, and in several other cases, which will be more particularly described in § 22.

a. The same double office is performed by gutturals beginning one syllable and yet inclining to complete the one before it, § 18. 2. c. In חַיָּה, for example, י belongs in a measure to both syllables. It properly begins the second, and yet it is preceded by a short vowel just as if it ended the first, which is accordingly to be reckoned an intermediate syllable, being in strictness neither simple nor mixed, but partaking of the nature of both.

Daghesh-Lene.

§ 21. The second class of signs added to the Hebrew text are those which are designed to guide in the pronunciation of the consonants. These are the diacritical point over Shin, Daghesh-lene, Daghesh-forte, Mappik, and Raphe. The use of the first of these has already been sufficiently explained, § 3. 1.

1. Daghesh-lene (דָּגֵשׁ קַל) is a point inserted in the six letters ב ג ד כ פ ת (technically called *B'ghadh K'phath*), to indicate the loss of their aspiration, e. g. בּ *bh*, בּ *b*; etc.

As these letters are always aspirated after a vowel-sound, however slight, and never as an initial utterance or when following a consonant, they invariably require Daghesh-lene whenever they are not immediately preceded by a vowel or a vocal Sh'va. It is consequently inserted in the initial aspirate of a word which begins a verse, בְּרֵאשִׁית Gen. 1:1, or which follows a word bearing a disjunctive accent (inasmuch as this represents a pause of longer or shorter duration), וּבְרִיתוֹ בָּאֵי ׀ Ex. 1:1, פֶּן ׀ עַתָּה Gen. 3:22, or ending in a consonant, מַצְלִיחַ דַּרְכִּי, אֶל־בְּנֵי Gen. 24:42; but not if it follows a word ending in a vowel and having a conjunctive accent, הָיְתָה תֹּהוּ, פְּנֵי תָהוֹם Gen. 1:2. The sacred name יְהֹוָה is followed by Daghesh-lene, even though it may have a conjunctive accent, Num. 10:29, Deut. 3:26, Josh. 10:30, 11:8, Ps. 18:21, because in reading the Jews always substitute for it the word אֲדֹנָי, which ends in a consonant. In a very few cases, however, e. g. אֲדֹנָי בָּם Ps. 68:18, קָרְאוֹ Isa. 34:11, שָׁלַי בָּהּ Ezek. 23:42, Daghesh-lene is not inserted after a vowel-letter, which retains its consonant sound.

2. Daghesh-lene is inserted in a medial or final aspirate preceded by a vowelless consonant, whether this be accompanied by silent Sh'va or Pattahh furtive, e. g. שָׂמַחְתָּ, כְּסָתְרָף; but not if it be preceded by a vowel or vocal Sh'va, whether simple or compound, e. g. עֲבָדָם, וּבְבֵית.

a. The primary signification of the name Daghesh is commonly explained from the Syriac ܕܓܫ (דְּגַשׁ), to which Castellus in his lexicon gives the sense of *piercing*. This is by some applied to the puncture or point which is its written sign, by others to its power of sharpening the sound of letters by removing their aspiration or doubling them. Buxtorf, however, in his Chaldee Lexicon, disputes the existence of such a root in either Syriac or Chaldee, alleging that in Prov. 12:18, the passage quoted to prove the word, the true reading is ܪܓܫܐ (רגשא). The six letters which receive Daghesh-lene in Hebrew have the same twofold pronunciation in Syriac, a red dot called Rukhokh (ܪܘܟܟܐ *softness*), being written beneath them when they were to be aspirated, and another called Kushoi (ܩܘܫܝܐ *hardness*), being written above them when they were not.

b. Grammarians are not agreed whether the aspirated or unaspirated sound of these consonants was the original one. There being no data for the settlement of the question, each decides it by his own theory of phonetic changes. The correctness of the Masoretic punctuation has sometimes been questioned in regard to this matter, on the ground of the improbability of such fluctuation in the sound of these letters in the same word. But besides the Syriac analogy just referred to, the Sanskrit language shows the almost unlimited extent to which euphonic changes may be carried by a people possessing a sensitive and discriminating ear. The Sanskrit aspirates, besides being subjected to other mutations which cannot here be detailed, regularly lose their aspiration when finals, and under certain conditions when medials, throwing it back, where this is possible, upon a previous letter. Bopp Kritische Grammatik, pp. 30. 42. Similar laws prevail to some extent in Greek, e. g. θρίξ, τριχός; τρέφω, θρέψω; θύω, ἐτύθην; οὐκ ἔχω, οὐχ ἕξω; μεθ' ὑμῖν.

§ 22. The absence of Daghesh-lene in an aspirate sometimes shows a preceding simple Sh'va to be vocal when this would not otherwise have been known. In most of the cases referred to, a letter originally belonging to the succeeding syllable is by the prefixing of a short vowel drawn back to complete the syllable before it; instead, however, of giving up its previous connection altogether, it forms an intermediate syllable, § 20. 2, the Sh'va remaining vocal though the antecedent vowel is short; thus, לְבַב *l'bhabh* with the prefix בְּ becomes בִּלְבַב *bil'bhabh*, not בְּלְבַב *bil-babh*.

a. The particular instances in which this may occur are the following, viz.: (1) The Kal imperative of verbs and the Kal infinitive with suffixes, e. g. עִבְדִי, עִבְדוּ, עִבְדָם, עָבְדֵנוּ from עֲבֹד; yet with occasional exceptions, as בְּאָסְפְּכֶם Lev. 23:39. (2) Those forms of Pe Guttural verbs in which the first radical assumes a short vowel in place of the silent Sh'va in the regular inflexion, e. g. יַעֲבְדוּ, תַּעֲבֹדֶם for תַּעַבְדֶּם, יַעַבְדוּ. (3) The construct plural of nouns עַבְדֵי from עֲבָדִים, כִּתְבוֹת from כְּתָבוֹת, חַרְבוֹת from חֲרָבוֹת; though with occasional exceptions, as רָשְׁפֵּי Cant. 8:6, but רִשְׁפֵּי Ps. 76:4, צִמְדֵּי Isa. 5:10, חָרְפוֹת Ps. 69:10, בִּרְכֵי Gen. 50:23, but בִּרְכֵיהֶם Judg. 7:6; בִּגְדֵי from בֶּגֶד are peculiar in omitting Daghesh in the singular with suffixes. (4) Three feminine nouns ending in וּת, מַלְכוּת from מֶלֶךְ, יַלְדוּת from יֶלֶד, עַבְדוּת (only occurring with suffixes) from עֶבֶד, but not בִּרְכוּת. Also a few other nouns of different forms, viz.: רִבְתָיִם but רִפְתִּי, שִׂפְכָה, כַּרְכֹּב, שַׂרְבִיט, מַרְבַּדִּים, אַבְרָן, יִקְתָאֵל Josh. 15:38, קְדַעְם Josh. 15:56. (5) After prefixes, as He interrogative, e. g. הֲיִדַעְתֶּם Gen. 29:5 from יְדַעְתֶּם, and inseparable prepositions, e. g. לְדָבִיר from דְּבִיר, בְּדָלַת from דֶּלֶת, כִּדְבַר from דָּבָר. Usage is not uniform in the case of Kal infinitives following inseparable prepositions, e. g. לִבְחוֹב, לִבְחוֹת; בְּגֵל, תְּגֵל, לִנְפֹּל; לְצָבָא Isa. 31:4, לִצְבֹא Num. 4:23, 8:24; בְּוֹבֹר, לִבְדֹת. (6) The suffixes of the second person ךָ, כֶם, כֶן, never receive Daghesh-lene, בְּקִרְבָּם, בִּנְךָ.

These rules are sometimes of importance in etymology; thus, כְּזָבוֹנֶיךָ Ezek. 27:12 must have as its ground form זְבוֹן, not זְבוֹן; and אַרְבָּם Hos. 7:6, רָחֵם Ps. 90:10 cannot be infinitives with suffixes, but must be from the segholates אֹרֶב, רַחַם.

b. The omission of Daghesh-lene in the final letter of תֹסֶף Prov. 30:6, abbreviated from תוֹסִיף or תוֹסֵף, is exceptional. The Daghesh occasionally occurring in initial aspirates after words ending in a vowel and having a conjunctive accent, is best explained not as an exception to the ordinary rules, but as Daghesh forte conjunctive, § 24, e. g. אַרְצָה כְּנַעַן Gen. 11:31 and elsewhere, אַרְצָה גֹּשֶׁן Gen. 46:28, גָּאֹה גָּאָה Ex. 15:1, 21, זֶה גָּאֱלָתִי Ex. 15:13, עָשִׂיתָ בָּם Deut. 16:1 (comp. כֹּה בָּנוּ Gen. 20:9), וְעָשִׂיתָ בָּם Deut. 31:29 (comp. וְאֵרְדָה לִּי Isa. 8:2), וַיְחִי כְּצִלֹּה Josh. 8:24, 10:20, עַלְיָה קָרֶץ Gen. 35:29, נִשְׁבְּעָה בוֹ Isa. 40:7. See also Gen. 39:12, Ex. 14: 4. 17, Isa. 10:9, Job 9:2. Ex. 15:11. 16, Ps. 35:10, Isa. 54:12, Jer. 20:9, Dan. 3:3. 5:11. The old strife as to the Daghesh in the word שְׁתַּיִם *two* is not yet settled. Kimchi explained it as Daghesh-lene upon the supposition that the word was abridged from אֱשְׁתַּיִם; Schultens as Daghesh-forte arising from an assimilated נ, contending that it was for שִׁנְתַּיִם from שְׁנָתַיִם; Nordheimer as an anomalous Daghesh-lene, introduced as a euphonic expedient to prevent the combination of an aspirated ת with a sibilant, such as is obviated in the Hithpael of verbs by a transposition that would here be inadmissible. The puzzle is still further perplexed by the circumstance that it once appears with the preposition מִן without the Daghesh, מִשְּׁתֵּי Judg. 16:28, and again with the same preposition with it, מִשְּׁתֵּיהֶם Jon. 4:11, the Methegh showing the Sh'va to be vocal, as might also be inferred from the fact that Daghesh-forte has been omitted.

Daghesh-Forte.

§ 23. 1. When the same consonant was repeated with a vowel or even the slightest hiatus intervening, so that successive movements of the organs of speech were required in the pronunciation, the Hebrews invariably wrote the letter twice. When, however, there was no interval between the reduplicated consonants, and the only audible result was a more protracted or vehement utterance of the same sound effected by a single effort of the organs, the letter was written but once. This fact the Masoretic punctuators have indicated by placing a point called Daghesh-forte (דָּגֵשׁ חָזָק) in the bosom of a letter so affected, to show that it is to be doubled in the pronunciation; thus, וַיִּמָּל *vayyimmāl*. Daghesh-forte may be found in any letter with the exception of the gutturals א ה ח ע, which on account of their weakness do not admit of reduplication. The letter ר, partaking of this with other peculiarities of the gutturals, receives it only in a very few exceptional cases, e. g. שֵׁרָאשֹׁ, מָרַּת.

2. The aspirates, when doubled, always at the same time lose their aspiration; thus, יִפָּקֵד *yippākēdh*. Daghesh-forte in these letters is readily distinguishable from Daghesh-lene by the consideration that a consonant cannot be pronounced double except after a vowel. A point in one of the aspirates is, therefore, Daghesh-forte if a vowel precedes, otherwise it is Daghesh-lene.

3. Daghesh-forte in ו may be distinguished from Shurek in the same way. Inasmuch as two vowels cannot come together in the same word, if a vowel precedes it is Daghesh-forte, if not it is Shurek.

> *a.* Some Grammarians speak of Daghesh-forte *implicitum* in the gutturals, by which they mean that these letters appear in certain cases to complete a foregoing syllable as well as to begin that in which they properly stand, in spite of the omission of Daghesh, which analogy would require them to receive. As these are included under what have already, § 20. 2. *a*, been explained as intermediate syllables, it is not thought necessary to employ an additional term.
>
> *b.* The Arabs have a sign of reduplication, Teshdid (ّ), which is written above the doubled letter. The Syrians have no written sign for this purpose, and it is disputed whether their letters were ever doubled in pronunciation. According to Asseman Biblioth. Orient. III. 2. p. 379, the Western differed from the Eastern Syrians in this respect, "Occidentales nullibi literas geminant."

§ 24. Different epithets have been applied to Daghesh-forte to describe its various uses or the occasions of its employment. 1. When separate letters, whether originally alike, or made so by assimilation, are by the inflection or formation of words brought into juxtaposition, the Daghesh-forte which represents such a doubling is called compensative; e. g. כָּרֵתִי, formed by appending the syllable תִי to the root כָּרַת; נָתַתִּי composed of the same syllable and the root נָתַן, whose last letter is changed to ת to conform with that which follows; סֹבְּבֵי from סָבַב. 2. When the reduplication is indicative of a particular grammatical form the Daghesh-forte is called characteristic, e. g. in the Piel, Pual, and Hithpael of verbs; as, הִלֵּךְ, הִתְהַלֵּךְ, and certain forms of nouns, as, גִּבּוֹר. 3. When it has arisen from the necessity of converting a previous simple syllable into a mixed one in order to preserve the quantity of a short vowel which it contains, it is Daghesh-forte conservative; e. g. יַסֵּב for יָסַב. 4. When the initial letter of a word is doubled under the influence of the final vowel of the word preceding, it is Daghesh-forte conjunctive; e. g. קוּמוּ צְּאוּ, יְהִיָה־לְּךָ, מַח־זֶּה. 5. When the last letter of an intermediate syllable is doubled in order to make the following hiatus or vocal Sh'va more distinct, it is Daghesh-forte dirimens or separative, because the letter which receives it is thus separated in part from the syllable to which it belongs; e. g. עִנְּבֵי *inn'bhē* for עִנְבֵי *in'bhē*. 6. When the first letter of a final syllable is doubled under the influence of a previous vowel bearing the accent (mostly a pause accent, § 36. 2. *a.*), for the sake of increased fullness and force of pronunciation, it is Daghesh-forte emphatic; e. g. חָדֵלּוּ for חָדְלוּ. In the first three uses named above Daghesh-forte is said to be essential, in the last three it is euphonic.

a. Daghesh-forte conjunctive occurs regularly after the pronoun מַה, e. g. מַה טּוֹב וּמַה־נָּעִים Ps. 133:1, and in a multitude of cases after final Kamets or Seghol in words accented on the penult or followed by Makkeph, § 43, c. g. לְקַחַת־זֹּאת Gen. 2:23, אָכַלְתָּ־שָּׁם Deut. 27:7, וְהָיְתָה לּוֹ Num. 25:13, קָנְאַתְ־צִּי Gen. 30:33; וְחִי־יָחְיֶה Num. 34:6, 7, 9, מְלֵאָה צָּאבּוֹ Ex. 13:1 (where the accent is on the ultimate), מַצְּנָה־לָּךְ Prov. 15:1 (in some editions), more rarely after other vowels, e. g. קוּמוּ צְּאוּ Gen. 19:14, לֹא וַיֹּאמְרוּ 1 Sam. 8:19, once after the liquid ר, e. g. לֹא וַיֹּאמֶר 1 Kin. 11:22. See also § 22. *b.* In a few instances words thus united are written as one, e. g. בַּמֶּה Ex. 4:2 for מַה זֶּה, so כָּלְּכֶם Isa. 3:15, בַּתְּלָאָה Mal. 1:13, בְּבֹאתְאָה

Isa. 27:8, and possibly אֶרְאֶלָּם Isa. 33:7. See Dr. Alexander's Commentary upon this passage.

b. Daghesh-forte separative occurs only in the following examples:

אֶפְרָה Hos. 3:2.	יִקְרַךְ 1 Sam. 28:10.	סֻבְּלוֹ Isa. 9:3, 10:27.
בְּרִקְרוֹתֶיךָ Ps. 45:10.	בְּסִחוֹתַיְכֶנָה (?) Ezek. 13:20.	עִנְּבֵי Deut. 32:32.
חֻגְּבָחִים Am. 5:25.	מַגְּלוֹתֶךָ Isa. 33:1.	כַּנְּתִּי 2 Sam. 23:27, Jer. 29:27.
הַבְצַעֲקָתָהּ Gen. 18:21.	מִשְׁחָרוֹ or מִשְׁחָרוֹ Ps. 89:45.	עֲצַבֵּיכֶם Isa. 58:3.
הִפְּתִיחַ Gen. 37:32.	מַגְּרוֹת Joel 1:17.	עַצְּרֵיכֶם Am. 5:21.
חֻלְּבָן Gen. 17:17.	מַמְּרֹרִים Job 9:18.	קַּבֵּי (?) Cant. 1:8.
הַדְּאִיתֶם 1 Sam. 10:24, 17:25, 2 Kin. 6:32.	מִזָּוְיֶךָ Nah. 3:17.	עִקְּבוֹת Ps. 89:52.
הַמְּרוֹתֶם Job 17:2.	מִקְּדָשׁ Ex. 15:17.	עִקְּבוֹתֶיךָ Ps. 77:20.
הַצְּפִינוֹ Ex. 2:3.	מִקְּרֵה Deut. 23:11.	עַשָּׁבוֹת Prov. 27:25.
הִדְּרִיפָהוּ (?) Judg. 20:43.	נְבֹּאא Job 30:8.	צִמְּתֻתֵנִי Ps. 119; 139.
הִתְּצְבָה 1 Sam. 1:6.	נְצֻּרָה Ps. 141:3.	צִמְּתַתוּנִי Ps. 88:17.
חָלְּקִי Isa. 57:6.	נְצֻּרָה Prov. 4:13.	קַשְּׁחוֹתָם (?) Ps. 37:15. Isa. 5:28.
יִקְּהַת Gen. 49:10.	נָתַקְּנֻהוּ Judg. 20:32.	שֻׁבְּלֵי Zech. 4:12.
לִיקְּהַת Prov. 30:17.	סֻבְּלוֹ Jer. 4:7.	שִׁבְּלוּל Ps. 58:9.

This list is corrected and enlarged from Gesen. Lehrg. pp. 86 ff. Those words which are followed by a note of interrogation (?) are found in some editions but not in others. Daghesh separative may be found after He interrogative in some instances not included in the above list.

c. Daghesh-forte emphatic occurs only in הֲלֻּלוּ Judg. 5:7, 1 Sam. 2:5; וַיְּחֻלּוּ Job 29:21; יָחַתּוּ or יָחְתּוּ Job 21:13; רִצָּתָהּ Isa. 33:12, Jer. 51:58; מֻלָּצָה Ezek. 21:15; נָקוֹשּׁוּ Ezek. 6:9; נָשַּׁחָה Jer. 51:30; נָתְּנָה Ezek. 27:19; קְבֻּלוּ (?) Isa. 19:6; and probably תְּהָתֻּלּוּ Job 13:9 (not in pause).

§ 25. In order to the distinct utterance of a reduplicated consonant, it must be followed as well as preceded by a vowel-sound. Daghesh-forte is consequently never written in a final vowelless letter, with the exception of the two words נָתַתְּ, אַתְּ, both of which end in aspirates whose pronunciation would be changed by the removal of the Daghesh. In every other instance the doubling is neglected, even though the letter be an aspirate, which will for this reason resume its aspiration; e. g. קַל, קַלּוּ; סֹב, סִבִּי; וַיִּחַתְּ abridged from וַיִּחַתְּ; וַיִּצַּף from וַיְצַפֶּה. In a medial letter with Sh'va Daghesh may be written, because the Sh'va being thus rendered vocal the reduplication can be made audible by means of the hiatus which it represents; it is, however, quite as frequently omitted, the Sh'va commonly remaining vocal as if it were inserted, and compound Sh'va being occasionally substituted for simple to indicate this fact, § 16. 3. *b.*; e. g. עֲוֵרִים for עִוְרִים, כְּסָאוֹ for כִּסְאוֹ, particularly after prefixes, as Vav conversive, the article and preposition מִ, so וַיְהִי, הַמְבַקֵּשׁ. It is seldom omitted from a medial aspirate on account of the change in its sound involved: yet even this is done occasionally, e. g. מִבְצִיר Judg. 8 : 2 for מִבְצִיר, תִּחְצוּ Isa. 22 : 10 for תִּתְצוּ, זִכְרוֹן from זִכָּרוֹן. In a few rare instances it is dropped from a letter followed by a vowel, when the laws of syllables will permit and the pronunciation will not be materially affected; e. g. תֵּעָגֵנָה Ruth 1 : 13 for תֵּעָגֶנָּה.

Mappik.

§ 26. Mappĭk (מַפִּיק *bringing out* or *uttering*), is a point in one of the letters א ה ו י, showing that it represents a consonant and not a vowel, or in other words that it does not quiesce in the preceding vowel-sign. It is unnecessary, however, to employ any notation for this purpose in the case of א ו and י, for their quiescence can be readily determined in all cases by the rules already given, § 13. Although it is much more extensively used in manuscripts, therefore, Mappik is in modern editions of the Hebrew Bible only inserted in final ה when it retains its consonantal power; e. g. אַרְצָהּ *artsāh*, אַרְצָה *artsā*, לְקָחָהּ *l'kāhhāh*, לְקָחָה *lak'hhā*. The point four times found in א, וַיָּבִיאוּ Gen. 43 : 26, Ezra 8 : 18, תָּבִיאוּ Lev. 23 : 17, רֹאֻה Job 33 : 21, though called a Daghesh in the Masoretic notes in the margin, is probably to be regarded as Mappik.

Raphe.

§ 27. Rāphe (רָפֶה *weak*), is a small horizontal stroke placed over a letter, and denotes the opposite of Daghesh-lene, Daghesh-forte, or Mappik, as the case may be. As no inconvenience can arise from its omission, it is only occasionally used in modern Bibles, and not with entire uniformity in the different editions. It is chiefly found where a Mappik has been omitted in ה, which according to analogy might be expected to be inserted, e. g. הִוָּסְדָה Ex. 9:18, וּשְׂעָרָה Lev. 13:4, בְּהֶרְאָה Num. 15:28, לָהּ Num. 32:42, מִשִּׁכְמָה Job 31:22 in some copies. In תַּעֲשֶׂה־לְּךָ Ex. 20:4, Deut. 5:8, it is the opposite of Daghesh-forte, and shows that ל may either be doubled agreeably to the point in its bosom or not. In לֹא תִּרְצָח Ex. 20:13, Deut. 5:17, it is the opposite of Daghesh-lene, and shows that the ת may either have its unaspirated sound, as the Daghesh indicates, or may be aspirated. It is often referred to in the marginal Masoretic notes even where it is no longer found in the text, e. g. Judg. 16:16, 28.

Accents

§ 28. The third class of Masoretic additions to the text are those which relate to the words. These are the accents, Makkeph, Methegh, and the K'ri. An accent (טַעַם) is written upon every word with a twofold design, 1st, of marking its tone-syllable, and 2dly, of indicating its relation to other words in the sentence. The great number of the accents has respect entirely to this second function, there being no difference in the quality of the stress laid upon particular syllables, such for example as is marked by the Greek acute, grave, and circumflex, but only that difference in its amount which arises from the unequal emphasis naturally laid upon the different members of a clause or period. The punctuators have attempted not only to indicate the pauses to be made in reading, as is done by the stops in use in other languages, but to represent to the eye the precise position held by each word in the structure of the sentence, and the various grades of attraction or repulsion arising from the relations whether co-ordinate or subordinate which subsist among them. Every sentence is fancifully regarded as a territory, which, partitioned into its several clauses, forms empires, kingdoms, and principalities, ruled by their respective sovereigns, each of whom has his own train of inferiors and dependants. The accents are accordingly divided into Disjunctives or Rulers (מְלָכִים), and Conjunctives or Servants (עֲבָדִים). The former indicate that the word upon which they are placed is more or less separated from those that follow; they mark thus the end of a clause or of the section of a clause over which they exert control. The latter indicate that the word over or under which they are written is connected with what follows and belongs to the clause or section ruled by the next succeeding Disjunctive.

a. The stress of voice denoted by the accent must not be confounded with quantity. An accented syllable may nevertheless be short, the energy with which it is pronounced not necessarily affecting its length.

b. The Jews made use of the accents as musical notes in the cantillation of the synagogue, whence they are also called נְגִינוֹת. In the judgment of some this is a part, and perhaps a leading part, of their original design. Their great variety, the frequent occurrence of accents of opposite powers upon the same word, and the distinct system of poetical accents, favor this opinion. Such as are curious to know the details may find the mode of their employment for this purpose explained at length in Bartoloccii Bibliotheca Magna Rabbinica, vol. iv. pp. 427–444.

§ 29. The Disjunctive accents may be divided into four classes of various rank or power, as follows, viz:

Class I. *Emperors.*

* 1. Sillûk   (׀)   סִלּוּק׃

* 2. Athnahh   (֑)   אֶתְנָח

Class II. *Kings.*

3.	S'gholta	(ˆ)	סְגֹלְתָּא	*postp.*
4.	Zakēph Katon	(׃)	זָקֵף קָטֹון	
5.	Zakēph Gadhol	(״)	זָקֵף גָּדֹול	
*6.	Tiphhha	(ˌ)	טִפְחָא	

Class III. *Lukes.*

*7.	R'bhī‘	(˙)	רְבִיעַ	
*8.	Shalsheleth	(ˈ)	שַׁלְשֶׁלֶת	
*9.	Zarka	(˜)	זַרְקָא	*postp.*
10.	Pashta	(`)	פַּשְׁטָא	*postp.*
11.	Y'thībh	(ˏ)	יְתִיב	*prep.*
12.	T'bhīr	(ˌ)	תְּבִיר	

Class IV. *Counts.*

*13.	Pazēr	(ʳ)	פָּזֵר	
14.	Karnē Pharā	(ᵗᵖ)	קַרְנֵי פָרָה	
15.	T'līsha Gh'dhola	(ʳ)	תְּלִישָׁא גְדֹולָה	*prep.*
16.	Geresh	(´)	גֶּרֶשׁ	
17.	G'rashayim	(˝)	גְּרָשַׁיִם	
*18.	P'sīk	(׀)	פָּסִיק׀	

The Conjunctive accents, or *Servants*, are the following, viz.:

*19.	Merka	(ˌ)	מֵרְכָא	
*20.	Munahh	(ˌ)	מוּנַח	
21.	Merka Kh'phula	(ˌˌ)	מֵרְכָא כְפוּלָה	
*22.	Mahpakh	(ˏ)	מַהְפַּךְ	
23.	Darga	(ˌ)	דַּרְגָּא	
*24.	Kudhma	(´)	קַדְמָא	
*25.	Yerahh ben Yōmō	(ᵥ)	יָרַח בֶּן־יֹומֹו	
26.	T'līsha K'tanna	(ˆ)	תְּלִישָׁא קְטַנָּה	*postp.*

a. Merka Kh'phula has sometimes been reckoned among the Disjunctives, as by Gesenius in his Lehrgebäude; but the absence of Dagheshlene in the word following that on which it stands in Ex. 5:15, Ezek. 14:4, proves that it is a Conjunctive.

b. According to their most probable significations, the names of the accents appear to be in part borrowed from their forms and in part from their uses. Thus the Disjunctives: Silluk, *end;* Athnahh, *rest;* Segholta, *bunch of grapes;* Zakeph, small and great, *causing suspension;* Tiphhha, *palm of the hand;* R'bhi", *square or reposing;* Shalsheleth, *chain;* Zarka, *dispersion;* Pashta, *expansion or letting down* (the voice); Y'thibh, *sitting still;* T'bhir, *interruption;* Pazer, *separator;* Karne Phara, *a heifer's horns;* T'lisha, great and small, *shield;* Geresh, *expulsion;* G'rashayim, *double Geresh;* P'sik, *cut off.* Conjunctives: Merka, *prolonging;* Munahh, (a trumpet) *at rest,* i. e., in its proper position; Merka Kh'phula, *double Merka;* Mahpakh, (a trumpet) *inverted;* Darga, *progress;* Kadhma, *beginning;* Yerahh ben-Yomo, *moon a day old.*

Other names are given to some of these accents, particularly where they occur in certain situations or combinations; thus Tiphhha is also called Tarhha (טַרְחָא), Munahh with P'sik is called L'gharmēh (לְגַרְמֵהּ), etc.

c. The classification of the Disjunctives, according to their respective powers and the laws of their consecution, has been the work of Christian writers, from whom all accurate investigations of the accentual system have proceeded. In fact, this whole subject is treated by the Jewish grammarians in the crudest and most perplexed manner. Buxtorf says, in his Thesaurus Grammaticus, p. 45: Accentuum ratio hactenus nec a quoquam nostrorum nec ab ipsis etiam Hebraeis sufficienter explicata est. The division exhibited above is the one now commonly adopted. The current names, Imperatores, Reges, Duces, Comites, are those used by Wasmuth in his Institutio Accent. Heb. 1664. Others have divided them differently. The learned Pfeiffer, author of the Dubiâ Vexata, distinguishes one Emperor, one Archduke, four Dukes, seven Counts, and five Barons. Boston, the well-known author of the Fourfold State, in an elaborate Latin treatise upon this subject left by him in manuscript and published shortly after his death, distributes them into three classes of superior and one of inferior rank. Mention is made, in a commendatory preface by Mill, the distinguished critic of the New Testament, of another manuscript in English, in which Boston applied his views practically in a twofold translation of the first twenty-three chapters of Genesis, with copious notes, both philological and theological. This, it is believed, has never been published. A curious little book upon the Canon by Ferdinand Parkhurst, London, 1660, makes six Regal and ten Principial Disjunctives. Y'thibh and P'sik being omitted altogether.

§ 30. 1. Fourteen of the accents are written over, and eleven under, the words to which they are attached. P'sik, whose only use is to modify the power of other accents, is written after the word to which it belongs, and in the same line with it. The place of the accents is either over or under the letter preceding the tone-vowel, with the exception of the prepositives Y'thibh and T'lisha Gh'dhola, which always accompany the initial letter of the word, and the postpositives S'gholta, Zarka, Pashta, and T'lisha K'tanna, which stand upon the final letter. Y'thibh is only used when the first is the tone-syllable. Pashta is repeated if the word on which it stands is accented on the penult, e. g. תֹּהוּ Gen. 1:2, or ends with two vowelless letters, e. g. וַיִּשְׁתְּ Ruth 3:7, or if the last letter has Pattahh furtive, e. g. יֹדֵעַ Gen. 33:13, and in some manuscripts and editions there is a like repetition of S'gholta and Zarka. When a word bears the other prepositive or postpositives, there is nothing to mark its tone-syllable unless this may chance to be the one upon which the nature of the accent in question requires it to be placed.

2. Silluk has the same form as Methegh, § 44; but the former invariably stands on the tone-syllable of the last word in the verse, while Methegh is never written under a tone-syllable. Pashta is likewise distinguished from Kadhma only by its position upon the last letter of the word, and after the superscribed vowel, if there be one, e. g. אֲשֶׁר Gen. 1:7, מַלְאֲכֵי Gen. 24:7, while Kadhma is placed upon the letter preceding the tone-vowel, e. g. אֲשֶׁר Gen. 2:19: where this chances to be a final letter the laws of consecution only can decide; thus, in זַרְעֲךָ Gen. 26:4, צֵאתְךָ Deut. 16:3, the accent is Pashta, but in וּלְזַרְעֲךָ Gen. 17:8, צֵאתְךָ 1 Sam. 29:6, it is Kadhma. Y'thibh is distinguished from Mahpakh by being written under the first letter of the word and taking precedence of its vowel if this be subscribed, e. g. עֵשֶׂב Gen. 1:11, פִּי Gen. 31:6, Deut. 10:17; Mahpakh belongs under the consonant which precedes the tone-vowel, and after its vowel-sign if this be subscribed, e. g. הַנָּהָר Gen. 2:14, בִּי Gen. 32:33, Deut. 4:7. When the initial syllable bears the tone and there is no subscribed vowel, the laws of consecution must decide; thus, in הִיא the accent is Y'thibh in Gen.

3:15, 44:17; Deut. 10:17; but Mahpakh in Josh. 17:1.

§ 31. The accents already explained are called the prosaic accents, and are found in all the books of the Old Testament with the exception of the Psalms (תְּהִלִּים), Proverbs (מִשְׁלֵי), and the poetic portion of Job (אִיּוֹב), whose initials form the technical word אֱמֶת. Here a different system of accentuation prevails. Thirteen of the prosaic accents, one-half of the whole number, nowhere occur in the books just named, viz.: S'gholta, Zakeph-Katon, and Zakeph-Gadhol of the Kings, Pashta, Y'thibh, and T'bhir of the Dukes, Karne Phara, T'lisha Gh'dhola, Geresh, and G'rashayim, of the Counts, Merka Kh'phula, Darga, and T'lisha K'tanna of the Conjunctives. Such as are common to both systems are in the previous table distinguished by an asterisk. The powers of some of these, however, are altered, so that a new arrangement of them is necessary; and they are supplemented by additional signs formed by combining the prosaic accents or assigning them unusual positions. The scale of the poetical or metrical accents thus constituted is as follows, viz.:

DISJUNCTIVE ACCENTS.

Class I.

1.	Silluk	(׃)	הַצָּבוּר׃
2.	Athnahh	(֑)	הַצָּבוּר
3.	Merka-Mahpakh	(֖)	הַצָּבוּר

Class II.

4.	R'bhi‛	(֗)	הַצָּבוּר	
5.	Pazer	(֡)	הַצָּבוּר	
6.	R'bhi‛ Geresh	(֝)	הַצָּבוּר	
7.	Tiphhha initial	(֖)	הַצָּבוּר	*prep.*
8.	Zarka	(֮)	הַצָּבוּר	*postp.*
9.	P'sik	(׀)	הַצָּבוּר׀	*postp.*

CONJUNCTIVE ACCENTS.

10.	Merka	(ֽ)	חַפְּכֽוֹר
11.	Merka-Zarka	(ֽ֮)	חַפְּכֽוֹר
12.	Mahpakh	(֤)	חַפְּכ֤וֹר
13.	Mahpakh-Zarka	(֤֮)	חַפְּכ֤וֹר
14.	Munahh	(֣)	חַפְּכ֣וֹר
15.	Munahh superior	(֬)	חַפְּכ֬וֹר
16.	Yerahh ben Yomo	(֪)	חַפְּכ֪וֹר
17.	Kadhma	(֙)	חַפְּכ֙וֹר
18.	Tiphhha	(֖)	חַפְּכ֖וֹר
19.	Shalsheleth	(֓)	חַפְּכ֓וֹר

a. It will be perceived that there are fewer Disjunctives but more Conjunctives than are exhibited by the prosaic accents. Merka-Mahpakh answers substantially to S'gholta; R'hibi‘-Geresh to Tiphhha before Silluk, and Tiphhha initial to Tiphhha before Athnahh. Tiphhha and Shalsheleth are transferred from the list of Disjunctives to that of the Conjunctives, whence it comes to pass that if a word bearing either of these accents terminates in a vowel, Daghesh-lene will not be inserted in a following initial aspirate, e. g. שֵׁ֣שָׁה בְּבֶ֫כֶם Ps. 31:10, מְבִ֣יא פְתָחִים Prov. 8:3, יִתְפְּשׂוּ בִמְזִמּוֹת Ps. 10:2.

b. P'sik, in the poetic as in the prosaic accents, is never used alone but always in conjunction with another accent. It serves to strengthen Disjunctives and to reduce the power of Conjunctives without disturbing the order of their consecution. It is thus used with Merka-Mahpakh Ps. 5:13, Pazer Ps. 10:14, Tiphhha initial Ps. 31:4, Mahpakh Ps. 5:9, Munahh Prov. 1:22, Merka Ps. 10:13, Kadhma Ps 10:5, Shalsheleth Ps. 7:6.

Position of the Accent

§ 32. The accent in Hebrew may fall either upon the ultimate or the penultimate syllable, but never at a greater remove from the end of the word. In the former case words are technically termed Milra (מִלְרַע *from below*), and in the latter Milêl (מִלְעֵיל *from above*).

1. The position of the accent may be considered in relation either to the syllabic or to the etymological structure of a word, that is to say, as affected by the nature of its syllables on the one hand or of the elements of which it is composed as a significant part of speech on the other. It is so far determined by the syllabic structure of words, that a long mixed syllable or a short simple syllable, whether in the ultimate or the penultimate, must receive the accent, § 18. 2. thus: רָב, שָׁלָה, וַתֶּעֱמֹדְנָה, יִצְחָק.

2. Considered in reference to their etymological structure, words exist in two conditions, (1.) their primary uninflected state, by which their essential and proper meaning is conveyed; (2.) with added affixes and prefixes, by which that meaning is variously modified. In their nude or primary state all words, whether primitives or derivatives, are accented upon the ultimate, and so continue to whatever flexion, involving no terminational appendages, they may be subjected. Thus, פָּקַד, פֹּקֵד, פֻּקַּד, פָּקֹד, יִפְקֹד, הִתְפַּקֵּד; זִכָּרוֹן, בְּנֵעֲלֵי; יוֹמָם; אַרְגְּמָן; מִדְבָּר, מִדְבָּר; זִכְרוֹן.

3. The only exception is a class of words called Segholates, in which the last vowel does not belong originally or essentially to the form, but is introduced for the sake of softening the pronunciation, § 61. 2; these are accented on the penultimate, as לֶגֶל, רֶגֶל, כֹּהֶנֶת, תֹּהוּ, בַּיִת, נֶצַח, סֵפֶר, מֶלֶךְ, יִשְׁתַּחוּ.

a. נֶעֱמְדָה Is. 50:8 is said to be the only instance of a word accented on the antepenult. The proper tone-syllable of this word is the ultimate, but upon the recession of the accent by § 35, the vowel next preceding, which has arisen from Sh'va and is unessential to the form, cannot receive it, so that it necessarily falls upon the one still further back.

§ 33. The additions which words may receive at the beginning or end affect the accent in proportion to the respective weight accorded to them. Additions to the end of words are of two sorts, which may be distinguished as affixes and suffixes. Affixes are so welded to the word or merged in it

§ 33   POSITION OF THE ACCENT.   43

that in the popular consciousness they have become an integral part of it, and their independent existence or separate origin is no longer thought of; such are the personal inflections of verbs and the terminations indicating gender and number in nouns and adjectives. Suffixes are not so intimately blended with the word to which they are attached as to have lost their individual identity and independent character, and consequently are of greater weight as respects the accent; such are the fragmentary pronouns appended to verbs, nouns, and prepositions.

1. If the appendage consists of a vowel (as ָה, ֶה, וּ, ִי, ְי, ְ־), or begins with one (as ה ָ, ִי ָ, ִיו ָ, ִים ָ, וֹת ָ, ָךְ, ֶ־, ָם, ָן, ֶ־ים, ֶ־ךְ), and can consequently only be pronounced by the aid of the final consonant of the word to which it is attached, it will attract the accent to itself or to its initial vowel from a noun, adjective, participle, or preposition, as דְּבָרִי, קְדָשִׁי, קְדָשִׁים; from דָּבָר דְּבָרִי, דְּבָרֶיךָ, דְּבָרָיו, דְּבָרִים, דְּבָרוֹ, from קֹדֶשׁ. Such an appendage to a verb, if a suffix, will so far accord with the rule just given as to carry the accent forward one syllable; but the accent will remain in its original position if it be an affix, unless it is either dissyllabic or causes the rejection of the vowel previously accented; הֶחֱרִים with a suffix הֶחֱרִימָם, but with an affix הֶחֱרִימוּ; עָבַד with a suffix עֲבָדוֹ, but with an affix עָבְדוּ, עָבְדִי; קָם, קָמָה, קָמוּ; קַל, אֲהֵבְתֶךָ, אַהֲבָה, אָהֵב; קָלִּיתִי, קַלּוּ, קַלָּה. It is to be observed, however, that a paragogic ָה or ֶה, § 61. 6, attached to nouns, pronouns, and adverbs, and occasionally a paragogic ִי does not disturb the position of the accent, e. g. אֶרֶץ, רַבָּתִי, שָׂפָה, אֵלֶּה, הֵמָּה; so נֹבְהָ, זֹב אַרְצָה Lam. 1:1, but מְלֵאֲתִי Isa. 1:21; neither does the feminine ending ֶת, which is a Segholate formation, e. g. מְדַבֶּרֶת, מְדַבֵּר.

a. Paragogic ָה receives the secondary accent Methegh in פַּדֶּנָה אֲרָם Gen. 28: 2, 5, 6, 7.

2. The appending of a simple syllable, such as the

suffixes עָךְ, נוּ, חוּ, הָ, מוֹ, or the verbal affixes תָּ, תִּי, נִי, עָה,. will not alter the position of the accent provided it originally stood upon the ultimate; if, however, its original place was the penult, or if the syllable in question be attached to the word by a union vowel, the accent must be carried forward one syllable to prevent its standing on the antepenult, which is never admissible: מָאַסְתָּ, מָאַס; כְּפָתְנִי, כְּפָתוּ, כְּפָהוּ, כְּפָה; מְאַסְתֶּנוּ; קָל, קָלוֹת, קָלִיתִי. Suffixes appended to a word ending with a consonant mostly require a connecting vowel, and consequently shift the position of the accent. Affixes, by reason of the less weight accorded to them, commonly do not. The suffix ךְ follows the general rule when preceded by a union vowel, but draws the accent upon itself when it is not, e. g. אָבִיךְ, יָדְךָ, יָדַךְ, לָךְ. A consonantal appendage to a long unaccented vowel, inasmuch as it converts the ultimate into a mixed syllable, necessarily draws the accent upon it from the penult, § 32. 1, e. g. יְמוּתִין, יְמוֹתִין; מְאַסְתֶּם, מְאַסְתִּיו, מָאַסְתִּי.

3. A mixed syllable, whether an affix as הֶם, תֶּן, or suffix as כֶּם, כֶּן, הֶם, הֶן, will attract the accent to itself, הֲלַכְתֶּם from הָלַךְ; מַלְכֵיהֶם, מַלְכְּכֶם, from מֶלֶךְ; הֲרֵמֹתֶם from הֵרִים. In the unusual form כְּפָהֶם 2 Sam. 23 : 6, the accent stands upon the union vowel.

4. The only prefixes which exercise any influence upon the position of the accent, are the Vav conversive of the future, which draws back the accent from a mixed ultimate to a simple penult, וַיֵּשֶׁב, וַיֹּאמֶר, יֹאמַר; and the Vav conversive of the preterite, which throws it forward from the penult to a simple ultimate, וְיָשַׁבְתָּ, יָשַׁבְתְּ, וְאָמַרְתָּ, אָמַרְתְּ, וַהֲשִׁיבוֹתִי.

<small>*a.* Some languages invariably accent the same part of the word; thus, Bohemian and Lettish the initial syllable, Polish and Lazian, one of the Caucasian tongues, the penult of all polysyllables. Others, in which more freedom is allowed, have no respect to the etymological structure of words, but are guided entirely by the character of their syllables. Thus, in Arabic and Latin words are accented according to the quantity of the penult; the accent is given to the penult if it is long, to the antepenult</small>

if the penult is short. In others still the etymological principle is the prevailing one, and this often has a wider scope than in Hebrew. Thus, in Greek the accent has the range of the last three syllables. In Sanscrit it may stand upon any syllable whatever even of the longest words. In English it is almost equally free, e. g. péremptorily, inconsiderátion, its removal from its primary position upon the radical portion of the word being conditioned by the respective weight of the formative syllables appended, e. g. pérson, pérsonate, pérsonally, persónify, personálity, personificátion.

§ 34. The location of the accent being thus influenced by the etymological structure of words, it may serve to distinguish words of like appearance but different formation. Thus, מֵתָה Gen. 30:1, בָּאָה Gen. 29:6, are participles, but מֵ֫תָה Gen. 35:18, בָּ֫אָה Gen. 29:9, are preterites, the feminine affix receiving the accent in one case but not in the other, § 33. 1. So בָּנוּ *they built* from בָּנָה, but בָּ֫נוּ *in us;* שָׁבוּ *they carried captive* from שָׁבָה, but שָׁ֫בוּ *they returned* from שׁוּב; אָחַז *he has seized,* but אֶחֱזֶ֫ה Job 23:9 *I shall see* from חָזָה; יֵרַע *it shall be evil* from רָעַע, יִרְעֶה *he shall feed* from רָעָה; מָרָה *he was rebellious,* מָ֫רָה *it was bitter* from מַר; קוּמִי *arise thou* (fem.), קוּמִ֫י *my rising up.*

§ 35. The position of the accent may be shifted from the following causes, viz.:

1. A Conjunctive is frequently removed from the ultimate to the penult if a Disjunctive immediately follows, whether upon a monosyllable or a dissyllable accented on the penult, in order to prevent the unpleasant concurrence of two accented syllables in closely connected words, e. g. קָ֫רָא לַיְלָה Gen. 1:5, בָּ֫נָה עִיר Gen. 4:17, אָ֫זְלַת יָד Deut. 32:36, וְרֹ֫אבְדוּ דָרֶךְ Ps. 2:12, לָ֫קַחַת לָךְ Isa. 36:8. In a few exceptional cases the secondary accent Methegh remains to mark the original tone-syllable, after the principal accent has been thrown back, לְבָ֫עֵר קָ֫יִן Num. 24:22, נָ֫בֵל צִיץ Isa. 40:7, הֲשָׁ֫מַע עָם Deut. 4:33.

2. The special emphasis given to the last word of a clause or section, and represented by what are called the

pause accents, § 36, 2, *a*, is sometimes rendered more distinct by a change of the accented syllable from the ultimate to the penult, e. g. כָּלוּ, כָּלוּ ; עָתָה, כַּתָּה ; אֵתָה, אַתָּה ; אָנֹכִי, אָנֹכִי ; or from the penult to the ultimate, particularly in the case of forms with Vav conversive of the future וַיֵּלֶךְ, וַיֵּלֶךְ ; so וַיֹּאמֶר, וַיָּקָם, וַיִּגְמֹל. The accent is in a few instances attracted to a short final syllable ending in a weak letter, which either loses its sound entirely, converting the syllable into a simple one, or requires considerable effort and energy of voice to make it distinctly heard, e. g. יֵרֶא Gen. 41 : 33 for יִרְאֶה; so תֵּרֶא Zech. 9 : 5, Mic. 7 : 10, חָשַׁע Ps. 39 : 14 for הֹשַׁע.

Consecution of Accents in Prose.

§ 36. 1. The second use of the accents is to point out the relation of words to one another. The Disjunctives indicate a greater or less separation between the word on which they stand and the following one; the Conjunctives indicate a connection. The greatest separation of all is effected by Silluk, which is written under the last word of every verse, and is followed invariably by two dots vertically placed (:), called Sōph Pāsūk (סוֹף פָּסוּק *end of the verse*). The next in power are Athnahh and S'gholta. When a verse was to be divided into two clauses, Athnahh was placed under the last word of the first clause, Silluk maintaining its position at the end of the verse. If it was to be divided into three clauses, which is the greatest number that any verse can have, the last word of the first clause receives S'gholta, the last word of the second Athnahh, and the last of all Silluk. Verses of one clause range from Gen. 26 : 6, containing three words, to such as Jer. 13 : 13 and 1 Chron. 28 : 1, containing more than twenty: the most common division is into two clauses, e. g. Gen. 1 : 1 אֱלֹהִים ... הָאָרֶץ; three clauses are much less frequent, Gen. 1 : 7 ; כֵּן . לָרָקִיעַ ... הָרָקִיעַ, 23 : 16, 24 : 30, 26 : 28.

a. In Job 1 : 8 S'gholta occurs in a verse of two clauses without Athnahh, probably because the accentuation is conformed to that of Job 2 : 3.

2. Each of these clauses is capable of subdivision to whatever extent its length or character may seem to demand by the Disjunctives Zakeph Katon, Zakeph Gadhol, R'bhi^a, Pazer, and T'lisha Gh'dhola, according to the number of sections to be made and the various degrees of their completeness. Thus, in Josh. 1 : 8 the clause of Athnahh is divided into five sections, בִּי . לַעֲשׂוֹת . . לַיְלָה . . . מִפִּיךָ . . . יָמוּשׁ, in 2 Kin. 1 : 6 into six, אֵלָיו . . יְהוָֹה . . בְּיִשְׂרָאֵל . שֹׁלֵחַ לִדְרֹשׁ . . . קְרוֹן. The choice of the accent to govern a particular section depends not only upon its power, but likewise upon its rank, the more exalted officer standing in ordinary cases nearer the sovereign. Accordingly toward the beginning of a clause an inferior Disjunctive will be used, even though the separation is such as would require an accent of much higher power to indicate it in a more advanced portion of the same clause. These accents, moreover, have not a fixed value like the stops in other languages; their power is not absolute but relative, and varies endlessly with the circumstances of the case. Athnahh in Gen. 1 : 1 marks the greatest division in the verse, but that is not sufficient to require a comma. In the next verse Zakeph Katon is equal to a semicolon in the first clause and less than a comma in the second. In Gen. 27 : 16 the separation indicated by R'bhi^a is wholly rhythmical.

a. Those accents which, as above described, mark the limits of clauses and sections, are denominated pause accents.

§ 37. In the sections thus created the accents are disposed relatively to the Disjunctive which marks its close. Each ruler has his servant and subordinate officer, whose

48 ORTHOGRAPHY. § 37

function it is to wait upon him. In other words, each Disjunctive is regularly preceded by a particular Conjunctive and inferior Disjunctive; and the train of accents in each section is formed by arranging the Disjunctives in their fixed order of succession with or without their regular Conjunctives until all its words are supplied. The trains proper to the different sections are shown in the following table:

	Disjunctives. Class I.	Conjunctives.	Disjunctives. Class II.	Conjunctives.	Disjunctives. Class III.	Conjunctives.	Disjunctives. Class IV.	Conjunctives.
Primary Sections.								
Secondary Sections.								
Unusual Sections.								

§ 38. CONSECUTION OF ACCENTS IN PROSE.

a. Accents of like forms are readily distinguishable in the table by the column in which they stand. Where perspicuity requires it the distinction will hereafter be made by appending their initial letters, thus: Kadhma ' ᵏ Pashta ' ᵖ, Mahpakh ' ᵐ, Y'thibh ' ʸ.

§ 38. *Explanation of the Table.*—The trains preceding the three principal accents are exhibited in the horizontal lines of the uppermost division; those of the ordinary dependent sections in the middle division, and those of rare occurrence at the bottom.

1. *Train of Silluk.*—If Silluk be immediately preceded by a Conjunctive, it will be Merka; if a Disjunctive precede it in the same section, with or without an intervening Merka, it will be Tiphhha, Gen. 1 : 1. If there be a Conjunctive before Tiphhha, it will be Merka, Gen. 1 : 1; if two Conjunctives, which occurs but fourteen times, they will be Merka Kh'phula and Darga, Gen. 27 : 25, Lev. 10 : 1, 2 Chron. 20 : 30. The next Disjunctive before Tiphhha, in the same section, will be T'bhir, Gen. 1 : 4. If T'bhir be preceded by one Conjunctive, it will be Darga, Gen. 1 : 12, or Merka, Gen. 1 : 26; if by two, the second will be Kadhma, 1 Sam. 15 : 33, or Munahh, Gen. 2 : 4; and if by three, the third will be T'lisha K'tanna, Gen. 2 : 19. The next Disjunctive before T'bhir, in the same section, will be Geresh, Gen. 26 : 11, 27 : 4, or G'rashayim, Ex. 23 : 4. If Geresh be preceded by one Conjunctive, it will be Kadhma, Gen. 24 : 7, or Munahh, Isa. 60 : 17; if by a second, it will be T'lisha K'tanna, Gen. 2 : 5, or Munahh with P'sik, Gen. 28 : 9; if by a third, it will be Munahh, 1 Sam. 14 : 34; if by a fourth, it will also be Munahh, Deut. 1 : 19.

a. The parentheses of the table contain alternate accents. Thus, Merka is substituted for Darga and for Mahpakh (before Pashta in the clause of Zakeph Katon) if no more than one vowel intervenes between the Conjunctive and the king which it precedes, e. g. Gen. 1 : 22, Gen. 1 : 24, 26; Gen. 5 : 17, Deut. 1 : 2, 35. Munahh is also regularly substituted for Kadhma, whenever the accent stands on the initial letter of the word, Gen. 25 : 8, Gen. 19 : 35; 1 Kin. 19 : 7, Deut. 1 : 28; Gen. 19 : 12.

Eccl. 5:7. G'rashayim takes the place of Geresh provided the accent is on the ultimate and it is not preceded by Kadhma either on the same or the previous word, Ex. 16:23, 36:3. When two accents are included in a parenthesis the meaning is that if an additional accent is required, these two will take the place of the one before the parenthesis. P'sik has no separate place in the consecution, but is joined with the other accents to modify their power. It is constantly associated with the Disjunctive Shalsheleth to add to its strength, and occasionally with the different Conjunctives to reduce their strength, but without disturbing the order of their consecution, e. g. with Merka Ex. 16:5, Munahh Gen. 46:2, Mahpakh Ex. 30:34, Kadhma Lev. 11:32, Darga Gen. 42:13, T'lisha K'tanna 1 Sam. 12:3.

2. *Train of Athnahh.*—If Athnahh be preceded by a Conjunctive, it will be Munahh, Gen. 1:1; if by a Disjunctive in its own section, it will be Tiphhha, Gen. 1:1. The accents which precede Tiphhha have already been mentioned in explaining the train of Silluk.

3. *Train of S'gholta.*—The first Conjunctive before S'gholta will be Munahh, Gen. 3:3; if there be two, the second will be Munahh, Lev. 8:31, or Merka, Gen. 3:14. The first Disjunctive in its section will be Zarka, Gen. 1:28; and if this be preceded by one Conjunctive, it will be Munahh, Gen. 1:7, or Merka, 1 Chron. 5:18; if by two, the second will be Kadhma, Gen. 30:16, 31:32; if by three, the second will be Munahh and the third Kadhma, Lev. 4:35. The next Disjunctive before Zarka will be Geresh, Gen. 24:7, or G'rashayim, Ex. 39:3. The accents preceding these have been explained in 1.

4. *Train of Zakeph Katon.*—The first Conjunctive before Zakeph Katon will be Munahh, Gen. 1:2; the second likewise Munahh, Gen. 27:45. The first Disjunctive will be Pashta, Gen. 1:2; or, if the proper place of the accent be the first letter of the word, Y'thibh, Gen. 1:11, 2:11. The first Conjunctive before Pashta will be Mahpakh, Gen. 1:9, or Merka, Gen. 1:2; the second, Kadhma, Gen. 39:19, or Munahh, Gen. 1:12; the third will be T'lisha K'tanna, Ezr. 3:11. The Disjunctive before Pashta will be

Geresh, Gen. 1 : 24, or G'rashayim, Gen. 1 : 11 ; the further consecution is explained in 1.

a. In some instances Pashta is found not in the train of Zakeph Katon, but seeming to govern an independent section, e. g. Ex. 29 : 20, Deut. 9 : 6, Josh. 10 : 11, 2 Sam. 14 : 7, 2 Chron. 18 : 23.

5. Zakeph Gadhol is mostly used instead of Zakeph Katon when no other accent precedes it in its own section, whether upon the same word or one before it : אַךְ בָּשָׂר Gen. 9 : 4 (in some editions), in which it is preceded by Munahh, is exceptional.

6. *Train of R'bhi^a.*—The first Conjunctive before R'bhi^a will be Munahh, Gen. 1 : 9 ; the second, Munahh commonly with P'sik, Gen. 2 : 5, or Darga, Gen. 6 : 15 ; the third, Munahh with P'sik, Gen. 7 : 23, 31 : 29, or Merka, Ex. 14 : 10. The Disjunctive before R'bhi^a will be Geresh, Ex. 16 : 3, or G'rashayim, Deut. 1 : 11, which are preceded as in 1.

7. *Train of Pazer.*—Pazer may be preceded by one Munahh, 1 Sam. 14 : 34, by two, Ezek. 9 : 2, by three, 1 Sam. 14 : 34, or by four, Isa. 66 : 20.

8. *Train of T"lisha Gh'dhola.*—T'lisha Gh'dhola is the weakest of the Disjunctives which are ever set to rule independent sections. Its weakness is in fact such, that it is sometimes drawn into the section of a stronger Disjunctive ; thus, in Gen. 1 : 12, Lev. 4 : 7, 1 Sam. 17 : 51, Isa. 9 : 5, Neh. 5 : 18, it takes the place of T'lisha K'tanna among the antecedents of Pashta, standing between it and Geresh or G'rashayim ; in Gen. 13 : 1, 21 : 14, Deut. 26 : 12, it stands similarly between T'bhir and Geresh or G'rashayim. And in many cases, perhaps in most, when it rules a section of its own, this is a mere subsection, not so much a division of one of the principal clauses as a fragment broken off from one of the larger sections at a point where T'lisha K'tanna would have stood had the connection been sufficiently close

to require a Conjunctive, e. g. Gen. 19 : 2, 1 Kin. 20 : 28. That this is not always so appears, however, from examples like 2 Sam. 14 : 32, Gen. 7 : 7, Isa. 66 : 19, Jer. 39 : 5, and particularly Gen. 31 : 52, where וְאָם־אַתָּה corresponds to the preceding אִם־אָ֠נִי. T'lisha Gh'dhola may be preceded by one Munahh, Gen. 27 : 46, by two, Josh. 2 : 1, by three, or by four, 1 Kin. 2 : 5.

9. Shalsheleth occurs but seven times, viz., Gen. 19:16, 24 : 12, 39 : 8, Lev. 8 : 23, Isa. 13 : 8, Am. 1 : 2, Ezr. 5:12, and in every instance stands upon the initial word of the verse, and is accompanied by P'sik. It has consequently no antecedents.

10. Karne Phara is only used sixteen times. Its section never contains less than three words: its immediate predecessor is always Yerahh ben Yomo, to which may be added one Munahh, Num. 35 : 5, Neh. 5 : 13, 13 : 5, 2 Chron. 24 : 5; two, 2 Kin. 10 : 5, Jer. 38 : 25, Est. 7 : 9, Neh. 1 : 6, 2 Chron. 35 : 7; three, Josh. 19 : 51, 2 Sam. 4 : 2, Jer. 13 : 13; four, 1 Chron. 28 : 1; or five, Ezek. 48:21.

§ 39. 1. The complete trains of the several accents contain one Disjunctive from each of the inferior orders, disposed in due succession of rank, with one Conjunctive immediately preceding the first class of Disjunctives, two Conjunctives preceding the second class, three the third class, four or more the fourth class. These trains are adapted to sections of different length and character by omitting such of the Conjunctives, and more rarely by repeating such of the Disjunctives, as the mutual relations of the words may seem to require, and breaking off the series as soon as every word in the section is supplied. Thus, while the general order of consecution is fixed and invariable, there is the utmost liberty and variety in particular cases.

a. In a very few instances the Conjunctives go beyond the number here assigned. Thus, Athnahh is preceded by two Munahhs in Ex. 3 : 4,

§ 39   CONSECUTION OF ACCENTS IN PROSE.   53

and, according to some editions, in Isa. 48:11. T'bhir is preceded by four Conjunctives, Josh. 10:11, 2 Chron. 22:11, Isa. 66:20; Pashta by four, Ex. 5:8, 2 Kin. 5:1, and even by five, Josh. 19:51.

2. If a section consists of but a single word, this will receive the appropriate Disjunctive, the entire antecedent series of the table being then omitted as unnecessary; thus, Silluk וַיָּמֹת: Gen. 5:5; Athnahh וַיֹּאמֶר Gen. 24:34; Zakeph Katon וּכְנַּעַה Isa. 1:30; R'bhi*a* וְהַמַּיִם Gen. 7:19; Pazer וַיֹּאמֶר Gen. 22:2; T'lisha Gh'dhola רַק Gen. 19:8. This, as has been already said, is the regular length of the sections of Zakeph Gadhol and Shalsheleth; but those of S'gholta are never composed of less than two words, and those of Karne Phara never of less than three.

3. In sections of greater length there is a disposition towards a regular alternation of Disjunctives and Conjunctives upon successive words, e. g. Gen. 23:11 : ˎ ˏ ˎ ˏ ˎ ˏ, Gen. 24:7 ˊ ˏ ˉ ˏ ˈ ʾ*k*, and consequently though two or more Conjunctives may be allowed before a particular Disjunctive, only the first of these is in the majority of cases employed. The actual relations of words may, however, so interfere with this regularity as on the one hand to cause the intervening Conjunctives to be dropped entirely, e. g. Gen. 1:22 ˎ ˏ ˎ ˏ, 1 Chron. 15:18 ˊ ˊ ˊ ˊ ˏˎ ˊ ˊ ˊ ˊ, or, on the other, to introduce as many Conjunctives as the table will admit, e. g. Gen. 3:14 ˊ ˏ ˏ ˉ ˏ ˏ ʾ*k*ˈ. But if either of the three primary sections consist of but two words, the first must have a Disjunctive accent, however close its relation may be to the second, e. g. וַיִּטַּע כֶּרֶם׃ Gen. 9:20, וְנִפְקְחוּ עֵינֵיכֶם Gen. 3:5, כֶּרֶם יִשְׁכָּבוּ Gen. 19:4.

a. In Gen. 24:15, where, however, editions differ, Silluk is in a section of two words immediately preceded by Merka.

b. Sometimes an excluded term of the series will take the place of the secondary accent Methegh, §44. Tiphhha is thus five times written upon the same word with Silluk, e. g. Num. 15:21, and eleven times with

Athnahh, e. g. Num. 28:26. Munahh, Gen. 21:17, for which Kadhma is sometimes substituted, Gen. 18:21, often stands upon the same word with Zakeph Katon. Kadhma is also joined in this manner with Munahh, Lev. 10:12, Merka, Judg. 21:21, Neh. 12:44, Mahpakh, Lev. 25:46, and Geresh, Ex. 16:15, 21:22, 35. Mahpakh with Munahh, Lam. 4:9.

4. Occasionally a subordinate Disjunctive or its alternate is repeated in the same section with or without its antecedents. Thus, T'bhir, Deut. 26:2 ֽ ֽ ֛ ֛, so Deut. 30:20, 1 Sam. 20:21, 2 Kin. 17:36. Zarka, 2 Kin. 1:16 ֘ ֮ ֘ ֮, so ver. 6, Gen. 42:21, Jer. 21:4, Neh. 2:12. Pashta, Gen. 24:14, 42, 48, 65; 1 Kin. 20:9. Pashta, Pashta and Y'thibh, 2 Kin. 10:30, Ezr. 7:25. Geresh and G'rashayim, Gen. 28:9.

a. There is a double accentuation of part of Gen. 35:22, and of the entire decalogue, both in Ex. 20:2-17, and Deut. 5:6-21, which involves a double vocalization in certain words, e. g. פֶּ֣ן Ex. 20:3, i. e. either פָּנָ֑י or פָּנָ֔י. Single words also occur with alternative accents, e. g. with G'rashayim or Geresh and T'lisha Gh'dhola הָ֛י Gen. 5:29, אָ֛רֶב Lev. 10:4, שֵׁ֗ב 2 Kin. 17:13, וְאֶצְלָ֤ה Ezek. 48:10, אָ֛ת Zeph. 2:15.

Poetic Consecution.

§ 40. 1. The principle of the consecution is the same in the poetic as in the prosaic accents, although there is considerable diversity in the details. There is a like division of verses into clauses and sections ruled by a Disjunctive at the end, which imposes upon them its own special train of accents. The sections are fewer, however, and the trains shorter than in prose, on account of the greater brevity of the sentences in poetry for the most part. But this reduction is more than compensated by the new complexity arising from the latitude allowed in the choice of Conjunctives, which it seems impossible to reduce to fixed rules, and is probably to be referred to their use as musical notes for the

§ 40　POETIC CONSECUTION.

cantillation of the synagogue. It should be added, that the embarrassment arising from this inherent complexity of the subject is seriously aggravated by the numerous discrepancies in the different editions of the Bible, by which the true accentuation in the three poetical books is often involved in doubt and uncertainty.

<small>a. In addition to availing himself of the researches of others, particularly of Nordheimer and Ewald in their discussions of this subject, the author has examined verse by verse the entire book of Proverbs and the first division of the Psalms (Ps. 1-41), as well as other selected Psalms and portions of Job. As the result, he confesses himself quite unable to disentangle the mystery; and as the only contribution he can make towards its solution he has concluded to present in detail, and in as convenient a form as possible, the facts observed, hoping that some future exploration may discover the principle of order, if any such principle there be, in this apparently inextricable confusion.</small>

2. Verses may consist of one, two, or three clauses, distinguished by the three Disjunctives of the first class. If the verse contain but one clause, Silluk will be written upon the last word, Ps. 4 : 1; if it contain two clauses, the division will be made by Athnahh, Ps. 1 : 4, or by Merka-Mahpakh, Ps. 1 : 2. 3 : 3, upon the last word of the first clause; if it contain three, the last word of the first will have Merka-Mahpakh, the last word of the second Athnahh, and the last word of the third Silluk, Ps. 1 : 1. Clauses may consist of a single section when no subdivision of them is necessary; or they may consist of two or more sections, when the subdivision is effected by R'bhiᵃ or Pazer, e. g. ׃֗ ֑ ֥ ֖ Ps. 18 : 51, ׃֗ ֑ ֥ ֨ Prov. 1 : 10, ֗ ֑ ֥ ֨ Ps. 41 : 7, ֗ ֑ ֥ ֥ ֖ Ps. 7 : 6,, ֗ ֑ ֥ ֥ ֖ Ps. 17 : 14.

§ 41. The order of the accents in the various sections is exhibited in the following table:

	Disjunctives. Class I.	Conjunctives.	Disjunctives. Class II.	Conjunctives.
Principal Sections.				
Subordinate Sections.				

Explanation of the Table.

a. *Train of Silluk.*—If Silluk is preceded by a single Conjunctive, it will be Munahh, Prov. 1:4, or Merka either alone as Prov. 1:2, or compounded with Zarka, Ps. 10:5, and P'sik, Ps. 10:3. If it be preceded by two Conjunctives, they will be ˌˌ Ps. 5:5, ˌˌ Ps. 10:6, ˌˌ Prov. 12:1 (in some editions), ˌˌ Prov. 25:26, ˌˌ Ps. 18:7, ˌˌ Ps. 36:1, or ˌˌ Prov.

§ 41   POETIC CONSECUTION.   57

8:13. If it be preceded by three Conjunctives, they will be , , Ps. 24:6, ,ₑ ' Ps. 10:2 (or ₄ₑ, 'Ps. 7:6). ,ₑₑ Prov. 26:25 (or ,ₑ. ˙ Ps. 28:8 or ,ₑ,. Prov. 29:13), ,, ˙ Ps. 4:8, ,ₑ 'Prov. 3:27, ᴶᴶ'. If it be preceded by four Conjunctives, they will be ,ₑ,', Ps. 89:2, ,ₑ. ˙, 'Ps. 32:5, or ᴶᴶ', Ps. 3:3 (in some editions ᴶᴶ'ₑ). If it be preceded by five Conjunctives, they will be ,ₑ,,', Job 32:6, 37:12 (in this latter example some editions substitute a Makkeph for Merka).

If Silluk be preceded by a Disjunctive in its own section, it will be R'bhiᵃ-Geresh, Ps. 1:1, 5:3, 10. R'bhiᵃ-Geresh may be preceded by one Conjunctive,, Ps. 5:4; by two,,, Ps. 8:2, or ,ₑ Ps. 31:10, 19; by three, ,,, or ,ₑ. Ps. 73:4.

There are occasional deviations from the Conjunctives of the table; thus, R'bhiᵃ-Geresh is in Ps. 34:8 preceded by ₑ ˙ 'ₑ. In some of these cases, however, editions differ in their notation of the accents. Thus, in Ps. 5:7 some editions have ,ₑ ˙ before Silluk, others ,, ˙; in Ps. 18:36, Prov. 30:17, some have ,, others ,; in Ps. 20:2 some have , ,ₑ; others ,ₑ; in Prov. 24:8 some have ,,, others ,, the two words being joined by Makkeph. So, again, some editions have in Ps. 9:11 ₑ before R'bhiᵃ-Geresh, in Ps. 18:44 ₑ, in Prov. 27:19 ,ₑ; in Prov. 21:17 ,,; while other editions do not depart in these passages from the order given in the table. Similar discrepancies exist in the other sections likewise.

b. *Train of Athnahh.*—Athnahh may be preceded by one Conjunctive, , Ps. 5:8 (or ,, Prov. 8:30, 34), , Ps. 5:3 (or ,, Ps. 35:21, , ˙ Ps. 69:2), ₑ Prov. 23:3, ₑ Ps. 14:3, Prov. 6:3 (or ,ₑ Prov. 16:10); by two,,, Ps. 6:8 (or ,, Ps. 7:17), ,ₑₑ Prov. 28:25, Ps. 5:2 (in some editions the latter example has ,ᴶ,), ,ₑ Ps. 14:5, ,, Prov. 11:12, 14:21, ,' Ps. 37:1, , Prov. 8:21, ₑ, Ps. 25:10; by three, ,,, Prov. 24:21, ,,ₑ Ps. 6:6 (or ,,, ˙ Ps. 9:10, or ,, ,ₑ Ps. 16:10), ,,, ' Ps. 10:17, ,ₑ ˙ Prov. 8:13, ,ₑ,ₑ Ps. 18:50, ,,ₑ ,ₑ Ps. 10:13, ᴶ' Prov. 6:27, ˙ ₑ Ps. 72:3; by four, ,,,ₑ Prov. 3:12, ,,, ₑ Prov. 24:16, ,ₑ,ₑ Ps. 34:7, ,, ' Ps. 32:2 (in some editions), ᴶ' ₑ Prov. 1:19, ˙ '₁ Ps. 65:2.

If Athnahh be preceded by a Disjunctive in its own section, it will be Tiphhha initial, Ps. 1:6, 26:4. Tiphhha initial may be preceded by one Conjunctive, , Ps. 5:6; by two, ,, Ps. 9:19 (or ,, ˙ Ps. 14:1, or ,, Ps. 16:9), , ˙ Ps. 32:11, ,, Ps. 35:14, 15, ,, ' Prov. 25:20; by three, ,ₑ,ₑ Ps. 23:6, ,, ,ₑ Ps. 27:1, ,, ' ₑ Ps. 12:5 (or ,, ', ˙ Prov. 27:14), ,ₑ' Ps. 9:14.

c. *Train of Merka-Mahpakh.*—Merka-Mahpakh may be preceded by one Conjunctive, which is almost always Yerahh ben Yomo, Ps. 1:1, though occasionally it is, in some editions at least, Merka, Ps.15:5, 35:10, or Mahpakh, Ps. 24:8, 31:10. If it be preceded by a Disjunctive in its own section, Zarka will be employed, Ps. 1:1, Prov. 1:11.

Zarka may be preceded by one Conjunctive, ‸ Ps. 12:7 (or ‸‸ Prov. 1:22)‸, ‸ Ps. 6:3, ‸‸ Ps. 12:3, ′ Ps. 31:12; by two, ‸ ′ Prov. 30:15 (in some editions ‸ ′), ‸‸ Ps. 24:10 (or ‸ ‸‸ Ps. 13:6), ‸ ‸‸ Ps. 21:10, ′ Ps. 27:2 (or ‸′ ″ Ps. 35:26), ′ ‴ Ps. 7:10; by three, ‸ ‸′ Ps. 29:9, ‸′ Ps. 31:14, ‸′ ″ Ps. 10:14; or by four, ‸‸‸′ Ps. 40:6.

d. Train of R'bhi.—R'bhi may be preceded by one Conjunctive, ‸ Ps. 5:1, ‸ Ps. 8:2 (or ‸ ″ Ps. 23:4, or ‸ Ps. 6:7), ‴ Prov. 28:22, ‴ Ps. 22:25, ′ Ps. 11:2 (or ‸ ′ Ps. 5:11); by two, ‸‸ Prov. 8:33, ‸‸ Ps. 28:7 (or ‸‸‸ Ps. 18:3), ‸ ′ Ps. 9:7, ‸ ″ Ps. 11:4, ‸ ′ Ps. 26:1, ‴ Ps. 27:6 (or ‴ Ps. 5:9), ‸ ′ Prov. 6:22, ‸ ″ Ps. 18:1 (or ‸ ′ ″ Ps. 7:7, or ‸ ′ ″ Ps. 39:5), ‸ ‴ Job 16:10; or by three, ‸ ‸ ′ Ps. 40:7, ‸ ‸′ Ps. 41:7 (or ″ ‸ ′ Ps. 39:6, or ″ ‸ ′ Ps. 3:8, or ‸ ‸ ″ Ps. 41:14), ′ ‸ ′ Ps. 19:14 (or ‴ ‸ ′ ″ Ps. 39:12), ‴ ′ ″ Ps. 40:11, ‸ ″ ′ Prov. 24:31.

e. Train of Pazer.—Pazer may be preceded by one Conjunctive, ‸ Ps. 89:20 (or ‸ Prov. 30:8),′ Ps. 32:5 (or ‸ ′ Ps. 17:14); by two, ‸‸ Ps. 5:10, Prov. 7:23 (or ‸‸‸ Ps. 28:5), ‸′ Ps. 13:3 (or ‸ ′ Prov. 27:10), ‸‸ Ps. 90:4, ‸ ′ Ps. 7:6, ‸ ′ Ps. 39:13, ‸‸ Ps. 11:2, ′ Ps. 5:12; or by three, ‸ ′ Ps. 22:35, 23:4, ‸‸‸ Prov. 25:29 (where some editions have ‸‸ ′).

§ 42. The trains of these several accents are adjusted to sections of varying length by expedients similar to those employed with the prose accents, viz.: 1. Omitting the Conjunctives in whole or in part. 2. Repeating the Disjunctives, e. g. ″ Ps. 14:1, ″ Ps. 17:14, or their equivalents, e. g. Tiphhha initial before ″ Ps. 7:10, before ′ Ps. 9:1; ″ before ″ Ps. 18:1, before ′ Ps. 22:15; ‴ before Tiphhha initial Ps. 16:17. 3. Writing two accents upon the same word, מִמַּֽעֲצוֹתֵיהֶ֑ם Ps. 5:11, הֽוֹרַ֗י Ps. 27:11, וַיַּ֥רְא Ps. 18:16. 4. Uniting two or more words by Makkeph, so that they require but a single accent. 5. Writing the different parts of a compound accent upon separate words; thus, Merka-Mahpakh אָמַ֥ל אָ֗נִי Ps. 6:3, Merka-Zarka כִּ֥י חָ֗פֵץ Ps. 22:9, Mahpakh-Zarka כִּ֗י בָאָ֔רֶץ Prov. 6:3.

a. Sometimes when two accents are written upon the same word, one is the alternate of the other; thus, בְּצֵעַ Prov. 1:19, may be either בֹּצֵעַ or בֹּצֵעַ according as the accent remains in its proper position in the ultimate, or is thrown back upon the penult in consequence of the next word being accented upon its initial syllable.

Makkeph.

§ 43. Makkeph (מַקֵּף *joining*) is a horizontal stroke by which two, three, or even four words may be united. אִם־תְּבַקְשֶׁנָּה, אֶתְנָן־לָךְ Gen. 30:31, יֶשׁ־לִי־כֹל Gen. 33:11, כָּל־עַל־דְּבַר־אֲשֶׁר Gen. 12:20, 25:5, Ex. 20:11, וְאֶת־כָּל־אֲשֶׁר־לוֹ Ex. 22:8, כָּל־עַל־בְּנֵי־שָׁחַץ Job 41:26. It belongs properly to the accentual system, words which are closely related being often connected in this manner in order to obviate the necessity of unduly multiplying Conjunctive accents. Thus, the first fifteen words of Ex. 22:8 are in this manner reduced to eight. Monosyllabic particles are frequently, and some almost constantly, linked with the succeeding or preceding word, of which they may be regarded as in a manner appendages; thus, אֶל, עַל, אֶת, כֹּל, אַל, פֶּן, גַּם, נָא, etc. Examples are not wanting, however, of longer words similarly united, e. g. שְׁלֹשֶׁת־עָרִים Deut. 19:15, נֶאֱשַׁר־הַיֶּלֶד 1 Kin. 17:21, אֲמַר־יְהֹוָה Isa. 31:4. This use of Makkeph is not to be confounded with that of the hyphen in modern languages between the members of a compound, as *self-same*, *master-builder*. Words united by Makkeph are still as separate as ever in character and signification; but they are pronounced together and are accented as though they formed but one word. Hence, whatever number of words be thus joined, the last only will receive an accent. And, as a further consequence, if a word preceding Makkeph properly ends in a long mixed syllable, this will, by the loss of the accent, be shortened, אֶת־שָׁנִי, הִתְהַלֶּךְ־לָךְ כָּלִיל, or failing this, will commonly receive the secondary accent Methegh, אִידְיִרְאֶה, שָׁם־יוֹסֵף.

a. Tsere remains before Makkeph in בֶּן־, נֵר־, עֵד־, עֵץ־ ; it sometimes remains and is sometimes shortened in שֵׁ־, שֵׁשׁ *six*, בָּ־ e. g. Gen. 16:13 שֶׁם־יִהְיֶה, but ver. 15 שְׁב־בְּלוֹ. It once remains according to some editions in אֶת־ Job 41:26, a word which is three times written אֶת without Makkeph, Ps. 47:5, 60:2, Prov. 3:12. Comp. § 19. 2, *a*.

b. Makkeph is occasionally found in the middle of a long word, which has been erroneously divided into two, e. g. יִפְח־פְּלָה Jer. 46:20, and perhaps פְּקַח־קוֹחַ Isa. 61:1. Sometimes words are thus divided without a Makkeph to unite the sundered parts, e. g. בַּךְ עֲלָים Lam. 4:3, בָּחַר בְּחִירָה 2 Chron. 34:6, and probably אֲהָבוּ הֵבוּ Hos. 4:18, לַחְשׁ פְּלוֹת Isa. 2:20. (See Dr. Alexander's Commentary on this passage.) The last two examples are plainly intended by the punctuators to be read as separate words. This might likewise be done in the preceding examples if they were pointed בַּךְ לֻלָים and בָּחַר בְּחִירָה.

METHEGH.

§ 44. Methegh (מֶתֶג *bridle*), a small perpendicular stroke under the initial letter of the syllable to which it belongs, is a secondary accent denoting a stress of voice inferior to the main accent. As this latter always has its place in Hebrew either upon the ultimate or the penult, distinctness was promoted and monotony relieved, especially in long words, by giving prominence to one or more of the antecedent syllables. There is a natural tendency to heighten the force of the accent by passing lightly over the immediately preceding syllable, this diminished force creating in its turn a new stress upon that next beyond it, and so on in alternate elevations and depressions to the beginning of the word. Agreeably to the principle just stated, Methegh regularly stands in polysyllables upon the second syllable before the accent, and again upon the fourth if the word have so many, e. g. וּמֵהַתִּיכוֹנוֹת, מִמִּסְגְּרוֹתֵיהֶם, בְּתֵיהֶם, יוֹצִיאֵנִי, יָאֱסֹף, הָאָדָם. And so upon two or more words connected by Makkeph, which are pronounced as one, e. g. יִרְאֶה־לּוֹ Gen. 22:8, כִּי־אִם־לָחֶם 1 Sam. 21:7.

a. Sometimes, however, particularly when the nature of the syllables requires it, § 32. 1, Methegh takes the place of the principal accent before

Makkeph irrespective of the position of the accent upon the following word, הַשְׁאִיר־לוֹ Num. 21:35, מִכֶּה־הַבָּשָׁן Num. 21:33, כָּכָה־בָּבֶל Jer. 34:1, וְכָל־שֵׂה־חוּם Gen. 30:32, הָלוֹא־וָה 1 Sam. 21:12, כִּי־לִי Ex. 19:5.

b. It is to be observed that the position of Methegh is determined by that of the tone-syllable, not by that of the accentual sign when these are not coincident, as frequently happens with prepositives and postpositives, e. g. הַגִּידֹתִי Deut. 4:26, הִירוּתֵינוּ Josh. 22:27, where the tone falls on the penult, לְחִיָּקִים Jer. 26:21, where the tone is upon the ultimate.

§ 45. The secondary accent is liable to be shifted from its normal position for the following reasons, viz.:

1. If the syllable which should receive it is mixed, it may be given in preference to an antecedent simple syllable, e. g. וָאֶשְׁתַּפְּלָה 2 Sam. 22:24, וּמָהִתְהַלֵּךְ Job 1:7, מֵהַתִּתְחֹלוֹת Ezek. 42:5, שְׁאָל־הָאִישׁ Gen. 43:7; or if none such precede, it may be omitted altogether, e. g. וַיִּמְצְאֵם Jer. 33:24, הַיִּזְרְעֵאלִי 1 Kin. 21:1, אֶת־כָּל־הַמִּצְוָה Deut. 6:25.

2. It is always given to simple syllables when followed by a vocal Sh'va, whether simple or compound, or a vowel which has arisen from Sh'va, the slight pronunciation proper to the Sh'va or its derivative giving new prominence to the preceding vowel, בְּשִׁקֲתוֹת, לַאֲשֶׁר, יֶהֱיֶה, יֹאמְרוּ Gen. 30:38, יֶחֱרְדוּ; sometimes to intermediate syllables, § 20. 2, e. g. סְבִיבַי Isa. 9:17, 10:34, עֲמָדְךָ Obad. ver. 11, particularly after He interrogative or when Daghesh-forte has been omitted as after the article, Vav conversive, and the preposition מִן, e. g. לַמְנַצֵּחַ, הַצְפַרְדְּעִים, בְּנֵרוֹת, הַלְלִי, הַתְשַׁלַּח, הָמָשֹׁל, וַיְהִי; rarely and only as an exception to a mixed syllable standing in the first place before the principal accent, e. g. תֶּדְשֵׁא Gen. 1:11, הַפָּתִים Ex. 12:7, Zech. 14:2.

a. It hence appears how Methegh comes to be of use in distinguishing the doubtful vowels, § 19, and to what extent it can be relied upon for this end. As it invariably accompanies the vowel of a simple syllable when followed by vocal Sh'va, it must always be found with *ă*, *ĭ*, and *ŭ* preceding Sh'va, inasmuch as this will necessarily be vocal. Initial ו *ŭ*, the unemphatic conjunction, is an exception, with which it is commonly not written, e. g. וּקְבָהּ Gen. 6:19, וּלְלֵאָה Gen. 31:4, though it is sometimes,

e. g. וְלְהַבְדִּיל Gen. 1:18, וְשֻׁבָּח Judg. 5:12. The absence of Methegh, except in the case just mentioned, is consequently conclusive evidence of the shortness of the vowel. As, however, short vowels in intermediate syllables, and in a few rare instances even in mixed syllables, may receive Methegh, the presence of this sign does not of itself determine the vowel to be long; the ultimate decision must in this case depend on other considerations.

3. When by the operation of the preceding rule Methegh comes to stand in the first place before the accent, another Methegh is nevertheless occasionally found in the second place, the two thus standing in immediate succession, e. g. בְּמָהְדָּהּ Gen. 32:22, וַיַּעֲלוּ Gen. 45:25; and even three occur upon successive syllables, e. g. וּמְסָעֲמָדָהּ Isa. 22:19. But commonly where there is more than one Methegh, their position relatively to each other is governed by the same rules as the position of Methegh generally with relation to the principal accent, e. g. וְאַחֲרִיתוֹ, וַתֵּשֶׁב, לִישׁוּעָתָךְ, מַחְבְּלִים.

4. Methegh is sometimes written under a letter with Sh'va, e. g. שְׁלַח־נָא Job 1:11, 2:5, הֲשִׂי־אֵשׁוֹ Job 19:6, נִתְּקָה Ps. 2:3, כְּמֵחָבֵת Jer. 49:18, בְּמֵעַי Ruth 1:11.

a. A Methegh so situated is called Gaya (גַּעְיָא *bellowing*) by Jewish grammarians, and, according to Elias Levita, it occurs eighty-four times, the number yielded by its name arithmetically reckoned. Methegh upon a short vowel before a compound Sh'va was called Ma'rīkh (מַאֲרִיךְ *prolonging*), with a short Hhirik it was called Hhīrūk (חִירוּק *gnashing*).

5. The place of Methegh is frequently supplied by an accent chosen agreeably to the laws of consecution, § 39. 3. *b.*, e. g. אֲנַחֲמָם Isa. 66:13, לֵאלֹהֵיהֶם Deut. 12:31, וְאֹסְפָם Zech. 7:14, וְלַצְּבָא Num. 10:28, וַיִּקְהָלוּ Josh. 22:12.

a. The want of consistency or of uniformity, which may be occasionally observed, in regard to the insertion or omission of Methegh, e. g. שֶׁאֲהֲבָה Cant. 1:7, שֶׁאֲהַבְתָּ Cant. 3:1; שֶׁלֹּה Cant. 6:5, שָׁהֶם Lam. 4:9;

עֲרֹבֹת Num. 31:12, עַרְבוֹת Josh. 4:13, and the discrepancies between different manuscripts and editions, e. g. אֶלֻּבָּח or אַלֻּבָה Gen. 45:28, שְׂאוּ־זִמְרָה or שְׂאוּ־זִמְרָה Ps. 81:3, if not arising in the first instance from clerical errors, are probably to be attributed to the inferior importance of the sign itself, whose place might be presumed to be sufficiently determined even if not written.

K'RI AND K'THIBH.

§ 46. Various notes extracted from the Masora (מָסוֹרָה *tradition*), a collection of remarks upon the text, are found in the margin of the Hebrew Bible, which are explained in the glossary at the end of most editions. The most important of these are the various readings known as the K'rī (קְרִי *read*), and K'thībh (כְּתִיב *written*). If in any instance traditional usage sanctioned a reading different from that which was written in the text or the K'thibh, the punctuators did not venture to alter the text itself for the sake of making the correction; they went no further than to connect with the letters of the text the vowels of the word to be substituted for it in reading or the K'ri, with a reference to the margin where the letters of the substitute might be found. Thus, with the word וַיֹּאמְרוּ Josh. 6:7 is connected the marginal note ויאמר קרי. The vowels here attached to the K'thibh belong not to it but to the unpointed word in the margin, which is accordingly וַיֹּאמֶר. The proper vowels for the pronunciation of the K'thibh are not written, but must be supplied from a knowledge of the form indicated by the letters, which in this case is וַיֹּאמְרוּ. Again, in ver. 9, תִּקְעוּ in the text refers to תקעי ק in the margin; the K'ri is here תִּקְעִי, and the K'thibh, whose vowels are left to be determined by the reader, תְּקָעוּ. Jer. 42:6 has אֲנוּ where the marginal note is אנחנו קרי; the K'ri is accordingly אֲנַחְנוּ, and the K'thibh אֲנוּ. In order to indicate that a given word was to be omitted in reading, it was left unpointed, and the note כתיב ולא קרי, *written but not read,* placed in the margin, e. g. חמש Ezek. 48:16, בא 2 Kin. 5:18, ידרך Jer. 51:3. If, on the other hand, a word was to be supplied, its vowels were inserted in the text and its letters placed in the margin, with the note קרי ולא כתיב, *read but not written,* e. g. Judg. 20:13 in the text ְ,ּ, and in the margin בְּנֵי, to be read בְּנֵי; so Jer. 31:38 בָּאִים. In 1 Kin. 21:8 the first letter of הַסְפָרִים is left unpointed as superfluous, and in Job 2:7 עַד, is explained by the margin to stand for וְעַד: so Jer. 18:23 וְיִהְיוּ for וְ‍הָיוּ.

a. The number of these marginal readings differs in different editions. Elias Levita states that there are 848. Others have computed them to be 1,000; others still, 1,200.

§ 47. Sometimes a different reading from that of the text is suggested by the points alone without a marginal note being added in explanation, as when a particular word or orthography is regularly substituted for another of frequent occurrence. These cases are presumed to be so familiar to the reader as to require no other index of their existence than the presence of the appropriate vowels. Thus, the divine name יהוה, which the Jews had a superstitious dread of pronouncing, was and still is read by them as if it were אֲדֹנָי Lord, whose points it accordingly receives, יְהֹוָה, unless these two names stand in immediate connection, when, to avoid repetition, it is read אֱלֹהִים and pointed יֱהֹוִה Gen. 15:2, Hab. 3:19. The antiquity of this superstition is attested by the Κύριος of the Septuagint, followed in the English as well as in other modern versions by the rendering LORD. The true sound of the name never having been noted, is now lost; the only clue that is left being its etymology and the form which it assumes in composition, § 62. 1, from which the conclusion has been variously drawn that it was יַהֲוָה, יִהְוָה, or יֶהֱוָה. The common pronunciation Jehovah is manifestly founded upon the error of combining the consonants of this word with the vowels of another and an entirely different one. There is, however, especially as it is uncertain whether *Yahve* or *Yah^{a}va*, or either of these, was its original sound, no good reason for abandoning the pronunciation familiar to the Christian world and hallowed by the association of constant usage for the sake of adopting another which is, or is supposed to be, phonetically more exact, any more than we need be guilty of the pedantry of preferring *Yeshayahu* to Isaiah because it approaches more nearly to the original pronunciation of the prophet's name. Other standing K'ris, unnoted in the margin, are הוא, the form of the pronoun of the third person feminine which is used throughout the Pentateuch; this is designed to be read היא, though the sound indicated by the letters is in all probability הוא. So יִשָּׂשכָר read יִשָּׂכָר, and יְרוּשָׁלַם read יְרוּשָׁלַיִם.

§ 48. In the absence of definite information respecting the origin and sources of these various readings, it is difficult to determine with absolute precision the weight to which they are respectively entitled. The current opinion of the ablest Hebraists, based upon a careful scrutiny of their internal character and the relation which ordinarily appears to subsist between them, is that while the K'ri may perhaps, in a few cases, correct errors in the K'thibh, and so restore the original reading, it is in the great majority of instances an explanatory gloss rather than an emendation. With the rare exceptions already suggested, the K'thibh is esteemed the true reading, the object of the K'ri being to remove orthographical anomalies, secure grammatical uniformity, substitute usual for unusual, prevailing for obsolete words and forms, and occasionally to introduce euphemistic expressions. While the K'ri is probably not to be esteemed the original reading, therefore, it deserves attention as the grammatical or exegetical comment of a steadfast tradition.

Accuracy of the Points.

§ 49. 1. All the Masoretic additions to the text designed to facilitate its reading have now been considered. The correctness of the pronunciation, which they yield, is vouched for not only by the esteem in which they are universally held by the Jews, but by the scrupulous minuteness of the system, its consistency with itself and with the vowel-letters of the text, its affinity with and yet independence of the vocalization of the kindred languages the Arabic and Syriac, and the veneration for the already established text which evidently characterized its authors, since they did not venture to change the text even in the slightest particular.

2. The only additional information which has come down to us respecting the true sound of Hebrew words, is furnished by the mode of writing proper names in the Septuagint version, and the few Hebrew words preserved by ancient authors, particularly Origen and Jerome. These have been subjected to an elaborate comparison with the Masoretic punctuation, and the result has been to establish their substantial agreement in the main, with, however, not a few remarkable points of divergence. In relation to this subject it should be observed, that the Hebrew pronunciation of the Seventy is inferred entirely from their mode of spelling proper names, not from words in living use in the language. The chances of inaccuracy, on the part of the translators, are here peculiarly great. Many names were not familiar and were of rare occurrence; and as no system of vowel notation then existed, they were left entirely to their independent knowledge of the sound of each individual word. These words were written by them in a foreign alphabet, whose sounds did not coincide precisely with those of the Hebrew, and in which the proper equivalents varied somewhat according to their combinations. The true sound was also de-

parted from sometimes because the laws of Greek euphony forbade its exact reproduction. The negligence with which they are chargeable elsewhere was also probably aggravated here, and in fact there are many instances in which they not merely deviate from the vowels but transpose or change the letters. Leaving out of view, therefore, such incidental discrepancies as are to be accounted for in the ways now suggested, a thorough and extended examination of the subject reveals, with all the general agreement, a number of regular and systematic deviations.

a. These are thus stated by Ewald, Lehrbuch, p. 116. (1.) An $\bar{e}$ or $\bar{\imath}$ derived from $\check{a}$ is written $\bar{a}$, as תֶּרַח Θαρα, בִּלְעָם Βαλααμ, גִּבְעוֹן Γαβαων, בְּרִים Μαριαμ; and on the other hand, a is sometimes written $\bar{e}$, אָהֳלִיבָמָה Ὀλιβεμα, קְנַז Κενεζ, גֵּת Γεθ, especially before ח, as קֹרַח Κορε, זָרַח Ζαρε. (2.) $\bar{e}$ is written for $\bar{\imath}$ and $\bar{o}$ for $\bar{u}$, חִתִּים Χετταιοι, גֵּיחוֹם Γεεννα, גִּדְעוֹן Γεδεων, מִצְרַיִם Μεσραιμ, אֲחַזְיָה Οχοζαθ, עֻזִּיָּה Οζια. (3.) for the diphthongal $\bar{e}$ and $\bar{o}$ their constituents ai and au are substituted, קַיִן Καιναν, נְבוֹ Ναβαυ. (4.) The vowel letters are softened into their homogeneous vowels וַיִּקְרָא ουικρα, וַיְדַבֵּר ουιδαβηρ. (5.) Vocal Sh'va is written as a full vowel, commonly a, or if an o follow, o, צְבָאוֹת Σαβαωθ, רְעוּאֵל Ραγουηλ, כְּרוּבִים Χερουβιμ, סְדֹם Σοδομα; the final vowel of Segholates is also written $\bar{o}$ if o precedes, מֹלֶךְ Μολοχ, עֹמֶר γομορ.

3. The regularity of these deviations seems to be best accounted for by the assumption that the pronunciation represented in the Septuagint is that which prevailed among the Jews in Egypt, which would naturally be less pure than that of Palestine represented in the vowel points, and which, moreover, betrays in the particulars recited above a strong leaning to Aramæan forms and sounds. Accordingly the view now commonly entertained is that the vowel notation of the Masorites is correct, at least in all essential particulars, and that it is properly to be put at the basis of all investigations into the phenomena of the language.

Orthographic Changes.

§ 50. The signs thus far described represent all the sounds of the Hebrew language. Its stock of words is formed by combining these in various significant ways. The laws of such combinations, and especially the mutations to which they are subject, or which they occasion, next demand attention. When a particular idea has been attached to a certain combination of sounds, its different modifications may naturally be expressed by slightly varying those sounds. This may take place,

1. By the substitution of one letter for another of like character, and for the most part of the same organ, e. g.:

הָיָה *to be, exist,* חָיָה *to live ;* נָבַע *to pour forth,* נָבָא the same idea applied to words, *to prophesy ;* עָנַק *to encircle the neck with an ornament,* חָנַק *to strangle,* אָנַק applied to sounds uttered in strangulation, *to groan ;* רָגַל *to go about as a spy,* רָכַל *to go about as a merchant ;* כָּנַס *to collect,* גְּנָזִים *treasures ;* גָּבִיעַ *a cup,* כּוֹבַע or קוֹבַע *a helmet* (of similar shape); רַךְ *tender, delicate,* רַק *thin ;* תָּכַן *to make straight,* תִּכֵּן to straighten the beam of the balance, *to weigh ;* בְּכוֹר *first born,* בִּכּוּר *first ripe,* בֹּקֶר the first portion of the day, *the morning ;* תָּלָה *to suspend,* דָּלָה applied to a bucket, *to let down ;* גָּזַר *to cut,* קָצַר *to reap ;* זָהָב *gold,* צָהֹב *yellow ;* כָּבַן *to conceal,* שָׁכַן and צָפַן *to hide away* as treasures, כָּפַן *to cover with boards ;* נָתַץ *to destroy* by tearing down, נָתַשׁ *to destroy* by uprooting ; טָבַח *to slay,* זָבַח *to sacrifice ;* חָבַל *to bind,* אָבַל *to bound ;* בָּרַח *to break up, flee, to break out, blossom,* פָּרַק *to break in pieces ;* קָצַב *to cut off,* חָצַב *to hew stone,* חָטַב *to cut wood ;* כָּתַר *to surround,* כָּתַר *to encircle the head with a crown ;* נָתַךְ *to pour out,* נָסַךְ *to pour in libation* or *in casting metals ;* צָהַר *to shine,* בָּהַר *to be pure ;* חָרַת *to engrave,* חָרַשׁ *to plough ;* בָּחַן *to prove,* בָּחַר *to approve, choose ;* שָׁתָה *to drink,* its causative הִשְׁקָה ; חָתַר *to break through,* חָקַר *to investigate ;* יָצַב *to place,* its reflexive הִתְיַצֵּב.

2. By the transposition of letters, e. g.:

פָּרַץ *to deal violently,* עָצַר *to urge ;* קָצַר *to cut with the sickle, reap,* חָרַץ *to cut with the teeth, bite ;* נָשַׁף *to blow,* נֶפֶשׁ *breath ;* כָּנַס *to collect,* נְכָסִים *riches,* מִסְכְּנוֹת *storehouses.*

3. By the addition of a letter:

Thus, from the letters צר, in which inheres the idea of compression, are formed צָרַר *to bind,* צוּר *to press together,* אָצַר *to heap up,* יָצַר *to be*

§ 51   ORTHOGRAPHIC CHANGES.   69

straitened, נָצַר *to guard, besiege,* צָר *to restrain,* חָצֵר *an enclosure;* from גז are formed גָּזַר *to cut*, גָּרַז *to cut off*, גוז *to cut loose, go away*, גָּזַז *to shear*, גָּזַל *to plunder*, גָּזִית *hewn stone;* פָּרַשׂ *to unfold, make distinct*, פֵּרְשׁוּ *to spread out;* כֶּרֶם *a vineyard*, כַּרְמֶל *a garden.*

§ 51. Such literal changes as those just recited not only serve to express new shades of meaning, but even where the meaning remains precisely the same, they may represent diversities of other sorts. Thus, the distinction may be,

1. In point of currency or style: One form of the word being in more common and familiar use, the other more rare and savoring, perhaps, of the elevated or poetic style, e. g.:

נָצַר *to guard*, נָצַר poetic; בְּרוֹשׁ *cypress*, בְּרוֹת once in poetry; סָגַר *to shut*, rarely סָכַר; סְעָרָה *storm*, שְׂעָרָה rare and poetic; סָכַךְ *to cover*, once שָׂכַךְ: דָּעַךְ *to be quenched*, once זָעַךְ; תָּעַב *to abhor*, once תָּאַב; סָכַל *to be foolish*, once כָּסַל; עַוְלָה *iniquity*, once עַלְוָה.

2. Of antiquity: The pronunciation of a word or its form may undergo changes in the lapse of time. Of the few instances of this sort, which our imperfect data enable us to fix upon with some measure of confidence, the following may be taken as specimens, e. g.:

To laugh in the Pentateuch צָחַק, in other books (Judg. 16:25 excepted) שָׂחַק; *to cry out* in the Pentateuch צָעַק, only once (Ex. 2:23) זָעַק which is the more frequent form in other books; כִּשְׂבָּה, כִּבְשָׂה *a lamb*, occur in the Pentateuch interchangeably with כֶּבֶשׂ, כֶּשֶׂב, which are the only forms found in other books; *a sceptre* שֵׁבֶט, but in the book of Esther שַׁרְבִיט; *Damascus* דַּמֶּשֶׂק, in Chronicles דַּרְמֶשֶׂק; *how* 1 Chron. 13:12, Dan. 10:17 הֵיךְ, in earlier books אֵיךְ.

3. Of Dialect: The same word may come to be pronounced differently by those who speak distinct though related languages. Thus, the Aramæan dialects, the Chaldee and Syriac, in very many words regularly substitute א for the Hebrew final ה, and the corresponding linguals for the Hebrew sibilants, צ being sometimes still further weakened by the loss even of the lingual sound to that of the guttural ע, e. g.:

Heb. תָּעָה *to wander*, Chald. טְעָא, Syr. ܛܥܐ; Heb. זָהָב *gold*, Chald. דְּהַב, Syr. ܕܗܒܐ; Heb. צוּר *a rock*, Chald. טוּר, Syr. ܛܘܪܐ; Heb. שָׁלֹשׁ *three*, Chald. תְּלָת, Syr. ܬܠܬ, Arab. ثَلَاثٌ; Heb. אֶרֶץ *the earth*, Arab. أَرْضٌ, Chald. אֲרַע, Syr. ܐܪܥܐ. Other consonant changes: Heb. בֵּן *a son*, Arab. إِبْنٌ, Chald. בַּר, Syr. ܒܪ; Heb. קָטַל *to kill*, Arab. قَتَلَ; Heb. רָקָב, Syr. ܢܩܒܐ; Heb. כִּסֵּא *a throne*, Chald. כּוּרְסֵי, Syr. ܟܘܪܣܝܐ, Arab. كُرْسِيٌّ; Heb. חֶלְקָה *a field*, Chald. חַקְלָא, Syr. ܚܩܠܐ, Eth. ሐቅል።.

4. Of simple euphony: An alternate form of a word may be produced to facilitate its pronunciation or make its sound more pleasing, e. g.:

אַרְגָּמָן, אַרְגְּוָן *purple*; שָׂנֵא, שָׂנָא *to hate*; לִשְׁכָּה, נִשְׁכָּה *chamber*, הֵיוָג, הֵוָג *Achan*; נְבוּכַדְרֶאצַּר, נְבוּכַדְנֶאצַּר *Nebuchadnezzar*; דֹּאֵג, דַּוָּג *Doeg*; אַלְגּוּמִּים, אַלְמֻגִּים *almug* or *algum trees*; מַתַּלְּעוֹת, מַלְתְּעוֹת *teeth*.

a. Mere varieties of orthography must not be mistaken for consonantal changes, e. g. לֹא occasionally for לוֹ and *vice versa*, probably שִׁבֳּלֻת for סִבֳּלֶת, and such permutations of gutturals as abound in the manuscripts of the Samaritans, who, making no distinction in the sounds of these letters, perpetually confounded them in writing, Gesen. Sam. Pent. p. 52. A like faulty pronunciation has been attributed to the Galileans, to which there is a probable allusion in Matt. 26:73. Buxtorf Lex. Chald. p. 434.

§ 52. The changes thus far described result in the production of distinct words, and belong to the domain of the lexicon rather than of the grammar. The lexicographer regards such words as cognate, and traces them back to their common source; but, in the view of the grammarian, they are totally distinct. The mutations with which the latter concerns himself are such as take place in the direct derivation and inflection of words. These are altogether euphonic, are more restricted in their character, and take place within far narrower limits, than those heretofore considered. When words are subjected to grammatical changes their sounds are brought into new connections, attended, it may be, with

§ 53   CONSONANT CHANGES.   71

a difficulty of utterance which demands some measure of relief, or they pass readily and naturally into other sounds, which are easier of pronunciation or more agreeable to the ear. The mutations thus induced are of three sorts, viz.: Consonant Changes, the Conversion of Consonants into Vowels, and Vowel Changes. These will require to be considered separately.

Consonant Changes.

§ 53. The first class of changes embraces those which affect the consonants. These mostly arise from the concurrence of two consonants, creating a difficulty in the pronunciation or yielding a sound displeasing to the ear. This may take place either at the beginning or the close of a syllable. Syllables in Hebrew may, and often do, begin with two consonants, § 18. 1; but the necessity of this is avoided in certain cases by the following expedients:

1. In the beginning of words the weak letter ה is sometimes prefixed with a short vowel, thus creating a new initial syllable to which the first consonant may be transferred.

a. The only instances of this are afforded by the second and seventh conjugations of verbs, the Niphal and Hithpael, e. g. הִקְטֵל = תִּקְטֵל for תְּקַטֵּל; הִתְקַטֵּל probably for תְּקַטֵּל § 82. 5. *b.* In אַהֲלֹךְ Ezek. 14:3 א is prefixed instead of ה. Prosthesis is more common in the domain of the lexicon, where א is always the letter used, e. g. זְרוֹעַ, אֶזְרוֹעַ *arm*; תְּמוֹל, אֶתְמוֹל *yesterday*. A prefixed א is even occasionally employed to soften the pronunciation without the necessity stated above, e. g. אֲבַטִּחִים, אֲנָפִים, אֲדַרְכֹּנִים, אוּזִּים. So in Chaldee אֲדַם *blood*, Heb. דָּם; אַגַּן *garden*, Heb. גַּן. In Arabic the concurrence of two consonants at the beginning of a word is regularly obviated by prefixing ا. Comp. Greek χθές, ἐχθές.

2. The first of the concurrent consonants, if it has a comparatively feeble sound, is sometimes dropped.

72 ORTHOGRAPHY. § 53

a. This occurs regularly in verbs whose first radical is י or נ, and in nouns derived from such verbs, e. g. שֵׁב for יְשֵׁב, דֵּעָה for יְדֵעָה, גּוּל for רְגוּל, חִי for חָיִי, תֵּן for נָתֵן Ezek. 2:10 for נָתְנִי, חָשַׁל Ezek. 1:4 for נַחְשַׁל, and perhaps בָּאר Am. 8:8 for בְּיָאֹר.

א is thus dropped in נַחְתּוּ for נִאֲחַתּוּ, שֶׁ for אֲשֶׁר; also in a few instances from the beginning of the second syllable of words, e. g. וָאֶבְדְּךָ Ezek. 28:16 for וָאַאֲבֶדְךָ; אֹזֶן Job 32:11 for אַאֲזִין; הָסוּרִים Eccl. 4:14 for הָאֲסוּרִים; מַצֹּת 2 Chron. 22:5 for מַאֲצֹּת; הָרַמִּים Ezek. 20:37 for הָאֲרַמִּים; מַצֹּלֶת 1 Kin. 5:25 with Daghesh-forte conservative for מַאֲצֹלֶת; אָחַז Prov. 8:17 for אֲאַחֵז; מֵזִין Prov. 17:4 for מַאֲזִין; שְׁלָתְךָ 1 Sam. 1:17 for שְׁאֵלָתְךָ. These examples likewise admit of a different explanation; א may give up its consonantal power, losing its sound in that of the preceding vowel, agreeably to § 57. 2 (2), after which it may readily be dropped altogether.

ש is occasionally dropped from the participles of the Pual or fourth conjugation, as לֻקַּח for מְלֻקָּח, ל in לְקַח for לִקַּח, ה in לַּח Ex. 3:2 for לֶהָבַת; לְשִׂיחָה Ex. 7:22 for לַהֲשִׂיחָה Ex. 7:11; and perhaps כ in סוּחֹה Gen. 49:11, which appears to be for כְּסוּחֹה.

b. The rejection of a consonant from the beginning of a syllable, when not immediately followed by another consonant, is exceptional; as רַד Judg. 9:11 for יָרַד; תַּחַת 2 Sam. 22:41 for נָתַחַת; חַר Ezek. 33:30 for הֶחָתַלְתִּי; הָאֲשֹׁות Neh. 3:13 for הָאֲשֹׁותִי; הִתְחַלְתִּי Judg. 9:9 for הֶחָתַלְתִּי, and perhaps שׁוּב Jer. 42:10, which seems to be for יָשׁוּב.

3. The second consonant is sometimes dropped, if it is a letter of feeble sound.

a. This is regularly the case with ה of the article and of verbal prefixes, and י as the final radical of verbs, e. g. לַבַּיִת for לְהַבַּיִת; יִקְטֵל for יְקַטְטֵל; גְּלִי for גָּלוּי.

It occurs besides in a few sporadic examples with these same letters, and more rarely still with א, ו, and ע, e. g. וִי for וְהִי, נִי for נְהִי Ezek. 2:10 for נְהִי, קְטַלְתֵּמוּ and יְקַטְלְמוּ, יְרוּשָׁלַיִם, יוֹשָׁט with Daghesh-forte conservative for יְקַטְלָנְהוּ and וַתָּלֹד Lam. 3:53 for וַיְרִדוּ, הָרוֹנֶךָ Gen. 3:16 for חֵרָיוֹנֵךְ; מַצֵּבֵנוּ Job 35:11 for מְאַצֵּבֵנוּ Ex. 26:24 for תֹּאֲמִים, וַתַּזְרֵנִי 2 Sam. 22:40 for וַתְּאַזְּרֵנִי; כִּי וְהֵאָזַרְנִי Isa. 3:24 for כִּוי, רָאֵל Isa. 13:20 for יַאֲהֵל, גְּוִי for גֵּוִי, רָמִים for רְאֵמִים as a particle of entreaty, probably for בִּי Am. 8:8 (K'thibh) for נָשְׁקָה; בֵּל בְּנֶשְׁקָה the name of a Babylonish deity for בֵּעַל. The conjecture that בֹּי Mic. 1:10 is for בְּעַכּוֹ *in Accho* is ingenious and favoured by the occurrence of בְּנַת *in Gath* in the parallel clause; but it is at variance with the points, which, upon this hypothesis, should be בֹּי.

b. In rare cases this rejection occurs even after a mixed syllable, whose final consonant is thus drawn forward, e. g. אָמָה for אֲמָה, חָמָה Job 29:6 for חֵמְאָה, חָצָב Ex. 2:4 for תִּתְחַצַּב and probably אֶפֶס Ps. 139:8 with Daghesh-forte conservative for אֶסְלַק.

§ 54. When the concurrence takes place at the close of a syllable, whether the second consonant belongs to the same syllable with the first as at the end of words, or to a different syllable as in the middle of words, the following changes may be produced.

1. An aspirate following another consonant loses its aspiration, § 21; or if it be brought into juxtaposition with its like so as to form a doubled letter, the aspiration of both will be removed, § 23. 2, unless the combination occurs at the end of a word, where the reduplication is not expressed, § 25. Thus, בַּתְּ for בַּתְּ, מַתְּ for מַתְתְ, הִתְתַּם for הִתַּם, לִבְבָךְ for לִבְּךָ, but רַב from רָבַב, מְשָׁרְתֵי 1 Kin. 1 : 15 for מְשָׁרֲתֵי or מְשָׁרְתֵי, מֲחַבַּת Ezek. 4 : 3 for מַחֲבַת, מִשְׁחַת Mal. 1 : 14 for מָשְׁחָת.

2. The first of two concurring consonants is in certain cases assimilated to the second, the doubling thus occasioned being expressed as in the case of letters originally alike by Daghesh-forte, except at the end of words, § 25, where Daghesh disappears or is only virtually present, being resumed upon the addition of a fresh vowel or syllable. This is most frequently the case with the liquid נ, rarely with ל and ר and only in particular words; so ת of the Hithpael of verbs before ד and ט, and in a few instances before sibilants and other letters, and ד at the end of a few words before ת. Thus, יִתֵּן for יִנְתֵן, מִתַּתִּ for מַתַּתִּי; יִקַּח for יִלְקַח, בַּדֻפָּה Ezek. 27 : 23 for כַּלָּה Am. 6 : 2; שֶׁלִּי for אֲשֶׁר לִי; יִדַּכְּאוּ for יִתְדַּכְּאוּ, יִשָּׂא for יִתְשָׂא, הִזַּכּוּ for הִתְזַכּוּ, תִּשּׁוֹמֵם for אַחַת, לָדַת for לָלֶדֶת, תִּתַּפֶּה for תִּתְפַּשֶּׂה; כַּת for הִנַּבְאוּ for הִתְנַבְּאוּ, תִּתְשׁוֹמֵם for אַחַרְתִּ.

a. So perhaps כ in מִכָּה according to Gesenius for מִכְבָּה and טַ for טַבְּ. Compare Greek συγγενής for συνγενής, τέτυμμαι for τέτυπμαι, and Eng. *il-logical, ir-religion, im-mature* formed by the negative prefix *in*.

3. A few isolated cases occur of the reverse process more common in Chaldee and Syriac, by which a doubled letter is resolved into two different consonants by the change of the

first or the second member of the reduplication to a liquid ר or נ, e.g. מְכַרְבָּל for מְכַבְבָּל, דַּרְמָשֶׂק for דַּמֶּשֶׂק, מְעַזְנָיָה Isa. 23:11 for מְעַנְּיָה, קִנְצֵי Job 18:2 in the judgment of some for קִצֵּי ends, though others make the נ a radical, and give the word the sense of snares. The conjecture that תְּמוּ Ps. 64:7, Lam. 3:22 is for תַּמּוּ is unnecessary and unwarranted.

4. When ת of the Hithpael of verbs would stand before a sibilant, it is transposed with ס and שׁ, and with צ it is in addition changed to ט. Thus, מִשְׁתַּמֵּר for מִתְשַׁמֵּר, יִשְׁתַּמֵּר for יִתְשַׁמֵּר, יִתְשַׁקֵּל for יִתְשַׁקֵּל, נִצְטַדָּק for נִתְצַדָּק.

a. In הִתְשׁוֹגַבְנָה Jer. 49:3 the transposition does not take place in consequence of the number of similar letters which would thus be brought into proximity. In the cognate languages ת is likewise transposed with ו and changed to ד: thus, Chald. חִזְדַּבַּן for הִתְזַבַּן; so, also, in Syriac and Arabic. The only example of a Hebrew verb whose first letter is ו appearing in this conjugation is הִוָּדְעוּ Isa. 1:16, where ת is assimilated agreeably to 2. Compare with these transpositions the frequent Doric change of ζ (= δσ) into σδ, as συρίσδω for συρίζω.

§ 55. The occurrence of a consonant at the end of a word may, inasmuch as the succeeding word must necessarily begin with one, be regarded as an additional case of the concurrence of consonants. As the contact is less close, however, than when they meet in the same word, it is less fruitful of changes than in the cases already considered.

1. There are three instances in which it has been doubtfully conjectured that a final ן has been assimilated to a following initial מ; viz. יְשִׁשּׂוּם Isa. 35:1 presumed to be for יְשׂוּשׂוּן; פִּדְיוֹם Num. 3:49 for פִּדְיוֹן Ex. 21:30, Ps. 49:9; סֻלָּם Gen. 28:12.

a. Final consonants are in Sanskrit perpetually modified by the initial letter of the following word. But it is by no means clear that this is so in Hebrew, even in the examples alleged, as the forms admit of a different explanation. See in regard to the first passage, Dr. Alexander's Commentary.

2. A few cases occur of the rejection of a letter, chiefly ן and מ, from the end of a word.

a. ן of the verbal endings וּן and יִן is almost always dropped, being only retained as an archaeic or emphatic form, and chiefly at the end of a clause, e. g. יִרְדְּיֻן Deut. 8:16, but mostly יִרְדּוּ; תְּדַבְּרוּן Gen. 32:20, commonly תְּדַבְּרוּ; תְּעַשִּׂין Ruth 3:4, commonly תַּעֲשִׂי. So, too, in some proper nouns, מְגִדּוֹן Zech. 12:11, מְגִדּוֹ Josh. 12:21; שִׁילוֹ, whose original ן is shown in the derivative שִׁילֹנִי and is perpetuated in the modern name *Seilûn*.

b. In like manner מ is rejected from the dual and plural terminations of nouns upon their entering into the close connection of the construct state with the following word, אָזְנֵי from אָזְנַיִם, בָּתֵּי from בָּתִּים.

c. If the feminine endings ת and הָ have, as is probable, a common origin, this may be best explained by the assumption that ה is in many cases rejected from the termination, leaving only the vowel, though it is always retained when any addition is made to the word: thus, the construct state חָכְמַת, absolute חָכְמָה, but with a suffix חָכְמָתִי; קְטָלָה (comp. אָזְלַת Deut. 32:36), קְטָלַתְנִי. It is to be observed here, that this phenomenon does not establish the possibility of an interchange between the consonants ה and ת, because ה in this case represents not *h* but the vowel *â*.

§ 56. A few other changes remain to be mentioned which are due to special causes.

1. Nun is often inserted in certain forms of verbal suffixes to prevent the hiatus between two vowels, יַעַבְרֶנְהוּ Jer. 5:22, or § 53. 3. *a.* יַעַבְרֵהוּ Isa. 33:21 for יַעַבְרֵהוּ, אֲרוֹמְמֶנְהוּ Ex. 15:2 for אֲרוֹמְמֵהוּ. Comp. Gr. ἀνόσιος and English indefinite article *an*.

2. Vav at the beginning of words is changed to י, e. g. יֶלֶד for וֶלֶד, יָלַד for וָלַד, יִקְטֹל for וִקְטֹל. The only exceptions are the four words וָו, וָזָר Prov. 21:8, וָלָד Gen. 11:30, וָלָד 2 Sam. 6:23 (K'ri), and the prefixes Vav Conjunctive and Vav Conversive.

3. Vav, though capable of being reduplicated, e. g. אִוֶּלֶד is in most instances relieved from this necessity by the substitution of י, or by doubling the following letter in its stead, e. g. אָקוּם or אֲקוֹמֵם for אֲקַוֵּם.

a. In one instance after such a change of ו to י, a following י suffers the contrary change to ו to prevent the triple recurrence of the same letter, אֲרִוְךָ Isa. 6:9 for אֲרִיְךָ.

4. Yodh before the plural termination ים. is in a few cases changed to א to prevent the conjunction of like sounds, תְּלוּאִים Hos. 11:7 for תְּלוּיִם Josh. 10:26; צְבוֹאִים Hos. 11:8 for צְבֹיִם Gen. 10:19; הוֹדָאִים from הוֹדָיִ; צְבָאוֹת (also צְבָאֹת) for צְבָיִים; בְּלוֹאֵי Jer. 38:12 for בְּלֹיֵי (or as some read, בְּלוֹיֵי) ver. 11.

a. In like manner ו is changed to א before וֹת in the word נָאוֹת for נְוֹת from נָוָה; it is consequently unnecessary to assume, as Gesenius does, a singular נָאָה which never occurs.

Change of Consonants to Vowels.

§ 57. The second class of changes is the conversion of consonants into vowels, or the substitution of the latter for the former. This occurs,

1. Occasionally in reduplicated syllables or letters, כּוֹכָב for כַּבְכָּב; טוֹטָפוֹת for טַפְטָפוֹת; בָּבֶל for בַּלְבֵּל Gen. 11:9; צְלָחוֹת 2 Chron. 35:13 from צַלַּחַת Prov. 19:24.

2. Much more frequently with the quiescents.

(1) A prefixed וְ is softened to its homogeneous vowel $\bar{u}$ before other labials or vowelless letters, e. g. וּדְבַר, וּבַיִת; the softening of an initial י to $\bar{\imath}$ only occurs in אִישִׁי 1 Chron. 2:13 for יִשַׁי ver. 12, אֵשׁ 2 Sam. 14:19, Mic. 6:10 for יֵשׁ.

(2) Medial or final quiescents without vowels of their own often lose their sound in that of a preceding vowel. This is invariably the case with ו and י following their homogeneous vowels, e. g. הוּלַד for הֻוְלַד § 59, בִּיהוּדָה for בְּיַהוּדָה, unless they are doubled, as צַוָּה, מַיְשִׁרֵי, and occasionally even

then, e. g. מֵימֵי for מֵימֵי. Final א always, and medial א frequently, gives up its consonant sound after any vowel whatever, e. g. מֹצָאת, מֹצָא, מָצָא for מֹצָאת.

a. Medial א regularly loses its consonantal power in the future Kal of Pe Aleph verbs, e. g. יֹאבַל; in אֹמֵר preceded by ל, thus לֵאמֹר; in אֱלֹהִים and certain forms of אָדוֹן preceded by the prefixes ב ל כ ו, thus, לֵאלֹהִים, לַאדֹנָי, לַאדֹנִי, לַאדוֹן but לַאדֹנָיו, לַאדֹנִי, לַאדֹנֵינוּ. The following examples are of a more individual character, e. g. נָאצָה for נֶאָצָה, וָאֶצְּפֶה 1 Kin. 11:39 for וָאֲצַפֶּה, הָאֲסֻפּוֹת Num. 11:4, בָּאזִקִּים Jer. 40:1, כְּאַבְאָתֵיהֶ Isa. 14:23. In a few cases this has led to a change of orthography, the א which is no longer heard being dropped, or another vowel letter substituted for it, e. g. יוֹכְלוּ Ezek. 42:5, and אוֹכִיל Hos. 11:4 from אָבַל, רִישׁוֹן Job 8:8 for רֹאשׁוֹן, רוֹשׁ Deut. 32:32 for רֹאשׁ, and the examples cited § 53. 2, *a*.

b. The consonant ה never loses its sound in that of a preceding vowel like the rest of the quiescents. The letter ה is often used to denote a vowel, but if in any word it properly expresses a consonant this is never converted into a vowel, or *vice versâ.* The exceptions are apparent not real, as in the frequent abbreviation of the ending יָהוּ in proper names to יָה, thus חִזְקִיָּהוּ, חִזְקִיָּה. The change here does not consist in the rejection of the vowel ו and the softening of the consonant ה, but the syllable הוּ is dropped, whereupon final Kamets is written by its appropriate vowel letter, § 11. 1, *a*, just as מִיכָיְהוּ after the rejection of יְהוּ becomes מִיכָה. So in those rare cases in which ה is substituted for the suffix ם, e. g. שְׂעָרָה Lev. 13:4 for שְׂעָרָם. The proper name פַּרְדָּאֵל Num. 34:28 is derived not from פָּרָה but פָּרַד, a root of kindred meaning, of whose existence, though otherwise unattested, this word is itself a sufficient voucher.

(3) Medial א often gives its vowel to a preceding vowelless letter and rests in its sound; י occasionally does the same with a homogeneous vowel, when preceded by a vowelless prefix.

a. Thus, א: רָאשִׁים for רֵאשִׁים, חַטָּאת for חֲטָאת; שָׁאטְךָ Ezek. 25:6 from שָׁאַט ver. 15; נְשֹׂא Ps. 139:20 for נָשׂוֹא, so יִשּׂוֹא Jer. 10:5; רְאוּבֵנִי from רְאוּבֵן; בֹּרְאָם Neh. 6:8 for בֹּדְאָם; הֹיא Isa. 51:20, תֵּאוֹ Deut. 14:5; וַיֹּאשֶׁר for וַיַּאֲשֵׁר; בַּאֲבִיר Isa. 10:13 for בְּאַבִּיר; חֹטְאִים 1 Sam. 14:33 for חֹטְאִים; יְאֶשֶׁר Zech. 11:5 for יַאֲשֶׁר; this even occurs after mixed syllables, e. g. מְלָאכָה for מְלָאכָה; נָאִיץ for נָאֵץ; לִקְרָאת for לִקְרֹאת, particularly in proper nouns יִשְׁמָעֵאל for יִשְׁמָעֵאל, יִזְרְעֵאל for יִזְרְעֵאל. So, פִּרְיֹנוֹ: Eccles. 2:13 for פִּרְיוֹנוֹ; וַיְלַלֵּת Jer. 25:36 for וִילֵלַת, לִיקְּהַת Prov. 30:17 for לִיקְהַת. There is no instance of this with ו, on the contrary, קְוֻצּוֹת Cant. 5:2, 12.

(4) At the end of words ו and י, when without a vowel of their own and preceded by a vowelless letter, invariably

quiesce in their homogeneous vowels, ו in an unaccented *û*, י in *î*, which draws the accent upon itself and frequently causes the dissolution of a previous syllable and the rejection of its vowel, יְהִי for יִהְיֶה; יִשְׁתַּחְוּ for יִשְׁתַּחֲוּ, בְּחִי for בֹּהִי for דָּמִי, פְּרִי for דָּמְיִ‎.

(5) When preceded or accompanied by heterogeneous vowels, ו and י are sometimes dropped, or if the vowel be *a*, they not unfrequently combine with it, forming the diphthongal *o* and *e*, § 62. 1, c. g. הוּצַּק for חֻיְצַק, גְּלֹה for גְּלִי, גָּלָה for גָּלְיָה, הֵקִים for הֵקְיִם, קָם for קַוְם, גְּלִי for הוֹשִׁיב for הוֹשְׁיִב, נָדוֹשׁ for נָדְוֹשׁ, מוֹת construct state of מָוֶת, בֵּית const. of בַּיִת, הֵילִיל for הַיְלִיל, יִגְלֶה for יִגְלְיֶה‎.

a. Vav rarely remains with a heterogeneous vowel unless accompanied by weak letters, by contrast with which it becomes comparatively strong, e. g. רָוַח‎, גִּוֵּר‎, חָוָה‎.

Vowel Changes.

§ 58. 1. The third class of changes embraces those which take place in the vowels. The primary office of the vowels is to aid in pronouncing the consonants, to which consequently they are quite subordinate, merely occupying, so to speak, the interstices between them. Their number and variety being greater, however, than is demanded for this single purpose, they have besides to a certain extent an independent value and meaning of their own in the constitution of words. (1) Changes of vowels, while they cannot like a difference of consonants create distinct verbal roots, are yet fruitful of those minor modifications of which etymology takes cognizance, such as the formation of derivatives and grammatical inflexions, e. g. גָּדַל *to be great*, גֹּדֶל *greatness*, גָּדוֹל *great;* קָטַל *he killed*, קְטֹל *to kill*, קְטֹל *kill thou*, קָטֹל *killing*, קָטוּל *killed;* סוּס *a horse*, סוּסָה *a mare*. (2) They may indicate differences in the forms of words which have arisen in the lapse of time; נַעַר in the Pentateuch means indifferently *girl* or *boy*, in later books *girl* is נַעֲרָה; הִיא in the Pentateuch *he* or *she*, in other books *she* is always הִיא; the form of the demonstrative הַלָּזֶה is found only in Genesis, הַלָּז in writers after the time of Moses, הַלֵּזוּ in Ezekiel; the plural of the demonstrative in the Pentateuch אֵל or אֵלֶּה, elsewhere, with a single exception, אֵלֶּה. The imperfect notation of the vowels in the original mode of writing by letters alone has, however, left us without the means of ascertaining to what extent such changes may have taken place. (3) They may indicate diversity of dialect, e. g. קְטַל *to kill*, Chald. קְטַל, Syr. ܩܛܠ, Arab. قَتَلَ, Ethiop. ቀተለ፡.

2. The vowel changes with which orthography is concerned, on the other hand, are purely euphonic, being in themselves void of significance, and springing solely from the natural preference for what is easier of utterance or more agreeable to the ear. Orthographically considered, vowels are either mutable or immutable, the latter being unaffected by those circumstances which occasion changes in the former. A vowel may be immutable by nature, or made so by position. A short vowel in a mixed syllable before the accent is ordinarily immutable by position, being beyond the reach of the common causes of mutation, e. g. מִשְׁפָּחָה, מִדְבָּר. Long vowels are immutable by nature in certain words or classes of words; but they are only distinguishable as such by a knowledge of the etymological forms which require them. It may, however, be observed, as a general though not an invariable rule, that the vowels of such words and forms as are prevailingly written with the vowel letters are less liable to mutation than those which are prevailingly written without them. Mutable vowels are liable to changes both of quantity, from long to short, and the reverse, and of quality from pure to mixed (*u* to *o*, *i* to *e*, *a* to *ĕ*) and the reverse, these changes being confined, except in rare in-

stances, to the cognate forms; thus, *i* never passes into *u* or *o*, nor these into *a*. Only as *ĕ* stands in relation to both *i* and *a*, it serves to mediate the interval between them, and thus accounts for the occasional changes of *i* to *a* or the reverse, e. g. הִקְטִיל, הִקְטַלְתְּ, הִקְטַלְתָּ; בַּת for בֶּנֶת, בִּתִּי; דָּם, דְּמָכֶם comp. יְדֵכֶם, יָד.

a. The exceptional change from *u* or *o* to *e* occurs only in the pronouns, e. g. קְטַלְתֶּם, before suffixes קְטַלְתּוּהָ; and in the particle אֵת, before suffixes אֹתִי. There are also a few examples of the change of short vowels in mixed syllables before the accent, e. g. מַרְכָּבָה, construct מִרְכֶּבֶת, plural מַרְכְּבוֹת.

§ 59. The mutations of vowels are due to one or other of the following causes, viz.: 1. Syllabic changes. 2. The influence of consonants. 3. The influence of vowels. 4. The accent. 5. The shortening or lengthening of words. As the vowel of unaccented mixed syllables is always short, and that of simple syllables long, § 18. 2, it is evident that a change in the character of a syllable will involve a corresponding change in its vowel, unless the accent interfere to prevent. Accordingly, when for any cause a mixed syllable becomes simple, its short vowel will be converted into a long one; and when a simple syllable becomes mixed, the reverse change will take place, e. g. הַר, הָרִים; קָמָה, קָמְתָּ. In the case of the vowels *i* and *u* there is frequently an additional change of quality, viz., of *ĭ* to *ē* and *ŭ* to *ō*, e. g. הֵקִים for הֵקִימוּ; כּוֹנֵן for כֹּנְנוּ in place of כֻּנַּן § 56. 3.

a. Daghesh-forte is thus resolved by the prolongation of the previous vowel in בּוֹרְחִים, בּוֹרְגִים; חֲמִישִׁי, חֲדָשִׁי; פִּלַּגְשִׁי, פִּלַּגְשֵׁי; קַרְלֹשׁ, קְטֻלּוֹשׁ; הִתְפַּקְּדוּ for הִתְפָּקְדוּ § 33. 2. *a*; מְרֻקָּשִׁים Eccles. 9:12 for יוּקְשִׁים; חִטְקִי, חָקִי; גִּלְיָתָה Lam. 1:8, if this is for גָּלְתָה see ver. 17; and if the conjecture of Gesenius (Thesaurus, p. 483) be correct as to the true reading in 1 Chron. 23:6, 24:3 יְחַלְּקֵם for יַחַלְּקֵם.

§ 60. Contiguous consonants may give rise to vowel changes by their individual peculiarities, as is the case with the gutturals, or by their concurrence. The peculiarities of the gutturals are fourfold, viz.:

1. A preference for the vowel Pattahh of the same organ, into which, consequently, a preceding or accompanying vowel is frequently converted, e. g. שָׁלַח for שָׁלֵח; פָּעַם for פָּעֵם; יִגְבַּה for יִגְבֹּהַ; שָׁמֵעַ for שָׁמֵעַ; טְנֵאָה from שָׂנֵא.

a. The instances in which this permutation occurs cannot easily be embraced under any general rules. In some cases it was optional; in others, usage decides for it or against it without, however, being absolutely uniform. The following statements embrace what is of most importance. (1) The stability of the vowel often depends upon the weight attached to it in the etymological form; thus, שְׁמַע in the imperative but not in the infinitive שְׁמֹעַ; יִשְׁמַע for יִשְׁמֵעַ, but שָׁמֵעַ not שָׁמַע for שֹׁמֵעַ. (2) The vowel preceding the guttural is more liable to change than that which succeeds it, e. g. יִשְׁלַח always, but יִרְעַל and תֶּחֱזַל; יִזְנַח but חֹסֶם; נָקַף but עֲבֹד. (3) An accented vowel is sometimes retained where one unaccented would suffer change, e. g. רָחֵל but וַיִּזְנַח; לֶחֶם and וַיִּזְנַח. (4) O and u are less subject to alteration than i and e, e. g. בַּעַל for בֹּעַל; a which is already cognate with the gutturals is mostly retained, though it occasionally becomes ā before ח, e. g. אָחִים from אָח, דִּבְנָתְהִ Job 31:24 (in most copies) from דִּבְעָה, יָרֵחַ from יְרֵחָה. (5) א in many cases prefers the diphthongal vowels e and o, thus שֵׁאֵל, אָמְרָתִי, וַיְצַאתִי, תִּמְצָאן, יֶאְסֹר but יַאַסְרוּם; יֹאכַל, רְבָא. (6) ר partakes of this preference for ā to a limited extent, e. g. יִרְאָה for יַפְסַר or נַפְסָר; וַיַּרְא from יִרְאָה.

2. The reception of Pattahh furtive, §17, at the end of a word after a long heterogeneous vowel (i. e. any other than a), or before a vowelless final consonant, e. g. רֵעַ, יַגְבִּיהַּ, נֹחַ, יָגַעְתָּ, רוּחַ.

a. This is necessary when the vowel preceding a final guttural cannot be converted into Pattahh. Sometimes the form with Pattahh and that with Pattahh furtive occur interchangeably. e. g. לְשַׁלַּח and לְשַׁלֵּחַ, or with a slight distinction, as אֲשַׁלַּח, in pause אֲשַׁלֵּחַ; מִזְבַּח, construct מִזְבֵּחַ. In a few instances a guttural preceding a final vowelless letter takes simple Sh'va instead of Pattahh furtive, e. g. לְקַחְתְּ 1 Kin. 14:3, and in most editions שָׁבַחְתְּ Jer. 13:25. As final א is always either quiescent or otiant, it never receives Pattahh furtive. The letter ר never takes it unless it be in a single instance, and that in a penultimate syllable יִרְדֹּף Ps. 7:6. which is probably to be read *yi*ᵃ*rdoph*; though it might be pronounced *yiraddoph*, which some conceive to be an anomalous form for יִרְדֹּף, after the analogy of יִצְחָק Gen. 21:6, the compound Sh'va being lengthened into a vowel followed by euphonic Daghesh, as in the related words

חֲבוּרָה Isa. 1:6, and חֲבָלָה Isa. 53:5, while others adopt the explanation of the old Jewish Grammarians, that it is a peculiar combination of the Kal יִרְדֹּף and the Piel יְרַדֵּף.

3. A preference for compound rather than simple Sh'va, § 16. 3, whether silent or vocal, inasmuch as the gutturals are more readily made audible at the beginning than at the close of a syllable, and the hiatus accompanying them assumes more of the complexion of a vowel than is usual with stronger consonants.

a. The gutturals occasionally retain simple Sh'va when silent. This is regularly done by a final radical ה, ח or ע, followed by a servile letter, e. g. גָּבַהְתְּ, יָדַעְנוּ, יִרְבְּעָם, מִשְׁפְּחֹתָם, מִשְׁפַּחְתּוֹ, with few exceptions as יָרְדְּנוּךְ Hos. 8:2, נִצְּלָנוּ Gen. 26:29, חֹקְבֵנוּ 2 Sam. 21:6. Other cases have more of a casual or sporadic character, and occur chiefly with the stronger gutturals ה and ח, מַחֲשְׁבוֹת, חֲתִיתָהּ, תִּחְלֹל, יֶחְיֶה, נֶחְפָּז, יָחְיֶה, but נַחְפְּשָׂה, יַחְבְּשׁוּ but נַחֲלָה, נָחְלָה, נַחְלָה from נַחַל *a brook;* more rarely with א and ע, נַעְלָם Lev. 4:13, בִּגְשָׁא 1 Kin. 15:16, בְּעָלָהּ Isa. 11:15, שָׂעְרָה Deut. 25:7 but in pause שַׂעְרָה Isa. 28:6, נֶאְדָּרִי Ex. 15:6; ר has for the most part simple Sh'va יְגָרְשׁוּ, רְבִית, though in a few instances it has compound בְּרֲבוֹ, וַיְקַרֲבֵהוּ.

b. (1) Among the compound Sh'vas the preference, unless there is some reason for choosing another, is ordinarily given to Hhateph Pattahh, as the simplest and most in accordance with the nature of the gutturals, and to this an antecedent Hhirik, when unessential to the form, is commonly made to correspond, e. g. עֲבֹד, יַעֲבֹד for יִקְטֹל. Sometimes, particularly with א (see 1. *a.* 5.) Hhateph Seghol is taken אֱלִלֹּת, אֱמוּנָה, אֱזָרָה, אֱסֹף, אֱדוֹם, חֶרְיָם, עֱזוּז, עֱנוּת, בֱּרִיךְ, יֹאחֱזוּךְ Joel 2:5, יֹאחֱזוּךְ Jer. 13:21, which not infrequently becomes Hhateph Pattahh upon the prolongation of the word אֲמָרְךָ, אֲמָר, Prov. 25:7, אֲמָתוֹ, אֲדוֹמִי, יֹאחֲזוּהוּ Judg. 10:2, or the carrying forward of its accent וְתָחֳרַמְתִּי, הָחֳרַבְתִּי, הָאֲבַדְתִּי.

(2) If, however, ŏ or ō, characteristic of the form, precede, this commonly determines the Sh'va to be selected. e. g. יַעֲמֹד for הַעֲמִיד, חָעֳמִיד for יַעֲמֹד, פָּעֳלִי for פָּעֳלִי; though sometimes Hhateph Pattahh is retained and the intermediate syllable, § 20. 2, resolved into a simple one by prolonging the vowels, e. g. הֶעֱרָה Josh. 7:7, הָעֳלוּ, פָּעֳלוּ Isa. 1:31. Hhirik may, however, remain short, e. g. תֶּחֱלָא, שֶׁחֲרִי Job 6:22, particularly if a Daghesh-forte has been omitted from the guttural, e. g. נֶאְסָה Jer. 3:8, though even in this case the assimilation sometimes takes place, e. g. יַחְמוּ Gen. 30:39 for יֶחֱמוּ, אַחֲרֵי Judg. 5:28 for אֶחֱרֵי. If a vowel has been rejected from the form, the corresponding Hhateph is generally preferred, e. g. כְּפָרִים from כֹּפֶר, חֲדָרִים, חֲדָרִי Ezek. 16:33, רָאִי Gen. 16:13; הֶשִׁיבוֹ 1 Kin. 13:20 from הָשִׁיב, הֲשִׁיבוֹ Gen. 37:22 from הָשִׁיב. There are occasional instances of the same word being variously written in this respect, e. g. אֲחוֹזִי Ruth 3:15, אֶחֱזוּ Cant. 2:15; יִתְאָרְהוּ and

יִתְאָרְֽהוּ Isa. 44:13; חֲמַרְמָ֫רוּ Job 16:16 (K'ri in some copies), חֳמַרְמָ֫רוּ Lam. 1:20, תֹּאֲרוּ Isa. 52:14, תֹּאֲרוּ 1 Sam. 28:14.

c. Before another guttural the compound Sh'va is frequently replaced by the corresponding short vowel, e. g. הַאֲלֵךְ for הֶאֱלֵךְ, הַעֲיֽרֹתִי for הֶעֱיֽרֹתִי, הַאֲחִיכֶם for הֶאֱחִיכֶם; and occasionally under א by a long vowel before other letters as well as gutturals, or by a short vowel with Daghesh, e. g. אֳהָלִים for אֹהָלִים, אֳרֳחֹתָיו, אֲבוֹס for אֵבוּס, אֱזוֹר for אֵזוֹר, אַסֵּר for אֱסֹר. This disposition to render the gutturals more audible by the aid of a vowel is further shown by their attracting to themselves the vowel of another letter, particularly in triliteral monosyllables, e. g. זָ֫רַע for זֶ֫רַע (וָ֫רַע), חֵטְא, נֶ֫טַע, בֶּ֫טַע, קֹ֫דַח 2 Kin. 12:9, בֹּאֲשׁ for בָּאֲשׁ, also קְרָאן Ex. 2:20 for קָרְאָן Ruth 1:20, תְּאֵהֲבוּ Prov. 1:22 for תֶּאֱהֲבוּ, תְּאָבְלֶ֫ה Job 20:26 for תֹּאכְלֵ֫הוּ, וַאֲסָפָרֵם Zech. 7:14 for וַאֲסָעֲרֵם, and by their sometimes causing an antecedent or accompanying vowel to be retained where analogy would require its rejection, e. g. מוֹצָאֵי for מֹצָאֵי from מֹצָא, הֵיאָךְ, מִשְׁעִי, סָרִיסִי and בַּחוּרִים from בָּחוּר comp. 1. *a.* (4), יִמְצָאֻהוּ Deut. 32:10; תִּכְלַת, מְבִלַּת.

4. An incapacity for being doubled, whence they never receive Daghesh-forte, and the previous syllable thus becoming a simple one, its vowel is generally lengthened, § 59, ă to ā, ĭ to ē, ŭ to ō, e. g. מָאֵן for מַאֵן, מֵאֵן for מִאֵן, יְבֹרַךְ for תְּעָרֵב, אֵחוּר, יְבֹרַךְ.

a. Sometimes an intermediate syllable, § 20. 2, is formed, and the vowel remains short. (1) This is commonly the case before ח, frequently before ה, less often before ע, rarely before א, never before ר, e. g. נִחַם, נָאֵץ, חִלַּב, בַּחֵר, שֵׁחוּ. (2) It is more likely to occur in the body of a word than after a prefix. e. g. יִחַלְתִּי Ps. 119:43 from יָחַל, but יַחְלֹף Job 38:24 from חָלַף. (3) When the guttural comes to stand at the end of the word the short vowel is often resumed, e. g. תִּחְרָב, תֶּחֱרָב Prov. 22:24 from חָצָר, Ps. 141:8 from תֶּעֱרֶה but תֶּחֱרָב Deut. 2:9. There are a very few instances in which Daghesh-forte is found in ר, e. g. שָׁבֻרָה פָּתַח Ezek. 16:4, מְרַת Prov. 14:10, מַעֲנֵה־רָךְ Prov. 15:1 (in some editions), שֶׁהֳרֹאשִׁי Cant. 5:2, see also § 24. *b.*

§ 61. The concurrence of consonants gives rise to the following vowel changes, viz.:

1. When two vowelless letters come together at the beginning of a syllable in contravention of the law in § 18, the impossible combination is relieved by giving to the first of them a short vowel. This, if there be no reason for preferring another, will be the briefest of the vowels, Hhirik, e. g.

חִזְקִי for חָזְקִי, בְּדְבַר for בִּדְבַר, דִּבְרֵי for דִּבְרֵי. If a vowel has been omitted from the word, the corresponding short vowel is frequently employed, e. g. מַלְכֵי for מִלְכֵי from מֶלֶךְ (מָלֵךְ); יָהֹן from יָחְנָה for יְחֶנֶה, חֶבֶל from חֶבְלֵי; מַלְכֹּה from מַלְכֹּי. Or if one of the consonants be a guttural, the vowel mostly conforms to the compound Sh'va, which it has or might have, e. g. לַחְבֹּר for לְחָבֹר, לְחָלִי for לַחֲלִי, יֶחֱזְקוּ for יַחֲזְקוּ, עֲבְדֵי for עַבְדֵי, פְּעָלֹה for פָּעֳלֹה, לְחָבֹר.

a. Vav before a guttural follows the rule just given; before י, and sometimes before ה or ח followed by י, it takes Hhirik; before other vowelless letters it gives up its consonant sound and quiesces in its homogeneous vowel Shurek, § 57. 2. (1), thus וּלְבַב, וַיְהִי, וַיְהִי, וַיַּעַבְדוּ and וְחָיָה, וְהָיָה, וְהִנֵּה.

b. In triliteral monosyllables or final syllables with the vowel Pattahh, the first letter sometimes receives an accented Seghol, to which the following Pattahh is then assimilated, e. g. פֶּתַח for פְּתַח construct of פָּתָח, בְּמַלְכַּת for בְּמַלְכַּת, the Seghols being liable to be changed to Pattahhs by the presence of a guttural מִשְׁפַּחַת for מִשְׁפְּחַת.

c. In בְּצַאֲבָם Gen. 32: 20 for בְּצַאֲבָם the vowelless letters belong to different syllables, and the introduction of the new vowel makes it necessary to lengthen the one before it.

2. Although two vowelless letters are admissible at the end of a word, § 18, the harshness of the combination is commonly relieved by the insertion of Seghol, e. g. יֶרֶב for יִרְבּ, לֶכֶת for לְכְתְּ. If either letter is a guttural, Pattahh is mostly used instead, e. g. יִתַן, פֹּעַל, נֵצַח. If either letter is י, its homogeneous vowel Hhirik is used; if the second letter is ו, it will rest in Shurek, § 57. 2. (4.), e. g. תֹּהוּ, פְּלִי, בַּיִת, but מָוֶת.

a. When the penultimate letter is ה or ח, it in a few instances takes Seghol, as אֹהֶל, בֶּהָן, לֶחֶם, חֶרֶב. When the final letter is א, it either remains otiant, § 16, or requires Seghol, שָׁוְא, וַיַּרְא, בָּרָא, פֶּרֶא; a penultimate א either quiesces in the antecedent vowel or attracts it to itself, § 60. 3. *c*, וַיֵּאוּ, שְׂאֵת or שְׂאֵת, רֹאשׁ. The alternate mode of facilitating the pronunciation of gutturals before a vowelless letter at the end of a word by means of Pattahh furtive, has been explained § 60. 2.

3. When the same letter is repeated with or without a mutable vowel intervening, there is often a contraction into

one doubled letter, and the vowel is rejected or thrown back upon the preceding consonant, e. g. יִסֹּב for יִסְבְּבוּ, יְסַבְבוּ for יְסֹבֵב (Daghesh-forte disappearing at the end of the word), לֵב for לֵבָב, יְכוּפֵּנוּ Job 31 : 15 for יְכוֹנְנֵנִי (see 4. below); if another consonant immediately follow the contracted letters, a diphthongal vowel ֵי or וֹ may be inserted to render the reduplication more audible and prevent the concurrence of three consonants, תְּסֻבְּבֶינָה, סַבּוֹתִי.

4. In accented syllables the diphthongal vowels *e* and *o* are employed before two consonants or a doubled consonant in preference to the pure *î* and *û*, e. g. קוּם, תָּשֵׁבְנָה; תָּשִׁיב, וַיֵּבְךְּ, קֹשֶׁט, הָסֵב, so תִּקְטֹלְנָה, תַּקְטִיל; קָמָה. This is still the case when at the end of a word an auxiliary Seghol or Pattahh has been inserted between the letters (according to 2.), e. g. מֵילִיק from מֵילִיק, פַּעַל, סֵפֶר, רָגֶז, or the reduplication of the doubled letter is no longer heard and the Daghesh-forte does not appear, § 25, e. g. הָסֵב comp. הִקְטִיל.

a. The vowel *ê* is in like circumstances often reduced to one of its constituents *a*, e. g. הִקְטַלְתִּי from הִקְטִיל, קְטָלְתִּי from קָטֵל, תֵּלַכְנָה from תֵּלֵךְ, הֵסַבּוּ, תִּזְבַּרְנָה, תֵּלַדְנָה, and occasionally to its other constituent *i*, e. g. הִתְקַדִּשְׁתֶּם from הִתְקַדֵּשׁ, יִרְבְּהֶם from יָרֵשׁ. The only example of Shurek in a Segholate form is חֲלֻצָּה Lev. 5 : 21.

5. In unaccented syllables *ĭ* and *ŭ* are preferred to *ĕ* and *ŏ* before doubled letters, אַתְּ, אִתִּי, אֶת-, תֵּת-, תִּתִּי; הַסְבֹּת from הֵסֵב; מִגְּשׁ comp. מָקוֹם, חָק, חֻקִּי, יְסֻבֵּנִי, וַיָּסָב; הֵסֵב, though such forms as מָגֵּה, כַּלַּת, עֻזְּךָ, חָגֵּנִי likewise occur.

6. A vowel is occasionally given to a final consonant to soften the termination of the word, and make the transition easier to the initial consonant of that which follows; thus, הֹלֵךְ, אַיֵּה, אִי, אֶלֶּה, אֶל, הֵמָּה, הֵם; גָּלָה for גֻּלְתָה; לַיְלָה, לַיִל, יְכַסְיֻמוּ Ex. 15 : 10; בְּצָמוֹ; חִתִּתוֹ, חַיַּת, מַגְבִּירֹהִי, מַגְבִּירֹהִי; הָפְכִי; Ex. 15 : 5.

a. These paragogic vowels have established themselves in the current forms of certain words, as לַיְלָה הֵמָּה, אַצָּה, אָבִי, אָחִי, פִּי. But,

with these exceptions, they are chiefly found in poetry. The vowels ִי
and וּ are mostly attached to words in what is called the construct state,
ה ָ to words in the absolute; and all of them to the feminine ending ה.
Examples of וּ: בְּנוֹ Num. 23:18, 24:3, 15, חֵיתוֹ several times, עָרָיו Ps.
114:8. Examples of ִי: אֲחֹתִי Hos. 10:11, אֹסְרִי Gen. 49:11, בְּנִי ibid.,
גְּבֶרְתִּי Gen. 31:39, דְּבָרָתִי Ps. 110:4, הֹפְכִי Ps. 114:8, יֹשֵׁב Ps. 123:1,
בְּגָעֳלָתִי Ps. 113:5, מַשְׁפִּילִי ver. 6, מְקִימִי ver. 7, הַשִּׁירִי ver. 8, בְּוֹשִׁיבִי
ver. 9, מִלְאֲתִי Isa. 1:21, מְאַדֶּרִי Ex. 15:6, יֹשְׁבִי Zech. 11:17, רַבָּתִי Lam.
1:1, עֲלָתִי ibid., שֹׁבְנִי Deut. 33:16. It is also attached to the first member
of the compound in many proper names, e.g. מַלְכִּי־צֶדֶק, עַבְדִּי־אֵל, to certain
particles, as בִּלְתִּי, זוּלָתִי, דִּי, and perhaps to such participial forms as
יֹשְׁבֵי Jer. 22:23. Or ה ָ: אֲרִימְתָה Ex. 15:16, אַרְצָה Isa. 8:23, Job 34:13,
37:12, חָרְסָה Judg. 14:18, יָשְׁבָתָה Ps. 3:3, 80:3, Jon. 2:10, לָיְלָה almost
constantly, מִיתָה Ps. 116:15, נָחֵלָה Num. 34:5, עָזְלָתָה Ps. 92:16
(K'ri), 125:3, Ezek. 28:15, Hos. 10:13, עֵלָתָה Job 5:16, עֵרָתָה Ps. 44:27,
63:8, 94:17, עָשָׂתָה Job 10:22, תֵּבֶלָתָה Josh. 19:43, Judg. 14:1, and regularly in the third person feminine of the preterite of לה verbs. In
modern Persian ī is similarly appended to nouns in close connection with a
following word, to remove the obstruction of the final consonant and serve
as a uniting link.

§ 62. The changes due to the influence of vowels may
arise from their concurrence or proximity.

1. Concurring vowels may coalesce; a uniting with a
forms a, uniting with i or u it forms the diphthongal e or o,
e. g. הָשְׁבִֹית Neh. 3:13 from הָאֲשָׁבִֹית after the rejection of א
by § 53. 2. b; בַּיִת after the softening of ִי to i becomes בֵּית;
קְטָלַהוּ by the rejection of ה becomes קְטָלוֹ; יְהֹו prefixed to
proper names is from יָהוּ for יַהְו, § 57. 2 (4).

2. One of them may be hardened into its corresponding
semi-vowel; $ī$ ִי with $ī$ ִי may form $ī$ ִי, or the first $ī$ may
be changed to iy, which, upon the reduplication of the י to
preserve the brevity of the antecedent vowel, § 24. 3, becomes
יִּי, e. g. עִבְרִי with יִם becomes עִבְרִיִּים or עִבְרִיִּם. So, ִי before ה, forms יָה, and before וֹ forms יוֹ, e. g. עִבְרִיָּה,
עִבְרִיּוֹת; in like manner וּ is changed before וֹ into uv, forming וּוֹ, which, by § 56. 3, becomes יוֹ, e. g. מַלְכִּיּוֹת, by the
substitution of וֹת for ת, מַלְכָיוֹת. $Ī$ ִי followed by $ū$ וּ forms
iv, הִמְשִׂירוּ for הִמְשִׂרוּ Josh. 14:8. פִּיו, חֲמִשׂוּוֹ; פִּיהוּ, קְטַלְתִּיו; קְטַלְתִּיהוּ,
$Ē$ ֵי before $ī$ ִי or $ū$ וּ is resolved into ay, which, joined with
the appropriate semi-vowels, becomes ָי and יו, the virtual

reduplication of the final consonant in the one case preserving the short vowel, which is lengthened in the other; thus סִיסָי with ִי becomes סוּסָי, and with הִי, סִיסָהִי. The same resolution of ִי occurs before final ךָ, forming ךָ ִי, and by § 61. 2 יָדֶ ךָ, thus נְעִילַי with ךָ becomes נְעִילָיִךָ.

a. Grammarians have disputed whether in such words as עִבְרִיִּים, מַלְכֻיּוֹת the point in י is Daghesh-forte or Mappik, § 26, and accordingly whether they are to be read *ibhriyyim, malkhuyyoth,* or *ibhrīyim, malkhūyoth.* If the explanation given above be correct, it is Daghesh-forte Conservative. Comp. קָם קַם.

b. Such forms as פָּרְיוֹ, פָּרְיוֹ, פָּרְיוֹ from פָּרִי are only apparent exceptions to the above rules. The word is properly פִּרְיִ, and to this the additions are made, the auxiliary Hhirik being dropped with the cessation of the cause from which it originated. § 57. 2. (4). In בָּרְאִים 2 Chron. 17 : 11 from בָּרְבִי and יָם, the vowels are kept separate by an interposed א.

c. In words of כֹּה formation, such as עָשֹׂה, עָשִׁי, עָשִׂים from עָשָׂה and ה,, ו, ים,, it might appear as though one vowel were rejected before another. But the correct explanation is that י is the true final radical, and the forms above given are for עָשִׂיָה, עָשִׂיֹו, עָשִׂיִם (like קָבָלִים) from which י is rejected by § 53. 3. In the same way עָשׂוּי, עָשׂוּי, etc., from עָשָׂה are for עָשׂוּיִ, עָשׂוּיָךְ. In such alternate forms as פָּרְיָה from פָּרַח, the radical י is retained by preserving the antecedent vowel, which, before Daghesh-forte Conservative, becomes Hhirik, § 61. 5.

§ 63. The following euphonic changes are attributable to the proximity of vowels, viz. :

1. Pattahh before a guttural is often changed to Seghol if another *a* follows, and the same change sometimes occurs after a guttural if another *a* precedes.

The particular cases are the following:

a. When (ַ) stands before a guttural with (ָ) always before ה, e. g. הָתֵב for הַתָב, בְּעֶתָה Prov. 21:22. הֶחָרָם, חִנְחַמְתִּי (also when ה has Hhateph Kamets, e. g. הֶחֳרָשִׁים, הֶחֳרַלְתִּי Judg. 9:9), often before ח and ע, particularly if it receives the secondary accent, e. g. הֶחָלִים for הַחָלִים, הֶעָה but לַחֲבָה, חֶעָרוּ; מֶה עָשִׂיתָ, הֶעָלָה, rarely before א and ר, Gen. 14: 10, נָאֲצוּת Neh. 9: 18, 26 but נָאֲצוֹתֶיךָ Ezek. 35:12.

b. When (ַ) before a guttural is followed by another consonant with (ְ) or (ֲ) יֶחְדָּל, יַחְדָּלוּ but יֶחְדְּלוּ, נֶחְבָּא but נַחֲבֵאת, יֶחֱבָא, once before the liquid ל, e. g. אֶבְלְךָ Ex. 33:3 for אַבְלְךָ, and once before נ, e. g. לְחֶנְנָה for לְחָנְנָה.

c. In וָאֶקְרָאָה 1 Sam. 28:15 and the combination עוֹלָם וָעֶד a similar change takes place after a guttural to prevent the repetition of the vowel *a*; so in יְרַשְּׁנָה Ps. 20:4, and אָנָה וָאָנָה after the liquid נ.

2. Pattahh is sometimes assimilated to a following Seghol, or to a preceding Kamets or Tsere.

a. The assimilation to (ֶ) takes place regularly in what are called Segholate forms, in which an auxiliary Seghol has by § 61. 2 been introduced between two vowelless letters, מֶלֶךְ for מַלְךְּ, דֶּרֶב for דַּרְבּ, אֶרֶץ for אַרְץ, but בַּיִת, פַּחַם; only before ו, which can combine with *a* and not with *e*, *a* is retained and lengthened to (ָ) by § 59, אָנֶיךָ, תָּוֶךְ. Rarely in other cases יַדְכֶם for יַדְכֶם, where the change is facilitated by the preceding י.

b. The assimilation to (ָ) occurs in a few cases after a guttural with ה prefixed, e. g. הָחָם for הַחָם, הָהָר for הַהָר, הָאָרֶץ for הַאָרֶץ.

c. The assimilation to (ֵ) occurs in the Kal future of Pe Yodh verbs where the alternate forms are יֵשֵׁב and יִיקַץ.

§ 64. The following vowel changes are due to the accent, viz.:

1. If a long vowel in a mixed syllable be deprived of its accent, it will be shortened, § 18, e. g. הִשָּׁמֶר הִשָּׁמֵר; יָשֹׁב, יָּשָׁב־; יֶחֱזֶה־, וַיֶּחֱזַב; וַיָּשָׂם, רָשֵׁם.

a. If a vowel preceding Makkeph is incapable of being shortened, it will receive the secondary accent Methegh, agreeably to § 43.

2. The accent prefers to be immediately preceded by a simple syllable and a long vowel. Accordingly an antecedent vowelless letter often receives what may be called a pretonic vowel. This is commonly the simplest of the long vowels *ā*, e. g. קָטַל, יָשֹׁב, לָקַחַת, יְחִדָּלִין, occasionally *ē*, e. g. תֵּאָבֵדוּן, יֵלָדוּן, שֵׂמֹאת, rarely *ō*, e. g. יִקְצֹרוּן. Such a vowel is sometimes inserted, even though a pre-existing mixed syllable is thereby destroyed, e. g. in the plurals of Segholates and of feminine nouns derived from them, מְלָכִים from מֶלֶךְ, מְלָכוֹת from מַלְכָּה.

§ 65. The special emphasis, with which the last word of a clause is dwelt upon, gives rise to certain vowel changes in connection with the pause accents, § 36. 2. *a*. These are (1) lengthening short vowels, viz., (ַ) and not infrequently (ֶ) which has arisen from (ִ) to (ָ), e. g. אָמַר, אָמָר; כָּתַבְתָּ, כָּתָבְתָּ; עֶבֶד, עָבֶד; אֶרֶץ, אָרֶץ; and bringing back Kamets

Hhatuph shortened from Hholem to its original length וַיָּמָת, וַיָּמָת. (2) Restoring vowels which have been dropped in the course of inflection, e. g. דִּבְרוּ, דִּבְרוּ; עָבְדוּ, עָבְדוּ; עָמְדוּ, עָמְדוּ. (3) Changing simple Sh'va in triliteral syllables and before the suffix ה to Seghol, e. g. יְחִי, בֵּיתָהּ; בֵּיתָהּ; שְׁכֶם, שֶׁכֶם; יְחִי. (4) Changing compound Sh'va to the corresponding long vowel, e. g. חֳלִי, חָלִי; (חֲצִי) חָצִי; אֲנִי, אָנִי, חֳלִי.

a. Pattahh sometimes remains without change, e. g. עַד Ps. 132:12, דִּבַּרְתְּ 2 Sam. 2:27, וַנִּצְּלוּ Jer. 7:10, גָּנַבְתִּי Prov. 30:9, צִדַּקְתִּי Job 34:5, אֲבֶלְתִּי Neh. 5:14. Seghol more frequently, מֶלֶךְ. צֶדֶק, דֶּרֶךְ, קֶרֶשׂ and הֶגֶה. Long vowels are mostly unaltered; only Tsere is in mixed syllables occasionally changed to Pattahh. e. g. הֶחֱזַק Isa. 18:5 for הֶחֱזֵק, so חָשַׁב Isa. 42:22, הַף Gen. 17:14, וַיִּגְמַל Gen. 21:8, יֵלֶךְ Gen. 25:34, which, in one word of Segholate formation, is converted to Seghol. e. g. לָשֵׁב, רָשֵׁב. Where the same word has alternate forms, one is sometimes selected as the ordinary and the other as the pausal form, thus יַחְפֹּץ, יֶחְפָּץ; שְׁבַלְתִּי, רָחָבָה, רְחָבָה, שָׁבַלְתִּי, דַּרְבֹּן Gen. 43:14; Eccl. 12:11, דָּרְבָן 1 Sam. 13:21; עוֹ, עָז Gen. 49:3, תֵּשֵׁב, תֵּשֵׁבְתְּ Lev. 26:34, 35; יְשַׁשֵּׂם, יְשַׂמֵּשׂ. Sometimes, instead of changing the Sh'va before ה to Seghol, its vowel is shifted, thus בָּהּ, בָּהּ; רֻדָּהּ, אָרְדָהּ, and in Ex. 29:35 אָכְלָה. The position of the pause accent, so far as it differs from that of the ordinary accent, has been explained § 35. 2.

b. Of the pause accents, or those which mark the limits of clauses and sections, the first class, viz., Silluk, Athnahh, and Merka with Mahpakh, almost always give rise to the vowel changes which have been described; the second and third classes, S'gholta. Zakeph Katon, Zakeph Gadhol, R'bhi' and Shalsheleth, e. g. וְיִקְרָא־לוֹ Isa. 13:8, do so frequently; the fourth class, Pazer, e. g. 2 Kin. 3:25, Prov. 30:4, and T'lisha Gh'dhola, e. g. Ezek. 20:21, but seldom. Pausal forms are occasionally found with other Disjunctives, thus, Tiphhha חֶם־לֶבָב Deut. 13:5, Pashta תִּשָּׂא־לוֹ ibid., Geresh שְׁלָל Ezek. 40:4, and even with Conjunctives, e. g. אֲנִי Isa. 49:18, הִצַּלְתִּי Ezek. 17:15, נְשׂוּא 2 Chron. 29:31.

§ 66. 1. The shortening and lengthening of words has an effect upon their vowels. The shortening may take place

(1) At the end of a word by the rejection of a vowel.

This occurs only with (ָ) or (ֵ) in certain forms of לה verbs, e. g. תֵּגֶל from תִּגְלָה, וַיְצִי, וַיָּגֶל for וִיצַוֶּה, וַיִּגְלֶה, וַתַּשְׁקְ for וַתַּשְׁקֶה. In the last two examples the short vowel is lengthened upon its receiving the accent, comp. § 64. 1. If the rejected vowel was preceded by two consonants, these will now stand together at the end of the word, and be liable to the changes described § 61. 2, e. g. הָרְפֵּה for חֵרָפֵת.

(2) In the body of a word by shortening a long vowel in a mixed syllable, which must, of course, be the one bearing the accent, § 32. 1, or rejecting a long vowel in a simple syllable before the accent (the pretonic vowel, § 64. 2), דָּבָר, מִקְדָּשׁ; מִלַּד, מָלֵד; מְקֻדָּשׁ; דְּבַר.

a. This is in general the only reduction possible. The vowel of a mixed syllable, if short already, is capable of no further abbreviation; and it cannot be rejected, or there would be a concurrence of vowelless consonants which the language seeks to avoid (תּוֹסְףְּ Prov. 30:6 is an exception). And the vowel of a simple syllable, if short, must have the accent, § 32. 1, which preserves it from rejection. The changes above recited are confined to the last two, or, in case the accent is upon the penult, the last three syllables of the word; for the antecedent portions of polysyllables are already abbreviated to the utmost. Contractions due to the peculiarities of certain letters, as the gutturals and quiescents, which have been before explained, are not here taken into the account, e. g. שָׁמַע, שְׁמַע; יָדַי, יָדַיִם; בּוֹת, בָּיִת.

b. Where the last vowel cannot be shortened, it sometimes experiences a change of quality from pure to diphthongal, such as is produced by the pressure of two following consonants, § 61. 4, e. g. יַבְדִּל, יַבְדֵּל; חוֹשִׁים, כִּיסֵי, סוּסִים; רָשׁוֹת, רָשׁוּת; רָשׁוֹת, רָשִׁית; הוֹשַׁב.

2. If a word be lengthened by additions at the end, its vowels are liable to changes in consequence.

(1) Such additions create a tendency to shorten the previous part of the word in the manner just described. For the normal length of words in Hebrew being dissyllabic, the genius of the language is opposed to transcending this limit any further than is absolutely necessary. If the addition is not of sufficient weight to affect the position of the accent, no abbreviation results. But if it is of weight enough to remove the accent, an abbreviation follows if it is possible for one to be made, e. g. דָּבָר, דְּבָרִים, דִּבְרֵיכֶם for דִּבְרֵיכֶם by § 61. 1.

(2) They produce changes in an ultimate mixed syllable. If the appendage begin with a consonant, the antecedent vowel will now be succeeded by two consonants and be liable to the changes consequent upon such a position, § 61. 4, e. g. תַּקְטֵלְנָה from תַּקְטִיל; קָמָה from קָם; הִקְטַלְתִּי from הִקְטִיל;

§ 66   VOWEL CHANGES.   91

קְטַלְתִּי from קְטֹל. If the appendage begin with a vowel, it will attach itself to the final consonant, which will in consequence be drawn away from its own syllable to begin the new one. This may occasion the following changes:

(*a*) If the preceding vowel is an auxiliary Seghol or Pattahh, introduced to facilitate the pronunciation of the second of two vowelless consonants, § 61. 2, it will be rejected, inasmuch as it is no longer required for this purpose, e. g. סִתְרוֹ from סֵתֶר, מַלְכּוֹ from מֶלֶךְ.

(*b*) If it be a short vowel, it must either be lengthened to adapt it to the simple syllable in which it now stands, or rejected on account of the disposition to abbreviate words upon their receiving accessions at the end, e. g. קְטָלָה and קָטְלָה from קָטֹל. The cases are very rare in which a short vowel remains unchanged in consequence of its having the accent, § 18. 2, e. g. מִדְבָּרָה 1 Kin. 19:15 from מִדְבָּר, חָשְׁמַלָּה Ezek. 8:2 from חַשְׁמַל.

(*c*) If it be a long vowel, it may be rejected, as יִקְטְלִי from יִקְטֹל, שְׁמִי from שֵׁם, or retained either unaltered, as מִשְׁפָּטִי from מִשְׁפָּט, הֲקִימוֹת from הֵקִים, or with a change of quality from pure to diphthongal or the reverse, מְתִיקָה from פָּלִיט, פְּלֵטִים from הֵקִים, הֲקִמוֹתִי, נָסוֹג from נְסִגֹּתִי, מָתוֹק.

TABLE SHOWING THE CHARACTER AND AFFINITIES OF THE VOWELS
AND THE ORDINARY LIMITS OF EUPHONIC CHANGES.

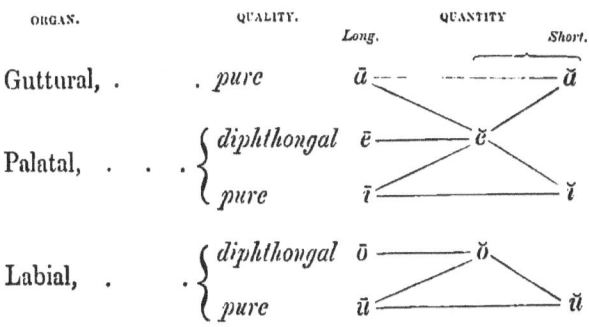

PART SECOND.

ETYMOLOGY.

Roots of Words.

§ 67. ETYMOLOGY treats of the various kinds of words, their formation and inflections. Three successive stages are here to be distinguished. The first is the root or radical portion of words. This embraces those fundamental sounds, in which the essential idea originally inheres. Roots do not enter, in their nude or primitive form, into the current use of language, but they constitute the basis upon which all actually occurring words, with the exception of the inorganic interjections, are constructed. The second stage is the word itself in its simple uninflected state; this is formed, if a primitive, directly from the root, if a derivative, from a pre-existing primitive, by certain changes or additions, which serve to convert the radical idea into the precise conception intended, which is as yet, however, expressed absolutely. The third and only remaining stage is the word as it appears in the actual utterances of speech, so modified by inflections as to suggest the definite qualifications of the idea, such as the tense of verbs, the gender and number of nouns, and the degree of adjectives, or its relations whether of agreement or subordination, such as the persons and modes of verbs and the cases of nouns.

§ 68. There are in Hebrew, as in most languages, two classes of roots, which may be denominated respectively pronominal and verbal. Pronominal roots form the basis of such words as express the relations of things to the speaker or to one another, viz., pronouns and certain prepositions, adverbs, and other particles. From verbal roots, which are by far the more numerous, spring words expressive of ideas, viz., verbs, nouns, and such particles as are derived from them. Verbal roots consist exclusively of consonants, and are almost invariably triliteral. The introduction of a vowel or vowels, even for the sake of pronouncing them, destroys their abstract radical character, and converts them into specific words of this or that description. Nevertheless, for reasons of convenience, the letters of the root are usually pronounced by the aid of the vowels belonging to them in the simplest form of the corresponding verb, which is mostly the third person singular of the preterite, e. g. קָטַל, מָלַךְ. This must not be suffered, however, to lead to the confusion of identifying that particular verbal form with the proper radical, nor of supposing the verb to be the radical part of speech from which nouns in all cases are derived: verbs and nouns are rather to be regarded as co-ordinate branches springing from a common root.

    a. The few quadriliterals and quinqueliterals which occur are mostly formed from pre-existing triliterals by the addition of a weak letter, or a letter similar to one of the original radicals, e. g. כִּרְסֵם *to lay waste* comp. כָּסַם; וְלָעָה *to burn* comp. לָעָה; שַׂרְעַפָּה *a branch* comp. סַרְעַפָּה; שַׂרְעַפִּים *thoughts* comp. סְעִפִּים; שַׁרְבִיט *a sceptre* comp. שֵׁבֶט; שַׁלְאֲנָן *tranquil* comp. שַׁאֲנָן; פִּרְשֵׂז *to spread* comp. פָּרַשׂ; or by blending two different roots, e. g. רַעֲנָן *to be fresh* composed of רָעַב and רַעֲנָן; פַּלְמוֹנִי *a certain one* = פְּלֹנִי אַלְמֹנִי; צְפַרְדֵּעַ *a frog* from צָפֹר *to leap* רָדָה (in Arabic) *a marsh*. Some, which are not thus reducible, may perhaps be of foreign origin.

    b. Many of the triliteral roots appear to be based upon pre-existing biliterals. Thus, the cognates גָּוַר, גָּזַל, גָּזַז, גָּזָה, גָּרָה, גּוּז, have in common the two letters גז with the associated idea of *cutting*, §50. 3. The frequent examples of this description, together with the fact of the existence of a few biliterals, e. g. אָב *father*, אָח *brother*, אֵם *mother*, have suggested the thought that the ultimate roots may in all cases have been biliterals, and that the triliterals were a secondary formation. Various ingenious but unsuccessful attempts have been made to demonstrate this position by an actual analysis, and to effect the reduction of all roots to two primitive letters. Still more extravagant and fanciful is the endeavour, which has actually been made, to explain the origin of roots from the individual letters of which they are composed, and to deduce their meanings from the names, the shapes, or other peculiarities of those letters. The existence of roots and the meanings attached to them must be accepted as ultimate facts. Some have arisen, no doubt, from the imitation of sounds in nature; but in most cases no satisfactory reason can be given why a given combination of sounds has that particular sense, which is in fact connected with it.

§ 69. The formation of words and their inflection are accomplished partly by internal changes and partly by external additions. The internal changes are the insertion of vowels and the reduplication of consonants in various significant ways, e. g. קָטַל, קֹטֶל, קָטֵל, קְטָל. The external additions are significant syllables welded to the root or to the word, either at the beginning or the end, e. g. קָטַל, קָטְלָה, יִקְטֹל, הִתְקַטַּלְנוּ.

a. The triliteral and exclusively consonantal character of Semitic roots is their most remarkable peculiarity in distinction from those of the Indo-European languages which are as prevailingly monosyllabic, the vowel being an essential constituent, while the number of consonants is variable. The fact of the vowel being an integral part of the root in these languages interferes with their employment of internal changes for purposes of derivation and inflection, and confines them almost entirely to external additions, e. g. *voco, vocabam, vocatio, vocabulum, vocito,* etc. The composition of words of which such large use is made in the Indo-European tongues, e. g. *ad-voco, in-voco,* etc., is almost unknown in Hebrew except in the formation of proper names.

b. Different languages differ greatly in their flexibility, that is to say, in the variety of words which may spring from a common root, and the number of forms which the same word may assume to express the various relations into which it enters. Relations, which in some languages are expressed by flection, as the cases of nouns, tenses of verbs, concord of adjectives, are in others indicated by additional words, as prepositions, auxiliary verbs, etc., or suggested by the order of words in the sentence.

c. Formative syllables, added either at the beginning or the end of words for the sake of inflection, are, in the ordinary consciousness of those who use the language, completely amalgamated with them, so that their separate origin and signification is never thought of. They are thus to be distinguished from those words which, by reason of their dependent character, are attached to others as prefixes or suffixes, but yet preserve their separate identity as prefixed conjunctions and prepositions and suffixed pronouns.

§ 70. The parts of speech in Hebrew are either declinable as pronouns, verbs, and nouns (including adjectives); or indeclinable, as the article, adverbs, prepositions, conjunctions, and interjections. As most if not all of the syllables employed in the formation and inflection of verbs and nouns are of pronominal origin, it will be necessary to consider the pronouns first.

a. The classification usual with the Jewish grammarians is into verbs (פְּעָלִים *actions*), nouns (שֵׁמוֹת *names*), and particles (מִלִּים *words*).

PRONOUNS.

PERSONAL PRONOUNS.

§ 71. The Hebrew pronouns are personal, demonstrative, relative, and interrogative or indefinite. The personal pronouns are the following, viz.:

	SINGULAR.		PLURAL.
1. I	אָנֹכִי, אֲנִי	We	אָנוּ, נַחְנוּ, אֲנַחְנוּ
2. { Thou *m.*	אַתָּה	Ye *m.*	אַתֶּם
{ Thou *f.*	אַתְּ, אַתִּי	Ye *f.*	אַתֵּן, אַתֵּנָה
3. { He	הוּא	They *m.*	הֵם, הֵמָּה
{ She	הִיא	They *f.*	הֵן, הֵנָּה

There are, it will be perceived, distinct forms for singular and plural in the three persons, and for masculine and feminine in the second and third. There is no form for the neuter, as that gender is not recognized in Hebrew.

a. (1) The alternate forms of the first person singular אָנֹכִי (in pause אָנֹכִי with the accent on the penult except Job 33:9), and אֲנִי (in pause אָנִי) are used interchangeably and with perhaps equal frequency. It has been observed, however, that while the former is the more common in the Pentateuch, it never occurs in the books of Chronicles, and but once in Ezekiel, viz., 36:28, a passage borrowed from the Pentateuch. The usual plural of this person is אֲנַחְנוּ; נַחְנוּ occurs but six times, viz., Gen.

42:11, Ex. 16:7, 8, Num. 32:32, 2 Sam. 17:12, Lam. 3:42; אַתָּ though common in later Hebrew, occurs but once in the Old Testament, viz., Jer. 42:6 K'thibh, where the K'ri substitutes the usual form.

(2) The second person masc. sing. אַתָּה (in pause occasionally אָתָּה Ps. 2:7, 25:27, 40:18, 70:6, but mostly אַתָּה) is in five instances written אַתְּ without the final. He, which is however restored in the K'ri, viz., 1 Sam. 24:19, Ps. 6:4, Job 1:10, Eccles. 7:22, Neh. 9:6, and in three instances אַתְּ without the final vowel Num. 11:15, Deut. 5:24, Ezek. 28:14. The feminine אַתְּ is occasionally written אַתִּי Judg. 17:2, 1 Kin. 14:2, 2 Kin. 4:16, 23, 8:1, Jer. 4:30, Ezek. 36:13; the K'ri invariably retrenches the superfluous י, though it is probable that the original pronunciation proper to this orthography was אַתִּי. The feminine plural אַתֵּן occurs only Ezek. 34:31, where a few manuscripts read אַתֶּן; the alternate form אַתֵּנָה occurs Gen. 31:6, Ezek. 13:11, 34:17; in Ezek. 13:20 most editions have אַתֵּנָה.

(3) The third person fem. sing. הִיא occurs but eleven times in the books of Moses, viz., Gen. 14:2, 20:5, 38:25, Lev. 2:15 (in some editions), 11:39, 13:10, 21, 16:31, 21:9, Num. 5:13, 14. In its stead is found הוּא a combination of the letters of the masculine with the vowel of the feminine. The explanation of this is that הוּא *hû* was at that early period of common gender and used indifferently for both masculine and feminine. As this primitive usage subsequently became obsolete, the word, when used for the feminine, was read הִיא *hî* according to the uniform practice of the later books, and the punctuators have suggested this by giving it the corresponding vowel, §47. According to Kimchi הִיא Ruth 1:13 and הֵנָּה 2 Sam. 4:6, Jer. 50:5, stand for the masculine plural; this assumption is unnecessary, however, as in the first passage the feminine may have the sense of the neuter "*these things*," and in the last two it is an adverb of place, meaning *here*.

b. (1) The pronoun אָנֹכִי unites the palatal found in the nominative singular of the first person in Indo-European languages, Gr. ἐγώ, Lat. *ego*, Goth. *ik*, with the nasal of its other parts Gr. μέ, νῶϊ, Lat. *me, nos*, Goth. *mik*. The same combination is found in the Coptic and the Phoenician. The Arabic and Syriac have retained only the abbreviated form in the singular and the prolonged form in the plural. The second person אַתָּה is based upon the lingual ת as the Doric τύ, Lat. *tu*, Ger. *du*, Eng. *thou*; and the third person הוּא upon the guttural ה as the Zend *hô*, Gr. ὁ. Lat. *hic*, Eng. *he*.

(2) Words in such constant and familiar use as the pronouns are subject to more or less irregularity in all languages. The original plural termination, as will be shown more fully hereafter in the case of verbs and nouns, is ם. In the first person מ is omitted to prevent the concurrence of nasals in the same syllable, אָנוּ, אֲנִי; the plural of the prolonged form seems to be best explained by supposing it to have been originally אֲנֹכִי, which was in the singular softened to אָנֹכִי by §57. 1, and in the plural by a transposition and weakening of the palatal to a guttural (comp. Gr. ἐγώ, Sans. *aham*). became אֲנַחְנוּ or by §53. 2, נַחְנוּ. The plurals of the second and third persons were originally אַתֵּם, הֵם, which are still

§ 72   PRONOUNS.   97

preserved in the Arabic, and have left their traces in the inflections of verbs, e. g. קְטַלְתּוּנִי, וְקִטְלוּן. The vowel *û*, however, which in the plurals of masculine nouns has been converted into *î*, has in the pronouns undergone a still further modification into the diphthongal *ĕ* הֶם or *ĕ* אֶתֶּם. The distinction of gender is indicated in the plural not by affixing the characteristic termination of that gender as in nouns, but by a change of the final nasal. An unaccented ה ָ is often added by § 61. 6. to relieve the harshness of the consonantal ending.

  c. In the technical language of the Jewish grammarians pronouns are called כִּנּוּיִים *cognomina*; the first person is מְדַבֵּר *the speaker*, the second נִצָּב *present*, the third נִסְתָּר *hidden* or *absent*.

§ 72. When the pronouns are used in their separate form as distinct words they have the forms already given. When, however, they stand in a relation of dependence to verbs, nouns, and particles, they are appended to them in the following abbreviated forms, called the pronominal suffixes:

		SINGULAR.		PLURAL.	
1.	Com.	ִי	ִנִי	נוּ	
2.	Masc.	ךָ		כֶם	
	Fem.	ךְ		כֶן	
3.	Masc.	הוּ		ם	הֶם
	Fem.	הָ	ָהּ	ן	הֶן

In the first person singular ִי is attached to nouns, and ִנִי to verbs. In the second person the palatal כ is substituted for the lingual ת of the separate pronoun. For a similar change in the first person see § 85. *a.* (1). The modifications in the forms of the suffixes, occasioned by the endings of the words to which they are attached, will be considered hereafter, §§ 101, 220. The third plural forms הָם, הֶן are used with plural nouns; ם, ן with verbs and singular nouns.

The suffixes of the second and third persons plural כֶם, כֶן, הֶם, הֶן are called *grave*, the rest are *light*. The former being mixed syllables, always receive the accent, § 33. 3, and tend more strongly to shorten the words to which they are attached than the latter.

7

Demonstrative Pronouns.

§ 73. 1. The ordinary demonstrative is—

           Masc. *Fem.*   *Common.*

SINGULAR, זֶה זֹאת *this*   PLURAL, אֵל אֵלֶּה *these*.

The poetic form זוּ is sometimes a demonstrative, Ps. 12:8, Hab. 1:11, but more frequently a relative (like the English *that*), in which case it is used without change for both genders and numbers. The feminine is occasionally written without the final ה and with a different vowel letter זֹה or זוֹ. The plural, coming from a different root, is sufficiently distinguished without the usual termination; אֵל occurs eight times in the books of Moses and once in 1 Chron. 20:8; in all other places the consonantal termination is softened by an appended הָ.

2. The singular of this pronoun is in a few instances compounded with ל either without any change of meaning, or, as Ewald and Nordheimer follow Jarchi in supposing, in the sense of the remote demonstrative *that*. Thus (with the article ה prefixed)—

                      Masc.   *Fem.*   *Com.*

SING. *this* or *that*   הַלָּזֶה   הַלֵּזוּ   הַלָּז

a. The first form occurs twice in Genesis (24:65, 37:19), the third six times in the post-Mosaic books as a masculine (Judg. 6:20, 1 Sam. 14:1, 17:26, 2 Kin. 23:17, Dan. 8:16, Zech. 2:8), and once as a feminine (2 Kin. 4:25), the second once in Ezekiel (36:35).

3. The personal pronoun of the third person הוּא is used for the remote demonstrative *that*.

Relative Pronoun.

§ 74. The relative *who, which* is אֲשֶׁר, which may be employed as a separate word, or may be shortened to a prefix שֶׁ

§ 75   INTERROGATIVE AND INDEFINITE PRONOUNS.   99

with Daghesh-forte compensative in the following letter, unless it be a guttural and consequently incapable of receiving it, § 23. 1. In a few instances the prefix שֶׁ takes the vowel (ֶ) followed by Daghesh-forte, Judg. 5:7, Cant. 1:7, Job 19:29; once it has (ָ) before א Judg. 6:17, and twice (ַ) Eccl. 2:22 (in some copies), 3:18. The relative suffers no change for gender or number either in its separate or its prefixed state. Its objective relation to verbs and particles and its possessive relation to nouns are expressed without changing the relative itself, or removing it from its position at the beginning of its clause by appending the appropriate pronominal suffix to the governing word, e. g. אֲשֶׁר שְׁלָחוֹ *who he sent him*, i. e. whom he sent, אֲשֶׁר זַרְעוֹ *which its seed*, i. e. whose seed. It may also receive an adverbial sense from being followed by the pronominal adverb שָׁם *there*, e. g. אֲשֶׁר — שָׁם *where*, אֲשֶׁר — שָׁמָּה *whither*, אֲשֶׁר — מִשָּׁם *whence*.

a. The prefix שֶׁ occurs to the exclusion of the full form of the relative in the Song of Solomon, and with great frequency in another production of Solomon's, Ecclesiastes. There are besides occasional examples of it in other books, e. g. Judg. 5:7, 6:17, 7:12, 8:26, 2 Kin. 6:11, 1 Chron. 5:20, Job 19:29, Ps. 122–124, 129, 133–137, 144, Lam. 2:15, 16. The word בְּשַׁגַּם Gen. 6:3 is in several ancient versions and in the common English translation rendered as though it were made up of the preposition בְּ, the relative שֶׁ and the particle גַּם *for that also;* but the most recent interpreters derive it from the verb שָׁגַג *to err*, and translate *in their erring*.

b. אֲשֶׁר or שֶׁ is also used for the conjunction *that.* Comp. Lat. *quod*.

INTERROGATIVE AND INDEFINITE PRONOUNS.

§ 75. 1. The pronouns מִי *who?* or *whoever* relating to persons, and מָה *what?* or *whatever* relating to things, are employed both as interrogatives and in an indefinite sense. They experience no change for gender or number.

The vowel of מה is regulated by the initial sounds of the succeeding word. Before a letter capable of receiving Daghesh-forte it is pointed מַה and the following letter is doubled, e. g. מַה־שְּׁמוֹ Ex. 3:13. Before the stronger gutturals ה and ח it also commonly receives (.), e. g. מַה־הִיא Ps. 39 : 5, מֶה חָטָאתִי Gen. 31 : 36. Before the weaker gutturals א, ע and ר, it commonly takes (ָ), e. g. מָה־אֵלֶּה Zech. 1 : 9, מָה עַבְדְּךָ 2 Kin. 8 : 13, מָה רְאִיתֶם Judg. 9 : 48. Before ה, ח, and ע with Kamets, and occasionally before other letters it takes (ֶ), § 63. 1. *a*, e. g. מֶה־הָיָה לוֹ Ex. 32 : 1, מֶה־חָטָאתִי Gen. 20 : 9, מֶה־עָשִׂיתִי ib., מֶה קוֹל 1 Sam. 4 : 14, מֶה מִּשְׁפָּט 2 Kin. 1 : 7. In a few instances the final vowel letter is omitted and the interrogative is joined with the following word, e. g. מַזֶּה Ex. 4 : 2, מַלָּכֶם Isa. 3 : 15, מַתְּלָאָה Mal. 1 : 13, מָהֶם Ezek. 8 : 6 K'thibh.

2. Another interrogative is formed by prefixing the particle אֵי to the pronoun זֶה, זֹאת, thus אֵי זֶה *which?* or *what?* 1 Kin. 13 : 12, Eccles. 11 : 6, אֵי לָזֹאת *for what? why?* Jer. 5 : 7.

3. The words פְּלֹנִי אַלְמֹנִי which are always used in combination, or contracted into one פְּלֹמֹנִי, are in usage equivalent to an indefinite or indeterminate pronoun, Eng. *a certain one*, Lat. *quidam*, Gr. ὁ δεῖνα; they are, however, derived not from pronominal but verbal roots.

Verbs.

THEIR SPECIES.

§ 76. 1. Hebrew verbs have seven different forms which have been denominated species or conjugations (בִּנְיָנִים *buildings*). These represent as many modifications of the verbal idea, and are as follows, viz.:

1.	קַל	Kal	Simple active.
2.	נִפְעַל	Niphal	" passive.
3.	פִּעֵל	Piël	Intensive active.
4.	פֻּעַל	Pual	" passive.
5.	הִפְעִיל	Hiphīl	Causative active.
6.	הָפְעַל	Hophal	" passive.
7.	הִתְפַּעֵל	Hithpaël	Reflexive.

a. The term *conjugations* was introduced by Reuchlin, and is very generally employed in Hebrew grammars and in those of the cognate languages. It must be borne in mind, however, that Hebrew conjugations are totally unlike the conjugations of Latin and Greek. The latter denote the various modes of inflection adopted by different roots. The former are modifications of the same root, which differ in meaning while their inflections are substantially alike. They correspond rather with voices or with derivative verbs, such as frequentatives and causatives, although they not infrequently require to be translated by words radically distinct. The term *species* proposed by Schultens, though less commonly adopted, is more descriptive.

2. Kal means *light*, and denotes that species in which no other than the three radical letters appear, and these only in their single power. The other species are called *heavy* (כְּבֵדִים), because burdened by the reduplication of the radicals or the addition of other letters. Their names are derived from פָּעַל *to do*, which was the model for inflection, the form assumed by this verb in each species serving as its designation. Unusual verbal forms are in like manner denoted by the corresponding forms imposed upon its radicals.

3. Other technical expressions, such as the names of the various classes of verbs, are also to be traced to this source. A verb whose first radical is a guttural, a Nun, or a Yodh, is called a Pe Guttural, Pe Nun (פ״ן), or Pe Yodh (פ״י) verb, Pe as the initial of פָּעַל becoming the technical designation of a first radical generally. So a verb whose second radical is Vav is called an Ayin Vav (ע״ו); one whose third radical is He, a Lamedh He (ל״ה); one whose second and third radicals are alike an Ayin Doubled (ע״ע), etc.

§ 77. The general idea of the several species already stated is liable to certain modifications in the variety of cases to which it is applied.

1. The Niphal is commonly the passive of Kal or of the simple idea of the verb, גָּנַב *to steal*, Ni. *to be stolen;* כָּתַב *to write*, Ni. *to be written*.

2. Sometimes, like the Greek middle voice which coincides with the passive in certain of its forms, it has a reflex-

ive signification, טָמַן *to hide*, Ni. *to hide one's self;* שָׁמַר *to keep*, Ni. *to keep one's self*, φυλάττεσθαι; נָחַם Ni. *to repent*, lit. *to grieve one's self*, μεταμέλεσθαι; or expresses reciprocal action, יָעַץ *to counsel*, Ni. *to take counsel together;* לָחַם Ni. *to fight*, μάχεσθαι, lit. *to devour one another*. In some verbs it has both a passive and a reflexive sense, מָכַר Ni. *to be sold* and *to sell one's self;* רָאָה Ni. *to be seen* and *to let one's self be seen, to appear*.

3. Sometimes when the Kal is intransitive and does not admit of a proper passive, the Niphal is either identical with it in signification, קָרַב K. and Ni. *to approach*, or retains a shade of its original force by representing the state or condition not absolutely as in Kal, but as something effected and involving a change from another previous condition, מָלֵא *to be full*, Ni. *to be filled*, הָיָה *to be*, Ni. *to become*.

§ 78. 1. The Piel gives new intensity to the simple idea of the verb, by which its meaning is variously modified according to the nature of the case, מָעַט *to be few*, Pi. *to be very few;* רָדָה *to follow*, Pi. *to follow ardently, to pursue;* פָּחַד *to fear*, Pi. *to fear constantly, to be timid;* שָׁאַל *to ask*, Pi. *to ask repeatedly and earnestly, to beg;* בָּרָא *to create*, as God, Pi. *to form* with pains and labour, as man; כָּתַב *to write*, Pi. *to write much* with the implication that it is to little purpose, *to scribble;* קָבַר *to bury*, Pi. *to bury great numbers*.

2. The energy resident in this species displays itself by signifying the producing or causing of that which is denoted by the simple idea of the verb, thus quickening intransitive verbs into transitives, and making such as were transitive before to be doubly so. In this, which is the more frequent case, it becomes virtually equivalent to a causative, אָבַד *to perish*, Pi. *to make to perish, to destroy;* לָמַד *to learn*, Pi. *to teach*, i. e. *cause to learn*. Both these senses are occasionally found united in the same verb, קָרַב Pi. *to be very near* and *to bring near;* שָׁחַת Pi. *to be very corrupt* and *to corrupt or destroy*.

3. Pual is the passive of Piel, and therefore can only exist when the sense of the latter is such that a passive is possible.

§ 79. 1. The Hiphil denotes the causing or producing of that which is signified by the simple form of the verb, and, as in the corresponding case of Piel, intransitive verbs become transitive, and such as admitted of one object before are now capable of receiving two: יָרַד *to descend*, Hi. *to cause to descend, bring down;* בּוֹא *to come*, Hi. *to bring;* רָאָה *to see*, Hi. *to show.*

2. In some verbs Hiphil has an intransitive sense, but in most of these cases there is either an ellipsis of the object or the idea of production and causation can still be obscurely traced, קָשַׁב Hi. *to be attentive*, prop. *to make (one's ear) attend;* מָתַק Hi. *to be sweet*, prop. *to cause sweetness;* שָׂכַל Hi. *to be wise*, prop. *to act wisely, exhibit wisdom;* אָמֵץ Hi. *to be brave*, prop. *to act bravely;* זָקֵן Hi. *to grow old*, prop. *to acquire age.* In a few instances both senses are found united in the same verb, פָּרַח Hi. *to cause to bud* and *to put forth buds;* אָרַךְ Hi. *to prolong* and *to be long;* עָשַׁר Hi. *to enrich* and *to grow rich;* שָׁמֵן Hi. *to make fat* and *to become fat* (comp. Eng. *fatten*).

3. Hophal is the passive of Hiphil.

a. When Kal has both a transitive and an intransitive sense, Hiphil, as the causative of the latter, becomes substantially identical with the former, נָטָה K. *to extend* or *to bend*, trans. and intrans., Hi. *id.* trans. In Job 23:11, Ps. 125:5, Isa. 30:11, where the Hiphil of this verb appears to be used intransitively in the sense of *turning aside*, there is an ellipsis of its proper object, *to bend (the steps).*

§ 80. 1. The Hithpael is reflexive or reciprocal of the idea of the verb, mostly as this is expressed in the Piel species (from which it is formed, § 82. 5), the particular shade of meaning being modified according to the circumstances of the case. (1) It indicates that the subject is likewise the direct object of the action, מִלֵּט Pi. *to deliver*, Hith. *to escape, deliver one's self;* צִדֵּק Pi. *to justify*, Hith. *to justify one's self;*

חִפֵּשׂ Pi. *to seek*, Hith. *to disguise one's self*, prop. *to let one's self be sought for;* חִלָּה Pi. *to make sick*, Hith. *to make one's self sick* whether in reality or in the esteem of others, i. e. *to feign sickness;* חָכַם Hith. *to show one's self wise* whether in reality or in his own conceit. (2) Or that he is the indirect object of the action, which is for his benefit, or relates entirely to him, פִּתַּח Pi. *to open*, Hith. *to open for one's self;* נָחַל Hith. *to inherit (for one's self);* חָנַן Pi. *to make gracious*, Hith. *to implore favour*, prop. *to make to be gracious to one's self.* (3) Or that the action is mutual between two or more parties, קִשֵּׁר Pi. *to bind*, Hith. *to conspire*, prop. *to band together;* רָאָה *to see*, Hith. *to look upon one another.*

2. This species is sometimes a mere passive like the Niphal שָׁכַח *to forget*, Hith. *to be forgotten;* כִּפֶּר Pi. *to atone*, Hith. *to be atoned;* עִתֵּד Pi. *to prepare*, Hith. *to be prepared.* In a few instances the reflexive and the passive senses are found in the same verb, מָכַר Hith. *to sell one's self* and *to be sold.*

 a. (1) The affinity between the Piel and Hiphil species is such as in very many verbs to render it unnecessary to retain them both, and one or the other has been allowed to fall into disuse. Where both exist, they are often nearly or quite synonymous, and are used indiscriminately, קָדַשׁ Pi. and Hi. *to sanctify,* or differ only in the frequency of their employment, שָׁלַח Pi. and Hi. (rare) *to send,* שָׁמַע Pi. (rare) and Hi. *to cause to hear.* In other cases they are distinguished by adhering to those significations of the species in which they depart palpably from one another, צָמַח Pi. (intens.) *to grow luxuriantly,* Hi. (caus.) *to make to grow,* סָכַל Pi. (caus.) *to make foolish,* Hi. (intrans.) *to act foolishly;* or by developing them from different significations of the root, בָּשַׁל Pi. *to cook* (food), Hi. *to ripen* (fruit); בָּרַךְ Pi. *to bless* (prop. to kneel in worship), Hi. *to cause to kneel* (as a physical act), עִצֵּם Pi. *to break the bones* (עֶצֶם), Hi. *to render strong;* or by restricting them to special applications, קָטַר Pi. *to burn incense* (to idols), Hi. *to burn incense* (to God); חָלַף Hi. *to change,* Pi. *to change* (the clothes); פָּשַׁט Hi. *to strip,* Pi. *to strip* (the slain in battle).
 (2) It is still less common to find both Niphal and Hithpael in the same verb. Where this does occur they are sometimes used interchangeably, at others a distinction is created or adhered to, שָׁפַךְ Ni. and Hith. *to be poured out;* דָּבַר Ni. and Hith. *to talk with one another;* בָּרַךְ Ni. *to be blessed,* Hith. *to bless one's self;* חָלַשׁ Ni. *to be ploughed,* Hith. *to keep (one's self) quiet;* קָשַׁר Ni. *to be bound,* Hith. *to conspire.*
 (3) When in particular verbs two species have substantially the same

sense, it sometimes happens that parts only of each are in use, one supplementing the deficiencies of the other, or that one of the active species, losing its proper passive, is supplied by another whose corresponding active is wanting. Thus יָכֹל *to be able* has a Kal preterite and infinitive; but its future is Hophal (strictly, *to be made able,* but in usage the equivalent of Kal); פָּסַח *to be pale,* נָגַשׁ *to draw near,* נָתַךְ *to be poured out,* have their futures in the Kal but their preterites in the Niphal; יָסַף *to add* has both a Kal and a Hiphil preterite, which are synonymous, but only a Hiphil future. Again, in בָּדַל *to separate* and שָׁמַד *to destroy,* the Kal has yielded to the Hiphil (strictly, *to cause separation, destruction*), but the Niphal is retained as its passive; רָחַץ *to bathe* and זָרַק *to sprinkle,* have in the active the Kal form and in the passive the Pual.

(4) All verbs are found in one or more of these species or conjugations, but very few in the whole of them. Of the 1,332 triliteral verbs in the Hebrew Bible, 530 appear in some one species only, 360 in two species, 235 in three, 118 in four, 70 in five, 12 in six, and but 7 in the entire number, viz.: בָּקַע *to cleave asunder,* גָּלָה *to uncover,* חָלָה *to be sick,* יָדַע *to know,* יָלַד *to bring forth,* פָּקַד *to visit,* רוּם *to be high.* The number of species in which a given verb appears, is sometimes limited by the necessity of the case, as when its meaning will not admit of the modifications denoted by all the species; or by usage, as when certain species are dropped as unnecessary, the ideas which they would convey being expressed in another manner; or by the circumstance that in the small volume of the Old Testament, examples may not occur of all the species which actually were in use.

b. Instances occur in which the active species, and less frequently the passives, derive their meanings not directly from the root, but from some noun which has sprung from it. These are called Denominatives. Thus, עָרַף K. *to break the neck* (עֹרֶף); עִשֵּׂר K. *to tithe* (עֶשֶׂר *ten*); לָבַן *to make bricks* (לְבֵנָה); נִלְבַּב Ni. *to be possessed of understanding,* or, according to others, *to be devoid of understanding* (לֵבָב *heart*); כִּהֵן Pi. *to act as priest* (כֹּהֵן); קִנֵּן Pi. *to build a nest* (קֵן); מְרֻבָּע Pu. part. *square* (אַרְבַּע *four*); מְשֻׁקָּד Pu. *almond-shaped* (שָׁקֵד); מְתֻלָּע Pu. *dyed scarlet* (תּוֹלָע); הִשְׁלִיג Hi. *to snow* (שֶׁלֶג); הֶאֱזִין Hi. *to give ear* (אֹזֶן); הִפַּח Hi. *to snare* (פַּח); הִמְלִיחַ Ho. *to be salted* (מֶלַח); הִתְיַהֵד Hith. *to make one's self a Jew* (יְהוּדִי); הִצְטַיֵּד Hith. *to supply one's self with provision* (צֵידָה). A verbal form may occasionally arise even from an adverb, נֶהְלְאָה Ni. part. *removed far away* (הָלְאָה), or an interjection, וַיַּהַס Hi. *and he stilled* (הַס *hush!*).

Perfect Verbs.

§ 81. There is one normal standard for the formation of these several species and their further inflection, to which all verbs conform unless prevented by the character of their radicals. There are no anomalous or irregular deviations from this standard, such as are found in other languages, for which no explanation can be given but the fact of their occurrence. Whatever deviations do occur result from the presence of letters in the root which do not admit of certain combinations and forms, and compel the adoption of others in their stead. Verbs are hence distinguished into perfect and imperfect. They are styled perfect when their radical letters are capable of entering into all those combinations and exhibiting all those forms which conformity with the standard requires. They are imperfect when the root contains a weak letter, § 7. 2, or is otherwise so constituted as to lead to a departure from the standard inflections.

§ 82. 1. In perfect verbs the Kal is formed by giving Pattahh, or more rarely one of its compounds, Tsere or Hholem, to the second radical as its essential or characteristic vowel, and to the first radical a pretonic Kamets, § 64. 2, thus: קָטֹל, כָּבֵד, קָטַל.

a. The number of verbs, perfect and imperfect, whose second radical has Tsere or Hholem, or as they are technically called *middle ē* and *middle ō*, is quite inconsiderable. They are mostly of an intransitive signification.

(1) The following have Tsere, viz.:

זָקֵן to be old.	כָּבֵד (Isa. 24:20 כָּבֵד) to be heavy.	מֵת to die.
חָפֵץ to delight.		נָבֵל to fade.
חָצֵב to hew.	יָשֵׁר to be right.	צָמֵא to thirst.
טָהֵר to be clean.	לָבֵשׁ and לָבַשׁ to put on.	קָמֵל (Isa. 33:9 קָבֵל) to wither.
טָמֵא to be unclean.	מָלֵא trans. or intrans. (Esth. 7:5 מָלָא trans.) to fill or be full.	
יָבֵשׁ to be dry.		שָׂנֵא to hate.
יָרֵא to fear.		שָׁפֵל to be brought low.

(2) The following have Tsere in pause, § 65. 3. *a*, or as a pretonic vowel, § 64. 2, before a suffix, but Pattahh in other cases. Such as only occur in pause or with suffixes are printed with Tsere.

אָהֵב to love.	גָּדֵל to be or become great.	חָדֵל to cease.
אָשֵׁם to be guilty.		חָמֵץ to be leavened.
בָּצֵק to swell.	דָּבֵק to cleave to.	חָנֵף to be profaned.
גָּבֵר to prevail.	דָּשֵׁן to grow fat.	חָסֵר to lack.

§ 82 PERFECT VERBS. 107

חָפֵר to blush (distin- עָצֵם to be strong. שָׂבֵעַ to be sated.
guished from חָפַר צָלֵחַ to come upon, to שָׂמֵחַ to rejoice.
to dig). prosper. שָׁכֵחַ to forget.
יָגֵף to be weary. קָדֵשׁ to be holy. שָׁכֵן to dwell.
יָרֵשׁ to possess. קָרֵב to come near. שָׁמֵם to be desolate.
נָעֵם to be pleasant. רָעֵב to be hungry. שָׁמֵעַ to hear.

Several others are marked with Tsere in the lexicon of Gesenius, in which that vowel does not occur.

(3) The following have Hholem:

אוֹר to shine. יָכֹל to be able. הֹ (Ps. 18:15 רֶה) to
בּוֹשׁ to be ashamed. יָקֹשׁ to snare. shoot.
טוֹב to be good. נוֹז (see §86. a) to flow. שָׁכֹל (Gen. 43:14 שָׁכֻלְתִּי)
יָגֹר to dread. קָטֹן to be small. to be bereaved.

2. The Niphal is formed by prefixing נ to the letters of the root; thus, נִקְטַל, which by § 61. 1. becomes נִקְטֹל.

3. The Piel and Pual are formed by doubling the second radical and attaching the appropriate vowels; thus, קִטֵּל, קֻטַּל.

4. The Hiphil and Hophal are formed by prefixing ה with the proper vowels; thus, הִקְטִיל, הָקְטַל.

5. The Hithpael is formed by prefixing הִת to the construct infinitive of the Piel; thus, הִתְקַטֵּל. If the first radical be one of the sibilants ס, שׂ or שׁ, the ת of the prefixed syllable will be transposed with it, הִשְׁתָּרֵג, הִשְׂתַּפֵּךְ, הִסְתַּבֵּל. If the first radical be צ, the ת will be transposed, and in addition changed to ט, e. g. הִצְטַדֵּק. If the first radical be one of the linguals ד, ט or ת, the ת will be assimilated or united to it by Daghesh-forte, הִטַּהֵר, הִדַּבֵּר, הִתַּמֵּם.

a. In one instance הִתְשֹׁטֲבָה Jer. 49:3 ת remains before שׂ without transposition, which would bring three linguals in close connection, and once it is assimilated to שׁ, Eccl. 7:16 תִּשּׁוֹמֵם, elsewhere תִּשְׁתּוֹמֵם; ת is likewise assimilated to the sibilant ז in the only Hithpael form in which that letter is the initial of the root הִזַּכּוּ Isa. 1:16. In one instance מִתְדַּפְּקִים Judg. 19:22 ת remains without assimilation before ד. The ת may either be assimilated or not to the initial נ of two verbs נָבָא, נָשָׂא, and the initial כ of two כּוּן, פָּאֵר. It is assimilated to the כ of כָּבַס, which occurs but twice in the Hithpael, to the נ of נָאֵץ, which only occurs once, and in one instance to ר, viz. אֲרוֹמָם Isa. 33:10 but תְּרוֹמֵם Dan. 11:36.

b. The seven species may, agreeably to their formation, be reduced to three with their derivatives, viz.:

Active	1. Kal	2. Piel	3. Hiphil
Passive		Pual	Hophal
Middle	Niphal	Hithpael	

(1) The prefixed letters of the Niphal and Hithpael נ and ת (with ה prosthetic, §53. 1. *a*) are probably in their origin fragmentary pronouns signifying *self;* whether they are referable to אֲנִי and אַתָּה of the first and second persons must be left to conjecture. The idea primarily suggested is that of performing an action upon one's self; but in the Niphal usually, and in the Hithpael occasionally, the reflexive signification has, as in certain tenses of the Greek middle and in the reciprocal verbs of some modern languages, given place to the passive. In the Aramæan the forms with a prefixed את have not only quite lost their original character as reflexives, but have superseded all other passives.

(2) The idea of causation in the Hiphil and Hophal, if the author may venture to offer his own opinion upon this perplexed subject, is not due, as in the Indo-European causatives, to the introduction of a syllable directly suggesting it. It appears to be primarily another intensive form, with which usage has ordinarily connected, as it frequently has with the Piel, the notion of productive energy or the quickening of an intransitive into a transitive. As in the Piel and its derivatives, the idea of intensity is suggested by giving a doubled and consequently more intense pronunciation to the central radical; so in the Hiphil, by a like symbolism, the power of the root is augmented by the accession of a new initial syllable, whether the weak letter ה is merely for the sake of pronouncing the vowel, which seems likely from the corresponding א in Aramæan and Arabic, or is itself significant, in which case it must be of pronominal origin, related possibly to הוא of the third person, and having a prepositional or intensive force.

(3) The distinction between active and passive in the intensive and causative species is made by the vowels alone, and that in a way perfectly simple, and yet as clearly marked as possible. Of the three pure vowels *i* and *u* offer the most striking contrast, and these are severally set in opposite syllables in the forms to be distinguished; *i* or its cognate *e* marks the second syllable of the actives, *u* or its cognate *o* the first syllable of the passives, the other syllable receiving in every case the simplest and only remaining vowel: thus. הִקְטִיל, קִטֵּל — קֻטַּל, הָקְטַל. For that *a* primarily belonged to the first syllable of both Piel and Hiphil is apparent from its retaining its place throughout these species with the exception of the preterite, and from its preservation in the cognate languages.

§ 83. If קָטַל *to kill* be taken as the representative of the regular verb, the various species with their significations will be as follows, viz.:

1. Kal	קָטַל	*to kill.*
2. Niphal	נִקְטַל	*to be killed.*
3. Piel	קִטֵּל	*to kill many* or *to massacre.*
4. Pual	קֻטַּל	*to be massacred.*
5. Hiphil	הִקְטִיל	*to cause to kill.*
6. Hophal	הָקְטַל	*to be caused to kill.*
7. Hithpael	הִתְקַטֵּל	*to kill one's self.*

a. It is in each case the third person masculine singular of the preterite which is given above, and the strict signification therefore is *he has killed,* etc. These being the simplest forms of the various species, however, and destitute of any sign of tense or person, are commonly used to represent the species; and in this sense the proper equivalent is the infinitive, which is the form used for designating verbs in English.

b. The verb קָטַל is well fitted for a model, and is now generally so employed. The consonants, which compose its root, have no peculiarities to interfere with its inflection, it has a signification capable of being carried through all the species, and as it exists likewise in the cognate languages, it offers a good basis for their comparison. It occurs, indeed, but three times in the Bible, Job 13:15, 24:14, Ps. 139:19, and in but one species; still the very rarity of its occurrence only restricts it more completely to its use as a representative or typical verb. The old Jewish model פָּעַל, §76. 2, is objectionable on account of its weak letter ע, and on account of the twofold sound of its initial radical פ, which, with its Daghesh-lene, might prove perplexing to beginners.

c. (1) The existence of other and less usual species is a needless assumption. The Poel, Pilel, Pilpel and the like, are not additional species but identical in character and signification with those already named. The more copious Arabic, with its nicer shades of distinction, has greatly multiplied the number of its species or conjugations, incorporating into its standard paradigm forms corresponding to some of these which the Hebrew only occasionally employs. In the latter language, however, they are at the utmost alternate forms substituted in place of the ordinary ones, and found for the most part in the imperfect verbs, to the nature of whose radicals they owe their peculiarities of structure. When, as is the case in a very few instances, there is a double form to a particular species in the same verb, usage has mostly created an arbitrary distinction between them, e. g. Pi. שֵׁרֵשׁ *to uproot* and שֹׁרֵשׁ *to take root;* Pi. קִיֵּם *to cause to stand,* applied to covenants and oaths, *to ratify,* and קוֹמֵם, in a physical sense, *to raise up;* Hi. הֵנִיחַ *to cause to rest, to set down,* and הִנִּיחַ *to leave, to let alone.* There is no objection to the employment of these names as convenient designations of particular modes of formation, provided it is understood that they mean nothing more.

(2) There are very few instances of what may be called compound species; thus, Niphal of Pual נְגֹאֲלוּ Isa. 59:3, Lam. 4:14, *to be exceed-*

ingly defiled, stronger than the simple Niphal נִגְאָל ; Niphal of Hithpael וְנִטְמֵאוּ Ezek. 23 : 48, נְכַּפֵּר Deut. 21 : 8, : נִשְׁתַּוָּה Prov. 27 : 15.

§ 84. To each of these species belong a preterite and future, two forms of the infinitive, an absolute and a construct, a participle, and, except to the Pual and Hophal which as pure passives cannot express a command, an imperative. The Kal has both an active and a passive participle, one more, consequently, than the other species. The preterite of each species is the form already described, § 83. The remaining parts are formed in the following manner, viz. :

1. The absolute infinitive is formed by changing the last vowel in Hiphil and Hophal to Tsere, and in each of the other species to Hholem, observing likewise that Hhirik in the penult of Piel and Hiphil is to be changed to Pattahh. (See Paradigm of the Perfect Verb.) This rule gives to Niphal the infinitive נְקֹטֹל, which form actually occurs, §91. *b*. If, however, the original Sh'va be suffered to remain after the prefixed נ, § 82. 2, thus, נְקְטֹל, a prosthetic ה will be required in order to its pronunciation, § 53. 1. *a*, after which נ will be assimilated to the following letter, § 54. 2, and a pretonic Kamets, § 64. 2, added to the ק in order to give full effect to the reduplication ; thus הִקָּטֹל, which is the form written in the paradigm.

2. The construct infinitive is formed from the absolute in the Kal by rejecting the pretonic Kamets, § 82. 1, in Niphal by changing the last vowel to Tsere, and in the remaining species by making the last vowel conform to the corresponding vowel of the preterite.

3. The future is formed from the construct infinitive by the appropriate personal prefixes ; if the first letter of the infinitive be ה, it is rejected, § 53. 3, and its vowel given to the prefix.

a. (1) Some verbs take Pattahh in the last syllable of the Kal future instead of the Hholem of the construct infinitive. This is particularly the case with intransitive verbs. Such as have Tsere in the preterite regularly take Pattahh in the future; of the list given §82. 1. a. (1) and (2) but three חָבַב, בָּלַל, שָׁבַב take Hholem, and two חָפֵץ and שָׂבַע take indifferently Hholem or Pattahh. Of verbs with middle o in the preterite three בּוֹשׁ, קָטֹן and שָׁדַד take Pattahh in the future; the rest either do not occur in the future, or have imperfect letters in their root which obscure their true formation.

(2) The following verbs with Pattahh in the preterite have Pattahh likewise in the Kal future. Those which do not occur in the Kal preterite, or occur only in forms which do not reveal the character of the vowel following the second radical, are distinguished by an asterisk. Verbs having a Pattahh in the future, which is due to imperfect letters in the root, (e. g. Pe Yodh, Ayin Guttural, Lamedh Guttural), are not included in this list.

אָבַל to mourn.	נָגַשׁ to come near.	רָבַץ to lie down.
*אָלַף to learn.	נָפַל (intrans.) to fall off.	רָגַז to rage or tremble.
*אָמַץ to be strong.		*רָטַב to be wet.
*אָנַף to be angry.	*נָסַךְ to be poured.	רָכַב to ride.
*הָבַל to become rain.	סָלַק (§86. b.) to ascend.	*רָפַד to spread.
חָזַק to be strong.	עָשַׁן to smoke.	*רָקַב to rot.
חָכַם to be wise.	*עָתַק to be removed.	שָׁכַב to lie down.
חָשַׁךְ to be dark.	*צָדַק to be righteous.	שָׁלַט to rule.
*כָּסַל to be foolish.	קָלַל to be lightly esteemed.	*שָׁלֵם to be complete.
לָמַד to learn.		*שָׁמֵן to grow fat.
מָתַק to be sweet.	*קָשַׁב to be attentive.	

(3) The following with Pattahh in the preterite have both Pattahh and Hholem in the future.

בָּגַד to deal treacherously.	חָמַם to be hot.	נָשַׁךְ to bite.
	חָנַן to be gracious.	פָּעַל to do.
גָּזַר fut. o, to tear, fut. a, to resolve.	*חָרַשׁ fut. o, to plough, fut. a, to be silent.	פָּשַׁט to strip off.
		קָסַם to use divination.
הָלַךְ (mostly fut. ê) to go.	עָרַף to tear.	קָצַר fut. o, to cut off, fut. a, to be short.
זָעַן to curse.	יָצַר to form.	
*חָבַשׁ to bind.	מָעַל to trespass.	שָׁבַת to rest.
*חָלַשׁ fut. o, to subdue, fut. a, to be weak.	נָדַד to flee.	תָּמַם to be finished.
	נָדַר to vow.	

b. Some imperfect verbs, chiefly Pe Yodh, take Tsere in the second syllable of the Kal future, e. g. יָשֵׁב, יִתֵּן.

4. The imperative has the same form with the construct infinitive except in Hiphil, where the last vowel is Tsere as in the infinitive absolute.

a. Where the Kal future has Pattahh or Tsere the imperative takes the same.

5. The Kal active participle takes the form קֹטֵל and the passive קָטוּל. The participle of the Niphal lengthens the last vowel of the preterite from Pattahh to Kamets; those of the other species are formed by prefixing מְ to the construct infinitive, rejecting ה where this is the initial letter, § 53. 3, and lengthening the last vowel where this is short.

§ 85. 1. The preterite and future are inflected through three persons, the imperative only in the second person, a command presupposing the form of direct address. There are also distinct forms for the singular and plural numbers and for the masculine and feminine genders. Verbal inflections are made by means of pronominal fragments added to the end of the preterite and imperative, and for the most part prefixed to the future.

a. The following are the fragments used for this purpose in the various parts of the verb:

Preterite (עָבַר).

(1) SINGULAR. 3rd pers. masc. The third person alone has no personal ending in any of its forms; as each of the others has such a termination, none was needed for the sake of distinction. Nothing more was required than to indicate the gender and number. The masculine singular is expressed by the simple form of the species with no appended sign whatever.

3 *fem.* The original feminine termination is ־ה, which, appended to the masculine, would give קָטְלַת, a form used before suffixes, § 101. 1, in Lamedh He verbs and occasionally elsewhere, § 86. *b*. Commonly, however, in verbs as in nouns and adjectives, the final ה is dropped, § 55. 2. *c*, and the previous vowel, which thus comes to stand in a simple syllable, is lengthened, קָטְלָה.

2 *masc.* The appended תָּ is derived from אַתָּה.

2 *fem.* תְּ from אַתְּ.

1 *com.* תִּי changed from כִּי of אָנֹכִי; compare the similar relation of the suffixes ךָ, כֶם to the pronouns אַתָּה, אַתֶּם § 72. The Ethiopic retains the *k* unaltered, *katalku*.

§ 85   PERFECT VERBS.

PLURAL. *3 com.* The original plural termination § 71. *b.* (2) is a nasal ם or ן preceded by the vowel וּ. The full ending וּן is still found in a very few instances, § 86. *b*, generally the ן is dropped, § 55. 2. *a.*

2 masc. תֶּם from אַתֶּם.

2 fem. תֶּן from אַתֶּן.

1 com. נוּ from אֲנוּ.

Future (עָתִיד).

(2) SINGULAR. *3rd pers. masc.* The prefixed י is from הוּא; the vowel *u*, which distinguishes the masculine pronoun, is changed to the corresponding semivowel וּ, and this at the beginning of words becomes י, § 56. 2.

3 fem. תּ, the sign of the feminine, is here prefixed.

2 masc. and fem. The prefixed תּ is from אַתָּה, אַתְּ, from the latter of which is derived the appended י ִ of the feminine.

1 com. The prefixed אֶ is from אֲנִי.

PLURAL. *3 masc. and 2 masc.* The same plural termination as in the preterite is appended to the corresponding singular forms.

3 fem. and 2 fem. The feminine plural is, as in the pronouns הֵנָּה, אַתֵּנָה, denoted by נָה appended to the singular, the 2 fem. sing. termination י ִ being dropped as superfluous.

1 com. The prefixed נ is from אֲנוּ.

Imperative (צִוּוּי), *etc.*

(3) No designation of the person is here necessary as the second is the only one in use. Gender and number are indicated by the same terminations as in the corresponding person of the future. The future forms will, in fact, in every case directly yield those of the imperative by rejecting the prefixed תּ, the sign of the second person, and restoring the ה in those cases in which it has been suppressed.

(4) The *Infinitive* (מָקוֹר *fountain*, whence other forms are derived) is an abstract verbal noun commonly masculine, but sometimes with a feminine termination.

(5) The *Participle* (בֵּינוֹנִי *intermediate* between the preterite and the future) shares the inflections of nouns and adjectives.

2. The inflections of the perfect verb in all the species are shown by the paradigm of קָטַל upon the next page.

PARADIGM OF

		KAL.	NIPHAL.	PIEL.	PUAL.
Pret.	3 m.	קָטַל	נִקְטַל	קִטֵּל	קֻטַּל
	3 f.	קָטְלָה	נִקְטְלָה	קִטְּלָה	קֻטְּלָה
	2 m.	קָטַלְתָּ	נִקְטַלְתָּ	קִטַּלְתָּ	קֻטַּלְתָּ
	2 f.	קָטַלְתְּ	נִקְטַלְתְּ	קִטַּלְתְּ	קֻטַּלְתְּ
	1 c.	קָטַלְתִּי	נִקְטַלְתִּי	קִטַּלְתִּי	קֻטַּלְתִּי
Plur.	3 c.	קָטְלוּ	נִקְטְלוּ	קִטְּלוּ	קֻטְּלוּ
	2 m.	קְטַלְתֶּם	נִקְטַלְתֶּם	קִטַּלְתֶּם	קֻטַּלְתֶּם
	2 f.	קְטַלְתֶּן	נִקְטַלְתֶּן	קִטַּלְתֶּן	קֻטַּלְתֶּן
	1 c.	קָטַלְנוּ	נִקְטַלְנוּ	קִטַּלְנוּ	קֻטַּלְנוּ
Infin.	absol.	קָטוֹל	הִקָּטֹל	קַטֵּל	קֻטֹּל
	constr.	קְטֹל	הִקָּטֵל	קַטֵּל	(קֻטַּל)
Fut.	3 m.	יִקְטֹל	יִקָּטֵל	יְקַטֵּל	יְקֻטַּל
	3 f.	תִּקְטֹל	תִּקָּטֵל	תְּקַטֵּל	תְּקֻטַּל
	2 m.	תִּקְטֹל	תִּקָּטֵל	תְּקַטֵּל	תְּקֻטַּל
	2 f.	תִּקְטְלִי	תִּקָּטְלִי	תְּקַטְּלִי	תְּקֻטְּלִי
	1 c.	אֶקְטֹל	אֶקָּטֵל	אֲקַטֵּל	אֲקֻטַּל
Plur.	3 m.	יִקְטְלוּ	יִקָּטְלוּ	יְקַטְּלוּ	יְקֻטְּלוּ
	3 f.	תִּקְטֹלְנָה	תִּקָּטַלְנָה	תְּקַטֵּלְנָה	תְּקֻטַּלְנָה
	2 m.	תִּקְטְלוּ	תִּקָּטְלוּ	תְּקַטְּלוּ	תְּקֻטְּלוּ
	2 f.	תִּקְטֹלְנָה	תִּקָּטַלְנָה	תְּקַטֵּלְנָה	תְּקֻטַּלְנָה
	1 c.	נִקְטֹל	נִקָּטֵל	נְקַטֵּל	נְקֻטַּל
Imper.	2 m.	קְטֹל	הִקָּטֵל	קַטֵּל	
	2 f.	קִטְלִי	הִקָּטְלִי	קַטְּלִי	
Plur.	2 m.	קִטְלוּ	הִקָּטְלוּ	קַטְּלוּ	wanting
	2 f.	קְטֹלְנָה	הִקָּטַלְנָה	קַטֵּלְנָה	
Part.	act.	קֹטֵל		מְקַטֵּל	
	pass.	קָטוּל	נִקְטָל		מְקֻטָּל

Perfect Verbs.

HIPHIL.	HOPHAL.	HITHPAEL.	KAL (*mid. ē*).	KAL (*mid. ō*).
הִקְטִיל	הָקְטַל	הִתְקַטֵּל	כָּבֵד	שָׁכֹל
הִקְטִילָה	הָקְטְלָה	הִתְקַטְּלָה	כָּבְדָה	שָׁכְלָה
הִקְטַלְתָּ	הָקְטַלְתָּ	הִתְקַטַּלְתָּ	כָּבַדְתָּ	שָׁכֹלְתָּ
הִקְטַלְתְּ	הָקְטַלְתְּ	הִתְקַטַּלְתְּ	כָּבַדְתְּ	שָׁכֹלְתְּ
הִקְטַלְתִּי	הָקְטַלְתִּי	הִתְקַטַּלְתִּי	כָּבַדְתִּי	שָׁכֹלְתִּי
הִקְטִילוּ	הָקְטְלוּ	הִתְקַטְּלוּ	כָּבְדוּ	שָׁכְלוּ
הִקְטַלְתֶּם	הָקְטַלְתֶּם	הִתְקַטַּלְתֶּם	כְּבַדְתֶּם	(שְׁכָלְתֶּם)
הִקְטַלְתֶּן	הָקְטַלְתֶּן	הִתְקַטַּלְתֶּן	כְּבַדְתֶּן	(שְׁכָלְתֶּן)
הִקְטַלְנוּ	הָקְטַלְנוּ	הִתְקַטַּלְנוּ	כָּבַדְנוּ	שָׁכֹלְנוּ
הַקְטֵל	הָקְטֵל	(הִתְקַטֵּל)	כָּבוֹד	שָׁכוֹל
הַקְטִיל	הָקְטֵל	הִתְקַטֵּל	כְּבֹד	שְׁכֹל
יַקְטִיל	יָקְטַל	יִתְקַטֵּל	יִכְבַּד	יִשְׁכַּל
תַּקְטִיל	תָּקְטַל	תִּתְקַטֵּל	תִּכְבַּד	תִּשְׁכַּל
תַּקְטִיל	תָּקְטַל	תִּתְקַטֵּל	תִּכְבַּד	תִּשְׁכַּל
תַּקְטִילִי	תָּקְטְלִי	תִּתְקַטְּלִי	תִּכְבְּדִי	תִּשְׁכְּלִי
אַקְטִיל	אָקְטַל	אֶתְקַטֵּל	אֶכְבַּד	אֶשְׁכַּל
יַקְטִילוּ	יָקְטְלוּ	יִתְקַטְּלוּ	יִכְבְּדוּ	יִשְׁכְּלוּ
תַּקְטֵלְנָה	תָּקְטַלְנָה	תִּתְקַטֵּלְנָה	תִּכְבַּדְנָה	תִּשְׁכַּלְנָה
תַּקְטִילוּ	תָּקְטְלוּ	תִּתְקַטְּלוּ	תִּכְבְּדוּ	תִּשְׁכְּלוּ
תַּקְטֵלְנָה	תָּקְטַלְנָה	תִּתְקַטֵּלְנָה	תִּכְבַּדְנָה	תִּשְׁכַּלְנָה
נַקְטִיל	נָקְטַל	נִתְקַטֵּל	נִכְבַּד	נִשְׁכַּל
הַקְטֵל		הִתְקַטֵּל	כְּבַד	
הַקְטִילִי		הִתְקַטְּלִי	כִּבְדִי	
הַקְטִילוּ	wanting	הִתְקַטְּלוּ	כִּבְדוּ	
הַקְטֵלְנָה		הִתְקַטֵּלְנָה	כְּבַדְנָה	
מַקְטִיל		מִתְקַטֵּל		
	מָקְטָל			

a. In order to a better understanding of the preceding paradigm, it should be observed that certain changes result from attaching the personal inflections to the verb, which are to be explained by the general laws of sounds and syllables.

(1) The prefixes of the future occasion no changes unless they stand before ה which is rejected, and its vowel given to the prefix, §53. 3, e. g. יְקַטֵּל for יְהַקְטֵל, or stand before a vowelless letter when the Sh'va of the prefix becomes Hhirik, §61. 1, thus forming a new syllable to which the initial radical is attached, e. g. יִקְטֹל for יְקְטֹל. Where א of the first person singular would receive Hhirik, it takes the diphthongal Seghol instead, §60. 1. *a* (5), e. g. אֶקְטֹל, אֲקַטֵּל.

(2) Terminations consisting of a vowel, viz., ה ָ and י ִ of the feminine singular and וּ of the plural, occasion the rejection of the vowel in the ultimate, §66. 2, which is no longer needed, except in the Hiphil whose long י ִ is retained in the preterite and future, and takes the place of (ֵ) in the imperative, e. g. קִטְלִי, קִטְלָה but הַקְטִילָה. In the Kal imperative the rejection takes place although it creates a necessity for the formation of a new syllable, קִטְלִי, קִטְלָה for קְטֹלִי, קְטֹלָה from קְטֹל, §61. 1.

(3) Terminations consisting of a consonant תְּ or of a simple syllable נָה, נוּ, תִּי, תָּ occasion no change, except the compression of the antecedent vowel, which now stands before two consonants, to (ַ) in the preterite, and from י ִ to (ֵ) in the future, תִּקְטַלְנָה, הִקְטַלְתְּ, §61. 4. But verbs with middle *o* retain the Hholem in the Kal preterite, יְכָלְתִּי.

(4) Terminations consisting of a mixed syllable כֶם, הֶן occasion the same compression of the vowel of the ultimate, and inasmuch as they always receive the accent, §33. 3, they likewise cause the rejection from the penult of the Kal preterite of the pretonic Kamets, which owes its existence to the proximity of the tone syllable, §82. 1, קְטַלְתֶּם from קָטַל.

Remarks on the Perfect Verbs.

KAL.

§ 86. *a.* PRETERITE. Verbs with middle Tsere exchange this for Pattahh upon the accession of a personal affix beginning with a consonant. Those with middle Hholem retain this vowel, unless it be deprived of the accent when it is shortened to Kamets Hhatuph, יָכֹלְתִּי, יָגֹרְתִּי, יָכֹלְתִּי, יְכָלְתִּי, וְיָבָלְתִּי. The second vowel, whatever it be, is regularly dropped before affixes beginning with a vowel, but here, as elsewhere throughout the paradigm, is restored and if need be lengthened on the reception of a pause accent, e. g. יָכֵלוּ, חָטְאָה, קָהֵרוּ. The words נָזֹלוּ Judg. 5 : 5, נָזְלוּ Isa. 63 : 19, 64 : 2, are by Kimchi, Mikhol fol. 5, regarded as Kal preterites from נָזַל *flowed*, in which case the second must be added to the list of forms with Daghesh-forte emphatic, §24. *c*, by Gesenius as Niphal preterites from זָלַל *shook*, comp. גָּבְלָה Gen. 11 : 7, נָבֹּא Am. 3 : 11 from בָּזַז, בָּנַן.

§ 87. REMARKS ON THE PERFECT VERBS. 117

b. SING. 3 *fem.* The old form with ת is found constantly in Lamedh He verbs, occasionally in Lamedh Aleph, and in two instances besides, אָזְלַת Deut. 32 : 36 (with the accent on the penult because of a following monosyllable, § 35. 1.), and שָׁבָ֫ת Ezek. 46 : 17 from שׁוּב. The vowel letter א is once written in place of ת, גָּבְרָא Ezek. 31 : 5 *K'thibh*, § 11. 1. *a*.

2 *masc.* The vowel letter ה is sometimes appended as in the pronoun אַתָּה from which the termination is taken, בְּגַדְתָּה Mal. 2 : 14, עֲזַבְתָּה Jer. 17 : 4 ; so in other species besides Kal, וּבְסַפְתָּה Gen. 31 : 30, יָדְעְתָּה Job 38 : 12 *K'thibh*, הִצַּבְתָּה Ps. 73 : 27. In the last example the ת of the root is united by Daghesh-forte with the ת of the personal affix ; this union regularly occurs between roots ending with ת and affixes beginning with the same letter וְצִוִּ֫תִי Job 23 : 17, חֹשַׁבְתְּ Ps. 89 : 45. הִשְׁבַּתִּי Isa. 16 : 10, חָשַׁבְתֶּם Ex. 5 : 5, לַתְּ Ezek. 28 : 8, לַתְּ Gen. 19 : 19, וְרָחַתְתִּי Jer. 49 : 37.

2 *fem.* The full termination תִּי of אַתִּי is frequently added in Jeremiah and Ezekiel and occasionally elsewhere, זָבַלְתִּי Ezek. 16 : 22, and repeatedly in the same chapter, יָרַדְתִּי Ruth 3 : 3 ; so in other species דִּבַּ֫רְתִּי Jer. 3 : 5, לְלֶדְתִּי Jer. 13 : 21. See also Jer. 4 : 19, 22 : 23, 46 : 11.

1 *com.* The vowel letter י is, contrary to the ordinary rule, § 11. 1. *a*, omitted in four instances in the K'thibh, though it is supplied by the K'ri, יָרַדְתְּ Ps. 140 : 13, Job 42 : 2, בָּנִיתְ 1 Kin. 8 : 48, עָשִׂיתְ Ezek. 16 : 59.

PLUR. 3 *com.* The full ending וּן only occurs in יְדָלוּן Deut. 8 : 3, 16 צָלוּן Isa. 26 : 16, and יִקְשָׁיוּן Isa. 29 : 21 from קוֹשׁ, the restoration of the Hholem before the pause accent causing the rejection of the Kamets, which is a pretonic vowel and can only remain in the immediate vicinity of the accent ; the form is thus sufficiently explained without the necessity of assuming it to be the future of a verb קוּשׁ which nowhere else occurs. An otiant א, § 16. 1, is twice added to this person, as is regularly the case in Arabic, חָלְבִיא Josh. 10 : 24, אָבִיא Isa. 28 : 12. The forms of similar appearance נָשִׁיא Ps. 139 : 20, יָרִיא Jer. 10 : 5, are in reality of different character as the א is in these a radical, whose vowel has been shifted to the preceding letter, § 57. 2. (3). The occasional omission of the vowel letter ו from the K'thibh, e. g. אָמְרָ 1 Sam. 13 : 19, קָמֻ Esth. 9 : 27, שָׁפְכָה Deut. 21 : 7, הָיָה Josh. 18 : 12. 14. 19 indicates a difference of reading. The words of the text are in the singular, and require the pointing אָמַר etc. שָׁפְכָה etc. ; the K'ri has substituted אָמְרוּ, שָׁפְכוּ etc. for the sake of a more exact concord of the verbs with their subjects, § 48.

2 *masc. and fem.* There is no example of a verb middle *ō* in the second person plural ; the forms in the paradigm are inferred from analogy, to indicate which they are enclosed in parentheses. In הִשְׁכַּלְכְתֶּן Am. 4 : 3, ן , is added to the 2 *fem.* as to the corresponding pronoun.

§ 87. INFINITIVE. The Hholem of the construct is usually written without ו, בְּגֹד Isa. 33 : 1, though not invariably, בֹּשׁ and שְׁבֹל כְּבֹשׁ and כְּבוֹשׁ, and before Makkeph is shortened to Kamets Hhatuph, § 64. 1, קְסָם־ Ezek. 21 : 26. 28. 34. The Hholem of the absolute infinitive is usually though not invariably written with ו, e. g. בְּגוֹד Isa. 48:8 but שְׁבָב Lev. 15:24, and is immutable. The construct infinitive has Pattahh in place of Hholem in שְׁכַב 1 Kin. 1:21 *et passim* and שְׂנֹא Eccles. 12:4. The feminine form of the construct infinitive occurs repeatedly in imperfect though it is of rare occurrence in perfect verbs, e. g. דִּבְקָה Deut. 11:22, 30:20, Josh. 22:5, שָׂנְאָה, אֲהֵבָה, יָרְאָה, הָאֵבָה Jer. 31:12, חָסְנָה Ezek. 16:5, עָצְאָה Lev. 15:32. In Pe Yodh and Lamedh He verbs the feminine is the customary form.

§ 88. FUTURE. 3 *masc.* The Hholem is commonly written without Vav, though often with it יִמְלֹךְ, יִכְתֹּב and יִכְתּוֹב, and before Makkeph is shortened to Kamets Hhatuph, § 64. 1, יִמְלָךְ־ Isa. 32:1, the Vav being in such cases rejected by the K'ri if found in the K'thibh, e. g. אֲבַתִּיב־ Hos. 8:12; in יִגְבּוֹל־ Josh. 18:20 the Hholem remains. The vowel of the last syllable is rejected, as is the case throughout the paradigm, upon the reception of a vowel affix, § 66. 2, unless retained or restored by the pause accent, § 65. 2, יִמְלֹכוּ Prov. 8:15, תִּלְמְדוּ Jer. 10:12; twice, however, instead of rejection Hholem is changed to Shurek יְשֻׁמּוּ Ex. 18:26, תֶּעֱבוּרִי Ruth 2:8. A like form appears in the K'thibh, Prov. 4:16 יִשְׂבּוּלוּ.

3 *fem.* The sign of the feminine is in two instances added both at the beginning and the end of the verb, viz.: תְּבוֹאָתָה Deut. 33:16, תֶּאֱתָיָן Job 22:21, paragogic ה, being appended to the former, § 97. 1, and a pronominal suffix to the latter. A like duplication of the sign of the second person feminine occurs in תְּבֹאת 1 Sam. 25:34 K'ri, where the K'thibh has the fuller ending תבאתי.

2 *fem.* ן is sometimes added to the long vowel with which this person ends תִּדְבָּקִין Ruth 2:8, תֵּרְדִין Ruth 3:4, תִּשְׁתַּפְּרִין 1 Sam. 1:14. Occasionally the feminine ending is omitted and the masculine form used instead, e. g. תִּבְרַת־ Isa. 57:8.

1 *com.* אֶסַּק Ps. 139:8, though by some grammarians referred to נָסַק, is probably for אֶסְלַק from סָלַק, the liquid ל being excluded, and Daghesh-forte conservative inserted in the previous letter, § 53. 3.

PLUR. 2 *masc. and* 3 *masc.* The full plural termination וּן is of more frequent occurrence here than in the preterite, the vowel of the second radical being either retained or rejected, יִקְצֹרוּן Ruth 2:9, תַּעֲבֹרוּן Josh. 24:15, יַחְדָּלוּן Ex. 9:29, יִשְׁאָלוּן Josh. 4:6, יִלְקְטוּן, יְשַׁבֵּחוּן Ps. 104:28, יִשְׁכָּבֻן 1 Sam. 2:22, Josh. 2:8, תִּשְׁמְרוּן Deut. 11:22, תֶּאְסְרָן Jer. 21:3; so in other species, יִרְבְּיוּן Job 19:23, יְקַצְּצוּן Job 21:21, תְּדַבְּרוּן Gen. 32:20 and תְּדַבֵּרוּן Ps. 58:2, תְּבַקְּשׁוּן 2 Kin. 6:19, תַּפְשִׁיטוּן Mic. 2:8, יִתְחַפְּצוּן Job 9:6. It is chiefly found at the end of a clause or verse, the pausal emphasis delighting in lengthened forms, or before words beginning with a weak letter, to separate the final vowel more completely from that of the following initial syllable. In the judgment of Nordheimer יְשִׂישׂוּם Isa. 35:1 preserves this ending in a still older form: Ewald thinks the final ן has been assimilated to the initial מ of the following word, § 55. 1; in all probability, however, ם is here, as it usually is, the 3 plur. suffix, and it is

§ 89   REMARKS ON THE PERFECT VERBS.   119

properly so rendered in the common English version *shall be glad for them*.

3 fem. In a very few cases the initial י of the masculine form is retained, the distinction of gender being sufficiently marked by the termination תְּבַלֵּדְנָה Dan. 8 : 22, יַחְמֵנָּה Gen. 30 : 38, יִשָּׁרְנָה 1 Sam. 6 : 12; or, on the other hand, the termination י of the masculine is retained, the gender being sufficiently indicated by the prefixed ת, תִּבְטְחוּ : Jer. 49 : 11, תִּקְרְבוּ Ezek. 37 : 7; sometimes the gender is neglected entirely and the masculine form used for the feminine, e. g. יְרָשְׁשׁוּ Hos. 14 : 1. The assumption that the 3 *fem. plur.* is used for the 3 *fem. sing.* in תִּקְרֶאנָה Ex. 1 : 10, תֵּרַדְנָה Job 17 : 16, תֵּרְבַּסְנָה Isa. 28 : 3, תִּשָּׁבַרְנָה Isa. 27 : 11, תִּשְׁלַחְנָה Judg. 5 : 26, is unnecessary; in the first passage מִלְחָמָה, the subject of the verb, is used in a collective sense, *wars shall occur;* the others are to be similarly explained with the exception of the last, where נָה may be the suffix with Nun epenthetic in place of the more usual form תִּשְׁלָחֶנָה *her hand — she puts it forth.* Comp. Obad. ver. 13.

2 and 3 fem. The vowel letter ה is occasionally in the Pentateuch, and more rarely in other books, omitted from the termination נָה, particularly when there are other vowel letters in the word, וַתְּבֶהָין Gen. 27 : 1, תָּבֹאןָ Gen. 30 : 38, וַתֵּלֶשְׁןָ Gen. 33 : 6, תִּוָּלֵדְןָ Ezek. 3 : 20, תָּחֲרִין nine times in the Pentateuch, three times in Ezekiel, and once in 1 Samuel.

When the root of the verb ends with ן this is united by Daghesh-forte with the affix נָה, § 25, תְּשֻׁבֹּנָה Ezek. 17 : 23, תְּקוֹנַנָּה Ezek. 32 : 16, or without Daghesh, תְּחֻנַּנִי Ruth 1 : 13, תֵּאָמַנְה Isa. 60 : 4, תְּרַנֵּנָּה Ps. 71 : 23 in most editions. So in the fem. plur. imperative, הַאֲזֵנָּה Gen. 4 : 23.

§ 89. IMPERATIVE. *Sing. masc.* The Hholem of the last syllable, as in the future and infinitive construct, is mostly written without ו, e. g. פְּקֹד, yet not always, שָׁפֹּט and שְׁטֹף; before Makkeph it is shortened to Kamets Hhatuph -מְלָךְ Judg. 9 : 14. It may perhaps be similarly shortened without Makkeph in סְעָד Judg. 19 : 5, comp. ver. 8, § 19. 2. *a*, or the vowel may be Kamets lengthened from Pattahh by the accent, which does occur, though rarely, with conjunctives, § 65. 3. *b*.

Fem. sing. and masc. plur. The vowel of the first syllable is commonly Hhirik, but under the influence of the rejected Hholem it is occasionally Kamets Hhatuph, § 61. 1, מָלְלִי Judg. 9 : 10, מָשְׁבוּ Ezek. 32 : 20 (but מִשְׁבוּ Ex. 12 : 21, for the Methegh see § 45. 2), כָּלוּ Zeph. 3 : 14, קָרְחִי Mic. 1 : 16, and (with ו retained in the K'thibh) קְסוֹמִי 1 Sam. 28 : 8, Judg. 9 : 12. Upon the restoration of the original vowel by the pause accent, the vowel under the first radical is dropped as no longer necessary, שְׁבוּ Zech. 7 : 9, בִּרְדוּ Nah. 2 : 9. When the third radical is an aspirate it rarely receives Dagesh-lene in this mood though preceded by Sh'va, § 22. *a*. (1); such cases as חָשְׂפִּי Isa. 47 : 2, אִסְפִּי Jer. 10 : 17, are exceptional.

Fem. plur. The final vowel ה, is dropped in שְׁמַעַן Gen. 4 : 23, § 90; occasionally ה is not written though the vowel remains, מְצֶאןָ Ruth. 1 : 9.

§ 90. PARTICIPLES. *Active.* The Hholem of the first syllable is written indifferently with or without Vav, בֹּגֵד and בּוֹגֵד, mostly without when additions are made to the word. In מוּכֶרֶת Prov. 25:19 Shurek is substituted for Hholem, unless, as Ewald suggests, it is a Pual participle with מ omitted; or, as others propose, it is to be taken as an abstract noun. The Tsere of the second syllable is written without י except סֹבְרֵי 2 Kin. 8:21; it is shortened to Seghol in הֹלֵם Isa. 41:7, upon the recession of the accent. תּוֹסִיפְךָ Ps. 16:5 and יֹסֵף Isa. 29:14, 38:5, Eccles. 1:18, have been improperly regarded as participles with Hhirik in place of Tsere. The former is the Hiph. fut. of the verb יָסַף, which is found in Arabic though it occurs only in this place in Hebrew, and means *thou wilt enlarge;* the latter is the ordinary Hiphil future of יָסַף, and the construction is elliptical, *I (am he who) will add,* see Dr. Alexander's Commentaries. Participles are rarely formed from neuter verbs, yet נֹבֵל *fading,* שָׁמֵם *desolate,* verbal adjectives of the same form with the preterites middle ē and ō being mostly used instead, מָלֵא *full,* זָקֵן *old,* יָגֵר *afraid.*

Passive. This, in the few cases in which it is in use in intransitive verbs, has the sense of the active, לָבֻשׁ and לְבוּשׁ *wearing,* שָׁכֵן and שָׁכוּן *dwelling,* בָּטֻחַ *trusting;* there are occasional instances of the same thing in transitive verbs, זָכוּר *remembering,* אָחוּז *holding.* The last vowel is with few exceptions as פְּסֻלִם Deut. 32:34, שְׁחֻם, נְקֻם written with Vav.

There are a very few instances in which participles appear to be inflected in the different persons by means of the terminations proper to the preterite. This, although common in Chaldee and Syriac, occurs in Hebrew only in the following examples:

2 *fem. sing.* יֹלַדְתְּ Gen. 16:11, Judg. 13:5, 7; and with the fuller ending מְקַנַּנְתִּי, יֹשַׁבְתִּי Jer. 22:23, שֹׁכַנְתִּי Jer. 51:13. The punctuators must have regarded these terminations as personal inflections, because the simple form of the feminine participle and that which it always has when joined with a noun of the third person, is יֹלֶדֶת Gen. 17:19, and with י paragogic in the K'thibh יֹשַׁבְתִּי Ezek. 27:3.

2 *masc. plur.* מִשְׁתַּחֲוִיתֶם Ezek. 8:16, the Hithpael participle of שָׁחָה. There is, it is true, an abruptness and difficulty in the construction, *they, ye were worshipping,* which can only be explained upon the assumption that after describing these bold transgressors in the third person, Ezekiel turns to them and directly addresses them in the second, or that his meaning is, not only they but ye too (the people) were worshipping in these your representatives. But in view of the frequent and sudden changes of person found in the prophets, and the unusual forms and bold constructions which abound in Ezekiel, almost any explanation seems preferable to an unauthorized change of the text, with most modern interpreters, to the ordinary plural מִשְׁתַּחֲוִים which is contained in a very few manuscripts, but not enough to overcome the presumption in favor of the more difficult reading; or the supposition of a mongrel word compounded of the two roots שָׁחָה *to worship,* and שָׁחַת *to corrupt,* in order to suggest the idea of a corrupt or corrupting service.

3 *plur.* : מְקַלְלוּנִי *they are cursing me*, Jer. 15 : 10. Kimchi explains this word as a compound of the roots קָלַל *to curse*, and קָלָה *to treat as vile;* Gesenius, as a confusing of two distinct readings, the participle מְקַלְלֻנִי and the preterite קִלְּלוּנִי; and Ewald changes the text to מְקַלְלֻנִי, though his conjecture is unsustained by a single manuscript, and Nun epenthetic never occurs with participles. The suggestion is here offered that the letters of the word may be regarded as the plural of the participle inflected after the manner of the preterite, with the added suffix, so that the proper pointing would be מְקַלְלֻנִי; the punctuators, however, have sought here, as not infrequently elsewhere, § 48, to establish a more exact agreement between the participle and its subject כֻּלֹּה by pointing the former as a singular, whereupon the Vav must be looked upon as epenthetic or superfluous, : מְקַלְלוּנִי as if for : מְקַלְלֻנִי. In fact, a few manuscripts omit the Vav, while others remark that it is superfluous; the weight of authority is certainly in favor of retaining it, though the other reading may be accepted as an explanatory gloss.

NIPHAL.

§91. *a.* PRETERITE SING. 3 *masc.* Some copies have נִגְלֶה Jer. 50 : 23 with Seghol under the prefixed Nun for נִגְלָה.

b. INFINITIVE. The following may be mentioned as examples of the shorter form of the absolute נִכְסֹה Gen. 31 : 30, הִלֹּה Judg. 11 : 25, נִגְלֹה 1 Sam. 2 : 27, נִקְרֹא 2 Sam. 1 : 6; of the longer form given in the paradigm חֲזֹתֹן Jer. 32 : 4, which once appears with prosthetic א In place of ה Ezek. 14 : 3 אִדָּרֵשׁ, § 53. 1. *a.* The construct infinitive usually has Tsere הִשָּׁמֵר Ezek. 16 : 36, but is in one instance הִזְדֶּה Ps. 68 : 3, formed as in Kal by rejecting the pretonic Kamets from the absolute. There are a few examples of the construct form used for the absolute הִשָּׁבֵר 1 Kin. 20 : 39, הִשָּׁמֵר Deut. 4 : 26. The prosthetic ה is commonly retained after prefixed prepositions לְהִשָּׁבֵר which are less closely connected with the word than the formative prefixes of the future; it is, however, rejected in the paradigm הִפָּצְלוּ Prov. 24 : 17, comp. בְּהִפָּצֵל Dan. 11 : 34. The Tsere of the last syllable of the construct infinitive, as well as of the future and imperative which are formed from it, is shortened to Seghol upon losing its accent, הִשָּׁמֶר Job 34 : 22, הִלָּחֶם Judg. 9 : 38, יִלָּכֵד Eccles. 7 : 26, rarely to Pattahh, חִיַּבַּע Job 18 : 4. In the Imperative הִשָּׁמֶר the form with Seghol is the usual one, that with Tsere only occurring in Isa. 7 : 4. The pretonic Kamets of this species is singular in not being liable to rejection on the shifting of the tone, e. g. הִנָּבְרָכֶם Ezek. 21 : 29, יִפָּרֵתוּן Ps. 37 : 9.

c. FUTURE SING. 1 *com.* The prefixed א occasionally has Hhirik, אִוָּשַׁע Ezek. 20 : 36, 1 Sam. 12 : 7, אִדָּרֵשׁ Ezek. 14 : 3, אִכָּבְדָה Ex. 14 : 4, 17.

PLUR. *fem.* Tsere rarely remains in the second syllable תֵּעָנֶינָה Ruth 1 : 13, being, as in the Piel preterite, commonly changed to Pattahh before the concurring consonants, תֵּאָכַלְנָה Jer. 24 : 2, so with a pause accent, תִּשָּׁבַבְנָה Isa. 13 : 16 K'ri, Zech. 14 : 2 K'ri, תֵּרָמַסְנָה Isa. 28 : 3; the first, as the original form, is, however, placed in the paradigm.

d. IMPERATIVE. Ewald regards נְקָבָה Isa. 43:9, Joel 4:11, וּכְלִי Jer. 50:5, as imperatives without the usual ה prosthetic; but this assumption is needless, for they can readily be explained as preterites.

e. PARTICIPLE. In 1 Sam. 15:9 וְנִבְזָה *contemptible,* is in form a Niphal participle from the noun בִּזָה *contempt.*

PIEL.

§ 92. *a.* The intensive species is usually formed by doubling the second radical; in וַיְפַלֵּל Ezek. 28:23, and the passive form אֻצַּל the third radical is doubled instead, an expedient resorted to repeatedly in Ayin Vav verbs and occasionally in Ayin guttural. In צִמְרַחוּנִי Ps. 88:17 both radicals are doubled; the entire second syllable is repeated in סְחַרְחַר Ps. 38:11, חֲמַרְמָרוּ Lam. 2:11, 1:20 a passive form, as shown by the Hhateph-Kamets, §82. 5. *b* (3), and in אֲהַבְיַהְבוּ Hos. 4:18, provided this is to be read as one word, §43. *b*; if, according to the division in the Masoretic text, הֵבוּ is a separate word, it is the imperative of יָהַב *to give,* though this is always elsewhere pointed הָבוּ. In יָפְיָפִיתָ Ps. 45:3, the first syllable is repeated, the ŏ under the first letter indicating it to be a passive form.

b. Intensity may likewise be denoted without a reduplication by inserting the long vowel Hholem in the first syllable of the root. This is often done in Ayin doubled verbs, but only in the following instances in others, *pret.* יֹרַדְתִּי 1 Sam. 21:3, שֹׁרֵשׁ Isa. 40:24, יֹרְאֶה Ps. 77:18, שׁוֹלַחְתִּי Isa. 10:13 *fut.* יֹסֵף Hos. 13:3, *inf. abs.* הֹלֹךְ and הֹלוֹל Isa. 59:13, *inf. const.* בּוֹשְׁשָׂם Am. 5:11, *part.* מְשֹׁפְטִי Job 9:15, מְלוֹשְׁנִי Ps. 101:5 K'thibh. These are called Poel forms by many grammarians, and those in the preceding paragraph Pilel, Pulal, Pealal, etc. They are in reality, however, only modified forms of the Piel, whose signification they share.

c. PRETERITE SING. 3 *masc.* The original Pattahh of the first syllable §82. 5. *b* (3) is preserved in נַשַּׁנִי Gen. 41:51. The second syllable has Seghol in דִּבֶּר (in pause), דִּבֵּר, פָּאֵר, כִּפֶּס (twice), Pattahh in גִּדַּל, אִבַּד (הֵגֵל in pause), חִתַּן, פִּלַּשׁ, קִלַּס, שִׁלַּם (in pause); שִׁלַּחַתִּי Isa. 19:21), and before Makkeph in ־לִמַּד, מִלַּט (: מִלֵּט in pause); *a* appears likewise in the pausal form קִצְּצָה Mic. 1:7. The Tsere is always retained in the infinitive construct and future, and with the exception of פַּלֵּג Ps. 55:10, in the imperative; though throughout the species it is shortened to Seghol upon losing the accent, קִבְּצָה Deut. 30:3, ־קַדֵּשׁ Ex. 13:2, יְשַׁלְּבָה Deut. 7:10.

d. INFINITIVE. The primitive form of the infinitive absolute is of rare occurrence, e. g. יַסֹּר Ps. 118:18, קַלֹּא 1 Kin. 19:10, רַסֹּא Ex. 21:19, בְּלִי Josh. 24:10. Most commonly it has Tsere in the second syllable like the infinitive construct, אַבֵּד Jer. 12:17, לַבֵּד Jer. 32:33, בַּלֵּשׁ Jer. 39:18, קַבֵּץ Mic. 2:12, שַׁלֵּם Ex. 21:36; and in one instance it has Hhirik in the first syllable like the preterite נִאֵץ 2 Sam. 12:14. There is no need of assuming a similar form for the infinitive construct in חַלֵּל Lev. 14:43, which can readily be explained as a preterite. Tsere of the construct is shortened to Seghol before Makkeph, ־דַּבֶּר Isa. 59:13, or on the recession of the accent, צָחָק Gen. 39:14, 17, and in one instance besides, לְכָה Judg. 5:8. There are a few examples of the construct infinitive with a feminine termination, יָסְרָה Lev. 26:18, זִמְרָה Ps. 147:1, שִׁלְּבֵת Isa. 6:13, צִדְקָתֶךָ Ezek. 16:52.

e. Future Sing. 1 com. א is commonly prefixed with Hhateph-Pattahh; it has, however, the diphthongal Hhateph-Seghol in אֱזָרְךָ Lev. 26:33, § 60. 3. *b*, and draws to itself the full vowel which has hence arisen to a preceding וֹ, in וְאֶסְבְּרֵם Zech. 7:14 for וַאֲסַבְּרֵם, § 60. 3. *c*.

Plur. 2 *and* 3 *fem.* Tsere under the second radical is sometimes changed to Pattahh, though not with the same frequency as in the Niphal, תִּרְבֶּצְנָה Isa. 13:18, but תִּרְבַּרְנָה Job 27:4, and in pause Prov. 24:2.

PUAL.

§ 93. *a.* Of the vowels proper to the first syllable of the passive, § 82. 5. *b* (3). Pual ordinarily has *ŭ*, which is preferred before a doubled consonant שֻׁלַּם, § 61. 5, and Hophal *o* before concurrent consonants הִפְקַד. This distinction is not steadfastly adhered to, however, and Pual occasionally appears with Kamets Hhatuph, כָּדְרָה Ezek. 16:4, צָדְדָה Nah. 3:7, כָּלּוּ Ps. 72:20, כֹּסּוּ Ps. 80:11, Prov. 24:31, יָחְבְּרָךְ Ps. 94:20, מֵאָדָם *passim*. This seems to furnish the best explanation of the disputed words תָּרְצְחוּ or תִּרְצְחוּ Ps. 62:4, בְּלָשׁוֹנִי Ps. 101:5 K'ri, תֶּאֱכָלֵהוּ Job 20:26. Gesenius regards these as Piel forms with (.) lengthened to (.) on the omission of Daghesh-forte, § 59. *a*; but the absence of Methegh, which Gesenius inserts without authority, shows the vowel to be *o* not *a*. Others think that תֶּאֱכָלֵהוּ is the Kal future for תֹּאכְלֵהוּ, the vowel being attracted to the guttural from the previous letter, § 60. 3. *c*. There is no difficulty, however, in regarding them all as Pual forms, and translating severally *may you be slain, armed with the tongue* (of a slanderer), *shall be made to consume him.* In Ps. 62:4 the reading of Ben Naphtali תִּרְצְחוּ is probably to be preferred to that of Ben Asher, which is found in the common text; the former is a Piel and has an active sense: (how long) *will ye slay or murder?* See Alexander and Delitzsch, *in loc.*

b. The vowel *ŭ* of the first syllable is occasionally written with Vav, וְגֻפָּה Ezek. 16:34, הֻפְּלוּ Ps. 78:63, יֻגַּד Judg. 18:29, 13:8, Job 5:7, מְאוּגָּל Ezek. 27:19, but mostly without it.

c. Preterite Sing. 3 *masc.* An instance of paragogic ה‍ָ appended to the preterite is found in עֻלְּפָה Ezek. 31:15.

d. Infinitive. The absolute form occurs in גֻּנֹּב Gen. 40:15; there is no example of the construct.

e. Participle. As מְסֻבָּר, מְסֻפָּד, מְשֻׁלָּח; in a few instances the initial מ is omitted, לֻקָּח 2 Kin. 2:10 for מְלֻקָּח, כֻּרְסָה (with Daghesh-forte euphonic) Ezek. 21:15, 16, יֻקָּשִׁים Eccles. 9:12 for מְיֻקָּשִׁים, § 59. *a*. Some of the forms in which this has been alleged may however be better explained as preterites.

HIPHIL.

§94. *a.* PRETERITE. The first vowel is usually Hhirik but occasionally Seghol, e. g. חִכְלַמְנוּם 1 Sam. 25:7, particularly in Pe guttural and a few Lamedh He verbs. Once א is prefixed instead of ה, : אַאֲלַפְתִּי Isa. 63:3; in Isa. 19:6 הֶאֱזְנִיחוּ is not a double Hiphil with both א and ה prefixed, but is a denominative from אֹזֶן, a derivative of זָן, which does not indeed occur in its simple form but is justified by the analogy of אָבִיב from בּוּב. ה takes the place of ה in הִרְגַּלְתִּי Hos. 11:3; so likewise the future תְּתָחֲלָה Jer. 12:5, and participle מְתָחֲרָה Jer. 22:15, though the corresponding preterite is הֶחֱרָה Neh. 3:20.

SING. 3 *masc.* The *i* of the second syllable is almost always written with Yodh, rarely without it, e. g. הִגִּד 1 Sam. 12:24, but in every other place הִגְדִּיל. So in the participle בַּגֹּלִם Job 11:3 but בַּגֹּלִים Judg. 18:7.

b. INFINITIVE. *Absolute.* The Tsere of the second syllable which before Makkeph is shortened to Seghol הַגֶּד־ Prov. 24:23, 28:21, is mostly written without י, thus הַשְׁבֵּ, הַבְדֵּל, הַכְבֵּד, הַקְדֵּשׁ, הַמְשֵׁל, הַסְכֵּן, הַקְטֵל, הַגְּלֵה, though sometimes with it הַשְׁכִּיר Am. 9:8 but הַשְׁמֵד Isa. 14:23, הַשְׁכֵּל and הַשְׁכִּיל, twice הַשְׁכִּים, nine times הַשְׁכֵּם, הִכְתִּיר, הַעֲצִיר. Hhirik in this syllable is rare and exceptional, הַשְׂכִּיל Ezek. 21:31, הַכְבִּיר Josh. 7:7. א is prefixed instead of ה in אַשְׁכִּים Jer. 25:3 and אַבְרֵךְ Gen. 41:43, provided the latter is a Hebrew and not a Coptic word.

Construct. The second vowel is commonly Hhirik written with י, הַשְׁכִּלְךָ, הַקְדִּישׁ rarely and as an exception without י, לַשְׁמֹר Isa. 23:11, or with Tsere הַגְנֵל Deut. 32:8, לַעֲשׂוֹ Deut. 26:12, Neh. 10:39, לַפְּנֵי Dan. 11:35. In a few instances the first vowel is Hhirik as in the preterite הִשְׁמֶדְךָ Deut. 7:24, 28:48, Josh. 11:14, 1 Kin. 15:29, הִרְגִּיעִי Jer. 50:34, הַדְרִיכָה Jer. 51:33, הַקְצוֹת Lev. 14:43. The initial ה is mostly retained after prefixed prepositions, though it is sometimes rejected, as לַשְׁמִית Am. 8:4 but לְהַשְׁבִּית Ps. 8:3, לַשְׁמֹר once but לְהַשְׁמִיר fifteen times.

c. FUTURE PLUR. In a very few instances Hhirik is rejected upon the addition of the masculine plural termination וַיַּדְבְּקוּ 1 Sam. 14:22, 31:2, וַיַּדְרְכוּ Jer. 9:2. There is no example of this without the presence of Vav conversive unless it be תַּחְבְּרוּ Job 19:3, which may be regarded as Kal.

d. IMPERATIVE SING. *masc.* The second syllable usually has Tsere without Yodh הַשְׁלֵךְ, הַשְׁלֵה, and before Makkeph, Seghol הָסֶךְ־ Job 22:21, הַגֶּד־ 1 Sam. 23:11, הַבֵּט־ Isa. 64:8. There are a very few examples with Hhirik in pause, : הוֹפִיעַ Ps. 94:1, to which some would add הוֹצִיא Isa. 43:8, but see Alexander, הוֹכִיחַ Prov. 19:25, הַגְלִיא Jer. 17:18.

e. PARTICIPLE. In מֹצִיא Ps. 135:7, Tsere is taken in place of Hhirik upon the recession of the accent; בְּסַפֵּחַ Isa. 53:3 is not a participle but a noun, Alexander *in loc.* Hhirik is, in a few exceptional cases occurring in the later books, rejected in the plural, בְּהִלְלִים Zech. 3:7 for מְהֻלָּלִים, בְּחָלְלִים Jer. 29:8, מַצְוָרִים 2 Chron. 28:23, מָצְרִים 1 Chron. 15:24 K'ri, 2 Chron. 7:6 K'ri. Comp. Chald. מְהַלְּלִין Dan. 3:25.

HOPHAL.

§ 95. *a.* The first vowel, though mostly Kamets Hhatuph הָבְלְכּוּ, הָבְלַךְ, הָשְׁלְכָה, is occasionally Kibbuts, both vowels even appearing in the same verb, הֻשַּׁבְ Ezek. 32:32, הָשְׁבְּתָה ver. 19, מֻצָּבָה 2 Kin. 4:32; הֻשְׁלַךְ Dan. 8:11, הֻבְלָבְךָ Isa. 14:19, הֻשְׁלַלְבִי Ezek. 16:5, מֻצַּב 2 Sam. 20:21; תָּקְרָא Lev. 6:15, מָקְצָר Mal. 1:11, הָפְקַד, מָפְקָדִים; רְבָשָׁלִים, מוּרָק, Ezek. 29:18.

b. PRETERITE. In הָחֲדַלְתִּי *am I obliged to leave?* Judg. 9:9, 11. 13, the characteristic הֻ is rejected after הֲ interrogative.

c. INFINITIVE. The absolute has Tsere in the second syllable, הָחְתֵל Ezek. 16:4, הֻלֵּד Josh. 9:24. The construct has Pattahh, הוּסַר Ezr. 3:11.

d. IMPERATIVE. This mood occurs twice, הָשְׁבְּתָה Ezek. 32:19, הָפְדִי Jer. 49:8.

e. PARTICIPLE. In מָחְצָצוֹת Ezek. 46:22 ה remains after the preformative מ.

HITHPAEL.

§ 96. *a.* PRETERITE. In two instances אֶת is prefixed instead of הִת, viz., אֶתְחַבַּר 2 Chron. 20:35, אֶתְהוֹלָלִי Ps. 76:6. In the verb פָּקַד Daghesh-forte is omitted in the second radical and the previous vowel lengthened, § 59. *a.*, הִתְפָּקְדוּ, הִתְפָּקֵד Judg. 20:15, 17, יִתְפָּקֵד Judg. 21:9, in addition to which the vowel of the prefixed syllable is *ŏ* in הָתְפָּקְדוּ Num. 1:47, 2:33, 26:62, 1 Kin. 20:27. In three verbs upon the assimilation of ת to the first radical, the prefix takes *ŭ*, § 61. 5, הֻדַּשְּׁנָה (the accentuation is unusual) Isa. 34:6, הֻנַּשְּׂאָה Deut. 24:4 (but in the future always יִנַּשֵּׂא Lev. 21:1 and repeatedly elsewhere), הֻכַּבֵּס (*inf. const.*) Lev. 13:55, 56. These are sometimes called Hothpaal and regarded as passives of Hithpael. Where both forms exist in the same verb, however, as in פָּקַד and נָשָׂא, there appears to be no distinction in their meaning; they seem rather to have arisen from a disposition to give to the Hithpael, where it has a passive signification, § 80. 2, the vowels of a proper passive species, § 82. 5. *b* (3). In הִתְגּוֹשֵׁשׁ Jer. 25:16, יִתְהוֹלָל Jer. 46:8 (elsewhere יִתְעַשֵּׁת), and מְגֹאָלִין Isa. 52:5, *ŏ* prolonged from *ŭ*, on account of the absence of Daghesh-forte, is for a like reason given to the first radical.

b. The last vowel of the preterite, infinitive construct, future, imperative and participle, is Tsere written without Yodh, הִתְנַבֵּל, הִתְהַלֵּל, הִתְקַדֵּשׁ *inf. const.*, הִתְפַּצֵּר *imper.*, מִתְבָּרֵךְ, which before Makkeph is shortened to Seghol, הִתְקַדֶּשׁ- Isa. 30:29, הִתְהַלֶּךְ- Gen. 6:9, יִתְבָּלַע- Job 6:16. Frequently, however. Pattahh is used, or, with a pause accent, Kamets, הִתְקַצָּף *pret.*, הִתְהַלָּךְ *pret.* and *imper.* (but *inf. const.* and *part.*

with ē, fut. *a* and *ē*). תִּתְקַדָּשׁוּ, יִתְהַלָּם, תִּתְפַּתֵּל, נִצְטַדָּק, יִתְרַחֲשׁוּ, תִּתְעַלָּמִי,
מִנַּצֵּץ, יִתְחַפֵּשׂוּ Mic. 1:10 K'ri; יִתְחַפְּשׂוּ Ezek. 27:30; יִתְפָּצְצוּ; יִתְלַכְּדוּ:
Isa. 52:5. Pattahh is also sometimes found in the feminine plural of the
future, תִּתְחַלַּכְנָה Zech. 6:7 but תִּשְׁתַּבַּכְנָה Lam. 4:1, where some copies
have תִּשְׁתָּפַכְנָה. Hhirik occurs instead of Pattahh in the preterites,
וְהִתְקַדִּשְׁתֶּם, וְהִתְגֻּדַּלְתִּי Ezek. 38:23, וְהִתְקַדִּשְׁתֶּם Lev. 11:44, 20:7, each of
which has Vav conversive, throwing the accent more strongly on the final
syllable.

c. There is no example of the infinitive absolute.

Paragogic and Apocopated Future and Imperative.

§ 97. The paucity of moods in Hebrew is partially compensated by modifications of the future, known as the paragogic and apocopated futures.

1. The paragogic or cohortative is formed from the ordinary future by appending the termination ָה, to the first person singular or plural, and in a very few instances to the third person singular, thus converting it from a simple declaration of futurity to an expression of desire or determination, אֶשְׁמֹר *I shall keep*, אֶשְׁמְרָה *I will surely keep* or *let me keep*, Ps. 39:2; נִתְּקָה *let us break*, נַשְׁלִיכָה *let us cast away*, Ps. 2:3; יָחִישָׁה *let him hasten*, Isa. 5:19.

a. The third person of the paragogic future occurs besides the example just given, in תְּבוֹאָה *let it come* Isa. 5:19, יֶחְשְׁכָה *be it dark* (by some explained as a noun, *darkness*) Job 11:17, יִרְצֶנָּה *may he accept* (as fat), or, according to Kimchi, *may he reduce to ashes*, Ps. 20:4, תַּהֲלֹמֵנָה Prov. 1:20, 8:3, and after Vav conversive וַתֶּעְגָּבָה Ezek. 23:20, and ver. 16 K'ri. It has also been suspected in יִקְרָחָה Lev. 21:5 K'thibh.

b. Instead of ָה, ה is appended in וָאֶקְרָאֶה 1 Sam. 28:15, יִדְרְשֶׁנָּה Ps. 20:4, § 63. 1. *c;* so in the imperative דְּעֶה or דְּעָה Prov. 24:14.

2. The apocopated or jussive future is an abbreviation of the second or third persons singular and expresses a wish or command, or with a negative, dissuasion or prohibition. In the perfect verb it has a separate form only in the Hiphil species, the י. of the ultimate being changed to (ֵ), or before Makkeph to (ְ), יַדְבִּיק *he will cause to cleave*, יַדְבֵּק *may he or let him cause to cleave;* תַּשְׂכִּיל *thou wilt understand*, תַּשְׂכֵּל

thou mayest understand or *understand thou*, Dan. 9 : 25, אַל־תַּשְׁלֶט־ *may it not* or *let it not rule*, Ps. 119 : 133. In some classes of imperfect verbs, as in the Ayin-Vav and particularly the Lamedh-He, it is used in other species still.

a. The only instances of the abbreviated future occurring in the first person are אָחֹזְק Isa. 42:6 and נֵרָא Isa. 41:23 K'thibh, where the K'ri has נִרְאֶה.

b. The paragogic and apocopated futures may be regarded as mutually supplementary, and as forming together something like a complete Optative or Subjunctive mood. The apocopated future has, it is true, no separate form for the *second fem. sing.* or the *second* and *third pers. plur.*, in which the verb has terminal inflections, but it may be regarded as coinciding in these with the ordinary future, except that it never has the final ן. So in those species in which it is indistinguishable from the ordinary future, it may yet be regarded as included under it. Neither the apocopated nor the paragogic futures occur in the strictly passive species, viz., the Pual and Hophal, self-determination and command both implying that the subject is the originator of the action. The more flexible Arabic has three varieties of the future in addition to the ordinary one, to express as many modifications or moods.

c. The apocopated future derives its name from the apocopation of the final letter by which it is characterized in ל״ה verbs; the brevity of its form is adapted to the energy and rapid utterance of a command. On the other hand, the speaker dwells upon the word expressive of his own desire or determination, thus giving rise to the prolonged form of the paragogic future. The appended ה, may perhaps be identical with a like termination added to nouns to indicate motion or direction, denoting as it does the direction of the speaker's will or wishes towards that which the verb expresses.

§ 98. 1. Paragogic ה, is sometimes appended to the masculine singular of the imperative, softening the command into an earnest entreaty or expression of strong desire, שְׁמַע *hear* (thou), שִׁמְעָה *oh, hear!* or *pray, hear!* הַקְשֵׁב *listen,* הַקְשִׁיבָה *pray, listen!* The addition of this vowel to the imperative and to the future causes, as in the regular inflections of the paradigm, § 86. *b.* (2), the rejection of the vowel of the ultimate syllable, except in the Hiphil where י. remains in the future and is restored in the imperative. In the Kal imperative this rejection occasions the concurrence of two vowelless consonants, the first of which must accordingly take a short vowel, § 61. 1; if the rejected vowel was Hholem this will be Kamets-Hhatuph, otherwise it will be the briefest of the vowels, Hhirik, זָב, זָכְרָה Jer. 49:11; זְכֹר, זָכְרָה 2 Chron. 6:42, שְׁכַב, שִׁכְבָה Gen. 39:7. 12.

a. In a few instances the vowel-letter remains in the K'thibh though invariably thrown out in the K'ri, e. g., צרושה K'thibh, צְרֻפָה K'ri Ps. 26:2, מלובח K'thibh, מְלֻבָּה K'ri Judg. 9:8; ואשקילה K'thibh, וָאַשְׁקֶלָה K'ri Ezr. 8:25; אשקובה K'thibh, אֲשֻׁקָה K'ri Isa. 18:4. This may not indicate, however, the retention of the full vowel but only of an audible remnant of it, § 13. *a*, which is likewise attested by the occasional appearance of Hhateph Kamets, אֲשֻׁקָה 1 Kin. 19:20, וָאֲשֻׁגְלָה Dan. 8:13 (in some copies) or Hhateph Pattahh וָאֲשֻׁקָלָה Ezr. 8:26, Jer. 32:9, and by the fact that the resulting Sh'va, even when simple, is always vocal, § 22. *a* (1). Occasionally Kamets-Hhatuph is found in the paragogic imperative when the vowel of the ordinary imperative is Pattahh; thus, קְלֹב Lev. 9:7, קָרְבָה Ps. 69:19, and on the contrary, מִכְרָה Gen. 25:31, *fut.* יִבְּר Ex. 21:7, נְצָלָה (with Daghesh separative) Ps. 141:3.

2. As the imperative is itself a shortened form there is little room for further abbreviation; it sometimes, however, suffers apocopation of the final ה, of the feminine plural, שְׁמַעַן Gen. 4:23 for שְׁמַעְנָה, § 61. 2, קְרָאן Ex. 2:20 for קְרֶאנָה, § 60. 3. *c*, and in Lamedh He verbs of final ה ֶ of the masculine singular, הַד 2 Kin. 6:18 for הִכֵּה Ezek. 6:11, גַּל Ps. 119:18 for גַּלֵּה; הֶרֶב Deut. 9:14 for הַרְפֵּה Judg. 11:37, but without any evident change of meaning.

VAV CONVERSIVE.

§ 99. 1. The primary tenses are supplemented by two others, formed in a peculiar manner by what is called Vav Conversive (וָו הִפּוּךְ). This prefix has the remarkable effect, from which its name is derived, of converting the ordinary future into a preterite and the ordinary preterite into a future. The following appear to be the reasons of this singular phenomenon. Past and future are relative and depend for their signification in any given case upon the point of time from which they are reckoned. This may be the moment of speaking, when all anterior to that moment will be past, and all posterior to it future. Or by some conventional method understood between the speaker and his hearers, an ideal present may be fixed distinct from the real present and the measurements of past and future made from the former. Now Vav Conversive placed before a future indicates that its tense is to be reckoned not from the actual present but from the time denoted by some previous word, whether verb, noun, or adverb. And when the stand-point is thus taken in the past, events may be described as future with reference to it, though they have actually taken place at the time of narration. Vav is properly the copula *and;* when this is prefixed to the future for the purpose already designated, it is followed by Pattahh and Daghesh-forte, which give to it the force of *and then* or *and so,* indicating that what follows is the sequel of what precedes. Consequently a narration begun in the preterite may be continued in the future with Vav Conversive, the opening words fixing the initial point from which all that come after proceed in regular succession; and the future so employed is converted into what may be called a continuative preterite. Thus, in the account of the creation in Gen. 1, the original condition of things is described in the preterite, ver. 2, *the earth was* הָיְתָה *without form and void.* The subsequent scene is then surveyed from this point. The next statement is accordingly made by a future with Vav Conversive, ver. 3, וַיֹּאמֶר *and God said,* in its primitive import, *and then God says* or *will say,* his speaking being future to the state of things previously described. This fixes a new stand-point from which the next step in the process is a fresh advance; it is hence followed by another future with Vav Conversive, ver. 4, וַיַּרְא *and he saw;* and so on, וַיַּבְדֵּל *and he divided,* ver. 5, וַיִּקְרָא *and he called,* etc.

a. The nature of this prefix would be more precisely expressed perhaps by calling it Vav Consecutive, as Ewald and others propose. But as Vav Conversive is the name in common use, and as this sufficiently characterizes its most striking effect, it is here retained. There have been various conjectures respecting its origin. In the judgment of some וַ is an abbreviation of the verb הָוָה was, hence וַיֹּאמֶר he was or it was (so that) he will say i. e. he was about to say or was saying, which is then likened to the Arabic combination of the preterite of the substantive verb with the future tense to express past action; but ו evidently has the sense of the conjunction and, וַיֹּאמֶר does not mean he said, but and he said. Others regard it as an abbreviation of וְהָיָה and he was; Ewald of זְאָו and then. Rödiger thinks that the vowel has no inherent significance, but is attached to the conjunction on account of the emphasis of its peculiar use. Perhaps the best suggestion is that of Schultens, Instit. p. 424, that וַיֹּאמֶר may be for וְהָיֹּאמֶר, by § 53. 3 ; הַ prefixed to a noun is the definite article, and points it out as one previously known; its use in this particular case is to define the time of the action of the verb before which it stands by pointing it out as known from what preceded. The vowel of this prefix is upon this hypothesis analogous both in its origin and its effects to the augment ε in Greek, or a in Sanskrit, by which a preterite is formed from a present or a future, τύπτω, ἔτυπτον; τύψω, ἔτυψα, and which is traced by Bopp to a pronominal root having a demonstrative sense, Vergleichende Grammatik pp. 786 ff. The fact that the Samaritan Pentateuch sometimes substitutes ה for ו conversive might seem to lend confirmation to this theory of its derivation. But as ה stands with equal frequency for ו copulative, and ו for the article ה, it is probable that these commutations are to be classed with the other numerous inaccuracies of this edition.

2. This employment of Vav Conversive to alter the meaning of the tenses by transporting the mind of the hearer or reader to an ideal present in the past or future is one of the most remarkable idioms of the Hebrew language, and one which may appear to be extremely arbitrary, as it certainly is in some of its applications, at least, quite difficult of conception and foreign to our habits of thought. It nevertheless imparts a beauty and a vividness to Hebrew description which are altogether peculiar and which are incapable of being adequately transferred to any other language. The narrator lives in the midst of that which he records, and watches its progress step by step telling what he sees. This peculiarity of the Hebrew tenses may perhaps be illustrated by an analogous though far more restricted usage in English, by which certain tenses may be transferred to another sphere than that which they describe if measured from the time of narration, without any confusion or liability to mistake resulting from it. Thus, the present may be used of past

events, as, Then the devil *taketh* him up into an exceeding high mountain and *sheweth* him, etc. .Or the present and the perfect may be used of what is still future, as, When thou *art converted* strengthen thy brethren; When he *is come* he will reprove the world of sin.

3. Vav Conversive, it has already been stated, is prefixed to the future with Pattahh and Daghesh-forte in the following letter, וַיֵּרֶד, וַתִּמְלִיכוּ, וַיִּקְבֹּץ. If the first letter of the future be Yodh with Sh'va, Daghesh is commonly omitted, § 25, but rarely if it be יְ, and never if it be תְּ, since its removal in this case would change the sound of the letter by restoring its aspiration, וַיְסַפֵּר, וַיְדַבֵּר but וַתְּדַבֵּר, וַיֶּאֱסֹף. Before א of the first person singular, which cannot receive Daghesh, § 23. 1, Pattahh is lengthened to Kamets, § 60. 4, וָאֵלֵךְ, וָאֲדַבֵּר. In the Hiphil י. is, with few exceptions, e. g. וָיַּחְשֵׁךְ Ps. 105: 28, compressed to (..) as in the apocopated future, וַתַּגְדֵּל, וַיַּקְשֵׁב, and before Makkeph it is shortened to (,) וַיַּגֶּד־. In the first person singular, however, י. remains in the Hiphil, and a paragogic ה, is not infrequently appended in all the species, e. g. וָאַשְׁלִיךְ, וָאֶשְׁלָה or וָאֶשְׁלְךָ; וָאָעִיד or וָאַדְבְּרָה; or וָאֲדַבֵּר, וָאֶמְלְטָה, וָאַשְׁמִיד; וָאַגֵּד; paragogic ה, also occurs though more rarely in the first pers. plur. וַנַּחֲלְמָה Gen. 41: 11, וַנִּבְקְשָׁה, וַנָּצִימָה Ezr. 8: 23, וַנִּפְשָׂה ver. 31.

a. The tendency to abbreviation produced by Vav Conversive is much more apparent in some classes of imperfect verbs. Thus, final ה is rejected from ל״ה verbs as in the apocopated future וַיִּגֶל, וַיֵּבְךְּ, וַיִּגָּל; the accent is drawn back from a mixed ultimate to a simple penult in the Kal and Hiphil of Ayin doubled verbs and of those which have a quiescent for their first or second radical, in consequence of which the vowel of the last syllable, if long, is shortened, § 64. 1, רָס, וַיֹּסֶף; וַיֹּאבַל, וַיָּשָׁב, וַיֹּשֶׁב; וַיָּקָם, רָקִים; וַיֵּלֶךְ, הָלִיךְ; וַיֹּשֶׁב, יוֹשֵׁב. The same drawing back of the accent and shortening of the ultimate syllable occurs in the Piel of the following verbs, whose middle radical is ר, וַיְבָרֵךְ, וַיְגָרֶשׁ but not in וַיְחָבֵּל; so in וַיְשׁוֹרֵר Hab. 3: 6, and the Hithpael וַיִּתְפַּשׂ Dan. 2: 1. It occurs also in the Niphal of a few verbs, which form the exception, however, not the rule, וַיִּפְּלֵחַ or וַיֵּאָסֵף, וַיִּנָּגֶף, וַיִּנָּגֶף but וַיִּפְתַּח, וַיִּשָּׁאֵה, וַיִּקְבֵר, וַיִּמָּלֵא, וַיִּלָּבֵד, etc. The first person singular is mostly exempted from shortening or change of accent, וָאֶשֵּׁב,

וָאָקִים or וְאָקִים, נָאָקִים, though it sometimes suffers apocopation in ל״ה verbs וָאֵרָא, וָאֲלִי. The prolonged plural ending וּן is very rarely used after Vav Conversive; it does, however, occur, e. g. וַתִּקְרָבוּן Deut. 1:22, וַתְּכַבְּדוּן Deut. 4:11, וַיַּחֲנוּן Judg. 11:18.

b. In a very few instances Vav Conversive takes Pattahh before א, its vowel being conformed to the compound Sh'va, which follows, e. g. וָאֶגְלֹשׁ Judg. 6:9, וָאֶמְלְתָהוּ 2 Sam. 1:10, וָאַבֶּשָּׁה Ezek. 16:10 but וָאֶבְשָׁה ver. 8, וָאֶרְחַלֵּל Job 30:26, וָאֲחַשְּׁבָה Ps. 73:16.

§ 100. 1. Vav Conversive prefixed to the preterite makes of it a continuative future or imperative, by connecting with it the idea of futurity or command expressed in a preceding verb. It is properly the conjunction וְ *and*, whose pointing it takes, its peculiar force being derived from its connecting power. Accordingly, in speaking of coming events, the stand-point is first fixed in the future by the opening words, and the description is then continued by the preterite with Vav Conversive. Thus, in Samuel's recital, 1 Sam. 10:1–8, of what was to happen to Saul, he first refers the whole to the future by the word, ver. 2, בְּלֶכְתְּךָ *upon thy departing*, and then proceeds with preterites with Vav prefixed, וּמָצָאתָ *thou shalt find*, וְאָמְרוּ *and they shall say*, ver. 3, וְחָלַפְתָּ *and thou shalt pass on*, etc. etc. In like manner injunctions begun in the imperative are continued in the preterite with Vav Conversive. Thus the Lord directed Elijah, 1 Kin. 17:3 לֵךְ (imper.) *go*, וּפָנִיתָ (pret.) *and turn*, וְנִסְתַּרְתָּ (pret.) *and hide*, וְהָיָה (pret.) *and it shall be*.

2. This prefix commonly has the effect of removing the accent to the ultimate in those forms in which it ordinarily stands upon the penult; and if the penult be a long mixed syllable, as in the Kal preterite of verbs with Ihholem, it will in consequence be shortened, וְגָכַלְתָּ, יָכֹלְתָּ.

a. The shifting of the accent, which served in some measure to indicate to the ear the alteration in the sense, takes place chiefly in the following cases, viz.:

(1) It occurs with great regularity in the first and second persons singular of every species, חָלַכְתָּ *thou hast gone*, וְחָלַכְתָּ *and thou shalt go*, וְחָלַכְתִּי *and I will go*, so וְדִבַּרְתִּי, וְהִשְׁבַּעְתִּי, וְהִתְחַלַּכְתִּי, though וְהִצַּלְתִּי Zeph. 1:17, except in לא and ל״ה verbs, where the accent usually re-

§ 101   VERBS WITH SUFFIXES.   133

mains in its original position although the usage is not uniform, וּפָנִ֫יתִי
Lev. 26 : 9. וּבָ֫אתִי 1 Kin. 18 : 12. וְהִרְבֵּ֫יתִיךָ 1 Chron. 4 : 10. וְהִשְׁתַּחֲוָ֫יתִי 1 Sam.
15 : 30, יָחֵ֫בִּיתִי Isa. 8 : 17 but וָאֶצְרָ֫ךְ Lev. 24 : 5, וּבָ֫אתָ Gen. 6 : 18, וְהִרְבֵּ֫יתִי
וְהִפְרֵ֫יתִי Lev. 26 : 9, וַתְּבִאֵ֫הוּ Ex. 26 : 33. In the first person plural of all
verbs the accent generally remains upon the penult, יָזְבֵ֫חֻ Ex. 8 : 23,
יְלַקְּחֻ֫נוּ, וְחַלַּקְנ֫וּ Gen. 34 : 17.

(2) It occurs, though less constantly, in the third feminine singular
and third plural of the Hiphil of perfect verbs, and of the various species
of Ayin-Vav and Ayin-doubled verbs. יִחְבַּדִּיל֫הַ Ex. 26 : 33, וְהֵבִיאָ֫ה Lev.
15 : 29, וְרָחַ֫ץ Isa. 11 : 2, יָקֵ֫לֹּוּ, וְחָלוּ Hab. 1 : 8 but וְהִתְחַלְּלוּ Ezek. 43 : 24,
וּפָ֫שׁוּ Hab. 1 : 8.

VERBS WITH SUFFIXES.

§ 101. Pronouns are frequently suffixed to the verbs of which they are the object. The forms of the suffixes have already been given § 72. It only remains to consider the changes resulting from their combination with the various parts of the verb.

1. The personal terminations of the verbs undergo the following changes :

Preterite.

SING. 3 *fem.* The old ending ת ִ, § 85. *a* (1), takes the place of ה ָ.

    2 *masc.* תָּ sometimes shortens its final vowel before the suffix נִי of the first person.

    2 *fem.* The old ending תִּי, § 86. *a*, instead of תְּ.

PLUR. 2 *masc.* תְּ from the old pronominal ending תֶּם, § 71. *b* (2), takes the place of תֶּם. The feminine of this person does not occur with suffixes.

Future.

PLUR. 2 and 3 *fem.* The distinctive feminine termination is dropped, and that of the masculine assumed, תִּקְטְל֫וּ for תִּקְטֹ֫לְנָה.

a. In several of these cases it would be more correct to say that it is the uncompounded state of the verb in which the change has taken place, and that before suffixes the original form has been preserved, the added syllable having as it were protected it from mutation.

2. Changes in the suffixes: The suffixes are joined directly to those verbal forms which end in a vowel; those forms which end in a consonant insert before the suffixes of the second pers. plur. כֶם, כֶן, and the second masc. sing. ךָ, a vocal Sh'va, and before the remaining suffixes a full vowel, which in the preterite is mostly *a* and in the future and imperative mostly *e*.

The 3 fem. sing. preterite inserts *ă* before the suffixes of the third pers. plural, and *ĕ* before the second fem. singular; when it stands before the third sing. suffixes הוּ, הָ, there is frequently an elision of ה, requiring Daghesh-forte conservative in the verbal ending ת to preserve the quantity of the previous short vowel, קְטָלַתְהוּ for קְטָלַתּוּ, קְטָלַתְהָ for קְטָלַתָּה, see § 57. 3. *b*.

When the third masc. sing. suffix הוּ is preceded by (ֹ), the ה may be elided and the vowels coalesce into וֹ, קְטָלוֹ for קְטָלָהוּ; when it is preceded by ִי, Shurek may be hardened to its corresponding semi-vowel ו, קְטָלְתִיו for קְטַלְתִּיהוּ § 62. 1.

When the third fem. suffix הָ is preceded by (ָ), final Kamets is omitted to prevent the recurrence of the same sound, קְטָלָהּ for קְטָלָהָ.

When הוּ, הָ of the third pers. singular are preceded by (ֵ), the vowel of union for the future, a נ, called Nun Epenthetic, is sometimes inserted, particularly in emphatic and pausal forms, to prevent the hiatus between the two vowels, (ֵ) being at the same time shortened to (ֶ); ה is then commonly elided and a euphonic Daghesh-forte inserted in the Nun, יִקְטְלֶנּוּ for יִקְטְלֵהוּ. The same shortening of the (ֵ) and insertion of Daghesh may occur in the first person singular and plural and the second masculine singular; this, like the preceding, takes place chiefly at the end of clauses.

§ 101   VERBS WITH SUFFIXES.   135

a. The Nun Epenthetic of the future and the Preterite vowel of union a, which is abbreviated to Sh'va before ךָ, כֶם, כֶן, may be relics of old forms of the verb still represented in the Arabic, where the Preterite ends in a, and one mode of the future has an appended Nun. Daghesh-forte in the suffixes of the first and second persons may be explained, as is usually done, by assuming the insertion and assimilation of Nun Epenthetic, יִקְטְלֶךָּ for יִקְטְלֶנְךָ; or it may be Daghesh-forte emphatic, § 24. 6, and the few cases in which Nun appears in these persons may be accounted for by the resolution of Daghesh, § 54. 3, instead of the Daghesh having arisen from the assimilation of Nun, so that יִקְטְלֶךָּ may be for יִקְטְלֶךָ instead of the reverse.

b. The suffixes, since they do not in strictness form a part of the word with which they are connected, are more loosely attached to it than the pronominal fragments which make up the inflections; hence vowels of union are employed with the former which serve to separate as well as to unite. Hence too the vocal Sh'va, inserted before the suffixes of the second person, does not so completely draw the final consonant of the verb to the appended syllable as to detach it from that to which it formerly belonged; this latter becomes, therefore, not a simple but an intermediate syllable, § 20. 2. A like distinction exists between prefixed prepositions, etc., and the personal prefixes of the future. The latter form part and parcel of the word, while the former preserve a measure of their original separateness. Hence when they form a new initial syllable by the aid of the first consonant of the word, this is properly a mixed syllable after a personal prefix but intermediate after a preposition, יִכְתּוֹב but בִּכְתוֹב, § 22. a. Hence, too, a liability to contraction in one case which does not exist in the other, יָקֵם but לְהָקֵם, יֵשֵׁל but בִּשֵׁל.

3. Changes in the body of the verb:

Except in the Kal preterite those forms which have personal terminations experience no further change from the addition of suffixes; those which are without such terminations reject the vowel of the last syllable before suffixes requiring a vowel of union and shorten it before the remainder, יִקְטְלֵהוּ, יִקְטְלֵנִי, יִקְטֹל, יְקַטְלוּנִי, יְקַטְלוּ; but ִי of the Hiphil species is almost always preserved, יַקְטִילֵנִי, הִקְטִילֵנִי.

In the Kal imperative and infinitive the rejection of the vowel occasions the concurrence of two vowelless letters at the beginning of the word, which impossible combination is obviated by the insertion of Hhirik to form a new syllable; or, if the rejected vowel was Hholem, by the insertion of Kamets Hhatuph.

In the Kal preterite, where both vowels are liable to mutation, a distinction is made by rejecting the first before suffixes and the second before personal inflections where this is possible, e. g. קָטַל, קְטָלָה, קְטָלוּ but קְטָלוֹ, קְטָלֵנִי. Accordingly upon the reception of a suffix the vowel of the second radical, whether it be a, e, or o, must be restored, and if need be lengthened, whenever, in the course of regular inflection, it has been dropped, and the vowel of the first radical, wherever it remains in the regular inflection, must be rejected.

a. Final mixed syllables, as shown in 2 *b*, ordinarily become intermediate upon appending כֶם, כֶן, הּ, and consequently take a short vowel notwithstanding the following vocal Sh'va. This is invariably the case before כֶם and כֶן, unless the word to which they are attached has a long immutable vowel in the ultimate which is of course incapable of being shortened; it is also usually the case before הּ, the principal exception, so far as verbal forms are concerned, being the *a* and *e* of the Kal preterite, *a* of the Kal future, and *i* of the Hiphil, נִזְרָהּ, גְּדָלָהּ, אֲהֵבָהּ, אַצִּלָהּ, אֲנַגְּלָהּ, חֲשִׁיבָהּ but הְּכַבְּדָהּ, הִצְּהָ, אָרְהָ.

§ 102. 1. The first and second persons of the verb do not receive suffixes of the same person with themselves, for when the subject is at the same time the object of the action the Hithpael species is employed or a reciprocal pronoun is formed from the noun נֶפֶשׁ *soul, self,* as נַפְשִׁי *myself.* Suffixes of the third person may, however, be attached to the third person of verbs, provided the subject and object be distinct.

a. There is a single example of a verb in the first person with a suffix of the first person, but in this case the pronoun expresses the indirect object of the verb, עֲשִׂיתִנִי *I have made for me,* Ezek. 29 : 3.

2. Neuter verbs and passive species, whose signification does not admit of a direct object, may yet receive suffixes expressive of indirect relations, such as would be denoted by the dative or ablative in occidental languages, צֻמְתֻּנִי *ye fasted for me* Zech. 7 : 5, תִּנָּשֵׁנִי *thou shalt be forgotten by me.* Isa. 44 : 21.

3. The infinitive may be viewed as a noun, in which case its suffix is to be regarded as a possessive, and represents the subject of the action; or it may be viewed as a verb when its suffix represents the object, e. g. קָטְלִי *my killing*, i. e. that which I perform, קָטְלֵנִי *killing me*. The participle may also receive the suffix either of a verb or a noun, the pronoun in either case denoting the object, רֹאִי *seeing me* Isa. 47 : 10, שֹׂנְאַי *hating me*, lit. *my haters*, Ps. 35 : 19.

a. The infinitive with a verbal suffix represents the subject in בְּשׁוּבֵנִי *at my returning*, Ezek. 47 : 7.

§ 103. The paradigm upon the next page exhibits certain portions of the regular verb קָטַל with all the suffixes.

a. The parts of the verb selected are sufficient representatives of all the rest, and by the aid of the rules already given will enable the student to determine any other required form for himself. The third person singular of the Hiphil preterite, which undergoes no change in the body of the verb, will answer *mutatis mutandis* for all the forms in that species ending with the final radical. The third singular of the Piel preterite, which suffers a change in its last syllable only, will in like manner answer for all the forms in that species ending with the final radical. The Kal preterite is given in all the persons, both on account of the peculiarity of that tense, which suffers changes in both its vowels, and in order to exhibit the changes in the personal terminations which apply equally to the preterites of the other species. The Kal infinitive and imperative are peculiar in forming a new initial syllable which echoes the rejected vowel. The third person singular of the Kal future affords a type of all the forms in that tense which end with the final radical; and the third plural of the same tense is a type of all the future forms in this and in the other species which have personal terminations appended. The participles undergo the same changes in receiving suffixes with nouns of like formation, and are therefore not included in this table.

Paradigm of the Perfect

		Singular.				
		1 com.	2 masc.	2 fem.	3 masc.	3 fem.
Kal Preterite.						
Sing.	3 masc.	קְטָלַנִי	קְטָלְךָ	קְטָלֵךְ	קְטָלָהוּ / קְטָלוֹ	קְטָלָהּ
	3 fem.	קְטָלַתְנִי	קְטָלַתְךָ	קְטָלָתֵךְ	קְטָלַתְהוּ / קְטָלַתּוּ	קְטָלָתָהּ
	2 masc.	קְטַלְתַּנִי / קְטַלְתָּנִי	—	—	קְטַלְתָּהוּ / קְטַלְתּוֹ	קְטַלְתָּהּ
	2 fem.	קְטַלְתִּינִי	—	—	קְטַלְתִּיהוּ / קְטַלְתִּיו	קְטַלְתִּיהָ
	1 com.	—	קְטַלְתִּיךָ	קְטַלְתִּיךְ	קְטַלְתִּיו	קְטַלְתִּיהָ
Plur.	3 com.	קְטָלוּנִי	קְטָלוּךָ	קְטָלוּךְ	קְטָלוּהוּ	קְטָלוּהָ
	2 masc.	קְטַלְתּוּנִי	—	—	קְטַלְתּוּהוּ	קְטַלְתּוּהָ
	1 com.	—	קְטַלְנוּךָ	קְטַלְנוּךְ	קְטַלְנוּהוּ	קְטַלְנוּהָ
Infinitive.		קָטְלֵנִי / קָטְלֵי	קָטְלְךָ	קָטְלֵךְ	קָטְלוֹ	קָטְלָהּ
Future.						
Sing.	3 masc.	יִקְטְלֵנִי / יִקְטְלֵי	יִקְטָלְךָ / יִקְטָלֶךָּ	יִקְטְלֵךְ	יִקְטְלֵהוּ / יִקְטְלֶנּוּ	יִקְטְלֶהָ / יִקְטְלֶנָּה
Plur.	3 masc.	יִקְטְלוּנִי	יִקְטְלוּךָ	יִקְטְלוּךְ	יִקְטְלוּהוּ	יִקְטְלוּהָ
Imperative.						
Sing.	2 masc.	קָטְלֵנִי	—	—	קָטְלֵהוּ	קָטְלָהּ
Piel Preterite.						
Sing.	3 masc.	קִטְּלַנִי	קִטֶּלְךָ	קִטְּלֵךְ	קִטְּלוֹ	קִטְּלָהּ
Hiphil Preterite.						
Sing.	3 masc.	הִקְטִילַנִי	הִקְטִילְךָ	הִקְטִילֵךְ	הִקְטִילוֹ	הִקְטִילָהּ

Verbs with Suffixes.

		Plural.		
1 com.	2 masc.	2 fem.	3 masc.	3 fem.
קְטָלָנוּ	קְטָלְכֶם	קְטָלְכֶן	קְטָלָם	קְטָלָן
קְטָלַתְנוּ	קְטָלַתְכֶם	קְטָלַתְכֶן	קְטָלַתַם	קְטָלָתַן
קְטַלְתָּנוּ	—	—	קְטַלְתָּם	קְטַלְתָּן
קְטַלְתִּ-נוּ	—	—	קְטַלְתִּים	קְטַלְתִּין
—	קְטַלְתִּי כֶם	קְטַלְתִּי כֶן	קְטַלְתִּים	קְטַלְתִּין
קְטָלוּנוּ	קְטָלוּכֶם	קְטָלוּכֶן	קְטָלוּם	קְטָלוּן
קְטָלוּתָנוּ	—	—	קְטָלוּתֻם	קְטָלוּתֻן
—	קְטָלוּכֶם	קְטָלוּכֶן	קְטָלוּם	קְטָלוּן
קָטְלֵנוּ	קָטְלְכֶם	קָטְלְכֶן	קָטְלָם	קָטְלָן
יִקְטְלֵנוּ / יִקְטְלֵפוּ	יִקְטְלְכֶם	יִקְטְלְכֶן	יִקְטְלֵם	יִקְטְלֵן
יִקְטְלוּנוּ	יִקְטְלוּכֶם	יִקְטְלוּכֶן	יִקְטְלוּם	יִקְטְלוּן
קָטְלֵנוּ	—	—	קָטְלֵם	
קָטְלֵנוּ	קָטְלְכֶם	קָטְלְכֶן	קָטְלָם	קָטְלָן
הִקְטִילָנוּ	הִקְטִילְכֶם	הִקְטִילְכֶן	הִקְטִילָם	הִקְטִילָן

Remarks on the Perfect Verbs with Suffixes.

PRETERITE.

§ 104. *a.* There are two examples of (ִ) as the union vowel of the preterite, יְסָרַ֫נִי Isa. 8:11, שְׁאֵלֵךְ Judg. 4:20. Daghesh-forte euphonic is sometimes inserted in the suffix of the first pers. sing., יִסְּרַ֫נִּי Ps. 118:18, חֲנָ֫נִּי Gen. 30:6.

b. The suffix of the second masc. sing. is occasionally ךָ, in pause : עֲזָרָ֑ךְ Isa. 55:5, so with the infinitive, חֲשֶׁכְרֶךָ Deut. 28:24, 45; and a similar form with the future may perhaps be indicated by the K'thibh in Hos. 4:6 אֲמָאסְאךָ; § 11. 1. *a,* where the K'ri has אֶמְאָסְךָ. With לֹא and לֹה verbs this form of the suffix is of frequent occurrence, : עָנְךָ Isa. 30:19, Jer. 23:37, הִפְרָאֶךָ Ezek. 28:15. In a few instances the final *a* is represented by the vowel letter ח, and the suffix is written בָה, הֲצִדְבָּה 1 Kin. 18:44, תֻּנְצְּבָה Prov. 2:11, יְבָרְכ֫וּבָה Ps. 145:10, רְעוּבָה Jer. 7:27.

c. The suffix of the second fem. sing. is commonly ךְ, : קְרָאֵךְ Isa. 54:6, שְׁאֵלֵךְ Isa. 60:9, except after the third fem. sing. of the verb, when it is הָ֑כִי, אֲהַבָּ֑תְךִי Ruth 4:15, שְׁדָדְתֵ֫כִי Isa. 47:10; sometimes, especially in the later Psalms, it has the form כִי corresponding to the pronoun אַתִּי, אוֹדְלֵכִי Ps. 137:6, הַמְעַטְּלֵכִי Ps. 103:4.

d. The suffix of the third masc. sing. is written with the vowel letter ה instead of ו in פֹּרְשֹׂה Ex. 32:25, קֹבֹה Num. 28:8, and in some copies אֲבִלֹה 1 Sam. 1:9, where it would be feminine; this form is more frequently appended to nouns than to verbs.

e. In a few instances the ה of the third fem. suffix is not pointed with Mappik, and consequently represents a vowel instead of a consonant, שְׂבֵרָה (with the accent on the penult because followed by an accented syllable) Am. 1:11. so with the infinitive, הַגְּבָרָה Ex. 9:18, הַצִּבָה Jer. 44:19, and the future, וַתְּחְלָה Ex. 2:3.

f. The suffix of the third masc. plur. receives a paragogic י once in prose, גֵּרַשְׁתֵּ֫ימוֹ Ex. 23:31, and repeatedly in poetry, תְּמַלָּאֵ֫מוֹ, הוֹרִישֵׁ֫מוֹ Ex. 15:9; once ה is appended, יְבַסְיֻ֫מוּ Ex. 15:5; הֶם is used but once as a verbal suffix, אֶצַרְיֵהֶם Deut. 32:26.

g. The suffix of the third fem. plur. ן is seldom used, יְדָעְתִּין Isa. 48:7, יְחִיתָן Hab. 2:17; more frequently the masculine ם is substituted for it, סְתָמוּם Gen. 26:15, 18, וַיְגָרְשׁוּם Ex. 2:17, יְרָאקְרוּם 1 Sam. 6:10. so Num. 17:3, 4, Josh. 4:8, 2 Kin. 18:13, Hos. 2:14, Prov. 6:21 ; הֶן is never used with verbs. When attached to infinitives a paragogic הָ is sometimes added to ן, בִּיאָנָה Ruth 1:19, לְרָחְתָּה Job 39:2.

h. Verbs, which have Tsere for the second vowel in the Kal preterite, retain it before suffixes, אֲהַבְךָ Deut. 7:13, לִבְשָׁם Lev. 16:4, שׂנֵאָה Deut. 24:3, יְרָאוּהוּ Job 37:24. The only example of a suffix appended to a preterite whose second vowel is Hholem, is יְכָלְתִּ֫יו Ps. 13:5 from יָכֹלְתִּי,

§ 105   PERFECT VERBS WITH SUFFIXES.   141

the Hholem being shortened to Kamets Hhatuph by the shifting of the accent. Tsere of the Piel species is mostly shortened to Seghol before הֶ, בֶּ, כֶּן, קִבְּצָךְ Deut. 30:3, יְקַבֶּצְךָ ver. 4, but occasionally to Hhirik, אֲאַמִּצְכֶם (the Methegh in most editions is explained by § 45. 2) Job 16:5, אֲרוֹמִמְךָ Isa. 25:1, מְקַדִּשְׁכֶם Ex. 31:13, פָּרִשְׁכֶם Isa. 1:15. Hhirik of the Hiphil species is retained before all suffixes with very few exceptions, וַיַּשְׁרֵנוּ 1 Sam. 17:25. Ps. 65:10; in יַגְּרְךָ Deut. 32:7, the verb has the form of the apocopated future.

i. The third fem. preterite sometimes takes the third masc. sing. suffix in its full form, גְּמָלַתְהוּ Prov. 31:12, אֲבָלַתְהוּ Ezek. 15:5, so in pause: אֲהֵבַתְהוּ 1 Sam. 18:28, אֲבָלָתְהוּ Gen. 37:20, סְמָכַתְהוּ Isa. 59:16. and sometimes contracted by the exclusion of ה, גְּמָלַתּוּ 1 Sam. 1:24, יְלָדַתּוּ Ruth 4:15, גְּנָבַתּוּ Job 21:18. The third fem. suffix is always contracted, אֲחָזַתָּה Jer. 49:24, חַלְּקָתָה Isa. 34:17, כְּבָשָׂתָה 1 Sam. 1:6. The suffix of the third masc. plural is ם ָ, not ם ַ, with this person of the verb, the accent falling on the penult. גְּבָלָתַם Gen. 31:32, מְצָאַתַם Ex. 18:8, נְצָלָתַם Ps. 119:129, טְרָפָתַם Isa. 47:14. In the intermediate syllable before ה the vowel is usually short in this person, יְלָדַתְהָ Jer. 22:26, אֲבָלָתְךָ Ezek. 28:18, though it is sometimes long, חִבְּלָתְךָ Cant. 8:5. as it regularly is in pause: יְלָדַתְךָ *ibid.;* so before נִי and נוּ of the first person, אֲבָלַתְנִי Ps. 69:10, מְצָאַתְהוּ Num. 20:14.

j. The second masc. sing. preterite usually takes Pattahh before נִי except in pause, חֲקַרְתַּנִי Ps. 139:1, חִתַּתַּנִי Job 7:14, יֹדַעְתַּנִי Ps. 22:2. It takes the third masc. sing. suffix either in its full form, כְּפַרְתַּהוּ Ezek. 43:20, or contracted, אֲסַפְתּוֹ 2 Kin. 5:6. שַׂמְתּוֹ Hab. 1:12, קַבֹּתוֹ (accent thrown back by § 35. 1) Num. 23:27, הֲקִטַּלְתּוֹ Ps. 89:44.

k. The second fem. sing. preterite assumes (ְ), commonly without Yodh, § 11. 1. *a,* before suffixes, and is accordingly indistinguishable from the first person except by the suffix which it receives, § 102. 1, or by the connection in which it is found, יְלִדְתִּנִי Jer. 15:10, לְבַבְתִּנִי Cant. 4:9, רְמִיתִנִי 1 Sam. 19:17, מְשִׁיתִהוּ Ex. 2:10; once it takes (ִ), הוֹרַדְתֵּנוּ Josh. 2:18, and in a few instances the masculine form is adopted in its stead, הִשְׁבַּעְתָּנוּ Josh. 2:17, 20, Cant. 5:9, יְלִדְתּוֹ Jer. 2:27 K'ri, הֲבֵאתוֹ 2 Sam. 14:10.

l. The plural endings of the verb may be written fully ו or defectively (ֻ), thus. in the third person. סְבָבוּנִי Ps. 18:6, כְּבָבֻנִי Hos. 12:1; the second צְמַתֻּנִי Zech. 7:5, הֱצַלְתִּנוּ Num. 20:5, 21:5; and the first וּדְבַשְׁנֻהוּ 1 Chron. 13:3.

FUTURE.

§ 105. *a.* The union vowel *a* is sometimes attached to the future, thus יִ ָ. תִּרְבְּקַנִי Gen. 19:19, יֶאֱהָבַנִי Gen. 29:32, יִרְאַנִי Ex. 33:20, Num. 22:33, יְדַבְּרַנִי Isa. 56:3, יַשְׂבְּעַנִי Job 9:18; נוּ יַכִּירֶנּוּ Isa. 63:16; ו (for הוּ ָ), יִרְדֵּהוּ Hos. 8:3, יִלְבָּדוּ Ps. 35:8, יִתְקָפוֹ Eccles. 4:12. וַיְשֻׁבוֹ 1 Sam. 21:14, so in the K'thibh, 1 Sam. 18:1 וַיֶּאֱהָבוּ, where the K'ri has וַיֶּאֱהָבֵהוּ; ה, (for הָ). וַיַּבִּיאֶהָ Gen. 37:33, תִּתְּנָה 2 Chron. 20:7, יְשָׁשׂ־לָהּ Isa. 26:5; ם, יִלְבָּשָׁם Ex. 29:30, רְשִׁישָׁם Deut. 7:15, יְרֵם Num. 21:30, יְרִם Ps.

142 ETYMOLOGY. §106

74:8, אֲמִילָם Ps. 118:10; וְ֫, יוֹשְׁבָן Ex. 2:17. In 1 Kin. 2:24 the K'ri has יוֹשִׁיבֵ֫נִי, while the K'thibh has the vowel letter י representing the ordinary e, יוֹשִׁיבֵ֫נִי.

b. The suffixes with Daghesh inserted occur chiefly in pause; thus יְ֫, יוֹדְלֵ֫נִי Jer. 50:44; יְ֫, תְּבָרְכֵ֫נִי Gen. 27:19, תְּבִיאֵ֫נִי Job 7:14, 9:34; ינ, (1st plur.), יְבִיאֵ֫נוּ Job 31:15; ה, אֶקְבָּצֵ֫ה Isa. 43:5, יִזְרֵ֫הָ Isa. 44:2, אֹרֵ֫הָ Ps. 30:13; גוּ (3 masc. sing.), תִּפְקְדֶ֫נּוּ. תִּבְחָגֶ֫נוּ Job 7:18, יְסֻבְּבֶ֫נוּ Job 41:2 K'ri, יִשָּׂאֶ֫נָּה Hos. 12:5; יְהְ, תְּדַשְּׁרֶ֫נָּה Ps. 65:10, or without Daghesh, תְּשַׁלְּחֶ֫נָּה Judg. 5:26, Obad. ver. 13; the unemphatic form of the suffix and that with Daghesh occur in conjunction, יְשָׂמֵ֫ילָה Isa. 26:5. There are a very few examples, found only in poetry, of נ inserted between the verb and the suffix without further change, יְבָרְכֶ֫נּוּ Ps. 50:23, אֶתְקָנֶ֫נּוּ Jer. 22:24, יְשָׁבְרֶ֫נְהוּ Jer. 5:22, יְבָרְכֶ֫נְהוּ Ps. 72:15, יִצְּרֶ֫נְהוּ Deut. 32:10, אֲרוֹמְמֶ֫נְהוּ Ex. 15:2.

c. The plural ending וּן is in a few instances found before suffixes. chiefly in pause, יְשָׁחֲרֻ֫נְנִי, יִקְרָאֻ֫נְנִי, יִמְצָאֻ֫נְנִי Prov. 1:28, יִשָּׂחֻ֫נּוּ Ps. 63:4, יִמְצָאֻ֫נְהוּ Ps. 91:12, יְשָׂרְתֻ֫נְהוּ Isa. 60:7, 10, יְבָרְכֻ֫נְהוּ Jer. 5:22, twice it has the union vowel a, תְּדָבָאֻ֫נְנִי Job 19:2, יְלַפְּדֻ֫נוֹ Jer. 2:24; Prov. 5:22.

d. When the second vowel of the Kal future is o, it is rejected before suffixes requiring a union vowel, compound Sh'va being occasionally substituted for it in the place of simple, אֶסְפֵּ֑ם Hos. 10:10, יְהָרְגֵ֫נוּ Num. 35:20, אֲצָרְךָ Isa. 27:3, יַעַקְבֵ֫נוּ Isa. 62:2, יִרְדְּפָהּ Ezek. 35:6, אֶכְתְּבֶ֫נָּה Jer. 31:33; once the vowel remains, but is changed to Shurek. תִּשְׁבֻ֑ם Prov. 14:3; a, on the other hand, is retained as a pretonic vowel. §64. 2. יִלְבָּשֵׁ֫נִי Job 29:14, יִלְבָּשָׁם Ex. 29:30, אֶלְבָּשָׁה Cant. 5:3, תֻּרְבְּקֵ֫נִי Gen. 19:19. Hholem is shortened before ךָ, כֶם, הֶם, though the vowel letter ו is occasionally written in the K'thibh, אֲעִירָה Jer. 1:5.

e. The following are examples of feminine plurals with suffixes: 2 fem. plur. תֵּרְאֶ֫נָה Cant. 1:6, 3 fem. plur. תְּחַשְּׁבָ֑נִי Job 19:15, אֹיְבֶ֫יהָ Jer. 2:19. The masculine form is sometimes substituted for the feminine, רְאָשׁוּרָ֫יו, יְהַלְלוּהָ Cant. 6:9.

INFINITIVE AND IMPERATIVE.

§106 a. Kal Infinitive. Before ךָ, כֶם, כֶן, Hholem is shortened to Kamets Hhatuph, אָכְלְךָ Gen. 2:17, גָּדְלוֹ (Methegh by §45. 2) Obad. ver. 11, אָכְלְכֶם Gen. 3:5, אָכְרֶכֶם Mal. 1:7. Pattahh remains in the single example, חַנֻּנְכֶם Isa. 30:18; sometimes the vowel of the second radical is rejected before these as it is before the other suffixes, and a short vowel given to the first radical, commonly Kamets Hhatuph, עָבְרְךָ Deut. 29:11, שָׁמְעֲךָ 2 Kin. 22:19, עָבְרְכֶם Deut. 27:4, once Kibbuts, קָצְרְכֶם Lev. 23:22, sometimes Hhirik, שִׁכְבָּה Gen. 19:33, 35 but שִׁבְתּוֹ Ruth 3:4, שִׁבְנוּ Zech. 3:1, גְּעֹלוּ 2 Sam. 1:10, פִּתְחוֹ Neh. 8:5, and occasionally Pattahh. רִתְקָהּ Ezek. 25:6. In the feminine form of the infinitive, as in nouns, the old feminine ending ת is substituted for ה, שִׁכְבָּתָהּ Isa. 30:19, חֻצָּבוֹ Hos. 7:4. The Niphal infinitive retains its pretonic Kamets before suffixes, הִנָּבְרָכֶם Ezek. 21:29.

b. Kal Imperative. The first radical commonly receives Kamets Hhatuph upon the rejection of Hholem, קְבָרֵ֫נִי, קָהֳלִ֫י Jer. 15:15, but occasionally it takes Hhirik, וּצְלָ֫ה (with Daghesh-forte euphonic) Prov. 4:13.

IMPERFECT VERBS.

§ 107. Imperfect verbs depart more or less from the standard already given, as the nature of their radicals may require. They are of three classes, viz.:

I. Guttural verbs, or those which have a guttural letter in the root.

II. Contracted verbs, two of whose radicals are in certain cases contracted into one.

III. Quiescent verbs, or those which have a quiescent or vowel letter in the root.

These classes may again be subdivided according to the particular radical affected. Thus there are three kinds of guttural verbs:

1. Pe guttural verbs, or those whose first radical is a guttural.

2. Ayin guttural verbs, or those whose second radical is a guttural.

3. Lamedh guttural verbs, or those whose third radical is a guttural.

There are two kinds of contracted verbs:

1. Pe Nun verbs, or those whose first radical is Nun, and is liable to be contracted by assimilation with the second.

2. Ayin doubled verbs, or those whose second and third radicals are alike, and are liable to be contracted into one.

There are four kinds of quiescent verbs:

1. Pe Yodh verbs, or those whose first radical is Yodh.

2. Ayin Vav and Ayin Yodh verbs, or those whose second radical is Vav or Yodh.

3. Lamedh Aleph verbs, or those whose third radical is Aleph.

4. Lamedh He verbs, or those in which He takes the place of the third radical.

The guttural differ from the perfect verbs in the vowels only; the first division of the contracted verbs differ only in the consonants; the quiescent and the second division of the contracted verbs differ from the perfect verbs in both vowels and consonants.

a. The third class of imperfect verbs may either be regarded as having a quiescent letter in the root, which in certain forms is changed into a vowel, or as having a vowel in the root, which in certain forms is changed into a quiescent letter. As the settlement of this question is purely a matter of theory, the usual name of quiescent verbs has been retained as sufficiently descriptive.

b. The origin of these various technical names for the different kinds of imperfect verbs is explained § 76. 3.

Pe Guttural Verbs.

§ 108. Gutturals have the four following peculiarities, § 60, viz.:

1. They often cause a preceding or accompanying vowel to be converted into Pattahh.

2. They receive Pattahh furtive at the end of a word after a long heterogeneous vowel or before a vowelless final consonant.

3. They take compound in preference to simple Sh'va.

4. They are incapable of being doubled, and consequently do not receive Daghesh-forte.

§ 109. Pe guttural verbs are affected by these peculiarities as follows, viz.:

1. The Hhirik of the preformatives is changed to Pattahh before the guttural in the Kal future, if the second vowel be Hholem, יַעֲמֹד for יִעֲמֹד; but if the second radical has Pattahh this change does not occur, because it would occasion a repetition of the same vowel in successive syllables, § 63. 1. b. In the Kal future a, therefore, in the Niphal preterite and participle, where the vowel of the second syllable is likewise a, and in the Hiphil preterite, where ĭ is characteristic and therefore less subject to change, Hhirik is compounded with Pattahh, or, in other words, is changed to the diphthongal Seghol, הֶחֱזַק, נֶעֱמַד, הֶעֱמִיד. Seghol accompanying א of the first person singular of the Kal future, § 60. 1. a (5), and Kamets Hhatuph, characteristic of the Hophal species, suffer no change. The same is true of Hholem in the first syllable of the Kal participle, Hhirik of the Piel preterite, and Kibbuts of the Pual species, for the double reason that these vowels are characteristic of those forms, and that their position after the guttural renders them less liable to mutation, § 60. 1. a (2); the second reason applies likewise to the Hhirik of the feminine singular and masculine plural of the Kal imperative, which, as the briefest of the short vowels, is besides best adapted to the quick utterance of a command, עִמְדִי, עִמְדוּ.

2. As the guttural does not stand at the end of the word, there is no occasion for applying the rule respecting Pattahh furtive; this consequently does not appear except in יַחַךְ, apocopated future of חָזָה, and in one other doubtful example, § 114.

3. Wherever the first radical should receive simple Sh'va the guttural takes compound Sh'va instead; this, if there be no reason for preferring another, and especially if it be preceded by the vowel Pattahh, will be Hhateph Pattahh, whose sound is most consonant with that of the gutturals; this is the case in the Kal second plural preterite, construct infinitive, future and imperative with Hholem, and in the Hiphil,

infinitives, future, imperative, and participle, יַעֲמֹד, עֲמָדְתֶּם.
If, however, the guttural be preceded by another vowel than
Pattahh the compound Sh'va will generally be conformed to
it; thus, after Seghol it becomes Hhateph Seghol as in the
Kal future and imperative ā, the Niphal preterite and participle, and the Hiphil preterite, הֶעֱמִיד, יֶחֱזַק, and after
Kamets Hhatuph it becomes Hhateph Kamets as in the
Hophal species, הָעֳמַד. If this compound Sh'va in the
course of inflection comes to be followed by a vowelless
letter, it is changed to the corresponding short vowel, § 61. 1,
thus, (ֱ) becomes (ֶ) in the second feminine singular and the
second and third masculine plural of the Kal future; (ֲ) becomes (ַ) in the third feminine singular and the third plural
of the Niphal preterite; and (ֳ) becomes (ָ) in the corresponding persons of the preterite and future Hophal, תָּעֳמְרִי,
הָעָמְדָה, נֶעֶמְדָה.

a. The simple Sh'va following a short vowel thus formed, remains
vocal as in the corresponding forms of the perfect verb, the new syllable
being not mixed but intermediate, and hence a succeeding aspirate will
retain its aspiration, thus יַעַמְדוּ *yaam'dhū*, not יַעַמְדוּ *yaamdū*, § 22. *a*.
In like manner the Kal imperative has עִמְדִי, עִמְדוּ, not עִמְדִי, עִמְדוּ, showing that even in the perfect verb קָטְלִי, קָטְלוּ were pronounced *kit'lī*,
kit'lā, not *kitlī*, *kitlā*.

4. The reduplication of the first radical being impossible
in the infinitive, future and imperative Niphal, the preceding
vowel, which now stands in a simple syllable, is lengthened
in consequence from Hhirik to Tsere, § 60. 4, הֵעָמֹד for הִעָמֹד.

§ 110. 1. The verb עָמַד *to stand*, whose inflections are shown
in the following paradigm, may serve as a representative of
Pe guttural verbs. The Piel, Pual, and Hithpael are omitted, as they present no deviation from the regular verbs.
The Niphal of עָמַד is not in use, but is here formed from
analogy for the sake of giving completeness to the paradigm.

Paradigm of Pe Guttural Verbs.

		KAL.	NIPHAL.	HIPHIL.	HOPHAL.
Pret.	3 m.	עָבַד	נֶעֱבַד	הֶעֱבִיד	הָעֳבַד
	3 f.	עָבְדָה	נֶעֶבְדָה	הֶעֱבִידָה	הָעָבְדָה
	2 m.	עָבַדְתָּ	נֶעֱבַדְתָּ	הֶעֱבַדְתָּ	הָעֳבַדְתָּ
	2 f.	עָבַדְתְּ	נֶעֱבַדְתְּ	הֶעֱבַדְתְּ	הָעֳבַדְתְּ
	1 c.	עָבַדְתִּי	נֶעֱבַדְתִּי	הֶעֱבַדְתִּי	הָעֳבַדְתִּי
Plur.	3 c.	עָמְדוּ	נֶעֶבְדוּ	הֶעֱבִידוּ	הָעָבְדוּ
	2 m.	עֲבַדְתֶּם	נֶעֱבַדְתֶּם	הֶעֱמַדְתֶּם	הָעֳבַדְתֶּם
	2 f.	עֲבַדְתֶּן	נֶעֱבַדְתֶּן	הֶעֱבַדְתֶּן	הָעֳבַדְתֶּן
	1 c.	עָבַדְנוּ	נֶעֱבַדְנוּ	הֶעֱבַדְנוּ	הָעֳבַדְנוּ
Infin.	Absol.	עָבוֹד	הֵעָמֹד	הַעֲבֵד	הָעֳבֵד
	Constr.	עֲבֹד	הֵעָבֵד	הַעֲבִיד	הָעֳבַד
Fut.	3 m.	יַעֲמֹד	יֵעָבֵד	יַעֲבִיד	יָעֳבַד
	3 f.	תַּעֲמֹד	תֵּעָבֵד	תַּעֲבִיד	תָּעֳבַד
	2 m.	תַּעֲמֹד	תֵּעָבֵד	תַּעֲבִיד	תָּעֳבַד
	2 f.	תַּעַבְדִי	תֵּעָבְדִי	תַּעֲבִידִי	תָּעָבְדִי
	1 c.	אֶעֱמֹד	אֵעָבֵד	אַעֲבִיד	אָעֳבַד
Plur.	3 m.	יַעֲמְדוּ	יֵעָבְדוּ	יַעֲבִידוּ	יָעָבְדוּ
	3 f.	תַּעֲמֹדְנָה	תֵּעָבַדְנָה	תַּעֲמֵדְנָה	תָּעֳמַדְנָה
	2 m.	תַּעַבְדוּ	תֵּעָבְדוּ	תַּעֲבִידוּ	תָּעָבְדוּ
	2 f.	תַּעֲמֹדְנָה	תֵּעָבַדְנָה	תַּעֲמֵדְנָה	תָּעֳמַדְנָה
	1 c.	נַעֲמֹד	נֵעָבֵד	נַעֲבִיד	נָעֳבַד
Imper.	2 m.	עֲמֹד	הֵעָבֵד	הַעֲבֵד	wanting
	2 f.	עִבְדִי	הֵעָבְדִי	הַעֲבִידִי	
Plur.	2 m.	עִמְדוּ	הֵעָבְדוּ	הַעֲבִידוּ	
	2 f.	עֲמֹדְנָה	הֵעָבַדְנָה	הַעֲמֵדְנָה	
Part.	Act.	עֹבֵד		מַעֲבִיד	
	Pass.	עָבוּד	נֶעֱבָד		מָעֳמָד

2. The Kal imperative and future of those verbs which have Pattahh in the second syllable may be represented by חֲזַק *to be strong.*

IMPERATIVE.

SINGULAR.		PLURAL.	
masc.	*fem.*	*masc.*	*fem.*
חֲזַק	חִזְקִי	חִזְקוּ	חֲזַקְנָה

FUTURE.

	3 *masc.*	3 *fem.*	2 *masc.*	2 *fem.*	1 *com.*
SING.	יֶחֱזַק	תֶּחֱזַק	תֶּחֱזַק	תֶּחֶזְקִי	אֶחֱזַק
PLUR.	יֶחֶזְקוּ	תֶּחֱזַקְנָה	תֶּחֶזְקוּ	תֶּחֱזַקְנָה	נֶחֱזַק

3. Certain verbs, whose first radical is א, receive Hholem in the first syllable of the Kal future after the following, which is distinctively called the Pe Aleph (פֵּ״א) mode.

FUTURE OF PE ALEPH VERBS.

	3 *masc.*	3 *fem.*	2 *masc.*	2 *fem.*	1 *com.*
SING.	יֹאכַל	תֹּאכַל	תֹּאכַל	תֹּאכְלִי	אֹכַל
PLUR.	יֹאכְלוּ	תֹּאכַלְנָה	תֹּאכְלוּ	תֹּאכַלְנָה	נֹאכַל

Five verbs uniformly adopt this mode of inflection, viz.: אָבַד *to perish,* אָבָה *to be willing,* אָכַל *to eat,* אָמַר *to say,* אָפָה *to bake;* a few others indifferently follow this or the ordinary Pe guttural mode, אָהֵב *to love,* אָחַז *to take hold,* אָסַף *to gather.*

REMARKS ON PE GUTTURAL VERBS.

§ 111. 1. The preformative of the Kal future *a* has (ִ) in one instance, וַתִּצְבַּם Ezek. 23:5. That of the Kal future *o* has (ֲ) in רֲחֵלָה Prov. 10:3, רֲחֵשָׁה Ps. 29:9. Three verbs with future *o,* חָלַם, חָרַם, חָשַׁד have Pat-

§ 111. REMARKS ON PE GUTTURAL VERBS.

tahh in the first syllable when the Hholem appears, but Seghol in those forms in which the Hholem is dropped, יַהֲרֹס Job 12:14, יַחֲלֹס 2 Kin. 3:25 but יַחְרְסוּ Ex. 19:21, 24; so with suffixes, יַחְלְצֵנִי Ps. 141:5, יֶחֶרְסָךְ Isa. 22:19, נֶחֱמָדָהוּ Isa. 53:2. חָפֵר has יַחְסְדוּ but יֶחְפָּרוּ.

2. *a.* If the first radical be א, which has a strong preference for the diphthongal vowels, § 60. 1. *a* (5), the preformative takes Seghol in most verbs in the Kal future, whether *a* or *o*, יֶאֱסֹף, יֶאֱסֹר, תֶּאֱזֹר, תֶּאֱחֹז as well as יֶאֱסֹף, יֶאֱבַל, תֶּאֱלֶה; in a few with future *a*, § 110. 3, it takes the other compound vowel Hholem when to complete the diphthongal character of the word the (ֱ) of the second syllable usually becomes (ֳ) in pause, and in a few instances without a pause accent, יֹאחֲזוּ, יֹאבֵד, יֹאבַר, and in two verbs it becomes (ֳ) after Vav conversive, וַיֹּאחֶז; וַיֹּאמֶר.

b. As א is always quiescent after Hholem in this latter form of the future, § 57. 2. (2) *a*, Pe Aleph verbs might be classed among quiescent verbs, and this is in fact done by some grammarians. But as א has the double character of a guttural and a quiescent in different forms sprung from the same root, and as its quiescence is confined almost entirely to a single tense of a single species, it seems better to avoid sundering what really belongs together, by considering the Pe Aleph as a variety of the Pe guttural verbs. In a few instances א gives up its consonantal character after (ֶ) which is then lengthened to (ֵ), תֵּאָחֵז Mic. 4:8. When thus quiescent after either Tsere or Hholem, א is always omitted in the first person singular after the preformative א, אֹחַר Gen. 32:5 for אֶאֱחַר, אֹהַב Prov. 8:17 for אֶאֱהַב, אֹכַל Gen. 24:33 for אֹאכַל, and occasionally in other persons, חֹלִי Jer. 2:36 for תֵּאֱזֹלִי; so יֵרֵא Deut. 33:21, תֹּבַא Prov. 1:10, תֹּסֶף Ps. 104:29, תֹּסְדוּ 2 Sam. 19:14, וַתֹּחֶז 2 Sam. 20:9, וַתֹּבֶהוּ 1 Sam. 28:24; in a few instances the vowel letter ו is substituted for it, יוֹבְלוּ Ezek. 42:5 for יֹאבְלוּ, אוֹמַר Neh. 2:7, Ps. 42:10.

c. A like quiescence or omission of א occurs in וַיֵּצֶל Num. 11:25 Hi. fut. for וַיֶּאֱצֶל, חָצִיל Ezek. 21:33 Hi. inf. for הַאֲצִיל, אָדוֹן Job 32:11 Hi. fut. for אַאֲזִין, בְּזוֹן Prov. 17:4 Hi. part. for מַאֲזִין, § 53. 2. *a*, בִּלְעִי Job 35:11 Pi. part. for מְאַלְּפֵנוּ, § 53. 3, חַזְתַּנִי 2 Sam. 22:40 Pi. fut. for תְּאַזְּרֵנִי, וָרֶב 1 Sam. 15:5 Hi. fut. for וַיָּאֶרֶב, הָתִיוּ Isa. 21:14 Hi. pret. for הֵאֱתָיוּ, תַּל Isa. 13:20 Pi. fut. for יְאַהֵל, and after prefixes לֵאמֹר for לֶאֱמֹר, the Kal infinitive of אָמַר with the preposition ל, וְאֶעֶבְדָּךְ Ezek. 28:16 Pi. fut. with Vav conversive for וָאֲאַבֶּדְךָ, וָאַכְשֵׁר Zech. 11:5 Hi. fut. with Vav conjunctive for וָאַאֲשִׁיר, הַסוּרִים Eccles. 4:14 Kal pass. part. with the article for הָאֲסוּרִים.

d. The diphthongal Hholem is further assumed by Pe Aleph roots once in the Niphal preterite, נֹאחֲזוּ Num. 32:30 for נֶאֶחֲזוּ, and five times in the Hiphil future, אֹבִידָה Jer. 46:8 for אַאֲבִידָה, אוֹכִיל Hos. 11:4 for אַאֲכִיל, אוֹצְרָה Neh. 13:13 for אַאֲצִירָה, וַיֹּאֶל 1 Sam. 14:24 abbreviated from וַיֹּאֲלֶה for וַיֹּאֲלֶה, וַיּוֹחַר, וַיֹּאחַר 2 Sam. 20:5 K'ri for וַיֹּאֱחַר.

e. א draws the vowel to itself from the preformative in תֶּאֱהָבוּ Prov. 1:22 Kal fut. for תֶּאֱהֲבוּ in pause תֶּאֱהָבוּ Zech. 8:17, Ps. 4:3, § 60. 3. *c.* Some so explain תְּאַכְּלֵהוּ Job 20:26, regarding it as a Kal future for

תֹּאבְלֵ֫הוּ with the vowel attracted to the א from the preformative; it is simpler, however, to regard it as a Pual future with Kamets Hhatuph instead of Kibbuts, as מְאֻדָּם Nah. 2:4, יְבֹרַךְ Ps. 94:20.

3. *a.* Kamets Hhatuph for the most part remains in the Kal infinitive and imperative with suffixes, as זָכְרִי, זָכְרֵךְ, עָבְדֵךְ, being rarely changed to Pattahh, as in חַבְלֵ֫הוּ Prov. 20:16, or Seghol, as אֶסְפֶה־ Num. 11:16, בְּרַךְ Job 33:5. In the inflected imperative Seghol occurs once instead of Hhirik, חֶשְׂפִּי־ Isa. 47:2, and Kamets Hhatuph twice in compensation for the omitted Hholem, עֲלִי Zeph. 3:14 but עֲלוּ Ps. 68:5, חָרְבוּ Jer. 2:12 but חִרְבוּ Jer. 50:27, though the *o* sound is once retained in the compound Sh'va of a pausal form, חֳרָבִי Isa. 44:27. Ewald explains תֶּעֶבָּרֵם Ex. 20:5, 23:24, Deut. 5:9, and נַעֲבָדֵם Deut. 13:3 as Kal futures, the excluded Hholem giving character to the preceding vowels; the forms, however, are properly Hophal futures, and there is no reason why the words may not be translated accordingly *be induced to serve.* In a few Kal infinitives with a feminine termination ה has (ָ), חָמְלָה Ezek. 16:5, חָמְצָהוֹ Hos. 7:4.

b. In a very few instances Pattahh is found in the first syllable of the Niphal and of the Hiphil preterite, נַעֲבָר Ps. 89:8, הַחֲיִתֶם Judg. 8:19.

§112. 1. The guttural invariably receives compound Sh'va in place of simple, where this is vocal in the perfect verb; and as in these cases it stands at the beginning of the word, it is more at liberty to follow its native preferences, and therefore usually takes (ֲ). In חֱיִיתֶם 2 plur. pret., חֲיוֹת inf., הֱיֵה imper. of הָיָה, the initial ה has (ֱ) under the influence of the following י; א receives (ֲ) in the second plural of the Kal preterite, and in the feminine and plural of the passive participle, אֲבַדְתֶּם, אֲבוּסִים, but commonly (ֲ) in the imperative and infinitive, §60. 3. *b,* אֱכֹל imper. and אֱכֹל inf., אֱחֹז and אֱחֹז inf., אֱמֹר imper., אֱמֹר inf. and imper. (but הַאֲזֵל Job 34:18 with ה interrogative), אֱכֹל, אֱכָה (with ה, paragogic אֱסְפָה), and in a very few instances the long vowel (ָ). §60. 3. *c,* אֵפוֹ Ex. 16:23 for אֵפוֹ, אֲרִיֵה Isa. 21:12.

2. Where the first radical in perfect verbs stands after a short vowel and completes its syllable, the guttural does the same, but mostly admits an echo of the preceding vowel after it, inclining it likewise to begin the syllable which follows. In the intermediate syllable thus formed, §20. 2, the vowel remains short, only being modified agreeably to the rules already given by the proximity of the guttural, which itself receives the corresponding Hhateph. The succession is, therefore, usually (ַ ֲ), (ֶ ֱ) or (ָ ֳ). In a very few instances this correspondence is neglected; thus, in תַּהֲלֹךְ 3 fem. fut. of הָלַךְ *to go* (comp. יִצְחַק from צָחַק *to laugh*) the Hhirik of the preformative remains and the guttural takes Hhateph Pattahh; in הַעֲלָה (once, viz., Hab. 1:15 for הֶעֱלָה) and הָעֳלָה Hiphil and Hophal preterites of עָלָה *to go up,* and הַעֲבַרְתָּ (once, viz., Josh. 7:7 for הֶעֱבַרְתָּ) Hi. pret. of עָבַר *to pass over,* the guttural is entirely transferred to the second syllable, and the preceding vowel is lengthened. The forms לִהְיוֹת, נִהְיָה, יִהְיֶה from הָיָה *to be,* and יִחְיֶה from חָיָה *to live,* are peculiar in having simple vocal Sh'va.

§ 112   REMARKS ON PE GUTTURAL VERBS.   151

3. Where (ֶ) or (ָ) are proper to the form these are frequently changed to (ֱ) or (ֲ) upon the prolongation of the word or the removal of its accent forward. Thus, in the Kal future, יֶאֱסֹף 2 Kin. 5:3, יַאַסְפוּ Ex. 4:29, יַאַסְפֵנִי Ps. 27:10, תַּאַסְפוּ Josh. 2:18; יַאַרְגוּ Isa. 59:5, תֶּאֱרְגִי Judg. 16:13; the Niphal, נֶאֱלַם 1 Kin. 10:3, נֶעֶלְמָה Nah. 3:11, נַעֲלָמִים Ps. 26:4; and especially in the Hiphil preterite with Vav conversive, הַאֲבַדְתָּ Job 14:19, וְהַאֲבַדְתֶּם Deut. 7:24, יַהֲבַדְתֶּם Deut. 9:3 (comp. הַאֲבַלְתֶּם Ps. 80:6), וְהַאֲבַדְתִּי Lev. 23:30; וְהַאֲבִלּוֹתִי Isa. 49:26; הֶחֱוִיתִי Neh. 5:16, וְהֶחֱוֵיתִי Ezek. 30:25; הֶעֱבַדְתִּיךָ Isa. 43:23, וְהֶעֱבַדְתִּיךָ Jer. 17:4; הֶאָזִין Deut. 1:45, וְהַאֲזַנְתָּ Ex. 15:26, וְהֶחְתַּתִּי Jer. 49:37; after Vav conjunctive, however, the vowels remain unchanged, וְהַחֲזוֹתִי 1 Sam. 17:35, וְהַחֲרַלְתִּי Ps. 50:21. The change from (ֶ) to (ֱ) after Vav conversive occurs once in the third person of the Hiphil preterite, וְהֶאֱזִין Ps. 77:2, but is not usual, e. g. וְהֶחֱרִיךָ . . . וְהִצְמִידוֹ Lev. 27:8. There is one instance of (ֱ) instead of (ֲ) in the Hiphil infinitive, הַחֲוִיקִי Jer. 31:32.

4. A vowel which has arisen from Sh'va in consequence of the rejection of the vowel of a following consonant, will be dropped in guttural as in perfect verbs upon the latter vowel being restored by a pause accent, עָבָדוּ, עָמְדוּ; רְעֵדוּ, יַעֲמֹדוּ.

5. Sometimes the silent Sh'va of the perfect verb is retained by the guttural instead of being replaced by a compound Sh'va or a subsidiary vowel which has arisen from it. This is most frequent in the Kal future, though it occurs likewise in the Kal infinitive after inseparable prepositions, in the Niphal preterite and participle, in the Hiphil species, and also though rarely in the Hophal. There are examples of it with all the gutturals, though these are most numerous in the case of ה, which is the strongest of that class of letters. In the majority of roots and forms there is a fixed or at least a prevailing usage in favour either of the simple or of the compound Sh'va; in some, however, the use of one or the other appears to be discretionary.

a. The following verbs always take simple Sh'va under the first radical in the species, whose initial letters are annexed to the root, viz.:

אָדַם Hi. *to be red.*	חָבַל K. Hi. *to be vain.*	חָגַר K. *to gird.*
אָדַר Ni. Hi. *to be illustrious.*	הָגָה K. Hi. *to meditate.*	חָדַל K. (not Ho.) *to cease.*
אָטַם Hi. *to close.*	חָדַשׁ K. *to thrust.*	חָצַב K. *to cut.*
*אָשַׁר K. *to shut.*	חָדַר K. Ni. *to honour.*	חָיָה K. (not Hi.) *to live.*
אָלַם K. *to learn.*	חָיָה K. Ni. *to be.*	
אָזַר K. *to gird on.*	*חָבַל K. *to injure, wound.*	חָכַם K. Hi. *to be wise.*
אָשַׁם K. Ni. (not Hi.) *to be guilty.*	חָבָא Ni. Hi. Ho. *to hide.*	*חָלַשׁ K. meaning doubtful.
	חָבַט K. *to beat off.*	
	חָבַר Hi. *to join together.*	

* ἅπαξ λεγόμενον.

152 ETYMOLOGY. § 112

חָמַד K. Ni. *to desire.*
חָמַל K. *to spare.*
חָמַס K. Ni. *to do violence to.*
חָמֵץ K. *to be leavened.*
חָמַר K. *to ferment.*
חָנַךְ K. *to dedicate.*
חָסַל K. *to devour.*
חָסַם K. *to muzzle.*
חָסֵר K. Hi. *to lack.*
חָפָה Ni. *to cover.*
חָפַז K. Ni. *to be panic-struck.*
חָפֵץ K. *to delight.*

חָפַר K. *to dig.*
חָפַר K. Hi. *to blush.*
חָפַשׂ K. Ni. *to search.*
חָצַב K. (not Hi.) *to hew.*
†חָקַר K. Ni. *to investigate.*
*חָרַג K. *to tremble.*
חָתָה K. *to take up.*
חָרָה Ni. *to be destined.*
חֻתַּל Ho. *to be swaddled.*
חָתַם K. Ni. Hi. *to seal.*
חָתַף K. *to seize.*
חָתַר K. *to break through.*
חָבַב K. *to love, dote.*

עָדָה K. *to put on as an ornament.*
עָדָה Hi. *to gather much.*
עָדַר Ni. *to be wanting.*
עָכַר K. Ni. *to trouble.*
עָפַל Hi. *to be presumptuous.*
עָשַׁשׁ K. Ni. *to pervert.*
עָשַׂר K. Hi. *to tithe.*
*עָתָה Ni. *to be burnt up.*
עָתַק K. Hi. *to be removed.*
עָתַר K. Ni. Hi. *to entreat.*

b. The following are used with both simple and compound Sh'va, either in the same form or in different forms, viz.:

אָסַר *to bind.*
הָפַךְ *to turn.*
חָבַל *to take in pledge.*
חָבַשׁ *to bind.*
חָזַק *to be strong.*
חָלָה *to be sick.*
חָלַק *to divide.*

חָסָה *to trust.*
חָשַׂךְ *to withhold.*
חָשַׂף *to uncover.*
חָשַׁב *to think.*
חָשַׁךְ *to be dark.*
עָבַר *to pass over.*
עָזַר *to help.*

עָטָה *to wear.*
עָטַר *to encircle.*
עָלַם *to conceal.*
עָצַר *to shut up, restrain.*
עָקַב *to supplant.*
עָשַׁן *to smoke.*
עָשַׁר *to be rich.*

c. The following have simple Sh'va only in the passages or parts alleged, but elsewhere always compound Sh'va, viz.:

אָהַב 2 Chr. 19:2, Pr. 15:9, *to love.*
אָזַר Ps. 65:7, *to gird.*
אָסַף Ps. 47:10, *to gather.*
הָלַךְ Ps. 109:23, *to go.*
חָלַם Job 39:4, Jer. 29:8, *to dream.*
חָלַף Job 20:24, *to change, pierce.*

חָרֵד Ezek. 26:18, *to tremble.*
חָשָׁה Hi. part. *to be silent.*
חָתַת Jer. 49:37, *to be dismayed.*
עָבַד Eccl. 5:8, *to serve.*
עָלִי Jer. 15:17, Ps. 149:5, and
עָלַץ Ps. 5:12, *to exult.*

All other Pe guttural verbs, if they occur in forms requiring a Sh'va under the first radical, have invariably compound Sh'va.

The use or disuse of simple Sh'va is so uniform and pervading in certain verbs, that it must in all probability be traced to the fixed usage of actual speech. This need not be so in all cases, however, as in other and less common words its occurrence or non-occurrence may be fortuitous; additional examples might have been pointed differently.

* ἅπαξ λεγόμενον.   † Except Ps. 44:22.

§ 113. 1. The Hhirik of the prefix is in the Niphal future, imperative and participle, almost invariably lengthened to Tsere upon the omission of Daghesh-forte in the first radical, נֵחָסַן, יֵאָצֵר Isa. 23: 18, יֵחָבֵט (the retrocession of the accent by § 35. 1) Isa. 28: 27, יֵחָלֵק Job 38: 24, נֵחָלֵץ Num. 32: 17, וַיֵּחָנֵק 2 Sam. 17: 23, which is in one instance expressed by the vowel letter י, תֵּיעָשֶׂה Ex. 25: 31. The only exception is בֶּהָרֵג (two accents explained by § 42. a) Ezek. 26: 15 for בְּהִהָרֵג, where the vowel remains short as in an intermediate syllable, only being changed to Seghol before the guttural as in the Niphal and Hiphil preterites. According to some copies, which differ in this from the received text, the vowel likewise remains short in אֶעֱנֶה Job 19: 7, חֶזְיֹנֹתִי Ezek. 43: 18, וַיַּחְלְקֵם 1 Chron. 24: 3, בְּעֶזְרָה Lam. 2: 11.

2. The initial ה of the Hiphil infinitive is, as in perfect verbs, rarely rejected after prefixed prepositions, as לַחֲלֹק Jer. 37: 12 for לְהַחֲלֹק, לְהַחֲרִיא Eccles. 5: 5, לְהַעֲבִיר 2 Sam. 19: 19, לְעָשׂ Deut. 26: 12, בַּעֲשׂ Neh. 10: 39, לבזוּי 2 Sam. 18: 3 K'thibh; and still more rarely that of the Niphal infinitive, בְּעֶזְרָה Lam. 2: 11 for בְּהֵעָזְרָה, בְּהֵהָרֵג Ezek. 26: 15.

§ 114. The letter ר resembles the other gutturals in not admitting Daghesh-forte, and in requiring the previous vowel to be lengthened instead, וַיֵּרְדֵם Jon. 1: 5, וַיַּרְגִּנוּ Ps. 106: 25. In other cases, however, it causes no change in an antecedent Hhirik, יִרְדֹּף Deut. 19: 6, יִרְאֶה 2 Sam. 7: 10, הִרְבַּבְתָּ Ps. 66: 12, except in certain forms of the verb רָאָה *to see*, viz., וַיֵּרֶא Kal future with Vav conversive, shortened from יִרְאֶה, הִרְאָה which alternates with הֶרְאָה as Hiphil preterite, and once with Vav conversive preterite, יַהְרְאִיתִי Nah. 3: 5. It is in two instances preceded by Hhirik in the Hiphil infinitive, הִרְאִיתִי, הִרְאִי Jer. 50: 34. In the Hophal species the participles מָרְדָּה Isa. 14: 6, מָרְבָּה Lev. 6: 14 take Kibbuts in the first syllable, but רָאָה, רָעַל have the ordinary Kamets Hhatuph. Resh always retains the simple Sh'va of perfect verbs whether silent or vocal, רְדָה Gen. 44: 4, רְדֹפוּנִי Ps. 129: 86, except in one instance, יֶרְדֹּף Ps. 7: 6, where it appears to receive Pattahh furtive contrary to the ordinary rule which restricts it to the end of the word, § 60. 2. a.

§ 115. The verb אָצַל reduplicates its last instead of its second radical in the Pual, אֲצָלֵל; חָלַל reduplicates its last syllable, חֲרַרְמְרוּ Lam. 2: 11, § 92. a. תִּרְגַּלְתִּי Hos. 11: 3 has the appearance of a Hiphil preterite with ת prefixed instead of ה.

חָלָל is a secondary root, based upon the Hiphil of הֵלֵל. See ע״ֹ verbs. For the peculiar forms of אָסַף and הָלַךְ see the פּ״י verbs, יָסַף and יָלַךְ.

Ayin Guttural Verbs.

§ 116. Ayin guttural verbs, or those which have a guttural for their second radical, are affected by the peculiarities of these letters, § 108, in the following manner, viz.:

1. The influence of the guttural upon a following vowel being comparatively slight, this latter is only converted into Pattahh in the future and imperative Kal, and the feminine plural of the future and imperative Niphal, Piel, and Hithpael, where the like change sometimes occurs even without the presence of a guttural, יִגְאַל for יִגְאֹל ; תִּגְאַלְנָה for תִּגְאֹלְנָה.

2. No forms occur which could give rise to Pattahh furtive.

3. When the second radical should receive simple Sh'va, it takes Hhateph Pattahh instead as the compound Sh'va best suited to its nature; and to this the new vowel, formed from Sh'va in the feminine singular and masculine plural of the Kal imperative, is assimilated, גַּאֲלִי for גְּאֲלִי.

4. Daghesh-forte is always omitted from the second radical in Piel, Pual, and Hithpael, in which case the preceding vowel may either remain short as in an intermediate syllable, or Hhirik may be lengthened to Tsere, Pattahh to Kamets, and Kibbuts to Hholem, § 60. 4, בֵּרַךְ, גֵּאֵל.

§ 117. The inflections of Ayin guttural verbs may be shown by the example of גָּאַל, which in some species means *to redeem*, and in others *to pollute*. The Hiphil and Hophal are omitted, as the former agrees precisely with that of perfect verbs, and the latter differs only in the substitution of compound for simple Sh'va in a manner sufficiently illustrated by the foregoing species.

a. The Pual infinitive is omitted from the paradigm as it is of rare occurrence, and there is no example of it in this class of verbs. As the absolute infinitive Piel mostly gives up its distinctive form and adopts that of the construct, §92. *d*, it is printed with Tsere in this and the following paradigms.

Paradigm of Ayin Guttural Verbs.

	KAL.	NIPHAL.	PIEL.	PUAL.	HITHPAEL.
Pret. 3 m.	גָּאַל	נִגְאַל	גֵּאַל	גֹּאַל	הִתְגָּאֵל
3 f.	גָּאֲלָה	נִגְאֲלָה	גֵּאֲלָה	גֹּאֲלָה	הִתְגָּאֲלָה
2 m.	גָּאַלְתָּ	נִגְאַלְתָּ	גֵּאַלְתָּ	גֹּאַלְתָּ	הִתְגָּאַלְתָּ
2 f.	גָּאַלְתְּ	נִגְאַלְתְּ	גֵּאַלְתְּ	גֹּאַלְתְּ	הִתְגָּאַלְתְּ
1 c.	גָּאַלְתִּי	נִגְאַלְתִּי	גֵּאַלְתִּי	גֹּאַלְתִּי	הִתְגָּאַלְתִּי
Plur. 3 c.	גָּאֲלוּ	נִגְאֲלוּ	גֵּאֲלוּ	גֹּאֲלוּ	הִתְגָּאֲלוּ
2 m.	גְּאַלְתֶּם	נִגְאַלְתֶּם	גֵּאַלְתֶּם	גֹּאַלְתֶּם	הִתְגָּאַלְתֶּם
2 f.	גְּאַלְתֶּן	נִגְאַלְתֶּן	גֵּאַלְתֶּן	גֹּאַלְתֶּן	הִתְגָּאַלְתֶּן
1 c.	גָּאַלְנוּ	נִגְאַלְנוּ	גֵּאַלְנוּ	גֹּאַלְנוּ	הִתְגָּאַלְנוּ
Infin. Absol.	גָּאוֹל	הִגָּאֵל	גֵּאֵל		
Constr.	גְּאֹל	הִגָּאֵל	גֵּאֵל		הִתְגָּאֵל
Fut. 3 m.	יִגְאַל	יִגָּאֵל	יְגֵאֵל	יְגֹאַל	יִתְגָּאֵל
3 f.	תִּגְאַל	תִּגָּאֵל	תְּגֵאֵל	תְּגֹאַל	תִּתְגָּאֵל
2 m.	תִּגְאַל	תִּגָּאֵל	תְּגֵאֵל	תְּגֹאַל	תִּתְגָּאֵל
2 f.	תִּגְאֲלִי	תִּגָּאֲלִי	תְּגֵאֲלִי	תְּגֹאֲלִי	תִּתְגָּאֲלִי
1 c.	אֶגְאַל	אֶגָּאֵל	אֲגֵאֵל	אֲגֹאַל	אֶתְגָּאֵל
Plur. 3 m.	יִגְאֲלוּ	יִגָּאֲלוּ	יְגֵאֲלוּ	יְגֹאֲלוּ	יִתְגָּאֲלוּ
3 f.	תִּגְאַלְנָה	תִּגָּאַלְנָה	תְּגֵאַלְנָה	תְּגֹאַלְנָה	תִּתְגָּאַלְנָה
2 m.	תִּגְאֲלוּ	תִּגָּאֲלוּ	תְּגֵאֲלוּ	תְּגֹאֲלוּ	תִּתְגָּאֲלוּ
2 f.	תִּגְאַלְנָה	תִּגָּאַלְנָה	תְּגֵאַלְנָה	תְּגֹאַלְנָה	תִּתְגָּאַלְנָה
1 c.	נִגְאַל	נִגָּאֵל	נְגֵאֵל	נְגֹאַל	נִתְגָּאֵל
Imper. 2 m.	גְּאַל	הִגָּאֵל	גֵּאֵל		הִתְגָּאֵל
2 f.	גַּאֲלִי	הִגָּאֲלִי	גַּאֲלִי	wanting	הִתְגָּאֲלִי
Plur. 2 m.	גַּאֲלוּ	הִגָּאֲלוּ	גַּאֲלוּ		הִתְגָּאֲלוּ
2 f.	גְּאַלְנָה	הִגָּאַלְנָה	גֵּאַלְנָה		הִתְגָּאַלְנָה
Part. Act.	גֹּאֵל		מְגֵאֵל		מִתְגָּאֵל
Pass.	גָּאוּל	נִגְאָל		מְגֹאָל	

Remarks on Ayin Guttural Verbs.

§ 118. 1. If the second radical is ר, the Kal future and imperative commonly have Hholem; but the following take Pattahh, אָרַךְ *to be long*, חָרֵב *to be dried* or *desolate*, חָרַד *to tremble*, חָרַף *to reproach, to winter*, חָרַץ *to sharpen*, עָרַב *to be sweet*, קָרַב *to come near*, קָרַם *to cover*; טָרַף *to tear in pieces*, has either Hholem or Pattahh; חָרַשׁ *to plough* has fut. *o*, *to be silent* has fut. *a*.

2. With any other guttural for the second radical the Kal future and imperative have Pattahh; only נָהַם *to roar*, and רָחַם *to love*, have Hholem; זָעַם *to curse*, בָּעַל *to trespass*, and פָּעַל *to do*, have either Pattahh or Hholem; the future of אָחַז *to grasp*, is יֶאֱחֹז or יֹאחֵז.

3. Pattahh in the ultimate is as in perfect verbs commonly prolonged to Kamets before suffixes, where Hholem would be rejected, אֲהֵבָהּ Prov. 4:6, יִשְׁחָטֵם 2 Kin. 10:14, אֶשְׁחָקֵם 2 Sam. 22:43, שָׁאֲלוּנִי Isa. 45:11, יֶאֱחָזֵנִי Gen. 29:32.

4. The feminine plurals of the Niphal and Piel futures have Pattahh with the second radical whether this be ר or another guttural, תִּבָּהַלְנָה Ezek. 7:27, תִּשְׁלַחְנָה Prov. 6:27, תֶּחֱרַגְנָה Ezek. 16:6, תְּנַאֲפְנָה Hos. 4:13, but Tsere occasionally in pause, תִּזְבָּחֵרְנָה Jer. 9:17.

§ 119. 1. With these exceptions the vowel accompanying the guttural is the same as in the perfect verb; thus the Kal-preterite *mid. ē* : אָהֵב Gen. 27:9, אָהַבְתָּ Deut. 15:16; infinitive יִלְּךְ 1 Sam. 7:8, סָחֹר Jer. 15:3, with Makkeph, ־כְּרָת 1 Kin. 5:20; Niphal infinitive, הִלָּחֵם Ex. 17:10, with suffixes, הִשָּׁעֶנְךָ 2 Chron. 16:7, 8, with prefixed בְּ, בְּנָלֹחַ Judg. 11:25, נִשְׁאַל 1 Sam. 20:6, 28, and once anomalously with prefixed א, אִדָּרֹשׁ Ezek. 14:3 (a like substitution of א for ה occurring once in the Hiphil preterite, אַגְאַלְתִּי Isa. 63:3); future יִצְחַב Ex. 14:14, with Vav conversive, וַיִּפְאַס Job 7:5, וַיִּקְהַל Ex. 32:1, וַיִּצְעַק Judg. 6:34, וַתִּבְחַר Ex. 9:15, וַתְּחִי Num. 22:25, or with the accent on the penult, וַיִּצְלַח Ex. 17:8, וַתֵּצֵא Gen. 41:8; imperative, הִלָּחֵם 1 Sam. 18:17, or with the accent thrown back, הִצָּרֵד Gen. 13:9; Hiphil infinitive, הַבְאֵשׁ 1 Sam. 27:12, הַרְחֵק Gen. 21:16, הַחֲרֵם Deut. 7:2, apocopated future, יֶרַב 1 Sam. 2:10, יַקְהֵל 1 Kin. 8:1 (in the parallel passage, 2 Chron. 5:2, יַקְהִיל), תֶּשְׁחִית Deut. 9:26, יֶבְרַח Ps. 12:4, with Vav conversive, וַיַּבְלַע 1 Kin. 22:54, וָאֶכְחֵד Zech. 11:8; imperative, הַקְתֵּב Ex. 28:1, with Makkeph, הַרְחֵב־ Ps. 81:11, הַוְשַׁע 2 Sam. 20:4, הַקְהֵל־ Deut. 4:10, with a pause accent the last vowel sometimes becomes Pattahh, הִרְחָק Job 13:21, הֶעֱבַר Ps. 69:24, though not always, הַקְהֵל Lev. 8:3. Hophal infinitive, הָחֳרֵב 2 Kin. 3:23. Tsere is commonly retained in the last syllable of the Piel and Hithpael, which upon the retrocession or loss of the accent is shortened to Seghol, בְּחַם Lev. 5:22, יָחֵם Hos. 9:2, צִחֵק Gen. 39:14, לְשָׁחֵת Ps. 104:26, יָלְדָה 74:10, וַיְשָׁרֵת Gen. 39:4, וַתִּתְחַצָּב Dan. 2:1, הִתְקָרֵב 2 Kin. 18:23, and occasionally before suffixes to Hhirik, פָּרְשֵׂךָ Isa. 1:15, מְבָרַכְךָ (fem. form for מְבָרַכְתְּךָ, § 61. 5) 1 Sam. 16:15 but לְרַחֲצָם Isa. 30:18, שַׁתְּחַב־

§ 120, 121 REMARKS ON AYIN GUTTURAL VERBS.

Ezek. 5:16; in a few instances, however, as in the perfect verb, Pattahh is taken instead, thus in the preterite, לָהֵם Mal. 3:19, רָחַם Ps. 103:13, רָחַק Isa. 6:12, אָרַשׂ Deut. 20:7, בָּרַךְ Gen. 24:1 (בְּרָךְ rarely occurs except in pause), סָלַע Isa. 25:11, and more rarely still in the imperative, קְלָב Ezek. 37:17, and future יִתְגָּרָב Prov. 14:10, יִתְגָּאָל; יִתְגָּאָל Dan. 1:8.

2. שָׁאַל, which has Kamets in pause, שָׁאֵל, שָׁאֲלוּ, but most commonly Tsere before suffixes, שְׁאֵלְךָ, שְׁאֵלֵנוּ, exhibits the peculiar forms, שְׁאֵלָתָם 1 Sam. 12:13, שְׁאֵלְתִּיו 1 Sam. 1:20, שְׁאֵלְתִּיהוּ Judg. 13:6, הִשְׁאִלְתִּיהוּ 1 Sam. 1:28.

3. Kamets Hhatuph sometimes remains before the guttural in the Kal imperative and infinitive with suffixes or appended ה, אֲהָבָם Hos. 9:10, גָּאֲלָהּ Ruth 3:13, מָאֳסָם Am. 2:4, מָאֳסָבָם (by § 61.1) Isa. 30:12, קָרְבָּם Deut. 20:2 (the alternate form being מָרְדָּם Josh. 22:16), רָחְצָה Ex. 30:18, רָחֳקָה Ezek. 8:6, and sometimes is changed to Pattahh, יְקָבֶץ Isa. 57:13, מָצֳלָם Ezek. 20:27, שָׁחֲטָה Hos. 5:2, אֲהָבָה Deut. 10:15, הֶאֱלָה Jer. 31:12, or with simple Sh'va under the guttural, צִדְקוֹ Ps. 68:8, יִשְׁבוֹ 2 Chron. 26:19. In יִצְמָה Num. 23:7, Kamets Hhatuph is lengthened to Hholem in the simple syllable. Once the paragogic imperative takes the form שְׁאָלָה Isa. 7:11, comp. שְׁבָה, סָלְחָה Dan. 9:19, רְפָאָה Ps. 41:5.

4. Hhirik of the inflected Kal imperative is retained before ר, בְּרָהוּ Josh. 9:6, and once before ח, שְׁחֵרוּ Job 6:22; when the first radical is א it becomes Seghol, אֱהָבוּ Ps. 31:24, אֱחֱזוּ Cant. 2:15; in other cases it is changed to Pattahh, זַעֲקִי Isa. 14:31, זַעֲקִי Judg. 10:14.

§ 120. 1. The compound Sh'va after Kamets Hhatuph is (ֳ), after Seghol (ֱ), in other cases (ֲ), as is sufficiently shown by the examples already adduced. Exceptions are rare, אֱחוּז Ruth 3:15, תִּשְׁחֲרִי Ezek. 16:33. יְתָאֲרֵהוּ y'tha°rēhū Isa. 44:13.

2. The letter before the guttural receives compound Sh'va in יִרְצָחָ Gen. 21:6; in נָאֱשָׂא Ezek. 9:8, this leads to the prolongation of the preceding vowel and its expression by the vowel letter א, § 11:1. a. This latter form, though without an exact parallel, is thus susceptible of ready explanation, and there is no need of resorting to the hypothesis of an error in the text or a confusion of two distinct readings, נְשָׂא and אֶשָּׂא.

3. Resh commonly receives simple Sh'va, though it has compound in some forms of בְּרַךְ, e. g. תְּבָרֲבוֹ Num. 6:23, בֵּרֲכוֹ Gen. 27:27.

§ 121. 1. Upon the omission of Daghesh-forte from the second radical the previous vowel is always lengthened before ר, almost always before א, and prevailingly before ע, but rarely before ה or ח. The previous vowel remains short in בָּעַת to terrify, כָּעַס to provoke, מָעַט to be few, נָעַר to shake, and צָעַק to cry. It is sometimes lengthened, though not always, in בָּאֵר to make plain, נָאֵף to commit adultery, נָאֵץ to despise, נָאַל to reject, שָׁאַל to ask; בָּעַר to consume, יָעָה to sweep away by a tempest, תָּעַב to abhor; בָּהַל to affright, כָּהָה to be dim, נָהַל to lead. It is also lengthened in קָהָה to be dull, which only occurs Eccl. 10:10. The only instances of

the prolongation of the vowel before ה are לָחֶם Pi. inf. Judg. 5:8, צִחֶן Pu.
pret. Ezek. 21:18, הֹחוּ Pu. pret. Ps. 36:13, הִתְרָחַצְתִּי Job 9:30, the first two
of which may, however, be regarded as nouns. Daghesh-forte is retained
and the vowel consequently remains short in בְּחֵה Ezek. 16:4, רָאֹה Job
33:21, unless the point in the latter example is to be regarded as Mappik, § 26.

2. When not lengthened, Hhirik of the Piel preterite commonly remains unaltered before the guttural, בִּחֲרוּ Job 15:18, שִׁחֲתָה Jer. 12:10,
though it is in two instances changed to Seghol, אֶחֲרוּ Judg. 5:28, יִחֶסְתַּנִי
Ps. 51:7.

3. When under the influence of a pause accent the guttural receives
Kamets, a preceding Pattahh is converted to Seghol, § 63.1.a, הִגֶּדְתִּי
Ezek. 5:13, יֶחְגָּם Num. 23:19, יִשְׁחָרוּ׃ Num. 8:7.

§ 122. 1. רֵגֵן and שַׁאֲנָן are Piel forms with the third radical reduplicated in place of the second; סְחַרְחַר doubles the second syllable; and אֲהַבוּ
תֵבוּ Hos. 4:18, is by the ablest Hebraists regarded as one word, the last
two radicals being reduplicated together with the personal ending, § 92. a.

2. שֹׁרֵשׁ and סֹעֵר have two forms of the Piel, שֵׁרֵשׁ and שָׁרָשׁ, סֵעֵר and
סֹעֵר, § 92. b.; and גָּעַשׁ two forms of the Hithpael, הִתְגָּעֲשָׁה, יִתְגֹּעֲשׁוּ Jer.
46:7, 8; מִצָּעֲךָ Isa. 52:5, follows the analogy of the latter; יַנְאֲצוּ Eccl.
12:5, is sometimes derived from נָאֵץ to despise, as if it were for יִנְאֲרִיץ;
such a form would however be unexampled. The vowels show it to be
the Hiphil future of נוץ or rather נָצֵץ to flourish or blossom, the א being
inserted as a vowel letter, § 11.1.a. נִגְאֲלוּ Isa. 59:3, Lam. 4:14 is a
Niphal formed upon the basis of a Pual, § 83. c. (2). דְּרוֹשׁ Ezra 10:16
is an anomalous infinitive from דָּרַשׁ, which some regard as Kal, others
as Piel.

Lamedh Guttural Verbs.

§ 123. Lamedh guttural verbs, or those which have a guttural for their third radical, are affected by the peculiarities of these letters, § 108, in the following manner, viz.:

1. The vowel preceding the third radical becomes Pattahh in the future and imperative Kal, and in the feminine plurals of the future and imperative Piel, Hiphil, and Hithpael, יִשְׁלַח.

2. Tsere preceding the third radical, as in the Piel and Hithpael and in some forms of the other species, may either be changed to Pattahh or retained; in the latter case the guttural takes Pattahh-furtive, § 17, after the long heterogeneous vowel, e. g. יְשַׁלֵּחַ or יְשַׁלַּח.

3. Hhirik of the Hiphil species, Hholem of the Kal and Niphal infinitives, and Shurek of the Kal passive participle, suffer no change before the final guttural, which receives a Pattahh-furtive, שָׁלֹחַ, הִשְׁלִיחַ.

4. The guttural retains the simple Sh'va of the perfect verb before all afformatives beginning with a consonant, though compound Sh'va is substituted for it before suffixes, which are less closely attached to the verb, שָׁלְחָה, שְׁלָחַהּ.

5. When, however, a personal afformative consists of a single vowelless letter, as in the second feminine singular of the preterite, the guttural receives a Pattahh-furtive to aid in its pronunciation without sundering it from the affixed termination, שָׁלַחַתְּ.

a. Some grammarians regard this as a Pattahh inserted between the guttural and the final vowelless consonant by § 61. 2, and accordingly pronounce שָׁלַחַתְּ *shalakhat* instead of *shala‘hht*. But as these verbs do not suffer even a compound Sh'va to be inserted before the affixed personal termination, it is scarcely probable that a full vowel would be admitted. And the Daghesh-lene in the final Tav and the Sh'va under it show that the preceding vowel sign is not Pattahh but Pattahh-furtive, § 17. *a*.

6. There is no occasion in these verbs for the application of the rule requiring the omission of Daghesh-forte from the gutturals.

§ 124. The inflections of Lamedh guttural verbs may be represented by שָׁלַח *to send*. The Pual and Hophal, which agree with perfect verbs except in the Pattahh-furtive of the second feminine preterite and of the absolute infinitive, are omitted from the paradigm. The Hithpael of this verb does not occur, but is here formed from analogy, the initial sibilant being transposed with ת of the prefix, according to § 82. 5.

a. Instead of the Niphal infinitive absolute with prefixed ה, which does not happen to occur in any verb of this class, the alternate form with prefixed נ, § 91. *b*, is given in the paradigm, נִשְׁלֹחַ being in actual use.

Paradigm of Lamedh Guttural Verbs.

	KAL.	NIPHAL.	PIEL.	HIPHIL.	HITHPAEL.
Pret. 3 m.	שָׁלַח	נִשְׁלַח	שִׁלַּח	הִשְׁלִיחַ	הִשְׁתַּלַּח
3 f.	שָׁלְחָה	נִשְׁלְחָה	שִׁלְּחָה	הִשְׁלִיחָה	הִשְׁתַּלְּחָה
2 m.	שָׁלַחְתָּ	נִשְׁלַחְתָּ	שִׁלַּחְתָּ	הִשְׁלַחְתָּ	הִשְׁתַּלַּחְתָּ
2 f.	שָׁלַחַתְּ	נִשְׁלַחַתְּ	שִׁלַּחַתְּ	הִשְׁלַחַתְּ	הִשְׁתַּלַּחַתְּ
1 c.	שָׁלַחְתִּי	נִשְׁלַחְתִּי	שִׁלַּחְתִּי	הִשְׁלַחְתִּי	הִשְׁתַּלַּחְתִּי
Plur. 3 c.	שָׁלְחוּ	נִשְׁלְחוּ	שִׁלְּחוּ	הִשְׁלִיחוּ	הִשְׁתַּלְּחוּ
2 m.	שְׁלַחְתֶּם	נִשְׁלַחְתֶּם	שִׁלַּחְתֶּם	הִשְׁלַחְתֶּם	הִשְׁתַּלַּחְתֶּם
2 f.	שְׁלַחְתֶּן	נִשְׁלַחְתֶּן	שִׁלַּחְתֶּן	הִשְׁלַחְתֶּן	הִשְׁתַּלַּחְתֶּן
1 c.	שָׁלַחְנוּ	נִשְׁלַחְנוּ	שִׁלַּחְנוּ	הִשְׁלַחְנוּ	הִשְׁתַּלַּחְנוּ
Infin. Absol.	שָׁלוֹחַ	נִשְׁלֹחַ	שַׁלֵּחַ	הַשְׁלֵחַ	—
Constr.	שְׁלֹחַ	הִשָּׁלַח	שַׁלַּח	הַשְׁלִיחַ	הִשְׁתַּלַּח
Fut. 3 m.	יִשְׁלַח	יִשָּׁלַח	יְשַׁלַּח	יַשְׁלִיחַ	יִשְׁתַּלַּח
3 f.	תִּשְׁלַח	תִּשָּׁלַח	תְּשַׁלַּח	תַּשְׁלִיחַ	תִּשְׁתַּלַּח
2 m.	תִּשְׁלַח	תִּשָּׁלַח	תְּשַׁלַּח	תַּשְׁלִיחַ	תִּשְׁתַּלַּח
2 f.	תִּשְׁלְחִי	תִּשָּׁלְחִי	תְּשַׁלְּחִי	תַּשְׁלִיחִי	תִּשְׁתַּלְּחִי
1 c.	אֶשְׁלַח	אֶשָּׁלַח	אֲשַׁלַּח	אַשְׁלִיחַ	אֶשְׁתַּלַּח
Plur. 3 m.	יִשְׁלְחוּ	יִשָּׁלְחוּ	יְשַׁלְּחוּ	יַשְׁלִיחוּ	יִשְׁתַּלְּחוּ
3 f.	תִּשְׁלַחְנָה	תִּשָּׁלַחְנָה	תְּשַׁלַּחְנָה	תַּשְׁלַחְנָה	תִּשְׁתַּלַּחְנָה
2 m.	תִּשְׁלְחוּ	תִּשָּׁלְחוּ	תְּשַׁלְּחוּ	תַּשְׁלִיחוּ	תִּשְׁתַּלְּחוּ
2 f.	תִּשְׁלַחְנָה	תִּשָּׁלַחְנָה	תְּשַׁלַּחְנָה	תַּשְׁלַחְנָה	תִּשְׁתַּלַּחְנָה
1 c.	נִשְׁלַח	נִשָּׁלַח	נְשַׁלַּח	נַשְׁלִיחַ	נִשְׁתַּלַּח
Imper. 2 m.	שְׁלַח	הִשָּׁלַח	שַׁלַּח	הַשְׁלַח	הִשְׁתַּלַּח
2 f.	שִׁלְחִי	הִשָּׁלְחִי	שַׁלְּחִי	הַשְׁלִיחִי	הִשְׁתַּלְּחִי
Plur. 2 m.	שִׁלְחוּ	הִשָּׁלְחוּ	שַׁלְּחוּ	הַשְׁלִיחוּ	הִשְׁתַּלְּחוּ
2 f.	שְׁלַחְנָה	הִשָּׁלַחְנָה	שַׁלַּחְנָה	הַשְׁלַחְנָה	הִשְׁתַּלַּחְנָה
Part. Act.	שֹׁלֵחַ		מְשַׁלֵּחַ	מַשְׁלִיחַ	מִשְׁתַּלֵּחַ
Pass.	שָׁלוּחַ	נִשְׁלָח			

Remarks on Lamedh Guttural Verbs.

§ 125. 1. The Kal future and imperative have Pattahh without exception; in one instance the K'thibh inserts ו, אסלוח Jer. 5:7, where the K'ri is אֶסְלַח־. The vowel *a* is retained before suffixes, remaining short in בְּצַעַ Am. 9:1, but usually lengthened to Kamets, יִבְקָעוּהָ 2 Chron. 21:17, יִשְׁלָעֵהוּ Gen. 23:11. In the paragogic imperative *a* may be retained, סָלְחָה, שְׁלָחָה Dan. 9:19, or rejected, and Hhirik given to the first radical, שִׁדְרָה־ Job 32:10, שְׁלְחָה Gen. 43:8. Hhirik appears in מִבְלָח Gen. 25:31, but verbs whose last radical is ר commonly take Kamets Hhatuph like perfect verbs both before paragogic ה, and suffixes, שָׁמְרָה־ 1 Chron. 29:18, קָשְׁרֵם Prov. 3:3.

2. The Kal infinitive construct mostly has *o*, לִבְלֹעַ Jon. 2:1, גְּנֹב; Num. 17:28, גְּעֹר Isa. 54:9, rarely *a*, שָׁלַח Isa. 58:9, גְּעַ Num. 20:3, מְשֹׁחַ 1 Sam. 15:1. With a feminine ending, the first syllable takes Kamets Hhatuph, גָּבְהָה Zeph. 3:11; so sometimes before suffixes, וְבֹחוֹ 2 Sam. 15:12, שָׁמְעִי Neh. 1:4, שָׁמְעָם Josh. 6:5, but more commonly Hhirik, בְּצַעַם Am. 1:13, פִּגְעוֹ Num. 35:19, פִּתְחֹה Neh. 8:5, rarely Pattahh, רַקְעֵךְ Ezek. 25:6.

3. Most verbs with final ח have Hholem in the Kal future and imperative. But such as have middle *ē* in the preterite take Pattahh, § 82. 1. *a*; and in addition the following, viz.: אָסַר to shut, אָמַר to say, הָדַר to honour, חָיַר to grow pale, נָחַת to shake, עָשַׁר to be rich, עָתַר to entreat, פָּגַע to slip away, צָפַר to press, שָׁבַר to drink or be drunken. The following have Pattahh or Hholem, גָּזַר to decree, נָדַר to vow, קָצַר fut. *o*, to reap, fut. *a*, to be short.

§ 126. 1. Tsere is almost always changed to Pattahh before the guttural in the preterite, infinitive construct, future and imperative; but it is retained and Pattahh-furtive given to the guttural in pause, and in the infinitive absolute and participle which partake of the character of nouns and prefer lengthened forms. Thus, Niphal: infin. constr., הִשָּׁמַע Esth. 2:8, הִפָּתַח Isa. 51:14, future, יִשָּׁבַע Ps. 9:19, יִתְפֶּשׂ Job 17:3, imperative, even in pause, הֵאָנְחָה. Piel: preterite, גִּלַּע Lev. 14:8, גֵּרַע 2 Chron. 34:4, infin. constr., בַּלַּע Hab. 1:13, בַּלַּע Lam. 2:8, future, יְפַלַּח Job 16:13, תְּכַבְּשׁ 2 Kin. 8:12, תְּנַגֵּעוּן Deut. 7:5, imperative, שַׁלַּח Ex. 4:23. Hiphil: apocopated future, יַבְלַח 2 Kin. 18:30, fut. with Vav conversive, יַצְלַח Judg. 4:23, fem. plur., תַּפְלַחְנָה Ps. 119:171, imperative, הוֹשַׁע Ps. 86:2, and even in pause, תַּצְלַח 1 Kin. 22:12. Hithpael: יִתְפַּלַּע Prov. 17:14, יִתְאַנְחוּ Dan. 11:40, הִשְׁתַּבַּח Ps. 106:47; this species sometimes has Kamets in its pausal forms, הִתְרַבְּקוּ Josh. 9:13, תִּתְרַגְּעוּ Ps. 107:27. On the other hand, the absolute infinitives: Piel, שַׁלֵּחַ Deut. 22:7. Hiphil, הַגְלֵחַ Isa. 7:11, Hophal, הָגְלֵחַ Ezek. 16:4. Participles: Kal, בֹּצֵעַ Deut. 28:52, but occasionally in the construct state with Pattahh, בֹּצַע Ps. 94:9, רֹגַע Isa. 51:15, רֹקַע Isa. 42:5, שֹׁסַע Lev. 11:7, Piel, מְזֹגַע 1 Kin. 3:3, Hithpael, מִשְׁתַּבַּע 1 Sam. 21:15. Tsere is retained before suffixes of the second person instead of being either changed to Pattahh or as in perfect verbs shortened to Seghol, Pi. inf. const. שַׁלְּחָה Deut. 15:18, fut. אֲשַׁלְּחָה Gen. 31:27. There is one instance of Pattahh in the Hiphil inf. const., הוֹבַח Job 6:26.

2. In verbs with final ה Pattahh takes the place of Tsere for the most part in the Piel preterite (in pause Tsere), and frequently in the Hithpael (in pause Kamets); but Tsere (in pause Tsere or Pattahh, §65.a) is commonly retained elsewhere, שִׁבַּר Ps. 76:4, :שִׁבְּרִי Ex. 9:25, תִּתְהַדָּר Prov. 25:6, הִתְאַגֵּר Ps. 93:1, יְאַשֵּׁר Gen. 22:14, יְאַשֵּׁר Gen. 10:19, :תְּקַבֵּר Zeph. 2:4. Two verbs have Seghol in the Piel preterite, דִּבֶּר (in pause, וַיְדַבֵּר) and כִּפֶּר.

§127. 1. The guttural almost always has Pattahh-furtive in the second fem. sing. of the preterite, שָׁמַעַתְּ Ruth 2:8, :שָׁמַעַתְּ Ezek. 16:28, הִגַּעַתְּ Esth. 4:14, הִמְלַחַתְּ Ezek. 16:4, scarcely ever simple Sh'va, לָקַחְתְּ 1 Kin. 14:3, שָׁכַחְתְּ Jer. 13:5, and never Pattahh (which might arise from the concurrence of consonants at the end of a word, §61.2), unless in לָבַחַת Gen. 30:5, and :נֹבַחַת Gen. 20:16, the former of which admits of ready explanation as a construct infinitive, and the latter may be a Niphal participle in the feminine singular, whether it be understood as in the common English version "*she was reproved*," or *it is adjudged* (i. e. justly due as a compensation) to thee; the latest authorities, however, prefer to render it *thou art judged*, i. e. justice is done thee by this indemnification. Pattahh is once inserted before the abbreviated termination of the feminine plural imperative, שְׁמַעַןָ Gen. 4:23 for שְׁמַעְנָה.

2. The guttural takes compound instead of simple Sh'va before suffixes, not only when it stands at the end of the verb, דְּגֶעְךָ Num. 24:11, יִשְׁבְּךָ Prov. 25:17, but also in the first plural of the preterite, שָׁבַחֲנוּ Ps. 44:18 (שָׁבַחֲנוּ ver. 21), יְרֵעֲנוּ Isa. 59:12, בָּלַעֲנוּהוּ Ps. 35:25, הֱקִימֲנוּ 2 Sam. 21:6, שְׁמַעֲנוּהָ Ps. 132:6; ר retains simple Sh'va before all personal terminations and suffixes, אָרְרְתְּ Judg. 4:20, אֲמַרְכֶּם Mal. 1:7, עֲבָדְכֶם Josh. 4:23.

3. In a few exceptional cases the letter before the guttural receives compound Sh'va, אֲפַשָּׂה Isa. 27:4, לְקַחְתּ Gen. 2:23.

§128. The Hiphil infinitive construct once has the feminine ending וּת, הַשְׁמְלוּת Ezek. 24:26; וַתִּגְבְּהֶינָה Ezek. 16:50 for וַתִּגְבַּהְנָה perhaps owes its anomalous form to its being assimilated in termination to the following word, which is a Lamedh He verb. In נשקה Am. 8:8 K'thibh for נִשְׁקָה the guttural ע is elided, §53.3.

PE NUN (פ״ן) VERBS.

§129. Nun, as the first radical of verbs, has two peculiarities, viz.:

1. At the end of a syllable it is assimilated to the fol-

lowing consonant, the two letters being written as one, and the doubling indicated by Daghesh-forte. This occurs in the Kal future, Niphal preterite and participle, and in the Hiphil and Hophal species throughout; thus, יִנְגַּשׁ becomes יִגַּשׁ, written יִגַּשׁ, so נִגַּשׁ for נִנְגַּשׁ, הִגִּישׁ for הִנְגִּישׁ. In the Hophal, Kamets Hhatuph becomes Kibbuts before the doubled letter, § 61. 5, הֻגַּשׁ for הָנְגַּשׁ.

2. In the Kal imperative with Pattahh it is frequently dropped, its sound being easily lost from the beginning of a syllable when it is without a vowel, גַּשׁ for נְגַשׁ, § 53. 2. A like rejection occurs in the Kal infinitive construct of a few verbs, the abbreviation being in this case compensated by adding the feminine termination ה; thus, גֶּשֶׁת for גֶּשֶׁת (by § 63. 2. a), the primary form being נְגֹשׁ.

a. In the Indo-European languages likewise, n is frequently conformed to or affected by a following consonant, and in certain circumstances it is liable to rejection, e. g. ἐγγράφω, ἐμβάλλω, συστρέφω.

§ 130. 1. The inflections of Pe Nun verbs may be represented by נָגַשׁ *to approach.* In the Piel, Pual, and Hithpael, they do not differ from perfect verbs. The last column of the paradigm is occupied by the Kal species of נָתַן *to give,* which is peculiar in assimilating its last as well as its first radical, and in having Tsere in the future.

a. The Kal of נָגַשׁ is used only in the infinitive, future, and imperative, the preterite and participle being supplied by the Niphal, which has substantially the same sense: the missing parts are in the paradigm supplied from analogy.

b. The future of נָתַן has Pattahh in one instance before Makkeph, וַיִּתַּן־ Judg. 16 : 5.

Paradigm of Pe Nun Verbs.

	KAL.	NIPHAL.	HIPHIL.	HOPHAL.	KAL.
Pret. 3 m.	נָגַשׁ	נִגַּשׁ	הִגִּישׁ	הֻגַּשׁ	נָתַן
3 f.	נָגְשָׁה	נִגְּשָׁה	הִגִּישָׁה	הֻגְּשָׁה	נָתְנָה
2 m.	נָגַשְׁתָּ	נִגַּשְׁתָּ	הִגַּשְׁתָּ	הֻגַּשְׁתָּ	נָתַתָּ
2 f.	נָגַשְׁתְּ	נִגַּשְׁתְּ	הִגַּשְׁתְּ	הֻגַּשְׁתְּ	נָתַתְּ
1 c.	נָגַשְׁתִּי	נִגַּשְׁתִּי	הִגַּשְׁתִּי	הֻגַּשְׁתִּי	נָתַתִּי
Plur. 3 c.	נָגְשׁוּ	נִגְּשׁוּ	הִגִּישׁוּ	הֻגְּשׁוּ	נָתְנוּ
2 m.	נְגַשְׁתֶּם	נִגַּשְׁתֶּם	הִגַּשְׁתֶּם	הֻגַּשְׁתֶּם	נְתַתֶּם
2 f.	נְגַשְׁתֶּן	נִגַּשְׁתֶּן	הִגַּשְׁתֶּן	הֻגַּשְׁתֶּן	נְתַתֶּן
1 c.	נָגַשְׁנוּ	נִגַּשְׁנוּ	הִגַּשְׁנוּ	הֻגַּשְׁנוּ	נָתַנּוּ
Infin. Absol.	נָגוֹשׁ	הִגֹּשׁ	הַגֵּשׁ	הֻגֵּשׁ	נָתוֹן
Constr.	גֶּשֶׁת	הִנָּגֵשׁ	הַגִּישׁ	הֻגַּשׁ	תֵּת
Fut. 3 m.	יִגַּשׁ	יִנָּגֵשׁ	יַגִּישׁ	יֻגַּשׁ	יִתֵּן
3 f.	תִּגַּשׁ	תִּנָּגֵשׁ	תַּגִּישׁ	תֻּגַּשׁ	תִּתֵּן
2 m.	תִּגַּשׁ	תִּנָּגֵשׁ	תַּגִּישׁ	תֻּגַּשׁ	תִּתֵּן
2 f.	תִּגְּשִׁי	תִּנָּגְשִׁי	תַּגִּישִׁי	תֻּגְּשִׁי	תִּתְּנִי
1 c.	אֶגַּשׁ	אֶנָּגֵשׁ	אַגִּישׁ	אֻגַּשׁ	אֶתֵּן
Plur. 3 m.	יִגְּשׁוּ	יִנָּגְשׁוּ	יַגִּישׁוּ	יֻגְּשׁוּ	יִתְּנוּ
3 f.	תִּגַּשְׁנָה	תִּנָּגַשְׁנָה	תַּגֵּשְׁנָה	תֻּגַּשְׁנָה	(תִּתֵּנָּה)
2 m.	תִּגְּשׁוּ	תִּנָּגְשׁוּ	תַּגִּישׁוּ	תֻּגְּשׁוּ	תִּתְּנוּ
2 f.	תִּגַּשְׁנָה	תִּנָּגַשְׁנָה	תַּגֵּשְׁנָה	תֻּגַּשְׁנָה	(תִּתֵּנָּה)
1 c.	נִגַּשׁ	נִנָּגֵשׁ	נַגִּישׁ	נֻגַּשׁ	נִתֵּן
Imper. 2 m.	גַּשׁ	הִנָּגֵשׁ	הַגֵּשׁ		תֵּן
2 f.	גְּשִׁי	הִנָּגְשִׁי	הַגִּישִׁי	wanting	תְּנִי
Plur. 2 m.	גְּשׁוּ	הִנָּגְשׁוּ	הַגִּישׁוּ		תְּנוּ
2 f.	גַּשְׁנָה	הִנָּגַשְׁנָה	הַגֵּשְׁנָה		(תֵּנָּה)
Part. Act.	נֹגֵשׁ		מַגִּישׁ		נֹתֵן
Pass.	נָגוּשׁ	נִגָּשׁ		מֻגָּשׁ	נָתוּן

164

Remarks on Pe Nun Verbs.

§ 131. 1. If the second radical be a guttural or a vowel letter, Nun becomes strong by contrast and is not liable to rejection or assimilation, נָהֲלוּ Num. 34:18, נָהַג 2 Kin. 4:24, הִנְחַנִי Gen. 24:48, אֲנָוֵהוּ Ex. 15:2. It is, however, always assimilated in the Niphal preterite of נִחַם *to repent*, and occasionally in נָחֵת *to descend*, e. g. יֵחַת Jer. 21:13, תֵּחַת Prov. 17:10, נְחִתוּ Ps. 38:3 but תִּנְחַת ibid., הִנָּחֵת Joel 4:11.

2. Before other consonants the rule for assimilation is observed with rare exceptions, viz.: תִּנָּשֵׂא Isa. 58:3, תִּנְדְּדִי Ps. 68:3, יִנְצֹר Jer. 3:5, יִנְצְרוּ Deut. 33:9 (and occasionally elsewhere), יִנְקַב־ Job 40:21, יִנְקְפוּ Isa. 29:1, הִנָּתֵךְ Ezek. 22:20, לִנְבֹּל (for לִהִנָּבֵל) Num. 5:22, בְּצַלְךָ (for בְּצִלְּךָ with Daghesh-forte separative, § 24. 5) Isa. 33:1, הִנָּתְקוּ Judg. 20:31.

3. Nun is commonly rejected from the Kal imperative with *a*, גַּשׁ 2 Sam. 1:15 (once before Makkeph, גֶּשׁ־ Gen. 19:9, in plural גְּשׁוּ 1 Kin. 18:30 and גֹּשׁוּ Josh. 3:9), שַׁל Ex. 3:5, בַּ Job 1:11, סַע Deut. 2:24, פְּתַח Ezek. 37:9, וּשְׁקָה Gen. 27:26, though it is occasionally retained, נְטֹלֵנוּ 2 Kin. 19:29, נְשָׂא Ps. 10:12, or by a variant orthography, נְסָה Ps. 4:7 but always elsewhere שָׂא. In imperatives with *o*, and in Lamedh He verbs which have ē in the imperative, Nun is invariably retained, נְטֹשׁ Prov. 17:14, נְצֹר Ps. 24:14, נְקֹם Num. 31:2, נְחֵן Ps. 58:7, נְקֵבָה Gen. 30:27, נְטֵה Ex. 8:1.

4. The rejection of Nun from the Kal construct infinitive occurs in but few verbs; viz.: גֶּשֶׁת (with suffix, גִּשְׁתּוֹ) from נָגַשׁ, פַּחַת from נָפַח, גַּעַת (twice) and גִּל from נָגַע, צֵאת (once) and נְשֹׁא from נָשָׂא has שְׂאֵת (by § 60. 3. *c*), with the preposition לְ, לָשֵׂאת by § 57. 2. (3), once שֵׁת (§ 53. 3) Job 41:17, once without the feminine ending. שׂוֹא Ps. 89:10, and twice נְשׂא; נָתַן has commonly תֵּת (for תִּתֵּה), with suffixes תִּתִּי, but נְתֹן Num. 20:21, and נְתָן־ Gen. 38:9.

5. The absolute infinitive Niphal appears in the three forms הִנָּתֹן Jer. 32:4, הִנָּתֹה Ps. 68:3, and נִגֹּף Judg. 20:39.

6. The ת of the prefix in the Hithpael species is in a few instances assimilated to the first radical, § 82. 5. *a*, הִנַּחַמְתִּי Ezek. 5:13, הִנַּבֵּאתִי Ezek. 37:10, Jer. 23:13, תִּנַּשֵּׂא Num. 24:7, Dan. 11:14, מִצַּיֵּץ Isa. 52:5.

§ 132. 1. The last radical of נָתַן is assimilated in the Niphal as well as in the Kal species, נִתַּן Lev. 26:25. The final Nun of other verbs remains without assimilation, תִּתֶּה, צָלַנְתְּ, שָׁבַנְתְּ, בָּנַתָה. In 2 Sam. 22:41 תִּתָּה is for נָתַתָּה which is found in the parallel passage Ps. 18:41. תִּתֶּן 1 Kin. 6:19, 17:14 K'thibh, is probably, as explained by Ewald, the Kal construct infinitive without the feminine ending (תֵּת) prolonged by reduplication, which is the case with some other short words, e. g. מִצְּצוּ from מָץ, מֵירָי for מֵי; others regard it as the infinitive תֵּת with the 3 fem. plur. suffix or with ן paragogic; Gesenius takes it to be, as always elsewhere, the

2 masc. sing. of the Kal future. תְּהִי Ps. 8:2, is not the Kal infinitive (Kimchi), nor the 3 fem. sing. pret. for נְתְהִי (Nordheimer), but the imperative with paragogic ה‎ֽ. See Alexander in loc.

2. The peculiarities of Pe Nun verbs are shared by לָקַח to take. whose first radical is assimilated or rejected in the same manner as נ. Kal inf. const. קַחַת (with prep. ל, לָקַחַת, to be distinguished from לְקַחְתְּ 2 fem. sing. pret.), once קַחְתּ‎ֽ (by §60. 3. c) 2 Kin. 12:9, with suffixes קַחְתִּי, fut. יִקַּח, imper. קַח, קְחִי rarely לְקָחִי, לְקַח, Hoph. fut. יֻקַּח, but Niph. pret. נִלְקַח. In Hos. 11:3 קָחָם is the masculine infinitive with the suffix for קַחְתָּם; the same form occurs without a suffix, קָח Ezek. 17:5, or this may be explained with Gesenius as a preterite for לָקֹחַ.

3. In Isa. 64:5 וַנָּבֶל has the form of a Hiphil future from נָבֵל, but the sense shows it to be from בָּלַל for נִבָּלֵל, Daghesh-forte being omitted and the previous vowel lengthened in consequence, §59. a.

AYIN DOUBLED (עע) VERBS.

§ 133. The imperfect verbs, thus far considered, differ from the perfect verbs either in the vowels alone or in the consonants alone; those which follow, differ in both vowels and consonants, § 107, and consequently depart much more seriously from the standard paradigm. The widest divergence of all is found in the Ayin doubled and Ayin Vav verbs, in both of which the root gives up its dissyllabic character and is converted into a monosyllable; a common feature, which gives rise to many striking resemblances and even to an occasional interchange of forms.

§ 134. 1. In explaining the inflections peculiar to Ayin doubled verbs, it will be most convenient to separate the intensive species Piel and Pual with their derivative the Hithpael from the other four. That which gives rise to all their peculiar forms in the Kal, Niphal, Hiphil, and Hophal species, is the disposition to avoid the repetition of the same sound by uniting the two similar radicals and giving the intervening vowel to the previous letter, thus, סָב for סָבַב, סֹב for סָבֹב § 61. 3.

2. In the Kal species this contraction is optional in the preterite; it is rare in the infinitive absolute though usual in

the construct, and it never occurs in the participles. With these exceptions, it is universal in the species already named.

§ 135. This contraction produces certain changes both in the vowel, which is thrown back, and in that of the preceding syllable.

1. When the first radical has a vowel (pretonic Kamets, § 82. 1), as in the Kal preterite and infinitive absolute, and in the Niphal infinitive, future and imperative, this is simply displaced by the vowel thrown back from the second radical, thus הָסֵב, הָסֹב; סֹב, סָבוֹב, סַב, סָבַב.

2. When the first radical ends a mixed syllable as in the Kal future, the Niphal preterite, and throughout the Hiphil and Hophal, this will be converted into a simple syllable by the shifting of the vowel from the second radical to the first, whence arise the following mutations:

In the Kal future יִסְבֹּב becomes יִסֹב with *i* in a simple syllable, contrary to § 18. 2. This may, however, be converted into a mixed syllable by means of Daghesh-forte, and the short vowel be retained, thus יִסֹּב; or the syllable may remain simple and the vowel be lengthened from Hhirik to Tsere, § 59, thus, in verbs fut. *a*, יֵמַר for יִמְרַר; or as the Hhirik of this tense is not an original vowel but has arisen from Sh'va, § 85. 2. *a* (1), it may be neglected and *â*, the simplest of the long vowels, given to the preformative, which is the most common expedient, thus יָסֹב. The three possible forms of this tense are consequently יִסֹב, יֵסֹב and יָסֹב.

In the Niphal preterite נִסְבַּב becomes by contraction נִסַּב. In a few verbs beginning with ח the short vowel is retained in an intermediate syllable, thus נִחַר for נִחְרַר; in other cases Hhirik is lengthened to Tsere, נֵחַן for נִחְנַן, or as the Hhirik is not essential to the form but has arisen from Sh'va, § 82. 2, it is more frequently neglected, and Kamets, the simplest of the long vowels, substituted in its place, thus נָסַב. The forms of this tense are, therefore, נָחַר, נֵחַן, נָסַב.

In the Hiphil and Hophal species the vowels of the prefixed ה are characteristic and essential. They must, therefore, either be retained by inserting Daghesh-forte in the first radical, or be simply lengthened; no other vowel can be substituted for them, הֵסֵב for הִסְבִּיב, יַסֵּב or יָסֹב for יָסְבָּב, חָסַב (Kibbuts before the doubled letter by § 61. 5) or הוּסַב for הָסְבַּב.

3. The vowel, which is thrown back from the second radical to the first, stands no longer before a single consonant, but before one which, though single in appearance, is in reality equivalent to two. It is consequently subjected to the compression which affects vowels so situated, § 61. 4. Thus, in the Niphal future and imperative Tsere is compressed to Pattahh, הִסָּב, הִסָּבֵב; יִסֹּב, יִסָּבֵב (comp. קָטֵל, קְטַלְתְּ) though it remains in the infinitive which, partaking of the character of a noun, prefers longer forms. So in the Hiphil long Hhirik is compressed to Tsere, הֵסֵב, הִסְבִּיב (comp. הִקְטִיל, הִקְטַלְתִּי).

§ 136. Although the letter, into which the second and third radicals have been contracted, represents two consonants, the doubling cannot be made to appear at the end of the word. But

1. When in the course of inflection a vowel is added, the letter receives Daghesh-forte, and the preceding vowel, even where it would be dropped in perfect verbs, is retained to make the doubling possible, and hence preserves its accent, § 33. 1, סַבָּה, יָסֹבּוּ.

2. Upon the addition of a personal ending which begins with a consonant, the utterance of the doubled letter is aided by inserting one of the diphthongal vowels, ō (וֹ) in the preterite, and e (ֵי) in the future. By the dissyllabic appendage thus formed the accent is carried forward, § 32, and the previous part of the word is shortened in consequence as much as possible, הֵסֵב, הֲסִבּוֹתִי; יָסֹב, תְּסֻבֶּינָה.

3. When by the operation of the rules already given, § 135. 2, the first radical has been doubled, the reduplication of the last radical is frequently omitted in order to

relieve the word of too many doubled letters. In this case the retention of the vowel before the last radical, contrary to the analogy of perfect verbs, and the insertion of a vowel after it, are alike unnecessary, and the accent takes its accustomed position, תִּסַּבְנָה‎, יִסֹּב‎.

§ 137. The Piel, Pual, and Hithpael sometimes preserve the regular form, as הִתְהַלֵּל‎, הָלַל‎, הִלֵּל‎. The triple repetition of the same letter thus caused is in a few instances avoided, however, by reduplicating the contracted root with appropriate vowels, as סִכְסֵךְ‎, הִתְקַלְקֵל‎. Or more commonly, the reduplication is given up and the idea of intensity conveyed by the simple prolongation of the root, the long vowel Hholem being inserted after the first radical for this purpose, as הִתְגּוֹלֵל‎, סוֹבֵב‎.

§ 138. In the following paradigm the inflections of Ayin doubled verbs are shown by the example of סָבַב‎ *to surround*. The Pual is omitted, as this species almost invariably follows the inflections of the perfect verb; certain persons of the Hophal, of which there is no example, are likewise omitted. An instance of Piel, with the radical syllable reduplicated, is given in סִכְסֵךְ‎ *to excite*.

a. The Hithpael of סָבַב‎ does not actually occur; but it is in the paradigm formed from analogy, the initial sibilant being transposed with the ת of the prefix, agreeably to § 82. 5.

b. In his Manual Lexicon, Gesenius gives to סִכְסֵךְ‎ the meaning *to arm*, but the best authorities prefer the definition subsequently introduced by him into his Thesaurus, *to excite.*

Paradigm of Ayin

	KAL.	NIPHAL.	PIEL.
Pret. 3 m.	סָבַב	סַב	נָסַב	סוֹבֵב
3 f.	סָבְבָה	סַבָּה	נָסַבָּה	סוֹבְבָה
2 m.	(סָבַבְתָּ)	סַבּוֹתָ	נְסַבּוֹתָ	סוֹבַבְתָּ
2 f.	(סָבַבְתְּ)	סַבּוֹת	נְסַבּוֹת	סוֹבַבְתְּ
1 c.	סָבַבְתִּי	סַבּוֹתִי	נְסַבּוֹתִי	סוֹבַבְתִּי
Plur. 3 c.	סָבְבוּ	סַבּוּ	נָסַבּוּ	סוֹבְבוּ
2 m.	(סָבַבְתֶּם)	סַבּוֹתֶם	נְסַבּוֹתֶם	סוֹבַבְתֶּם
2 f.	(סָבַבְתֶּן)	סַבּוֹתֶן	נְסַבּוֹתֶן	סוֹבַבְתֶּן
1 c.	סָבַבְנוּ	סַבּוֹנוּ	נְסַבּוֹנוּ	סוֹבַבְנוּ
Infin. Absol.	סָבוֹב	סֹב	הִסּוֹב	סוֹבֵב
Constr.	סְבֹב	סֹב	הִסֵּב	סוֹבֵב
Fut. 3 m.	יָסֹב	יִסַּב	יִסַּב	יְסוֹבֵב
3 f.	תָּסֹב	תִּסַּב	תִּסַּב	תְּסוֹבֵב
2 m.	תָּסֹב	תִּסַּב	תִּסַּב	תְּסוֹבֵב
2 f.	תָּסֹבִּי	תִּסַּבִּי	תִּסַּבִּי	תְּסוֹבְבִי
1 c.	אָסֹב	אֶסַּב	אֶסַּב	אֲסוֹבֵב
Plur. 3 m.	יָסֹבּוּ	יִסַּבּוּ	יִסַּבּוּ	יְסוֹבְבוּ
3 f.	תְּסֻבֶּינָה	תִּסַּבְנָה	תִּסַּבְנָה	תְּסוֹבֵבְנָה
2 m.	תָּסֹבּוּ	תִּסַּבּוּ	תִּסַּבּוּ	תְּסוֹבְבוּ
2 f.	תְּסֻבֶּינָה	תִּסַּבְנָה	תִּסַּבְנָה	תְּסוֹבֵבְנָה
1 c.	נָסֹב	נִסַּב	נִסַּב	נְסוֹבֵב
Imper. 2 m.	סֹב		הִסַּב	סוֹבֵב
2 f.	סֹבִּי		הִסַּבִּי	סוֹבְבִי
Plur. 2 m.	סֹבּוּ		הִסַּבּוּ	סוֹבְבוּ
2 f.	סֻבֶּינָה		הִסַּבְנָה	סוֹבֵבְנָה
Part. Act.	סֹבֵב			מְסוֹבֵב
Pass.	סָבוּב		נָסָב	

Doubled Verbs.

HIPHIL.	HOPHAL.	HITHPAEL.	PIEL.
הֵסֵב	הוּסַב	הִסְתּוֹבֵב	סִבְבֵךְ
הֵסַבָּה	הוּסַבָּה	הִסְתּוֹבְבָה	סִבְבָה
הֲסִבּוֹתָ		הִסְתּוֹבַבְתָּ	סִבַּבְתָּ
הֲסִבּוֹת		הִסְתּוֹבַבְתְּ	סִבַּבְתְּ
הֲסִבּוֹתִי		הִסְתּוֹבַבְתִּי	סִבַּבְתִּי
הֵסֵבּוּ	הוּסַבּוּ	הִסְתּוֹבְבוּ	סִבְבוּ
הֲסִבּוֹתֶם		הִסְתּוֹבַבְתֶּם	סִבַּבְתֶּם
הֲסִבּוֹתֶן		הִסְתּוֹבַבְתֶּן	סִבַּבְתֶּן
הֲסִבּוֹנוּ		הִסְתּוֹבַבְנוּ	סִבַּבְנוּ
הָסֵב			סַבֵּךְ
הָסֵב		הִסְתּוֹבֵב	סַבֵּךְ
יָסֵב	יוּסַב	יִסְתּוֹבֵב	יְסַבֵּךְ
תָּסֵב	תּוּסַב	תִּסְתּוֹבֵב	תְּסַבֵּךְ
תָּסֵב	תּוּסַב	תִּסְתּוֹבֵב	תְּסַבֵּךְ
תָּסֵבִּי	תּוּסַבִּי	תִּסְתּוֹבְבִי	תְּסַבְבִי
אָסֵב	אוּסַב	אֶסְתּוֹבֵב	אֲסַבֵּךְ
יָסֵבּוּ	יוּסַבּוּ	יִסְתּוֹבְבוּ	יְסַבְבוּ
תְּסִבֶּינָה		תִּסְתּוֹבַבְנָה	תְּסַבֵּבְנָה
תָּסֵבּוּ	תּוּסַבּוּ	תִּסְתּוֹבְבוּ	תְּסַבְבוּ
תְּסִבֶּינָה		תִּסְתּוֹבַבְנָה	תְּסַבֵּבְנָה
נָסֵב	נוּסַב	נִסְתּוֹבֵב	נְסַבֵּךְ
הָסֵב		הִסְתּוֹלֵב	סַבֵּךְ
הָסִבִּי	wanting	הִסְתּוֹבְבִי	סַבְבִי
הָסֵבּוּ		הִסְתּוֹבְבוּ	סַבְבוּ
הֲסִבֶּינָה		הִסְתּוֹבַבְנָה	סַבֵּבְנָה
מֵסֵב	מוּסָב	מִסְתּוֹבֵב	מְסַבֵּךְ

171

Remarks on Ayin Doubled Verbs.

§ 139. 1. The uncontracted and the contracted forms of the Kal preterite are used with perhaps equal frequency in the third person; the former is rare in the first person, וְזַמֹּתִי Zech. 8:14, 15, בַּלּוֹנוּ Deut. 2:35, and there are no examples of it in the second; רֹבּוּ Gen. 49:23 and רַמּוּ Job 24:24 are preterites with Hholem, § 82.1. In Ps. 118:11, סַבּוּנִי גַם־סְבָבוּנִי the uncontracted is added to the contracted form for the sake of greater emphasis. Compound Sh'va is sometimes used with these verbs instead of simple to make its vocal character more distinct, § 16. 1. *b*, גִּלָּה Gen. 29:3, 8, צָלֲלוּ Ex. 15:10, הֲקָלוֹךְ Isa. 64:10, עֲנָנִי Gen. 9:14, תְּקָבֶנּוּ Num. 23:25.

2. The following are examples of the contracted infinitive absolute, קֹב Num. 23:25, שֹׁל Ruth 2:16, סוֹר Isa. 24:19, הֵךְ (with a paragogic termination) ibid.; of the uncontracted, אָרוֹר, גָּלוֹן, חָנוֹן, בָּזוֹז, שָׁדוֹד, פָּתוֹת, כָּתוֹת; of the infinitive construct, גֹּז and גָּז, סֹבּ and סֹב, עָדֵד, בֹּז, חֹם, once with *u* as in Ayin Vav verbs, בּוֹר Eccles. 9:1, and occasionally with *a*, רָד־ Isa. 45:1, שָׁךְ Jer. 5:26, בָּלָּם (with 3 plur. suf.) Eccl. 3:18, חַנֻּבְּם Isa. 30:18 (חָנַם Ps. 102:14); לַחְמָם Isa. 17:14, though sometimes explained as the noun לֶחֶם with the suffix *their bread*, is the infinitive of חָמַם *to grow warm*; בְּשִׁשָּׁם Gen. 6:3 Eng. ver. *for that also*, as if compounded of the prep. בְּ, the abbreviated relative and שָׁם, is by the latest authorities regarded as the infinitive of שָׁגַג *in their erring*; חֻלּוֹ Job 29:3 has Hhirik before the suffix. 'The feminine termination יתּ is appended to the following infinitives, חָלוֹת Ps. 77:10, Job 19:17, שַׁמּוֹת Ezek. 36:3, וַשּׁוֹתִי Ps. 17:3. The imperative, which is always contracted, has mostly Hholem, סֹב, רוֹם and חֹם but sometimes Pattahh, גַּל Ps. 119:22 (elsewhere גֹּל), פְּצֵה Ps. 80:16. Fürst regards חַת as a contracted participle from חָתַת, analogous to the Ayin Vav form קָם.

3. The following uncontracted forms occur in the Kal future, יֶחֱנַנּוּ Am. 5:15, יִדּוֹר and יִדֹּד from נָדַד; in the Niphal, יִצָּבֵב Job 11:12; Hiphil, חַשְׁשָׁם Mic. 6:13, מִשְׁמָמִים Ezek. 3:15, וְהַחְתַּתִּי Jer. 49:37, and constantly in רָגַן and יָלַל; Hophal, יֻלַּד Job 20:8 from נָדַד. In a few instances the repetition of the same letter is avoided by the substitution of א for the second radical, יִמְאֲסוּ = יִמַּסּוּ Ps. 58:8 and perhaps also Job 7:5, מַמְאִיר = מַמְרִיר Ezek. 28:24, Lev. 13:51, 52, שַׁאֲסִיךְ = שֹׁסַיִךְ Jer. 30:16 K'thibh. Comp. in Syriac ܐܦܘ part. of ܥܦ. According to the Rabbins בְּזָוָא = בְּזוֹז Isa. 18:2, but see Alexander in loc.

§ 140. 1. Examples of different forms of the Kal future: (1) With Daghesh-forte in the first radical, יִתֹּם, יֹשֹּׁם, יִקֹּד, יִשֹּׁב, אֶלֹּת, יִלֹּה; or with *a* as the second vowel, יִגַּל, יִמַּל; יִקַּמּוּ. (2) With Tsere under the personal prefix, יֵחַם, יֵחַת, יֵמַר, יֵבֵל, תֵּקַל, יֵחַמּוּ, *ē* being once written by means of the vowel letter י, אֵיתַם. (3) With Kamets under the personal prefix, יָחֹן, יָרֹב, יָלֹז, יָצֹר, יָרֹק, יָרֹד, יָדֹץ, יָשֹׁח; this occurs once with fut. *a*, יַחַד Prov. 27:17. With Vav Conversive the accent is drawn

§ 140   REMARKS ON AYIN DOUBLED VERBS.   173

back to the simple penult syllable in this form of the future, and Hholem is consequently shortened, § 64. 1, וַיָּחָן, וַיָּחָם, וַיָּעָז, וַיָּמָר, וַיָּלֶן. There are a few examples of û in the future as in Ayin Vav verbs, יָרוּן Prov. 29 : 6, יָרִיעַ Isa. 42 : 4, Eccles. 12 : 6, תָּחֵם Ezek. 24 : 11 and perhaps יָגֹר Gen. 49 : 19, Hab. 3 : 16, יָשׁוּד Ps. 91 : 6, though Gesenius assumes the existence of גוּר and שׁוּד as distinct roots from גָּדַד and שָׁדַד.

2. The Niphal preterite and participle: (1) With Hhirik under the prefixed נ, נִגְרוֹת Job 20 : 28, נִחַל, נִחַר, נִחָת. (2) With Tsere under the prefix, נֵחַלְתִּי Jer. 22 : 23, נֶאֱרִים Mal. 3 : 9, נֵחַמִּים Isa. 57 : 5. (3) With Kamets under the prefix, נָסַב, נָגַל, נָחַר, נָבַר; sometimes the repetition of like vowels in successive syllables is avoided by exchanging a of the last syllable for Tsere, נָגֵל and נָקֵל, נָמֵס and נָמֵס, נָסֵבָּה Ezek. 26 : 2, or for Hholem as in Ayin Vav verbs, נָבוֹז Eccl. 12 : 6, נָבוֹז Am. 3 : 11, נָבוֹג Nah. 1 : 12, נָבֹל Isa. 34 : 4.

3. The Niphal future preserves the Tsere of perfect verbs in one example, תֵּחֵל Lev. 21 : 9, but mostly compresses it to Pattahh, יִחַד, יִגַּל, יִחַר, יִסַב, יִמַס, יָשֹׁם, אֶצָּה; like the preterite it sometimes has Hholem, תָּבוֹז Isa. 24 : 3, תָּבוֹק ibid. If the first radical is a guttural and incapable of receiving Daghesh, the preceding Hhirik is lengthened to Tsere, יֵחַר, יֵחַם, תֵּלִיץ, תֵּרֹשׁוּ, אֵחָל. The Kal and Niphal futures, it will be perceived, coincide in some of their forms; and as the signification of these species is not always clearly distinguishable in intransitive verbs, it is often a matter of doubt or of indifference to which a given form should be referred. Thus, יִגַּל, יִסַּב, יָשֹׁם are in the Niphal according to Gesenius, while Ewald makes them to be Kal, and Fürst the first two Niphal and the third Kal.

4. The Niphal infinitive absolute: הִבּוֹז Isa. 24 : 3, הִבּוֹק ibid., or with Tsere in the last syllable, הִשֵּׁם 2 Sam. 17 : 10. The infinitive construct: הִשֵּׁם Ps. 68 : 3, הֵחַל Ezek. 20 : 9, and once with Pattahh before a suffix, הֵחַלּוֹ Lev. 21 : 4. The imperative: הִגָּרוּ Isa. 52 : 11, הֵרֹמּוּ Num. 17 : 10.

5. In the Hiphil preterite the vowel of the last syllable is compressed to Tsere, הֵסֵב, הֵחֵל (in pause הֵפֵר, so הֵשִׁמּוּ, הֵחֵמּוּ), or even to Pattahh, הֵסַבּוּ, הֵחַק, הֵקַל, הֵחַל, הֵתַל, הֵסַר, הֵבַד, הֵחַל, הֵשַׁח, הֵחַלּוּ. Both infinitives have Tsere, thus the absolute: הָחֵל, הָחֵם, הָפֵר, הָפַח, הָחֵל; the construct: הָתֵם, הָסֵב, הָחֵל, (הָצֵל) הָצֵיר Zech. 11 : 10), הָחֵל, הָחֵם, in pause הָחֵם, חָבֵי, with a final guttural, הָרַע, חָרַב. The imperative: הָסֵב, הָחֵל, הָחֵל, הָשֵׁעַ; הָשִׁמּוּ Job 21 : 5 is a Hiphil and not a Hophal form as stated by Gesenius, the first vowel being Kamets and not Kamets Hhatuph. Futures with a short vowel before Daghesh-forte in the first radical: יָחֵל, יָגֵר, יַבֵּשׁ, יָגָל, יָחַבּוּ, יְמַגֵּר, יַסֵּב; with a long vowel, יָחֵל, יָחֵל and יָרֵב, חָקֵל יָזִיעַ (ê expressed by the vowel letter א, § 11. 1. a) Eccles. 12 : 5. When in this latter class of futures the accent is removed from the ultimate, whether by Vav Conversive or any other cause, Tsere is shortened to Seghol, וַיָּסֶךְ, וַיָּדַר, וַיָּפַר, וַיָּדַק, וַיָּגַל, תָּחֶל, and in one instance to Hhirik, וַתָּרֵץ Judg. 9 : 53 (וַתָּרִץ would be from רוּץ) before a guttural it becomes Pattahh, וַיָּרַע, יָחַד. יֵצַר. Participles: מֵסֵב, מֵפֵר, מֵחֵל, מֵצֵל Ezek. 31 : 3, בָּרַב Prov. 17 : 4. In a very

few instances the Hhirik of the perfect paradigm is retained in the last syllable of this species as in Ayin Vav verbs, מָלִיךְ Judg. 3:21, רָשִׁים Jer. 49:20, וַנָּשִׁים Num. 21:30.

6. Hophal preterites: הוּגָּל, הֻגְּדָה, הֻגְּדָה, הָמְלוּ; futures: יֻגַּשׁ, יֻגַּר, יוּלַד; participles: מוּפָז, מֻגָּד, or in some copies מֻגָּד 2 Sam. 23:6; infinitive with suffix, הֻשַּׁמָּה Lev. 26:34, with prep., בְּהֻשַּׁמָּה ver. 43.

§ 141. 1. Upon the addition of a vowel affix and the consequent insertion of Daghesh-forte in the last radical, the preceding vowel and the position of the accent continue unchanged, זַכּוּ, רַבּוּ, נָשַׁמָּה (distinguished from the fem. part. נָשַׁמָּה), יְתַלּוּ; if the last radical does not admit Daghesh-forte a preceding Pattahh sometimes remains short before ח, but it is lengthened to Kamets before other gutturals, וְרָעֵב, מָרָה (100. 2), חָבְּרוּ, שָׁחַח and שָׁחוּ. When the first radical is doubled, Daghesh is omitted from the last in the Kal fut. o, יְתַמּוּ, יָקֹדּוּ, יְתַמּוּ, and occasionally elsewhere יָבֹהוּ Hi. fut. הֻמַּבּוּ Ho. pret. Other cases are exceptional, whether of the shifting of the accent, רָבוּ Ps. 3:2, רַבִּי Ps. 55:22, קֹלּוֹ Jer. 4:13, and consequent shortening of the vowel, אֻגִּי Jer. 7:29 for אֻגִּי, רָעִי, רָעוּ for רֹעִי, רֹעוּ, עֲדָדָיו Jer. 49:28 (with the letter repeated instead of being simply doubled by Daghesh, so likewise in יְשָׁדְדֵם Jer. 5:6, חָנְנֵנִי Ps. 9:14), for שֹׁדוּ; the omission of Daghesh, נָבֹחַ 1 Sam. 14:36, תָּעֻזְנָה Prov. 7:13, חֻנְּצוּ Cant. 6:11, 7:13, יְתַקְּפוֹ Job 19:23, קַבָּה Num. 22:11, 17 (Kal imper. with ה, parag. for קַבָּה shortened by Makkeph from קָבָה-, so אָרָה- ora Num. 23:7), or in addition, the rejection of the vowel, רוּמוּ K. fut. Gen. 11:6 for רָאוּמוּ, נֵרְדָה Gen. 11:7 K. fut. for נֵרְדָה Isa. 19:3 Ni. pret. for נִבְקָה or נִבְקָה, נָסְבָה, Ezek. 41:7 Ni. fut. for נָסְבָה; נָזֹלּוּ Judg. 5:5 according to Gesenius for נָזֹלּוּ Ni. pret. of זָלַל to shake, according to others K. pret. of נָזַל to flow; וַתְּצֵלְנָה Ezek. 36:3 for נָצֵלְנָה (Ewald) from צָלַל to enter, or for וַתְּצֵלְנָה Ni. fut. of צָלַל to go up, Ezek. 7:24 Ni. pret. for נָחֲלוּ, נָחֲרוּ Cant. 1:6 Ni. pret. for נָחֲרוּ. Once instead of doubling the last radical ל is inserted, דַּלְיוּ Prov. 26:7 for דָּלּוּ, comp. דִּרְיוֹשׁ Ezr. 10:16 for דָּרוֹשׁ.

2. Upon the insertion of a vowel before affixes beginning with a consonant, the accent is shifted and the previous part of the word shortened if possible; thus, with o in the preterite, קָלוֹתִי, וַאֲרוּחִי (Kamets before ר which cannot be doubled), הָצַרְתִּי, הָדַרְקוֹת, נְמַלְתִּי, בְּגוּנוּ, סַמֹּתֶם (the vowel remaining long before ר), חָתֹחַתִּי (Pattahh instead of compound Sh'va on account of the following guttural, § 60. 3. c), הָחֱלוֹתִי, once with a, נְאֻנִי Mic. 2:4; with e in the future, תִּחְלֶאנָה, תִּצְלֶאנָה, תִּסְפְּרֶינָה. If the first radical be doubled, Daghesh is omitted from the last, and the customary vowel is in consequence not inserted, תִּשְׁלְנָה, תִּשְׁקְנָה; other cases are rare and exceptional, גְּנַבְתִּי, נְכָלְתֶם, תָּבוּנוּ, נָתַלְתִּי, הַסְּרִחָה which is first plur. pret. for תָּבוּ not third plur. for תָּבוּ (Ewald), § 54. 3; שַׂבּוּתִי Deut. 32:41, חַמּוֹתִי Isa. 44:16, דַּלּוֹתִי Ps. 116:6, have the accent upon the ultimate instead of the penult.

3. Before suffixes the accent is always shifted, and if possible the vowels shortened, הֲדָפַנִי, יְשָׁלוּ, יְסָבּוּךָ from יָשַׁבוּ, יְסָבַּהוּ, יְסָבַּהוּ from יְסָבֵנִי

§ 141.   REMARKS ON AYIN DOUBLED VERBS.   175

from הָרִים, הַהָרִים from הָהָר; in יָחֹנּוּ Gen. 43:29, Isa. 30:19, from יָחֹן, הַפְרְכָם Lev. 26:15 from הָפֵר, the original vowels have been not only abbreviated but rejected, and the requisite short vowel given to the first of the concurring consonants, § 61. 1. In a very few instances a form resembling that of Ayin Vav verbs is assumed, Daghesh being omitted from the last radical and the preceding vowel lengthened in consequence, חוּקִּי Prov. 8:29 for חֻקִּי ver. 27, הֲתִימְךָ Isa. 33:1 for הֲתִמְּךָ, הֲשִׁמוֹתִיהוּ Ezek. 14:8 for הֲשִׁמּוֹתִיהוּ, הַגִּילוּגָה Lam. 1:8 for הִלּוּצָה Hi. pret. of זָלַל, יְחִיתַן Hab. 2:17 for יְחִתֵּן Hi. fut. of חָתַת with 3 fem. plur. suf., אֲרִקֵם 2 Sam. 22:43 in a few editions for אֲדִקֵּם. Nun is once inserted before the suffix in place of doubling the radical, קָבְנוֹ Num. 23:13 for קָבוֹ.

§ 141. 1. Of the verbs which occur in Piel, Pual, or Hithpael, the following adopt the forms of perfect verbs, viz.:

אָרַר to curse.	רָבַב to cry.	קָנַן to make a nest.
בָּזַז to plunder.	כָּתַת to smite, break.	קָצַץ to cut off.
בָּרַר to purify.	לָבַב to take away the heart.	רָבַב to be many.
גָּשַׁשׁ to grope.		רָכַךְ to be tender.
זָקַק to refine.	לָקַק to lick.	שָׂדַד to harrow.
חָמַם to warm.	מָשַׁשׁ to feel, to grope.	שָׂרַר to rule.
חָצַץ to divide.	עָזַז to leap.	שָׁנַן to sharpen.
חָתַת to be broken.	פָּלַל to judge, to intercede.	תָּמַם to be perfect.
טָלַל to cover.		

2. The following, which are mostly suggestive of a short, quick, repeated motion, reduplicate the radical syllable, viz.:

חָרַר to burn.	מָהַהּ to linger.	שָׁעַע to sport, delight.
כָּרַר to dance.	סָבַב to excite.	שָׁקַק to run.
לָהַהּ to be mad.	צָפַף to chirp.	תָּלַל to mock.

3. The following insert Hholem after the first radical, viz.:

אָנַן to complain.	נָדַד to fly.	רָצַץ to break.
בָּלַל to mix.	נָסַס to lift up.	שָׁחַח to sink.
בָּקַק to empty.	סָפַף to occupy the threshold.	שָׁלַל to spoil.
גָּדַד to cut.		שָׁמֵם to be desolate or amazed.
גָּרַר to sweep away.	צָרַר to bind.	
דָּמַם to be still.	קָסַס to cut off.	תָּפַף to beat.
חָתַת to break loose	קָשַׁשׁ to gather.	

4. The following employ two forms, commonly in different senses, viz.:

גִּלְגֵּל and גּוֹלֵל to roll.   חָנַן to make gracious, הוֹנֵן to be gracious.
הָלַל to praise, הוֹלֵל to make mad.
חָלַל to profane, חוֹלֵל to wound.   מָלַל to speak, מוֹלֵל to mow.

סָבַב to change, סוֹבֵב to surround. קָלַל to curse, קִלְקֵל to whet.
עָנַן to gather clouds, כּוֹנֵן to prac- רָצַץ and רוֹצֵץ to crush.
tise sorcery. שָׁדַד and שׁוֹדֵד to treat with vio-
פּוֹרֵר to burst, פִּרְפֵּר to shake to pieces. lence.

5. The following use different forms in different species, viz.:

חֹקֵק Pi. to decree, Pu. חֻקַּק. רָנַן Pi. to shout, Hith. הִתְרוֹנֵן.*
מָדַד Pi. to measure, Hith. הִתְמֹדֵד. רָשַׁשׁ Pi. to break, Pu. רֻשַּׁשׁ.
מָרַר Pi. to make bitter, Hith. הִתְמַרְמֵר. שָׁנַן Pi. to inculcate, Hith. הִשְׁתּוֹנֵן
סָלַל Pi. to exalt, Hith. הִסְתּוֹלֵל. to pierce.
עָלַל Pi. to maltreat, Hith. הִתְעַלֵּל
and הִתְעוֹלֵל.

6. The following examples exhibit the effect of gutturals upon reduplicated forms: Preterite, שַׁעֲשַׁע Isa. 11:8; Infinitive, לְהִתְחָרֹה Prov.
26:21, הִתְמַהְמֵהַּ Ex. 12:39; Future, אֶשְׁתַּעֲשָׁע Ps. 119:47, יְשַׁעֲשָׁע Ps.
94:19; Imperative, הִשְׁתַּעֲשְׁעוּ Isa. 29:9; Participle, מְתַעְתֵּעַ Gen. 27:12,
מִתְלַהְלֵהַּ Prov. 26:18.

§ 142. 1. The Pual species adheres to the analogy of perfect verbs
with the exception of the preterites, נוֹדָד Nah. 3:17, כּוֹלַל Lam. 1:12, the
future תְּשֻׁעֲשָׁעוּ Isa. 66:12, and the participles, מְגוּלָלָה Isa. 9:4, מְחֹלָל
Isa. 53:5.

2. יְעֹרָרוּ Isa. 15:5 is for יְעֹרְרוּ Pi. fut. of עָרַר, § 57. 1. תִּתְבָּרַר 2 Sam.
22:7 is contracted for תִּתְבָּרָר Ps. 18:27, probably with the view of assimilating it in form to the preceding תִּתַּמָּם; in regard to תִּתַּפָּל in the
same verse, Nordheimer adopts the explanation of Alting that it is a similar contraction of the Hithpael of פָּלַל thou wilt show thyself a judge, but as
it answers to תִּתְפַּתָּל Ps. 18:27, the best authorities are almost unanimous
in supposing a transposition of the second radical with the first and its
union with ת of the prefix.

3. חָלַל and הָלַל. The prefixed ה remains in the Hiphil future of חָלַל,
e. g. הֶחֱלוּ, יְהָחֵלּוּ, יָהֵלּוּ and in the derivative nouns תְּחִלִּים, תַּחֲלוּאוֹת,
whence these forms are in the lexicons referred to the secondary root יָחַל.

PE YODH (פּ״י) VERBS.

§ 143. In quiescent verbs one of the original radicals is
א, ו or י, which in certain forms is converted into or ex-
changed for a vowel. As א preserves its consonantal character when occupying the second place in the root, and also

---

* מְתִרוֹנֵן Ps. 78:65 is not from רוּן (Gesenius) but from רָנַן, see
Alexander in loc.

§ 144 PE YODH VERBS. 177

(with the exception of the Pe Aleph future, § 110. 3, and a few occasional forms, § 111. 2) when it stands in the first place, verbs having this letter as a first or second radical belong to the guttural class; those only in which it is the third radical (Lamedh Aleph) are properly reckoned quiescent. On the other hand, if the first, second, or third radical be either Yodh or Vav, the verb is classed as quiescent. All verbs into which either ו or י enter as a first radical are promiscuously called Pe Yodh, as the modes of inflection arising from these two letters have been blended, and Yodh in either case appears in the Kal preterite from which roots are ordinarily named, § 83. *a*. In the second radical the Vav forms (Ayin Vav) preponderate greatly over those with Yodh (Ayin Yodh). In the third radical the Yodh forms have almost entirely superseded those with Vav, though the current denomination of the verbs is derived from neither of these letters but from He (Lamedh He), which is used to express the final vowel of the root in the Kal preterite after the proper radical has been rejected.

a. Verbs whose third radical is the consonant ה belong to the guttural class, e. g. גָּבַהּ, תָּמַהּ, and are quite distinct from the quiescent verbs לה in which ה always represents a vowel, e. g. פָּנָה, גָּלָה.

§ 144. 1. In Pe Yodh verbs the first radical is mostly Yodh at the beginning, § 56. 2, and Vav at the close of a syllable. It is accordingly Yodh in the Kal, Piel, and Pual species, and commonly in the Hithpael, יָשַׁב, יֵשֵׁב, יֻשַּׁב, הִתְיַשֵּׁב. It is Vav in the Niphal and commonly in the Hiphil and Hophal species, הוּשַׁב, הוֹשִׁיב, נוֹשַׁב.

2. In the Kal future, if Yodh be retained, it will quiesce in and prolong the previous Hhirik, and the second radical will take Pattahh, e. g. יִירַשׁ; if the first radical be rejected the previous Hhirik is commonly lengthened to Tsere, יֵקַר, the Pattahh of the second syllable being sometimes changed to Tsere to correspond with it, § 63. 2. *c*, e. g. יֵשֵׁב; in a few instances Hhirik is preserved by giving Daghesh-forte to the

12

second radical as in Pe Nun verbs, the following vowel being either Pattahh or Hholem, יִצֹּק, יִצַּר.

3. Those verbs which reject Yodh in the Kal future, reject it likewise in the imperative and infinitive construct, where it would be accompanied by Sh'va at the beginning of a syllable, § 53. 2. *a*, the infinitive being prolonged as in Pe Nun verbs by the feminine termination, שֶׁבֶת, שָׁבַת.

§ 145. 1. In the Niphal preterite and participle Vav quiesces in its homogeneous vowel Hholem, נוֹשָׁב, נוֹשַׁב; in the infinitive, future, and imperative, where it is doubled by Daghesh-forte, it retains its consonantal character, הִוָּשֵׁב, יִוָּשֵׁב.

2. In the Hiphil Vav quiesces in Hholem, הוֹשִׁיב, יוֹשִׁיב; a few verbs have Yodh quiescing in Tsere, הֵיטִיב, וַיֵּטִיב; more rarely still, the first radical is dropped and the preceding short vowel is preserved, as in Pe Nun verbs, by doubling the second radical, יַצִּיע, הִצִּיג.

3. In the Hophal Vav quiesces in Shurek, הוּשַׁב, יוּשַׁב; occasionally the short vowel is preserved and Daghesh-forte inserted in the second radical, יֻצַּג.

<small>*a*. The Hholem or Tsere of the Hiphil arises from the combination of *a*, the primary vowel of the first syllable in this species, § 82. 5. *b*. (3), with *u* or *i*, into which the letters ו and י are readily softened, § 57. 2. (5). The Hholem of the Niphal is to be similarly explained: the Hhirik of this species, which has arisen from Sh'va and cannot combine with Vav, is exchanged for the simplest of the vowels *a* (comp. נְפֹל, נְקוֹם), and the union of this with ו forms ô. The Hophal retains the passive vowel *u*, which is occasionally found in perfect verbs, § 95. *a*.</small>

§ 146. The inflections of Pe Yodh verbs may be represented by those of יָשַׁב *to sit* or *dwell*. The Piel, Pual, and Hithpael are omitted from the paradigm, as they do not differ from perfect verbs. The alternate form of the Kal future is shown by the example of יָבֵשׁ *to be dry*.

Paradigm of Pe Yodh Verbs.

	KAL.	NIPHAL.	HIPHIL.	HOPHAL.	KAL.
Pret. 3 m.	יָשַׁב	נוֹשַׁב	הוֹשִׁיב	הוּשַׁב	יָבֵשׁ
3 f.	יָשְׁבָה	נוֹשְׁבָה	הוֹשִׁיבָה	הוּשְׁבָה	יָבְשָׁה
2 m.	יָשַׁבְתָּ	נוֹשַׁבְתָּ	הוֹשַׁבְתָּ	הוּשַׁבְתָּ	יָבַשְׁתָּ
2 f.	יָשַׁבְתְּ	נוֹשַׁבְתְּ	הוֹשַׁבְתְּ	הוּשַׁבְתְּ	יָבַשְׁתְּ
1 c.	יָשַׁבְתִּי	נוֹשַׁבְתִּי	הוֹשַׁבְתִּי	הוּשַׁבְתִּי	יָבַשְׁתִּי
Plur. 3 c.	יָשְׁבוּ	נוֹשְׁבוּ	הוֹשִׁיבוּ	הוּשְׁבוּ	יָבְשׁוּ
2 m.	יְשַׁבְתֶּם	נוֹשַׁבְתֶּם	הוֹשַׁבְתֶּם	הוּשַׁבְתֶּם	יְבַשְׁתֶּם
2 f.	יְשַׁבְתֶּן	נוֹשַׁבְתֶּן	הוֹשַׁבְתֶּן	הוּשַׁבְתֶּן	יְבַשְׁתֶּן
1 c.	יָשַׁבְנוּ	נוֹשַׁבְנוּ	הוֹשַׁבְנוּ	הוּשַׁבְנוּ	יָבַשְׁנוּ
Infin. Absol.	יָשׁוֹב		הוֹשֵׁב		יָבוֹשׁ
Constr.	שֶׁבֶת	הִוָּשֵׁב	הוֹשִׁיב	הוּשַׁב	יְבֹשׁ
Fut. 3 m.	יֵשֵׁב	יִוָּשֵׁב	יוֹשִׁיב	יוּשַׁב	יִיבַשׁ
3 f.	תֵּשֵׁב	תִּוָּשֵׁב	תּוֹשִׁיב	תּוּשַׁב	תִּיבַשׁ
2 m.	תֵּשֵׁב	תִּוָּשֵׁב	תּוֹשִׁיב	תּוּשַׁב	תִּיבַשׁ
2 f.	תֵּשְׁבִי	תִּוָּשְׁבִי	תּוֹשִׁיבִי	תּוּשְׁבִי	תִּיבְשִׁי
1 c.	אֵשֵׁב	אִוָּשֵׁב	אוֹשִׁיב	אוּשַׁב	אִיבַשׁ
Plur. 3 m.	יֵשְׁבוּ	יִוָּשְׁבוּ	יוֹשִׁיבוּ	יוּשְׁבוּ	יִיבְשׁוּ
3 f.	תֵּשַׁבְנָה	תִּוָּשַׁבְנָה	תּוֹשֵׁבְנָה	תּוּשַׁבְנָה	תִּיבַשְׁנָה
2 m.	תֵּשְׁבוּ	תִּוָּשְׁבוּ	תּוֹשִׁיבוּ	תּוּשְׁבוּ	תִּיבְשׁוּ
2 f.	תֵּשַׁבְנָה	תִּוָּשַׁבְנָה	תּוֹשֵׁבְנָה	תּוּשַׁבְנָה	תִּיבַשְׁנָה
1 c.	נֵשֵׁב	נִוָּשֵׁב	נוֹשִׁיב	נוּשַׁב	נִיבַשׁ
Imper. 2 m.	שֵׁב	הִוָּשֵׁב	הוֹשֵׁב		יְבַשׁ
2 f.	שְׁבִי	הִוָּשְׁבִי	הוֹשִׁיבִי	wanting	יְבָשִׁי
Plur. 2 m.	שְׁבוּ	הִוָּשְׁבוּ	הוֹשִׁיבוּ		יְבָשׁוּ
2 f.	שֵׁבְנָה	הִוָּשַׁבְנָה	הוֹשֵׁבְנָה		יְבַשְׁנָה
Part. Act.	יֹשֵׁב		מוֹשִׁיב		יָבֵשׁ
Pass.	יָשׁוּב	נוֹשָׁב		מוּשָׁב	יָבוּשׁ

Remarks on Pe Yodh Verbs.

§147. 1. The following verbs retain Yodh in the Kal future, viz.:

יָבֵשׁ to be dry.	יָסַךְ to be poured.	יָרֵא to fear.
יָגַע to toil.	יָעַד to appoint.	יָרָה to cast.
יָחַר to delay.	יָעַף to be weary.	יָרַשׁ to possess.
יָנָה to oppress.	יָעַץ to counsel.	יָשַׂם to put.
יָנַק to suck.	יָפָה to be beautiful.	יָשֵׁן to sleep.

The concurrence of Yodhs in the third person of the future is sometimes prevented by omitting the quiescent יֵבֹשׁ, יֵרְאוּ, יֵשְׁנוּ, the long vowel receiving Methegh before vocal Sh'va, and thus distinguishing the last two words from the Lamedh He forms, יִרְאוּ from רָאָה and יִשְׁנוּ from שָׁנָה, § 45. 2.

2. The following have Tsere under the preformative; those in which the second vowel is likewise Tsere are distinguished by an asterisk:

יָדַע to know.	* יָלַד to bear.	יָקַע to be dislocated.
יָחַד to be joined.	* יָצָא to go out.	* יָרַד to go down.
יָחַם to conceive.	יָצַר to be straitened.	* יָשַׁב to sit, dwell.

The second syllable has Pattahh in תֵּלַד Jer. 13:17, Lam. 3:48, and in the feminine plurals, תֵּלַדְנָה, תֵּרַדְנָה; תֵּצֶאנָה has Seghol after the analogy of Lamedh Aleph verbs; תִּשְׁבֻּנֶה (with the vowel-letter י for ē) occurs only in the K'thibh, Ezek. 35:9, and of course has not its proper vowels. In יִירְדוּ Ps. 138:6 the radical Yodh remains and has attracted to itself the Tsere of the preformative. Comp. § 60. 3. c.

3. The following insert Daghesh-forte in the second radical, viz.: יָסַר to chastise, instruct, יָצַת to burn. In תִּירְהוּ Isa. 44:8 short Hhirik remains before a letter with Sh'va; יִרְבֵּנִי Job 16:11 is explained by some as a Kal future, by others as a Piel preterite.

4. The following have more than one form: יָטַב to be good fut. יֵיטַב, once תֵּיטְבִי Nah. 3:8; יָצַק to pour, יִצֹּק, once וַיִּצֶק 1 Kin. 22:35; יָצַר to form, יִצֹּר and וַיִּצֶר; יָקַד to burn, יֵקַד Isa. 10:16, and תִּיקַד Deut. 32:22; יָקַץ to awake, יִיקַץ once יֶקַץ 1 Kin. 3:15; יָקַר to be precious, יִיקַר and יֵקַר, or with a vowel letter for ē, וַיִּיקַר; יָשַׁם to be desolate, תֵּשַׁם once תִּישַׁמְנָה Ezek. 6:6; יָשַׁר to be right, יִישַׁר, once יְשַׁרְנָה (3 fem. plur., § 88) 1 Sam. 6:12. Some copies have יִגְעוּ Isa. 40:30 for יִיגָעוּ.

5. In futures having Tsere under the preformative, the accent is shifted to the penult after Vav Conversive in the persons liable to such a change, viz.: 3 sing., 2 masc. sing., and 1 plur., Tsere in the ultimate being in consequence shortened to Seghol, וַיֵּרֶד, וַיֵּלֶד. Pattahh in the ultimate becomes Seghol in וַיֵּצֶר, וַיִּיצֶר (with a postpositive accent) Gen. 2:7, 19, וַיִּישֶׁם Gen. 50:26; but וַיֵּשֶׁב, וַיִּירַשׁ, וַיִּישַׁן, וַיִּיקַץ, וַיִּירַשׁ, only once before a

§ 148–150   REMARKS ON PE YODH VERBS.   181

monosyllable, § 35. 1, וַיִּקַ֑ץ Gen. 9:24. The accent remains on the ultimate in the Lamedh Aleph form וַיֵּצֵא, unless the following word begins with an accented syllable, e. g. וַיֵּ֥צֵא Gen. 4:16, 8:18. The pause restores the accent in all these cases to its original position, וַיֵּ֔שֶׁב Ruth 4:1, וַתֵּ֖חַד Ps. 139:1, וַיֵּ֑רֶד Ps. 18:10, § 35. 2.

§ 148. 1. Kal construct infinitives with Yodh: יְלֹד and with a feminine ending רִבְצַת, לֶדֶת, יְסֹד with suf. יְסָדִי, once with prep. לִיסֹד 2 Chron. 31:7, Daghesh conservative after ז, § 14. a; יְרְאַת, § 87, once יְרֹא Josh. 22:25 and with prep. לְרֹא 1 Sam. 18:29 from יְרָא; יְרוֹת once יְרוֹא 2 Chron. 26:15 from יָשׁוֹן, יָרֹה.

2. Infinitives without Yodh: דֵּעָה (with suf. דַּעְתִּי), דֵּעָה Ex. 2:4, and without the feminine termination דֵּעַ (with suf. לְדְתִּי) and לֵדָה, once עֵת 1 Sam. 4:19, § 54. 2, צֵאת (with suf. צֵאתִי), צֵעָה (with suf. דָּרָה), רָדָה (with suf. רִדְתִּי) once רָדָה Gen. 46:3, רֶשֶׁת (with suf. שִׁבְתָּם), שֶׁבֶת (with suf. שִׁבְתִּי) once שְׁבָתִי Ps. 23:6). Yodh is perhaps dropped from the absolute infinitive שׁוֹב Jer. 42:10, which is usually explained to be for יְשׁוֹב; it may, however, be derived from the Ayin Vav verb שׁוּב.

3. Imperatives with Yodh: יְרָה, יְרָא, יְרָד. Without Yodh: דַּע (with ה parag. דְּעָה Prov. 24:14), הַב (with ה parag. הָבָה; for הֲבוּ Hos. 4:18, see § 92. a). צֵא (צֵאָה, fem. plur. צְאֶינָה Cant. 3:11), שֵׁב (שְׁבָה, שֵׁבָה). With both forms: צֵק and רֵק (רְקוּ), רֵד (רְדָה), twice יְרַד Judg. 5:13, רֵשׁ and רְשָׁה.

§ 149. 1. The Niphal of יָרַד has û instead of ô, נוּגֵּי Zeph. 3:18, נוֹגוֹת Lam. 1:4; נוֹלְדוּ 1 Chron. 3:5, 20:8 has û followed by Daghesh. וַיִּצֶת, which according to Gesenius is from יָצַת has î; Ewald assumes the root to be צָתַת, and refers to it likewise the Kal future and the Hiphil ascribed to יָצַת, § 147. 3. and § 150. 4. In that case the Daghesh in יִצַּתָּה Isa. 33:12, Jer. 51:58, will not require the explanation suggested in § 24. c, but the K'thibh הוֹצִיחִית 2 Sam. 14:30 will be unexplained. נוֹקֵשׁ Ps. 9:17 is not the Niphal preterite or participle of יָקֹשׁ, but the Kal participle of נָקַשׁ.

2. Yodh appears in the Niphal future of two verbs instead of Vav, וַיִּיָּחֶל Gen. 8:12, 1 Sam. 13:8 K'ri, יִיָּרֶה Ex. 19:13. In the first person singular א always has Hhirik, אִוָּדַע, אִוָּגֵל, אִוָּכֵר, אִוָּרֵשׁ, אִוָּשֵׁעַ, אִוָּתֵר.

§ 150. 1. In the Hiphil the following verbs have Yodh preceded by Tsere, viz.: יָטַב to be good, יָלַל to howl, יָמַן to go to the right, יָמַר to change, יָנַק to suck. Yodh is likewise found in הֵימִשְׁנִי Judg. 16:26 K'thibh, and in the following instances in which the prefix has Pattahh as in perfect verbs, הֵיסִירָם Hos. 7:12, הֵישִׁירוּ Prov. 4:25, הַיְשֵׁר Ps. 5:9 K'ri (K'thibh הוֹשֵׁר), הַיְצֵא Gen. 8:17 K'ri (K'thibh הוֹצֵא), מֵימִינִים 1 Chron. 12:2.

2. In יְרִיבֻ Job 24:21 (elsewhere וְיֵיטִיב) and יְלִיל (once אֲילִילַת Mic. 1:8), the radical Yodh attracts to itself the vowel of the preformative, comp. § 147. 2. He remains after the preformative in יְהֵילִילוּ Isa. 52:5, יְהוֹדֶה Neh. 11:17, Ps. 28:7, יְהוֹשִׁיעַ 1 Sam. 17:47, Ps. 116:6. Both Yodh and Vav, quiescing in their appropriate vowels, are liable to omission, הַבְרִשׁוּ, הֹלִיד, הֵנִיקָה, הֵמִין, and once the vowel Tsere is dropped before a suffix, תְּנִיקָהוּ Ex. 2:9 for תֵּינִיקֵהוּ.

3. Vav conversive draws the accent back to the penultimate Tsere or Hholem of the Hiphil future in the persons liable to be affected by it, § 147. 5, and shortens the final vowel, וַיֹּשֶׁב, וַיָּרֶם, וַיֵּינַק, וַיּוֹשַׁב; but with a pause accent : וַיֹּתַר Ruth 2:14.

4. The following verbs insert Daghesh in the second radical in the Hiphil, viz.: יָצַג to set, place, יָצַע to spread, יָצַק to pour, except : מוּצֶקֶת 2 Kin. 4:5 K'ri (K'thibh מִיצֶקֶת), יָצַת to burn, except הוּצְּתָה 2 Sam. 14:30 K'thibh.

5. In the Hophal a few examples occur of ŭ followed by Daghesh, יֻגַּד Ex. 10:24, יֻצַּע Isa. 14:11, Esth. 4:3, מוּסָּד Isa. 28:16, מֻצָּק Job 11:15; and a few of Hholem, הוֹלָד Lev. 4:23, 28, יוֹלָא Prov. 11:25 for יוֹרֶא from יָרָה. The construct infinitive : הוּסַד Ezr. 3:11, and with the feminine termination הוּלֶּדֶת Ezek. 16:4, חֻלֶּדֶת Gen. 40:20, Ezek. 16:5.

§ 150. 1. In the Kal preterite Yodh is once dropped, לֵד Judg. 19:11 for יָלַד. Hhirik occurs with the second radical of יָלַד and יָרַשׁ in the first and second persons singular with suffixes, and in the second person plural, which is perhaps due to the assimilating power of the antecedent Yodh, e. g. יְרִשְׁתֶּם, יְרִשְׁתָּהּ, וִילִדְתַּנִי.

2. In the Piel future the prefix Yodh of the third person is contracted with the radical after Vav conversive, וַיְיַבְּשֵׂהוּ Nah. 1:4 for וַיְיַבְּשׁוֹ. וַיִּלַח Lam. 3:33, וַיַּלוּ Lam. 3:53, וַיְשַׁלֵּם 2 Chron. 32:30 K'ri (K'thibh וַיִּשְׁרָם).

3. Three verbs have Vav in the Hithpael, הִתְיַלֵּד, הִתְיַצֵּב, הִתְוַדָּה; ת is assimilated to the following ו and contracted with it in נִוַּסְּרוּ Ezek. 23:48 for נִתְוַסְּרוּ a peculiar Niphal formed on the basis of a Hithpael, § 83. c. (2). In תֵּרָצַב Ex. 2:4 for תִּתְיַצֵּב Yodh is rejected and its vowel given to the preceding letter, § 53. 3. b.

§ 151. 1. הָלַךְ and יָלַךְ. הָלַךְ to go in the Hiphil and for the most part in the infinitive construct, future and imperative Kal follows the analogy of Pe Yodh verbs, as though the root were יָלַךְ. Thus, Kal inf. const. לֶכֶת (לְבַת, with suf. לֶכְתִּי) rarely הֲלֹךְ; fut. יֵלֵךְ (once with the vowel letter י for ē, אֵילְכָה Mic. 1:8, fem. pl. תֵּלַכְנָה), occasionally in poetry יַהֲלֹךְ (3 fem. sing. תֶּהֱלָךְ); imper. לֵךְ (with ה parag. לְכָה, or without the vowel letter לְךְ, fem. pl. לֵכְנָה and לֵכֶן) once הֲלִכוּ Jer. 51:50. Hiphil: הוֹלִיךְ once in the imper. הֵילִיכִי Ex. 2:9, and once in the participle מַהֲלִכִים Zech. 3:7 for מַהְלִיכִים, § 94. e.

2. אָסַף to gather and יָסַף to add are liable to be confounded in certain forms. In the Hiphil future of יָסַף, ō is twice represented by the vowel letter א, וַיֹּאסֶף 1 Sam. 18:29, תֹּאסְפוּן Ex. 5:7; אָסַף drops its א in the Kal future, when it follows the Pe Aleph inflection, § 110. 3, which it does only in the following instances, וַיֹּסֶף 2 Sam. 6:1, אֹסְפָה Ps. 104:29, אָסְפָה Mic. 4:6, אֹסְפֵךְ 1 Sam. 15:6, where the Hhirik, being abbreviated from Tsere, is short, notwithstanding the Methegh in the intermediate syllable, § 45. 2. a. The apoc. Hiph. fut. of יָסַף when joined with the negative particle אַל is accented on the penult, אַל־תּוֹסֶף Deut. 3:26, and in one instance the vowel of the ultimate is dropped entirely, אַל־תּוֹסְףְּ Prov. 30:6.

3. הוֹשַׁבְתִּים Zech. 10:6 is probably, as explained by Gesenius and Hengstenberg, for הוֹשַׁבְתִּים from יָשַׁב to dwell, though Ewald derives it from שׁוּב to return, as if for הֲשִׁיבוֹתִים, and Kimchi supposes it to be a combination of both words suggesting the sense of both, in which he is followed by the English translators, *I will bring them again to place them.*

הֹבִאישׁ Isa. 30:5 "is regarded by Gesenius as an incorrect orthography for הוֹבִישׁ; but Maurer and Knobel read it הִבְאִישׁ and assume a root בָּאַשׁ synonymous with בּוּשׁ". Alexander in loc.

חוֹמִירָה Ps. 16:5, see §90.

Ayin Vav (עו) and Ayin Yodh (עי) Verbs.

§152. Yodh and Vav, as the second radical of verbs, have the following peculiarities, viz:

1. They may be converted into their homogeneous vowels *i* and *u*.

2. They may be rejected when accompanied by a heterogeneous vowel, which is characteristic of the form. Yodh forms are confined to the Kal of a few verbs; in the other species Vav forms are universal.

a. Yodh is never found as a quiescent middle radical in any species but Kal: it enters as a consonant into the Piel of two verbs, and the Hithpael of two, §161. 1, the Niphal of הָיָה *to be*, and the Hiphil of חָיָה *to live.*

§153. 1. In the Kal preterite and active participle and in the Hiphil and Hophal species, the quiescent is rejected and its vowel given to the preceding radical. Thus,

Kal preterite: קָם for קָוַם where *ā*, which arises from blending *ă* with the pretonic Kamets, §62. 1, is in partial compensation for the contraction, מֵת for מָוֵת, בּשׁ for בּוּשׁ, רָב for רִיב. For an exceptional formation, see §158. 1.

Active participle: קָם for קָוֵם, מֵת for מָוֵת, בּשׁ for בּוּשׁ, רָב for רִיב, the ordinary participial form being superseded by that of another verbal derivative, as is the case in some perfect verbs of a neuter signification, §90.

Hiphil and Hophal: הָקִים for הִקְוִים, יָקִים for יַקְוִים, הוּקַם for הָקַם, the short vowel of the prefix being prolonged in a simple syllable, § 59.

2. In the Kal construct infinitive, future, imperative and passive participle, the quiescent is softened into its homogeneous vowel, קִים, רִיב; in the future the preformative commonly takes the simplest of the long vowels $\bar{a}$, יָקִים, יָרִיב, comp. יָסֹב.

3. In the Kal absolute infinitive and in the Niphal species a similar softening of ו occurs, which, with the accompanying or preceding a, forms $\bar{o}$, § 57. 2. (5), קוֹם (kōm= kaūm) for קָוֹם; נָקוֹם for נָקַם, the prefix usually taking the simplest of the long vowels $\bar{a}$; יָקוֹם for יָקַם.

4. In the first and second persons of the Niphal and Hiphil preterites $\bar{o}$ (וֹ) is inserted before the affixed termination in order to preserve the long vowel of the root from the compression incident to standing before two consonants, § 61. 4; in the feminine plurals of the Kal future $\breve{e}$ (יְ,) is sometimes inserted for a similar reason, this prolongation of the word being attended by a shifting of the accent and a consequent rejection of the pretonic vowel of the first syllable, תְּקוּמֶינָה, הֲקִימוֹת, נְקוֹמוֹתָם. In the Niphal preterite, when the inserted וֹ receives the accent, the preceding ו is for euphony changed to י, e. g. נְקִימוֹתִי.

5. In the Kal and Hiphil species the apocopated future takes the diphthongal vowels $\bar{o}$ and $\bar{e}$ in distinction from the ordinary future, which has the pure vowels $\bar{u}$ and $\bar{\imath}$, § 65. 2. b, thus יָשֹׁב, יָשֵׁב. With Vav Conversive the accent is drawn back to the simple penult, and the vowel of the last syllable is shortened, וַיָּשָׁב, וַיֵּשֶׁב.

§ 154. 1. In the Piel, Pual, and Hithpael, the form of perfect verbs is rarely adopted, the second radical appearing as ו, e. g. עַוֵּד, or as י, e. g. קַיֵּם.

2. Commonly the third radical is reduplicated instead

of the second, which then quiesces in Hholem, Pi. קוֹיֵם,
Pu. קוֹיָם, Hith. הִתְקוֹיֵם.

a. In the Pual *o* is the passive vowel here adopted in preference to *u*: in the Piel and Hithpael it arises from the combination of *u*, to which ו is softened, with the antecedent *a*, קוֹיֵם for קֻוְיֵם; §82. 5. *b* (3).

3. Sometimes the quiescent letter is omitted from the root, and the resulting biliteral is reduplicated, Pi. כִּלְכֵּל, Pu. כָּלְכַּל.

a. The two forms of the intensive species, which depart from the regular paradigm, precisely resemble in appearance those of Ayin doubled verbs, though constructed upon a different principle, as already explained.

§ 155. The inflections of Ayin Vav verbs are shown in those of קוּם *to stand* or *rise*, in the following paradigm; the divergent forms of Ayin Yodh verbs in the Kal species are exhibited by רִיב *to contend*.

a. Ayin Vav and Ayin Yodh verbs are named not from the Kal preterite, in which the quiescent is rejected, but from the construct infinitive, the simplest form in which all the radicals appear.
b. No Hophal forms occur in those persons in which the inflective terminations begin with a consonant. The same is true of the Ayin Yodh imperative.

Paradigm of Ayin Vav

	KAL.	NIPHAL.	PIEL.	PUAL.
Pret. 3 m.	קָם	נָקוֹם	קוֹבֵם	קוֹבַם
3 f.	קָבָה	נָקוֹבָה	קוֹבְמָה	קוֹבְמָה
2 m.	קַבְתָּ	נְקוּמֹתָ	קוֹבַמְתָּ	קוֹבַמְתָּ
2 f.	קַבְתְּ	נְקוּמוֹת	קוֹבַמְתְּ	קוֹבַמְתְּ
1 c.	קַבְתִּי	נְקוּמֹתִי	קוֹבַמְתִּי	קוֹבַמְתִּי
Plur. 3 c.	קָבוּ	נָקוֹבוּ	קוֹבְמוּ	קוֹבְמוּ
2 m.	קַבְתֶּם	נְקוֹבֹתֶם	קוֹבַמְתֶּם	קוֹבַמְתֶּם
2 f.	קַבְתֶּן	נְקוֹבֹתֶן	קוֹבַמְתֶּן	קוֹבַמְתֶּן
1 c.	קַבְנוּ	נְקוּבוֹנוּ	קוֹבַמְנוּ	קוֹבַמְנוּ
Infin. Absol.	קוֹם	הָקוֹם		
Constr.	קוּם	הָקוֹם	קוֹבֵם	
Fut. 3 m.	יָקוּם	יִקּוֹם	יְקוֹבֵם	יְקוֹבַם
3 f.	תָּקוּם	תִּקּוֹם	תְּקוֹבֵם	תְּקוֹבַם
2 m	תָּקוּם	תִּקּוֹם	תְּקוֹבֵם	תְּקוֹבַם
2 f.	תָּקוּמִי	תִּקּוֹמִי	תְּקוֹמְמִי	תְּקוֹמְמִי
1 c.	אָקוּם	אִקּוֹם	אֲקוֹבֵם	אֲקוֹבַם
Plur. 3 m.	יָקוּבוּ	יִקּוֹבוּ	יְקוֹבְמוּ	יְקוֹבְמוּ
3 f.	תְּקוּמֶינָה	תִּקּוֹרַדְנָה	תְּקוֹבֵמְנָה	תְּקוֹבַמְנָה
2 m.	תָּקוּבוּ	תִּקּוֹבוּ	תְּקוֹבְמוּ	תְּקוֹבְמוּ
2 f.	תְּקוּמֶינָה	תִּקּוֹרַדְנָה	תְּקוֹבֵמְנָה	תְּקוֹבַמְנָה
1 c.	נָקוּם	נִקּוֹם	נְקוֹבֵם	נְקוֹבַם
Imper. 2 m.	קוּם	הָקּוֹם	קוֹבֵם	wanting
2 f.	קוּבִי	הִקּוֹבִי	קוֹמְמִי	
Plur. 2 m.	קוּבוּ	הִקּוֹבוּ	קוֹבְמוּ	
2 f.	קֹבְנָה	הִקּוֹבְנָה	קוֹבֵמְנָה	
Part. Act.	קָם		מְקוֹבֵם	
Pass.	קוּם	נָקוֹם		מְקוֹבָּם

AND AYIN YODH VERBS.

HIPHIL.	HOPHAL.	HITHPAEL.	KAL.	
הֵקִים	הוּקַם	הִתְקוֹמֵם	רַב	
הֵקִימָה	הוּקְמָה	הִתְקוֹמְמָה	רַבָּה	
הֲקִימוֹתָ	(הוּקַמְתָּ)	הִתְקוֹמַמְתָּ	רַבְתָּ	רִיבוֹת
הֲקִימוֹת	(הוּקַמְתְּ)	הִתְקוֹמַמְתְּ	רַבְתְּ	
הֲקִימוֹתִי	(הוּקַמְתִּי)	הִתְקוֹמַמְתִּי	רַבְתִּי	רִיבוֹתִי
הֵקִימוּ	הוּקְמוּ	הִתְקוֹמְמוּ	רַבּוּ	רִיבוּ
הֲקִימוֹתֶם	(הוּקַמְתֶּם)	הִתְקוֹמַמְתֶּם	רַבְּתֶם	
הֲקִימוֹתֶן	(הוּקַמְתֶּן)	הִתְקוֹמַמְתֶּן	רַבְּתֶן	
הֲקִימוֹנוּ	(הוּקַמְנוּ)	הִתְקוֹמַמְנוּ	רַבְנוּ	
הָקֵם			רוֹב	רִיב
הָקִים		הִתְקוֹמֵם	רָב	
יָקִים	יוּקַם	יִתְקוֹמֵם	יָרִיב	
תָּקִים	תּוּקַם	תִּתְקוֹמֵם	תָּרִיב	
תָּקִים	תּוּקַם	תִּתְקוֹמֵם	תָּרִיב	
תָּקִימִי	תּוּקְמִי	תִּתְקוֹמְמִי	תָּרִיבִי	
אָקִים	אוּקַם	אֶתְקוֹמֵם	אָרִיב	
יָקִימוּ	יוּקְמוּ	יִתְקוֹמְמוּ	יָרִיבוּ	
תְּקִימֶנָה	(תּוּקַמְנָה)	תִּתְקוֹמֵמְנָה	תָּרֹבְנָה	
תָּקִימוּ	תּוּקְמוּ	תִּתְקוֹמְמוּ	תָּרִיבוּ	
תְּקִימֶנָה	(תּוּקַמְנָה)	תִּתְקוֹמֵמְנָה	תָּרֹבְנָה	
נָקִים	נוּקַם	נִתְקוֹמֵם	נָרִיב	
הָקֵם		הִתְקוֹמֵם	רִיב	
הָקִימִי	wanting	הִתְקוֹמְמִי	רִיבִי	
הָקִימוּ		הִתְקוֹמְמוּ	רִיבוּ	
הָקֵמְנָה		הִתְקוֹמֵמְנָה	(רֹבְנָה)	
מֵקִים		מִתְקוֹמֵם	רָב	
	מוּקָם		רוֹב	

REMARKS ON AYIN VAV AND AYIN YODH VERBS.

§ 156. 1. Medial Yodh and Vav remain without quiescence or rejection in a few verbs, whose root contains another feeble consonant by contrast with which these letters acquire new strength. This is always the case in Lamedh He verbs, e. g. הָיָה, נָוָה; so likewise in the following guttural verbs and forms, גָּוַע *to expire*, יַחֲרִיוּ׃ Isa. 29:22, יִצְיָחוּ׃ Isa. 42:11, אָיַב *to be an enemy*, עוֹיֵל 1 Sam. 18:9 K'ri (K'thibh עָוֵל), כָּרָה Jer. 4:31, which are confined to the Kal species, and in רָוָה *to be airy or refreshing*, which is besides found in the Pual participle.

2. The Kal preterite has Pattahh in two instances as in Ayin Vav verbs, גָּז Zech. 4:10, שָׁם Isa. 44:18 but שָׂם Lev. 14:42. It has Tsere in מֵת *to die*, נֵר Isa. 17:11 but נָרוּ Jer. 50:3, and Hholem in אוֹר *to shine*, בּוֹשׁ *to be ashamed*, טוֹב *to be good*, § 82. 1. a, and in בָּא Jer. 27:18, elsewhere בָּאוּ, יָרוּ Isa. 1:6, Ps. 58:4, elsewhere יָרוּ. Hhirik once occurs instead of Pattahh in the second person plural, שַׁמְתֶּם Mal. 3:20. The following participles have Tsere, צֵר, מֵת, מֵץ, לֵץ, לֵצִים; the following have Hholem, בּוֹשִׁים, בּוֹשִׁים, קוֹמִים 2 Kin. 16:7 (comp. קוֹמְרִים Ex. 32:25 in the Samaritan copy), elsewhere קָמִים.

3. The vowel letter א is written for a, § 11. 1. a, once in the preterite, קָאַט Hos. 10:14, and occasionally in the participle, לָאט Judg. 4:21, רֵאמוֹת Prov. 24:7, רֵאשׁ 2 Sam. 12:1, 4, Prov. 10:4, 13:23, שַׁאֲנִים *despising* Ezek. 16:57, 28:24, 26, to be distinguished from שָׁטִים *rowing* Ezek. 27:8, 26. The consonant א is once introduced in place of the omitted ו, רָאֲמָה Zech. 14:10 for רָמָה; the ancient versions favour the assumption, that כַּאֲרִי Ps. 22:17 is in like manner for כָּרִים *piercing*, though the most recent and ablest expositors take it to be a preposition and noun *like the lion*. Alexander in loc.

4. The accent regularly remains upon the radical syllable before affixes consisting of a vowel or a simple syllable, though with occasional exceptions, e. g. קָאָה Lev. 18:28, רָבוּ Gen. 26:22, שָׂבוּ Gen. 40:15, תָּרוּ Num. 13:32. In a few instances it is shifted by Vav conversive preterite, § 100. 2, וְלָשׂוּ Obnd. ver. 16, וְסָפוּ Am. 3:15, וְנָחָה Isa. 11:2, וְרָוָה Isa. 7:19 but יָבֹאוּ ibid., וּבָאָה Zech. 5:4, וְלָן ibid., where the feminine ending is הָ֫ instead of הָ; so in the passive participle, זוּרָה Isa. 59:5 for זוּרָה.

§ 157. 1. Hholem is in a few instances found instead of Shurek in the construct infinitive, בּוֹא, בּוֹשׁ Judg. 3:25, מוֹט, נוֹחַ and גוֹחַ, נוֹס Isa. 7:2, elsewhere נוּס, עוּז Isa. 30:2, which is not from עָוַז שֹׁב Josh. 2:16, elsewhere שׁוּב, and with suf. רוֹמָם Ezek. 10:17, גּוֹחִי Ps. 71:6, which is not the participle from גָּוַח (Gesenius), גֹּחִי *my breaking forth*, i. e. the cause of it Ps. 22:10, see Alexander in loc.; Gesenius explains this form as a participle, but is obliged in consequence to assume a transitive sense which nowhere else belongs to the verb.

2. The following imperatives have Hholem, אוֹרִי Isa. 60:1, בֹּא, בּוֹשׁ,

§ 158. AYIN VAV AND AYIN YODH VERBS.

גְּחִי Mic. 4 : 10, הוֹשִׁי Mic. 4 : 13. With paragogic ה, קוּמָה or קֻמָה, שׁוּבָה or שֻׁבָה. Examples of the feminine plural, קֹמְנָה, שֹׁבְנָה.

3. The following futures have Hholem. יָבוֹא, יָדוֹן Gen. 6 : 3, elsewhere יָדִין, נָסוֹג Ps. 80 : 19, יָחוֹם and יָחוּם, יָבוֹשׁ where the Hhirik of the perfect paradigm is lengthened to Tsere under the preformative. Examples of the feminine plural : הְּבֹאֶינָה and תְּבֹאנָה, תְּבוּשֶׁינָה, תְּפוּצֶינָה and Zech. 1 : 17 תְּפוּצֶינָה (in some editions without Daghesh), תְּשׁוּבֶינָה and תְּשֹׁבְנָה, הְּבוּשֶׁנָה, תָּאֹרְנָה Ezek. 13 : 19. The accent is shifted and Kamets rejected from the preformative upon the addition of a suffix or paragogic Nun, the latter of which is particularly frequent in this class of verbs both in the Kal and Hiphil future, יְשׁוּגֶּנִי, אֶזְעָקָה, תְּעוּרְךָ, יָסֻבּוּ, תְּבוּאַתוּן, יְקוֹמְוּן, תְקוּמִי Ezek. 4 : 12, with Daghesh euphonic in the ב which is omitted in some copies. Apocopated future : יָלֵד, יָשֹׁב and יָרֵב-, יָגֹל, תָּקֹם, יָקֹם, יָקָם with the accent thrown back to the penult יָקָם. Future with Vav conversive : וַיָּדֶן (in pause וַיִּקַּח), וַיָּרֶשׁ (= וַיִּירַשׁ), וַיָּגֶל, וַיָּקֶם, וַיָּרֶץ, וַיָּצֻם, the last vowel is changed to Pattahh before a final guttural, וַיָּנַח, and sometimes before ר or after an initial guttural וַיָּנַר but וַיָּעַף he was weary, וַיַּחַם he flew, וַיֵּחַם ; the vowel of the preformative is likewise changed to Pattahh in יַחְשׁוּ Job 31 : 5, וַיָּרֶב 1 Sam. 14 : 32, וַיָּשַׂם 1 Sam. 15 : 19 but וַיָּשֶׂם 1 Sam. 25 : 14.

§ 158. 1. The verbs which exhibit peculiar Ayin Yodh forms in Kal, with unimportant exceptions, either do not occur in the Hiphil or retain the same signification in both these species. This has led some grammarians to entertain the opinion that these are not Kal but abbreviated Hiphil forms, while others suppose that the Hiphil in these verbs is a secondary formation, and has arisen from the Kal future having the form of the Hiphil. Only three examples occur of quiescent Yodh in the Kal preterite, רִיבוֹתִי Job 33 : 13 (כ'ר לָבָתִי Lam. 3 : 58), בִּינֹתִי Dan. 9 : 2 (כ'ר בָּתָה Ps. 139 : 2) דִּילוּם Jer. 16 : 16.

2. The following verbs have י in the Kal future and imperative, בִּין to understand, גִּיחַ (once גָּחִי Mic. 4 : 10) to break forth, גִּיל (once יָגֵל Prov. 23 : 24 K'thibh) to exult, דִּין (once יָדוֹן Gen. 6 : 3) to judge, לִין to lodge, רִיב to contend, שִׂים to muse, שִׂים (once יָשׂוּם Ex. 4 : 11) to put, שִׁית (once יְשִׁיתוּ Isa. 35 : 1) to rejoice, שִׁיר (once יָשׁוֹר Job 33 : 27) to sing, שִׁית to place ; חוּל or חִיל to twist, writhe, has both Yodh and Vav. To these are to be added גִּירוּ Jer. 4 : 3, Hos. 10 : 12, חוּשָׁי Ps. 71 : 12 K'thibh, K'ri חוּשָׁה as always elsewhere ; יָאִיץ to urge, יָצִיץ to flourish, לָרִיד to wander, are in the Hiphil according to Gesenius : but as the corresponding preterites are not Hiphil but Kal, and there are no other forms of the Kal future, they might with equal propriety be regarded as Kal futures of Ayin Yodh roots ; the second of them is so regarded by Ewald. Apocopated futures : יָקֶם, יָגֵל and לָגֶל, רָבָה, יָשֵׂם, יָשֵׁת, תָּקֶל, יָקֶם and תֵּלֶן : With Vav conversive : וַיָּגֶל, וָאָגֶל, וַיָּלֶן, וַיָּתֵן, וַתָּחֶל, וַיָּנַח, וַיָּשַׁר. With paragogic Nun and suffixes : יְשִׁימָם. הְּחִי־לוּן, יְגִילוּן. Feminine plural : תְּלִילַנָה.

3. The infinitives show a stronger disposition to adopt Vav forms. Yodh is only retained in the following absolute infinitives : בִּין Prov. 23 : 1, גִּיחַ and גֹּחַ, גִּיל Prov. 23 : 24 K'ri (גֹּל K'thibh), רִיב Jer. 50 : 34, else-

where רֵב. Construct infinitives: לִין, דִּין Gen. 24:23, elsewhere לוּן, לִיב once = רוּב Judg. 21:22 K'thibh, שִׂיחַ and שׂוּחַ, שִׂים Job 20:4, 2 Sam. 14:7 K'ri, elsewhere שׂוֹשׂ, שִׁיר 1 Sam. 18:6 K'ri (K'thibh שׁוּר), שִׁית, also with suf. הֲדִישׁוֹ Deut. 25:4, elsewhere הוּשׁ. In the difficult verse Hos. 7:4 מְבִיר has been variously explained, as the Kal infinitive preceded by the preposition בְּן or as the Hiphil participle. The only certain instance of a Kal passive participle of Ayin Yodh verbs is שׂוּפָה 2 Sam. 13:32 K'ri (K'thibh שִׂיבַת); some explain שִׂים Num. 24:21, Obad. ver. 4, as a passive participle, others as an infinitive.

4. Ayin Yodh verbs adopt the Vav forms in all the derivative species, e. g. נָזִיד, רוּשַׁת, הִתְבּוֹנֵן, נָבוֹן, רְבִילְחוּ, נְבִלֹּתִי; נָזִיד cooked, i. e. pottage, is the only instance of a Niphal participle with Yodh.

§ 159. 1. Examples of the Niphal preterite: נָבוֹג, נָבוֹץ, נָסוֹג; נָאוֹר, the accidental Hhirik of the perfect paradigm is preserved in נְמוֹל by means of Daghesh-forte in the first radical; in נָלוֹז it is lengthened to Tsere before the guttural; in : נֵעֹר Jer. 48:11 the radical ו is rejected, which gives it the appearance of an Ayin doubled verb. Inflected forms: נְפוֹצֹתֶם, (part. fem. נְבוֹכָה), נְבֹכֶּה, נָבֹגוּ, נְבֹוֹתָ, נְבֹלּוֹתָ, נְסוּגֹתִי, נְפוֹגֹתִי, נְקוֹלֹתָם.

2. Infinitive absolute: הִמּוֹל. Construct: הִמּוֹל, הִסּוֹחַ, with ה rejected after the preposition לֵאוֹר Job 33:30, § 91. b; once it has Shurek, הִדּוֹשׁ Isa. 25:10. Imperative, הִמֹּלוּ, הִלוֹן.

3. Future: יָלִין, יָמוּשׁ יִמּוֹל יָלוֹן Ps. 72:17 K'ri (K'thibh יִנִּין), יִלֵּשׁוּ, נָבֹרִים, נְסוֹגִים, נְפֹצִים, נָלוֹן, נָבוֹן. Participle: נָבוֹן, נָלוֹז, נֵאֹתוּ, נָאוֹר, נָלוֹז, נְמוֹלִים.

§ 160. 1. The short vowel of the perfect paradigm is in a few instances preserved in the Hiphil by doubling the first radical, thus הֲנִיחַ and הֵלִיץ, הֵסִית and הֵסִית, הֵגֵל, יָלִיץ, יָלִין, and יָתִיר, and וַיָּחֶל 2 Sam. 22:33.

2. Hiphil preterite inflected: הֱצִיקָה, הֵבִינוּ, הֵרִיבוּ and הֵרִיבוּ, with syllabic affixes: הֲבִינוֹת, הֲבִינוֹשׁ, הֲרִימוֹת and הֵכַלְתָּ, הֲרִילָם and הֱכִילָם, וַהֲפִיצוֹתִי, הֲשִׁיבֹתִי, or when the first radical is a guttural, הֱצִירוֹתִי, הֱעִידֹת and הֱעִידֹתָ, or without the inserted Hholem, הֵקַפְתְּ, הֵסַבְתִּי and הֲנִיחוֹתִי, הֵבַנּוּ and הֱבִיאוֹנִי, הֵבֵאתֶם and הֵקֵאתֶם, הֲסַאוֹ, § 61.4. a. With suffixes, הֱבִיאוֹ, הֲסִירָה, הֱשִׁירְהָ, הֲסִירֵנִי, הֲקֵמֹתָם.

3. Hiphil future inflected: וַיָּלֶשׁ, הָלִישׁוּ, feminine plural תְּשֹׁבְנָה, תְּהִימֶנָה, תְּקִימֶנָה. With Nun paragogic and suffixes: יְרִימוּן, יְרִימַם. Apocopated future: יָלֵן, יָסֵב, יָפֶת, יָקֵל. With Vav conversive: וַיָּרֶב, וַיָּאִיר and וַיָּאֵד, וַיִּלֶן, וַיִּפֶן, if the last radical be a guttural, וַיַּנַּח, וַיָּנַח, or א, וַיָּבֵא once וַיָּבִיא and once וַיַּבִּיא; upon the reception of a suffix the vowel is restored to its original length, וַתְּשִׁיבֵם, וַיְרִיבִיחוּ.

4. Hiphil infinitive absolute: הָקֵם, הָשֵׁב, הָסֵת, הָנֵחַ once הָקִים Jer. 44:25; construct, הֲסִירְךָ, הֲרִימִי, הָגֵל, הָסִית, הָשִׁיב, הָקִים, with suffix הֲכִרְדָּם, הֲנִיפְךָ and once with a feminine termination הַנְפָת Isa. 30:28.

5. In a few instances *u* is found in the Hophal before Daghesh-forte or Sh'va, הֻנִּיחָה Zech. 5:11, הֻכָּה Ezek. 41:9, 11 but הוּצַּת Lam. 5:5, and in some editions הֻקַּם 2 Sam. 23:1, יֻטַּל Job 41:1, הֻכָּתוֹ 2 Sam. 21:9, though others read הָכָּתוֹ, יָטַל, הָקַם.

§ 161. 1. The following verbs, which are only found in one or more of the three reduplicated species, double the middle radical either as Vav or as Yodh, viz.: חָיַב *to render liable*, כָּלַל *to do wickedly*, עָוַר *to blind*, עָוַת *to pervert*, שָׁוַע *to cry for help*, הִצְטַיָּדְנוּ Josh. 9:12, יִצְטַיָּרוּ Josh. 9:4; so also קָם fut. יָקוּם and יְקוֹלֵל, עָלַד fut. יְיַלֵּד, which have quiescent Vav in other species, and רָוַח, which has consonantal Vav likewise in the Kal.

2. The following omit the quiescent in the Piel and double the resulting biliteral, כִּלְכֵּל *to sustain*, בְּאַשְׁתֵּיהֶ Isa. 14:23, מְצַלְצְלָה Isa. 22:17, מְזַוְזֶיךָ Hab. 2:7, יְאַפְצֵנִי Job 16:12 but יְפֹצֵץ Jer. 23:29, קָרְקַר Num. 24:17 and מִקַּרְקַר Isa. 22:5, תְּשַׁגְשְׁגִי Isa. 17:11; יְעֵרֵי Isa. 15:5 is for יְעַרְעֵרוּ, § 57. 1; יְכַלְכְּלוּ Job 39:3 is perhaps for יְכַלְכְּלוּ from כּוּל, comp. אֶסְפֵּף Ps. 139:8 for אֶסְפֹּף, § 88, though Gesenius conjectures that it is an erroneous reading for לְכַלְכֵּל from כּוּל. The only Hithpael formed by a like reduplication is תִּתְחַתַּל Esth. 4:4, elsewhere הִתְחוֹלֵל.

3. Other verbs double the third radical in the Piel and Hithpael. Examples of the feminine plural: תִּתְבּוֹשַׁשְׁנָה, תִּתְרַגַּגְנָה, תִּקְלֹטְנָה, תִּצּוֹלַדְנָה. Hholem is changed to *u* before the doubled letter in the contracted form, וַיְכוּנְנוּ Job 31:15 for וַיְכוֹנְנֶנּוּ, § 61. 3. Fürst explains תְּכוּנְנֶהָ Isa. 61:6 as in like manner for תְּכוֹנְנֶהָ, while Gesenius makes it a Kal future, used in this single instance in a transitive sense. בּוֹשַׁשְׁכֶם Am. 5:11 is probably a variant orthography for בּוֹסַסְכֶם, § 92. b.

4. The following are the only examples of the Pual in Ayin Vav verbs, viz.: With ר doubled, מְכֹרָר Eccles. 1:15, מְרֻוָּרִים Jer. 22:14. Reduplicated biliteral, כָּלְכְּלוּ 1 Kin. 20:27. The third radical reduplicated, חוֹלַל *to be born*, כּוֹנְנוּ Ezek. 28:13. Ps. 37:23, תְּרוֹמַמְנָה Ps. 75:11 and מְרֹמָם Neh. 9:5, יֹרַד Isa. 16:10, יְרוֹעָעוּ Job 26:11, מְשׁוֹלָבֹת Ezek. 38:8.

5. תְּזוֹצִתִילָם Jer. 25:34 is an anomalous preterite from פּוּץ *to scatter*, with ת prefixed and inflected after the analogy of Niphal; some copies have the noun תְּפוֹצִתִילָם *your dispersions*.

In וְהֻטַּבְתִּי Ezek. 36:11 for וְהֵטַבְתִּי from טוֹב, Tsere is retained under the prefix as though the word were from the related Pe Yodh verb יָטַב, e. g. וְהֵיטַבְתִּי. On the other hand, in וַתֵּנִקֵהוּ Ex. 2:9 from יָנַק, Tsere is rejected as though it were from an Ayin Vav verb.

Lamedh Aleph (ל״א) Verbs.

§ 162. 1. Aleph, as the third radical of verbs, retains its consonantal character only when it stands at the beginning of a syllable, הַמְצִיאוּ, מָצְאָה.

2. At the end of the word it invariably quiesces in the preceding vowel, § 57. 2. (2), מְצָא, מָצָא, הִמְצִיא. If this vowel be Pattahh, as in the Kal and Niphal preterites and in the Pual and Hophal species, it is in the simple syllable lengthened into Kamets, § 59, מָצָא for מָצַא, נִמְצָא for נִמְצַא; so likewise in the Kal future and imperative, where א as a guttural requires *a*, יִמְצָא for יִמְצַא, מְצָא for מְצַא. A like prolongation of Pattahh to Kamets occurs before medial א in the first and second persons of the Kal preterite, מָצָאתָ, מְצָאתֶם.

3. With the single exception just stated, medial א quiesces in the diphthongal vowel *e* before syllabic affixes; thus, in the first and second persons of the preterites of the derivative species in Tsere, נִמְצֵאת, הִמְצֵאתִי, in the feminine plurals of all the futures and imperatives in Seghol, מְצֶאןָ, תִּמְצֶאןָ.

a. This *e* may arise from the diphthongal preferences of א, § 60. 1. *a* (5); or it may be borrowed from the corresponding forms of ל״ה verbs, between which and ל״א verbs there is a close affinity and a strong tendency to mutual assimilation. In Chaldee and Syriac no distinction is made between them.

§ 163. This class of verbs is represented in the following paradigm by מָצָא *to find;* the Piel and Hithpael, though wanting in this verb, are supplied from analogy. The Pual and Hophal are omitted because they are of rare occurrence, and they present no peculiarities but such as are common to the other species.

a. In their ordinary inflection Lamedh Aleph verbs differ from the perfect paradigm in the vowels only.

Paradigm of Lamedh Aleph Verbs.

	KAL.	NIPHAL.	PIEL.	HIPHIL.	HITHPAEL.
Pret. 3 m.	מָצָא	נִמְצָא	מִצֵּא	הִמְצִיא	הִתְמַצֵּא
3 f.	מָצְאָה	נִמְצְאָה	מִצְּאָה	הִמְצִיאָה	הִתְמַצְּאָה
2 m.	מָצָאתָ	נִמְצֵאתָ	מִצֵּאתָ	הִמְצֵאתָ	הִתְמַצֵּאתָ
2 f.	מָצָאת	נִמְצֵאת	מִצֵּאת	הִמְצֵאת	הִתְמַצֵּאת
1 c.	מָצָאתִי	נִמְצֵאתִי	מִצֵּאתִי	הִמְצֵאתִי	הִתְמַצֵּאתִי
Plur. 3 c.	מָצְאוּ	נִמְצְאוּ	מִצְּאוּ	הִמְצִיאוּ	הִתְמַצְּאוּ
2 m.	מְצָאתֶם	נִמְצֵאתֶם	מִצֵּאתֶם	הִמְצֵאתֶם	הִתְמַצֵּאתֶם
2 f.	מְצָאתֶן	נִמְצֵאתֶן	מִצֵּאתֶן	הִמְצֵאתֶן	הִתְמַצֵּאתֶן
1 c.	מָצָאנוּ	נִמְצֵאנוּ	מִצֵּאנוּ	הִמְצֵאנוּ	הִתְמַצֵּאנוּ
Infin. Absol.	מָצוֹא	נִמְצֹא	מַצֹּא	הַמְצֵא	
Constr.	מְצֹא	הִמָּצֵא	מַצֵּא	הַמְצִיא	הִתְמַצֵּא
Fut. 3 m.	יִמְצָא	יִמָּצֵא	יְמַצֵּא	יַמְצִיא	יִתְמַצֵּא
3 f.	תִּמְצָא	תִּמָּצֵא	תְּמַצֵּא	תַּמְצִיא	תִּתְמַצֵּא
2 m.	תִּמְצָא	תִּמָּצֵא	תְּמַצֵּא	תַּמְצִיא	תִּתְמַצֵּא
2 f.	תִּמְצְאִי	תִּמָּצְאִי	תְּמַצְּאִי	תַּמְצִיאִי	תִּתְמַצְּאִי
1 c.	אֶמְצָא	אֶמָּצֵא	אֲמַצֵּא	אַמְצִיא	אֶתְמַצֵּא
Plur. 3 m.	יִמְצְאוּ	יִמָּצְאוּ	יְמַצְּאוּ	יַמְצִיאוּ	יִתְמַצְּאוּ
3 f.	תִּמְצֶאנָה	תִּמָּצֶאנָה	תְּמַצֶּאנָה	תַּמְצֶאנָה	תִּתְמַצֶּאנָה
2 m.	תִּמְצְאוּ	תִּמָּצְאוּ	תְּמַצְּאוּ	תַּמְצִיאוּ	תִּתְמַצְּאוּ
2 f.	תִּמְצֶאנָה	תִּמָּצֶאנָה	תְּמַצֶּאנָה	תַּמְצֶאנָה	תִּתְמַצֶּאנָה
1 c.	נִמְצָא	נִמָּצֵא	נְמַצֵּא	נַמְצִיא	נִתְמַצֵּא
Imper. 2 m.	מְצָא	הִמָּצֵא	מַצֵּא	הַמְצֵא	הִתְמַצֵּא
2 f.	מִצְאִי	הִמָּצְאִי	מַצְּאִי	הַמְצִיאִי	הִתְמַצְּאִי
Plur. 2 m.	מִצְאוּ	הִמָּצְאוּ	מַצְּאוּ	הַמְצִיאוּ	הִתְמַצְּאוּ
2 f.	מְצֶאנָה	הִמָּצֶאנָה	מַצֶּאנָה	הַמְצֶאנָה	הִתְמַצֶּאנָה
Part. Act.	מֹצֵא		מְמַצֵּא	מַמְצִיא	מִתְמַצֵּא
Pass.	מָצוּא	נִמְצָא			

REMARKS ON LAMEDH ALEPH VERBS.

§ 164. 1. Verbs having Tsere as their second vowel, § 82. 1. *a*, retain it in the first and second persons of the Kal preterite, מָצָאתָ, קָרָאתְ, שָׂנֵאתִי.

2. Quiescent א is occasionally omitted from the body of the word, e. g. Kal pret. יָצָתִי Job 1:21 for יָצָאתִי, צָבִתִי Num. 11:11, צָלִתִי Judg. 4:19, פָּלֵט Job 32:18, בָּא 1 Sam. 25:8 for בָּאָה: fut. תִּשֶּׂנָה and תִּשֶּׂאנָה; יֹלֵדָה Deut. 28:57 part. fem. sing. for יֹלֵדָאה, בְּשֵׁתִי Job 41:17 for מַשְׂאֵתוֹ const. inf. with prep. and suf. from נָשָׂא. Niph. pret. נַחְבְּתָה Josh. 2:16, וְנִשְׂאָה Lev. 11:43. Otiant א, § 16. 1, may in like manner be dropped from the end of the word after quiescent Vav or Yodh. e. g. חֹטִי Gen. 20:6 for חוֹטִא, וַיָּבוֹ 1 Kin. 12:12 for יָבֹא, מַחְטִי 2 Kin. 13:6, הַחֲטִי Jer. 32:35, יְרֵ Ps. 141:5, רָשִׁי Ps. 55:16, אָבִי 1 Kin. 21:29, Mic. 1:15, בְּלִי 2 Sam. 5:2, and in three other passages; תָּבִי Ruth 3:15 is Hiph. imper. fem. for תָּבִיאִי, § 62. 2.

3. The vowel following א is in a few instances given to a preceding vowelless consonant, and the א becomes otiant or quiescent, § 57. 2 (3), וְנִשָּׁא Ps. 139:20 for נָשׂוּא, יִרְאוּ Jer. 10:5 for יִרְאוּ, רְאוּ imp. for רְאוּ, יֹצֵא Eccles. 10:5 Kal part. fem. for יֹצְאָה, חֹטְאִים 1 Sam. 14:33 for חוֹטְאִים, בֹּרֵא Neh. 6:8 Kal part. with suf. for בֹּרְאָה, נִרְפָּא Ezek. 47:8 for נִרְפְּאוּ; and, on the contrary, quiescent א attracts to itself the vowel of the preceding consonant in קָרְאוּ Ex. 2:20 Kal imp. for קִרְאוּ and קֹרֵאנָה Cant. 3:11 for קְרֶאנָה from יָצָא.

4. Final א resumes its consonantal character upon the addition of suffixes וָאֶשָּׂא, receiving (ָ) before ךָ, כֶם and כֶן, in consequence of which a previous Tsere or Sh'va is converted into Pattahh, § 60. 1. שְׂנָאֲךָ, אֲצָאֲךָ, חֲטָאֲךָ, מָצָאֲךָ Pi. inf., שַׂנַּאֲכֶם, בָּכֶם Kal inf. for בְּכֶם, § 61. 1. *c*.

5. Kamets in the ultimate is mostly retained before suffixes and paragogic ה, וְיִרְאָה, רְפָאָה Ps. 41:5, וְאֶקְרָאֶה 1 Sam. 28:15, but נְסָבָּאָה Isa. 56:12. Tsere is rejected אֶצֶאָה Neh. 2:13, 2 Chron. 1:10, or retained only in pause : אֵצֵאָה Judg. 9:29.

§ 165. 1. He is, in a few instances, substituted for א, רָפֹה Ps. 60:4 for רָפָא, הַחֲרֵה Jer. 19:11 for הַחֲרָא, וָלֹה Ps. 4:7 for וְלֹא, § 3. 1. *a*, גְּבֵה Jer. 49:10 for גָּבָא, וְחָבֵה 1 Kin. 22:25, 2 Kin. 7:12 for הֶחָבָא, יִצֶּה Job 8:21 for יְמַלֵּא.

2. Sometimes א remains, but the vowels are those of ה"ל forms. כִּלֵּאתִי Ps. 119:101 for כִּלִּיתִי, חֹטֶא Eccl. 8:12, 9:18. Isa. 65:20 for חֹטֶה, נֹשֵׂא 1 Sam. 22:2, Isa. 24:2, טִילֵּא Eccl. 7:26, יָשֶׁה 1 Kin. 9:11, Am. 4:2 Pi. pret. for וְנָשָׂא, רָפָה Ps. 143:3 for רִפָּה, כִּלָּה Jer. 51:34 for כִּלֵּא, רְפָאתִי 2 Kin. 2:21 for רִפִּיתִי, רְפָאוּ Jer. 51:9 for רָפְאָה, יְנַסֶּא Job 39:24 for יְנַסֶּה, הִפְלָא Deut. 28:59 Hiph. pret. for הִפְלִיא, מֹצִיא Ps. 135:7 Hiph. part. const. for מֹצִיא from יָצָא; to which may be added הַשְּׁאָרִינָה Ezek. 23:49, תִּמְצֶאנָה Jer. 50:20, with י inserted as in ה"ל verbs.

§ 166–168   LAMEDH HE VERBS.   195

3. Sometimes the לה form is adopted both in consonants and vowels, כְּלֹה Ezek. 28:16 for כָּלָא, כְּלֹה 1 Sam. 6:10, נְשׁה Ezek. 39:26, כְּלֹתִי 1 Sam. 25:33 for כְּלֹאתִי, צָמֹה Ruth 2:9 for צָמְאָה, רָפֹה Gen. 23:6 for רָפָא, תִּרְפֶּינָה Job 5:18 for תִּרְפֶּאנָה comp. Jer. 8:11, 51:9, 2 Kin. 2:22, נְשׂוּי Ps. 32:1 for נְשׂוּא, נְבֵיתָ Jer. 26:9 for נִבֵּאתָ, הִתְנַבִּית 1 Sam. 10:6, הִתְנַבּוֹת 1 Sam. 10:13, הִצְרִיתָהּ 2 Sam. 3:8, צָבִיתָ Isa. 29:7 for צְבָאֶיהָ; מַקְנֶה Ezek. 8:3 is by some interpreters thought to be for מַקְנֶא *provoking to jealousy*, and by others explained in the sense of the לה verb *selling* (Israel to their foes).

§ 166. 1. The 3 fem. preterite has the old ending ת, § 86. *b*, in חָטָאת Ex. 5:16 for חָטְאָה, קָרָאת Deut. 31:29, Isa. 7:14, Jer. 44:23, הַבָּאת Gen. 33:11 Hoph. from בּוֹא, נִפְלָאת Ps. 118:23 (נִפְלְאָת Deut. 30:11 is the feminine participle), to which the customary ending ה is further added in נִפְלָאתָה 2 Sam. 1:26, הָתְפָּאָתָה Josh. 6:17 for הָתְפָּאָת.

2. A feminine termination ה, ת, or as in לה verbs וֹת, is occasionally added to the construct infinitive, e. g. Kal, קְרֹאת, רְאֹה, שְׂנֹאה, בְּרֹאה from קָרָא *to meet*, distinguished from קְרֹא and קְרֹאת Judg. 8:1 from קָרָא *to call*, מְלֹאת and מְלֹא never מְלֹאת Prov. 8:13, with suf. חַטָּאֹה Ezek. 33:12. Niphal, הִנָּבֵאות Zech. 13:4. Piel, מַלֹּאות and כַּלֵּא, קִנֹּאתוֹ 2 Sam. 21:2; בַּשֹּׂאוֹת Ezek. 17:9 is a Kal inf. const., formed as in Chaldee by prefixing בְ.

3. There are two examples of the Niphal infinitive absolute, נִקְרֹא 2 Sam. 1:6 and הִמָּצֵא Ex. 22:3: the analogy of the former has been retained in the paradigm for the sake of distinction from the construct. Piel infinitive absolute: בָּרֹא, רַפֹּא, קַטֹּא. Hiphil inf. abs.: הַחְטֵא, הַשֵּׁא.

4. The Hiphil future with Vav conversive commonly has Tsere in the ultimate, though Hhirik also occurs וַתַּחְבָּא, וַיַּחְבֵּא, וַיַּקְרָא and וַיּוֹצֵא, וַיָּבֵא, once וַיָּבִיא Ezek. 40:3, and once וַיָּבִיא Neh. 8:2.

5. Kamets sometimes occurs in the ultimate of the Hithpael future, יִתְנַשֵּׂא Num. 23:24 but תִּתְנַשֵּׂא Ezek. 29:15, so יִתְחַבָּא, יִמָּצָא, תִּתְפַּלָּא, יִתְמַלְּאוּן; more rarely in the preterite, חִטַּבְּאָה.

§ 167. 1. The following are the only Pual forms which occur. Pret.: קֹרָא, הֻבָּאוּ, רֻבָּאוּ. Fut.: יְרֻבָּא. Part.: מְרֻבָּא, מְשֻׂנָּאָה, מְשֻׂלָּאִים, מְסֻלָּאִים, מְשֻׁלָּאוֹת, with suf. מְקֹרָאֵי.

2. The following are the only Hophal forms: Pret. הוּבָאָה, הָחְבָּאוּ, הוּבָּאוּ, הָבָאת, הוּבָא. Fut.: יוּבָא, יוּבָאוּ. Part.: מוּבָא, מוּבָאת.

3. For the anomalous forms, תְּבוֹאָתָה Deut. 33:16, תְּבוּאָתֵהוּ Job 22:21, תָּבֹאת 1 Sam. 25:34 (K'thibh הבאתי), see § 88 (sing. 3 fem.)

Lamedh He (לה) Verbs.

§ 168. In these verbs the third radical, which is Yodh or Vav, does not appear at the end of the word except in the

Kal passive participle, e. g. גָּלוּי; in all other cases it is rejected or softened, the resulting vowel termination being usually expressed by the letter ה, § 11. 1. *a*.

In the various preterites ה stands for the vowel *a*, and is hence pointed הָ .

In the futures and participles it stands for *ĕ*, and is pointed הֶ .

In the imperatives it stands for *ē*, and is pointed הֵ .

In the absolute infinitives it stands for *ō* or *ē*; in the Kal it is pointed הֹ, in the Hiphil and Hophal הֵ, in the Niphal and Piel הֹ or הֵ. There are no examples in Pual and Hithpael.

The construct infinitives have the feminine ending וֹת.

a. In this class of verbs the Yodh forms have almost entirely superseded those with Vav. The latter are confined to the construct infinitive where וֹת, occurring in all the species, is best explained by assuming ו to be radical (comp. רָאֹה Ezek. 28:17 as an alternate of רְאוֹת) and to a few other sporadic cases, viz.: a single Kal preterite, שַׁלַּוְתִּי Job 3:25, the reduplicated forms of three verbs, נָאֲוָה , כְּמֵהַּ , הִשְׁתַּחֲוָה, and the peculiar form, אַרְיֵה Isa. 16:9.

b. In the Kal preterite, Yodh is rejected after the heterogeneous vowel Pattahh, § 57. 2. (5), which is then prolonged to Kamets in the simple syllable, בָּנָה for בָּנַי. As Pattahh is likewise the regular vowel of the ultimate in the preterites of Niphal and Hophal, and occasionally appears in Piel, § 92. *c*, and Hithpael, § 96. *b*, the final Kamets of these species may be similarly explained. The ending, thus made uniform in the other species, passed over likewise into the Hiphil preterite, which it did the more readily since *a* belongs at least to some of its persons in the perfect verb. Yodh is in like manner rejected after the heterogeneous Hholem of certain infinitives, while it leaves the homogeneous Tsere of others unmodified.

c. The futures, imperatives, and participles of certain of the species have *e* as the normal vowel of their ultimate; in this Yodh can quiesce, leaving it unchanged. Those of the other species (except the Hiphil, which is once more attracted into conformity with the rest) have or may have *a* in the ultimate; this, combined with the *i* latent in י, will again form *e*. In the future this becomes *ĕ* (ֶ) in distinction from the ending *ē* (ֵ) of the more energetic imperative; and the absolute is distinguished from the construct state of the participle in the same way.

§ 169. 1. Before personal endings beginning with a vowel the last radical is occasionally retained as י, particularly in prolonged or pausal forms, יֶחֱסָיוּן ; חָסָיוּ , חָסָיָה ; it is, however, commonly rejected and its vowel given to the antecedent consonant, גָּלוּ for גָּלָיוּ, תִּגְלִי for תִּגְלָיִי; in like manner the preterite 3 fem., which in these verbs retains the primary characteristic ה , § 86. b, גָּלָת for גָּלָיָת, to which is further appended the softened ending ה , thus גָּלְתָה, in pause גָּלָתָה.

<small>a. The ה of the 3 fem. pret. is frequently explained as a second feminine ending added after the first had lost its significance in the popular consciousness. It might, perhaps with equal propriety, be regarded as paragogically appended, § 61. 6, comp. such nouns as עֶזְרָתָה, יְשׁוּעָתָה, אֵימָתָה, in order to produce a softer termination and one more conformed to that which obtains in the generality of verbs. Nordheimer's explanation of the ה as hardened from ה , גָּלְתָה for גָּלְתָּה, labours under the double difficulty that there is neither proof nor probability for the assumption that the consonant ת could be exchanged for ה , and that ה in the preterite of these verbs is not a radical nor even a consonant, but simply the representative of the vowel a.</small>

2. Before personal endings beginning with a consonant the third radical י remains but is softened to a vowel, so that in the Kal preterite it quiesces in Hhirik, in the Pual and Hophal preterites in Tsere, in the Niphal, Piel, Hiphil, and Hithpael preterites in either Hhirik or Tsere, and in the futures and imperatives of all the species in Seghol, גָּלִית, תִּגְלֶינָה, גָּלִיתִי.

3. Forms not augmented by personal endings lose their final vowel before suffixes, e. g. גְּלִי, גְּלֵה from גָּלָה, יִגְלְךָ from יִגְלֶה, הַגְלֵךְ from הִגְלָה. The preterite 3 fem. takes its simple form, e. g. גָּלְתָהוּ or גָּלַתּוּ, and in pause גָּלָתָה.

§ 170. The Lamedh He verbs will be represented by גָּלָה *to uncover, reveal,* which is used in all the species.

Paradigm of Lamed ה

	KAL.	NIPHAL.	PIEL.
Pret. 3 m.	גָּלָה	נִגְלָה	גִּלָּה
3 f.	גָּלְתָה	נִגְלְתָה	גִּלְּתָה
2 m.	גָּלִיתָ	נִגְלֵיתָ	גִּלִּיתָ
2 f.	גָּלִית	נִגְלֵית	גִּלִּית
1 c.	גָּלִיתִי	נִגְלֵיתִי	גִּלִּיתִי
Plur. 3 c.	גָּלוּ	נִגְלוּ	גִּלּוּ
2 m.	גְּלִיתֶם	נִגְלֵיתֶם	גִּלִּיתֶם
2 f.	גְּלִיתֶן	נִגְלֵיתֶן	גִּלִּיתֶן
1 c.	גָּלִינוּ	נִגְלֵינוּ	גִּלִּינוּ
Infin. Absol.	גָּלֹה	נִגְלֹה	גַּלֵּה
Constr.	גְּלוֹת	הִגָּלוֹת	גַּלּוֹת
Fut. 3 m.	יִגְלֶה	יִגָּלֶה	יְגַלֶּה
3 f.	תִּגְלֶה	תִּגָּלֶה	תְּגַלֶּה
2 m.	תִּגְלֶה	תִּגָּלֶה	תְּגַלֶּה
2 f.	תִּגְלִי	תִּגָּלִי	תְּגַלִּי
1 c.	אֶגְלֶה	אֶגָּלֶה	אֲגַלֶּה
Plur. 3 m.	יִגְלוּ	יִגָּלוּ	יְגַלּוּ
3 f.	תִּגְלֶינָה	תִּגָּלֶינָה	תְּגַלֶּינָה
2 m.	תִּגְלוּ	תִּגָּלוּ	תְּגַלּוּ
2 f.	תִּגְלֶינָה	תִּגָּלֶינָה	תְּגַלֶּינָה
1 c.	נִגְלֶה	נִגָּלֶה	נְגַלֶּה
Imper. 2 m.	גְּלֵה	הִגָּלֵה	גַּלֵּה
2 f.	גְּלִי	הִגָּלִי	גַּלִּי
Plur. 2 m.	גְּלוּ	הִגָּלוּ	גַּלּוּ
2 f.	גְּלֶינָה	הִגָּלֶינָה	גַּלֶּינָה
Part. Act.	גֹּלֶה		מְגַלֶּה
Pass.	גָּלוּי	נִגְלֶה	

He Verbs.

PUAL.	HIPHIL.	HOPHAL.	HITHPAEL.
גֻּלָּה	הִגְלָה	הָגְלָה	הִתְגַּלָּה
גֻּלְּתָה	הִגְלְתָה	הָגְלְתָה	הִתְגַּלְּתָה
גֻּלֵּיתָ	הִגְלֵיתָ	הָגְלֵיתָ	הִתְגַּלֵּיתָ
גֻּלֵּית	הִגְלֵית	הָגְלֵית	הִתְגַּלֵּית
גֻּלֵּיתִי	הִגְלֵיתִי	הָגְלֵיתִי	הִתְגַּלֵּיתִי
גֻּלּוּ	הִגְלוּ	הָגְלוּ	הִתְגַּלּוּ
גֻּלֵּיתֶם	הִגְלִיתֶם	הָגְלֵיתֶם	הִתְגַּלֵּיתֶם
גֻּלֵּיתֶן	הִגְלִיתֶן	הָגְלֵיתֶן	הִתְגַּלֵּיתֶן
גֻּלֵּינוּ	הִגְלֵינוּ	הָגְלֵינוּ	הִתְגַּלֵּינוּ
(גֻּלֹּה)	הַגְלֵה	הָגְלֵה	(הִתְגַּלֹּה)
גֻּלּוֹת	הַגְלוֹת	(הָגְלוֹת)	הִתְגַּלּוֹת
יְגֻלֶּה	יַגְלֶה	יָגְלֶה	יִתְגַּלֶּה
תְּגֻלֶּה	תַּגְלֶה	תָּגְלֶה	תִּתְגַּלֶּה
תְּגֻלֶּה	תַּגְלֶה	תָּגְלֶה	תִּתְגַּלֶּה
תְּגֻלִּי	תַּגְלִי	תָּגְלִי	תִּתְגַּלִּי
אֲגֻלֶּה	אַגְלֶה	אָגְלֶה	אֶתְגַּלֶּה
יְגֻלּוּ	יַגְלוּ	יָגְלוּ	יִתְגַּלּוּ
תְּגֻלֶּינָה	תַּגְלֶינָה	תָּגְלֶינָה	תִּתְגַּלֶּינָה
תְּגֻלּוּ	תַּגְלוּ	תָּגְלוּ	תִּתְגַּלּוּ
תְּגֻלֶּינָה	תַּגְלֶינָה	תָּגְלֶינָה	תִּתְגַּלֶּינָה
נְגֻלֶּה	נַגְלֶה	נָגְלֶה	נִתְגַּלֶּה
wanting	הַגְלֵה	wanting	הִתְגַּלֵּה
	הַגְלִי		הִתְגַּלִּי
	הַגְלוּ		הִתְגַּלּוּ
	הַגְלֶינָה		הִתְגַּלֶּינָה
מְגֻלֶּה	מַגְלֶה	מָגְלֶה	מִתְגַּלֶּה

SHORTENED FUTURE AND IMPERATIVE.

§ 171. 1. The final vowel ה ָ is rejected from the futures when apocopated or when preceded by Vav conversive. The concurrence of final consonants thence resulting in the Kal and Hiphil is commonly relieved by inserting an unaccented Seghol between them, § 61. 2, to which the preceding Pattahh is assimilated in the Hiphil, § 63. 2. *a*, the Hhirik of the Kal either remaining unchanged or being lengthened to Tsere in the simple syllable.

	KAL.	NIPHAL.	PIEL.	HIPHIL.	HITHPAEL.
Future.	יִגְלֶה	יִגָּלֶה	יְגַלֶּה	יַגְלֶה	יִתְגַּלֶּה
Apoc. Fut.	יִגֶל or יֵגֶל	יִגָּל	יְגַל	יֶגֶל	יִתְגַּל
Vav. Conv.	וַיִּגֶל or וַיֵּגֶל	וַיִּגָּל	וַיְגַל	וַיֶּגֶל	וַיִּתְגַּל

2. The final vowel ה ָ is sometimes rejected from the imperative in the Piel, Hiphil, and Hithpael species, e. g. Pi. גַּל for גַּלֵּה, Hiph. הֶגֶל for הַגְלֵה, Hith. הִתְגַּל for הִתְגַּלֵּה.

REMARKS ON LAMEDH HE VERBS.

§ 172. 1. Kal preterite: The third person feminine rarely occurs with the simple ending ת ְ, עָשְׂתָ Lev. 25:21, הִית 2 Kin. 9:37 K'thibh; so in the Hiphil, הֶחְלְאָת Ezek. 24:12, הִרְצָת Lev. 26:31, and Hophal, הָגְלָת Jer. 13:19. Yodh is occasionally retained before asyllabic affixes, חָסָיָה Ps. 57:2, the only instance in which the feminine has the ending usual in other verbs, חָסָיוּ Deut. 32:37, נָבְיוּ Ps. 73:2 K'ri; so in the imperative, בְּצָיוּ Isa. 21:12; future, יִשְׁתָּיוּן, יֶחֱסָיוּן, יֶחֱזָיוּן, יִבְלָיוּן, אֱתָיוּ, רָאִיתִי, יִרְדְּיוּן, רִבְּלוּ, תִּדְצָיוּן, רְשָׁיוּ, Niphal preterite, נְשִׂיוּ, Piel future, יְדַמְּיוּן, יְכַסְּיֻנִי, Hiphil future, תִּגְלִיוּן, imperative, הָתָיוּ for הַאְתָיוּ.

2. Infinitive: Vav is sometimes written for the final vowel of the infinitive absolute instead of ה, שָׁתוֹ, רָאוֹ, קָנוֹ, עָשׂוֹ, מָרוֹ, הָרוֹ, הָגוֹ, גְּלוֹ, בָּלוֹ, ח, and in a few instances the feminine termination is added, רָאִית, אֱלִית, שְׁתוֹת. There are also examples of the omission of this termination from the construct infinitive, כַּסּוֹת and פַּסּוֹת, קָנֹה, רָאֹה, שְׁתֹה; once it has the form רָאִיָה Ezek. 28:17.

3. Future: There are a very few examples of Tsere as the last vowel of the future, תִּרְאֶה Dan. 1:13, תַּעֲשֶׂה Josh. 7:9, וַיַּעֲשֶׂה Josh. 9:24, תֶּהֱיֶה Jer. 17:17; so in the Piel, תְּגַלֶּה Lev. 18:7 ff.; and, on the other

§ 173   REMARKS ON LAMEDH HE VERBS.   201

hand, there is one instance of an imperative ending in Seghol, viz., the Piel, רְבָה Judg. 9:29. The radical י remains and rests in Hhirik in וְתִזְגִּי (3 fem.) Jer. 3:6, in the Hiphil, הֶחֱוִיתִי (2 masc.) Jer. 18:23, and in the Kal imperative, חֲבִי (2 masc.) Isa. 26:20. Yodh appears once as a consonant before a suffix, וַיֶּאֱתָיוּ Job 3:25, and once before ה paragogic, אֶהֱבָיָה Ps. 77:4, which is very rare in these verbs, but perhaps displaces the final vowel in אֲשִׂיחָה Ps. 119:117, and the Hithpael, נִשְׁתַּעֲשָׁע Isa. 41:23. In a few instances י is restored as a quiescent before suffixes, יְחַיֵּינוּ Hos. 6:2, חַפָּיְנִי 1 Kin. 20:35, וְכַסְּיֻבוֹ Ps. 140:10 K'ri, אַפְאֵיהֶם Deut. 32:26. Examples of the feminine plural: וַתַּעֲלֶינָה, תַּחֲלֶיךָ, תְּדַלְּנָה, תִּבְכֶּינָה, תֶּצֱלֶינָה and תֶּצְלֶינָה.

4. The future of a few verbs when apocopated or preceded by Vav conversive simply drops its last vowel, either retaining Hhirik under the personal prefix or lengthening it to Tsere, וַיִּפְתְּ, וַיִּשְׁבְּ, וַיִּגְבְּ, וַיִּרְדְּ, וַיֵּשְׁתְּ, וַיֵּשְׁתְּ; so in the Pe Nun forms, וַיִּט and וַיֵּט, וַיָּט, and Pe Yodh וַיֵּרֶד, with Pattahh-furtive under the first radical of the Pe guttural, יַרַח, § 17, or the vowel of the personal prefix changed to Pattahh, § 60. 1, וַיֵּרֶא, but וַתֵּרֶא, וַיַּרְא. Most commonly Seghol is inserted between the concurring consonants, וַיִּפֶן and וַיֵּפֶן, וַיִּזֶן, וַיִּגֶל, וַיְגֶל, וַיֹּהַל, וַיֵּבֶל and וַיִּפֶן and וַיֵּגֶל, וַיֵּתַל, וַיֵּרַא, וַיְּשֶׁת, or Pattahh if one of the consonants is a guttural, § 61. 2; thus, in Ayin guttural verbs, וַיֵּשְׁתְּ, וַיֶּחֱזֶה, וַיֵּרַד, וַיֵּחַתּ, in Pe guttural וַיַּחַן from יַחֲרֶה, § 60. 1. a. (3), יַחַר from יֶחֱרֶה, or with the additional change of the vowel of the prefix to Pattahh, וַיַּחַן, וַיָּחָן from יֶחֱיֶה, יַחְיֶה from יֵחָצֵא, וַיַּצַּב Isa. 59:17 (in 1 Sam. 15:19, 14:32 K'ri, this same form is from עוּט or לִיט, § 157. 3), וַיֵּטְשְׁ, וַיֵּלְךְ, וַיִּפֶן. The rejection of the final vowel takes place frequently even in the first person singular, which in other verbs is commonly exempt from shortening, § 99. 3. a, וָאֵפֶן, וָאֵרֶא and וָאֶרְאֶה, וָאֶחַד, וָאֵלֶךְ, וָאֵשְׁתְּ, וָאֵשְׁקְ and וָאֶעֱשֶׂה. In a few instances the final vowel is retained in other persons after Vav conversive, e. g. וַיַּעֲשֶׂה 1 Kin. 16:25, וַיִּבְכֶּה 2 Kin. 1:10, וַיִּבְנֶה Josh. 19:50, וַתִּבְכֶּה 1 Sam. 1:9, וַיִּגְלֶה 1 Kin. 16:17, וַיִּרְאֶה 1 Sam. 17:42, וַיִּפְרֶה 2 Kin. 6:23, תֶּשִׁי Deut. 32:18 is fut. apoc. of שָׁיָה as יְחִי or יְחִי of הָיָה.

5. The passive participle drops the final י in צָפוּ Job 15:22 for צָפוּי, עָשׂוּ Job 41:25 for עָשׂוּי, and .fem. plur. נְשִׂיּוֹת Isa. 3:16 K'thibh (K'ri וּנְשִׂיּוֹת), עָשׂוּיוֹת 1 Sam. 25:18 K'thibh.

§ 173. 1. In the Niphal preterite Yodh may quiesce in either Tsere or Hhirik, though the former is more frequent, נִגְלֵיתִי and נִגְלִיתִי, נִגְלֵיתָ and נִגְלִינוּ and נִגְלִיתִי, נִשְׁבֵּיתָ and נְבַעְתָּם, נִגְלִינוּ.

2. Examples of the infinitive absolute: נִגְלֹה, נִדְמֹה, הִקָּחֹה. Construct: הֵעָשׂוֹת and הִגָּלוֹת, הִגָּלוֹת, הֵרָאוֹת and הֵרָאֹה; with suffixes, הֵעָשׂוֹתוֹ, הִגָּלוֹתוֹ, once as though it were a plural noun, הִגָּלוֹתָם Ezek. 6:8, so the Kal infin., בִּנְיֹתְךָ Ezek. 16:31, once with a preposition, לִבְנוֹת Ex. 10:3.

3. Future apocopated and with Vav conversive: וַתִּגְלֶה, תֵּפֶל, וָאֵפֶת, וַיֵּפֶת, חֵפְשׁ, וַיֵּקְשׁ, וַיֵּרָא, and in one verb with Pattahh before ה, וַיַּחַן Gen. 7:23, Ps. 109:13, though some editions omit the Daghesh-forte in the former passage, thus making it a Kal future.

§ 174. 1. Piel: Two verbs, נָאָה *to be becoming* and נָחָה *to draw* (the bow), having a guttural for their second radical, double the third instead, which in the reduplication appears as Vav, though the general law is adhered to requiring its rejection from the end of the word and the substitution of the vowel letter ה. The only forms which occur are, of the former, the preterite נָאֲוָה Ps. 93:5, נָאוּ Cant. 1:10, Isa. 52:7, and of the latter the participle plur. constr. כְּנַחֲוֵי Gen. 21:16. There are three examples of Hholem inserted after the first radical, § 92. *b*, שׁוֹשִׁיתִי Isa. 10:13 from שָׁסָה, the שׂ being an orthographic equivalent for ס, § 3. 1. *a*, and in the infinitive, הֲלֹו Isa. 59:13.

2. In the first person singular of the Piel preterite י sometimes quiesces in Tsere; in all the other persons, however, and even in the first singular, when a suffix is added, it invariably quiesces in Hhirik, גִּלֵּיתִי and כִּלִּיתִים, בָּלִיתִי, בְּלִיתִי and בְּלִיתִיךָ, קִוִּיתִי, once קְוִיתִי, גִּלִּיתִי.

3. Infinitive absolute: הָלֹו, חֹלוֹ, כָּלֹה, נָקֵה, כַּלֵּה, קַוֵּה and קֹה. The construct always ends in וֹת with the exception of כַּלֵּה also בְּלוֹת, and חַלִּי Hos. 6:9.

4. Future: in אֶרְיֶה Isa. 16:9 from רָיָה, the second radical is doubled as י, § 153. 1, and the third appears as ו, § 56. 3. *a*; אֶבְכֶּה Ex. 33:3 is for אֶבְכָּה, § 63. 1. *b*. With Vav conversive: וַיֵּבְךְּ, וַיֶּרֶב, וַיֵּלֶךְ, וַיִּצֶר, וַיַּתְּ; so in the first person singular, וָאֵבְךְּ, וָאֵצֵא; once Pattahh is lengthened to Kamets, וָיְהִי 1 Sam. 21:14; so in pause, תִּגֶּל Prov. 25:9.

5. The imperative has Seghol in a single instance, רְבֶה Judg. 9:29 and sometimes drops its final vowel, גַּל, חַל, בַּן, נַס, צִי and צָוֵה.

6. Pual infinitive construct with suffix: עֻוֹּתִי Ps. 132:1.

§ 175. 1. Hiphil preterite: The prefixed ה has occasionally Seghol, הֶרְאִיתִיךָ, הֶרְאָה, הֶחְפָּה, הֶגְלָא, הֶגְלָה and הִגְלָה. Yodh may quiesce in Hhirik or Tsere, הִגְלֵיתִי, הִגְלִיתִי, הֱוֵיתִי, הֱוַיתִי. Yodh once remains as a quiescent in the 3 masc. sing., הֶחֱלִי Isa. 53:10, and once in the 3 masc. plur., הֶחְסָיוּ Josh. 14:8 for הֶחֱסִיו, § 62. 2.

2. The infinitive absolute has Kamets in הַרְבָּה by way of distinction from הַרְבֵּה and הַרְבֵּה Jer. 42:2, which are always used adverbially. Construct: The prefixed ה has Hhirik in one instance, הִקְצוֹת Lev. 14:43; לְהַשְׁאוֹת 2 Kin. 19:25 K'thibh is for לְהַשְׁאוֹת.

3. The future, when apocopated or preceded by Vav conversive, sometimes simply rejects its final vowel, וַיֵּפֶן, וַיָּרָא, וַיֶּרֶד, וַיַּשְׁקְ, וַיּוֹר from יָרָה, וַיְוֵ from נָוָה, וַיַּט from נָטָה, וַיַּךְ from נָכָה; commonly, however, Seghol is inserted between the concurring consonants, וַיַּאֱל from אָלָה, § 111. 2. *a*, וַיֶּגֶל, וָלֶן, וַיַּחְמֶס, וַיֶּרֶב, וַיִּגֶר, וַתֵּרֶא. or Pattahh if one of the consonants is a guttural, וַיַּחַד, וַיַּחַל, וַיַּחַת. Occasionally the final vowel remains, וַיִּגְלֶה 1 Kin. 16:17, 18:42, וַתִּרְבֶּה Ezek. 23:19; once the radical י appears quiescing in Hhirik, תֶּחְדִּי (2 masc. apoc. for תֶּחְדֶּה) Jer. 18:23. The retention or rejection of the vowel is optional in the first person singular, וָאַרְבֶּה, וָאַשְׁקֶה, וָאֶצֶּה and וָאַךְ from נָכָה, וָאַצֵּל, אַשׁ from נָטָה.

§ 176, 177   REMARKS ON LAMEDH HE VERBS.   203

4. The imperative is sometimes abbreviated, הִרְבֵּה and הֶרֶב, הַרְפֵּה and הֶרֶף, הַעַל for הַעֲלֵה, הַטֵּה and הַט, הַפֵּה and הַף; חָזְ־ (accent on the ultimate) Ps. 39:14 is for חֲזֵה, the same word Isa. 6:9 is from שָׁעָה, § 140. 5.

5. Hophal infinitive absolute: הֻפְלֵה Lev. 19:20.

§ 176. 1. Hithpael: One verb שָׁחָה reduplicates its third radical, which appears as ו, הִשְׁתַּחֲוָה to worship, fut. יִשְׁתַּחֲוֶה, with Vav conv. וַיִּשְׁתַּחוּ for וַיִּשְׁתַּחֲוִי, § 61. 2, plur. וַיִּשְׁתַּחֲווּ, infin. הִשְׁתַּחֲוֹת, and once with suf. הִשְׁתַּחֲוָיָתִי 2 Kin. 5:18, the accent being thrown back by a following monosyllable. For the inflected participle, מִשְׁתַּחֲוִיתֶם Ezek. 8:16, see § 90, page 120.

2. In the preterite י mostly quiesces in Tsere in the first person singular, and in Hhirik in the other persons, הִתְאַוֵּיתִי, הִשְׁתַּחֲוֵיתִי, הִתְפָּתַּיְתָ, הִשְׁתַּעֲרָה, הִתְעַלְּרִית, הִתְרַפִּיתָ, הִתְכַּסִּיתָ, הִשְׁתַּחֲוִיתֶם.

3. The future apocopated and with Vav conversive: וַיִּרֶב, יִרְבֶּה, תִּתְדַּל, יִתְרֵב, תִּשְׁבֶּה, or with Kamets in the accented syllable, תֵּגֶר, וַיִּהְאוּ, so always in pause, וַיִּרְהַל; וַתִּרְבֶּס Gen. 24:65.

4. The shortened imperative: הִתְחַל, הִתְגָּר.

§ 177. 1. הָיָה to be, fut. יִהְיֶה. Hhirik being retained before the guttural under the influence of the following Yodh, whence the Sh'va, though vocal, remains simple; so in the inf. const. with prep. בִּהְיוֹת, לִהְיוֹת, though without a prefix it is הֱיוֹת, once הֱיֵה Ezek. 21:15. The apocopated future יְהִי (in pause יֶחִי) and with Vav conversive וַיְהִי, is for יִהְי, the vowel of the prefix returning to the Sh'va from which it arose, § 85. 2. a (1), page 116, when the quiescence of the middle radical gives a vowel to the first. The same thing occurs in the peculiar form of the future יְהוּא Eccl. 11:3, where the second radical appears as ו, which it sometimes does in the imperative, הֱלָח and הֲוֵה Gen. 27:29 or הֱוֵא Job 37:6, and in the participle הֹוֶה Neh. 6:6, Eccl. 2:22, fem. הוָֹיָה Ex. 9:3.

2. חָיָה to live. The root חָיַי is usually inflected as a Lamedh He verb pret. חָיָה, fut. יִחְיֶה, apoc. יְחִי. with Vav conversive וַיְחִי, though in the preterite 3 masc. it occasionally takes an Ayin doubled form, חַי, e. g. Gen. 3:22, 5:5, and once in the 3 fem. an Ayin Yodh form חָיְתָה Ex. 1:16, or it may be explained as an Ayin doubled form with Daghesh-forte omitted, § 25.

3. In a few instances א is substituted for the third radical in Lamedh He verbs, רָצָאתִי Ezek. 43:27, אָתָא Isa. 21:12, נָשָׂא Jer. 23:39, רוּא 2 Chron. 26:15, תֹּבֹא Prov. 1:10 from אָבָה, וַיֵּרָא Deut. 33:21 from אָתָה, וַיִּחְלָא 2 Chron. 16:12. גָּא Lam. 4:1. שָׂא 2 Kin. 25:29. יִשְׁלָא Eccl. 8:1, תְּלָאוּם 2 Sam. 21:12 K'ri for תְּלֻאִים, תְּלוּאִים Hos. 11:7, Deut. 28:66 for תְּלוּיִים, § 56. 4, הַמּוֹרָאִים וַיֹּלִאוּ 2 Sam. 11:24 from רָלָה; the vowels are those of Lamedh Aleph verbs in אָתָא Jer. 3:22 for אָתִינוּ, תִּכְלָא 1 Kin. 17:14 for תִּכְלֶה, יִקְרָא Dan. 10:14 for יִקְרֶה; and the full Lamedh Aleph form is adopted in וַיַּפְרִיא Hos. 13:15 for יַפְרֶה.

Doubly Imperfect Verbs.

§ 178. Verbs which have two weak letters in the root, or which are so constituted as to belong to two different classes of imperfect verbs, commonly exhibit the peculiarities of both, unless they interfere with or limit one another. Thus, a verb which is both פ״א and ל״ה will follow the analogy of both paradigms, the former in its initial and the latter in its second syllable. But in verbs which are both ע״ו and ל״ה the ו is invariably treated as a perfect consonant, and the ל״ה peculiarities alone preserved. All such cases have been remarked upon individually under the several classes of verbs to which they respectively belong.

Defective Verbs.

§ 179. 1. It has been seen in repeated instances in the foregoing pages that verbs belonging to one class of imperfect verbs may occasionally adopt forms from another and closely related class. Thus a ל״א verb may appear with a ל״ה form, or an ע״ו verb with an ע״ע form or *vice versâ*. The occurrence of an individual example, or of a few examples of such divergent forms, may be explained in the manner just suggested without the assumption of an additional verb as their source. Sometimes, however, the number of divergent forms is so considerable, or the divergence itself so wide, that it is simpler to assume two co-existent roots of the same signification, and differing only in the weak letter which they contain, than to refer all to a single root.

a. Thus, כָּלָא means *to shut up* or *restrain*, and כָּלָה *to be finished:* yet a few ל״ה forms occur in the sense not of the latter but of the former verb. They are accordingly held to be from כָּלָא, but assimilated in inflection to the ל״ה paradigm. On the other hand, קָרָא means *to call*, and קָרָה *to meet;* but so many ל״א forms are found with this latter signification that it seems necessary to assume a second root קָרָא having that meaning. The verb *to run* is ordinarily רוּץ; but רָצָא Ezek. 1: 14 is too remote from an וֹ form to be referred to that root; hence it is traced to another verb רָצָא of the same sense. No clear line of distinction can be drawn between the cases in which divergent forms are to be traced to a single root, and those in which the assumption of a second is admissible or necessary. This must be decided in detail, and the best authorities not infrequently differ in their judgment of particular examples.

2. Where two verbs exist which are thus radically connected and identical in signification, it not infrequently happens that they are defective or mutually supplementary, that is to say, that one of them is in usage restricted to certain parts or species, the remainder being supplied by the other.

a. The following are examples of defective verbs: טוֹב *to be good*, used in the Kal species only in the preterite, the corresponding future is from יָטַב; יָרֵא Kal pret. *to fear*, the fut. and imper. from גּוּר; יָרַק Kal pret. and inf. *to spit*, fut. from רָקַק; נָפַץ Kal pret. and inf. *to break* or *disperse*, fut. and imp. from פּוּץ; נָכַר Kal pret. *to be alienated*, fut. from נָכַר; שָׂרָה K. pret. *to be a prince*, fut. from שׂוּר; רָבַב Kal pret. and inf. *to be many*, fut. from רָבָה which is used throughout the species; יָחַם Kal fut. *to be hot*, pret. and inf. from חָמַם, which is also used in the future; יָעַץ *to counsel*, borrows its Kal imper. from לַב; קוּם Kal fut. *to awake*, pret. from the Hiphil of יָקַץ, which is also used in inf. imper. and fut.; נָצַב *to place*, the reflexive is expressed by הִתְיַצֵּב from יָצַב; שָׁתָה *to drink*, the causative is הִשְׁקָה from שָׁקָה; הוֹבִישׁ from יָבֵשׁ is used as the causative of בּוֹשׁ *to be ashamed*, as well as הִבְרִישׁ; הָלַךְ *to go*, derives many of its forms from יָלַךְ; יָהַב *to give*, is only used in the Kal imperative, it is supplemented by נָתַן of totally distinct radicals.

Quadriliteral Verbs.

§ 180. Quadriliteral verbs are either primitives formed from quadriliteral roots, whose origin is explained, § 68. *a*, or denominatives, the formative letter of the noun or adjective being admitted into the stem along with the three original radicals. The former class adopt the vowels and inflections of the Piel and Pual species, while the latter follow the Hiphil.

a. The only examples of quadriliteral verbs are the following, viz.: Piel pret. פִּרְשֵׂז *he spread*. Job 26 : 9, where the original Pattahh of the initial syllable of the Piel, § 82. 5. *b* (3), is preserved; fut. with suf. יְכַרְסְמֶנָּה *he shall waste it*, Ps. 80:14. Pual pret. רֻטֲפַשׁ *it freshened*, Job 33:25, the Methegh and the Hhateph Pattahh being used to indicate that the Sh'va is vocal, and that the form is equivalent to רֻטֲפַשׁ; part. מְחֻסְפָּס *scaled off* or *resembling scales*, Ex. 16:14, בְּכַרְבֵּל *clothed*, 1 Chron. 15:27. Hiphil pret. הֶאֱזְנִיחוּ *they stank*, Isa. 19:6 for הֶאֱזְנִיחוּ as נִבְמְרוּ for נִכְמְרוּ, derived from אָזְנָה *putrescent*, which is simpler than to make it with Gesenius a double or anomalous Hiphil from זָנַה, § 94. *a*, comp. Alexander in loc.; fut. אַשְׂמְאִילָה *I will turn to the left*, Gen. 13:9; תַּשְׂמְאִילוּ Isa. 30:21, part. מַשְׂמְאִלִים 1 Chron. 12:2 from שְׂמֹאל *the left hand*, elsewhere reduced to a triliteral by the rejection of א, לְהַשְׂמִיל 2 Sam. 14:19, חֲשַׂבְלִי Ezek. 21:21. To these may be added the form, which occurs several times in the K'thibh בַּחֲצֹצְרִים 1 Chron. 15:24, etc., and מַחְצְרִים 2 Chron. 5:12, for which the K'ri substitutes מַחְצְרִים or מְחַצְּרִים. As it is a denominative from חֲצֹצְרָה *a trumpet*, it has been suspected that the form first mentioned should be pointed בַּחֲצֹצְרִים; the other, if a genuine reading, is probably to be read בַּחֲצֹרְלִים.

Nouns.

THEIR FORMATION.

§ 181. Nouns, embracing adjectives and participles as well as substantives, may be primitive, i. e. formed directly from their ultimate roots, or derivative, i. e. formed from preexisting words. Those which are derived from verbs are called verbals; those which are derived from nouns are called denominatives. The vast multiplicity of objects to which names were to be applied and the diversity of aspects under which they are capable of being contemplated, have led to a variety in the constitution of nouns greatly exceeding that of verbs, and also to considerable laxity in the significations attached to individual forms. But whatever complexity may beset the details of this subject, its main outlines are sufficiently plain. All nouns are, in respect to their formation, reducible to certain leading types or classes of forms, each having a primary and proper import of its own. The derivation of nouns, as of the verbal species, from their respective roots and themes calls into requisition all the expedients, whether of internal or external changes, known to the language, § 69. Hence arise four classes of nouns according as they are formed by internal changes, viz.:

1. The introduction of one or more vowels.

2. The reduplication of one or more of the letters of the root. Or by external changes, viz.:

3. The prefixing of vowels or consonants at the beginning of the root.

4. The affixing of vowels or consonants at the end.

a. The mass of nouns are to be regarded as primitives and not as derived from their cognate verbs. Many roots are represented by nouns alone, without any verbs from which they could have sprung, e. g. אָב *father*, אֶרֶץ *earth*. And where verbs of kindred meaning do exist, it is probable that they are not the source or theme of the nouns, but that both spring alike directly from their common ▼oot, as מָלַךְ *to reign*, and מֶלֶךְ *king* from the root מלך. Since, however, these roots or elemental themes are destitute of vowels, and consequently are incapable of being pronounced in their primitive or abstract state, it is customary and convenient in referring to them to name the verb which though a derivative form has the advantage of simplicity and regularity of structure, and is often the best representative of the radical signification. Accordingly, מֶלֶךְ *king* may be said to be derived from the root מָלַךְ *to reign*, that is, it is derived from the root מלך of which that verbal form is the conventional designation, §68.

b. Infinitives, participles, nouns which follow the forms of the secondary or derived species, §187. 2. *a*, and some others, are evidently verbals. Most nouns of the fourth class, as well as some others, are denominatives.

CLASS I.—*Nouns formed by the insertion of vowels.*

§ 182. The first class of nouns, or those which are formed by means of vowels given to the root, embraces three distinct forms, viz.:

1. Monosyllables, or those in which the triliteral root receives but one vowel.

2. Dissyllables, in which the second is the principal vowel and the first a pretonic Kamets or Tsere.

3. Dissyllables, in which the first is the principal vowel and the second a mutable Kamets or Tsere.

1. *Triliteral Monosyllables.*

§ 183. The formative vowel may be given either to the second radical קְטֹל, קְטִיל, קְטֹל, or to the first, קֶטֶל,

קְטֶל, קֹטֶל; in the latter case an unaccented Seghol is commonly interposed between the concurring consonants, § 61. 2, to which a preceding Pattahh is assimilated, § 63. 2. *a*, קָטֶל, קֶטֶל, קֹטֶל. Forms thus augmented by the introduction of an auxiliary vowel are termed Segholates.

a. In this and the following sections קטל is used as a representative root in order more conveniently to indicate to the eye the formation of the different classes of nouns. No root could be selected which would afford examples in actual use of the entire series of derivative forms; קטל has but one derivative קֶטֶל *slaughter*, and this only occurs in Obad. ver. 9.

b. As *ĭ*, *ŏ*, and *ŭ* rarely or never occur in mixed accented syllables, § 19, they are excluded from monosyllabic nouns. Every other vowel is, however, found with the second radical, thus *ă*, מְעַט *a little* prop. *paucity*, דְּבַשׁ *honey*, גֶּבֶר *man*; *ā*, אֱיָל *strength*, כְּתָב *writing*, שְׁאָר *residue*; *ĕ*, שֶׁכֶם *shoulder*, סְנֶה *bush*; *ē*, יְלֵל *howling*, בְּכִי *grief*, זְאֵב *a wolf*; especially *ī*, *ō*, and *ū*, which occur with greater frequency than any others. When the first radical receives the vowel, *ĭ* and *ŭ* are likewise excluded, inasmuch as they rarely or never stand before concurrent consonants, § 61. 4. Few of these nouns remain without the auxiliary Seghol גַּיְא *a valley*, שָׁוְא *vanity*, חֵטְא *sin*, נֵרְךְּ *spikenard*, קֹשְׁטְ *truth*. Kamets is only found before Vav, § 63. 2. *a*, § 65, מָוֶת, and in pause, אָבֶן, קָדֶם.

c. When the second radical receives the vowel, there is a concurrence of consonants at the beginning of the word, which is sometimes relieved by prefixing א, § 53. 1. *a*, with a short vowel, mostly *ĕ*, § 60. 1. *a* (5); but occasionally *ă*, אֶצְבַּע *finger* for צְבַע, אֶשְׁנָב *lattice*, אַבְּטִיחַ *bell*, אֶזְרוֹעַ and זְרוֹעַ *arm*, אֶתְמוֹל and תְּמוֹל *yesterday*.

§ 184. These nouns, standing at the first remove from the root, express as nearly as possible its simple idea either abstractly, e. g. אֱלִיל *emptiness*, שְׁכֹל *bereavement*, עֹזֶר *strength*, צֶדֶק *righteousness*, עֵזֶר *help*, גֹּדֶל *greatness*, or as it is realized in some person or object which may be regarded as its embodiment or representative, גְּבִיר *lord* from גָּבַר *to be mighty*, אֱנוֹשׁ *man* from אָנַשׁ *to be sick*, גְּבוּל *boundary*, נֶסֶךְ *libation* prop. *pouring out*, עֵמֶק *valley* prop. *depth*, חֹמֶץ *vinegar* prop. *sourness*.

a. That the position of the formative vowel before or after the second radical does not materially affect the character of the form, appears from the following considerations: (1.) The sameness of signification already exhibited, and which may be verified in detail. (2.) The occasional appearance of the same word in both forms, e. g. גֶּבֶר and גְּבַר *man*, נַעַר

§ 185   FORMATION OF NOUNS.   209

and נֶטַע *plant*, כֶּלֶא and כְּלִיא *prison*, צֹהַר and בֹּהוֹן *thumb*, נִצָּה and נְצוּחָה *brightness*. (3.) The concurrence of both forms in the Kal construct infinitive קְטֹל and קְטָלָה, § 87, קְטָלָה and קְטָלָבּ. (4.) The fact that Segholates may arise alike from קְטָל and קֹטֶל, § 61. 1. *b*. (5.) The cognate languages; monosyllables in Arabic, whose vowel precedes the second radical, answer to those whose vowel succeeds the same radical in Aramæan, and both to the Hebrew Segholates, e. g. עֶבֶד *servant*, Aram. עַבְדָּ, Arab. عَبْدٌ.

b. The presence of imperfect letters in the root may occasion the following modifications:

א״פ *roots*. Aleph, as a first radical, sometimes receives a long vowel (ֹ) instead of Sh'va (ְ), § 60. 3. *c*, אֵמוּן *fidelity* for אֱמוּן, אֵזוֹר *girdle* for אֱזוֹר.

ע״ל *Guttural* and ל״ע *Guttural*. If the third radical be a guttural, Pattahh is substituted for the auxiliary Seghol. § 61. 2, בֶּטַח *confidence*, שֵׁמַע *hearing*, גֹּבַהּ *height*; if the second radical be a guttural, the preceding vowel if Hholem remains unchanged, otherwise it also commonly becomes Pattahh נַעַר *young man*, נַעַר *youth*, פַּחַד *fear* but אֹהֶל *tent*, לֶחֶם *bread*.

פ״ and פ״נ *roots*. A vowelless י or נ is in a few instances rejected from the beginning of a word, § 53. 2. *a*, יְבוּל *produce* for יְבוּל, סוֹד *familiarity* for יְסוֹד, שֵׂיא *elevation* for נְשִׂיא, הִי *lamentation* for נְהִי, particularly in feminines and secondary derivatives; thus, רֶשֶׁת, חָמָה, עֵצָה, צָרָה drop an initial Yodh, and קִבָּה an initial Nun. Nun may also experience assimilation when it is a second radical, אַף *anger* for אַנְף, לִישׁ *cup* for לִנְשׁ.

ל״ו and ל״י *roots*. In Segholates י is preceded by Kamets עַיִל (according to Kimchi עָיִל in Ezek. 28 : 18) *wickedness*, תָּוֶךְ *midst*, unless the last radical is a guttural, רֶוַח *space*; ו is preceded by Pattahh and followed by Hhirik, לַיִל *night*, עַיִן *eye*. These letters frequently give up their consonantal character and become quiescent, § 57. 2. Vav is rejected in a few words as פִּי *brand* for פְּוִי, אִי *island* for אֱוִי, רִי *watering* for רְוִי, § 53. 3.

ל״ה *roots*. In a very few instances the proper final radical is rejected, as it is in verbs, and the final vowel written ה, as סְנֶה *bush*, בָּכָה *weeping*, הָגָה *thought*. When י appears as the radical, it prefers the form בְּרִי *weeping*, פְּרִי *fruit*, כְּלִי *vessel*; ו retains its consonantal character in חֶלְו *winter*, שְׂלָו *quail*, or it may be changed to its cognate vowel *û*, which combines with the preceding *a* to form *o*, § 62. 1, דִּיו (for d'yaû) *ink*, תְּאוֹ *antelope*. In Segholates י quiesces in Shurek, § 57. 2. (4), שָׂחוּ *swimming* for שָׂחְי, בֹּהוּ *emptiness*; the lexicon of Gesenius contains the forms מְדוּ *garment*, קֵצֶה *end*, שְׁלִי *security*, but these words only occur in the plural or with suffixes, and the absolute singular is quite as likely to have been שָׂלוּ, קָצוּ, מָדוּ.

2. *The main vowel in the ultimate.*

§ 185. 1. The second form of this class is a dissyllable with one of the long vowels in the second which is its prin-

14

cipal syllable, and in the first a pretonic Kamets, for which T'sere is occasionally substituted when the second vowel is Kamets, thus קְטָל or קָטָל‎, קָטֵל‎, קָטִיל‎, קָטוֹל‎, קָטִיל‎.

2. These are properly adjectives, and have for the most part an intransitive signification when the vowel of the ultimate is $\bar{a}$, $\bar{e}$, or $\bar{o}$, and a passive signification when it is $\bar{\imath}$ or $\bar{u}$, קָטֹן‎, קָטָן‎ and קָטֹן‎ *small*, דָּשֵׁן‎ *fat*, נְחוּשׁ‎ *made of brass*, בָּחִיר‎ *chosen*. Those with $\bar{a}$ and $\bar{\imath}$ in the ultimate are, however, prevailingly and the others occasionally used as substantives, and designate objects distinguished by the quality which they primarily denote, יָרָק‎ *herbs* prop. *green*, שֵׁכָר‎ *strong drink* prop. *intoxicating*, נָמֵר‎ *leopard* prop. *spotted*, צָנִיף‎ and צְנִיף‎ *turban* prop. *wound around*, כָּבוֹד‎ *glory, that which is glorious*.

a. The intransitive adjectives supply the place of Kal active participles to neuter verbs, § 90, and in ע״ע verbs they have superseded the regular formation, § 153. 1, קַם‎ for קָלַם‎. Kal passive participles are verbals with $\bar{u}$. This formation with $\bar{\imath}$ in the ultimate is adopted in several names of seasons, אָבִיב‎ *Abib, the time of ears of corn*, אָסִיף‎ *ingathering* prop. *the being gathered*, בָּצִיר‎ *vintage*, זָמִיר‎ *pruning-time*, חָרִישׁ‎ *ploughing-time*, קָצִיר‎ *harvest*.

b. Adjectives with $\bar{o}$ commonly express permanent qualities, those with $\bar{e}$ variable ones, גָּדוֹל‎ *great*, גָּדֵל‎ *growing great;* חָזָק‎ *strong*, חָזֵק‎ *becoming strong;* קָרוֹב‎ *near*, קָרֵב‎ *approaching;* רָחוֹק‎ *remote*, רָחֵק‎ *receding*. Hence the former are used of those physical and moral conditions which are fixed and constant, such as figure, colour, character, etc., אָרֹךְ‎ *long*, עָגֹל‎ *round*, עָמֹק‎ *deep*, גָּבֹהַּ‎ *high;* אָדֹם‎ *red*, בָּרֹד‎ *spotted*, נָקֹד‎ *speckled*, יָרֹק‎ *green*, עָקֹד‎ *striped*, צָחֹר‎ *white*, שָׂרֹק‎ *bay*, שָׁחֹר‎ *black;* מָתוֹק‎ *sweet*, טָהוֹר‎ *pure*, קָדוֹשׁ‎ *holy*. And the latter are employed of shifting and evanescent states of body and of mind, צָמֵא‎ *thirsty*, רָעֵב‎ *hungry*, שָׂבֵעַ‎ *sated*, יָעֵף‎ *weary*, אָבֵל‎ *grieving*, חָפֵץ‎ *desiring*, חָרֵד‎ *fearing*, עָלֵז‎ *exulting*.

c. The active signification asserted for the form קָטוֹל‎ in a few instances cannot be certainly established; יָקוֹשׁ‎ or יָקוּשׁ‎ *fowler*, is intransitive in Hebrew conception as is shown by the construction of the corresponding verb, comp. Lat. *aucupari, aucupatus*. Other alleged cases are probably not nouns but absolute infinitives of Kal, בָּחוֹן‎ Jer. 6:27 may as well be rendered *I have set thee to try* as *for a trier* (of metals); חֲבָלִים‎ Isa. 1:17 is not *oppressor* nor *oppressed* but *wrong-doing*, τὸ ἀδικεῖν, see Alexander in loc.; and even עָשׁוֹק‎ Jer. 22:3 may in like manner be *oppression* instead of *oppressor*.

d. ל״ה roots are restricted to forms with i, in which the radical י quiesces, טָרִי‎ *fresh*, עָנִי‎ *afflicted*, נָקִי‎ or נָקִיא‎ with otiant א, § 16. 1, *pure*,

§ 186   FORMATION OF NOUNS.

or with *a* which combines with it to form *ĕ*, ה ַ ‍, שָׂדַי and שָׂדֶה *field*, רָאֶה *fair*, גֵּאֶה *high*; in a few nouns this final vowel is dropped, דָּג *fish* for דָּגֶה, תָּו *mark* for תָּוֶה, עֵץ *tree* for עָצֶה, בֵּן *son* for בְּנֶה, פֶּה *mouth* for פֵּיֶה, unless, indeed, these and the like are to be regarded as primitive biliterals. Vav, as a final radical, may be preceded by *a*, עָנָו *meek*, or *ē*, שָׁלֵו *secure*.

3. *The main vowel in the penult.*

§ 186. 1. The third form of this class is a dissyllable having an immutable vowel, mostly Hholem, though occasionally Shurek or Tsere in the first, which is its principal syllable, and a mutable Kamets or Tsere in the second, thus קוֹטָל, קוֹטֵל, קִיטָל, קִיטֵל, קוּטָל.

2. These indicate the agent, and are either active participles, קוֹטֵל *killing*, or substantives, חוֹתָם *signet-ring* prop. *sealer*, אוֹיֵב *enemy, one practising hostility*, שׁוּעָל *fox* prop. *digger*, כֵּילָף *hammer* prop. *pounder*, הֵילֵל *morning star* prop. *shining one*.

a. A number of nouns, indicative of occupation, follow the participial form, which thus serves to express permanent and professional activity, בּוֹקֵר *herdsman*, חֹבֵל *sailor* prop. *rope-handler*, חוֹרֵשׁ *ploughman*, יוֹצֵר *potter* prop. *former*, כּוֹבֵס *fuller*, כֹּהֵן *priest*, כֹּרֵם *vine-dresser*, סוֹחֵר *merchant*, סוֹפֵר *scribe*, רוֹכֵל *trafficker*, רֹעֶה *shepherd*, רֹפֵא *physician*, רֹקֵחַ *dealer in unguents*, רֹקֵם *embroiderer*, שֹׁמֵר *watchman*, שׁוֹעֵר *porter* prop. *gate-keeper*, שׁוֹפֵט *judge*.

b. In a very few instances *u* in the first syllable is shortened and followed by Daghesh-forte conservative, עֻגָּב and עָגָב *pipe*, פּוּךְ *pit*.

c. ע״ע *roots*. The contraction of ע״ע and the quiescence of ע״י roots, by reducing them to biliteral monosyllables, obliterates to a considerable extent the distinctions which have been described and which are possible only in triliterals. The contracted forms which arise from ע״ע roots are סֹב, סָב, סֹב, סֹב, § 183. *b*. Of these סֹב = סְבַב belongs to the monosyllabic formation, and is chiefly used of abstracts, בֹּר *purity*, רֹב *multitude*, תֹּם *integrity*, עֹל *yoke*; and סָב = סָבַב to the first species of dissyllables, embracing adjectives and concrete nouns, תָּם *perfect*, חָג *feast*; while סֹב and סָב may arise indifferently from either, מַק *rottenness* is an abstract noun for מָקֵק, but רַךְ *tender* is an adjective for רָכָךְ, Kamets being compressed to Pattahh before the doubled letter, comp. § 135. 3; לֵב *heart* is for the dissyllable לְבַב, but חֵן *favour* for the monosyllable חָנַן.

ע״ו and ע״י *roots*. Nouns from quiescent ע״ו and ע״י roots may be divided into three pairs of forms, קָם, קוּם; רִיב, קוּם; רִיב. Of these the last pair (with the exception of Kal passive participles) belong to the primitive monosyllabic formation, רִיב *strife*, טוּב *goodness*, the first pair to the first species of dissyllables, לָשׁ *poor,* זֵר *proud,* אֵל *God* prop. *the mighty one,* and the second pair may belong to either, רֵישׁ = רָישׁ *poverty,* רָק = רֵיק *empty,* אָוֶן = אוֹן *strength,* טוֹב = בָּוֹת *good.*

CLASS II.—*Nouns with reduplicated radicals.*

§ 187. 1. The simple form proper to adjectives is explained § 185; it may be converted into an intensive by doubling the middle radical, retaining the long vowel of the second syllable and giving a short *i* or *a* to the first. This reduplicated or intensive form denotes what is characteristic, habitual, or possessed in a high degree. Adjectives of this nature are sometimes used as descriptive epithets of persons or things distinguished by the quality, which they denote, חַלָּשׁ *very weak,* פִּקֵּחַ *seeing* prop. (having eyes) *wide open,* צַדִּיק *righteous,* גִּבּוֹר *mighty man,* חַנּוּן *full of grace,* רַחוּם *merciful.*

a. As a general though not an invariable rule, the first syllable has Pattahh when a pure vowel *a, i,* or *u* stands in the ultimate, but Hhirik when the ultimate has one of the diphthongal vowels *ē* or *ō.* Several nouns with *a* in the second syllable are descriptive of occupations or modes of life, comp. § 186. 2. *a,* אִכָּר *husbandman,* דַּיָּג *fisherman,* דַּיָּן *judge,* חָרָשׁ (= חַלָּשׁ) *workman,* טַבָּח *cook,* מַלָּח *seaman* (from מֶלַח *salt*), סַבָּל *bearer of burdens,* צַיָּד *hunter,* קַשָּׁת *bowman,* גַּנָּב *thief,* not a mere equivalent to גוֹנֵב one who steals, but one who steals habitually, who makes stealing his occupation.

b. Since the idea of intensity easily passes into that of excess, the form קַטֵּל is applied to deformities and defects, physical or moral, אִלֵּם *dumb,* גִּבֵּן *hump-backed,* חֵרֵשׁ (= חֵרֵשׁ) *deaf,* עִוֵּר *blind,* פִּסֵּחַ *lame,* קֵרֵחַ *bald,* עִקֵּשׁ *perverse.*

c. In a few instances instead of doubling the second radical, the previous Hhirik is prolonged, § 59. *a,* קִמּוֹשׁ and קִימוֹשׁ *nettle* prop. *badly pricking,* קִיטוֹר *smoke,* שִׁיחוֹר *the Nile* prop. *very black,* צִינוֹק *prison,* בִּידוּד *spark,* כִּידוֹר *battle,* נִיצוֹץ *spark.*

d. The following double the third radical in place of the second, פֹּרְחָה *brood,* רַעְנָן *green,* שַׁאֲנָן *quiet,* נָאוָה *comely* from נָאָה, the last radical appearing as י, § 169, אֻמְלָל *feeble,* where the long vowel Tsere is inserted to prevent the concurrence of consonants.

e. ע״ע and more rarely ע״ו roots reduplicate the biliteral formed by their contraction, גַּלְגַּל and גִּלְגָּל *wheel* prop. *roller,* חִתְחַת *frightful,* זַרְזִיר *girt,* קָדְקֹד *crown of the head* prop. *dividing* (the hair); so fem. חַלְחָלָה *severe pain,* טַלְטֵלָה *casting down,* גֻּלְגֹּלֶת *skull,* and plur. כַּלְכַּלּוֹת *baskets,* כְּנִלִּים *turning*

§ 188   FORMATION OF NOUNS.   213

upside down from לְיָ = לְיָה, לֻגְלָאוֹת (sing. לֻגְלִי) *loops* and לֻגְלִים (sing. probably לֻגְלָה = לֻגְלִי) *winding stairs* from לְיָ = לְוָ; a root לוּל is needlessly assumed by Gesenius. Sometimes the harsh concurrence of consonants is prevented by the insertion of a long vowel, צִלְצָל (const. צִלְצָל) *cymbal* prop. *tinkling*, בְּרָרָה and כְרוּלָה *stark naked, totally destitute*, קַלְקַל *despicable*, or the softening of the former of the two consonants to a vowel, §57.1, כּוֹכָב *star* for כַּבְכָּב, טוֹטָפוֹת *bands* worn on the forehead for חֶרְקָלוֹן, שַׁעֲטָפוֹת (with the ending וֹן added) *ignominy* for קַלְקָלוֹן, בָּבֶל *Babylon* for בַּלְבָּל, or its assimilation to the succeeding consonant, כִּבָּר *something circular, a circuit* for כִּרְבָּר. The second member of the reduplication suffers contraction or change in שַׁרְשָׁה *chain* for שַׁרְשָׁלָה and קַרְקַע *floor* for קַרְקַר.

2. Abstracts are formed with a doubled middle radical by giving *ū* to the second syllable and *ĭ* to the first, חִבֻּק *folding* the hands, שִׁלּוּם *retribution*, שִׁקּוּץ *abomination*, and in the plural כִּפֻּרִים *atonement*, פִּקּוּדִים *commandments*, שִׁלּוּחִים *divorce*.

a. These may be regarded as verbals formed from the Piel. A like formation is in a few instances based upon other species, e. g. Hiphil הִתּוּךְ *melting* from נָתַךְ, הֲפוּגָה *cessation* from the ע״ע root פוּג, Niphal נִפְתּוּלִים *wrestlings:* נִחוּמִים when derived from the Niphal means *repentings*, when from the Piel *consolations*.

c. ע״ע roots reduplicate the biliteral to which they are contracted, חַרְחֻר *inflammation*, שַׁעֲשֻׁעִים *delight*.

c. A few roots, which are either ע״ע or ע guttural, or have a liquid for their third letter, double the last radical with *ū* in the final syllable, נַעֲצוּץ *thorn-hedge*, סָארוּר (= סָארוּר) *ruddy glow*, תַּמְרוּרִים *upright columns* designed for way-marks, שַׁעֲרוּרָה *horror*, נַאֲפוּפִים *adulteries*, גְּבֻנִּים *ridges*, also with *ō* or *ī* in the last syllable, נִיחֹחַ *acquiescence*, נַהֲלֹל *pasture*, כְּבְרִיר *shower*, כְּבְרִיר *obscuration*, שַׂעֲרִיר (K'thibh שערור) *tapestry*, חַכְלִיל whence חַכְלִילִי *dark*. The concurrence of consonants is relieved in שַׁבְּלוּל (in some editions) *snail* by Daghesh-forte separative.

§ 188. A few words reduplicate the two last radicals. These may express intensity in general, פְּקַח־קוֹחַ *complete opening*, יְפֵה־פִיָּה *very beautiful*, or more particularly repetition, הִפַּכְפַּךְ *twisted* prop. *turning again and again*, חֲלַקְלַק *slippery*, עֲקַלְקַל *crooked*, פְּתַלְתֹּל *perverse*, אֲסַפְסֻף *mixed multitude* prop. *gathered here and there*, חֲבַרְבֻּרוֹת *spots* or *stripes*, חֲפַרְפָּרוֹת *moles* prop. *incessant diggers*. As energy is consumed by repeated acts or exhibitions and so gradually weakened, this form becomes a diminutive when applied to adjectives of colour, אֲדַמְדָּם *reddish*, יְרַקְרַק *greenish*, שְׁחַרְחֹר *blackish*.

a. The first of two concurring consonants is softened to a vowel in חֲצֹצְרָה *trumpet* for חֲצַרְצְרָה, and probably זְוָאֵל Lev. 16:8 for זְלֹזֵל.
b. פ״ו roots drop their initial radical, הַבְהָבִים *gifts* from יָהַב, צֶאֱצָאִים *offspring, issue* from יָצָא.

Class III.—*Nouns formed by prefixes.*

§ 189. The third class of nouns is formed by prefixing either a vowel or a consonant to the root. In the following instances the vowel ă is prefixed with ā in the ultimate to form adjectives of an intensive signification, אַכְזָב *utterly deceitful*, אַכְזָר *violent*, אֵיתָן (= אַיְתָן) *perennial*, אַזְנָח (only represented by a derivative, § 94. *a*) *very foul, fetid*, אֲשָׁמָן *exceedingly gross or thick* (applied to darkness, Isa. 59 : 10), or verbal nouns borrowing their meaning from the Hiphil species, אַזְכָּרָה *memorial*, אַחְוָה *declaration*.

a. This form corresponds with اَفْعَل the Arabic comparative or superlative. Its adoption for Hiphil derivatives corroborates the suggestion, § 82. 5. *b* (2), respecting the formation of the Hiphil species and the origin of its causal idea.
b. The letter א is merely the bearer of the initial vowel and has no significance of its own in these forms; ה is substituted for it in הֵיכָל (= אַיְכָּל) *palace, temple* prop. *very capacious* from יָכֹל in the sense of its cognate כּוּל *to contain.* So, likewise, in a few verbals with feminine terminations, הַשְׁמִיעוּת Ezek. 24 : 26 *causing to hear* used for the Hiph. infin., § 128, הַצָּלָה *deliverance* from נָצַל, הֲנָחָה *grant of rest* (= הֲנָיחָה) from נוּחַ.
c. The short vowel prefixed with א to monosyllables of the first species, as explained § 183. *c*, has no effect upon the meaning, and does not properly enter into the constitution of the form.

§ 190. The consonants prefixed in the formation of nouns are מ, ת, and י. They are sometimes prefixed without a vowel, the stem letters constituting a dissyllable of themselves, מִקְטָל, מְסֻבָּב, תְּבַלֻּל, תְּאַשֵּׁר; more commonly they receive ă or ĭ followed by a long vowel in the ultimate, e. g. מִקְטָל, מַקְטֵל.

a. Pattahh commonly stands before ê, î, and û, and Hhirik before a and ô, unless the first radical is a guttural or an assimilated Nun when Pattahh is again preferred, מַאֲכָל *food,* מַטָּע *planting,* מַשּׂוֹר *saw,* תַּחְמָס *a species of bird,* יַהֲלֹם *a kind of gem.* Seghol is occasionally employed before a guttural or liquid followed by *a,* § 63. 1. *b,* בְּחָקְ *depth,* מֶרְכָּב *chariot,* מֶלְקָחַיִם *pair of tongs.* These rules are not invariable, however, as will appear from such forms as מִזְבֵּחַ, מִסְפֵּד, מִסְפָּר, מִלְקוֹשׁ, מִקְוָה. A few words have *â* in the ultimate, מַחֲלָת *harp,* חֶנֶק *strangling.* The insertion of Daghesh-forte separative in the first radical is exceptional, מִקְדָּשׁ Ex. 15:17, מִמְּרֹרִים Job 9:18, מִצְּנֵרוֹת Joel 1:17.

b. פּ״י roots. The first radical appears as י resting in Hhirik or Tsere, מִישׁוֹר and מֵישָׁר *rectitude,* תִּירוֹשׁ *new wine,* תֵּימָן *south,* or as י resting in Hholem or Shurek, מוֹעֵד *appointed time,* מוּסָר *correction,* תּוֹשָׁב *sojourner,* תּוּגָה *sorrow.* In a few instances it is rejected, תֵּבֵל *world,* or assimilated to the following radical, מַצָּע *bed,* מַדָּע *knowledge.*

ע״ו and ע״י roots. The root is reduced to a monosyllabic biliteral by the quiescence or rejection of the second radical, the prefix receiving Sh'va, מְצָד *citadel,* מְחִם *sound place,* תְּהוֹם *ocean,* רְקוֹם *living thing.* or more commonly a pretonic Kamets or Tsere, מָאוֹר *luminary,* מָדוֹן, דִּין and דִּין *strife,* בְּרוֹן *race,* יָרִיב *adversary.* The feminine form is almost always adopted after ת, תְּשׁוּעָה *salvation,* תְּרוּמָה *oblation.*

ע״ע roots. The root is mostly contracted to a biliteral and the vowel compressed to *ă, ä, ĕ* or *ŏ,* § 61. 4, the prefix sometimes receiving Sh'va which gives rise to a Segholate form, § 61. 1. *b,* מֶכֶס *tribute* for מְכָס, מָמֶר *bitterness* for מָמָר, תֶּבֶל *defilement* for תָּבָל, מֹרֶךְ *fear* for מָרָךְ, תֹּרֶן *mast* for תָּרָן; more frequently it receives a pretonic Kamets or Tsere, מָסָךְ *covering,* מָגֵן *shield,* מָצוּר *fortress,* צֵר *anguish.* In מַצָּץ *running,* the short vowel of the perfect root is preserved by means of Daghesh-forte in the first radical. ת is almost always followed by the feminine ending. תָּהֳלָה *folly,* תְּחִלָּה *beginning,* תְּפִלָּה *prayer.*

ל״ה roots. The ultimate has ה, מַדְוֶה *disease,* מִרְעֶה *pasture,* which is apocopated in a few words, מַשֵּׂל *lifting up,* מַעַל *higher part,* יַעַן and יַעַן *on account of,* and always disappears before the feminine ending ה . § 62. 2. *c,* מַעֲלָה *ascent,* מִצְוָה *commandment,* תִּקְוָה *hope,* תְּלָאָה *weariness.* Before the feminine termination ת the final radical appears as quiescent י or ו, תַּרְבִּית *interest,* תַּזְנוּת *whoredom,* תַּחֲנוֹת *encamping,* מַרְעִית *pasture.* Yodh is retained as a consonant after *ă,* מַחֲלָיִם *diseases.*

§ 191. The letter מ is a fragment of the pronoun מִי *who* or מָה *what.* Nouns, to which it is prefixed, denote

1. The agent *who* does what is indicated by the root, as the participles, § 84. 5, formed by an initial מ, and a few substantives, מַשְׂכִּיל *didactic psalm* prop. *instructor,* מַפָּל (from נָפַל) *chaff* prop. *what falls off.*

2. The instrument *by which* it is done, מַפְתֵּחַ *key* from

פָּתַח to open, מַלְמֵד goad from לָמַד to learn, מַשּׂוֹר saw from נָשַׂר to saw.

3. The place or time *in which* it is done, מִזְבֵּחַ *altar* from זָבַח *to sacrifice*, מַרְבֵּץ *lair*, מַלְבֵּן *brick-kiln*, מוֹשָׁב *period of residence*.

4. The action or the quality *which* is expressed by the root, מַטְבֵּחַ *slaughter*, מִסְפֵּד *mourning*, מַדְוֶה *sickness*, מְשֻׁגָּה *error*, מִישׁוֹר *straightness*. Verbals of this nature sometimes approximate the infinitive in signification and construction, as מַהְפֵּכָה *overturning*, מַשֹּׁאוֹת Ezek. 17:9, §166. 2. In Chaldee the infinitive regularly takes this form, e. g. מִקְטַל *to kill*.

5. The object upon *which* the action is directed or the subject in *which* the quality inheres, מַאֲכָל *food* from אָכַל *to eat*, מִזְמוֹר *psalm* from זָמַר *to sing*, מַלְקוֹחַ *booty* from לָקַח *to take*, מַשְׁמַנִּים *fat things* from שָׁמֵן *to be fat*, מִצְעָר *that which is small*, מֶרְחָק *that which is remote*.

a. These different significations blend into one another in such a manner that it is not always easy to distinguish the precise shade of meaning originally attached to a word: and not infrequently more than one of these senses co-exist in the same word. Thus, מָאוֹר *luminary*, may suggest the idea of agency, *dispenser of light*, or of place, *reservoir of light;* מַאֲכֶלֶת *knife*, may be so called as an agent, a *devourer*, or as an instrument, *used in eating;* מִקְדָּשׁ means both a *holy thing* and a *holy place;* מִמְכָּר *sale* and *something sold* or *for sale;* מַמְלָכָה *royal authority* and *kingdom;* מוֹצָא *the act, place, and time of going forth* and *that which goes forth;* מוֹשָׁב *the place and time of sitting or dwelling* as well as *they who sit or dwell.*

§ 192. Nouns formed by prefixing י or ת denote persons or things to which the idea of the root is attached.

1. י is identical in origin with the prefix of the 3 masc. future in verbs, and is largely used in the formation of names of persons, יִצְחָק *Isaac*, יִפְתָּח *Jephtha*, but rarely in forming appellatives, יָרִיב *adversary* prop. *contender*, יָסוּר *apostate* prop. *departer*, יַלְקוּט *bag* prop. *gatherer*, יְקוּם *living thing* prop. *that (which) stands*, יִצְהָר *fresh oil* prop. *that (which) shines*.

2. ת, probably the same with the prefix of the 3 fem. future of verbs, which is here used in a neuter sense, is employed in the formation of a few concrete nouns, תִּדְהָר oak prop. *that (which) endures*, תַּכְרִיךְ *cloak* prop. *that (which) wraps up*, תַּנּוּר *furnace* prop. *that (which) burns*, תַּפּוּחַ *apple* prop. *that (which) exhales* fragrance. But it more frequently appears in abstract terms like the feminine ending in other forms, תָּבוּן *understanding*, תַּמְרוּר *bitterness*, תַּעֲנוּג *delight*. It is very rarely found in designations of persons, and only when they occupy a relation of dependence and subordination, and may consequently be viewed as things, תַּלְמִיד *learner*, תּוֹשָׁב *one dwelling* on another's lands, *tenant, vassal*.

a. The great majority of nouns with ת prefixed have likewise a feminine ending, תַּרְדֵּמָה *deep sleep*, תְּשׁוּעָה *salvation*, תִּפְאָרֶת *beauty*, תַּרְמִית *fraud*.

CLASS IV.—*Nouns formed by affixes.*

§ 193. The nouns formed by means of an affixed letter or vowel are chiefly denominatives. The consonant ן appended by means of the vowel ō, or less frequently ā, forms

1. Adjectives, אַחֲרוֹן *last* from אַחַר *after*, רִאשׁוֹן *first* from רֹאשׁ *head*, תִּיכוֹן *middle* from תָּוֶךְ *midst*, נְחֻשְׁתָּן *brazen* from נְחֹשֶׁת *brass*. A very few are formed directly from the root, אֶבְיוֹן *poor*, עֶלְיוֹן *most high*, אַלְמֹן *widowed*.

2. Abstract substantives, the most common form of which is קִטָּלוֹן, e. g. עִוָּרוֹן *blindness*, בִּטָּחוֹן *confidence*, עִצָּבוֹן *pain*, יֵרָקוֹן *paleness*, though various other forms likewise occur, e. g. אֲבַדּוֹן and אָבְדָן *destruction*, פְּרָזוֹן *dominion*, כִּשְׁרוֹן *success*, קָרְבָּן *offering*.

a. In a few words the termination וֹן has been thought to be intensive, שַׁבָּת *sabbath*, שַׁבָּתוֹן *a great sabbath*, זֵד *proud*, זָדוֹן *exceedingly proud*, and once diminutive אִישׁ *man*, אִישׁוֹן *little man*, i. e. the *pupil* of the eye, so called from the image reflected in it. The word יְשֻׁרוּן *Jeshurun* from יָשָׁר *upright*, is by some explained as a diminutive or term of endearment, while others think that the termination וּן has no further meaning than to make of the word a proper name, comp. זְבֻלוּן. See Alexander on Isaiah 44:2.

b. ן is occasionally affixed with the vowel ê, גַּרְזֶן axe, צִפֹּרֶן nail.

c. A few words are formed by appending ם, e. g. עַבְדָּן and פִּדְיֹן ransom, סֻלָּם ladder from סָלַל to lift up, חַרְטֹם sacred scribe from חֶרֶב stylus, דָּרוֹם south from דָּרַר to shine; or ל, e. g. כַּרְמֶל garden from כֶּרֶם vineyard, גִּבְעֹל calyx or cup of a flower from גָּבִיעַ cup, קַרְסֹל ankle from קֶרֶם joint, חַרְגֹּל locust from חָרַג indicative of tremulous motion, עֲרָפֶל thick darkness from עָרִיף cloud, בַּרְזֶל iron probably from בָּלַז to pierce.

§ 194. The vowel ִי forms adjectives indicating relation or derivation.

1. It is added to proper names to denote nationality or family descent, עִבְרִי Hebrew, יְבוּסִי Jebusite, פְּלִשְׁתִּי Philistine, אֲרַמִּי Aramean, מִצְרִי Egyptian, יִשְׂרְאֵלִי Israelitish, an Israelite, דָּנִי Danite, קְהָתִי Kohathite, גֵּרְשֻׁנִּי Gershonite.

2. It is also added to other substantives, צְפֹנִי northerner, פְּנִימִי foreigner, פַּרְזִי villager, רַגְלִי footman, עִתִּי timely, inner from the plural פָּנִים; to a few adjectives, אַכְזָרִי and אַכְזָר violent, אֱוִילִי and אֱוִיל foolish, and even to prepositions, תַּחְתִּי lowest from תַּחַת, לִפְנַי front from לִפְנֵי+ִי., § 62. 2.

a. The feminine ending ה is dropped before this ending. יְהוּדִי Jew from יְהוּדָה, בְּרִיתִי Beriite from בְּרִיעָה, or the old ending ת takes its place, בַּעֲכָתִי Maachathite from בַּעֲכָה, or נ is inserted between the vowels, שֵׁלָנִי Shelanite from שֵׁלָה. Final ִי combines with the appended ִי. into ִי, § 62. 2, לֵוִי Levite and Levi, שׁוּנִי Shunite and Shuni.

b. In a very few instances וֹ takes the place of ִי., e. g. חוֹלִי white stuffs, הוֹלִי basket, לוּלִי loop, and perhaps חַלּוֹנַי, in a collective sense windows, חֲשׂוּפַי uncovered, כְּלַי which Gesenius derives from גָּבַל and takes to mean cunning; if, however, it is derived from כָּלָה, § 187. 1. c, and means spendthrift, the final Yodh will be a radical.

MULTILITERALS.

§ 195. 1. Quadriliteral nouns are for the most part evenly divided into two syllables, עַקְרָב scorpion, גִּזְבָּר treasurer, חֶרְמֵשׁ sickle, גַּלְמוּד barren. Sometimes the second radical receives a vowel, that of the first radical being either rejected, דְּמָשֶׂק damask, חֲנָמַל frost, סְמָדַר vine blossom, or preserved by the insertion of Daghesh-forte, חַלָּמִישׁ flint, עַכָּבִישׁ

spider, פִּלֶּגֶשׁ and פִּילֶגֶשׁ *concubine*. Occasionally the third radical has Daghesh-forte, בְּטַל *bat*, סְנַפִּיר *fin*.

2. Words of five or more letters are of rare occurrence and appear to be chiefly of foreign origin, אַרְגָּמָן *purple*, צְפַרְדֵּעַ *frog*, שַׁעַטְנֵז *cloth*, אֲחַשְׁתְּרָן *mule*, אֲחַשְׁדַּרְפָּן *satrap*.

3. Compound words are few and of doubtful character, צַלְמָוֶת *shadow of death*, מְאוּמָה *anything* prop. *what and what*, בְּלִימָה *nothing* prop. *no what*, בְּלִיַּעַל *worthlessness* prop. *no profit*, מַאֲפֵלְיָה *darkness of Jehovah*, שַׁלְהֶבֶתְיָה *flame of Jehovah*, except in proper names, מַלְכִּי־צֶדֶק *Melchizedek, king of righteousness*, עֹבַדְיָהוּ *Obadiah, serving Jehovah*, יְהוֹיָקִים *Jehoiakim, Jehovah shall establish*.

GENDER AND NUMBER.

§ 196. There are in Hebrew, as in the other Semitic languages, but two genders, the masculine (זָכָר) and the feminine (נְקֵבָה). The masculine, as the primary form, has no characteristic termination; the feminine ends in ה‎ָ or ת‎ָ, e. g. קָטֵל *masc.*, קְטִילָה or קֹטֶלֶת *fem.*

a. The only trace of the neuter in Hebrew is in the interrogative, מָה *what* being used of things as מִי *who* of persons. The function assigned to the neuter in other languages is divided between the masculine and the feminine, being principally committed to the latter.

b. The original feminine ending in nouns as in verbs, § 85. 1. *a* (1), appears to have been ת, which was either attached directly to the word, קְטֶלֶת which, by § 61. 2, becomes קְטָלֶת, or added by means of the vowel *a*, קְטָלָת or קְטָלָה, which by the rejection of the consonant from the end of the word, § 55. 2. *c*, becomes קְטָלָה. The termination ת‎ָ or ת‎ֶ is still found in a very few words, בָּרֶקֶת *emerald*, קָאַת *pelican*, שִׁפְחַת *company* 2 Kin. 9:17, מָחֳרָת *morrow*, מְנָת *portion*, קְצָת *end*, בְּצַלְתְּ Josh. 13:13, and the poetic forms, זִמְרָת *song*, נַחֲלָת *inheritance*, עֶזְרָת *help*, פֹּרָת *fruitful*, נוּמָת *sleep*. Two other words, חַיַּת Ps. 74:19 and גְּוִיַּת Ps. 61:1, have been cited as additional examples, but these are in the construct state, which always preserves the original ת final; it is likewise always retained before suffixes and paragogic letters, § 61. 6. *a*, רְשֻׁבָתָהּ, רְשֻׁבָתָה, חַיָתוֹ.

c. The feminine ending ת‎ָ receives the accent and is thus readily distinguished from the unaccented paragogic ה ָ . In a few instances grammarians have suspected that forms may perhaps be feminine, though the punctuators have decided otherwise by placing the accent on the penult, e. g. בֹּצְרָה *burning* Hos. 7:4, גְּלִילָה *Galilee* 2 Kin. 15:29, קְדָרָה *destruction* Ezek. 7:25, רָחָמָה *vulture* Deut. 14:17, שְׁפֵלָה *low* Ezek. 21:31.

d. The vowel letter א, which is the usual sign of the feminine in Chaldee and Syriac, takes the place of ה in דָּשָׁא *threshing* Jer. 50:11, חָרְדָא *terror* Isa. 19:17, חֵמָא *wrath* Dan. 11:44, לְבִיָּא *lioness* Ezek. 19:2, מַשְׂרָא *mark* Lam. 3:12, מָרָא *bitter* Ruth 1:20, קָרְחָא *baldness* Ezek. 27:31, שֵׁנָא *sleep* Ps. 127:2. No such form is found in the Pentateuch unless it be זְלָא *loathing* Num. 11:20, where, however, as Ewald suggests, א may be a radical since it is easy to assume a root זָלָא cognate to זוּל. The feminine ending in pronouns of the second and third persons, and in verbal futures is ִ י ; an intermediate form in *e* appears in זוּלְחִי Isa. 59:5 and עֲשָׂרָה the numeral *ten*, or rather *teen*, as it only occurs in numbers compounded with the units. For like unusual forms in verbs see § 86. *b.* and § 156. 4.

e. The sign of the feminine in the Indo-European languages is a final vowel, corresponding to the vowel-ending in Hebrew; the Latin has *a*, the Greek α or η, the Sanskrit *î*. And inasmuch as the feminine in Hebrew covers, in part at least, the territory of the neuter, its consonantal ending ה may be compared with *t*, the sign of the neuter in certain Sanskrit pronouns, represented by *d* in Latin, *id, illud, istud, quid;* in English *it, what, that.* This distinctive neuter sign has, however, been largely superseded in Indo-European tongues by *m* or *v*, which is properly the sign of the accusative, *bonum*, καλόν, the passivity of the personal object being allied to the lifeless non-personality of the neuter, Bopp Vergleich. Gramm. § 152. In curious coincidence with this, the Hebrew sign of the definite object is אֶת prefixed to nouns; and its principal consonant is affixed to form the inferior gender, the neuter being comprehended in the feminine.

§ 197. It is obvious that this transfer to all existing things, and even to abstract ideas, of the distinction of sex found in living beings, must often be purely arbitrary. For although some things have marked characteristics or associations in virtue of which they might readily be classed with a particular sex, a far greater number hold an indeterminate position, and might with quite as much or quite as little reason be assigned to either. It hence happens that there is no general rule other than usage for the gender of Hebrew words, and that there is a great want of uniformity in usage itself.

§ 197   GENDER AND NUMBER OF NOUNS.   221

a. The following names of females are without the proper distinctive feminine termination:

אֵם *mother.*   אָתוֹן *she-ass.*   פִּילֶגֶשׁ *concubine.*   שֵׁגַל *queen.*

So the names of double members of the body, whether of men or animals, which are feminine with rare exceptions:

אֹזֶן *ear.*   זְרוֹעַ *arm.*   כַּף *palm.*   קֶרֶן *horn.*
אֶצְבַּע *finger.* יָד *hand.*   כָּתֵף *shoulder.* רֶגֶל *foot.*
בֹּהֶן *thumb.*   יָרֵךְ *thigh.* עַיִן *eye.*   שֵׁן *tooth.*
בֶּרֶךְ *knee.*   כָּנָף *wing.*   צֵלָע *side.*   שׁוֹק *leg.*

The following nouns are also feminine:

אָח *brazier.*   כּוֹס *cup.*   עָיִשׁ *Great Bear.* צֹהַר *light.*
אֲשִׁית *footstep.* כִּכָּר *circuit.* עֶרֶשׂ *couch.*   צֵלָע *side.*
בְּאֵר *well.*   נֹגַהּ *brightness.* עֲשֵׂת *workmanship.* רִבּוֹא *myriad.*
בֶּטֶן *belly.*   נַעַל *shoe.*   פַּת *morsel.*   תֵּבֵל *world.*
חֶרֶב *sword.*   עִיר *city.*

b. The following nouns are of doubtful gender, being sometimes construed as masculine and sometimes as feminine. Those which are commonly masculine are distinguished thus (*); those which are commonly feminine are distinguished thus (†).

† אֶבֶן *stone.*   דֶּרֶךְ *way.*   *מִבְצָר *fortress.*   † פַּעַם *time (repe-*
*אוֹר *light.*   *הֵיכָל *temple.*   *מִזְבֵּחַ *altar.*   *tition).*
אוֹת *sign.*   *הָמוֹן *multitude.* מַחֲנֶה *camp.*   צָפוֹן *north.*
אֳנִי *fleet.*   זָקָן *beard.*   *מַטֶּה *rod.*   קֶשֶׁת *bow.*
אָרוֹן *ark.*   חַלּוֹן *window.*   *מָקוֹם *place.*   † רוּחַ *spirit.*
אֹרַח *path.*   חָצֵר *court.*   נְחֹשֶׁת *brass.*   † רְחֹב *street.*
† אֶרֶץ *earth.*   יוֹבֵל *jubilee.*   † נֶפֶשׁ *soul.*   *רֶחֶם *womb.*
† אֵשׁ *fire.*   יָמִין *right hand.*   סִיר *pot.*   *רֹתֶם *juniper.*
*בֶּגֶד *garment.*   יָתֵד *peg.*   † קֶמַח *flour.*   שְׁאוֹל *hell.*
*בַּיִת *house.*   *כָּבוֹד *glory.*   עָב *cloud.*   *שֵׁבֶט *sceptre.*
גָּדֵר *wall.*   דַּד *pail.*   *עַם *people.*   שַׁבָּת *sabbath.*
גַּיְא *valley.*   *כֶּרֶם *vineyard.*   † עֶצֶם *bone.*   שֶׁמֶשׁ *sun.*
גַּן *garden.*   *לֵב *heart.*   עֶרֶב *evening.*   שַׁעַר *gate.*
† גֶּפֶן *vine.*   לֶחֶם *bread.*   † עֵת *time (dura-*   תְּהוֹם *ocean.*
*גֹּרֶן *threshing-* † לָשׁוֹן *tongue.*   *tion).*   *תֵּימָן *south.*
    floor.   *מַאֲכָל *food.*   *פָּנִים *face.*   *תַּעַר *razor.*
† דֶּלֶת *door.*

Gesenius ascribes only one gender to a few of these words, but עָב is once fem. Prov. 12:25; so בְּאֶבֶל fem. Hab. 1:16, מִבְצָר fem. Hab. 1:10, מִזְבֵּחַ fem. Ezek. 43:13, עֶצֶם masc. Ezek. 24:10. The list might be reduced by referring the vacillation in gender, wherever it is possible, to the syntax rather than the noun. Verbs, adjectives, and pronouns, which belong to feminine nouns may in certain cases, as will be shown hereafter, be put in the masculine as the more indefinite and primary form. While, on the other hand, those which belong to masculine names of inanimate objects are sometimes put in the feminine as a substitute for the neuter.

c. Some species of animals exhibit a distinct name for each sex, the feminine being formed from the masculine by the appropriate termination, פָּר *bullock*, פָּרָה *heifer*, עֵגֶל *calf*, fem. עֶגְלָה, כֶּבֶשׂ *lamb*, fem. כִּבְשָׂה. or being represented by a word of different radicals, חֲמוֹר *ass*, fem. אָתוֹן. When this is not the case, the name of the species may be construed in either gender according to the sex of the individual spoken of, as גָּמָל *camel*, בָּקָר *cattle*, צִפּוֹר *bird*, or it may have a fixed gender of its own irrespective of the sex of the individual; thus, כֶּלֶב *dog*, זְאֵב *wolf*, שׁוֹר *ox*, are masculine, אַרְנֶבֶת *hare*, יוֹנָה *dove*, רָחֵל *sheep*, are feminine.

d. The names of nations, rivers, and mountains are commonly masculine, those of countries and cities feminine. Accordingly, such words as אֱדוֹם *Edom*, מוֹאָב *Moab*, יְהוּדָה *Judah*, מִצְרַיִם *Egypt*, כַּשְׂדִּים *Chaldees*, are construed in the masculine when the people is meant, and in the feminine when the country is meant.

§ 198. The feminine ending is frequently employed in the formation of abstract nouns, and is sometimes extended to the formation of official designations (comp. *his Honour, his Excellency, his Reverence*), פֶּחָה *governor*, בְּנָת *colleague*, קֹהֶלֶת *preacher*, and of collectives (comp. *humanity* for *mankind*), דָּג *a fish*, דָּגָה *fish*, עָנָן *a cloud*, עֲנָנָה *clouds*, עֵץ *a tree*, עֵצָה *timber*, אֹרֵחַ *a traveller*, אֹרְחָה *caravan*, צְלֵלָה Zeph. 3 : 19 *the halting*, פְּלֵיטָה *the escaped*.

a. (1) The feminine ending added to Segholates gives new prominence to the originally abstract character of this formation, רֶשַׁע and רִשְׁעָה *wickedness*, distinguished by Ewald as τὸ ἄδικον and ἀδικία, חֶרְפָּה *shame*, עַצְלָה *slothfulness*.

(2) So to monosyllables whose second radical receives the vowel, צְדָקָה *righteousness*, which is more abstract and at the same time used more exclusively in a moral sense than the Segholate, צֶדֶק *rightness*, אֲפֵלָה *darkness*, equivalent to אֹפֶל, נְגֹהָה (= נֹגַהּ) *brightness*, יְשׁוּעָה (= יֵשַׁע) *salvation*. Or nouns of this description might be supposed to have sprung from the adjectives belonging to the second form of Class I., the pretonic vowel falling away upon the addition of the feminine ending, אָפֵל *dark*, אֲפֵלָה *the dark*, τὸ σκοτεινόν, יְשׁוּעָה *the being saved* from יָשׁוּעַ, פְּלִילָה *justice* from פָּלִיל *judge*. The following nouns, descriptive of the station or functions of a particular class, follow this form, מֶלֶךְ *king*, מְלוּכָה *kingly office* or *sway*, נָבִיא *prophet*, נְבוּאָה *prophecy*. כֹּהֵן *priest*, כְּהֻנָּה *priesthood* or *priestly duty*, רֹכֵל *merchant*, רְכֻלָּה *traffic*.

§ 198   GENDER AND NUMBER OF NOUNS.   223

(3) The feminine ending occasionally gives an abstract signification to reduplicated forms, עִוֵּר *blind*, עִוֶּרֶת *blindness*, גִּבֵּחַ *having a bald forehead*, גַּבַּחַת *baldness in front*, חַטָּא *sinner*, חַטָּאת and חֲטָאָה *sin*, בַּלָּהָה *terror*, קַלָּסָה *scoffing*, חַלְחָלָה *anguish*, or to those which have a prefixed letter מ, מַהְפֵּכָה *overthrow*, מֶמְשָׁלָה *dominion*, מְהוּמָה *confusion*, or particularly ת, תְּשׁוּעָה *salvation*, תְּעוּדָה *testimony*, תִּקְוָה *hope*, תְּלָאָה *weariness*.

(4) It is likewise added to forms in ־ִי, פְּלִילִיָּה *judgment*, עֲלִילִיָּה *working*, רֵאשִׁית *beginning*, אַחֲרִית *end*, שְׁאֵרִית *remnant*, the termination ־ִית being often found in place of ־ִי, חָפְשִׁית 2 Chron. 26:21 K'ri, חָפְשׁוּת K'thibh, *disease* prop. *freedom* from duty, חָפְשִׁי *free*, חַבְצֶלֶת *redness*, חֲכַלְלִי *red*, מְרִירוּת *bitterness*, מְרִירִי *bitter*, כְּבֵדוּת *heaviness*, אַלְמְנוּת *widowhood*, and occasionally ־ִית, חָבְמִית *wisdom*, הוֹלֵלוּת *folly*, though the latter may perhaps be a plural as it is explained by Gesenius. Ewald suggests a connection between the final ־ִי of the relative adjective, which thus passes into ו and even to וֹ in this abstract formation, and the old construct ending ־ִי and וֹ. The further suggestion is here offered that both may not improbably be derived from the pronoun הוּא, which was originally of common gender, §71. a (3). Thus, חַיְתוֹ־אֶרֶץ Gen. 1:24 *beast of earth* is equivalent to חַיַּת הוּא אֶרֶץ *beast viz. that of earth*, and מַלְכִּי־צֶדֶק (which may be for מַלְכּוֹ as the plural ending ים. for ים, § 199. e), is equivalent to מֶלֶךְ הוּא צֶדֶק *king viz. that of righteousness*. The appended pronominal vowel thus became indicative of the genitive relation; and its employment in adjectives, involving this relation, is but an extension of this same use, יִשְׂרְאֵלִי *of or belonging to Israel, Israelitish*. The further addition of the feminine ending in its abstract sense, has mostly preserved the vowel from that attenuation to *i* which it has experienced at the end of the word, comp. § 101. 1. a. אַלְמְנוּת *widowhood* prop. *the state of a widow*, אַלְמָן, חָכְמוֹת *wisdom* prop. *the quality belonging to the wise* חָכָם. The rare instances in which the termination ־ִית is superimposed upon ־ִי, viz.: קַדְמֹנִיּוּת, אַכְזְרִיּוּת, may belong to a time when the origin of the ending was no longer retained in the popular consciousness. The termination ־ִית or ־וּת in abstracts derived from ל״ה roots is of a different origin from that just explained and must not be confounded with it; ־ִי or ־ו is there the final radical softened to a vowel, § 168, as שְׁבִית or שְׁבוּת *captivity* from שָׁבָה *to lead captive*.

b. In Arabic, nouns of unity, or those which designate an individual, are often formed by appending the feminine termination to masculines which have a generic or collective signification. This has been thought to be the case in a few words in Hebrew, אֳנִי *fleet*, אֳנִיָּה *ship*, שֵׂעָר *hair*, שַׂעֲרָה *a hair*, دَبٌّ *swarm*, דְּבוֹרָה *a bee*.

c. Some names of inanimate objects are formed from those of animated beings or parts of living bodies, which they were conceived to resemble, by means of the feminine ending, taken in a neuter sense, אֵם *mother*, אִמָּה *metropolis*, יָרֵךְ *thigh*, יַרְכָּה *hinder part, extremity*, כַּף *palm* of the hand, כַּפָּה *palm-branch*, מֵצַח *forehead*, מִצְחָה *greave*, פֶּה *mouth*, פֵּאָה *edge*.

§ 199. There are three numbers in Hebrew, the singular (לְשׁוֹן יָחִיד), dual (לְשׁוֹן שְׁנַיִם), and plural (לְשׁוֹן רַבִּים). The plural of masculine nouns is formed by adding ים ָ, or defectively written ִם, to the singular, סוּס *horse*, סוּסִים *horses*, צַדִּיק *righteous* (man), צַדִּיקִים or צַדִּיקִם *righteous* (men). The plural of feminine nouns is formed by the addition of וֹת, also written ֹת, the feminine ending of the singular, if it has one, being dropped as superfluous, since the plural termination of itself distinguishes the gender, כּוֹס *cup*, כּוֹסוֹת *cups*, בְּתוּלָה *virgin*, בְּתוּלוֹת and בְּתוּלֹת *virgins*, חַטָּאת *sin*, חַטָּאוֹת *sins*; in two instances the vowel-letter א takes the place of ו, § 11. 1. *a*, שֹׁראת Ezek. 31 : 8, בְּצֹאתָ Ezek. 47 : 11.

a. The masculine plural sometimes has ין ִ, instead of ים ָ, e. g. מֶלֶךְ oftener than מְלָכִים in the book of Job, מְלָכִין Prov. 31 : 3, רוֹזְנִין 2 Kin. 11 : 13, עָרִין Mic. 3 : 12, שַׁעֲשֻׁעִין Lam. 1 : 4, חַטָּאִין Ezek. 4 : 9, יָמִין Dan. 12 : 13. This ending, which is the common one in Chaldee, is chiefly found in poetry or in the later books of the Bible.

b. Some grammarians have contended for the existence of a few plurals in ִי without the final ם, but the instances alleged are capable of another and more satisfactory explanation. Thus, בְּרֵי 2 Kin. 11 : 4, כְּרָתִי, פְּלָתִי 2 Sam. 8 : 18, שָׁלִישִׁי 2 Sam. 23 : 8, and חֵצִי 1 Sam. 20 : 38 K'thibh (K'ri חִצִּים), are singulars used collectively; עַמִּי 2 Sam. 22 : 44, Ps. 144 : 2, Lam. 3 : 14, and רִמּוֹנִי Cant. 8 : 2, are in the singular with the suffix of the first person; מִנִּי Ps. 45 : 9 is not for מִנִּים *stringed instruments*, but is the poetic form of the preposition מִן *from*; כָּאֲרִי Ps. 22 : 17 is not for כָּאֲרִים *piercing*, but is the noun אֲרִי with the preposition כְּ *like the lion*, § 156. 3.

c. There are also a few words which have been regarded as plurals in ִי. But חֲלָלַי Zech. 14 : 5 and עָלַי Judg. 5 : 15, are plurals with the suffix of the first person. In חוֹזַי 2 Chron. 33 : 19, which is probably a proper name, and גֹּבַי Am. 7 : 1, Nah. 3 : 17, which is a singular used collectively, final י is a radical as in שְׂרֵי = שְׂרָה. חוֹרָי Isa. 19 : 9 is a singular with the formative ending ִי, § 194. *b*; חַלֹּנָה Jer. 22 : 14 and חֲשֻׁפַי Isa. 20 : 4, might be explained in the same way, though Ewald prefers to regard the former as an abbreviated dual for חַלּוֹנַיִם *double* (i. e. *large and showy*) *windows*, and the latter as a construct plural for חֲשׂוּפֵי, the diphthongal ê being resolved into *ay*, comp. § 57. 2 (5). דְּלָיַי Ezek. 13 : 18 is probably a dual for דָּלַיִם, though it might be for the unabridged singular דָּלָה, which, however, never occurs. The divine name שַׁדַּי *Almighty* is best explained as a singular; the name אֲדֹנָי *Lord* is a plural of excellence, § 201. 2, with the suffix of the first person, the original signification being *my Lord*.

d. In a few words the sign of the feminine singular is retained before the plural termination, as though it were one of the radicals, instead of being dropped agreeably to the ordinary rule, דֶּלֶת *door* pl. דְּלָתוֹת. So, כֶּסֶת *pillow*, קֶשֶׁת *bow*, שֹׁקֶת *trough*, חֲנִית *spear*, אַלְמָנוּת *widowhood*, כְּרִיתוּת *divorce*, זְנוּנִים *whoredom*, שָׂפָה *lip* pl. שְׂפָתוֹת. To these must be added שָׁחִית, provided it be derived from שָׁחָה in the sense of *pit*; it may, however, signify *destruction*, from the root שָׁחַת, when the final ת will be a radical. See Alexander on Psalm 107 : 20.

e. The original ending of the plural in nouns, verbs, and pronouns, seems to have been נָ, § 71. *b*. (2). In verbs the vowel has been preserved, but the final nasal has been changed or lost, יִקְטְלוּן or יִקְטְלוּ, § 85. 1. *a*. (1). In masculine nouns and pronouns the final nasal has been retained, but the vowel has been attenuated to ־ִ or *e*, סוּסִים, הָם, אַתֶּם : the Arabic has *úna* for the nominative and *ína* for the oblique case. If we suppose ת, the sign of the feminine, to be added to נָ, the sign of the plural, the vowel will regularly be changed to ־ִ before the two consonants, § 61. 4; then if the nasal be rejected before the final consonant, agreeably to the analogy of בַּת for בַּנְת and כּוֹס for כּוֹנְס, the resulting form will be ־וֹת, the actual ending of the feminine plural. If the sign of the plural, like all the other inflective letters and syllables, is of pronominal origin, this ם, which is joined to words by the connecting vowel ־ִ, may perhaps be related to מָה taken indefinitely in the quantitative or numerical sense of *quot* or *aliquot*, comp. Zech. 7 : 3; and the adverbial or adjective ending ־ָם or ־ָם may in like manner be referred to the same in its qualitative sense, comp. Ps. 8 : 5, so that רֵיקָם *vacue*, would strictly be *quà vacuus*. The pronoun seems in fact to be preserved without abbreviation in the Syriac ܐܝܡܡܐ = יוֹמָם *interdiu*.

§ 200. The gender of adjectives and participles is carefully discriminated, both in the singular and in the plural, by means of the appropriate terminations. But the same want of precision or uniformity which has been remarked in the singular, § 197, characterizes likewise the use of the plural terminations of substantives. Some masculine substantives take וֹת in the plural, some feminines take ים, and some of each gender take indifferently ים or וֹת.

a. The following masculine nouns form their plural by adding וֹת: those which are distinguished by an asterisk are sometimes construed as feminine.

אָב *father.*	* אֹרַח *path.*	* גֹּרֶן *threshing-floor.*	חִזָּיוֹן *vision*
אַגָּן *bowl.*	אַרְמוֹן *palace.*		חֲלוֹם *dream.*
אוֹב *familiar spirit.*	אֶשְׁכֹּל *cluster.*	דָּרְבָן *goad.*	חִשָּׁבוֹן *invention.*
	בּוֹר *pit.*	זָנָב *tail.*	טֶפַח *handbreadth*
אוֹצָר *treasure.*	גָּג *roof.*	חוּץ *street.*	כִּסֵּא *throne.*
* אוֹת *sign.*	גּוֹרָל *lot.*	חָזֶה *breast.*	לוּחַ *tablet.*

לַיִל night.   נֹאד bottle.   צִנּוֹר tube.   רַתּוֹק chain.
*מִזְבֵּחַ altar.   נֵר lamp.   *צִפּוֹר bird.   שֻׁלְחָן table.
מָטָר rain.   עוֹר skin.   צְרוֹר bundle.   שֵׁם name.
מַעֲשֵׂר tithe.   עָפָר dust.   קוֹל voice.   שׁוֹפָר trumpet.
*מָצוֹר summit.   עֵשֶׂב herb.   קִיר wall.   עַמּוּד pillar.
*מָקוֹם place.   שַׂר leader.   קְרָב war.   *תְּהוֹם deep.
מַקֵּל staff.   *צָבָא host.   *רְחוֹב street.

b. The following feminine nouns form their plural by adding ים: those marked thus (†) are sometimes masculine:

† אֶבֶן stone.   † דֶּרֶךְ way.   כֻּסֶּמֶת spelt.   פִּשְׁתָּה flax.
אֵלָה terebinth.   דָּת law.   לְבֵנָה brick.   פַּת morsel.
אַלְמָנָה widowhood.   זְמוֹרָה branch.   מִלָּה word.   רָחֵל sheep.
אִשָּׁה woman.   זְנוּת whoredom.   נְמָלָה ant.   שְׂעוֹרָה barley.
גַּחֶלֶת coal.   חִטָּה wheat.   סְאָה measure.   שִׁבֹּלֶת ear of corn.
† גֶּפֶן vine.   חֲשֵׁכָה darkness.   עֵז she-goat.   שִׁטָּה acacia.
דְּבֵלָה fig-cake.   יוֹנָה dove.   עִיר city.   תְּאֵנָה fig.
דְּבוֹרָה bee.   † כַּד pitcher.   פִּלֶגֶשׁ concubine.

Also בֵּיצִים eggs which is not found in the singular.

c. The following nouns form their plural by adding either ים or וֹת:

MASCULINE NOUNS.

אֵילָם porch.   לֵב heart.   מַעֲדָן delicacy.   פֶּרֶץ breach.
אֲרִי lion.   מָאוֹר light.   מַעְיָן fountain.   צַוָּאר neck.
דּוֹר generation.   מִגְדָּל tower.   מִשְׁכָּב bed.   קֶבֶר grave.
זֶבַח sacrifice.   מוֹסָד foundation.   מִשְׁכָּן dwelling.   קָנֶה reed.
זִכָּרוֹן memorial.   מוֹסֵר bond.   נָהָר river.   קַרְדֹּם axe.
יוֹם day.   מוֹשָׁב seat.   סַף basin.   שָׂדֶה field.
יַעַר forest.   מִזְרָק bowl.   עָוֹן iniquity.   שָׁבוּעַ week.
כִּיּוֹר laver.   מַכְאוֹב pain.   עָקֵב heel.   תַּעֲנוּג delight.
כִּנּוֹר harp.   מַסְמֵר nail.

FEMININE NOUNS.

אֵימָה terror.   אֲשִׁישָׁה grape-cake.   נַעַל shoe.   פַּרְסָה hoof.
אֲלֻמָּה sheaf.   אֲשֵׁרָה Astarte.   עֲרֵמָה heap.   שָׁנָה year.
אֻמָּה people.   חֲנִית spear.

NOUNS CONSTRUED IN EITHER GENDER.

אֹהֶל, אֲהָלִים aloes.   חַלּוֹן window.   מַטֶּה rod.   עֶצֶם bone.
בֶּגֶד garment.   חָצֵר court.   נֶפֶשׁ soul.   עֵת time.
גַּב rim.   כִּכָּר circle.   סִיר thorn.   פַּעַם foot.
הֵיכָל temple.   מִבְצָר fortress.   עָב cloud.   צֵלָע side.
זְרוֹעַ arm.   מַחֲנֶה camp.   עֲבֹת cord.

§ 201   GENDER AND NUMBER OF NOUNS.   227

d. The two forms of the plural, though mostly synonymous, occasionally differ in sense as in Latin *loci* and *loca*. Thus כִּכָּרִים is used of round masses of money, *talents*, כִּכָּרוֹת of bread, round *loaves*; סִירִים *thorns*, סִירוֹת *hooks*; עֲקֵבִים *heels*, עֲקֵבוֹת *foot-prints*; פְּעָמִים *footsteps* of men, פְּעָמוֹת *feet* of articles of furniture. Comp. § 198. *c*. Sometimes they differ in usage or frequency of employment: thus יָמוֹת *days*, שָׁנוֹת *years*, are poetical and rare, the customary forms being יָמִים, שָׁנִים.

e. Nouns mostly preserve their proper gender in the plural irrespective of the termination which they adopt; though there are occasional exceptions, in which feminine nouns in ־ים are construed as masculines, e. g. נָשִׁים *women* Gen. 7:13, מִלִּים *words* Job 4:4, נְמָלִים *ants* Prov. 30:25, and masculine nouns in וֹת are construed as feminines, e. g. מִשְׁכָּנוֹת *dwellings* Ps. 84:2.

f. In explanation of the apparently promiscuous or capricious use of the masculine and feminine endings, it may be remarked that the termination ־ים in strictness simply indicates the plural number, and is indeterminate as to gender, § 199. *e*, though the existence of a distinct form for the feminine left it to be appropriated by the masculine. The occurrence of ־ים in feminine nouns, and even in the names of females, as נָשִׁים *women*, עִזִּים *she-goats*, may therefore, like the absence of the distinctive feminine ending from the singular, be esteemed a mere neglect to distinguish the gender by the outward form. The occurrence of the feminine ending in a masculine noun, whether singular or plural, is less easily accounted for. Such words may perhaps, at one period of the language, have been regarded as feminine, the subsequent change of conception, by which they are construed as masculines, failing to obliterate their original form. Such a change is readily supposable in words, which there is no natural or evident reason for assigning to one sex rather than the other; but not in אָבוֹת *fathers*, which can never have been a feminine. One might be tempted in this case to suspect that וֹת was not the sign of the plural, comp. אֲחוֹת *sister*, חֲמוֹת *mother-in-law*, but that ו belonged to the radical portion of the word, and that ת was appended to form a collective, *fatherhood*, § 198, which has in usage taken the place of the proper plural. More probably, however, the idea of official dignity, which was so prominently attached to the paternal relation in patriarchal times, is the secret of the feminine form which אָב assumes in the plural, comp. פְּרָעוֹת *leaders*, קֹהֶלֶת *preacher*, while its construction as a masculine springs so directly out of its signification as to remain unaffected. And this suggests the idea that the like may have happened to names of inanimate objects. They may receive the feminine ending in its neuter sense to designate them as things, § 198. *c*, while at the same time they are so conceived that the masculine construction is maintained.

§ 201. 1. Some substantives are, by their signification or by usage, limited to the singular, such as material nouns taken in a universal or indefinite sense, אֵשׁ *fire*, זָהָב *gold*, אֲדָמָה *ground*; collectives, טַף *children*, עוֹף *fowl*, עַיִט *birds of* prey, בָּקָר large cattle (noun of unity שׁוֹר an ox), צֹאן small cattle (noun of unity שֶׂה a sheep or goat); many abstracts, יֶשַׁע salvation, עַוֶּרֶת blindness. On the other hand some are found only in the plural, such as nouns, whose singular, if it ever existed, is obsolete, מַיִם water, פָּנִים face or faces, שָׁמַיִם heaven, מֵעִים bowels, מְתִים men, מְרַאֲשׁוֹת adjacent to the head, and abstracts, which have a plural form, חַיִּים life, אֲהָבִים love, רַחֲמִים mercy, תַּחְבֻּלוֹת government.

a. The intimate connection between a collective and an abstract is shown by the use of the feminine singular to express both, § 198. In like manner the plural, whose office it is to gather separate units into one expression, is used to denote in its totality or abstract form that common quality which pervades them all and renders such a summation possible, comp. τὰ δίκαια *right*, τὰ ἄδικα *wrong*. Some abstracts adopt indifferently the feminine or the plural form, אֱמוּנָה and אֱמוּנִים *fidelity*, גְּאֻלָּה and גְּאוּלִים *redemption*, חַיָּה and חַיִּים *life*, חֲשֵׁכָה and חֲשֵׁכִים *darkness*, מִלֻּאָה and מִלֻּאִים *setting* of gems.

b. The form קְטוּלִים is adopted by certain words which denote periods of human life, בְּתוּלִים *childhood*, נְעוּרִים *childhood*, עֲלוּמִים *youth*, בְּחוּרִים *adolescence*, בְּתוּלִים *virginity*, כְּלוּלוֹת *period of espousals*, זְקֻנִים *old age*.

c. Abstracts, which are properly singular, are sometimes used in the plural to denote a high degree of the quality which they represent, or repeated exhibitions and embodiments of it, גְּבוּרָה *might*, גְּבוּרוֹת *deeds of might*.

2. There are a few examples of the employment of the plural form when a single individual is spoken of, to suggest the idea of exaltation or greatness. It is thus intimated that the individual embraces a plurality, or contains within itself what is elsewhere divided amongst many. Such plurals of majesty are אֱלֹהִים *God* the supreme object of worship, אֲדֹנָי *Supreme Lord* prop. *my Lord*, § 199. *c*, and some other terms referring to the divine being, בּוֹרְאֶיךָ Eccles. 12:1, גְּבוֹהִים Eccles. 5:7, עֹשַׂיִךְ Isa. 54:5, קְדוֹשִׁים Hos. 12:1; also, אֲדֹנִים (rarely with a plural sense) *lord*, בְּעָלִים (when followed by a singular suffix) *master*, בְּהֵמוֹת *Behemoth*, *great beast*, and possibly תְּרָפִים *Teraphim*, which seems to be used of a single image, 1 Sam. 19:13, 16.

§ 202. The dual is formed by adding ־ַיִם to the singular

of both genders, ה as the sign of the feminine remaining unchanged, and ה, reverting to its original form ת,, § 196. *b*, יָד *hand* du. יָדַיִם, דֶּלֶת *door* du. דְּלָתַיִם, שָׂפָה *lip* du. שְׂפָתַיִם.

a. The dual ending in Hebrew, as in the Indo-European languages, Bopp Vergleich. Gramm. § 206, is a modified and strengthened form of the plural ending. The Arabic goes beyond the Hebrew in extending the dual to verbs and pronouns. The Chaldee and Syriac scarcely retain a trace of it except in the numeral two and its compounds.

§ 203. The dual in Hebrew expresses not merely two, but a couple or a pair. Hence it is not employed with the same latitude as in Greek of any two objects of the same kind, but only of two which belong together and complete each other. It is hence restricted to

1. Double organs of men or animals, אָזְנַיִם *ears*, אָזְנַיִם *nostrils*, קַרְנַיִם *horns*, כְּנָפַיִם *wings*.

2. Objects of art which are made double or which consist of two corresponding parts, נְעָלַיִם *pair of shoes*, מֹאזְנַיִם *pair of scales*, מֶלְקָחַיִם *pair of tongs*, דְּלָתַיִם *folding doors*.

3. Objects which are conceived of as constituting together a complete whole, particularly measures of time or quantity, יוֹמַיִם *period of two days, biduum*, שְׁבֻעַיִם *two weeks, fortnight*, שְׁנָתַיִם *two years, biennium*, סָאתַיִם *two measures*, כִּכְּרַיִם *two talents*, דְּרָכַיִם Prov. 28:6, 18 *double way* (comp. in English *double dealing*), נַהֲרַיִם *pair of rivers*, i. e. the Tigris and Euphrates viewed in combination.

4. The numerals שְׁנַיִם *two*, כִּפְלַיִם *double*, מָאתַיִם *two hundred*, אַלְפַּיִם *two thousand*, רִבּוֹתַיִם *two myriads*, שִׁבְעָתַיִם *sevenfold*, כִּלְאַיִם *of two sorts*.

5. A few abstracts, in which it expresses intensity, עַצְלְתַיִם *double-slothfulness*, מְרָתַיִם *double-rebellion*, צָהֳרַיִם *double-light*, i. e. *noon*, רִשְׁעָתַיִם *double-wickedness*.

a. Names of objects occurring in pairs take the dual form even when a higher number than two is spoken of. שְׁלֹשׁ שִׁנַּיִם 1 Sam. 2:13 *the three teeth*, אַרְבַּע כְּנָפַיִם Ezek. 1:6 *four wings*, שֵׁשׁ כְּנָפַיִם Isa. 6:2 *six wings*,

שִׁבְעָה עֵינָיִם Zech. 3:9 *seven eyes,* כָּל־הַיָּדַיִם וְכָל־בִּרְכַּיִם *all the hands and all knees* Ezek. 7:17. Several names of double organs of the human or animal body have a plural form likewise, which is used of artificial imitations or of inanimate objects, to which these names are applied by a figure of speech, § 198. *c,* קַרְנַיִם *horns,* קַרְנוֹת *horns* of the altar, כְּנָפַיִם *wings,* כְּנָפוֹת *extremities,* כְּתֵפַיִם *shoulders,* כְּתֵפוֹת *shoulder-pieces* of a garment, עֵינַיִם *eyes,* עֲיָנוֹת *fountains,* רַגְלַיִם *feet,* רְגָלִים *times* prop. beats of the foot. In a few instances this distinction is neglected, שְׂפָתַיִם and שְׂפָתוֹת *lips,* יָדַיִם and יָדוֹת *sides,* יַרְכָתַיִם *extremities.*

b. The dual ending is in a very few words superadded to that of the plural, חוֹמוֹת *walls* of a city. חֹמָתַיִם *double walls,* לוּחוֹת *boards,* לֻחֹתָיִם *double boarding* of a ship, גְּדֵרֹתַיִם name of a town in Judah, Josh. 15:36.

c. The words מַיִם *water* and שָׁמַיִם *heaven* have the appearance of dual forms, and might possibly be so explained by the conception of the element of water as existing in two localities, viz. under and above the firmament, Gen. 1:7, and heaven as consisting of two hemispheres. They are, however, commonly regarded as plurals, and compared with such plural forms in Chaldee as עֲלָיִן Dan. 5:9 from the singular שְׁיָא. In יְרוּשָׁלַיִם *Jerusalem,* or as it is commonly written without the Yodh יְרוּשָׁלִָם, the final Mem is not a dual ending but a radical, and the pronunciation is simply prolonged from יְרוּשָׁלִָם, comp. Gen. 14:18, Ps. 76:3, though in this assimilation to a dual form some have suspected an allusion to the current division into the upper and the lower city.

§ 204. It remains to consider the changes in the nouns themselves, which result from attaching to them the various endings for gender and number that have now been recited. These depend upon the structure of the nouns, that is to say, upon the character of their letters and syllables, and are governed by the laws of Hebrew orthography already unfolded. These endings may be divided into two classes, viz.:

1. The feminine ת, which, consisting of a single consonant, causes no removal of the accent and produces changes in the ultimate only.

2. The feminine ה ָ, the plural ים and וֹת, and the dual יִם ַ, which remove the accent to their own initial vowel, and may occasion changes in both the ultimate and the penult.

§ 205. Nouns which terminate in a vowel undergo no change on receiving the feminine characteristic ת, מוֹאָבִי

§ 206   GENDER AND NUMBER OF NOUNS.   231

Moabite, מוֹאֲבִית *Moabitess*, מֹצֵא *finding* fem. מֹצֵאת, חֹטֵא *sinner*, חַטָּאת *sin*, § 198. Nouns which terminate in a consonant experience a compression of their final syllable, which, upon the addition of ת, ends in two consonants instead of one, § 66. 2, and an auxiliary Seghol is introduced to relieve the harshness of the combination, § 61. 2. In consequence of this the vowel of the ultimate is changed from ā or ă to ĕ, § 63. 2. *a*, from ē or ī to ĕ, or in a few words to ē, and from ō or ū to ŏ, § 61. 4. נִשְׁבָּר *broken* fem. נִשְׁבֶּרֶת, אֲדַמְדָּם *reddish* fem. אֲדַמְדֶּמֶת, הֹלֵךְ *going* fem. הֹלֶכֶת, גְּבִיר *master*, גְּבִרֶת *mistress*, חָמֵשׁ *five* fem. חֲמֵשֶׁת, אִישׁ *man*, אִשָּׁה *woman*, § 214. 1. *b*, נָפוֹץ *scattered* fem. נְפוֹצֶת, חֲיִשָׁה and נְחֹשֶׁת *brass*. When the final consonant is a guttural, there is the usual substitution of Pattahh for Seghol, שֹׁמֵעַ *hearing* fem. שֹׁמַעַת, מַגִּיעַ *touching* fem. מַגַּעַת.

   a. In many cases the feminine is formed indifferently by ת or by ה ָ ; in others usage inclines in favor of one or of the other ending; though no absolute rule can be given upon the subject. It may be said, however, that adjectives in ִי almost always receive ת; active participles, except those of ע״ע, ע״וּ and ל״ה verbs, oftener take ת than ה ָ ; ת is also found, though less frequently, with the passive participles except that of Kal, from which it is excluded.

   b. A final ן, ד or ה is sometimes assimilated to the feminine characteristic ת and contracted with it, § 54, בַּת for בִּנְת *daughter*, מַתָּת for מַתְּנָה *gift*, אֱמֶת for אֱמֶנְת *truth*, אַחַת for אֶחָדְת *one*, מִשְׁרַת 1 Kin. 1:15 for מְשָׁרַתְתְּ *ministering*, מָשְׁחָת Mal. 1:14 for מָשְׁחָתְתְּ *corrupt*, מַחֲבַת for מַחֲבֶתְתְּ *pan*. The changes of the ultimate vowel are due to its compression before concurring consonants.

   c. The vowel ū remains in תְּשׂוּמֶת Lev. 5:21 *deposit*, and the proper name תַּנְחֻמֶת *Tanhumeth*. From אָח *brother*, חָם *father-in-law* are formed אָחוֹת *sister*, חָמוֹת *mother-in-law*, the radical ו, which has been dropped from the masculine, retaining its place before the sign of the feminine, comp. § 101. 1. *a* ; נִפְלֵאת *difficult* Deut. 30:11 is for נִפְלָאֲת from נִפְלָא.

§ 206. The changes which result from appending the feminine termination ה ָ , the plural terminations ים and וֹת, and the dual termination יִם ַ , are of three sorts, viz. :

  1. Those which take place in the ultimate, when it is a mixed syllable.

2. Those which take place in the ultimate, when it is a simple syllable.

3. Those which take place in the penult.

§ 207. When the ultimate is a mixed syllable bearing the accent, it is affected as follows, viz.:

1. Tsere remains unchanged, if the word is a monosyllable or the preceding vowel is Kamets, otherwise it is rejected; other vowels suffer no change, מֵת *dead* fem. מֵתָה, pl. מֵתִים; יָרֵךְ *thigh* du. יְרֵכַיִם, שָׁלֵם *complete* fem. שְׁלֵמָה, pl. שְׁלֵמִים, f. pl. שְׁלֵמוֹת; הֹלֵךְ *going* fem. הֹלְכָה, pl. הֹלְכִים, f. pl. הֹלְכוֹת.

a. The rejection of Tsere is due to the tendency to abbreviate words which are increased by additions at the end, § 66. 1. It is only retained as a pretonic vowel, § 64. 2, when the word is otherwise sufficiently abbreviated, or its rejection would shorten the word unduly. Tsere is retained contrary to the rule by שִׁלֵּשִׁים, רִבֵּעִים *children of the third and fourth generations*, by a few exceptional forms, e. g. גְּבֵרָה Jer. 3:8, 11, מִשְׁבֵּלָה Ex. 23:26, גְּאֵלָה Cant. 1:6, שׁוֹאֵלָה Isa. 51:1, and frequently with the pause accents, § 65, e. g. יוֹלֵדָה Isa. 21:3, שׁוֹעֵלִים Lam. 1:16, שׁוֹמֵמוֹת: Isa. 49:8, אֹבֵדִים Ex. 28:40, סַנְוֵרִים Gen. 19:11, 2 Kin. 6:18 (once with Tiphhha), בְּצֵלְפִים: Isa. 2:20, פַּרְדֵּסִים Eccles. 2:5, מַצֵּרוֹת Isa. 2:4. It also appears in several feminine substantives, both singular and plural, e. g. מַהְפֵּכָה *overthrow*, מוֹעֵצוֹת *counsels*, תּוֹעֵבָה *abomination*, מַשְׁעֵנָה *staff*, מְכַשֵּׁפָה *witch*. On the other hand, the following feminines reject it though preceded by Kamets, יָעֵל *wild-goat*, fem. יַעֲלָה, יָעֵן *ostrich*, fem. יַעֲנָה, יָרֵךְ *thigh*, fem. יְרֵכָה. It is also dropped from the plural of the monosyllable בֵּן *son*, and its place supplied by a pretonic Kamets, בָּנִים *sons*, בָּנוֹת *daughters*, the singular of the feminine being בַּת for בִּנְתְּ, § 205. *b*; so מַזְלֵג *fork* pl. מִזְלָגוֹת.

b. Kamets in the ultimate is retained as a pretonic vowel, לָבָן *white*, fem. לְבָנָה, pl. לְבָנִים, f. pl. לְבָנוֹת; מִבְצָר *fortress*. pl. מִבְצָרִים and מִבְצָרוֹת, only disappearing in a few exceptional cases, שֵׂעָר *hair*, fem. שַׂעֲרָה, *quail*, pl. שַׂלְוִים, מִגְרָשׁ *pasture*, pl. מִגְרָשִׁים once מִגְרְשׁוֹת and מִצְבָּרוֹת *fords*, בְּכָר *talent* du. כִּכְּרַיִם but in pause כִּכָּרָיִם, נָהָר *river* du. נְהָרַיִם. The participles, נָבָא *prophesying* pl. נִבָּאִים, נִגְאָל *polluted* pl. נִגְאָלִים, ל"א *found* pl. נִמְצָאִים adopt the vowels of ה"ל forms, § 165. 2; but with the pause accents Kamets returns, נִפְצָעִים Ezek. 13:2, נִמְצָאִים: Ezr. 8:25. The foreign word פַּרְבָּר *suburbs* forms its plural irregularly פַּרְוָרִים.

c. Hholem and Hhirik commonly suffer no change; but in a few words Shurek takes the place of the former, and in one Tsere is substituted for the latter, § 66. 2 (3), מָגוֹר *terror* pl. מְגוּרִים, מָעוֹן *habitation* pl. מְעוֹנִים, מָתוֹק *sweet* fem. מְתוּקָה, pl. מְתוּקִים, צוֹק *distress* fem. צוּקָה, מָלוֹן *lodging* fem. מְלוּנָה, מָנוֹס *flight* fem. מְנוּסָה, מָנוֹחַ *rest* fem. מְנוּחָה, מָצוֹר *fortification* fem. מְצוּרָה, עָמֹק *deep* fem. עֲמוּקָה, Prov. 23:27 and רָחוֹק, צָפֹק,

§ 207 GENDER AND NUMBER OF NOUNS. 233

chain pl. רַתּוּקוֹת 1 Kin. 6:21 K'ri; פָּלִיט *escaped* pl. פְּלֵיטִים or פְּלֵטִים fem. פְּלֵטָה or פְּלֵיטָה.

d. Hholem is dropped from the plural of צִפּוֹר *bird* pl. צִפֳּרִים, as well as from the plural of nouns having the feminine characteristic ה in the singular; thus גֻּלְגֹּלֶת *skull*, by the substitution of the plural ending וֹת for ת֯, § 199, becomes גֻּלְגָּלוֹת, מַחֲלֹקֶת *course*, pl. מַחְלְקוֹת, or with Hhateph-Kamets under a doubled letter, § 16. 3. b, כֻּתֹּנֶת *coat* pl. כֻּתֳּנֹת, שִׁבֹּלֶת *ear of corn*, pl. שִׁבֳּלִים; in two instances a pretonic Kamets is inserted, בַּצֹּרֶת *drought* pl. בַּצָּרוֹת, עַשְׁתֹּרֶת *Astarte* pl. עַשְׁתָּרוֹת.

e. Seghol in nouns with the feminine characteristic ה affixed mostly follows the law of the vowel from which it has sprung, § 205; if it has been derived from Tsere it is rejected, if from any other vowel it is still in some instances rejected, though more commonly it reverts to its original form and is retained, יוֹנֶקֶת *sucker* (from יוֹנֵק) pl. יוֹנְקוֹת, אִגֶּרֶת *epistle* (from אִגָּר) pl. אִגָּרוֹת, מַאֲכֶלֶת *knife* (from מַאֲכָל) pl. מַאֲכָלוֹת, אֲדַמְדֶּמֶת *reddish* (from אֲדַמְדָּם) pl. אֲדַמְדַּמּוֹת, מֵינִקֶת *nurse* (from מֵינִיק) pl. מֵינִיקוֹת, קַשְׂקֶשֶׂת *scale* pl. קַשְׂקַשִּׂים and קַשְׂקַשּׂוֹת. Pattahh, which has arisen from a Seghol so situated under the influence of a guttural, follows the same rule, טַבַּעַת *ring* pl. טַבָּעוֹת, נֹגַעַת (from נֹגֵעַ) *touching* pl. נֹגְעוֹת.

f. A few nouns with quiescents in the ultimate present apparent exceptions, which are, however, readily explained by the contractions which they have undergone. Thus חוֹחַ for חָוָח, § 57. 2 (5). *thorn*, has its plural חוֹחִים or חָוָחִים; יוֹם (יָוָם) *day*, pl. יָמִים (יְוָמִים); מָדוֹן (מְדָוָן) *strife*, pl. מְדָנִים (מְדָוָנִים); שׁוֹר (שָׁוָר) *ox*, pl. שְׁוָרִים for דּוּד or דּוֹד, § 186. 2. c, *pot*, pl. דּוּדִים or הוּדִים, § 208. 3; שׁוּק (שָׁוָק or שׁוֹק) *street*, pl. שְׁוָקִים, עָר, עַר or עִיר) *city*, pl. once עָרִים Judg. 10:4 usually contracted to עָרִים (רָאשׁ) *head*, pl. רָאשִׁים (רְאָשִׁים). So סְאָה *measure* becomes in the dual סָאתַיִם for סְאָתַיִם and מֵאָה *one hundred*, du. מָאתַיִם for מְאָתַיִם; מְלָאכָה (מַלְאָכָה, § 57. 2 (3)), *work*, probably had in the absolute plural מְלָאכוֹת, whence the construct is מַלְאֲכוֹת.

2. The final consonant sometimes receives Daghesh-forte before the added termination, causing the preceding vowel to be shortened from $\bar{a}$ to $\breve{a}$, from $\bar{e}$ or $\bar{\imath}$ to $\breve{\imath}$, and from $\bar{o}$ or $\bar{u}$ to $\breve{u}$, § 61. 5. This takes place regularly in nouns which are derived from contracted עע roots, תָּם *perfect* fem. תַּמָּה, יָם *sea* pl. יַמִּים; מָגֵן (from גָּנַן) *shield*, pl. מָגִנִּים and מְגִנּוֹת, fem. מְגִנָּה; חֹק *statute* pl. חֻקִּים, fem. חֻקָּה, pl. חֻקּוֹת, or in whose final letter two consonants have coalesced, אַף for אַנְף du. אַפַּיִם *nose;* עֵז for עֶנְז *she-goat* pl. עִזִּים; עֵת for עֶדְתְ *time* pl. עִתִּים and עִתּוֹת; אִישׁ for. אֱנֹשׁ *man*, אִשָּׁה *woman*, and it not infrequently occurs in other cases.

a. Nouns with Pattahh in the ultimate with few exceptions double their final letter, being either contracted forms, דַּל *weak* pl. דַּלִּים fem. דַּלָּה pl.

גַּלּוֹת, or receiving Daghesh-forte conservative in order to preserve the short vowel. אֲגַם *pool* pl. אֲגַמִּים; so אוֹפָן *wheel*, הֲדַס *myrtle*, מְעַט *few*, חֲרָדָה *frightful*, יְרַקְרַק *greenish*, מַאֲוַיֵּי *desire*. Before gutturals Pattahh may be retained in an intermediate syllable. לַח *fresh* pl. לַחִים, or lengthened to Kamets, § 60. 4, שַׂר *prince* pl. שָׂרִים fem. שָׂרָה; so אֶצְבָּעוֹת *fingers*, אַרְבָּעָה *four*, כּוֹבָעִים *helmets*, מְצָרִים *straits* and הֲדָאִים *baskets*, לֻלָאת *loops*, which do not occur in the singular, but are commonly referred to הַגְּדִי לֻלָּאִי, § 194. *b*, ו being changed to א as in § 208. 3. *d*; also שַׁד *breast*, which omits Daghesh du. שָׁדַיִם. Pattahh is in the following examples changed to Hhirik before the doubled letter, § 58. 2, בַּז *prey* fem. בִּזָּה, חַת *fear* fem. חִתָּה, גַּת *wine-press* pl. גִּתּוֹת, בַּד *garment* pl. בַּדִּים and מִדִּים, מַס *tribute*, סַף *basin*, פַּת *morsel*, צַל *side*, גַּלְגַּל *wheel*, סַלְסִלּוֹת *baskets*, סַמְסְמִים *palm-branches*, מוֹרַג *threshing-sledge* pl. מוֹרִגִים or by the resolution of Daghesh-forte, § 59. *a*. It is rejected from צֶלְצַל *cymbal* pl. צֶלְצְלִים, זִן *sort* pl. זִנִים, גַּרְגְּרִים *berries*, probably from גַּרְגַּר and מְתִים *men*, from the obsolete singular, מַת. The plural of עַם *people* is עַמִּים and in a very few instances with the doubled letter repeated, עֲמָמִים; so הַר *mountain* pl. הָרִים and הֲרָרִים Deut. 8:9. צֵל *shadow* pl. צְלָלִים, חֹק *statute* pl. חֻקִּים, and twice in the construct, חִקְקֵי־ Judg. 5:15, Isa. 10:1, which implies the absolute form חְקָקִים.

b. The final letter is doubled after Kamets in the following words besides those from ע״ע roots, אוּלָם *porch* pl. אֻלַמִּים; so אֶזְנָן *hire*, גָּמָל *camel*, זְמָן *time*, חֲשֵׁכָה *darkness*, מֶרְחָק *distance*, קָטָן *small*, רַעֲנָן *green*, שַׁאֲנָן *quiet*, שׁוֹשָׁן *lily*, שָׁפָן *coney*, to which should perhaps be added עַקְרָב Deut. 8:15 *scorpion*, though as it has a pause accent in this place which is the only one where it is found with Kamets, its proper form may perhaps have been עֲקָרָב, § 65. The Niphal participle נִכְבָּד *honored* has in the plural both נִכְבָּדִים and נִכְבַּדִּים. Several other words, which only occur in the plural, are in the lexicons referred to singulars with Kamets in the ultimate; but the vowel may, with equal if not greater probability, be supposed to have been Pattahh. Kamets is shortened to Pattahh before ח, which does not admit Daghesh-forte, in the plurals of אָח *brother* pl. אַחִים, חָח *hook*, בִּטְחָה *confidence*, § 60. 4. *a*.

c. The following nouns with Hholem in the ultimate fall under this rule, in addition to those derived from ע״ע roots, גִּבְעֹן *peak* pl. גִּבְעֹנִים, חַרְטֹם *sacred scribe*, חַרְצֹב *band*, לְאֹם *nation*, עֵירֹם *naked*, and several adjectives of the form קָטֹל, which are mostly written without the vowel-letter ו, § 14. 3, e. g. אָדֹם *red* fem. אֲדֻמָּה, אֲדֻמִּים, אָיֹם *terrible*, אָרֹךְ *long*, etc.; אַשְׁפֹּת *dunghill* takes the form אַשְׁפַּתּוֹת in the plural.

d. There are only two examples of doubling when the vowel of the ultimate is Shurek, חֲרֻלִּים Prov. 24:31 *nettles* or *brambles* from חָרוּל, רְאֻיוֹת Esth. 2:9 from רָאוּי Kal pass. part of רָאָה.

e. אִישׁ (אֱנָשׁ) *man* is not contracted in the plural אֲנָשִׁים *men*; in the feminine, for the sake of distinction, the initial weak letter is dropped, נָשִׁים *women*, which is used as the plural of אִשָּׁה *woman*; אִישִׁים *men* and אִשּׁוֹת *women* are rare and poetic. אֵת *ploughshare* has either אִתִּים or אֵתִים in the plural.

§ 208. 1. Segholate nouns, or those which have an unaccented vowel in the ultimate, drop it when any addition is made to them, § 66. 2. (1). As this vowel arose from the concurrence of vowelless consonants at the end of the word, the necessity for its presence ceases when that condition no longer exists. Segholates thus revert to their original form of a monosyllable ending in concurrent consonants, § 183.

2. Monosyllables of this description receive the feminine ending with no further change than the shortening due to the removal of the accent, in consequence of which ŏ becomes ŭ or more rarely ŭ, ē becomes ĭ or more rarely ĕ; ĕ may be restored to ŭ from which it has commonly arisen, § 183, or like ē it may become ĭ or ĕ, עֶצֶם (עֹצֶם) *strength* fem. עָצְמָה, חֹפֶשׁ (חֻפְשׁ) fem. חָפְשָׁה *freedom*, אֹמֶר (אָמַר) *saying* fem. אִמְרָה and אָמְרָה, מֶלֶךְ (מַלְךְ) *king* מַלְכָּה *queen*, טֶבַח *slaughter* fem. טִבְחָה.

a. Nouns having either of the forms קְטָלָה, קִטְלָה, קָטְלָה, קֻטְלָה, are consequently to be regarded as sprung from monosyllables with the vowel given to the first radical.

3. Before the plural terminations a pretonic Kamets is inserted, and the original vowel of the monosyllable falls away, מֶלֶךְ (מַלְךְ) *king* pl. מְלָכִים, מַלְכָּה *queen* pl. מְלָכוֹת, אֹמֶר (אָמַר) *saying* pl. אֲמָרִים, אִמְרָה *id.* pl. אֲמָרוֹת, פֹּעַל (פֹּעֶל) *work*, pl. פְּעָלִים, חֵטְא *sin* pl. חֲטָאִים.

a. Pretonic Kamets is not admitted by the numerals עֶשְׂרִים *twenty* from עֶשֶׂר *ten*, שִׁבְעִים *seventy* from שֶׁבַע *seven*, תִּשְׁעִים *ninety* from תֵּשַׁע *nine*. The words בְּטְנִים *pistachio-nuts*, הָבְנִים *ebony*, צֶאֱלִים Job 40:21, 22, רַחֲמִים *mercies*, שִׁקְמִים and שִׁקְמוֹת *sycamores*, which do not occur in the singular, have been regarded as examples of a like omission. But there need be no assumption of irregularity if the first is taken with Fürst from בִּטְנָה, the second with Gesenius from הָבְנִי, and the others are explained after a like analogy. Quadriliteral Segholates also receive pretonic Kamets in the plural כִּנְבָן pl. כִּנְבָּזִים *merchants*, unless the new letter creates an additional syllable, in which case the introduction of Kamets would prolong the word too much, פִּלֶגֶשׁ *concubine* pl. פִּלַגְשִׁים, צִפֹּרֶן *nail* צִפָּרְנִים.

b. The superior tenacity of Hholem, § 60. 1. *a* (4), is shown by the occasional retention of o, not only as a compound Sh'va under gutturals, אֹרַח *way* pl. אֳרָחוֹת, so חֹדֶשׁ *month*, חֹרֶשׁ *thicket*, עֹמֶר *sheaf*, עֹפֶר *fawn*; but as

Kamets-Hhatuph in קֹדֶשׁ *holiness* pl. קֳדָשִׁים and קְדָשִׁים, שֹׁרֶשׁ *root* pl. שָׁרָשִׁים, § 19. 2, or as a long vowel in אֹהֶל *tent* pl. אֲרָוֹת, אֳהָלִים *stall* pl. אֲרָוֹת, § 60. 3. c, or shifted to the following letter so as to take the place of the pretonic Kamets in בֹּהֶן *thumb* pl. בְּהוֹנוֹת, נֹגַהּ *brightness* pl. נְגֹהוֹת, § 184. a. Comp. פֶּסֶל (פְּסֶל) *graven image* pl. פְּסִילִים. In other nouns it is rejected, בֹּקֶר *morning* pl. בְּקָרִים; so גֹּרֶן *threshing-floor*, כֹּפֶר *cypress*, קֹמֶץ *handfull*, רֹמַח *spear*, רֹתֶם *juniper*, שֹׁבֶל *hollow of the hand*.

c. Middle Vav quiesces in the plural of the following nouns: מָוֶת *death* pl. מוֹתִים, עָוֶל *iniquity* pl. עוֹלָה. Gesenius regards אוֹנִים Prov. 11:7, Hos. 9:4, as the plural of אָוֶן, while others derive it from אוֹן, translating it *riches* in the former passage and *sorrow* in the latter, the primary idea out of which both senses spring being that of *toil*. Middle Yodh quiesces in the plural of אַיִל *ram* pl. אֵילִים, זַיִת *olive* pl. זֵיתִים, לַיִל *night* pl. לֵילוֹת, but not in חַיִל *strength* pl. חֲיָלִים, עַיִן *fountain* pl. עֲיָנוֹת, עַיִר *ass-colt* pl. עֲיָרִים, תַּיִשׁ *goat* pl. תְּיָשִׁים. The plural of גַּיְא *valley* is גֵּאָיוֹת by transposition from the regular form גֵּיאָיוֹת which is twice found in the K'thibh 2 Kin. 2:16, Ezek. 6:3; בַּיִת *house* has as its plural בָּתִּים, whether this be explained as for בְּנָתִים from בָּנָה *to build* or for בְּתָתִים from בּוּת *to lodge*. Middle Yodh always quiesces before the feminine and dual endings, צַיִד *provision* fem. צֵידָה, עַיִן *eye* du. עֵינַיִם.

d. Monosyllables in י, from ל״ה roots belong properly to this formation, § 57. 2 (4) and § 184. *b*, and follow the rules given above both in the feminine (חֲלִי) חֶלְי *necklace* fem. חֶלְיָה, and the plural (אֲרִי) אֳרִי *lion* pl. אֲרָיוֹת and אֲרָיִים, גְּדִי *kid* pl. גְּדָיִים, or with the change of י to א, § 56. 4, which also occurs in verbs, § 177. 3, חֲלִי *necklace* pl. חֲלָאִים, *simple* pl. פְּתָיִים and פְּתָאִים, צְבִי *gazelle* pl. צְבָיִים, צְבָאִים and צְבָאוֹת; in like manner צְבָאִים *branches*, לְבָאִים *lions* are referred to צְבִי and לְבִי though these singulars do not occur; כְּלִי (כֶּלִי) *utensil* does not receive Kamets in the plural כֵּלִים.

4. The dual sometimes takes a pretonic Kamets like the plural, but more frequently follows the feminine in not requiring its insertion, דֶּלֶת (דַּלְתְּ) *door* du. דְּלָתַיִם, דֶּרֶךְ (דַּרְכְּ) *way* du. דְּרָכַיִם, קֶרֶן (קַרְנְ) *horn* du. קַרְנַיִם and קְרָנַיִם, לְחִי, מְתָנַיִם, צְלָעַיִם, לֶחִי (לֶחְיְ) *cheek* du. לְחָיַיִם, בֶּרֶךְ (בַּרְכְּ) *knee* du. בִּרְכַּיִם, so מְתָנַיִם, צְלָעַיִם, צָהֳרַיִם, עַרְבַּיִם.

§ 209. When the ultimate is a simple syllable, the following cases occur, viz:

1. Final ה, is rejected before the feminine and plural endings, יָפֶה *beautiful* fem. יָפָה f. pl. יָפוֹת, מַעֲשֶׂה *work* pl. מַעֲשִׂים; so מַחֲנֶה *camp* du. מַחֲנַיִם.

a. The last radical in words of this description is properly י, which is rejected after a vowelless letter, § 62. 2. *c*, so that יָפָה is for יָפְיָה and

§ 209   GENDER AND NUMBER OF NOUNS.   237

בְּצָשִׁים for מַעֲשׂוֹרִים. In a very few instances the radical י remains. e. g. עֹלָה Cant. 1:7 from עֹלֶה (עֹלִי) מִרְחִים Isa. 25:6 from מִרְחָה (מִרְחָי) and is even strengthened by Daghesh-forte, § 207. 2, בִּיבֶה Lam. 1:16 from בּוֹכָה, פּׂרִיָה and פֹּרָה, § 196. b. fem. of פֶּרֶה, הָרָיוֹת Hos. 14:1, elsewhere הָרוֹת, פֶּה mouth, edge pl. פִּים, פִּיוֹת and פִּיּוֹת, or changed to א, § 56. 4, טָלֶה (טָלִי) young lamb טְלָאִים (טְלָיִים), so that it is not necessary to assume a singular טְלִי which no where occurs, חֶלְבָּה Ps. 10:8 חֵלְכָאִים ver. 10. See Alexander in loc.

2. Final י may combine with the feminine and plural endings, so as to form יָה., יִים., יוֹת., or it may in the masculine plural be contracted to ים., § 62. 2, עִבְרִי Hebrew pl. עִבְרִים and עִבְרִיִּים fem. עִבְרִיָּה f. pl. עִבְרִיּוֹת; צִי ship pl. צִים and צִיִּים, חָפְשִׁי free pl. חָפְשִׁים, נָקִי pure pl. נְקִיִּים. So nouns in ית. upon the exchange of the feminine singular for the plural termination עַמּוֹנִית Ammonitess pl. עַמּוֹנִיּוֹת, חִתִּית Hittitess חִתִּיּוֹת.

a. In עַרְבִיאִים 2 Chron. 17:11 Arabians from עַרְבִי an א is interposed, elsewhere עַרְבִים; דָּלִיּוֹת branches, זָוִיּוֹת corners and מְנַקִּיּוֹת bowls, which do not occur in the singular, are assumed to be from דָּלִית, זָוִית and מְנַקִּית.

b. A few monosyllables in י. form their feminines in this manner, though in the masculine plural they follow the rule before given, § 208. 3. d, גְּדִי kid fem. גְּדִיָּה, לְבִי lion, לְבִיָּא lioness, § 196. d, צְבִי gazelle fem. צְבִיָּה (and צְבִיָּא and צְבִיָה are used as proper names), שְׁתִי drinking fem. שְׁתִיָּה.

3. There are few examples of final ה or ו with added endings. The following are the forms which they assume: שְׁקִי drink pl. שִׁקּוּיִם, מַלְכוּת kingdom pl. מַלְכִיּוֹת, § 62. 2, עֵדוּת testimony pl. עֵדְוֹת, אָחוֹת sister pl. אֲחָיוֹת and אֲחָיוֹת for אֲחָוֹת, רִבּוֹ and רִבּוֹא myriad pl. רִבּוֹת, רִבּאוֹת and רִבֹּאוֹת; the dual רִבֹּתַיִם inserts the sign of the feminine.

a. חֲנִיּוֹת or חֲנֻיוֹת Jer. 37:16 cells is referred to the assumed singular חָנוּת; נְשׁוּיוֹת Isa. 3:16 K'thibh and בְּשׂוּוֹת 1 Sam. 25:18 K'thibh are formed from נָשׂוּ, עָשׂוּ abbreviated Kal passive participles, § 172. 5, but in the absence of the appropriate vowel points their precise pronunciation cannot be determined.

b. Nouns ending in a quiescent radical א may be regarded as terminating in a consonant, since this letter resumes its consonantal power upon an addition being made to the word. Comp. § 162. נִצְאָ found fem. נִצְאָה, פֶּרֶא wild ass pl. פְּרָאִים.

§ 210. The changes, which occur in the penult, arise from the disposition to shorten the former part of a word, when its accent has been carried forward by accessions at the end, § 66. 1. They consist in the rejection of Kamets or Tsere, גָּדוֹל *great* fem. גְּדוֹלָה pl. גְּדוֹלִים f. pl. גְּדוֹלוֹת, דָּבָר *word* pl. דְּבָרִים, זִכָּרוֹן *memorial* pl. זִכְרֹנוֹת, כָּנָף *wing* du. כְּנָפַיִם, מֵשִׁיב *restoring* pl. מְשִׁיבִים fem. מְשִׁיבָה, מֵצַר *distress* pl. מְצָרִים, לֵוִי *Levite* pl. לְוִיִּים, except from nouns in ה‍ָ, in which the place of the accent is not changed by the addition of the terminations for gender and number, § 209. 1, יָפֶה *beautiful* fem. יָפָה pl. יָפוֹת, שָׂדֶה *field* pl. שָׂדוֹת, קָשֶׁה *hard* pl. קָשִׁים, מֵעֶה pl. מֵעִים and מֵעוֹת *bowels*, נָכֶה *smitten* pl. נְכִים. Other penultimate vowels are mostly exempt from change.

a. Kamets, which has arisen from Pattahh in consequence of the succeeding letter not being able to receive Daghesh-forte, as the form properly requires, is incapable of rejection. Such a Kamets is accordingly retained without change before ר, e. g. חָרָשׁ for חָרָּשׁ, § 187. 1. *workman* pl. חָרָשִׁים, so פָּרָשׁ *horseman*, בָּרִיחַ *fugitive*, סָרִיס (const. סְרִיס) *eunuch*, עָרִיץ *terrible*, חָרוּץ *violent*, חָרוּץ *diligent*, or shortened to Pattahh before ח, § 60. 1. *a* (4), בָּחוּר *young man* pl. בַּחוּרִים. Kamets is also retained in certain ע"ע and ל"ה derivatives as a sort of compensation for the reduction of the root by contraction or quiescence, e. g. מָגֵן *shield* pl. מָגִנִּים and מָגִנּוֹת, מָצוֹד *fortress* pl. מְצָדִים, דָּלִית *branch* pl. דָּלִיּוֹת, זָוִית *corner* pl. זָוִיּוֹת. Other instances of its retention are rare and exceptional, בָּגוֹד *treacherous* fem. בָּגוֹדָה, שָׁבִיעַ (const. שְׁבַע) *week* pl. שָׁבָעִים and שָׁבֻעוֹת but du. שְׁבֻעַיִם, שָׁלִישׁ *warrior* pl. שָׁלִישִׁים.

b. When Kamets following a doubled letter is rejected, and Dagheshforte is omitted in consequence, § 25, the antepenultimate vowel is in a few instances changed from Hhirik to Seghol, § 61. 5, חִזָּיוֹן *vision* pl. חֶזְיוֹנוֹת, עִשָּׂרוֹן *a tenth* pl. עֶשְׂרֹנִים, but זִכָּרוֹן *memorial* pl. זִכְרֹנוֹת.

c. Tsere is not rejected if it has arisen from Hhirik before a guttural in a form which properly requires Daghesh-forte, חֵרֵשׁ for חִרֵּשׁ, § 187. 1. *b*, *deaf* pl. חֵרְשִׁים, or if it is commonly represented by ר, § 14. 3, כֵּלַח or פֵּילַח, § 186, *hammer* pl. פֵּילַשּׁוֹת, or a radical י quiesces in it, אֵיתָן or אֵתָן (from יָתַן) § 189) *perennial* pl. אֵיתָנִים or אֵתָנִים, הֵיכָל *temple* pl. הֵיכָלִים, and הֵיכָלוֹת, and מֵישָׁרִים and מֵישָׁרִים *rectitude*, זֵידוֹנִים (from זֵד or זֵיד) *proud*. Other cases are rare and exceptional, e. g. אֲבֵלִים Neh. 3 : 34 *feeble*.

d. Hholem is almost invariably retained in the penult, yet it yields to the strong tendency to abbreviation in the following trisyllables: אַשְׁדּוֹדִית *Ashdoditess* pl. אַשְׁדֳּדִיּוֹת Neh. 13 : 23 K'ri (K'thibh אשׁדודיוֹת). עַמּוֹנִית *Ammonitess* pl. עַמֳּנִיּוֹת id. (K'thibh עמוניות, 1 Kin. 11 : 1 צַמֳּנִיּוֹת),

§ 211 GENDER AND NUMBER OF NOUNS. 239

Sidonian f. pl. צִדְנִיֹּת where long Hhirik becomes Tsere before concurrent consonants, § 61. 4.

e. When the penult is a mixed syllable containing a short vowel, it is ordinarily not subject to change, § 58. 2. The tendency to the greatest possible abbreviation is betrayed, however, in a few examples by the reduction of the diphthongal Seghol to Pattahh, comp. § 60. 3. *b*, אֶשְׁכֹּל *cluster* pl. אֶשְׁכֹּלוֹת Cant. 7 : 8. מֶרְכָּב *chariot* fem. מֶרְכָּבָה pl. מַרְכָּבוֹת, מִרְחָק *distance* pl. מֶרְחַקִּים and מֶרְחַקִּים, or of Pattahh to the briefest of the short vowels Hhirik, comp. § 207. 2. *a*, זַלְעָפָה *fury* pl. זַלְעָפוֹת, מַזְלֵג *fork* pl. מִזְלָגוֹת, § 190. *a*, צַלַּחַת *dish* pl. צַלָּחוֹת by the resolution of Daghesh-forte for צַלְּחוֹת, § 59. *a*; אַחֵר for אַחֵר *other* has in the plural אֲחֵרִים, אֲחֵרוֹת as if from אָחָר, גַּחֶלֶת *coal* has pl. גֶּחָלִים by § 63. 1.

§ 211. In forming the plural of nouns, which have a feminine ending in the singular, the latter must first be omitted before the rules already given are applied. Thus, מַמְלָכָה *kingdom* by the omission of the feminine ending becomes מַמְלָךְ, hence, by § 207. 1, its plural is מַמְלָכוֹת; so מַלְכָּה *queen* becomes מַלְךְ, and by § 208. 3. its plural is מְלָכוֹת; אִגֶּרֶת *epistle* becomes אִגֵּר, and by § 207. 1. its plural is אִגְּרוֹת. As precisely the same changes result from appending the feminine ה, and the plural endings, except in the single case of Segholate nouns or monosyllables terminating in concurrent consonants, § 208, nouns in ה, become plural with no further change than that of their termination; only in the exceptional case referred to a pretonic Kamets must be inserted. Nouns in ת, after omitting the feminine ending, are liable to the rejection or modification of the vowel of the ultimate in forming the plural, as explained § 207. 1. *d*. and *e*. On the other hand, as the dual ending is not substituted for that of the feminine singular, but added to it, no such omission is necessary in applying the rules for the formation of the dual, it being simply necessary to observe that the old ending ת, takes the place of ה, , § 202. Thus שָׁנָה (שָׁנָת) *year*, by § 210, becomes in the dual שְׁנָתַיִם, דֶּלֶת *door*, by § 208. 4, du. דְּלָתַיִם, נְחֹשֶׁת *brass* du. נְחֻשְׁתַּיִם.

a. In the following examples a radical, which has been rejected from the singular, is restored in the plural, אָמָה (for אֲמָתָה) *maid-servant* pl.

240 ETYMOLOGY. § 212–214

אֲמָהוֹת, מְנָת (for מְנָיָת from מָנָה) *portion* pl. מְנָיוֹת and גְּנָאוֹת, comp. § 208. 3. *d*, קְצָת (for קְצָיָת from קָצָה) pl. קְצָוֹת; in like manner בְּנוֹת *colleagues* is referred to the assumed singular בְּנָת. פֶּחָה (פַּחֲוָה) *governor* has in the plural both פַּחֲווֹת (const. פַּחֲוֹת) and פַּחוֹת.

The Construct State.

§ 212. When one noun stands in a relation of dependence on another, the second or specifying noun is, in occidental languages, put in the genitive case; in Hebrew, on the other hand, the second noun undergoes no change, but the first is put into what is commonly called the construct state (סָמוּךְ or נִסְמָךְ *supported*). A noun which is not so related to a following one is said to be in the absolute state (מֻפְרָד *cut off*). Thus, דָּבָר *word* is in the absolute state; but in the expression דְּבַר הַמֶּלֶךְ *verbum regis, the word of the king,* דְּבַר is in the construct state. By the juxtaposition of the two nouns a sort of compound expression is formed, and the speaker hastens forward from the first noun to the second, which is necessary to complete the idea. Hence results the abbreviation, which characterizes the construct state.

a. The term *absolute state* was introduced by Reuchlin; he called the construct *the state of regimen.*

§ 213. The changes, which take place in the formation of the construct, affect

1. The endings for gender and number.

2. The final syllable of nouns, which are without these endings.

3. The syllable preceding the accent.

§ 214. The following changes occur in the endings for gender and number, viz.:

1. The feminine ending ה ָ is changed to ת ַ, שִׁפְחָה *handmaid* const. שִׁפְחַת; the ending ת remains unchanged, מִשְׁמֶרֶת *observance* const. מִשְׁמֶרֶת.

§ 215. THE CONSTRUCT STATE OF NOUNS.

a. The explanation of this appears to be that the construct state retains the old consonantal ending ה ָ , the close connection with the following noun preserving it as if in the centre of a compound word, § 55. 2. *c;* whereas in the isolation of the absolute state, the end of the word is more liable to attrition and the consonant falls away.

b. Some nouns in ה ָ preceded by Kamets adopt a Segholate form in the construct, בְּמַלְכָה *kingdom* const. מַמְלֶכֶת instead of מַמְלָכֵת § 61. 1. *b.* מֶמְשָׁלָה *dominion* const. מֶמְשֶׁלֶת, מְלָאכָה *work* const. מְלֶאכֶת, מֶרְכָּבָה *chariot* const. מֶרְכֶּבֶת, עֲטָרָה *crown* const. עֲטֶרֶת, לֶהָבָה *flame* const. לֶהָבַת, עֲשָׂרָה *ten* const. עֲשֶׂרֶת, or with the Segholah changed to Pattahhs under the influence of a guttural, מִשְׁפָּחָה *family* const. מִשְׁפַּחַת, אַרְבָּעָה *four* const. אַרְבַּעַת; so דְּבֵלָה *fig-cake* const. דְּבֶלֶת; אִשָּׁה *woman*, though it occurs in the absolute, Deut. 21:11, 1 Sam. 28:7, Ps. 58:9, is mostly used as the construct of אֵשֶׁת . On the other hand, חֵמָת *bottle* has in the construct חֵמַת Gen. 21:14 (the accent thrown back by § 35. 1) as if from חֵמָה .

2. The ending ים ִ of the masculine plural and יִם ַ of the dual are alike changed to י ֵ , עַמִּים *nations* const. עַמֵּי, קַרְנַיִם *horns* const. קַרְנֵי; וֹת of the feminine plural suffers no change קֹלוֹת *voices* const. קֹלוֹת .

a. The compression of *î* to *ê* regularly takes place upon its being followed by concurrent consonants, § 61. 4. This is here suggested as the explanation of the change of vowel in the plural. It results from the close connection of the construct state, which as it were, unites the two words into one compound term; thus, בָּתִּים *houses* joined to גָּזִית *hewn stone* would become בָּתִּים־גָּזִית, and by the dropping of the nasal, according to § 55. 2. *b,* בָּתֵּי גָזִית *houses of hewn stone.* Comp. § 199. *e.* In the dual the final nasal is likewise rejected, and *ay* combines to form the diphthongal *ê,* § 57. 2 (5).

b. In a very few instances the vowel ending of the masculine plural construct is added to feminine nouns בְּמָתֵי (the accent invariably thrown back by § 35. 1), commonly in the K'thibh במותי const. of בָּמוֹת *highplaces,* מֵרְאַשֹׁתָי 1 Sam. 26:12; this takes place regularly before suffixes, § 220. 2.

§ 215. 1. In a mixed final syllable Kamets is commonly shortened to Pattahh: so is Tsere when preceded by Kamets; other vowels remain without change, יָד *hand* const. יַד , מוֹשָׁב *seat* const. מוֹשַׁב, צַוָּאר *neck* const. צַוַּאר, זָקֵן *old* const. זְקַן , לֵב *heart* const. לֶב-, גִּבּוֹר *mighty man* const. גִּבּוֹר .

a. Kamets remains in the construct of אוּלָם *porch,* כְּתָב *writing,* מַתָּן *gift.* עָב *cloud* (once const. עַב Ex. 19:9), פִּתְגָם *decree* and יָם *sea,* e. g. יַם־הַמֶּלַח *sea of salt,* except in the phrase יַם סוּף *sea of weed,* i. e. *Red Sea;* חָלָב *milk* becomes חֲלֵב, and לָבָן *white* לְבֶן־ Gen. 49:12 in the construct.

16

b. Tsere remains in חָמֵשׁ *five* const. חֲמֵשׁ, יָוֵן *mire* const. יְוֵן, רֹפַח, breathing const. רְפַח, עָקֵב *heel* const. עֲקֵב, in the ע"ו derivative מָגֵן *shield* const. מָגֵן and in כָּלֵב found in several proper names. It is occasionally shortened to Seghol before Makkeph in אֵבֶל *mourning* const. אֶבֶל־, עֵת *time* const. עֵת, עֶת־ and עֶת־, שֵׁם *name* const. שֵׁם, שֶׁם־ and שֶׁם־: בֵּן *son*, which in the absolute retains Tsere before Makkeph, Gen. 30:19, Ezek. 18:10, has in the construct בֵּן, בֶּן־ or בֶּן־. Tsere is shortened to Pattahh in a few cases not embraced in the rule, viz.: קֵן *nest* const. קַן־, מַקֵּל *rod* const. מַקֵּל and מַקֵּל, אֹבֵד Deut. 32:28 *perishing* const. of אֹבֵד, the Kal participles of Lamedh guttural verbs, § 126. 1, and the following nouns with prefixed מ in several of which a preceding Pattahh is likewise changed to Hhirik, § 190. *a*, מַעֲשֵׂר *tithe* const. מַעְשַׂר, מִסְפֵּד *mourning* const. מִסְפַּד, מַפְתֵּחַ *key* const. מַפְתַּח and מַפְתַּח, מַרְבֵּץ *lair* const. מַרְבַּץ, מָרוֹם, מִרְזַח *clamour* const. מָרוֹם, מַשְׁבֵּר *matrix* const. מַשְׁבַּר, מַשְׁחָת *corruption* const. מִזְבֵּחַ *altar* const. מִזְבַּח, מִשְׁחָת.

c. Hholem is shortened to Kamets-Hhatuph before Makkeph in the construct of monosyllables from ע"ו roots, חֹק *statute* const. חָק־ and חָק־, rarely in other words גָּדֹל־ Prov. 19:19, Ps. 145:8, Nah. 1:3 (in the last two passages the K'thibh has גדול), טְהָר־ Job 17:10, Prov. 22:11, קְנָם־ Ex. 30:23, שְׁלָשׁ־ Ex. 21:11; this becomes Pattahh before the guttural in גְּבָהּ־ for גְּבֹהּ־ construct of גָּבֹהּ *high*. כֹּל *kol* construct of כֹּל *all* occurs twice, viz.: Ps. 35:10, Prov. 19:7, without a Makkeph following, § 19. 2. *a*; it must not be confounded with כָּל *kal* Isa. 40:12 *he comprehended* pret. of כּוּל.

d. The termination ִי becomes ִי in the construct, § 57. 2 (5), דַּי *enough* const. דֵּי, חַי *life* const. חֵי.

e. Three monosyllabic nouns form the construct by adding a vowel, אָב *father* const. אַב Gen. 17:4, 5, elsewhere אֲבִי, אָח *brother* const. אֲחִי, רֵעַ *friend* const. רֵעֶה 2 Sam. 15:37, 1 Kin. 4:5, or רֵעֵה 2 Sam. 16:16, Prov. 27:10 K'thibh. These may be relics of the archaic form of the construct, § 218, or the monosyllables may be abridged from ל"ה roots, § 185. 2. *c*.

2. In a simple final syllable ה‎ָ is changed to ה‎ֵ, שֶׂה *sheep* const. שֵׂה, רֹעֶה *shepherd* const. רֹעֵה, שָׂדֶה *field* const. שְׂדֵה; other vowels remain unchanged.

a. This is an exception to the general law of shortening, which obtains in the construct. It has, perhaps, arisen from the increased emphasis thrown upon the end of the word, as the voice hastens forward to that which is to follow. In like manner the brief and energetic imperative ends in Tsere in ל"ה verbs, while the future has Seghol, § 168. *c*. An analogous fact is found in the Sanskrit vocative. The language of address calls for a quick and emphatic utterance; and this end is sometimes attained by shortening the final vowel, and sometimes by the directly opposite method of lengthening it. Bopp Vergleich. Gramm. § 205.

b. פֶּה *mouth* has פִּי in the construct.

c. Nouns ending in quiescent א preserve their final vowel unchanged in the construct, יָרֵא *fearing* const. יְרֵא, צָבָא *host* const. צְבָא.

§ 216. 1. Kamets and Tsere are commonly rejected from the syllable preceding the accent, מָקוֹם *place* const. מְקוֹם, שָׁנָה *year* const. שְׁנַת, שָׁנִים *years* const. שְׁנֵי, אוֹצָרוֹת *treasures* const. אוֹצְרוֹת, יָדַיִם *hands* const. יְדֵי, לֵבָב *heart* const. לְבַב, חֵמָה *wrath* const. חֲמַת.

a. Kamets preceding the accented syllable is retained (1) when it has arisen from Pattahh before a guttural in consequence of the omission of Daghesh-forte, חָרָשׁ (for חַרָּשׁ) *workman* const. חָרַשׁ, פָּרָשׁ (מַפָּרָשׁ) *horseman* const. פָּרַשׁ, פֹּרֶכֶת (פֹּרֶּכֶת) *vail* const. פָּרֹכֶת, צָרָה (צַרָּה) *distress* const. צָרַת; (2) in words from עי and עו roots, עָרִים (from עָיר) *cities* const. עָרֵי, בָּאִים (from בּוֹא) *coming* const. בָּאֵי; (3) under מ prefixed to עי roots, מָסָךְ (from סָכַךְ) *covering* const. מְסַךְ, מָגֵן (from גָּנַן) *shield* const. מָגֵן, מָעוֹז (from עָזַז) *fortress* const. מָעוֹז, (4) in לה derivatives of the form גָּלוּת (from גָּלָה) *exile* const. גָּלוּת, הָגוּת *meditation* const. הָגוּת. (5) in the construct dual and plural of triliteral monosyllables or Segholates from לא and לה roots, לְחָיַיִם (from לְחִי) *cheeks* const. לְחָיֵי, גְּדָיִים (from גְּדִי) *kids* const. גְּדָיֵי, חֲטָאִים (from חֵטְא) *sins* const. חֲטָאֵי; (6) in the following nouns in most of which it stands immediately before or after a guttural, § 60. 3. *c,* אָלָה *curse,* מִצְוָה *care,* תְּעָלָה *conduit,* and the plurals דּוּדָאֵי, דְּבָרַי Lev. 7: 38, צֶאֱצָאֵי, מוֹצָאֵי, מוֹרָשֵׁי, בָּשָׂרַי, קָרְבָּנַי, חָרָשֵׁי 2 Kin. 12:8, מִפְלָאֵי Ezek. 27: 9, מִשְׁפְּטֵי Job 34: 25, מִקְרָאֵי, עֲבָדַי Eccles. 9: 1, חוֹשְׁבֵי.

b. Tsere is retained in words in which it is commonly represented by the vowel-letter י, or has י quiescing in it, הֵיכָל *temple* const. הֵיכַל, and in addition in the following, אֵבוּס *crib* const. אֵבוּס, so אֵזוֹר *girdle,* אֵשׁוּן *thread,* נֵכָר *foreign land* const. נֵכַר, אֲבֵדָה *loss* const. אֲבֵדַת, so אֵשָׁה Isa. 58: 10 *darkness,* בְּרֵכָה *pool,* גְּנֵבָה Ex. 22: 2 *theft,* מַגֵּפָה *plague,* מַהְפֵּכָה *overthrow,* מְכֵרָה Gen. 49: 5 *sword,* מַסֵּכָה *molten-image,* מְרֵרָה Job 16: 13 *gall,* עֲרֵמָה *heap,* צֵאָה *excrement,* תְּאֵנָה *fig-tree,* תַּרְדֵּמָה *deep sleep,* and the plurals אֲבֵלֵי *mourning* from אֲבֵלִים (אָבֵל), so חֲפֵצֵי *desiring,* יְשֵׁנֵי *sleeping,* שְׂמָתֵי, and טְמָתֵי *rejoicing,* שְׂכֵחֵי *forgetting,* זְאֵבֵי *wolves* from זְאֵבִים (זְאֵב); יְגֵעִי *weary* becomes יְגִיעֵי in the construct, and פְּלֵטִים *escaped* פְּלִיטֵי.

c. Hholem is rejected from the syllable before the accent in אַרְמְנוֹת const. pl. of אַרְמוֹן *palace,* אֶשְׁכְּלוֹת and אֶשְׁבְּלֹת const. pl. of אֶשְׁבּוֹל *cluster,* תְּאוֹמֵי Cant. 4: 5 and תָּאֳמֵי Cant. 7: 4 *twins,* בָּמֳתֵי from בָּמוֹת *highplaces,* see § 214. 2. *b;* it is changed to û in מַטְמֻנֵי from מַטְמֹנִים *treasures,* comp. § 88.

d. Medial Vav and Yodh, though they may retain their consonantal power in the absolute, quiesce in Hholem and Tsere in the construct, חָוָה *midst* const. תּוֹךְ, חַוּוֹת *cups* const. קְשׂוֹת, בַּיִת *house* const. בֵּית, עֲיָנוֹת *fountains* const. עֵינוֹת, גַּיְא *valley* const. גֵּיא, pl. גֵּאָיוֹת § 208. 3. *c,* const. גֵּאָיוֹת Ezek. 35: 8. Exceptions are rare, עָוֶל (according to Kimchi עֲוֹל) Ezek. 28: 18 *iniquity,* מִדְיָנָיו Prov. 19: 13 *contentions* צַוָּאר *neck* const. צַוְּארֵי and צַוְאֲרֵי.

e. A few nouns of the forms קָטֵל, קָטֹל, קָטוּל have קְטֹל or קְטֶל in the construct instead of קְטָל, § 61. 1. *b,* גָּדֵר *wall* const. גְּדֶר, גָּזֵל *robbery* const.

יָרֵךְ, יֶרֶךְ thigh const. יֶרֶךְ, כָּבֵד heavy const. כְּבַד and כָּבֵד, כָּתֵף shoulder const. כֶּתֶף, עָשָׁן smoke const. עֲשַׁן and עֶשֶׁן, צֵלָע side const. צֶלַע and צֵלַע; אָרֵךְ long is only found in the construct, the corresponding absolute was probably אָרֵךְ; כּוֹבַע helmet simply shifts its accent in the construct, כּוֹבַע. On the other hand, while most Segholate nouns suffer no change in the construct, a few adopt the form קְטַל, חָדָר chamber const. חֲדַר, זֶרַע seed const. once זְרַע־ Num. 11:7 elsewhere זֶרַע־, נֶטַע plant const. נְטַע, שָׁגָר foetus const. שְׁגַר, שֶׁבַע seven const. שְׁבַע, תֵּשַׁע nine const. תְּשַׁע; in like manner הֶבֶל vanity const. הֲבֵל.

2. When this rejection occasions an inadmissible concurrence of vowelless consonants at the beginning of a syllable, § 61.1, it is remedied by inserting a short vowel between them, commonly Hhirik, unless it is modified by the presence of gutturals, צִלְצָל tinkling const. צִלְצַל for צְלְצַל, דְּבָרִים words const. דִּבְרֵי for דְּבְרֵי, צְדָקָה righteousness const. צִדְקַת, pl. צְדָקוֹת const. צִדְקוֹת, בְּהֵמָה beast const. בֶּהֱמַת, חֲכָמִים wise const. חַכְמֵי. In the construct plural and dual of Segholates, however, the vowel is frequently regulated by the characteristic vowel of the singular which has been dropped, comp. § 208. 2, מְלָכִים from מֶלֶךְ (מַלְכּ) kings const. מַלְכֵי, שְׁבָטִים (שֵׁבֶט) tribes const. שִׁבְטֵי, גְּרָנוֹת (גֹּרֶן) threshing-floors const. גָּרְנוֹת, חֲרָפוֹת (חֶרְפָּה) reproaches const. חֶרְפוֹת, דְּלָתַיִם (דֶּלֶת) folding doors const. דַּלְתֵי, yet not invariably שְׁעָלִים or דְּלָתֵי) handfuls const. שַׁעֲלֵי, שֹׁקֶת trough (pl. שְׁקָתוֹת) const. שָׁקְתוֹת.

a. When in the construct plural the introduction of a new vowel is demanded by the concurrence of consonants, the syllable so formed is an intermediate one, so that the following Sh'va is vocal, and the next letter, if an aspirate, does not receive Daghesh-lene, thus, דְּלָתוֹת, מַלְכֵי, דִּלְתֵי, חָרְבּוֹת, מַלְכֵי, דִּלְתֵי not חָרְבּוֹת, § 22. a. 3. Exceptions are infrequent, as אֶלָּתִּךְ Deut. 3:17, חֶסְדֵּי Lam. 3:22 but חַסְדֵי Ps. 89:2, חָרְפּוֹת Ps. 69:10, עַרְפֵּי Ezek. 17:9, כִּסְפֵּי Gen. 42:25, 35, כַּסְפֵּי Lev. 23:18, צִמְדֵּי־ Isa. 5:10, קַשְׁתֹת Neh. 4:7, רִשְׁפֵּי Cant. 8:6 but רִשְׁפֵּי־ Ps. 76:4. In a few instances Daghesh-forte separative is inserted to indicate more distinctly the vocal nature of the Sh'va, § 24. 5, חַלְבֵּי Isa. 57:6, בִּגְבֵּי Lev. 25:5, בִּגְבֵּי Isa. 58:3, כִּקְבֵי Gen. 49:17, רִבְבוֹת Ps. 89:52, כְּשֹׂבוֹת Prov. 27:25, or compound Sh'va is taken instead of simple for the same reason, שִׁקֲתוֹת Gen. 30:38. The presence or absence of Daghesh-lene in the dual construct depends upon the form of the absolute, thus שִׂפְתֵי from שְׂפָתַיִם lips but בִּרְכֵּי from בִּרְכַּיִם knees. When the concurring consonants belong to different syllables a new vowel is not needed between them; one is sometimes inserted, however, after a guttural, מַעַרְבֵי, מַעַרְבוֹת but מַחְשְׁבוֹת. In the opinion of Ewald מִקְדְּשֵׁי Ezek. 7:24 is for מִקְדָּשַׁי from מִקְדָּשִׁים, and מִקְצֹעֹת Ex. 26:23, 36:28 for מִקְצֹעֹת; they may be better explained, however, as Piel and Pual participles.

b. The second syllable before the accent rarely undergoes any change. In a very few instances Seghol becomes Hhirik or Pattahh, the pure vowels being reckoned shorter than the diphthongal, comp. §210. *e.* מֶרְכָּבָה *chariot* const. מִרְכֶּבֶת. The changes in לֶהָבָה *flame* const. לֶהֶבֶת pl. לְהָבוֹת const. לַהֲבוֹת, גֶּחָלִים *coals* const. גַּחֲלֵי are due to the influence of the proximate vowels, § 63. 1; those in הִגָּיוֹן *vision* const. חֶזְיוֹן, כְּחֻלֹּת, *coals* const. כְּחֻלֹּת are consequent upon the dropping of Daghesh-forte, § 61. 5; that in אֹהָלִים (from אֹהֶל) *tents* const. אָהֳלֵי arises from the conversion of a simple into an intermediate syllable, § 59.

§ 217. The following table of the declension of nouns will sufficiently exemplify the rules which have been given.

a. The left-hand page is occupied by masculine nouns and the right-hand by feminine, the latter being, with few exceptions, derived from the former, or preserving, as in בֵּצָה צֵץ, תּוֹרָה תּוֹר an outward correspondence though the roots are different. There is thus shown the formation of the feminine from the masculine, as well as that of the plural from the singular and the construct from the absolute of both numbers and genders. A few examples are added of the formation of the dual and of the inflections of adjectives and participles. The Piel and Hithpael participles follow the analogy of the Kal; the Niphal is followed by the Pual, Hophal, and Hiphil, the last of which has in the sing. fem. מַקְטִילָה or מַקְטֶלֶת and in the plural מַקְטִילוֹת, מַקְטִילִים.

Declension

	Singular.		Plural.	
	Absol.	Constr.	Absol.	Constr.
Garden.	גַּן	גַּן	גַּנִּים	גַּנֵּי
Fish.	דָּג	דַּג	דָּגִים	דְּגֵי
Guard.	מִשְׁמָר	מִשְׁמַר	מִשְׁמָרִים	מִשְׁמְרֵי
Vengeance.	נָקָם	נְקַם	נְקָמִים	נִקְמֵי
Cloud.	עָנָן	עֲנַן	עֲנָנִים	עַנְנֵי
Heart.	לֵבָב	לְבַב	לְבָבִים	לִבְבֵי
Flower.	נֵץ	נֵץ	נִצִּים	נִצֵּי
Tree.	עֵץ	עֵץ	עֵצִים	עֲצֵי
Wall.	גָּדֵר or גָּדֵר		גְּדֵרִים	גִּדְרֵי
Suckling.	יוֹנֵק	יוֹנֵק	יוֹנְקִים	יוֹנְקֵי
Interpreter.	מֵלִיץ	מֵלִיץ	מְלִיצִים	מְלִיצֵי
Statute.	חֹק	חָק	חֻקִּים	חֻקֵּי
Turtle-dove.	תּוֹר	תּוֹר	תּוֹרִים	תּוֹרֵי
Memorial.	זִכָּרוֹן	זִכְרוֹן	זִכְרוֹנִים	זִכְרוֹנֵי
King.	מֶלֶךְ	מֶלֶךְ	מְלָכִים	מַלְכֵי
Hiding-place.	סֵתֶר	סֵתֶר	סְתָרִים	סִתְרֵי
Strength.	עֹצֶם	עֹצֶם	עֲצָמִים	עָצְמֵי
Death.	מָוֶת	מוֹת	מוֹתִים	מוֹתֵי
Hebrew.	עִבְרִי	עִבְרִי	עִבְרִיִּים or עִבְרִים	עִבְרִיֵּי
Appearance.	מַרְאֶה	מַרְאֵה	מַרְאִים	מַרְאֵי

	Singular.		Dual.		Plural.	
	Absol.	Constr.	Absol.	Constr.	Absol.	Constr.
Palm.	כַּף	כַּף	כַּפַּיִם	כַּפֵּי	כַּפּוֹת	כַּפּוֹת
Hand.	יָד	יַד	יָדַיִם	יְדֵי	יָדוֹת	יְדוֹת
Wing.	כָּנָף	כְּנַף	כְּנָפַיִם	כַּנְפֵי	כְּנָפוֹת	כַּנְפוֹת
Tooth.	שֵׁן	שֵׁן	שִׁנַּיִם	שִׁנֵּי		
Foot.	רֶגֶל	רֶגֶל	רַגְלַיִם	רַגְלֵי	רְגָלִים	
Ear.	אֹזֶן	אֹזֶן	אָזְנַיִם	אָזְנֵי		
Eye.	עַיִן	עֵין	עֵינַיִם	עֵינֵי	עֵינוֹת	עֵינוֹת
Lip.	שָׂפָה	שְׂפַת	שְׂפָתַיִם	שִׂפְתֵי	שְׂפָתוֹת	שִׂפְתוֹת

OF NOUNS.

	SINGULAR.		PLURAL.	
	Absol.	Constr.	Absol.	Constr.
Garden.	גַּנָּה	גַּנַּת	גַּנּוֹת	גַּנּוֹת
Fish (collective.)	דָּגָה	דְּגַת	דָּגוֹת	דְּגוֹת
Observance.	מִשְׁמֶרֶת	מִשְׁמֶרֶת	מִשְׁמָרוֹת	מִשְׁמְרוֹת
Vengeance.	נְקָמָה	נִקְמַת	נְקָמוֹת	נִקְמוֹת
Cloud (collective.)	עֲנָנָה	עֲנַנַת	עֲנָנוֹת	עַנְנוֹת
Sin.	חַטָּאת	חַטַּאת	חַטָּאוֹת	חַטֹּאות
Flower.	נִצָּה	נִצַּת	נִצּוֹת	נִצּוֹת
Counsel.	עֵצָה	עֲצַת	עֵצוֹת	עֲצוֹת
Wall.	גְּדֵרָה	גְּדֶרֶת	גְּדֵרוֹת	גְּדֵרוֹת
Sucker.	יוֹנֶקֶת	יוֹנֶקֶת	יוֹנְקוֹת	יוֹנְקוֹת
Poem.	מְלִיצָה	מְלִיצַת	מְלִיצוֹת	מְלִיצוֹת
Statute.	חֻקָּה	חֻקַּת	חֻקּוֹת	חֻקּוֹת
Law.	תּוֹרָה	תּוֹרַת	תּוֹרוֹת	תּוֹרוֹת
Skull.	גֻּלְגֹּלֶת	גֻּלְגֹּלֶת	גֻּלְגָּלוֹת	גֻּלְגְּלוֹת
Queen.	מַלְכָּה	מַלְכַּת	מְלָכוֹת	מַלְכוֹת
Hiding-place.	סִתְרָה	סִתְרַת	סְתָרוֹת	סִתְרוֹת
Strength.	עָצְמָה	עָצְמַת	עֲצָמוֹת	עַצְמוֹת
Kingdom.	מַלְכוּת	מַלְכוּת	מַלְכֻיּוֹת	מַלְכֻיּוֹת
Hebrew-woman.	עִבְרִית	עִבְרִית	עִבְרִיּוֹת	עִבְרִיּוֹת
Vision.	מַרְאָה	מַרְאַת	מַרְאוֹת	מַרְאוֹת

ADJECTIVES AND PARTICIPLES.

	SINGULAR.		PLURAL.	
	Masc.	Fem.	Masc.	Fem.
Many.	רַב	רַבָּה	רַבִּים	רַבּוֹת
Small.	קָטֹן	קְטַנָּה	קְטַנִּים	קְטַנּוֹת
Heavy.	כָּבֵד	כְּבֵדָה	כְּבֵדִים	כְּבֵדוֹת
Great.	גָּדוֹל	גְּדוֹלָה	גְּדוֹלִים	גְּדוֹלוֹת
Deep.	עָמֹק	עֲמֻקָּה	עֲמֻקִּים	עֲמֻקּוֹת
Kal act. part.	קֹטֵל	קֹטְלָה or קֹטֶלֶת	קֹטְלִים	קֹטְלוֹת
Kal pass. part.	קָטוּל	קְטוּלָה	קְטוּלִים	קְטוּלוֹת
Niphal part.	נִקְטָל	נִקְטָלָה or נִקְטֶלֶת	נִקְטָלִים	נִקְטָלוֹת

Paragogic Vowels.

§ 218. The termination ִי or וֹ is sometimes added to nouns in the construct singular, § 61. 6, בְּנִי Gen. 49:11 for בֶּן, מְלֵאֲתִי Isa. 1:21 for מְלֵאַת, רַבָּתִי Lam. 1:1 for רַבַּת, מַשְׁפִּילִי Ps. 113:6 for מַשְׁפִּיל, חַיְתוֹ Gen. 1:24 for חַיַּת. This occurs chiefly in poetry and is regarded as an archaism. These vowels for the most part receive the accent, and commonly occasion the rejection of Pattahh or Tsere from the ultimate.

a. Examples of this antique formation of the construct are likewise preserved in proper names, as מַלְכִּי־צֶדֶק *Melchizedek*, מְתוּשֶׁלַח *Methuselah*. Respecting the origin of these vowel endings, see § 198. *a* (4).

§ 219. 1. The unaccented vowel ָה, added to nouns indicates motion or direction towards a place, צָפוֹנָה *northward*, נֶגְבָּה *southward*, שָׁמַיְמָה *heavenward*, הַבַּיְתָה *to the house*, οἴκονδε, הָהָרָה *to the mountain*, whence it is called He directive or He local. The subsidiary vowel of Segholates is rejected before this ending, § 66. 2 (1), but other vowels are mostly unaffected, מִדְבָּר from מִדְבָּרָה, אֶרֶץ from אַרְצָה, גֹּרֶן from גָּרְנָה, מִדְבָּרָה 1 Kin. 19:15 from the construct state מִדְבַּר.

a. He directive is appended to the adverb שָׁם *there*, שָׁמָּה *thither*, and to the adjective חָלִיל *profane* in the peculiar phrase חָלִילָה *ad profanum* i. e. *be it far from*, etc. It is rarely used to indicate relations of time, יָמִים יָמִימָה 1 Sam. 1:3 *from days to days* i. e. *yearly*, שְׁלִשִׁתָה Ezek. 21:19 *for the third time*, עַתָּה *now* prop. *at (this) time*. For the sake of greater force and definiteness a preposition denoting direction is sometimes prefixed to words, which receive this ending, so that the latter becomes in a measure superfluous, לְמַעְלָה *upwards*, לְמַטָּה *downwards*, לַמִּזְרָחָה 2 Chron. 31:14 *to the east*, לִשְׁאוֹלָה Ps. 9:18 *to Sheol*, comp. ἀπὸ μακρόθεν.

b. The ending ָה rarely receives the accent מִזְרָחָה Deut. 4:41; in פַּדֶּנָה אֲרָם it receives in some editions an alternate accent, § 42. *a*, in others the secondary accent Methegh, § 33. 1. *a*. In הָרָה Gen. 14:10 and פַּנָּה *a* is changed to *e* before this ending, § 63. 1, in דִּלְנָה Ezek. 25:13, נֹבֶה 1 Sam. 21:2 the vowel of the ending is itself changed to *e*.

c. He directive is probably to be traced to the same origin with the definite article הַ, whose demonstrative force it shares. The syllable הַ is prefixed to a noun to single out a particular thing from all others of like kind as the object of attention. Appended to a word its weak guttural would be rejected and its vowel prolonged to הָ , § 53. 3; and in this form it is added to nouns to point out the object or direction of motion, and to verbs to indicate the object of desire, § 97. 1. In Chaldee this appended vowel forms what is called the emphatic state, and has the sense of the definite article, מֶלֶךְ *king*, מַלְכָּה or מַלְכָּא *the king.*

2. Paragogic ה, is sometimes appended to nouns, particularly in poetry, for the purpose of softening the termination without affecting the sense, § 61. 6.

Nouns with Suffixes.

§ 220. The pronominal suffixes, whose forms are given § 72, are appended to nouns in the sense of possessive pronouns, לְיָד *hand*, יָדִי *my hand*, etc. They suffer, in consequence, the following changes, viz:

1. Of the suffixes, which begin with a consonant, ךָ, כֶם, כֶן of the second person are connected with nouns in the singular by a vocal Sh'va, נוּ of the first person plural and ךְ of the second fem. singular by Tsere, and הוּ, ָה, ם, ן of the third person by Kamets; הָ is invariably contracted to וֹ, rarely written הֹ, § 62. 1, and הָ, to ה, , § 101. 2.

a. There is one example of a noun in the construct before the full form of the pronoun, יְמֵי־הִיא *her days* Nah. 2:9.

b. First person: נוּ is in a few instances preceded by Kamets, מָרְדָּכֳנוּ Ruth 3:2, קִרְמָנוּ Job 22:20.

Second person. The final vowel of ךָ is occasionally expressed by the vowel letter ה, יְרָדְכָה Ex. 13:16, בְּשִׂמְחָה Jer. 29:25. In pause the Sh'va before ךָ becomes Seghol, § 65, גַּבֶּךָ Gen. 33:5, כַּפֶּךָ Ps. 139:5, or Kamets may be inserted as a connecting vowel, particularly after nouns in ה, , whereupon the final Kamets is dropped to prevent the recurrence of like sounds, חָזְךָ Ps. 53:6. In the feminine the connecting vowel *e* is rarely written י, שִׁלְשֹׁתֵיךְ Ezek. 5:12; י,, which belongs to the full form of the pronoun, § 71. *a* (2), is sometimes added to the suffix, רֵעְיָתִי Jer. 11:15, בְּתוּלַבִּי Ps. 116:19, נשׁיבאל 2 Kin. 4:7 K'thibh, where the K'ri has יְשִׁיאֵל. Sometimes the distinction of gender is neglected in the plural and כֶם is used in place of the feminine, אֲבִיכֶם Gen. 31:9, אֶוְנְכֶם, בְּנֵיכֶם Jer. 9:19; ה, is sometimes added to the feminine suffix as to the full pronoun, וְמָתְכָנָה Ezek. 23:49.

Third person. The connecting vowel before הוּ and הָ is occasionally *e*, לְמִינֵהוּ Gen. 1:12, פְּיִלַּגְשׁוֹ Judg. 9:24, מֹשֵׁהוּ Nah. 1:13, אוּלֵהוּ Job 25:3. so רָעֵהוּ from רֵעַ and מֵרְבָּהוּ from מֶלֶךְ and frequently with nouns in ה, קָצֵהוּ; e does not occur before the plural ם unless it is represented by the vowel-letter י in מִזְבְּחוֹתֵיו 2 Chron. 34:5 K'thibh, where the K'ri has מִזְבְּחֹתָם; it is once found in the fem. plural קִרְבָּה Gen. 41:21. The form ה' in the masc. sing. is commonly reckoned an archaism, אָהֳלֹה Gen. 12:8, שִׁירֹה Ps. 42:9, כֵּלֹה Jer. 2:21, so several times in the K'thibh עִירֹה, סוּתֹה Gen. 49:11, תְּבוּאָתֹה Ex. 22:4, כְּסוּתֹה Ex. 22:26, נִסְבָּה Lev. 23:13, שִׁלֻּשֹׁה 2 Kin. 9:25, תְּבוּאָתֹה Ezek. 48:18, where the K'ri in each instance substitutes וֹ. In a few instances the consonant is rejected from the feminine, ה being retained simply as a vowel-letter; where this occurs it is commonly indicated in modern editions of the Bible by Raphe, שָׂרָה Lev. 13:4, חֶמְאָה Num. 15:28, or by a Masoretic note in the margin, אֲחֻזָּה Isa. 23:17, 18 for אֲחֻזָּתָהּ; once א is substituted for ה, בְּלֹא Ezek. 36:5. The longer forms of the plural suffixes הֵם, הֵן are rarely affixed to nouns in the singular, לְבָדְהֵן Gen. 21:28, מִלְּבַדְהֵן Ezek. 13:17, שְׁבוּתְהֵן Ezek. 16:53, or with the connecting vowel Kamets, כְּלָהֵם 2 Sam. 23:6, or with ה, appended, כְּלִּהֵנָה 1 Kin. 7:37, תֹּצְבַהֵנָה Ezek. 16:53. The vowel ה is also sometimes added to the briefer form of the fem. plural, לְבַדְנָה Gen. 21:29, כֵּלָּהּ Gen. 42:36. The distinction of gender is sometimes neglected in the plural, ם or הֵם being used for the feminine, כֻּלָּם Cant. 4:2, 6:6 for כֻּלָּן, יְדֵיהֶם Job 1:14 for יְדֵיהֶן.

c. The nouns אָב *father*, אָח *brother*, פֶּה *mouth* take the ending י, before suffixes, as they do likewise in the construct state, אָבִיךָ, אֲבִיהֶם; י of the first person coalesces with this vowel, פִּי, אָחִי, אָבִי and הוּ of the third person, commonly becomes ו §62. 2, פִּיו, אָחִיו more frequent than אֲבִיהוּ, אָחִיהוּ, פִּיהוּ. In גֵּוִי Zeph. 2:9 the vowel-letter י of the first person suffix is dropped after the final י of the noun.

2. The masculine plural termination ים, and the dual יִם, are changed to י before suffixes as in the construct state; the same vowel is likewise inserted as a connective between suffixes and feminine plural nouns, §214. 2. *b*. This י remains unchanged before the plural suffixes; but before ךָ the second masc. singular and ךְ third fem. singular it becomes יִ, and before the remaining suffixes the diphthongal vowel is resolved into יֶ, which combined with י the first singular forms יַ, with ךְ the second feminine יִךְ, and with הוּ the third masculine יו, §62. 2.

a. In a very few instances suffixes are appended to feminine plurals without the vowel י or its modifications, תְּחֻנַּתִי 2 Kin. 6:8 for תַּחֲנֹתַי, עֵדֹתִי Ps. 132:12 for עֵדֹתַי, מַפַּתְךָ Deut. 28:59 for מַכּוֹתֶיךָ, אֲחִיוֹתָהּ Ezek.

§ 221 NOUNS WITH SUFFIXES. 251

16:52 for אֲחִיוֹתָיִךְ, אֲבוֹתָם and אֲבוֹתֵיהָם, אוֹתָהּ Ps. 74:4, חַטֹּאתָם, חַרְבּוֹתָם, מִזְבְּחֹתָם, מַצֵּבֹתָם. On the other hand, suffixes proper to plural nouns are occasionally appended to feminine nouns in the singular, perhaps to indicate that they are used in a plural or collective sense, חֲמִשִׁתָיו Lev. 5:24, תְּהִלֹּתָיךְ Ps. 9:15, שִׁנְאָתָיו Ezek. 35:11, עֲצָתֶיךָ Isa. 47:13.

b. The vowel-letter י is not infrequently omitted after plural and dual nouns, דְּרָכֶהָ Ex. 33:13 for דְּרָכֶיהָ, יָדָם Ps. 134:2 for יְדֵיהֶם, מִידוֹ Ex. 32:19 K'thibh (K'ri מִיָּדָיו), עֲבָדוֹ 1 Sam. 18:22 K'thibh (K'ri עֲבָדָיו), גּוֹיֵהֶם Gen. 10:5 for גּוֹיֵיהֶם, חֶלְבֵּהֶן Gen. 4:4 for חֶלְבֵּיהֶן.

c. Second person. The vowel ִ remains unchanged before the fem. sing. ךְ in אֲשָׁרַיִךְ Eccl. 10:17 and with ָ_ appended: מַלְאָכֵבַח Nah. 2:14. Sometimes, as in the full pronoun, י is appended to the fem. sing. suffix and ה_ to the plural, תְּחַלּוּאָיְכִי Ps. 103:3, חַיָּיְכִי ver. 4, פִּסְתּוֹתֵיכָנָה Ezek. 13:20.

Third person. The uncontracted form of the masc. sing. יהו occurs in גְּבוּרֹתֵיהוּ Nah. 2:4 for גְּבֹרָיו, יְלָדֵיהוּ Hab. 3:10, כֵּילָיהוּ Job 24:23; *ēhū = aihu* by transposition of the vowels becomes *auhi = ôhî* וָחִי which is found once תַּגְמוּלוֹהִי Ps. 116:12, and is the ordinary form of this suffix in Chaldee. The final *a* of the fem. sing. is once represented by א, אֲתִיקֵירָא Ezek. 41:15. In a few instances ה is appended to the plural of either gender, אֱלֹהֵיתֵבָה Ezek. 40:16, גְּוִיֹּתֵיהֵנָה Ezek. 1:11, and וֹ to the abbreviated masc. ם, אֱלֹהֵימוֹ Deut. 32:37, וְבָחֵימוֹ ver. 38, בַּפֵּימוֹ Job 27:23, פְּנֵימוֹ Ps. 11:7.

3. The suffixes thus modified are as follows, viz.:

Appended to	SINGULAR.					PLURAL.			
	1 *c*.	2 *m*.	2 *f*.	3 *m*.	3 *f*.	1 *c*.	2 *m*.	2 *f*.	3 *m*.	3 *f*.
Sing. Nouns	ִי	ךָ	ךְ	וֹ	הָ	נוּ	כֶם	כֶן	ם	ן
Dual and Plur. Nouns	ַי	ֶיךָ	ַיִךְ	ָיו	ֶיהָ	ֵינוּ	ֵיכֶם	ֵיכֶן	ֵיהֶם	ֵיהֶן

§ 221. Certain changes likewise take place in nouns receiving suffixes, which arise from the disposition to shorten words, which are increased at the end, § 66.1. These are as follows, viz.:

1. The grave suffixes, § 72, כֶם, כֶן, הֶם, הֶן shorten the nouns, to which they are attached, to the greatest possible extent. Before them, therefore, nouns of both genders and all numbers take the form of the construct, לֵב heart, לְבַבְכֶם *your heart*, לְבָבָן *their hearts*; שָׂפָה *lip* du. שִׂפְתֵיהֶם pl. שִׂפְתוֹתֵיהֶם *their lips*.

a. דָּם *blood* becomes דִּמְכֶם and יָד *hand* יֶדְכֶם.

2. Feminine nouns, both singular and plural, take the construct form before the light suffixes likewise, with the exception that in the singular the ending הָ becomes ת, in consequence of the change from a mixed to a simple syllable, § 59, שָׂפָה *lip*, שְׂפָתוֹ *his lip*, שְׂפָתָם *their lip*, שִׂפְתוֹתֶיךָ *thy lips*, שִׂפְתוֹתָיו *his lips*.

a. If the construct has a Segholate form it will experience the change indicated in 5, מֶמְשָׁלָה const. מֶמְשֶׁלֶת suf. מֶמְשַׁלְתּוֹ. If two consonants have coalesced in the final letter, it will receive Daghesh-forte agreeably to 6, בִּתּוֹ from בַּת, אֲמָתוֹ from אָמָה; מְבַצְתָהּ 1 Sam. 16:15 from the fem. of מְבַצֶּת, § 205. *b*.

b. In a few exceptional instances the absolute form is preserved before suffixes, נְבֵלָתִי Isa. 26:19 from נְבֵלָה but נִבְלָתְךָ, נִבְלָתוֹ; יַעְרַת Cant. 2:10 from יַעְרָה const. יַעְרַת; so אֱלָתִי, גְּדֻלָּתָיו, תְּחִלָּתָיו, שְׁבוּעֹתָם but const. שְׁבֻעַת, comp. מֵעֵירָתָהּ const. עֵירַת.

3. Masculine nouns, both singular and plural, on receiving light suffixes take the form which they assume before the absolute plural termination, לֵב *heart*, לְבָבִי *my heart*, לְבָבְךָ *thy heart*, לְבָבֵנוּ *our hearts*.

a. Tsere in the ultimate is shortened to Hhirik or Seghol before ךָ, כֶם, כֶן, e. g. בִּנְךָ, מְסַדְּרְכֶם, מִקֶּלְכֶם, or with a guttural to Pattahh, אֹהַבְךָ, גָּאֳלְכֶם, though with occasional exceptions, אַבְנֵטְךָ Isa. 22:21, שֹׁלֵחֲךָ 1 Sam. 21:3, כְּסָאֲךָ from כִּסֵּא. Before other suffixes it is rejected from some monosyllables, which retain it in the plural, שְׁמוֹ from שֵׁם plur. שֵׁמוֹת, בְּנוֹ from בֵּן plur. בָּנִים but גֵּוִי, דַּלִּי, גֵּרִי, רֵעֶךָ.

4. Dual nouns retain before light suffixes the form which they have before the absolute dual termination, שְׂפָתַי *my lips*, שְׂפָתֵינוּ *our lips*, אָזְנַי *my ears*, אָזְנֵינוּ *our ears*; קַרְנַיִם and קַרְנַיִם *horns*, קַרְנָיו and קַרְנָיו *his horns*.

5. Segholate nouns in the dual and plural follow the preceding rules, but in the singular they assume before all suffixes, whether light or grave, their original monosyllabic form as before the feminine ending ה ָ , § 208, מֶלֶךְ *king*, מַלְכִּי *my king*, מַלְכְּכֶם *your king*; אֹזֶן *ear*, אָזְנִי *my ear*; in like manner יוֹנֶקֶת *sucker*, יוֹנַקְתּוֹ *his sucker*.

a. When the first radical has Hholem in the absolute, Hhateph-Kamets or Kamets-Hhatuph is sometimes given to the second radical before suffixes, פְּעָלוֹ and עָבְלוֹ from סֶבֶל קִצְבָּהּ Hos. 13:14, with Daghesh-forte separative. קַבְלוֹ Ezek. 26:9, קִצְבוֹ 1 Kin. 12:10, סִבְלוֹ Isa. 9:3, קַבְלוֹ Jer. 4:7; בֶּגֶד garment has בִּגְדוֹ, בִּגְדוֹ instead of בִּגְדוֹ, בִּגְדוֹ.

b. Middle Yodh and Vav mostly quiesce in ê and ô before suffixes, עֵירִי from עַיִן eye, מוֹתִי from מָוֶת death; but כִּירֹה Gen. 49:11 from עַיִר young ass, שִׁירֹה Isa. 10:17 from שַׁיִת thorn, עַוְלוֹ Ezek. 18:26, 33:13 from עָוֶל iniquity.

c. Triliteral monosyllables sometimes shift their vowel from the second radical to the first, thus assuming the same form with Segholates, comp. § 184. a. דִּבְשִׁי from דְּבַשׁ, שִׂבְרִי from שֶׂבֶר but כְּרֵשׂוֹ from כְּרֵשׂ; בֶּלְיֶךָ from כְּלִי; סָרְיְךָ, פְּרְיָהּ, סָרְבָם but פְּרִיָם from פְּרִי; שִׁבְיְךָ, שֶׁבְיָם but שְׁבִיכֶם from שְׁבִי. By a like transposition נַגְפֶּכֶם Ezek. 36:8 is for נֻגַפְכֶם from כָּנָף.

d. The noun אֶשֶׁר blessedness, which only occurs in the plural construct and with suffixes, preserves before all suffixes the construct form, אַשְׁרֵי , אַשְׁרֵיךָ, אַשְׁרָיו not אֲשָׁרֶיךָ .

6. Nouns in whose final letter two consonants have coalesced, or which double their final letter in the plural, § 207. 2, receive Daghesh-forte likewise before suffixes, the vowel of the ultimate being modified accordingly, עֻזִּי and עֻזִּי from עֹז (root עָזַז), בִּתְּכֶם from בַּת (בִּנְתְּ), אֶתְנַנָּהּ from אֶתְנָן (pl. אֶתְנַנִּים).

a. אֶשְׁנָב lattice, כַּרְמֶל garden, מִשְׂגָּב refuge, which do not occur in the plural, take Daghesh-forte before suffixes; שַׁבָּת has in the plural שַׁבָּתוֹת but before suffixes שַׁבְּתוֹ, שַׁבְּתֹכֶם; כֵּן (root כָּנַן) base has כַּנִּי.

b. In a very few instances a final liquid is repeated instead of being doubled by Daghesh, comp. § 207. 2. a, חַרְרִי Jer. 17:3, חַרְרֵי Ps. 30:8, הָרָרִם Gen. 14:6 from הָר; צַלְלוֹ Job 40:22 and צִלְלִי from צֵל; שָׁתֶּךָ Ezek. 16:4 and שָׁרְרֵךְ Cant. 7:3. Once Daghesh-forte is resolved by the insertion of נ, מְעֻנְזֶיהָ Isa. 23:11 for מְעֻזֶּיהָ, § 54. 3.

7. Nouns ending in ה‎ָ drop this vowel before suffixes as before the plural terminations, § 209. 1, שָׂדֶה field שָׂדִי, מִקְנֶה cattle מִקְנָה; שָׂדְךָ, שָׂדְהוּ.

a. The vowel e commonly remains as a connecting vowel before suffixes of the third person singular, § 220. 1. b; and in a few instances the radical י is restored, giving to singular nouns the appearance of being plural, עֶשְׂיָהּ Isa. 22:11, מְעַפֶּיךָ Hos. 2:16, נוֹטֵיהֶם Isa. 42:5, שֶׂה sheep becomes שֵׂיוּ or שֵׂיְהוּ.

§ 222. The following examples of nouns with suffixes will sufficiently illustrate the preceding rules:

Paradigm of Nouns with Suffixes.

Singular.

		heart		king		queen		hand	
Const.		לֵבַב		מֶלֶךְ		מַלְכַּת		יַד	
Sing. 1 c. my	"	לְבָבִי	"	מַלְכִּי	"	מַלְכָּתִי	"	יָדִי	
2 m. thy	"	לְבָבְךָ	"	מַלְכְּךָ	"	מַלְכָּתְךָ	"	יָדְךָ	
2 f. thy	"	לְבָבֵךְ	"	מַלְכֵּךְ	"	מַלְכָּתֵךְ	"	יָדֵךְ	
3 m. his	"	לְבָבוֹ	"	מַלְכּוֹ	"	מַלְכָּתוֹ	"	יָדוֹ	
3 f. her	"	לְבָבָהּ	"	מַלְכָּהּ	"	מַלְכָּתָהּ	"	יָדָהּ	
Plur. 1 c. our	"	לְבָבֵנוּ	"	מַלְכֵּנוּ	"	מַלְכָּתֵנוּ	"	יָדֵנוּ	
2 m. your	"	לְבַבְכֶם	"	מַלְכְּכֶם	"	מַלְכַּתְכֶם	"	יֶדְכֶם	
2 f. your	"	לְבַבְכֶן	"	מַלְכְּכֶן	"	מַלְכַּתְכֶן	"	יֶדְכֶן	
3 m. their	"	לְבָבָם	"	מַלְכָּם	"	מַלְכָּתָם	"	יָדָם	
3 f. their	"	לְבָבָן	"	מַלְכָּן	"	מַלְכָּתָן	"	יָדָן	

Plural. Dual.

		hearts		kings		queens		hands	
Const.		לִבְבֵי		מַלְכֵי		מַלְכוֹת		יְדֵי	
Sing. 1 c. my	"	לְבָבַי	"	מְלָכַי	"	מַלְכוֹתַי	"	יָדַי	
2 m. thy	"	לְבָבֶיךָ	"	מְלָכֶיךָ	"	מַלְכוֹתֶיךָ	"	יָדֶיךָ	
2 f. thy	"	לְבָבַיִךְ	"	מְלָכַיִךְ	"	מַלְכוֹתַיִךְ	"	יָדַיִךְ	
3 m. his	"	לְבָבָיו	"	מְלָכָיו	"	מַלְכוֹתָיו	"	יָדָיו	
3 f. her	"	לְבָבֶיהָ	"	מְלָכֶיהָ	"	מַלְכוֹתֶיהָ	"	יָדֶיהָ	
Plur. 1 c. our	"	לְבָבֵינוּ	"	מְלָכֵינוּ	"	מַלְכוֹתֵינוּ	"	יָדֵינוּ	
2 m. your	"	לִבְבֵיכֶם	"	מַלְכֵיכֶם	"	מַלְכוֹתֵיכֶם	"	יְדֵיכֶם	
2 f. your	"	לִבְבֵיכֶן	"	מַלְכֵיכֶן	"	מַלְכוֹתֵיכֶן	"	יְדֵיכֶן	
3 m. their	"	לִבְבֵיהֶם	"	מַלְכֵיהֶם	"	מַלְכוֹתֵיהֶם	"	יְדֵיהֶם	
3 f. their	"	לִבְבֵיהֶן	"	מַלְכֵיהֶן	"	מַלְכוֹתֵיהֶן	"	יְדֵיהֶן	

NUMERALS.

§ 223. 1. The Hebrew numerals (שְׁמוֹת הַמִּסְפָּר) are of two kinds, cardinals and ordinals. The cardinals from one to ten are as follows, viz.:

	MASCULINE.		FEMININE.	
	Absol.	Constr	Absol.	Constr.
One	אֶחָד	אַחַד	אַחַת	אַחַת
Two	שְׁנַיִם	שְׁנֵי	שְׁתַּיִם	שְׁתֵּי
Three	שְׁלֹשָׁה	שְׁלֹשֶׁת	שָׁלֹשׁ	שְׁלֹשׁ
Four	אַרְבָּעָה	אַרְבַּעַת	אַרְבַּע	אַרְבַּע
Five	חֲמִשָּׁה	חֲמֵשֶׁת	חָמֵשׁ	חֲמֵשׁ
Six	שִׁשָּׁה	שֵׁשֶׁת	שֵׁשׁ	שֵׁשׁ
Seven	שִׁבְעָה	שִׁבְעַת	שֶׁבַע	שְׁבַע
Eight	שְׁמֹנָה	שְׁמֹנַת	שְׁמֹנֶה	שְׁמֹנֶה
Nine	תִּשְׁעָה	תִּשְׁעַת	תֵּשַׁע	תְּשַׁע
Ten	עֲשָׂרָה	עֲשֶׂרֶת	עֶשֶׂר	עֶשֶׂר

a. אֶחָד is for אַחָד. § 63. 1. *a;* the Seghol returns to Pattahh from which it has arisen, upon the shortening of the following Kamets in the construct and in the feminine, אַחַת for אַחְדְּתְ, § 54. 2, but in pause אֶחָד; אָחֹד occurs in the absolute in Gen. 48: 22, 2 Sam. 17: 22, Isa. 27: 12, Ezek. 33: 30, Zech. 11: 7, and once חָד Ezek. 33: 30. The plural אֲחָדִים is also in use in the sense of *one*, Gen. 11: 1, Ezek. 37: 17, or *some*, Gen. 27: 44, 29: 20. Comp. Span. *unos.*

שְׁתַּיִם is for שִׁנְתַּיִם; for the Daghesh in ת see § 22. *b;* this is once omitted after Daghesh-forte, בִּשְׁתֵּי Judg. 16: 28.

A dual form is given to some of the units to denote repetition, אַרְבַּעְתָּיִם *fourfold,* שִׁבְעָתַיִם *sevenfold.*

שִׁבְעָה occurs once with a paragogic syllable, שִׁבְעָנָה Job 42: 13, and once with a suffix in the form שְׁבַעְתָּם 2 Sam. 21: 9 K'ri.

2. In all the Semitic languages the cardinals from *three* to *ten* are in form of the singular number, and have a feminine termination when joined to masculine nouns, but omit it when joined to feminine nouns. The explanation of this

curious phenomenon appears to be that they are properly collective nouns like *triad*, *decad*, and as such of the feminine gender. With masculine nouns they appear in their primary form, with feminine nouns, for the sake of distinction, they undergo a change of termination.

a. An analogous anomaly meets us in this same class of words in Indo-European tongues. The Sanskrit cardinals from *five* to *ten*, though they agree in case with the nouns to which they belong, are in form of the neuter gender and in the nominative, accusative and vocative they are of the singular number. In Greek and Latin they are not declined.

§224. The cardinals from *eleven* to *nineteen* are formed by combining עָשָׂר or עֶשְׂרֵה modifications of the numeral *ten* with the several units, those which end in ה, preserving the absolute form and the remainder the construct. Thus,

	MASCULINE.		FEMININE.	
Eleven	עָשָׂר	אַחַד	עֶשְׂרֵה	אַחַת
	עָשָׂר	עַשְׁתֵּי	עֶשְׂרֵה	עַשְׁתֵּי
Twelve	עָשָׂר	שְׁנֵים	עֶשְׂרֵה	שְׁתֵּים
	עָשָׂר	שְׁנֵי	עֶשְׂרֵה	שְׁתֵּי
Thirteen	עָשָׂר	שְׁלֹשָׁה	עֶשְׂרֵה	שָׁלֹשׁ
Fourteen	עָשָׂר	אַרְבָּעָה	עֶשְׂרֵה	אַרְבַּע
Fifteen	עָשָׂר	חֲמִשָּׁה	עֶשְׂרֵה	חֲמֵשׁ
Sixteen	עָשָׂר	שִׁשָּׁה	עֶשְׂרֵה	שֵׁשׁ
Seventeen	עָשָׂר	שִׁבְעָה	עֶשְׂרֵה	שֶׁבַע
Eighteen	עָשָׂר	שְׁמֹנָה	עֶשְׂרֵה	שְׁמֹנֶה
Nineteen	עָשָׂר	תִּשְׁעָה	עֶשְׂרֵה	תֵּשַׁע

a. The origin of עַשְׁתֵּי, the alternate of אֶחָד in the number *eleven*, is obscure. R. Jona thinks it to be an abbreviation for עַד שְׁתֵּי עָשָׂר *next to twelve*. Comp. Lat. *undeviginti*, *nineteen*. Kimchi derives it from עָשָׁת *to think*, *ten* being reckoned upon the fingers, and *eleven* the first number which is mentally conceived beyond.

חֲמֵשׁ עָשָׂר *fifteen* occurs Judg. 8:10, 2 Sam. 19:18, and שְׁמֹנַת עָשָׂר *eighteen* Judg. 20:25.

§225. 1. The tens are formed by adding the masculine

plural termination to the units, עֶשְׂרִים *twenty* being, however, derived not from *two* but from *ten* עֶשֶׂר.

Twenty	עֶשְׂרִים	Sixty	שִׁשִּׁים
Thirty	שְׁלֹשִׁים	Seventy	שִׁבְעִים
Forty	אַרְבָּעִים	Eighty	שְׁמֹנִים
Fifty	חֲמִשִּׁים	Ninety	תִּשְׁעִים

a. These numbers have no distinct form for the feminine, and are used indifferently with nouns of either gender. עֶשְׂרֹת Ex. 18 : 21, 25, Deut. 1 : 15 means not *twenty* but *tens*.

2. The units are added to the tens by means of the conjunction וְ *and*; the order of precedence is not invariable, though it has been remarked that the earliest writers of the Old Testament commonly place the units first, e. g. שְׁתַּיִם וְשִׁשִּׁים *two and sixty* Gen. 5 : 18, while the latest writers as commonly place the tens first, שִׁשִּׁים וּשְׁנַיִם *sixty and two* Dan. 9 : 25.

§ 226. Numerals of a higher grade are מֵאָה *one hundred*, אֶלֶף *one thousand*, רְבָבָה, רִבּוֹ or רִבּוֹא *ten thousand*. These are duplicated by affixing the dual termination מָאתַיִם *two hundred*, אַלְפַּיִם *two thousand*, רִבּוֹתַיִם or שְׁתֵּי רִבּוֹת *twenty thousand*. Higher multiples are formed by prefixing the appropriate units שְׁלֹשׁ מֵאוֹת *three hundred*, שְׁלֹשֶׁת אֲלָפִים *three thousand*, שֵׁשׁ רִבֹּאוֹת *sixty thousand*, אֶלֶף אֲלָפִים *one million*.

§ 227. 1. The ordinals are formed by adding ִי. to the corresponding cardinals, the same vowel being likewise inserted in several instances before the final consonant; רִאשׁוֹן *first* is derived from רֹאשׁ *head*.

First	רִאשׁוֹן	Sixth	שִׁשִּׁי
Second	שֵׁנִי	Seventh	שְׁבִיעִי
Third	שְׁלִישִׁי	Eighth	שְׁמִינִי
Fourth	רְבִיעִי	Ninth	תְּשִׁיעִי
Fifth	חֲמִישִׁי or חֲמִשִּׁי	Tenth	עֲשִׂירִי

The feminine commonly ends in יתָ., occasionally in יָּה..

a. There are two examples of the orthography רִאשׁוֹן Josh. 21:10, Job 15:7, and one of רִישׁוֹן Job 8:8, in all of which the K'ri restores the customary form.

2. There are no distinct forms for ordinals above ten, the cardinal numbers being used instead.

3. Fractional numbers are expressed by the feminine ordinals, שְׁלִישִׁית *one third,* רְבִיעִית *one fourth,* etc., and by the following additional terms, חֲצִי *one half,* רֶבַע and רֹבַע *one quarter,* חֹמֶשׁ *one fifth,* עִשָּׂרוֹן *one tenth.*

Prefixed Particles.

§228. The remaining parts of speech are indeclinable, and may be comprehended under the general name of particles. These may be divided into

1. Prefixed particles, which are only found in combination with a following word, viz. the article, He interrogative, the inseparable prepositions, and Vav conjunctive.

2. Those particles, which are written as separate words, and which comprise the great majority of adverbs, prepositions, conjunctions, and interjections.

a. No word in Hebrew has less than two letters; all particles of one letter are consequently prefixes. There is one example of two prefixes combined constituting a word הַל Deut. 32:6, though editions vary.

The Article.

§229. 1. The Definite Article (הֵא הַיְדִיעָה) consists of ה with Pattahh followed by Daghesh-forte in the first letter of the word to which it is prefixed, מֶלֶךְ *a king,* הַמֶּלֶךְ *the king.*

a. As the Arabic article ال is in certain cases followed by a like doubling of the initial letter, some have imagined that the original form of the Hebrew article was הַל and that the Daghesh-forte has arisen from the assimilation of ל and its contraction with the succeeding letter. Since, however, there is no trace of such a form, it seems better to acquiesce in the old opinion, which has in its favour the analogy of other languages, that the article הַ is related to the personal pronoun הוּא, whose principal consonant it retains, and that the following Daghesh is conservative, § 24. 3; comp. the demonstrative particle הָא and הָא *behold!* In הוֹירד Jer. 29 : 23 K'thibh (if read הַיּוֹרֵד) the article may perhaps be found in an unabridged form; the K'ri has הַיּוֹרֵד. The Arabic article is supposed to be found in the proper name אַלְמוֹדָד Gen. 10 : 26, אֶלְגָּבִישׁ *hail*, the equivalent of גָּבִישׁ, and possibly in אַלְקוּם Prov. 30 : 31.

b. There is, properly speaking, no indefinite article in Hebrew, although the numeral אֶחָד *one* is so employed in a few instances, as נָבִיא אֶחָד *a prophet* 1 Kin. 20 : 13.

2. If the first letter of the word have Sh'va, Daghesh-forte may be omitted except from the aspirates, § 25, הַיְאֹר, הַכְּתֻנֶת, הַבְּרָכָה but הַמְדַבֵּר.

3. Before gutturals, which cannot receive Daghesh-forte, § 60. 4, Pattahh is lengthened to Kamets; the short vowel Pattahh is, however, commonly retained before ח and ה, and sometimes before ע, the syllable being converted into an intermediate, § 20. 2. *a*, instead of a simple one, הָאֹהֶל, הָהָר, הָעַיִט Gen. 15 : 11, הָרֶשַׁע but הַחֹשֶׁךְ, הַהוּא, הַעַיִט Jer. 12 : 9.

a. The article very rarely has Kamets before ח, הָחִי Gen. 6 : 19, הָחַצְנִים Isa. 17 : 8; in a very few instances initial א quiesces in the vowel of the article, הָאֲסַפְסֻף Num. 11 : 4.

4. Before ה with Kamets or Hhateph-Kamets, Pattahh is changed to Seghol: before ה or ע with Kamets, it is likewise changed to Seghol if it stands in the second syllable before the accent, and consequently receives the secondary accent Methegh, הֶעָרִים, הֶהָרִים, הֶחֳדָשִׁים, הֶחָכָם, הֶתָג.

a. This change very rarely occurs before א, הֶאֱזוּר Mic. 2 : 7. When ה is followed by Kamets-Hhatuph, Pattahh remains הַחָכְמָה.

b. The article does not usually affect the vowels of the word before which it stands; in הַר *mountain* and עַם *people*, however, Pattahh is changed to Kamets to correspond with the vowel of the article הָהָר, הָעָם, so אֶרֶץ *earth* but הָאָרֶץ. The plurals of אֹהֶל *tent* and קֹדֶשׁ *holiness* without the article are אֹהָלִים Gen. 25 : 27, קָדָשִׁים Ex. 29 : 37, but with the article הָאֹהָלִים (for בְּהָאֹהָלִים) Judg. 8 : 11, הַקֳּדָשִׁים Ex. 26 : 33, § 208. 3 *b*;

קָאָת *pelican* Isa. 34:11, Zeph. 2:14, is pointed הַקָּאָת Lev. 11:18, Deut. 14:17 upon receiving the article.

5. When preceded by the inseparable prepositions the letter ה of the article is mostly rejected, and its vowel given to the preposition, § 53. 3, בַּשָּׁמַיִם for בְּהַשָּׁמַיִם, see § 231. 5.

HE INTERROGATIVE.

§ 230. 1. The letter ה (הֵא הַשְּׁאֵלָה) may also be prefixed to words to indicate an interrogation; it is then pointed with Hhateph-Pattahh, הֲנֵלֵךְ *shall we go?* הֲלֹא־הוּא *is he not?*

2. Before a vowelless letter this becomes Pattahh, § 61. 1, הַכְזוֹנָה Gen. 34:31, הַלְמַעַנְךָ Job 18:4, הַצֳרִי Jer. 8:22.

a. The new syllable thus formed is an intermediate one, § 22, and the succeeding Sh'va remains vocal, as is shown by the absence of Dagheshlene in such forms as הַיְרָאָם Gen. 29:5. In order to render this still more evident recourse is frequently had to Daghesh-forte separative, § 24. 5, הַלְּבֵן Gen. 17:17, הַתִּצְבַּקְתָּה 18:21, Methegh, § 45. 2, הַמִּשֹּׁל Judg. 9:2, הַתִּלְשַׁע Job 38:35, or compound Sh'va, § 16. 3. *b*, הַבְּרָכָה Gen. 27:38.

b. He interrogative has Pattahh and Daghesh-forte in one instance before a letter with a vowel of its own, הַיֵּיטַב Lev. 10:19.

3. Before gutturals it likewise usually becomes Pattahh, הַאֵלֵךְ Ex. 2:7, הַאֲשֶׁר 2 Kin. 6:22, הַהֵימִיר Jer. 2:11, הַעַט Hag. 1:4.

a. There are a few examples of He interrogative with Kamets before א, הָאָדָם Judg. 6:31, הָאֶפְרָתִי Judg. 12:5, הָאִישׁ Neh. 6:11.

4. Before gutturals with Kamets it is changed to Seghol, הֶאָמֹר Ezek. 28:9, הֶהָיְתָה Joel 1:2, הֶחָכָם Eccles. 2:19.

INSEPARABLE PREPOSITIONS.

§ 231. 1. The prepositions בְּ *in*, כְּ *according to*, לְ *to*, are regularly prefixed with Sh'va, בְּרֵאשִׁית *in the beginning*, כְּכֹל *according to all*, לְאַבְרָהָם *to Abraham*.

2. Before vowelless letters this Sh'va is changed to Hhirik, בִּדְבַר for כִּדְבָר, לִמְשֹׁל for לְמָשָׁל, בִּרְקִיעַ for בְּרָקִיעַ.

3. Before gutturals with compound Sh'va it is changed to the corresponding short vowel, בַּחֲרִי, כֶּאֱכֹל, לַאֲרִי.

a. Initial א quiesces in the following words after the inseparable prepositions, § 57. 2. (2) *a*, אָדוֹן *master* when connected with singular suffixes, אֲדֹנָי *Lord*, אֱלֹהִים *God*, and also in the inf. const. אֱמֹר *to say* after לְ, בֵּאלֹהִים for בְּאֱלֹהִים, לֵאלֹהִים, לַאדֹנָיְהָ, בַּאדֹנָיו, בַּאדֹנָי the Seghol lengthened to Tsere in the simple syllable, לֵאלֹהוֹ but לֵאלֹהִים, לֶאֱמֹר but לֵאמֹר, בֶּאֱמֹר, כֶּאֱמֹר. Before the divine name יהוה the inseparable prepositions are pointed as they would be before אֲדֹנָי or אֱלֹהִים, whose vowels it receives, § 47, לַיהוָֹה Gen. 4:3, לַיהוָֹה Ps. 68:21.

b. In a very few instances א with Pattahh and י with Hhirik give up their vowel to the preposition and become quiescent, כַּאבִּיר Isa. 10:13 for כְּאבִּיר, כִּירָתוֹן Eccles. 2:13 for כְּירָתוֹן.

4. Before monosyllables and before dissyllables, accented upon the penult, these prepositions frequently receive a pretonic Kamets, § 64. 2, לָנֶפֶשׁ, כָּזֹאת, בָּאֵלֶּה.

a. This regularly occurs with the Kal construct infinitive of פֹּ״ו, פֹּ״י, ע״ו and ע״ו verbs when preceded by לְ, e. g. לָגֶשֶׁת, לָחֵת, לָרֶדֶת, לָרֹב, לָרִיב; also with different forms of the demonstrative זֶה and with personal suffixes; and with monosyllabic or Segholate nouns when accompanied by disjunctive and especially pause accents. Before the pronoun מָה *what* they are commonly pointed בַּמָּה, כַּמָּה, לָמָה or followed by a guttural, לָמָה.

5. Before the article its ה is rejected and the vowel given to the preposition, לָהָאָרֶץ for לָאָרֶץ, כְּהַדָּבָר for כַּדָּבָר, בְּהֶהָרִים for בֶּהָרִים.

a. ה not infrequently remains after כְּ, כְּהַיּוֹם Gen. 39:11, more rarely after the other prepositions, לְהַדָּע 2 Chron. 10:7. The initial ה of the Hiphil and Niphal infinitives is occasionally rejected in like manner, לַשְׁבִּית Am. 8:4 for לְהַשְׁבִּית, בִּפְשְׁלוֹ Prov. 24:17 for בְּהִפָּשְׁלוֹ.

§ 232. The preposition מִן *from*, though used in its separate form, may also be abbreviated to a prefix by the assimilation and contraction of its final Nun with the initial letter of the following word, which accordingly receives Daghesh-forte, מִדֶּרֶךְ for מִן דֶּרֶךְ. Before ח Hhirik is commonly retained in an intermediate syllable, but before other gutturals it is lengthened to Tsere, מֵעַם, מֵהָלוֹם, מֵאֶרֶץ, מִן חוּץ for מֵחוּץ.

a. מִן is sometimes poetically lengthened to מִנִּי, and once has the form of a construct plural, מִנֵּי Isa. 30:11.

§ 233. These prepositions are combined with the pronominal suffixes in the following manner:

SINGULAR.

1 c.	בִּי	לִי	כָּמוֹנִי	בִּמְֶנִּי, בִּי, מֶנִּי
2 m.	בְּךָ, בָּךְ	לְךָ, לָךְ	כָּמוֹךָ	בִּמְךָ, מִמֶּךָּ
2 f.	בָּךְ	לָךְ		מִמֵּךְ
3 m.	בּוֹ	לוֹ	כָּמוֹהוּ	בִּמְנוּ, מִמֶּנּוּ, מִמֶּנְהוּ
3 f.	בָּהּ	לָהּ	כָּמוֹהָ	בִּמְנָּה

PLURAL.

1 c.	בָּנוּ	לָנוּ	כָּמוֹנוּ	מִמֶּנּוּ
2 m.	בָּכֶם	לָכֶם	כְּמוֹכֶם, כָּכֶם	מִכֶּם
2 f.	בָּכֶן	לָכֶן	—	מִכֶּן
3 m.	בָּהֶם, בָּם	לָהֶם, לָמוֹ	כְּמוֹהֶם, כָּהֶם	מֵהֶם, מִנְּהֶם
3 f.	בָּהֶן, בָּהֵן	לָהֶן	—	מֵהֶן

a. The syllable מוֹ inserted between כְּ and the suffixes, and which is in poetry sometimes added to בְּ, כְּ and לְ without suffixes to convert them into independent words, לָמוֹ, כְּמוֹ, בְּמוֹ, is commonly thought to be related in its origin to the pronoun מָה *what*, so that כָּמוֹנִי would in strictness denote *like what I am*, i. e. *like me*. The preposition מִן, with the exception of some poetical forms, reduplicates itself before the light suffixes, מִמֶּנִּי = מִנְמְנִי. Comp. a similar reduplication of a short word, מֵימֵי or מֵי construct of מַיִם *water*.

Vav Conjunctive.

§ 234. The conjunction *and* is expressed by ו prefixed with Sh'va, וְחֹשֶׁךְ, וְהָאָרֶץ. Before one of the labials ב, מ, פ, § 57. 2 (1), or before a vowelless letter Vav quiesces in

§ 235   SEPARATE PARTICLES.   263

Shurek, וּבֵין, וּמְלֹא, וּפְנִים, וּלְהַבְדִּיל. Before a vowelless
Yodh it receives Hhirik, in which the Yodh quiesces, וִינַקְּמֵם,
וִיהִי. Before a guttural with compound Sh'va it receives the
corresponding short vowel, וַאֲנִי, וֶאֱזוּז, וַחֲלִי. Before monosyllables and dissyllables accented on the penult it frequently
receives a pretonic Kamets, וָרֹבּוּ, וְלַיְלָה, וָרָע.

a. After Vav with Shurek, compound Sh'va is sometimes substituted for simple Sh'va in order to indicate more distinctly its vocal
character, וָהֳבֹא Gen. 2:12, וְהָקֳדָשׁ Ezek. 26:21, וּסְעָדָה 1 Kin. 13:7,
וְצֳלָתִי Jer. 22:20.

b. Vav receives Hhirik before He followed by Yodh in the forms
וִיהִיתֶם, וִיהִיוּ, וִיהִיָם, וִיהִיתָ 2 plur. preterite and imperative of the verbs
הָיָה *to be* and חָיָה *to live;* before the 2 masc. sing. imperative of the
same verbs it has Seghol, וֶחְיֵה, וֶחְיֵה for וְחָיָה, וְהָיָה.

c. א quiesces after Vav conjunctive as after the inseparable prepositions, § 231. 3. *a,* in אֲדוֹן *master* when connected with singular suffixes,
אֲדֹנִי *Lord* and אֱלֹהִים *God,* וַאדֹנִי, וַאדֹנַי, וֵאלֹהֵי, וֵאלֹהֵינוּ the Seghol
being lengthened to Tsere in the simple syllable. Hence also וִיהֹוָה
when יהוה has the vowels of אֲדֹנָי. A very few instances occur in which
א with Pattahh and י with Hhirik give up their vowel to Vav conjunctive
and become quiescent, וַאבְשׁוֹר Zech. 11:5 for וַאבְשָׁר, וִילְלַת Jer. 25:36
for וִילְלַת.

SEPARATE PARTICLES.

ADVERBS.

§ 235. 1. A few adverbs of negation, place and time, are
commonly classed as primitive, although they are probably
related to pronominal roots, as אַל and לֹא *not,* שָׁם *there,*
אָז *then.*

a. It is natural to suspect that the pronominal root ל, which gave rise
to the near demonstrative אֵל, אֵלֶּה *these* and to the prepositions indicative
of nearness or approach, ל *to,* אֶל *unto,* and which has a remote demonstrative force in הָלְאָה *yonder, beyond,* may also be the basis of לֹא and אַל
the idea of remoteness taken absolutely forming a negation. The same
idea, in a less absolute sense, may be traced in the conditional conjunction
לוּ *if.* The pronoun זֶה, of which probably שֶׁ is originally only a modification (comp. the relative use of זוּ, § 73. 1), is plainly connected with אָז
at that time and שָׁם *in that place.*

2. Derivative adverbs are formed

(1.) By affixing the terminations ם, or ם׳, אָמְנָם and אָמְנָם truly from אֹמֶן truth, חִנָּם gratuitously from חֵן grace, יוֹמָם by day from יוֹם day, רֵיקָם in vain from רִיק empty, פִּתְאֹם suddenly from פֶּתַע moment, שִׁלְשׁוֹם the day before yesterday from שָׁלֹשׁ three.

(2.) By abbreviation, as אַךְ surely, only from אָכֵן.

(3.) By composition, as מַדּוּעַ why? from מַה יָדוּעַ quid edoctus, מִלְמַעְלָה from above from מִן, לְ and מַעְלָה.

3. Besides those adverbs, which are such originally and properly, other parts of speech are sometimes used as adverbs. Thus

(1.) Nouns, מְאֹד mightily, exceedingly prop. might, סָבִיב around prop. circuit, עוֹד again prop. repetition, אֶפֶס no more prop. cessation; with a preposition, בִּמְאֹד exceedingly, לְבַד apart prop. to separation, or a suffix יַחְדָּו together prop. in its union. Compare the adverbial accusative and adverbial phrases of Greek and other languages.

(2.) Absolute infinitives, which are really verbal nouns, הֵיטֵב well prop. recte faciendo, הַרְבֵּה much, מַהֵר quickly.

(3.) Adjectives, particularly in the feminine, which is used as a neuter, טוֹב well, רִאשֹׁנָה at first, שֵׁנִית the second time, רַבָּה and רַבַּת much, יְהוּדִית in Jewish i. e. Hebrew, אֲרָמִית in Aramaic, נִפְלָאוֹת wonderfully.

(4.) Pronouns, זֶה here, now prop. this place, this time, הֵנָּה hither prop. to these places, with a preposition כֹּה thus prop. according to it, כֵּן so perhaps for כָּהֵן according to these things, though others explain it as an adverbial use of the participle כֵּן right, true, פֹּה here probably for בּוֹ in this (place).

§ 236. A few adverbs are capable of receiving pronominal suffixes, as הֵן or הִנֵּה behold, עוֹד yet, אַי where, to which may be added אַיִן there is not prop. non-existence and יֵשׁ

there is prop. *existence.* As the idea of action or of existence is suggested by them, they take the verbal suffixes, frequently with נ epenthetic. Thus

1. הִנֵּה. *First person* הִנְּנִי, הִנְנִי and הִנֵּנִי; הִנְנוּ, הִנֵּנוּ and הִנֵּנוּ. *Second person* masc. הִנְּךָ once הִנֶּכָּה; הִנְּכֶם, fem. הִנָּךְ. *Third person* הִנּוֹ and הִנֵּהוּ; הִנָּם.

2. עוֹד. *First person* עוֹדֶנִּי and עוֹדִי; once with *plur.* עוֹדֵינוּ Lam. 4:17 K'ri. *Second person* masc. עוֹדְךָ fem. עוֹדָךְ. *Third person* masc. עוֹדֶנּוּ, עוֹדָם fem. עוֹדֶנָּה.

3. אִי, *Second person* אַיֶּכָּה. *Third person* אַיּוֹ, אַיָּם.

4. אַיִן. *First person* אֵינֶנִּי. *Second person* masc. אֵינְךָ, אֵינְכֶם, fem. אֵינֵךְ. *Third person* masc. אֵינֶנּוּ, אֵינָם and אֵינֵמוֹ fem. אֵינֶנָּה.

5. יֵשׁ. *Second person* יֶשְׁךָ, יֶשְׁכֶם and יֶשְׁכָם. *Third person* יֶשְׁנוֹ.

PREPOSITIONS.

§ 237. 1. The simple prepositions in most common use, besides the inseparable prefixes, § 231, are chiefly אַחַר *behind, after,* אֶל־ *to, unto,* אֵצֶל *beside,* אֵת *with,* בֵּין *between,* בִּלְתִּי *without,* בְּעַד *through,* זוּלַת *except,* יַעַן *on account of,* מוּל or מוֹל *over against,* נֶגֶד *in presence of,* נֹכַח *in front of, before,* עַד *unto,* עַל *upon,* עִם *with,* תַּחַת *under.* Most of these appear to have been originally nouns; and some of them are still used both as nouns and as prepositions.

2. Other prepositions are compound, and consist of

(1.) Two prepositions, as מֵאַחֲרֵי *from after,* מֵאֵת and מֵעִם *from with,* מֵעַל *from upon,* מִתַּחַת *from under,* לְמִן *from,* לְנֶגֶד and לְנֹכַח *before,* אֶל־מוּל *toward.*

(2.) A preposition and a noun לְבַד and מִלְּבַד *besides* from בַּד *separation,* לִפְנֵי *before* and מִפְּנֵי, מִלִּפְנֵי *from before* from פָּנִים *face,* בִּגְלַל and בַּעֲבוּר *for the sake of,* בְּיַד *by* prop.

by the hand of, אֶל־עֵ֫בֶר *beyond,* מֵעֵ֫בֶר לְ *from beyond,* לְעֻמַּת *in conjunction with,* לְמַ֫עַן *and* עַל־עֵ֫קֶב *on account of,* כְּפִי, לְפִי, *and* עַל־פִּי *according to* prop. *at the mouth of.*

(3.) A preposition and an infinitive, לִקְרַאת *toward* prop. *to meet.*

(4.) A preposition and an adverb, בִּלְעֲדֵי and מִבַּלְעֲדֵי *without* from בַּל *not* עַד *unto,* לְ מֵהָ֫לְאָה *beyond,* בִּבְלִי *without.*

§ 238. 1. The prepositions take suffixes in the same manner as singular nouns, e. g. אֶצְלִי *beside me,* זוּלָתִי, כְּמִי, *except* אַחַר *after,* אֶל־ *to,* עַד *unto,* עַל *upon* and תַּ֫חַת *under,* which before suffixes assume the form of nouns in the masculine plural, e. g. אַחֲרָיו, אַחֲרֶיהָ, אַחֲרַי; בֵּין *between* adopts sometimes a singular, sometimes a masculine plural, and sometimes a feminine plural form, e. g. בֵּינִי, בֵּינוֹ and בֵּינוֹתֵ֫ימוּ, בֵּינֵ֫ימוּ and בֵּינָיו.

a. The plural form אַחֲרֵי occurs without suffixes more frequently than אַחַר; אֶלֵי, בַּלֵּי also occur in poetry.

b. תַּ֫חַת in a very few instances takes a verbal suffix, תַּחְתֵּ֫נִי 2 Sam. 22 : 37, 40, 48; with the 3 masc. plur. suffix it is תַּחְתָּם oftener than תַּחְתֵּיהֶם.

2. The preposition אֵת *with* is to be distinguished from אֵת the sign of the definite object, which is prefixed to a pronoun or definite noun, to indicate that it is the object of an active verb. With pronominal suffixes the ת of the preposition is doubled and its vowel shortened to Hhirik, thus אִתִּי, אִתְּךָ, אִתְּכֶם; the sign of the accusative becomes אוֹת before suffixes or before grave suffixes commonly אֶת, thus, אוֹתָם rarely אֹתָם, אוֹתְכֶם rarely אֶתְכֶם, אֶתְהֶם and אֹתִי.

a. Sometimes, particularly in the books of Kings, Jeremiah, and Ezekiel, the preposition takes the form אוֹתְךָ, אוֹתִי.

Conjunctions.

§ 239. 1. In addition to the prefixed copulative וְ, § 234, the following are the simple conjunctions in most common use, אוֹ *or*, אַף *also*, אִם *and* לוּ *if*, אֲשֶׁר *and* כִּי *that, because*, פֶּן *lest*.

2. Compound conjunctions are formed by combining

(1.) Two conjunctions כִּי אִם *but*, אַף כִּי *how much more* prop. *also that*.

(2.) The conjunction כִּי or אֲשֶׁר with a preposition, as כַּאֲשֶׁר *as*, לְמַעַן אֲשֶׁר *in order that*, יַעַן אֲשֶׁר and עֵקֶב אֲשֶׁר *because*, עַד כִּי *until*, תַּחַת כִּי *because*.

(3.) An adverb with a preposition or conjunction, בְּטֶרֶם *before*, לָכֵן or עַל־כֵּן *therefore*, לוּלֵי *unless* from לוּ *if* לֹא *not*.

INTERJECTIONS.

§ 240. The Hebrew interjections, like those of other languages, are of two sorts, viz.:

1. Natural sounds expressive of various emotions, as אָח, הָהּ, אֲהָהּ *ah! oh!* הֶאָח *aha!* הוֹי *ho! woe!* אוֹיָה, אִי, אֲבוֹי *woe!* אַלְלַי *alas!* הַס *hush!*

2. Words originally belonging to other parts of speech, which by frequent use were converted into interjections, הָבָה *come!* prop. *give*, לְכָה *come!* prop. *go*, הִנֵּה *behold!* prop. a demonstrative adverb, חָלִילָה *far be it!* בִּי *pray!* from בְּעִי *entreaty*, נָא *now! I pray thee!*

PART THIRD.

SYNTAX.

§ 241. 1. Syntax treats of sentences or of the manner in which words are employed in the utterance of thought. Its office, therefore, is to exhibit the several functions of the different parts of speech in the mechanism of the sentence, the relations which they sustain to each other, and how those relations are outwardly expressed.

2. Every sentence must embrace first a subject or the thing spoken of, and secondly, a predicate or that which is said about it. Upon these two simple elements is built the entire structure of human speech.

THE SUBJECT.

§ 242. The subject of every sentence must be either a noun, as בָּרָא אֱלֹהִים *God created* Gen. 1 : 1, or a pronoun, as אֲנִי קָדוֹשׁ *I* (am) *holy* Lev. 11 : 44; This includes infinitives, which are verbal nouns, עֲנוֹשׁ לַצַּדִּיק לֹא־טוֹב *to punish the just is not good* Prov. 17 : 26, and adjectives and participles when used substantively, לֹא־יָבוֹא טָמֵא *an unclean* (person) *shall not enter* 2 Chron. 23 : 19, לֹא הַמֵּתִים יְהַלְלוּ־יָהּ *the dead shall not praise the Lord* Ps. 115 : 17.

a. The subject of a sentence may be a noun preceded by the preposition מִן in a partitive sense, יָצְאוּ מִן־הָעָם *there went out* (some) *of the people* Ex. 16 : 27, or by the particle of comparison כְּ, כְּנֶגַע נִרְאָה (something) *like a plague has appeared* Lev. 14 : 35.

b. When the subject is an infinitive, it is mostly, as in English, preceded by the preposition לְ to, טוֹב לְהֹדוֹת (it is) *good to give thanks* Ps. 92:2, unless it is in the construct before a following noun לֹא־טוֹב הֱיוֹת הָאָדָם לְבַדּוֹ *man's being alone (is) not good* Gen. 2:18.

c. The subject is very rarely an adverb, הַרְבֵּה נָפַל מִן־הָעָם *many* (prop. *much*) *of the people have fallen* 2 Sam. 1:4.

§ 243. The subject may be omitted in the following cases, viz.:

1. When it is sufficiently plain from the connection, הַעוֹד עֻפָּה *is there yet with thee* (a corpse)? Am. 6:10, or is obvious in itself, אִתּוֹ יְלָדָה (his mother) *bare him* 1 Kin. 1:6. The personal pronouns are for this reason rarely used before verbal forms, which of themselves indicate the person, אָמַרְתִּי *I said*, אָמַרְתָּ *thou saidst*, unless with the view of expressing emphasis or opposition, הֵמָּה כָּרְעוּ וְנָפָלוּ וַאֲנַחְנוּ קַמְנוּ *they are brought down and fallen, but we are risen* Ps. 20:9.

2. When it is indefinite; thus, if an action is spoken of and it is not known or is not stated by whom it is performed. The third person plural may be so employed, וַיַּגִּדוּ לְשָׁאוּל *and they told Saul* 1 Sam. 18:20, or third person singular, comp. the French *on* and German *man*, קָרָא שְׁמָהּ בָּבֶל *one called its name Babel* i. e. *its name was called Babel*, or the second person singular, particularly in laws or in proverbs, the language of direct address being employed while every one who hears is intended, לֹא־תַעֲשֶׂה־לְךָ פֶסֶל *thou shalt not make unto thee a graven image* Ex. 20:4, הָבִיאָה לַמּוּסָר לִבֶּךָ *apply thine heart unto instruction* Prov. 23:12.

a. Sometimes the word אִישׁ *man* is used as an indefinite subject, כֹּה אָמַר הָאִישׁ בְּלֶכְתּוֹ וגו׳* *a man said thus, when he went*, etc. 1 Sam. 9:9, and sometimes the participle of the following verb, וְשֹׁמֵעַ חֹשֵׁשׁ *and the hearer shall hear* 2 Sam. 17:9, חָרְשׁוּ חֹרְשִׁים *ploughers ploughed* Ps. 129:3.

b. The third person plural indefinite seems to be used sometimes without any thought of the real agency concerned in the action spoken of, and where the English would require a passive construction, לֵילוֹת עָמָל מִנּוּ־לִי *wearisome nights are appointed to me* lit. *they have appointed* Job 7:3.

* וגו׳ is an abbreviation for וְגוֹמֵר *et completio, and so forth*, § 9. 1.

3. When the construction is impersonal; in this case the third person singular masculine is the form commonly adopted, אַל־יֵרַע בְּעֵינֶיךָ *let it not be grievous in thy sight* Gen. 21:12, אָז הוּחַל *then it was begun* i. e. *men began*, though the feminine is also employed on account of its special affinity with the neuter, וַתֵּצֶר לְיִשְׂרָאֵל *and Israel was distressed* lit. *it was strait to Israel* Judg. 10:9.

§ 244. 1. The subject may be extended by connecting two or more nouns or pronouns and thus forming what is called a compound subject, וַיְכֻלּוּ הַשָּׁמַיִם וְהָאָרֶץ וְכָל־צְבָאָם *and the heavens and the earth and all their host were finished* Gen. 2:1, וַאֲנִי וְהַנַּעַר נֵלְכָה *and I and the lad will go* Gen. 22:5.

2. Or it may be extended by adding to the noun an article, adjective, demonstrative pronoun, pronominal suffix, or another noun with which it may be either in apposition or in construction. When thus united with other qualifying words the noun alone is called the grammatical subject, the noun, together with its adjuncts, is called the logical subject.

The Article.

§ 245. The definite article is used in Hebrew as in other languages to particularize the object spoken of, and distinguish it from all others. It is accordingly prefixed in the following cases, viz.:

1. When the thing referred to is one which has been mentioned before, *and God said, Let there be* רָקִיעַ *a firmament, etc., and God made* הָרָקִיעַ *the firmament* Gen. 1:6, 7.

2. When it is defined by accompanying words, as a relative clause, אַשְׁרֵי הָאִישׁ אֲשֶׁר לֹא הָלַךְ וגו׳ *blessed is the man who has not walked*, etc., Ps. 1:1, an adjective, הַמָּאוֹר הַגָּדֹל *the greater light*, הַמָּאוֹר הַקָּטֹן *the lesser light* Gen. 1:16, or a demonstrative pronoun, הַר *a mountain*, הָהָר הַזֶּה *this mountain*, הָהָר הַהוּא *that mountain*, or by being directly ad-

dressed, הַמֶּלֶךְ *O king* 1 Sam. 17:55, הַשָּׁמַיִם *O heavens*, הָאָרֶץ *O earth* Deut. 32:1.

3. When it is obviously suggested by the circumstances, or may be presumed to be well known: *she emptied her pitcher into* הַשֹּׁקֶת *the trough* Gen 24:20, viz., the one which must have been by a well used for watering cattle; *Abimelech looked through* הַחַלּוֹן *the window* Gen. 26:8, i. e. of the house in which it is taken for granted that he was; *let us go to* הָרֹאֶה *the* (well-known) *seer* 1 Sam. 9:9.

a. The article is accordingly used as in Greek and in some modern languages in place of an unemphatic possessive pronoun: *she took* הַצָּעִיף *the veil* Gen. 24:65, i. e. the one which she had, or, according to the English idiom, *her veil;* David took הַכִּנּוֹר *the harp* i. e. *his harp* 1 Sam. 16:23, so the LXX. ἐλάμβανε Δαυὶδ τὴν κινύραν.

b. With words denoting time it expresses the present as that which would most readily occur to the mind, הַיּוֹם *the day* i. e. that which is now passing, *to-day* Gen. 4:14, הַלַּיְלָה *the night* i. e. *to-night* Gen. 30:15, הַשָּׁנָה *the year* i. e. *this year* Jer. 28:16, הַפַּעַם *the time* i. e. *this time* Gen. 29:35, unless another idea is more naturally suggested by the context, וַיְהִי הַיּוֹם *and it came to pass on the day* i. e. at the period before spoken of, *at that time* 1 Sam. 1:4, Job 1:6.

4. When it is distinguished above all others of like kind or is the only one of its class, הַבַּיִת *the house* viz. of God, the temple Mic. 3:12, הָאָדוֹן *the Lord* Isa. 1:24, הָאֱלֹהִים *the* (true) *God*, הַשָּׁמַיִם *the heavens*, הָאָרֶץ *the earth* Gen. 1:1, הַשֶּׁמֶשׁ *the sun* Gen. 15:12.

5. When it is an appellative noun used in a generic or universal sense, הַחֶרֶב *the sword devoureth one as well as another* 2 Sam. 11:25; *they shall mount up with wings* כַּנְּשָׁרִים *as the eagles* Isa. 40:31, and sometimes when it is a material or abstract noun, in which case the English idiom does not admit the article, *where there is* הַזָּהָב *gold* Gen. 2:11 LXX. τὸ χρυσίον; *thy wine mixed* בַּמַּיִם *with water* Isa. 1:22, *where shall* הַחָכְמָה *wisdom be found?* Job 28:12 LXX. ἡ δὲ σοφία κτλ; *they smote the men* בַּסַּנְוֵרִים *with blindness* Gen. 19:11.

a. The article is thus used with adjectives to denote the class, which they describe, *God shall judge* אֶת־הַצַּדִּיק וְאֶת־הָרָשָׁע *the righteous and the wicked* Eccl. 3:17; *the proverb of* הַקַּדְמֹנִי *the ancients* 1 Sam. 24:14; and with Gentile nouns, which are properly adjectives, §194. 1, הָאֱמֹרִי *the Amorite,* הַכְּנַעֲנִי *the Canaanite,* Gen. 15:21.

b. The Hebrew infinitive does not receive the article; דַּעַת, which is the only exception, see Gen. 2:9 and elsewhere, may be regarded as a noun. In a very few instances the article is prefixed to finite tenses of the verb with the force of a relative pronoun, הֶהָלְכוּא *who went* Josh. 10:24, הַיּוּלַּד *that shall be born* Judg. 13:8, הִתְקְדִּישׁ *which he sanctified* 1 Chron. 26:28, הַנִּמְצְאוּ *who are present* 1 Chron. 29:17, בְּהַבִּיא *into* (the place) *which he prepared* 2 Chron. 1:4; so also 2 Chron. 29:36, Ezr. 8:25, 10:14, 17, Isa. 56:3, Jer. 5:13, Dan. 8:1. It is once prefixed to a preposition, הַעֲלֶיהָ *what* (was) *upon it* 1 Sam. 9:24.

c. In the uses of the article, as stated above, Nos. 4 and 5 are really varieties of No. 3, since the prominent member of a class is the best known and most readily suggested, and when a word is used generically it designates a definite and well-known class of objects which is to be distinguished from every other class.

d. The Hebrew article is sometimes found where the English requires the indefinite article or none at all; but it must not on that account be supposed that it ever loses its proper force or becomes equivalent to an indefinite article. The difference of idiom is due to a difference in the mode of conception. Thus, in comparisons the Hebrew commonly conceived of the whole class of objects of which he spoke, while we mostly think of one or more individuals belonging to the class, כַּקֵּן *as* (the) *a nest,* Isa. 10:14, כַּסֵּפֶר *as* (the) *a scroll* Isa. 34:4, *like rending* הַגְּדִי (the) *a kid* Judg. 14:6, *as* הַדְּבֹרִים (the) *bees do* Deut. 1:44, כַּשָּׁנִים *as* (the) *scarlet,* כַּשֶּׁלֶג *as* (the) *snow,* כַּתּוֹלָע *as* (the) *crimson,* כַּצֶּמֶר *as* (the) *wool* Isa. 1:18. Cases also not infrequently occur in which the article may either be inserted or omitted with equal propriety and without any material change of sense, according as the noun is to the mind of the speaker definite or indefinite. In speaking of the invasion of his father's flocks, David says, הָאֲרִי *the lion and* הַדּוֹב *the bear came* 1 Sam. 17:34, because he thinks of these as *the* enemies to be expected under the circumstances; had he thought of them indefinitely as beasts of prey he would have said, without the article, *a lion and a bear.* It is said, Gen. 13:2, that Abram was very rich בַּמִּקְנֶה בַּכֶּסֶף וּבַזָּהָב *in* (the) *cattle, in* (the) *silver, and in* (the) *gold,* since these are viewed as definite and well-known species of property; but in Gen. 24:35 *he hath given him* צֹאן וּבָקָר וְכֶסֶף וְזָהָב *flocks and herds and silver and gold,* these are viewed indefinitely in Hebrew as in English.

§ 246. Nouns are definite without the article in the following cases, viz.:

1. Proper nouns, which are definite by signification, אַבְרָהָם *Abraham,* כְּנַעַן *Canaan,* יְרוּשָׁלַם *Jerusalem.*

a. Proper names, originally applied in an appellative sense, sometimes retain the definite article, הַבַּעַל *the lord*, Baal, הַשָּׂטָן *the adversary*, Satan, הַנָּהָר *the river, the Euphrates*, הַיַּרְדֵּן *the descending* (stream), *the Jordan*, הַלְּבָנוֹן *the white* (mountain), *Lebanon*, הַכַּרְמֶל *the garden*, Carmel, הַכִּכָּר *the circuit* of the Jordan, הַמִּצְפָּה *the watch-tower*, Mizpah, הָאָדָם and אָדָם *the* (first) *man*, Adam, הָאֱלֹהִים and אֱלֹהִים *the* (true) *God*. In חֲצִי שֵׁבֶט הַמְנַשֶּׁה *the half tribe of Manasseh* Deut. 3:13 and often elsewhere, the article makes more prominent the definiteness of the entire expression: it also occurs without the article, e. g. Num. 32:33.

2. Nouns with suffixes, which are rendered definite by the appended pronoun, אָבִינוּ *our father*, שְׁמוֹ *his name*, but in Greek ὁ πατὴρ ἡμῶν, τὸ ὄνομα αὐτοῦ.

a. There are a few instances in which, for special reasons, the article is prefixed to nouns having suffixes. It is emphatic in הַחֲצִי *the* (other) *half of them* Josh. 8:33, opposed to a preceding חֲצִיוֹ *one half of them;* so in בְּעֻבְרָתָהּ Isa. 24:2. In מִכְסַת הָעֶרְכְּךָ *the worth of thy estimation* Lev. 27:23, it serves to indicate more clearly the definiteness of the entire expression; so בְּתוֹךְ הָאֹהֶל *in the midst of my tent* Josh. 7:21, בְּתוֹךְ הַדִּבְרוֹ *in the midst of its fold* Mic. 2:12, כָּל־הַנָּשִׁים הָרוֹת *the whole of the women with child* 2 Kin. 15:16; in לַמַּעֲנֵהוּ Prov. 16:4 it distinguishes the noun מַעֲנֶה from the preposition לְמַעַן.

b. A suffix which is the direct object of a participle does not supersede the necessity of the article, הַמַּכֵּהוּ *the* (one) *smiting him* Isa. 9:12, הַמַּעַלְךָ *the* (one) *bringing thee up* Ps. 81:11, הַמְעַטְּרֵכִי *the* (one) *crowning thee* Ps. 103:4.

3. Nouns in the construct state before a definite noun, whether this has the article כּוֹכְבֵי הַשָּׁמַיִם *the stars of heaven* Gen. 26:4, רַגְלֵי הַכֹּהֲנִים *the feet of the priests* Josh. 3:13, is a proper name, שִׁבְטֵי יִשְׂרָאֵל *the tribes of Israel* Ex. 24:4, דְּבַר יְהֹוָה *the word of Jehovah* Gen. 15:1, has a pronominal suffix, בִּכּוּרֵי מַעֲשֶׂיךָ *the first-fruits of thy labours*, נְשֵׁי־בָנָיו *the wives of his sons* Gen. 7:13, or is itself definite by construction, מְעָרַת שְׂדֵה הַמַּכְפֵּלָה *the cave of the field of Machpelah* Gen. 23:19, אֲרוֹן בְּרִית־יְהֹוָה *the ark of the covenant of Jehovah* Josh. 3:3.

a. Nouns in the construct are occasionally found with the article, הָאֹהֱלָה שָׂרָה *to the tent of Sarah* Gen. 24:67, הָאֵל בֵּית־אֵל *the God of Bethel* Gen. 31:13, הַיָּתֵד הָאֶרֶג *the pin of the web* Judg. 16:14, כָּל הַתּוֹעֵבֹת הַגּוֹיִם *all the abominations of the nations* 1 Kin. 14:24, הַקֶּבֶר אִישׁ־הָאֱלֹהִים *the grave of the man of God* 2 Kin. 23:17, כָּל־הַמַּמְלְכוֹת הָאָרֶץ *all the king-*

doms of the earth Jer. 25:26, הַסֵּפֶר הַמִּקְנָה *the bill of the purchase*, Jer. 32:12, הָאֵפֶן שֹׁבְמָה Jer. 48:32; see Josh. 3:11, 8:11, 1 Chron. 15:27, 2 Chron. 8:16, 15:8, Ezr. 8:29, Isa. 36:8, Ezek. 45:16, 47:15, Zeph. 3:19, Zech. 4:7, Ps. 123:4; also 1 Sam. 26:22 K'thibh, 2 Kin. 7:13 K'thibh, where the K'ri omits the article.

b. Gentile nouns, derived from a compound proper name, frequently receive the article before the second member of the compound, בְּנֵי־הַיְמִינִי *the Benjamite* Judg. 3:15, בֵּית־הַשִּׁמְשִׁי *the Bethshemite* 1 Sam. 6:14, בֵּית הַלַּחְמִי *the Bethlehemite* 1 Sam. 16:18, אֲבִי הָעֶזְרִי *the Abiezrite* Judg. 6:11, though this last word also appears in the abbreviated form הָאִיעֶזְרִי Num. 26:30.

§ 247. The article is frequently omitted in the brief and emphatic language of poetry, where it would be required in prose, מַלְכֵי־אָרֶץ *kings of* (the) *earth* Ps. 2:2, לִפְנֵי שֶׁמֶשׁ *in the presence of* (the) *sun* Ps. 72:17, אָמַר שֹׁמֵר אָתָה בֹקֶר (the) *watchman says,* (the) *morning comes* Isa. 21:12; *to give* וְקֹדֶשׁ וְצָבָא *both sanctuary and host to be trampled* Dan. 8:13.

a. Occasional instances occur of its being dropped from familiar or frequently repeated expressions in prose, עַד אַחֲרִית שָׁנָה *to year's end* Deut. 11:12, בְּאֹהֶל מוֹעֵד *in* (the) *tabernacle of* (the) *congregation* Ex. 27:21 (comp. English *in church*), שַׂר־צָבָא (the) *captain of* (the) *host* 1 Kin. 16:16, לְמוּאֵל מֶלֶךְ *king Lemuel* Prov. 31:1; also in geographical and architectural details, such technical terms as וּגְבוּל *and* (the) *border* Josh. 13:23, וְרֹחַב *and* (the) *breadth* 2 Chron. 3:3.

b. When two definite nouns are connected by *and* the article is commonly repeated; it may, however, particularly in poetry, stand only before the first and be understood with the second, *woe unto* הַחֹקְקִים *the* (persons) *decreeing unrighteous decrees* וּמְכַתְּבִים *and writing,* etc. Isa. 10:1, הַנֵּבֶל וְכִנּוֹר *O psaltery and harp* Ps. 57:9. Still more rarely a pronominal suffix may be attached to the first only of two words to which it belongs, עָזִּי וְזִמְרָת *my strength and song* Ex. 15:2.

§ 248. There is no indefinite article in Hebrew; indefinite nouns are sufficiently characterized as such by the absence of the article. Thus, נָהָר *a river* Gen. 2:10, גַּם־רֶכֶב גַּם־פָּרָשִׁים *both chariots and horsemen* Gen. 50:9, חָלָב וּדְבָשׁ *milk and honey* Ex. 3:8, עוּל יָמִים *an infant of days* Isa. 65:20.

a. The numeral אֶחָד *one* is occasionally employed in the sense of an indefinite article, סַל אֶחָד *a basket* Ex. 29:3, אִישׁ אֶחָד *a man* Judg. 13:2, or in the construct before a plural noun, אַחַת הַנְּבָלוֹת *one of the foolish women* i. e. *a foolish woman* Job 2:10.

ADJECTIVES AND DEMONSTRATIVES.

§ 249. 1. Adjectives and participles, qualifying a noun, are commonly placed after it and agree with it not only in gender and number but in definiteness, that is to say, if the noun is indefinite they remain without the article, but if the noun is made definite, whether by the article or in any of the ways specified in § 246, they receive the article, בֵּן חָכָם *a wise son* Prov. 10:11, חָתָן יֹצֵא *a bridegroom going out* Ps. 19:6, הָאָרֶץ הַטּוֹבָה *the good land* Deut. 1:35, רַחֲמֶיךָ הָרַבִּים *thy manifold mercies* Neh. 9:19. If more than one adjective accompany a definite noun, the article is repeated before each of them, הַשֵּׁם הַנִּכְבָּד וְהַנּוֹרָא *the glorious and fearful name* Deut. 28:58.

a. The adjective רַבִּים *many* is in a few instances, for the sake of greater emphasis, prefixed to the noun which it qualifies, רַבִּים בָּנִים *many sons* 1 Chron. 28:5, רַבּוֹת עִתִּים *many times* Neh. 9:28, so Ps. 32:10, 89:51, Jer. 16:16. Other instances are rare, נָכְרִיָּה מַעֲשֵׂהוּ *his strange work*, בְּדָבְרוֹ *his strange task* Isa. 28:21, צַדִּיק עַבְדִּי *my righteous servant* Isa. 53:11, בֹּגֵדָה אֲחוֹתָהּ *her treacherous sister* Jer. 3:7, 10.

b. Some exceptional cases occur, in which an adjective qualifying a definite noun does not receive the article, הָעֲגָלָה חֲדָשָׁה *the new cart* 2 Sam. 6:3, הַגֶּפֶן נָכְרִיָּה *the strange vine* Jer. 2:21, Ezek. 39:27, Dan. 8:13, 11:31, or when the noun is made definite by a suffix, אֲחִיכֶם אַחֵר *your other brother* Gen. 43:14, הַכֶּבֶשׂ אֶחָד *the one lamb* Num. 28:4, Ezek. 34:12, Hag. 1:4. In דִּבָּתָם רָעָה *an evil report respecting them* Gen. 37:2, the suffix denotes the object and the noun is really indefinite. Comp. § 246. 2. *b.*

c. On the other hand, the article is sometimes dropped from the noun, but retained before the adjective, חָצֵר הַגְּדוֹלָה *the great court* 1 Kin. 7:12, אִישׁ הֶעָשִׁיר *the rich man* 2 Sam. 12:4, בּוֹר הַגָּדוֹל *the great well* 1 Sam. 19:22, Neh. 9:35, Ps. 104:18, Jer. 27:3, 32:14, 40:3 K'thibh, Ezek. 9:2, Zech. 4:7; so with the ordinal numbers, יוֹם הַשִּׁשִּׁי *the sixth day* Gen. 1:31, 2:3, Ex. 20:10, Deut. 5:14, Judg. 6:25, Jer. 38:14.

2. Demonstrative pronouns follow the same rule of position and agreement, only the nouns which they qualify are invariably definite, § 245. 2, הַיּוֹם הַזֶּה *this day* Gen. 7:13, הַדְּבָרִים הָאֵלֶּה *these things* Gen. 15:1, הָאֲנָשִׁים הָהֵמָּה *those men* Num. 9:7. If both an adjective and a demonstrative

qualify the same noun, the demonstrative is placed last, הָאָרֶץ הַטּוֹבָה הַזֹּאת Deut. 9:6, הַשָּׁנִים הַטֹּבוֹת הַבָּאֹת הָאֵלֶּה *these good years that* (are) *coming* Gen. 41:35.

a. The demonstrative זֶה occasionally stands emphatically before its noun, זֶה מֹשֶׁה *this Moses* Ex. 32:1, where it is probably contemptuous like the Latin *iste*, זֶה לַחְמֵנוּ *this our bread* Josh. 9:12, Judg. 5:5, 1 Sam. 17:55, 56, זֶה הָעָם *this people* Isa. 23:13, Hab. 1:11. The demonstrative both follows the noun and is repeated after the adjective in הַגּוֹיִם הָאֵלֶּה הַנִּשְׁאָרִים הָאֵלֶּה *these nations these that remain* Josh. 23:7, 12.

b. The article is sometimes omitted from the demonstrative, הַדּוֹר זוּ *this generation* Ps. 12:8, בַּלַּיְלָה הוּא *in that night* Gen. 19:33, 30:16, 32:23, 1 Sam. 19:10, particularly if the noun is made definite by means of a suffix, שְׁבֻעָתִי זֹאת *this my oath* Gen. 24:8, אֹתֹתַי אֵלֶּה *these my signs* Ex. 10:1, 11:8, Deut. 11:18, Josh. 2:14, 20, Judg. 6:14, 1 Kin. 22:23, 2 Chron. 18:22, 24:18, Jer. 31:21.

c. The article is still more rarely dropped from the noun, מְעַט דְּבַשׁ הַזֶּה *this small quantity of honey* 1 Sam. 14:29, אִישׁ אֶפְרָתִי הַזֶּה *that Ephrathite* 17:12, חֳלִי זֶה *this sickness* 2 Kin. 1:2, 8:8.

NUMERALS.

Cardinal Numbers.

§250. 1. The numeral אֶחָד *one* is treated like other adjectives, and follows the rules of position and agreement already given, מָקוֹם אֶחָד *one place* Gen. 1:9, הַיְרִיעָה הָאַחַת *the one curtain* Ex. 26:2.

a. In a very few instances the noun is in the construct before the numeral *one*, מִשְׁפַּט אֶחָד *one law* Lev. 24:22, אֲרוֹן אֶחָד *a chest* 2 Kin. 12:10, פַּחַת אֶחָד *one governor* Isa. 36:9, comp. §254. 6. *b.*

2. The other cardinal numbers are joined to nouns as follows, viz.:

(1.) They commonly stand before the noun to which they belong and in the absolute state, אַרְבָּעָה מְלָכִים *four kings* Gen. 14:9, שִׁשִּׁים עִיר *sixty cities* Deut. 3:4, מֵאָה צִמּוּקִים *a hundred cakes of raisins* 2 Sam. 16:1, שֵׁשֶׁת אֲלָפִים פָּרָשִׁים *six thousand horsemen* 1 Sam. 13:5.

(2.) Such as have a distinct form for the construct (viz.

2–10, מֵאָה *hundred*, אַלְפֵי *thousands*) may also stand before the noun in the construct state, שְׁנֵי בָנִים *two sons* prop. *two of sons* Gen. 10:25, אַרְבַּעַת יָמִים *four days* Judg. 11:40, מְאַת אֲדָנִים *a hundred sockets* Ex. 38:27, שְׁלֹשֶׁת אַלְפֵי גְמַלִּים *three thousand camels* Job 1:3.

a. The numbers *two, three, four*, and *seven*, occur with the suffixes of pronouns which are in apposition with them, שְׁנֵינוּ אֲנַחְנוּ *we, both of us* 1 Sam. 20:42, שְׁתֵּיהֶן *they two* or *both of them* 1 Sam. 25:43, שְׁלָשְׁתְּכֶם *ye three*, שְׁלָשְׁתָּם *they three* Num. 12:4, אַרְבַּעְתָּם *they four* Dan. 1:17, שִׁבְעָתָם *they seven* 2 Sam. 21:9 K'ri. The following numerals occur with pronominal suffixes having a possessive sense, חֲמִשֶּׁיךָ *thy fifty*, חֲמִשָּׁיו *his fifty* 2 Kin. 1:10, חֲמִשֵׁיהֶם *their fifties* ver. 14, אַלְפִּי *my thousand* Judg. 6:15, אַלְפֵיכֶם *your thousands* 1 Sam. 10:19, רִבְבֹתָיו *his ten thousands* 1 Sam. 18:7.

(3.) Less frequently the numerals stand after the noun in the absolute state, מַעֲלוֹת שֶׁבַע *seven steps* Ezek. 40:22, אֲתֹנֹת עֶשְׂרִים *twenty she-asses* Gen. 32:16, כִּכָּרִים מֵאָה־אֶלֶף *a hundred thousand talents* 1 Chron. 22:14.

§ 251. 1. The units (including *ten*), whether they stand singly or are compounded with other numbers, agree with their nouns in gender, שָׁלֹשׁ דְּלָתוֹת *three leaves* Jer. 36:23, שְׁלֹשָׁה סַלֵּי חֹרִי *three baskets of bread* Gen. 40:16, אַרְבָּעָה עָשָׂר כְּבָשִׂים *fourteen lambs* Num. 29:15; the other numerals observe no distinction of gender.

a. When the units qualify מֵאוֹת *hundreds* or אֲלָפִים *thousands*, their gender is determined by that of these words respectively. In שְׁלֹשֶׁת נְשֵׁי־בָנָיו *the three wives of his sons* Gen. 7:13, the masculine adjective is probably to be explained by the fact that the noun, though in reality feminine, has a masculine termination.

2. Nouns accompanied by the units (2–10) are almost invariably plural, while those which are preceded by the tens (20–90) or numbers compounded with them (21, etc.), are commonly put in the singular, אַרְבָּעִים יוֹם וְאַרְבָּעִים לָיְלָה *forty days and forty nights* Gen. 7:4, אַרְבַּע וּשְׁלֹשִׁים שָׁנָה *four and thirty years* Gen. 11:16, עֶשְׂרִים שָׁנָה וְשֶׁבַע שָׁנִים *twenty years and seven years* Gen. 23:1.

a. This phenomenon is probably to be accounted for upon a principle analogous to that by which the anomalous terminations for gender in the numerals has been explained, §223. 2. When the numeral has itself a plural form, as it has in the tens, the plurality of the entire expression is sufficiently indicated without giving a plural ending to the noun likewise. But with the units which have a singular termination, the noun must take a plural form. It may be observed, however, that this peculiarity chiefly affects a certain class of nouns, viz. those which are most frequently numbered, and in which, consequently, the tendency to abbreviate the expression by retrenching the plural ending is most strongly manifested. These are such as אִישׁ *man,* and various measures of time, space, weight, etc., e. g. שָׁנָה *year,* יוֹם *day,* אַמָּה *cubit,* שֶׁקֶל *shekel*. These nouns are also found, though less constantly, in the singular with *hundreds* and *thousands,* תְּשַׁע מֵאוֹת שָׁנָה *nine hundred years* Gen. 5:5, אֶלֶף אַמָּה *a thousand cubits* Num. 35:4, and with the numbers from 11 to 19, חֲמִשָּׁה עָשָׂר שֶׁקֶל *fifteen shekels* Lev. 27:7. Comp. in German *hundert Fuss lang, funfzig Pfund schwer,* and in English *twenty head of cattle, a ten foot pole.*

b. The numbers from 2 to 10 are very rarely found with singular nouns, שְׁמֹנֶה שָׁנָה *eight years* 2 Kin. 22:1, שָׁלֹשׁ אמה *three cubits* 25:17 K'thibh where the K'ri has אַמּוֹת. The tens are occasionally followed by the plural שְׁמֹנִים בְּנֵי־חַיִל *thirty companions* Judg. 14:11, שְׁלֹשִׁים מֵרֵעִים *eighty sons of valour* 2 Chron. 26:17, אַרְבָּעִים וּשְׁנֵי יְלָדִים *forty-two children* 2 Kin. 2:24. When the noun precedes the numeral it is always put in the plural.

c. In enumerations of familiar objects the noun is sometimes omitted, when the meaning is sufficiently plain from the connection, עֲשָׂרָה זָהָב *ten* (shekels) *of gold* Gen. 24:22, שְׁלֹשׁ מֵאוֹת כֶּסֶף *three hundred* (shekels) *of silver* Gen. 45:22, שְׁתֵּי־לֶחֶם *two* (loaves) *of bread* 1 Sam. 10:4, שֵׁשׁ־שְׂעֹרִים *six* (ephahs) *of barley* Ruth 3:15. In measurements, the word אַמָּה *cubit* is occasionally preceded by the preposition בְּ, thus אַרְבַּע בָּאַמָּה *four by the cubit* i. e. four cubits.

3. Compound numbers may either proceed from the higher to the lower denomination, אֶלֶף מָאתַיִם חֲמִשִּׁים וְאַרְבָּעָה *a thousand two hundred fifty and four* Neh. 7:34, or the reverse, שֶׁבַע וּשְׁלֹשִׁים וּמְאַת שָׁנָה *seven and thirty and a hundred years* Ex. 6:16. The noun sometimes stands at the beginning or end of the entire series as in preceding examples, and sometimes it is repeated after each numeral, מֵאָה שָׁנָה וְעֶשְׂרִים שָׁנָה וְשֶׁבַע שָׁנִים *a hundred years and twenty years and seven years* Gen. 23:1.

4. Numeral adjectives may receive the article when they represent an absolute number, or the noun is not expressed;

but when they are joined to a definite noun the latter alone receives the article, הַשְּׁנַיִם (*the*) *two are better than* הָאֶחָד (*the*) *one* Eccles. 4:9, הָאַרְבָּעִים *the forty* Gen. 18:29, חֲמִשִּׁים הַצַּדִּיקִם *the fifty righteous* ver. 28, שְׁתֵּי בְנֹתָיו *his two daughters* 19:30, אַרְבָּעִים הַיּוֹם *the forty days* Deut. 9:25.

a. When compound numbers 11, 12, etc., receive the article, it may be given to the first member of the compound, הַשְּׁנַיִם עָשָׂר *the twelve* 1 Chron. 25:19. 27:15, 1 Kin. 6:38, or to the second, שְׁנֵים הֶעָשָׂר אִישׁ *the twelve men* Josh. 4:4, 1 Kin. 19:19. In the example just cited the article is given to the numeral instead of to the noun, but in הַבָּקָר שְׁנֵים־עָשָׂר *the twelve oxen* 1 Kin. 7:44, the general rule is observed. In הַיְלָדִים הָאֵלֶּה אַרְבַּעְתָּם *these four children* Dan. 1:17, the numeral following a definite noun receives a pronominal suffix referring to it.

Ordinal Numbers, etc.

§ 252. 1. The ordinal numbers follow the general law of adjectives in position and agreement with the substantive, to which they belong, בֵּן שֵׁנִי *a second son* Gen. 30:7, בַּשָּׁנָה הַשְּׁלִישִׁית *in the third year* 1 Kin. 18:1.

2. The lack of ordinals above *ten* is supplied by using the cardinals instead, which are then commonly preceded by the noun in the construct state, שְׁנַת עֶשְׂרִים וָשֶׁבַע *the twenty-seventh year* 1 Kin. 16:10, although this order is not always observed, שְׁלֹשׁ־עֶשְׂרֵה שָׁנָה *thirteenth year* Gen. 14:4.

a. A fuller form of expression is sometimes employed, e. g. בִּשְׁנַת שְׁלֹשִׁים וּשְׁמֹנֶה שָׁנָה *in the thirty-eighth year* prop. *in the year of thirty-eight years* 1 Kin. 16:29, 2 Kin. 15:1.

b. In dates the cardinals are used for the day of the month and sometimes for the year, even though the number is below ten; the words day and month are also frequently omitted, בִּשְׁנַת שֶׁבַע *the seventh year* 2 Kin. 12:1, אַרְבָּעָה לַחֹדֶשׁ הַתְּשִׁיעִי *the fourth* (day) *of the ninth month* Zech. 7:1, בַּשְּׁבִיעִי *in the seventh* (month) ver. 5.

3. When the ordinals are used to express fractional parts, § 227. 3, they stand before the noun, שְׁלִשִׁית הַהִין *the third of a hin* Num. 15:6.

4. Distributive numbers are formed by repeating the cardinals, שְׁנַיִם שְׁנַיִם *two by two* Gen. 7:9, שִׁבְעָה שִׁבְעָה *by*

sevens ver. 2. The numeral adverbs *once, twice*, etc., are expressed by the feminine of the cardinals, אַחַת *once*, שְׁתַּיִם *twice* 2 Kin. 6:10, Ps. 62:12, or by means of the noun פַּעַם *stroke* or *beat*, פַּעֲמַיִם *twice* Gen. 27:36, עֶשֶׂר פְּעָמִים *ten times* Job 19:3 or רְגָלִים *steps*, שָׁלֹשׁ רְגָלִים *three times* Ex. 23:14.

a. This use of these nouns has arisen from the method of counting by beats or taps with the hand or foot.

APPOSITION.

§ 253. When one noun serves to define or to describe another it may be put in apposition with it. This construction, of which a more extended use is made in Hebrew than in occidental languages, may be employed in the following cases, viz.:

1. When both nouns denote the same person or thing, הַמֶּלֶךְ דָּוִד 2 Sam. 6:16, or less commonly, דָּוִד הַמֶּלֶךְ 13:39 *king David*, אִשָּׁה אַלְמָנָה *a woman* (who was) *a widow* 1 Kin. 7:14.

2. When the second specifies the first by stating the material of which it consists, its quantity, character or the like, הַבָּקָר הַנְּחֹשֶׁת *the oxen the brass* i. e. *the brazen oxen* 2 Kin. 16:17, שָׁלֹשׁ סְאִים קֶמַח *three measures* (consisting of) *meal* Gen. 18:6, שֶׁבַע־שָׁנִים רָעָב *seven years* (of) *famine* 2 Sam. 24:13, שְׁלֹשֶׁת שָׁבֻעִים יָמִים *three weeks* (of) *days* Dan. 10:3, יָמִים מִסְפָּר *days* (which are) *a number*, i. e. such as can be readily numbered, a few Num. 9:20, אֲמָרִים אֱמֶת *words* (which are) *truth* Prov. 22:21.

a. In this latter case the closer connection of the construct state might, with equal propriety, be employed, §254. 4, etc. The following examples will show with what latitude the rule of apposition is occasionally applied, מַיִם לַחַץ *water* (which is) *affliction* i. e. identified with it or characterized by it 1 Kin. 22:27, יַיִן תַּרְעֵלָה *wine* (which is) *intoxication* i. e. produces it Ps. 60:5, בְּקָר רֹעִי *pasture-cattle* i. e. those whose characteristic it is that they have been in the pastures 1 Kin. 5:3; *bearing*

הָאָרוֹן הַבְּרִית *the ark* viz. *the covenant*, which was the thing of chief consequence about the ark Josh. 3:14, *a hundred thousand* אֵילִים צֶבֶר 2 Kin. 3:4, which is by some understood to mean *wool-bearing rams* i. e. characterized by the production of wool; according to others, the first word denotes the quantity and the second the material, *rams* (of) *wool* i. e. as much as rams have, *fleeces*.

b. Proper nouns, which have no construct state, may be followed by qualifying nouns in a loose sort of apposition, בֵּית לֶחֶם יְהוּדָה *Bethlehem* (in) *Judah* 1 Sam. 17:12, compare in English, Princeton, New Jersey; פְּתוֹר אֲרַם נַהֲרַיִם *Pethor* (in) *Mesopotamia* Deut. 23:5, גַּת־פְּלִשְׁתִּים *Gath* (of) *the Philistines* Am. 6:2; *the destined possessor of my house is* דַּמֶּשֶׂק אֱלִיעֶזֶר *Damascus* (in the person of its citizen) *Eliezer* Gen. 15:2, אֱלֹהִים צְבָאוֹת *God* (of) *Hosts* Ps. 80:5, 8, 15, 20; when אֱלֹהִים is regarded as an appellative noun instead of a proper name, this divine title becomes אֱלֹהֵי צְבָאוֹת Ps. 89:9.

THE CONSTRUCT STATE AND SUFFIXES.

§ 254. When one noun is limited or restricted in its meaning by another, the first is put in the construct state; if the limiting word be a personal pronoun it is suffixed to the noun. The relation thus expressed corresponds, for the most part, to the occidental genitive or to that denoted in English by the preposition *of*. The primary notion of the grammatical form is simply the juxtaposition of two nouns, or the union of a noun and a pronoun, to represent the subordination of one to the other in the expression of a single idea, § 212. The particular relation, which it suggests, is consequently dependent on the meanings of the words themselves, and is in each case that which is most naturally suggested by their combination. Thus, the second noun or the pronominal suffix may denote

1. The *possessor* of that which is represented by the preceding noun, הֵיכַל יְהוָה *the temple of Jehovah* 1 Sam. 1:9, רְכוּשָׁם *their substance* Gen. 12:5. This embraces the various degrees of relationship, בֶּן־אַבְרָהָם *son of Abraham* Gen. 25:12, אִשְׁתֶּךָ *thy wife* Gen. 12:5.

2. The *whole*, of which the preceding word denotes a part,

אֶבְיֹנֵי עַמֶּךָ *the poor of thy people* Ex. 23:11, וְנִכְבַּדֵּי־אָרֶץ *the honourable of the earth* Isa. 23:9.

a. The construct relation, when thus employed, indicates that the part singled out from the whole possesses the quality referred to in an eminent degree. The first word is sometimes an abstract noun, קוֹמַת אֲרָזָיו *the height of his cedars* i. e. *his highest cedars* 2 Kin. 19:23. Here too belong the superlative expressions, קֹדֶשׁ קָדָשִׁים *holy of holies,* שִׁיר הַשִּׁירִים *the song of songs,* עֶבֶד עֲבָדִים *servant of servants,* one that is a servant by way of eminence when compared with all others.

3. An individual of the class denoted by the preceding noun, thus serving the purpose of a more exact *designation,* אֶרֶץ מִצְרַיִם *the land of Egypt* Gen. 41:19, נְהַר־פְּרָת *the river (of) Euphrates* Gen. 15:18, עֲצֵי אֲרָזִים *cedar trees,* 2 Chron. 2:7, תּוֹלַעַת יַעֲקֹב *worm (of) Jacob* Isa. 41:14, אַנְשֵׁי הַתָּרִים *men (who are) merchants* 1 Kin. 10:15.

4. The *material* of which the preceding noun is composed, נֶזֶם זָהָב *a ring of gold* Gen. 24:22, כְּלִי־עֵץ *vessel of wood* Lev. 11:32, עֵדֶר הָעִזִּים *the flock of goats* Cant. 4:1.

5. The *measure* of its extent, value, duration, etc., מַהֲלַךְ שְׁלֹשֶׁת יָמִים *a journey of three days* Jon. 3:3, מִשְׁקַל כִּכָּר *the weight of a talent* 1 Chron. 20:2, מְתֵי מִסְפָּר *men of number* i. e. readily numbered, few, Gen. 34:30, אֲחֻזַּת עוֹלָם *a possession of perpetuity* Gen. 17:8.

6. An *attribute,* by which it is characterized, גִּבּוֹר חַיִל *mighty man of valour* Judg. 11:1, עֵץ פְּרִי *tree of fruit* Gen. 1:11, גֵּיא חִזָּיוֹן *valley of vision* i. e. distinguished as the one where visions are received Isa. 22:1, צֹאן הַהֲרֵגָה *the flock of slaughter* i. e. which is to be slaughtered Zech. 11:4.

a. It will be observed that the Hebrew uses nouns to express many of the ideas for which adjectives are employed in other languages; thus, in the examples under Nos. 4, 5, and 6, *vessel of wood* for *wooden vessel, possession of perpetuity* for *perpetual possession, mighty man of valour* for *valiant mighty man, flock of slaughter* for *grex mactanda.* This both arises from and explains the comparative paucity of adjectives in Hebrew: though even where corresponding adjectives exist the other construction is frequently preferred, בִּגְדֵי קֹדֶשׁ *garments of holiness* Ex. 28:2, זִבְחֵי־צֶדֶק *sacrifices of righteousness,* קָדוֹשׁ *holy* and צַדִּיק *righteous* being used with

§ 254 THE CONSTRUCT STATE AND SUFFIXES.

less latitude and with a stricter regard to the ethical idea which they involve. Attributives are frequently formed by prefixing such words as אִישׁ *man*, בַּעַל *lord*, בֶּן *son*, בַּת *daughter*, to abstract nouns or other substantives, thus, אִישׁ תֹּאַר *a man of form* i. e. *comely* 1 Sam. 16:18, אִישׁ־דְּבָרִים *man of words* i. e. *eloquent* Ex. 4:10, בַּעַל הַחֲלֹמוֹת *the possessor of dreams* i. e. *dreamer* Gen. 37:19, בֶּן־שְׁמֹנַת יָמִים *son of eight days* i. e. *eight days old* Gen. 17:12, בֶּן־מָוֶת *son of death* i. e. *deserving to die* 1 Sam. 20:31, בְּנֵי־בְלִיַּעַל *sons of worthlessness* i. e. *wicked* Deut. 13:14, בַּת־תִּשְׁעִים שָׁנָה *daughter of ninety years* i. e. *ninety years old* Gen. 17:17.

b. Occasionally in poetry an adjective instead of agreeing with its substantive is treated as though it were an abstract noun, כְּלֵי הַקָּטָן *vessels of small* (capacity) Isa. 22:24, מֵי מְלֹא *waters of fulness* Ps. 73:10, כָּל־בֵּית הַגָּדוֹל perhaps *every house of great* (size), though others render *every great* (man's) *house* Jer. 52:13. So sometimes an adverb, מְתֵי מְעָט *few men* Deut. 26:5, עֹלַת תָּמִיד *continual burnt-offering* Num. 28:6, דְּמֵי חִנָּם *blood* (shed) *causelessly* 1 Kin. 2:31, צָרֵי יוֹמָם *enemies in the day time* Ezek. 30:16, אֶבֶן דּוּמָם *dumb stone* Hab. 2:19, or adverbial phrase, אֱלֹהֵי מִקָּרֹב *a God nigh at hand*, אֱלֹהֵי מֵרָחֹק *a God afar off* Jer. 23:23.

7. The *source* from which the preceding noun is derived, תּוֹרַת יְהֹוָה *the law of Jehovah* Ex. 13:9, סֵפֶר מֹשֶׁה *the book of Moses* 2 Chron. 25:4, חוֹלַת אַהֲבָה *sick from love* Cant. 2:5.

8. The *subject* by which an action is performed, or in which an attribute inheres, אַהֲבַת יְהֹוָה *the love of God* i. e. exercised by him 1 Kin. 10:9, חָכְמַת שְׁלֹמֹה *the wisdom of Solomon* 1 Kin. 5:10.

9. The *object*, upon which an action is directed, יִרְאַת אֱלֹהִים *the fear of God* Gen. 20:11, מֶמְשֶׁלֶת הַיּוֹם *the rule of the day* Gen. 1:16.

a. After nouns, which express or imply action, the following noun or suffix denotes the subject or the object as the sense or the connection may demand, קִנְאַת יְהֹוָה *the zeal of Jehovah*, which he feels Isa. 37:32, קִנְאַת־עָם *zeal of the people*, which is felt for them Isa. 26:11; זַעֲקַת סְדֹם *the cry against Sodom* Gen. 18:20, זַעֲקַת־דָּל *the cry of the poor* Prov. 21:13; חֲמָסוֹ *his wrong* i. e. done by him Ps. 7:17, חֲמָסִי *my wrong* i. e. done to me Gen. 16:5; דֶּרֶךְ־יָם *the way of the sea* i. e. leading to it 1 Kin. 18:43, דֶּרֶךְ יָרָבְעָם *the way of Jeroboam* i. e. in which he walked 1 Kin. 16:26.

b. Active participles are frequently put in the construct state before their object, מְשִׁיבַת נָפֶשׁ *restoring the soul* Ps. 19:8, אֹהֲבֵי שְׁמֶךָ *loving thy name* Ps. 5:12, בָּאֵי שַׁעַר *entering the gate* Gen. 23:10. So even before an infinitive which they govern, מַשְׁכִּימֵי קוּם *being early to rise* Ps. 127:2. Passive participles may be in the construct before the subject of the action, מֻכֵּה אֱלֹהִים *smitten of God* Isa. 53:4, יְלוּד אִשָּׁה *born of a woman*

Job 14:1, or before the secondary object, if the verb is capable in the active of having a double object, חֲגֻרַת־שָׂק *girded with sackcloth* Joel 1:8, לְבֻשׁ הַבַּדִּים *clothed with linen* Ezek. 9:11. When a noun follows the infinitive it may be in construction with it as its subject, כִּקְרֹא מֶלֶךְ *on the king's reading* 2 Kin. 5:7, הוֹרִישׁוֹ *his driving out* Num. 32:21, or be governed by it as its object, קְרֹא־שְׁמוּאֵל *to call Samuel* 1 Sam. 3:8, הוֹרִישָׁם *to drive them out* Deut. 7:17.

10. The respect in which a preceding attribute holds, so that it answers the purpose of *specification*, טְמֵא־שְׂפָתַיִם *unclean as to lips* Isa. 6:5, קְשֵׁי־לֵב *hard hearted* Ezek. 3:7, קְרֻעֵי בְגָדִים *rent as to garments*, 2 Sam. 13:31.

a. This answers to what is known as the Greek accusative, πόδας ὠκύς; the English has in certain cases adopted the Hebrew idiom, so that we can say *swift of foot, blind of an eye*, etc.

§ 255. 1. When the relation between two nouns is expressed by an intervening preposition, the first commonly remains in the absolute state: it may, however, particularly in poetry, be put in the construct, הָרֵי בַגִּלְבֹּעַ *mountains in Gilboa* 2 Sam. 1:21, נְבִיאֵי מִלִּבָּם *prophets out of their own heart* Ezek. 13:2, כְּדֵי בָנוּ *according to the ability in us* Neh. 5:8.

2. A noun is sometimes put in the construct before a succeeding clause with which it is closely connected: thus, before a relative clause, מְקוֹם אֲשֶׁר *the place where*, etc., Gen. 39:20, עַל־דְּבַר אֲשֶׁר *for the reason that* Deut. 22:24, particularly when the relative is itself omitted, בְּיַד־תִּשְׁלַח *by the hand of* (him whom) *thou wilt send* Ex. 4:13, תְּחִלַּת דִּבֶּר־יְהוָֹה *the beginning of* (what) *Jehovah spake* Hos. 1:2, or before the conjunction וְ *and*, חָכְמַת וָדַעַת *wisdom and knowledge* Isa. 33:6, שְׁכֻרַת וְלֹא מִיָּיִן *drunken and not with wine* Isa. 51:21.

3. Three, four, or even five nouns are sometimes joined together in the relation of the construct state, רָאשֵׁי בֵית־אֲבֹתָם *the heads of the houses of their fathers* Ex. 6:14, מִסְפַּר שִׁבְטֵי בְנֵי־יִשְׂרָאֵל *the number of the tribes of the children of Israel* Josh. 4:5, פְּרִי־גֹדֶל לְבַב מֶלֶךְ־אַשּׁוּר *the fruit of the greatness of heart of the king of Assyria* Isa. 10:12.

a. In a very few instances, only occurring in poetry, two words of like meaning are united in the construct before the same noun, נַהֲרֵי נַחֲלֵי דְבָשׁ *rivers, brooks of honey* Job 20 : 17, נוֹשְׁקֵי רוֹמֵי־קָשֶׁת Ps. 78 : 9, if rendered as it is by some *armed with, shooting the bow,* though נוֹשְׁקֵי may be in construction not with קָשֶׁת but with רוֹמֵי *armed ones of those who shoot the bow, armed bowmen.* See Alexander *in loc.*

§ 256. When two words are in the construct relation they must stand in immediate conjunction, and no other word can be suffered to come between them as it would obscure the sense. Hence an adjective, participle or demonstrative, qualifying a noun in the construct state, cannot stand immediately after it, but must be placed after the governed noun, מַעֲשֵׂה יְהוָה הַגָּדוֹל *the great work of Jehovah* Judg. 2 : 7, עֲטֶרֶת זָהָב גְּדוֹלָה *a great crown of gold* Esth. 8 : 15. So an article or suffix, belonging to a noun in the construct, must be attached not to it but to the governed noun, גִּבּוֹרֵי הַחַיִל *the mighty men of valour* Josh. 1 : 14, אֱלִילֵי זְהָבוֹ *his idols of gold* Isa. 2 : 20, שֵׁם קָדְשִׁי *my name of holiness* i. e. *my holy name* Lev. 20 : 3.

a. When the governing and the governed noun are of the same gender and number it may be doubtful to which of them the following adjective is to be referred, thus אֲחִי יֶפֶת הַגָּדוֹל Gen: 10 : 21 may either mean *the elder brother of Japheth* or *the brother of Japheth the elder.*

b. In a very few instances, only occurring in poetry, a noun with a suffix stands in the construct before a following word, מַרְכְּבֹתֶיךָ יְשׁוּעָה *thy chariots of salvation* Hab. 3 : 8, מַחְסִי־עֹז *my refuge of strength* Ps. 71 : 7, דַּרְכֵּךְ זִמָּה *thy way of lewdness* Ezek. 16 : 27, though these are rather to be regarded as instances of apposition in the wide sense, § 253. 2. Nouns in the construct occasionally receive the article, § 246. 3. *a.*

c. In the following passages a brief word intervenes between כֹּל, which, though properly a noun signifying *totality,* is in usage equivalent to a pronominal adjective *all, every,* and the noun which it governs, כָּל־תִּשָּׂא עָוֹן *take away all iniquity* Hos. 14 : 3, so 2 Sam. 1 : 9, Job 27 : 3, and perhaps Isa. 38 : 16; but see Alexander *in loc.* Like the Greek πᾶς, when followed by a definite noun כֹּל means *the whole* or *all,* כָּל־הָעָם *all the people,* כָּל־הָאָרֶץ *the whole earth,* when followed by an indefinite noun *every,* כָּל־בַּיִת *every house;* though here as elsewhere the poets may omit the article, which would be necessary in prose, כָּל־רֹאשׁ *the whole head* Isa. 1 : 5. Connected with a negative adverb it forms a universal negation *no,* or if the words be rendered separately our idiom requires us to translate כֹּל by *any,* כָּל־מְלָאכָה לֹא־יֵעָשֶׂה *no work shall be done* Ex. 12 : 16,

אֶרֶן כָּל־חָדָשׁ *there is no new thing* Eccl. 1:9, לֹא יוּכַל כָּל־אֱלֹהַּ *neither can any god* 2 Chron. 32:15. Comp. οὐ δικαιωθήσεται πᾶσα σάρξ Rom. 3:20.

d. He paragogic may be attached to a noun in the construct state, מִזְרְחָה שָׁמֶשׁ *toward the rising of the sun* Deut. 4:41, Gen. 24:67.

§ 257. The preposition לְ *to, belonging to*, with or without a preceding relative pronoun, may be substituted for the construct relation in its possessive sense, הַצֹּאן אֲשֶׁר לְאָבִיהָ *her father's sheep* prop. *the sheep which belonged to her father* Gen. 29:9, comp. צֹאן אֲבִיהֶם Gen. 37:12, הַבַּיִת לֶאֱלִישָׁע *the house of Elisha* 2 Kin. 5:9, comp. Latin *pater mihi*. This is particularly the case

1. When the first noun is omitted לְדָוִד (a psalm) *of David* Ps. 11:1, אַמְנוֹן לַאֲחִינֹעַם *Amnon* (son) *of Ahinoam* 2 Sam. 3:2.

2. When the first noun is indefinite and the second definite, בֵּן לְיִשַׁי *a son of Jesse* 1 Sam. 16:18 (בֶּן־יִשַׁי 2 Sam. 20:1 is *the son of Jesse*, § 246.3), עֶבֶד לְשַׂר הַטַּבָּחִים *a servant of the captain of the guard* Gen. 41:12.

a. Hence the frequent use of לְ (*Lamedh auctoris*) in the titles of the Psalms and other compositions, מִזְמוֹר לְדָוִד *a psalm of David* i. e. belonging to him as its author, תְּפִלָּה לַחֲבַקּוּק *a prayer of Habakkuk.*

3. When the first noun is accompanied by a numeral adjective, especially in dates, חֲמִשָּׁה־עָשָׂר יוֹם לַחֹדֶשׁ *the fifteenth day of the month* 1 Kin. 12:32, בַּשָּׁנָה הַחֲמִישִׁית לַמֶּלֶךְ *in the fifth year of the king* 1 Kin. 14:25, בִּשְׁנַת שָׁלֹשׁ לְאָסָא *in the third year of Asa* 1 Kin. 15:33.

4. When several genitives are connected together, סֵפֶר דִּבְרֵי הַיָּמִים לְמַלְכֵי יְהוּדָה *the book of the Chronicles of the kings of Judah* 1 Kin. 15:23.

The Predicate.

§ 258. 1. The predicate of a sentence, if a substantive, adjective, or pronoun, may be connected with its subject without an intervening copula, their mutual relation being sufficiently suggested by simply placing them together, כָּל־נְתִיבוֹתֶיהָ שָׁלוֹם *all her paths* (are) *peace* Prov. 3 : 17, טוֹב הָעֵץ *the tree* (was) *good* Gen. 3 : 6, זֶה הַדֶּרֶךְ *this* (is) *the way* Isa. 30 : 21.

2. Or the pronoun הוּא of the third person may be used as a copula, הַנָּהָר הָרְבִיעִי הוּא פְרָת *the fourth river is Euphrates* prop. *it* (is) *Euphrates* Gen. 2 : 14, מָה־אֵלֶּה *what are these?* Zech. 4 : 5, אַתָּה־הוּא מַלְכִּי *thou art my king* Ps. 44 : 5, הָאֲנָשִׁים הָאֵלֶּה שְׁלֵמִים הֵם *these men are peaceable* Gen. 34 : 21.

3. Or the verb הָיָה *to be* may be employed for a like purpose, particularly if the idea of past or future time is involved, הָאָרֶץ הָיְתָה תֹהוּ *the earth was desolate* Gen. 1 : 2, הַבָּקָר הָיוּ חֹרְשׁוֹת *the oxen were ploughing* Job 1 : 14.

a. Verbs which denote some modification of being are sometimes employed in the same way; thus, *his eyes* הֵחֵלּוּ כֵהוֹת *began* (to be) *dim* 1 Sam. 3 : 2; וַיָּחֶל נֹחַ אִישׁ הָאֲדָמָה *and Noah began* (to be) *a husbandman* Gen. 9 : 20; כְּהֲתִמְךָ שׁוֹדֵד *when thou ceasest spoiling* Isa. 33 : 1, *the hair* הָפַךְ לָבָן *has turned white* Lev. 13 : 3; *so to be called, to be esteemed,* etc.

b. Simple existence or non-existence is predicated by means of the particles יֵשׁ and אַיִן, the latter of which retains its absolute form when following the noun, but takes the construct form אֵין when it precedes the noun either immediately or separated from it by intervening words, יֶשׁ גֹּאֵל *there is a kinsman* Ruth 3 : 12, אָדָם אַיִן *there was not a man* Gen. 2 : 5, אֵין מֶלֶךְ *there was no king in Israel* Judg. 21 : 25. These particles may also be used as copulas with the personal pronouns, when the predicate is a participle, אֵינְךָ מְשַׁלֵּחַ *thou art not letting go* Ex. 8 : 17, יֶשְׁךָ מוֹשִׁיעַ *thou art saving* Judg. 6 : 36.

§ 259. 1. A noun in the predicate may receive the same adjuncts as in the subject, § 244.

2. Adjectives and demonstrative pronouns in the predicate agree with the nouns to which they relate in gender and number, but differ from qualifying adjectives and demonstratives, § 249, in standing before the noun and in not receiving the article, though the noun be definite, טוֹב הַדָּבָר *the word is good* Deut. 1 : 14, רַבִּים רַחֲמָיו *his mercies are great* 1 Chron. 21 : 13, אֵלֶּה תוֹלְדוֹת הַשָּׁמַיִם *these are the generations of the heavens* Gen. 2 : 4.

a. A predicate adjective may also, though less frequently, stand after the noun, הַנַּעֲרָה יָפָה *the damsel was fair* 1 Kin. 1:4, וְהָב הָאָרֶץ הַהִוא טוֹב *and the gold of that land is good* Gen. 2:12.

b. If the sense require the predicate to be made definite, it will receive the article, פִּי הַמְדַבֵּר *my mouth is the* (one) *speaking* Gen. 45:12.

Comparison of Adjectives.

§ 260. 1. Adjectives have no distinct form for the comparative or superlative. Comparison is expressed by means of the preposition מִן *from* placed after the adjective, טוֹבָה חָכְמָה מִפְּנִינִים *wisdom is better than rubies* prop. is good from rubies, differs from them and by implication is superior to them in point of goodness, Prov. 8:11; צַדִּיק אַתָּה מִמֶּנִּי *thou art more righteous than I*, 1 Sam. 24:17.

2. The superlative degree may be expressed

(1.) By adding כֹּל *all* to the comparative particle מִן, גָּדוֹל מִכָּל־בְּנֵי־קֶדֶם *great from all the sons of the east* i. e. *the greatest of all*, etc., Job 1:3.

(2.) By an emphatic use of the positive, so as to imply the possession of the attribute in an eminent degree, קָטֹן בָּנָיו *the least of his sons* prop. *the little* (one) 2 Chron. 21:17, הַיָּפָה בַּנָּשִׁים *O fairest among women* Cant. 1:8, הַקָּטֹן *the least*, הַגָּדוֹל *the greatest* 1 Chron. 12:14, טוֹבָם *the best of them* Mic. 7:4.

a. When the predicate is a verb instead of an adjective, comparison may be expressed in the same manner, אֶגְדַּל מִמֶּךָּ *I will be greater than thou* prop. *great from thee* Gen. 41:40, וַיֶּחְכַּם מִכָּל־הָאָדָם *and he was the wisest of all men* 1 Kin. 5:11. In a few passages, chiefly occurring in the book of Ecclesiastes, comparison is made by means of the adverb יוֹתֵר *more*, חָכַמְתִּי אֲנִי אָז יֹתֵר *I was then more wise* Eccl. 2:15.

b. The construction with מִן may also be used to denote excess, גָּדוֹל עֲוֹנִי מִנְּשֹׂא *my iniquity is too great to be forgiven* prop. *greater than* (it is possible) *to forgive* Gen. 4:13, מְעַט מִמְּךָ *too little for thee* Job 15:11.

c. A comparative sense is commonly ascribed to מִן in the following passages, in which an adjective, suggested by the context. must be supplied, יָשָׁר מִמְּסוּכָה *the upright* (is sharper) *than a thorn-hedge* Mic. 7:4, מֵאֶפֶס *less than nothing* Isa. 40:17, 41:24, Ps. 62:10, Isa. 10:10, Job 11:17; in some of these cases, however, מִן may have the sense of *from* or *of*, and denote that from which any thing is derived or of which it forms a part.

Verbs.

§ 261. 1. The doctrine of the Hebrew tenses rests upon a conception of time radically different from that which prevails in our own and in other Indo-European languages. Time is conceived of, not as distributed into three portions, viz.: past, present, and future, but as consisting of the past and future only. The present is, in this view, an inappreciable moment, without extension or cognizable existence, the mere point of contact between two boundless periods of duration, or the instant of transition from one to the other, and, as such, not entitled to be represented by a distinct verbal form. Every action or state of being is accordingly viewed as belonging to the past or to the future; and such as do not belong exclusively to one, may be referred indifferently to either.

2. Within these two grand divisions of time no account is made of those minuter distinctions, in the expression of which we are accustomed to employ such a variety of tenses, nor of those modal differences which are with us indicated by the indicative, subjunctive, and potential, except to that limited extent to which these may be regarded as covered by the paragogic and apocopated futures, § 264. Whatever is, or is conceived of as past, must be put in the preterite; the future is used for all that is, or is conceived of as future, while all subordinate modifications or shades of meaning are either suggested by accompanying particles, or, without being precisely indicated, are left to be inferred from the connection.

The Primary Tenses.

§ 262. The preterite is accordingly used of
1. The past, whether our idiom would require the abso-

lute past tense, i. e. the historical imperfect, *in the beginning God* בָּרָא *created*, etc., Gen. 1:1, *God* נִסָּה *tempted Abraham* Gen. 22:1; or one of the relative tenses, viz. the past viewed in relation to the present, i. e. the perfect, *what is this that* עָשִׂית *thou hast done* Gen. 3:13, *thee* רָאִיתִי *have I seen righteous* Gen. 7:1; the past in relation to another past, i. e. the pluperfect, *God ended his work which* עָשָׂה *he had made* Gen. 2:2; *and they did so as the Lord* צִוָּה *had commanded* Ex. 7:10; or the past in relation to a future, i. e. the future perfect, *when the Lord* רָחַץ *shall have washed away*, etc., Isa. 4:4, *until the time that she which travaileth* יָלָדָה *shall have brought forth* Mic. 5:2; or a conditional mood, *except the Lord of hosts had left unto us a very small remnant* הוֹתִיר *we should have been as Sodom* Isa. 1:9, *I would there were a sword in mine hand, for now* הֲרַגְתִּיךָ *I would have killed thee* Num. 22:29; or an optative, denoting something which was to have been desired but which nevertheless did not occur, לוּ־מַתְנוּ *O that we had died* Num. 14:2, לוּ חָכְמוּ *O that they had been wise that they* (fut.) *would consider this* Deut. 32:29, or a subjunctive (the Jordan was dried up), *that* יְרָאתֶם *ye might fear the Lord*, at that time and thenceforward *forever* Josh. 4:24.

a. In all these cases the verbal form merely expresses in the general that the action belongs to the past, but whether this is to be taken absolutely, relatively, or conditionally, must be learned from the circumstances of the case or from accompanying words. The proper English imperfect is expressed in Hebrew not by the preterite but by the participle, וְהוּא יֹשֵׁב *and he* (was) *sitting* Gen. 18:1, §266. 3.

b. In promises, contracts, etc., the preterite is sometimes employed, where we might have expected the future, because the inward act or purpose is intended rather than its outward execution, *unto thy seed* נָתַתִּי *I have given this land* Gen. 15:18, the grant was made though they were not yet put in possession; accordingly, when the latter idea is prominent, the future is used of the same transaction, *unto thy seed* אֶתֵּן *I will give this land* Gen. 12:7, 26:3. Comp. Gen. 4:14, 23:11, 13.

2. The present, regarded as the continuation or natural sequence of a pre-existing action or condition. Anything

begun in the past and continued in the present may be considered to belong to the past and accordingly spoken of in the preterite, *give me a little water for* צָמֵתִי *I am thirsty* Judg. 4:19 prop. I have been thirsty and (it is implied) I am so still; *the earth* מָלְאָה *is full of violence* prop. *has been and still is full* Gen. 6:13; *now* יָדַעְתִּי *I know that Jehovah is the greatest of all the gods* Ex. 18:11, prop. *I have known*, the knowledge being in fact contemporaneous with the information upon which it was based. Comp. in Latin *novi, memini, odi*.

a. It is comparatively a matter of indifference whether the preterite or the future be used to designate the present. That which now exists may either be regarded as continued from the past or as perpetuated in the future; and as it is contemplated under one or the other of these aspects, will the tense be determined accordingly. Thus, the question *whence come ye* is in Gen. 42:7 מֵאַיִן בָּאתֶם *whence have ye come*, but in Josh. 9:8 מֵאַיִן תָּבֹאוּ *whence are ye coming* or *will ye come;* because, in the former instance, the past action of coming is uppermost in the mind of the speaker, and in the latter this action is regarded as having not yet ceased.

3. Permanent facts or general truths; these, though true for all time, are gathered from experience and observation, and hence may be appropriately referred to the past, *an ox* יָדַע *knoweth his owner* Isa. 1:3, oxen always have done so and it is implied that they always will; *the Lord* רִחַם *pitieth them that fear him* Ps. 103:13.

a. The future is used in this case with the same frequency and propriety as the preterite, *An ox will know his owner* expresses the same general truth as *an ox has known his owner;* only in the former case attention is chiefly drawn to its future, and in the latter to its past realizations, § 263. 3.

4. The future, when viewed as past; the prophets, in their inspired descriptions of events which had not yet come to pass, often transport themselves to the time when they shall have been accomplished: and, surveying the future from this ideal point of view, they give to their predictions the form of a recital of what has already taken place, *Babylon*

נָפְלָה *has fallen* Isa. 21:9, *he* נָשָׂא *hath borne our griefs* Isa. 53:4, *for I* הֲשַׂפְתִּי *have made Esau bare* Jer. 49:10.

a. The counterpart of this prophetic preterite is the use of the future in vivid descriptions of the past, in which the writer appears, in imagination, to live over again what has already taken place, § 263. 5.

§ 263. The future is used in speaking of

1. The future, whether absolutely, אֶעֱשֶׂה *I will make of thee a great nation* Gen. 12:2, or relatively to something in the past, *he took his eldest son who* יִמְלֹךְ *was to reign* 2 Kin. 3:27, *Elisha was fallen sick of his sickness whereof* יָמוּת *he was to die* 2 Kin. 13:14; or conditionally, (would that I had died) *for I would have lain down* (pret.) *and* אֶשְׁקוֹט *would be at rest* Job 3:13; *but* (if it were my case) *I* אֶדְרֹשׁ *would seek unto God* Job 5:8; or optatively in the various grades of desire, determination, permission, or command, *so* יֹאבְדוּ *may all thine enemies perish* Judg. 5:31; *O that my grief* יִשָּׁקֵל *might be weighed* Job 6:2; *all that thou commandest us* נַעֲשֶׂה *we will do* Josh. 1:16; *deeds that* יֵעָשׂוּ *ought not to be done* Gen. 20:9; *of the fruit of the trees of the garden* נֹאכֵל *we may eat* Gen. 3:2, לֹא תֹאכְלוּ *ye shall not eat* ver. 3, *mine ordinances* תִּשְׁמְרוּ *ye shall keep* Lev. 18:4; or subjunctively, especially after conjunctions signifying *that, in order that, lest,* etc., (bring the venison) לְמַעַן תְּבָרֶכְךָ *in order that my soul may bless thee* Gen. 27:25, *against thee have I sinned that* תִּצְדָּק *thou mightest be justified* Ps. 51:6.

a. When employed in requests, the future is frequently accompanied by the particle נָא, thus, יְדַבֶּר־נָא *let thy servant speak, I pray thee* Gen. 44:18, יִגְמָר־נָא *let the wickedness of the wicked cease, I pray* Ps. 7:10.

b. The future is idiomatically used with טֶרֶם and בְּטֶרֶם *not yet, before,* whether the period referred to is past or future, the time denoted by the particle being antecedent to the action of the verb. Thus, referring to the past, *I ate of all* בְּטֶרֶם תָּבוֹא *before thou camest* Gen. 27:33, *the lamp of God* טֶרֶם יִכְבֶּה *had not yet gone out* 1 Sam. 3:4; to the future, *that my soul may bless thee* בְּטֶרֶם אָמוּת *before I die* Gen. 27:4, טֶרֶם יִקְרָאוּ *before they call, I will answer* Isa. 65:24. There are three examples of the use of the preterite with these particles, the reference being to past time, 1 Sam. 3:7, Ps. 90:2, Prov. 8:25.

2. The present, when it is conceived of as extending into the future, *comfort my people* יֹאמַר *saith your God* Isa. 40:1, the divine utterance though begun is not yet finished; הֲלוֹא תֵדְעוּ *do ye not know?* ver. 21, are you ignorant, and is this ignorance to continue? *why* תִבְכִּי *weepest thou?* 1 Sam. 1:8.

3. General truths or permanent facts, when the attention is directed to their validity for all time to come, *righteousness* תְּרוֹמֵם *exalteth a nation* Prov. 14:34, it does so now and always will; *a son* יְכַבֵּד *honoureth his father* Mal. 1:6.

4. Constant or habitual acts or states viewed as continuing for an indefinite period from the time spoken of, even though they may have ceased at the time of speaking, and so belong entirely to the past, *a mist* יַעֲלֶה *used to go up from the earth* Gen. 2:6, i. e. not only at the moment of time previously referred to but from that onward; *thus Job* יַעֲשֶׂה *did continually* Job 1:5; *the daughters of Israel* תֵּלַכְנָה *were in the habit of going from time to time* Judg. 11:40; so Gen. 29:2, Ex. 13:22, Num. 11:5, 1 Sam. 2:19.

5. The past, when the speaker or writer assumes an ideal point of vision prior to its occurrence, and so regards it as future. Thus, a historian in animated description, as we might use the present, אָז יָשִׁיר־מֹשֶׁה *then sings Moses* Ex. 15:1, *Balak* יַנְחֵנִי *brings me from Aram* Num. 23:7; or a poet, who lives in the midst of that of which he sings, יֹאבַד יוֹם אִוָּלֶד בּוֹ *let the day perish on which I am to be born* Job 3:3, where the speaker, by a bold figure, places himself before his birth, and prays that the day which was to give him existence might be annihilated, so that he might be saved from the misery of living; לָמָּה לֹא מֵרֶחֶם אָמוּת *why may I not die from the womb?* ver. 11, where his position is shifted to the time immediately after his birth; יוֹדִיעַ דְּרָכָיו לְמֹשֶׁה *he makes known his ways unto Moses* Ps. 103:7.

a. The intermingling of different tenses in relation to the same subject, which is so frequent in poetry, foreign as it may be to our modes of thought, does not justify the conclusion that they are used promiscuously or without regard to their distinctive signification. Thus the preterite and the future are frequently combined in order to give greater emphasis and compass to the statement made, by asserting it at once of both the grand divisions of time, *the wicked who* שַׁדּוּנִי *have wasted me, my deadly enemies* יַקִּיפוּ *will surround me* Ps. 17:9. *fire* אָכְלָה *devoured before them, and after them a flame* תְּלַהֵט *shall consume* Joel 2:3. Or the writer may place himself in the midst of an event, and regard part as having already taken place and part as yet to be performed; thus, in Ex. 15:14, 15, *the nations* שָׁמְעוּ *have heard* יִרְגָּזוּן *they will be afraid; pangs* אָחַז *have seized upon the inhabitants of Philistia; then the dukes of Edom* נִבְהֲלוּ *were troubled, the mighty men of Moab trembling* יֹאחֲזֵמוֹ *shall seize them, all the inhabitants of Canaan* נָמֹגוּ *have melted.* Or a verb may be put in the future to show that the action which it denotes, though in reality past, is subsequent to, or a consequence of, a preceding preterite, *they were both naked* וְלֹא יִתְבֹּשָׁשׁוּ *and were not ashamed* Gen. 2:25, Deut. 2:12.

§ 264. The apocopated and paragogic forms of the future are mostly used in their respective persons, § 97, to express its optative, conditional, or subjunctive senses, § 263. 1. The negative imperative is made by prefixing אַל *not* to the apocopated future, אַל־תָּרַע *harm not* Ps. 105:15; לֹא תָרֵעַ would mean *you shall not harm.*

a. These modified forms of the future, although they give a more distinct expression to the modal senses just indicated, are not essential to that end, since the same shades of meaning may be and often are suggested by the simple future. Instances are more rare, and only found in poetry, in which the apocopated or paragogic forms are used, when simple futurity is intended, Job 13:27, 24:25.

The Secondary Tenses.

§ 265. The secondary tenses agree in signification with their respective primaries. The future with Vav conversive, forming a secondary preterite, § 99. 1, has the same variety of senses with the primary or proper preterite, and is in fact a simple substitute for it. In like manner, the secondary future or the preterite with Vav conversive, § 100. 1, is a substitute for the primary future. A narrative or a paragraph, which begins with one of the primary tenses, is mostly continued by means of the corresponding secondary tense, provided the verb stands at the beginning of its clause, so that it can be attached to the conjunction, which is an essential part of the secondary formation. If, for any reason, this order of the words is interrupted or prevented, the primary tense must again be used. Thus, Gen. 22:1, *God* נִסָּה *tempted Abraham* וַיֹּאמֶר *and said* ... וַיֹּאמֶר *and he said* ... ver. 3, וַיַּשְׁכֵּם *and he rose up early* ... וַיַּחֲבֹשׁ *and saddled* ... וַיִּקַּח *and took* ... וַיְבַקַּע *and clave* ... וַיָּקָם *and rose up* וַיֵּלֶךְ *and went unto the place* אֲשֶׁר־אָמַר־לוֹ *of which God had told him.* Gen. 17:5, *thy name* לֹא־יִקָּרֵא *shall not be called Abram* וְהָיָה *and it shall be* ... ver. 6, וְהִפְרֵתִי *and I will make thee fruitful* ... וּנְתַתִּיךָ *and I will make nations of thee* וּמְלָכִים מִמְּךָ יֵצֵאוּ *and kings shall come out of thee.*

a. The future with Vav conversive describes an act subsequent to or contemporary with the time denoted by the words with which it is connected. It can, therefore, only relate to the past when it is preceded by a preterite with a past signification, or by some other word or phrase which refers to past time, *in the year of king Uzziah's death* וָאֶרְאֶה *(and) I saw* Isa. 6:1. But if it be preceded by a future tense, it has a future signification. יָשְׂחָק *he shall deride every stronghold* יִצְבֹּר *and shall heap up earth* וַיִּלְכְּדָהּ *and take it* Hab. 1:10, *who* יַעֲשֶׂה *shall do evil* ... וַיֵּלֶךְ וַיַּעֲבֹד *and shall go and serve other gods* Deut. 17:2, 3; unless a pause intervenes in which a preterite is to be supplied, as in Hab. 2:1, 2, *I will watch to see what he will say to me* ... וַיַּעֲנֵנִי יְהֹוָה *and (after I had thus watched) the Lord answered me.* The future with Vav conversive occurs in a preterite sense at the beginning of certain books, because they were regarded by their authors as supplements or continuations of preceding histories. וַיְהִי *And it came to pass* Josh. 1:1, Judg. 1:1, 1 Sam. 1:1, etc., etc.

b. The preterite with Vav has a future signification only after a future tense or an expression suggestive of futurity, e. g. *in thy distress* וּבַצַּר לְךָ *when there shall come upon thee all these things* Deut. 4:30; or as the initial word of a prophecy, which is regarded as linked with other disclosures of the future previously made, וְהָיָה *and it shall come to pass* Isa. 2:2. After an imperative it commonly has an imperative sense, this being one of the significations of the future, § 263. 1, *go unto Pharaoh* וְאָמַרְתָּ *and say to him* prop. *and thou shalt say* Ex. 7:26. When a preterite precedes, the Vav is not conversive, *thy servant was keeping his father's sheep* וּבָא *and there came* ... וַיָּבֹא *and took* ... וְיָצָאתִי *and I went out* ... וְהִכִּתִיו *and smote him*, etc., 1 Sam. 17:34, 35, unless it involves a reference to what is to take place hereafter, *I have blessed him* (the blessing is of course prospective), וְהִפְרֵיתִי *and I will make him fruitful,* וְהִרְבֵּיתִי *and I will multiply him* Gen. 17:20.

Participles.

§ 266. The participles being properly verbal nouns, do not in strictness involve any definite notion of time, and the connection must decide whether they are to be referred to the past, present, or future, thus נֹפֵל means *falling* Num. 24 : 4, *fallen* Judg. 4 : 22, or *about to fall* Jer. 37 : 14. Their principal uses are the following, viz. :

1. They express what is permanent or habitual, § 186. 2. *a*, (the Lord) אֹהֵב *loveth righteousness and justice* Ps. 33 : 5, *a generation* הֹלֵךְ *goeth, and a generation* בָּא *cometh, and the earth* עֹמָדֶת *abideth for ever* Eccles. 1 : 4. Passive participles so used suggest not only a constant experience of what is denoted by the verb, but in addition a permanent quality as the ground of it, נוֹרָא not only *feared* but *worthy to be feared,* מְהֻלָּל *worthy to be praised,* נֶחְמָד *desirable.*

2. When a particular time is intended the active participles most commonly relate to the present or to the proximate future, and passive participles to the past, מָה־אַתָּה רֹאֶה *what seest thou?* Jer. 1 : 11, הִנְנִי מֵבִיא *behold, I am about to bring the flood* Gen. 6 : 17, נֹתֵן *giving* נָתוּן *given,* מֵשִׁיב *restoring* מוּשָׁב *restored.*

a. The active participles of neuter verbs, which have no passive forms, are used in both a past and a present sense, מֵת *dying* and *dead,* נֹפֵל *falling* and *fallen;* this is less frequently the case with active verbs, *who then is he* הַצָּד־צַיִד *that hath hunted venison* Gen. 27 : 33; *these are the gods* הַמַּכִּים *that smote Egypt* 1 Sam. 4 : 8. Participles of passive form but active sense are ordinarily used of the present or proximate future, נִלְחָם *fighting.*

3. In narrations and predictions the time of the participles is reckoned not from the moment of speaking but from the period spoken of, *the two angels came* ... וְלוֹט יֹשֵׁב *and Lot* (was) *sitting in the gate of Sodom* Gen. 19 : 1; *he spake to his sons-in-law* לְקֹחֵי בְנֹתָיו *who* (were) *to marry his daughters* ver. 14; *he came to Shiloh* ... וּמַדָּיו קְרֻעִים *with his clothes*

rent 1 Sam. 4 : 12 ; *thou shalt meet a company of prophets* יֹרְדִים *coming down* 1 Sam. 10 : 5 ; *they shall declare his righteousness unto a people* נוֹלָד (who shall then be) *born* Ps. 22 : 32, 102 : 19, Judg. 13 : 8.

a. The period to which a participle is to be referred is sometimes determined by connecting with it the past or future tense of the substantive verb, *Moses* הָיָה רֹעֶה *was keeping the flock of Jethro* Ex. 3 : 1, *his throne* יִהְיֶה נָכוֹן *shall be established for ever* 1 Chron. 17 : 4.

Infinitive.

§ 267. The infinitive is an abstract verbal noun, and, like the participles, partakes of the character both of a noun and a verb. As a noun it may be the subject of a proposition, § 242, or it may be governed by a verb, noun, or preposition; it may also be put in the construct state before a noun denoting either its subject or its object.

a. The Infinitive as a subject: אָלֹה וְכַחֵשׁ וְרָצֹחַ וְגָנֹב וְנָאֹף (there is) *cursing and lying and killing and stealing and committing adultery* Hos. 4 : 2, עֲשׂוֹת מִשְׁפָּט *to do justice* (is) *a joy to the righteous* Prov. 21 : 15.

b. The construct infinitive is used after verbs, nouns, and prepositions, and when governed by a verb or noun it is usually though not invariably preceded as in English by the preposition לְ *to,* אוּכַל לְהִלָּחֶם בּוֹ *I shall be able to fight with him* Num. 22 : 11, עֵת לָלֶדֶת וְעֵת לָמוּת *a time to be born and a time to die* Eccl. 3 : 2; לְ is seldom omitted in prose but often in poetry, *I know not* (how) צֵאת וָבֹא *to go out and to come in* 1 Kin. 3 : 7, מֵאַנְתְּ הִכָּלֵם *thou hast refused to be ashamed* Jer. 3 : 3, עֵת סְפוֹד וְעֵת רְקוֹד *a time to mourn and a time to dance* Eccles. 3 : 4, עֲתִידִים עֹרֵר *ready to rouse leviathan* Job 3 : 8. Various prepositions may precede the infinitive, as לְ *to,* בְּ *in,* כְּ *like, at,* מִן *from,* עַד *until,* עַל *upon,* לְמַעַן *in order to,* יַעַן *because of,* לִפְנֵי *before,* etc.

c. The absolute infinitive is rarely governed by a verb, לִמְדוּ הֵיטֵב *learn to do well,* אַשְּׁרוּ חָמוֹץ *redress wrong* Isa. 1 : 17, *until he knows* מָאוֹס *to refuse the evil,* וּבָחוֹר *and to choose the good,* 7 : 15, וְלֹא־אָבוּ בִדְרָכָיו הָלוֹךְ *and they would not walk in his ways,* 42 : 24, *thou wilt make us offscouring* וּמָאוֹס *and refuse* Lam. 3 : 45.

d. The infinitive in the construct before its subject, בְּהִבָּרְאָם *in their being created* i. e. *when they were created; in the day* עֲשׂוֹת יְהֹוָה אֱלֹהִים *of the Lord God's making earth and heaven* Gen. 2 : 4 ; *there was no water* לִשְׁתֹּת הָעָם *for the drinking of the people* Ex. 17 : 1 ; וְשַׁבְתִּי *and my dwelling* (shall be) i. e. *I shall dwell* Ps. 23:6. Before its object, שֹׂאֵת פְּנֵי־רָשָׁע *the accepting of the person of the wicked* Prov. 18:5, תֵּת־כֹּחָהּ *to yield its strength* Gen. 4:12.

§ 268. The absolute infinitive, expressing as it does the abstract idea of the verb irrespective of tense, number, or person, may be used instead of any of the finite forms of the verb, when the sense is duly qualified by the context. Thus, it may take the place of

1. The preterite or the future, when one of those tenses immediately precedes, וַיִּתְקְעוּ *and they blew the trumpets* וְנָפוֹץ *and brake the pitchers* prop. (there was) *a breaking of the pitchers* Judg. 7:19; *all this* רָאִיתִי וְנָתוֹן אֶת־לִבִּי *I have seen and applied my heart* Eccl. 8:9; יִקְנוּ *they shall buy fields for money* וְכָתוֹב *and write the papers* וְחָתֹם *and seal* (them) וְהָעֵד *and take witnesses* Jer. 32:44.

a. This rarely occurs when no verb precedes in the same sentence, הֲרֹב עִם־שַׁדַּי יִסּוֹר (shall) *the fault-finder contend with the Almighty* Job 40:2, הַחַיּוֹת רָצוֹא וָשׁוֹב *the living creatures ran and returned* Ezek. 1:14, שַׁבֵּחַ אֲנִי *I praised* Eccl. 4:2.

2. The imperative, when it stands at the beginning of a sentence, זָכוֹר *remember the sabbath-day* prop. (let there be) *a remembering* Ex. 20:8, הָלוֹךְ וְדִבַּרְתָּ *go and say* 2 Sam. 24:12.

§ 269. The dependence of one verb upon another is most distinctly expressed by putting the second verb in the infinitive. The second verb may, however, be in form co-ordinated with the first by being put in the same or an equivalent tense with or without a copulative, the true relation between the verbs being left to be inferred from their obvious signification, הוֹאִיל הָלַךְ *he was willing, walked* i. e. *he was willing to walk* or *walked willingly* Hos. 5:11, לֹא אוֹסִיף עוֹד אֲרַחֵם *I will no more add to pity* i. e. *will not again pity* Hos. 1:6, מַשְׁכִּים הָלֹךְ *being early to go* or *going early* Hos. 6:4, *how* אוּכַל וְרָאִיתִי *shall I endure and see* i. e. *endure to see* Esth. 8:6.

§ 270   OBJECT OF VERBS.   299

a. This co-ordination most frequently occurs when the second verb expresses the principal idea and the first simply qualifies it, so that the latter might be rendered by an adverb. Though even in this case the second verb is often put in the infinitive, וַיֹּסֶף שַׁלַּח Gen. 8:10 *and he added to send* or וַיֹּסֶף וַיִּשְׁלַח 1 Sam. 19:21 *and he added and sent* for *he sent again.*

b. In the following instances the verbs thus co-ordinated have different subjects, אוּכַל נַכֶּה־בּוֹ *I shall be able, we shall smite him* i. e. I shall with your aid be able to smite him, Num. 22:6. לֹא הוֹסִיף יִקְרָאוּ־לָךְ *thou shalt not add they shall call thee* i. e. thou shalt no more be called by them, Isa. 47:1, 5; or are in different tenses, לֹא יָדַעְתִּי אֲכַנֶּה *I know not* (how) *I shall flatter* i. e. how to flatter, Job 32:22; יָדַעְתִּי וְאֶמְצָאֵהוּ *O that I knew and might find him* i. e. how to find him, Job 23:3.

Object of Verbs.

§ 270. The object of a transitive verb ordinarily stands after both the verb and its subject, and if it is an indefinite noun is distinguished simply by its position or by its relation to the verb as determined by its meaning; if a definite noun, or a demonstrative, relative, or interrogative pronoun, it may, at the pleasure of the writer, be further distinguished by prefixing to it אֵת the sign of the definite object; if a personal pronoun, it is suffixed either to אֵת or to the governing verb.

a. Considerable liberty is allowed in respect to the position of words, particularly in poetry; although, according to the natural order in Hebrew, the verb stands first, its subject next, and its object last, בָּרָא אֱלֹהִים אֵת הַשָּׁמָיִם *God created the heavens* Gen. 1:1, this is liable to any alteration that emphasis may require; the subject may precede the verb, and the object may stand between them or before them both.

b. A noun, which is the direct object of a verb, may receive אֵת, whether it is definite by signification, as a proper noun, *God tempted* אֶת־אַבְרָהָם *Abraham* Gen. 22:1, or is made so by the article, *God saw* אֶת־הָאוֹר *the light* Gen. 1:4, a pronominal suffix, *take, now,* אֶת־בִּרְכָתִי *my blessing* Gen. 33:11, or construction with a definite noun, *Jacob called* אֶת־שֵׁם הַמָּקוֹם *the name of the place* Gen. 35:15. The particle אֵת is not essential in any of these cases and is often omitted, particularly in poetry. If several definite nouns are connected together as the object of a verb, or if a verb has more than one definite object, אֵת may be repeated before each of them, *I have given* אֶת־הָאָרֶץ הַזֹּאת *this land*... אֶת־הַקֵּינִי *the Kenite* וְאֶת־הַקְּנִזִּי *and the Kenizzite,* etc., etc., Gen. 15:18-21; *they stripped* אֶת־יוֹסֵף *Joseph* אֶת־כֻּתָּנְתּוֹ *of his coat* אֶת־כְּתֹנֶת הַפַּסִּים *the full-length coat*

Gen. 37:23; or it may stand before a part of them only. Deut. 12:6, or it may be omitted altogether, Deut. 11:14. In a very few instances the article is dropped after אֶת, which of itself indicates the definiteness of the noun, *he reared up for himself* אֶת־הַמַּצֵּבָה *the pillar* 2 Sam. 18:18; *and carver strengthened* אֶת־צֹרֵף *gilder* Isa. 41:7, where the omission of the article is poetic, §247.

c. Pronouns with אֶת: אֶת־זֶה *this ye shall eat* Lev. 11:9; אֶת־זֶה *put this* (fellow) *in the prison* 1 Kin. 22:27; אֵת אֲשֶׁר *whom they have cast into the prison* Jer. 38:9; אֵת אֲשֶׁר־עָשָׂה *he knew what his youngest son had done to him* Gen. 9:24; אֶת־מִי חֵרַפְתָּ *whom hast thou reproached?* Isa. 37:23; it does not occur before the neuter מָה. It is also extended sometimes to the following words, which partake to a certain degree of the pronominal character, כֹּל *all, every,* Gen. 1:29, אִישׁ *any one, each* Ex. 21:28, אֶחָד *one* 1 Sam. 9:3. With personal pronouns, וַיְבָרֶךְ אֶתְהֶם Gen. 32:1, or וַיְבָרְכֵם Gen. 48:20 *and he blessed them.*

§ 271. Many verbs, which are not properly transitive, are nevertheless capable of a transitive construction; thus

1. Verbs signifying plenty or want: הַבַּיִת מָלֵא הָאֲנָשִׁים *the house was full* (of) *men* Judg. 16:27, שָׂבַעְתִּי עֹלוֹת אֵילִים *I am sated* (with) *burnt-offerings of rams* Isa. 1:11, חָסַרְנוּ כֹל *we lacked every thing* Jer. 44:18. Here belongs that peculiar Hebrew idiom, which expresses abundance by such phrases as the following: *the hills* תְּלַכְנָה חָלָב *shall run* (with) *milk* Joel 4:18, *mine eye* יָרְדָה מַּיִם *runneth down* (with) *water* Lam. 1:16; עָלָה כֻלּוֹ קִמְּשׂוֹנִים *it had all come up* (with) *thorns* i. e. was overgrown with them, Prov. 24:31.

2. Verbs signifying motion may have for their object the place which it immediately concerns, whether it be directed upon it, to it, or from it, וַנֵּלֶךְ אֵת כָּל־הַמִּדְבָּר *and we went* (through) *all the wilderness* Deut. 1:19, and figuratively, הֹלֵךְ צְדָקוֹת *walking* (in) *righteousness* Isa. 33:15, וַיָּבֹאוּ הָעִיר *and they came into the city* Josh. 8:19, יָצְאוּ אֶת־הָעִיר *they went out* (of) *the city* Gen. 44:4.

3. Intransitive verbs may, as in other languages, govern their cognate noun, חָלַמְתִּי חֲלוֹם *I have dreamed a dream* Gen. 37:9; וַיִּסְפְּדוּ־שָׁם מִסְפֵּד *and they lamented there a lamentation* Gen. 50:10; הֶבֶל תֶּהְבָּלוּ *ye will be vain a vanity* i. e. *utterly vain* Job 27:12; or even one from a different root if

it be related or analogous in signification, חָמָה גְדוֹלָה קִנֵּאתִי *I have been zealous a great fury* Zech. 8:2, אִישַׁן הַמָּוֶת *I shall sleep death* i. e. the sleep of death, Ps. 13:4.

4. Any verb may take as its object a noun which defines the extent of its application, חָלָה אֶת־רַגְלָיו *he was diseased in his feet* 1 Kin. 15:23; *only* הַכִּסֵּא אֶגְדַּל *in the throne will I be greater than thou* Gen. 41:40; תֹּאבְדוּ דֶרֶךְ *ye perish as to the way* i. e. lose the way Ps. 2:12.

a. By an impersonal construction of passive verbs their subject is sometimes converted into the object, which in fact it logically is, יֻתַּן אֶת־הָאָרֶץ *dandum est terram, let the land be given* Num. 32:5, וַיֻּגַּד לְרִבְקָה אֶת־דִּבְרֵי עֵשָׂו *and it was told to Rebekah* (i. e. some one told her) *the words of Esau* Gen. 27:42, so Gen. 17:5, Ex. 10:8, Lev. 10:18, 2 Sam. 21:11, etc. This construction is sometimes extended to neuter verbs in familiar phrases, which have become associated with an active idea, אַל יֵרַע בְּעֵינֶיךָ אֶת־הַדָּבָר *let not be evil in thine eyes* (i. e. do not regard as evil) *the thing* 2 Sam. 11:25, 1 Sam. 20:13, Josh. 22:17, Neh. 9:32. In 2 Kin. 18:30 תֻּנָּתֵן אֶת־הָעִיר *the city shall be given,* the verb agrees with עִיר notwithstanding its reception of the sign of the object: אֵת is omitted in the parallel passage, Isa. 36:15.

b. A noun, about which a statement is to be made, sometimes stands absolutely and is preceded by the sign of the object, אֶת־הַבַּרְזֶל נָפָל *as for the iron, it fell* 2 Kin. 6:5; אֶת־כָּל־אֵלֶּה אַנְשֵׁי חָיִל *as for all these* (they were) *men of valour* Judg. 20:44; אֶת־חֻקּוֹתַי *as for my statutes they did not walk in them* Ezek. 20:16. Some regard אֵת as the sign of the object in such passages as בָּא הָאֲרִי וְאֶת־הַדּוֹב 1 Sam. 17:34, and refer to the fact that the Arabic conjunction is followed by the accusative when it is used in the sense of *together with;* more probably, however, אֵת is the preposition *with,* § 238.2, and the passage is to be rendered *the lion came and* (that too) *with the bear,* so Num. 3:26, 1 Sam. 26:16, 1 Kin. 11:25, etc.

§ 272. 1. When a noun or pronoun is regarded as the indirect object of a verb, the relation is indicated by means of the appropriate preposition.

2. Many verbs vary their construction without any material difference of meaning according to the form of the conception in the mind of the speaker or writer, being followed by one preposition or by another or by none at all, as he views the relation as direct or indirect, and if the latter, under one aspect or another: thus, *they went out from the city* may be expressed by the direct relation, יָצְאוּ אֶת־הָעִיר Gen. 44:4,

or by the indirect, רָצְאוּ מִדְּהָעִיר Josh. 8:22; נִלְחֹם to fight is followed by עִם with Josh. 10:29, by בְּ in (בָּהּ in eam) ver. 31, by עַל against ver. 38, by אֵת Judg. 12:4.

a. A number of verbs are indifferently construed with a direct object or with לְ to, in reference to, thus, אָהַב to love any one and to have love to any one, רָפָא to cure and to perform a cure for any one, הוֹשִׁיעַ to save and to grant salvation to any one, שָׁחַת to destroy and to bring destruction to any one.

b. As the object of an action may, in certain cases, be regarded as the instrument with which it is performed, some transitive verbs also admit a construction with בְּ with, thus תִּקְעוּ שׁוֹפָר blow the trumpet Hos. 5:8, וַיִּתְקַע בַּשּׁוֹפָר and he blew with the trumpet Judg. 3:27; פָּרַשׂ הַיָּדַיִם to spread forth the hands Ps. 143:6, but followed by בְּ to spread forth with the hands Lam. 1:17.

3. By a condensed style of expression (*constructio praegnans*) prepositions are sometimes connected with verbs, to whose meaning they are not strictly conformed; thus, motion may be suggested by the preposition though the verb of itself implies no such idea, חִלַּלְתָּ לָאָרֶץ *thou hast profaned to the ground* i. e. profaned by casting to the ground, Ps. 89:40, פָּחֲדוּ אִישׁ אֶל־רֵעֵהוּ *they trembled one unto another* i. e. one turned tremblingly to another, Jer. 36:16, מִקַּרְנֵי רֵמִים עֲנִיתָנִי *thou hast answered* (by saving) *me from the horns of the unicorns* Ps. 22:22.

§ 273. Some verbs have more than one object, viz.:

1. The causatives of transitive verbs: וְהַאֲכַלְתִּי אֶת־מוֹנַיִךְ אֶת־בְּשָׂרָם *and I will make thy oppressors eat their own flesh* Isa. 49:26; לֹא הֶרְאָנוּ אֶת־כָּל־אֵלֶּה *he would not have caused us to see all these things* Judg. 13:23; וַיַּנְחִלֶהָ אֶת־יִשְׂרָאֵל *he shall cause Israel to inherit it* Deut. 1:38.

2. Verbs whose action may be regarded under different aspects as terminating upon different objects, or which, under the rules already given, may take a direct object of more than one kind, *all* אֲשֶׁר צִוָּה אֹתוֹ *which God commanded him* Gen. 6:22; לְהוֹרֹת אֶת־בְּנֵי יִשְׂרָאֵל אֵת כָּל־הַחֻקִּים *to teach the children of Israel all the statutes* Lev. 10:11; הִכִּיתָ אֶת־כָּל־אֹיְבַי לֶחִי *thou hast smitten all my enemies on the cheek* Ps. 3:8;

שְׂאוּ־יְדֵכֶם קֹדֶשׁ *lift up your hands to the sanctuary* Ps. 134 : 2; וְהָמָם מְהוּמָה *and he shall discomfit them a discomfiture* Deut. 7 : 23.

3. The instrument of an action, the material used in its performance, its design, or its result, is often regarded as its secondary or remote object, וַיִּרְגְּמוּ אֹתוֹ אֶבֶן *and they overwhelmed him with stones* Lev. 24 : 23; וְחָגַרְתָּ אֹתָם אַבְנֵט *and thou shalt gird them with a belt* Ex. 29 : 9; *thy seed* אֲשֶׁר־תִּזְרַע אֶת־הָאֲדָמָה *with which thou shalt sow the ground* Isa. 30 : 23; וַיִּיצֶר אֶת־הָאָדָם עָפָר *and he formed the man of dust* Gen. 2 : 7; אֲשֶׁר שְׁלַחְתִּיו *for which I have sent it* Isa. 55 : 11; וַיִּבְנֶה אֶת־הָאֲבָנִים מִזְבֵּחַ *and he built the stones into an altar* 1 Kin. 18 : 32.

a. The person affected by an action, of which he is not the immediate object, is occasionally regarded as its remote object, though not so frequently as in English, אֶרֶץ הַנֶּגֶב נְתַתָּנִי *thou hast given me the land of the south* Judg. 1:15, comp. in the same verse, וְנָתַתָּה לִי; רָעָה גְּמָלוּךְ *they did thee evil* Gen. 50 : 17, comp. וַיִּשְׁכְּרוּ אֶת־מֶלֶךְ מַעֲכָה גָּמְלוּ לָהֶם רָעָה Isa. 3:9; אֶלֶף אִישׁ *and they hired of the king of Maacah a thousand men* 1 Sam. 10:6. The same thing occurs in a few instances after intransitive verbs, גָּדַלַנִי *he grew up to me as to a father* Job 31 : 18; צַמְתֻּנִי *did ye fast unto me* Zech. 7 : 5.

4. Some verbs may govern the subject and predicate of a subordinate clause, לָדַעַת רֶשַׁע כֶּסֶל *to know wickedness (to be) folly* Eccl. 7 : 25, the latter, if it be an adjective or participle, will remain without the article, § 259. 2, שָׁמֹעַ שָׁמַעְתִּי אֶפְרַיִם מִתְנוֹדֵד *I have heard Ephraim bemoaning himself* Jer. 31 : 18, אֹתְךָ רָאִיתִי צַדִּיק *thee have I seen righteous* Gen. 7 : 1.

5. If an active verb is capable of governing a double object, its passive may govern the more remote of them, וּנְמַלְתֶּם אֵת בְּשַׂר עָרְלַתְכֶם *and ye shall be circumcised in the flesh of your foreskin* Gen. 17 : 11, וַתִּמָּלֵא הָאָרֶץ אֹתָם *and the land was filled with them* Ex. 1 : 7, קָרוּעַ כֻּתָּנְתּוֹ *rent as to his coat* i. e. *with his coat rent* 2 Sam. 15 : 32, שָׁלוּחַ קָשָׁה *sent (or charged) with a painful message* 1 Kin. 14 : 6.

Adverbial Expressions.

§ 274. The predicate of a proposition may be further qualified

1. By adverbs, which commonly stand after the words to which they refer, וְהִנֵּה־טוֹב מְאֹד *and behold* (it was) *very good* Gen. 1:31; וַיִּכְעַס הַרְבֵּה *and he was greatly provoked* Neh. 3:33; *I am* שְׂכָרְךָ הַרְבֵּה מְאֹד *thy exceeding great reward* prop. *thy reward very much* Gen. 15:1.

a. Adjectives belonging to the subject may of course be qualified in the same manner as though they were found in the predicate.

2. By nouns used absolutely to express the relations of time, place, measure, number, or manner.

a. Thus, time when: עֶרֶב וָבֹקֶר וְצָהֳרַיִם *evening and morning and noon will I pray* Ps. 55:18; *tarry here* הַלַּיְלָה *to-night* Num. 22:8; *Gideon came* רֹאשׁ הָאַשְׁמֹרֶת *at the beginning of the watch.* Time how long: *and he shall shut up the house* שִׁבְעַת יָמִים *seven days* Lev. 14:38; *the land rested* שְׁמוֹנִים שָׁנָה *eighty years* Judg. 3:30.

b. The place where: the absolute use of nouns in this sense is confined almost entirely to the familiar words, פֶּתַח *at the door of* Gen. 18:1, Judg. 9:35, בֵּית *at the house of* Gen. 38:11, Num. 30:11, and a few proper names, בֵּית לֶחֶם *at Bethlehem* 2 Sam. 2:32, בֵּית־אֵל *at Bethel* Hos. 12:4.

c. Measures of space: שָׁלוֹשׁ אַמּוֹת גָּבְהָהּ *three cubits high* Ezek. 41:22; *he went* דֶּרֶךְ יוֹם *a day's journey* 1 Kin. 19:4.

d. Number: שֶׁבַע פְּעָמִים שֻׁב *return seven times* 1 Kin. 18:43; *he offered sacrifices* מִסְפַּר כֻּלָּם *according to the number of them all* Job 1:5.

e. Manner, answering to the Greek adverbial accusative: *ye shall dwell* בֶּטַח *in security* Deut. 12:10; *ye shall not go* רוֹמָה *loftily* Mic. 2:3; *the tribes went up* עֵדוּת לְיִשְׂרָאֵל *according to a law of Israel* Ps. 122:4; *thou shalt not go there* יִרְאַת שָׁמִיר *for fear of briers* Isa. 7:25; *to serve him* שְׁכֶם אֶחָד *with one consent* prop. *shoulder* Zeph. 3:9.

3. By nouns preceded by a preposition forming a qualifying phrase.

a. For the meanings and usage of the several prepositions see the lexicon.

Neglect of Agreement.

§ 275. The general rule that verbs, adjectives, and pronouns agree in gender and number with the noun to which they respectively relate, is subject to some remarkable exceptions; the principal of which are the following, viz.:

1. When the predicate adjective or verb precedes the noun it often prefers a primary to a secondary form, that is to say, the masculine may be used instead of the feminine and the singular instead of the plural. The reason of this is that the attention is not so particularly drawn to the accidents of gender and number in the subject until it is uttered, and consequently the predicate is not required to conform so precisely to it.

a. Thus, the masculine for the feminine: לֹא־נָשָׂא אֹתָם הָאָרֶץ *the land could not bear them* Gen. 13:6, רָחוֹק מֵרְשָׁעִים יְשׁוּעָה *salvation is far from the wicked* Ps. 119:155, חִרְדוּ שַׁאֲנַנּוֹת *tremble ye careless women* Isa. 32:11. The singular for the plural: יָבֹא דְבָרֶיךָ *let thy words come to pass* Judg. 13:12, יָשָׁר מִשְׁפָּטֶיךָ *upright are thy judgments* Ps. 119:137, אֲנוּשָׁה מַכּוֹתֶיהָ *her wounds are incurable*, or the singular may be understood distributively, *each of her wounds is incurable* Mic. 1:9. The masculine singular for the feminine plural: לֹא רָגַב כְּלִמּוֹת *reproaches cease not* Mic. 2:6, עַד־יַעֲבֹר הַוּוֹת *until calamities be overpast* Ps. 57:2, וַיְהִי־לוֹ נָשִׁים *and there were to him wives* 1 Kin. 11:3.

b. When the predicate consists of several verbs or adjectives, one of which precedes and the rest follow the noun, the latter must agree with it, while the first may be put in its primary form, יְהִי מְאֹרֹת *let there be lights* ... וְהָיוּ לְאֹתֹת *and let them be for signs* Gen. 1:14, וַיְהִי אֲנָשִׁים הָיוּ טְמֵאִים *and there were men who were defiled* Num. 9:6. In 1 Kin. 10:12 two verbs are put in the masc. sing. with a plural subject.

c. The predicate, even when it follows the subject, occasionally departs from it in gender or number, retaining its primary form; this takes place with passive or neuter verbs of familiar occurrence, and which are probably used impersonally as the same verbs are elsewhere, §271.4.*a*, *the sons of Jacob* אֲשֶׁר יֻלַּד־לוֹ *whom* (his wives) *had born to him* prop. *there had been born to him* Gen. 35:26, comp. Gen. 4:18, 46:22, 27, בְּנֵי־בַיִת הָיָה לִי *there was to me* (i. e. I had) *house-born servants* Eccles. 2:7, comp. Gen. 47:24, Ex. 12:49, 28:7, Num. 9:14, 15:29, Deut. 18:2, 1 Chron. 24:28, 2 Chron. 17:13, כַּלָּפָה הָיָה *it was dark* prop. *darkness* Gen. 15:17. The disposition to recur to their primary form discovers itself in a very few instances in qualifying adjectives when separated from the noun to which they belong, רוּחַ גְּדוֹלָה וְחָזָק *a great and strong wind* 1 Kin. 19:11; in Ps. 63:2, בְּאֶרֶץ־צִיָּה וְעָיֵף quoted by Nordheimer as an additional example the second adjective may agree not with אֶרֶץ but with the preceding noun, בְשָׂרִי *for thee longs my flesh, in a dry land, and weary.* Alex. *in loc.*

2. Collective nouns may have verbs, adjectives, and pronouns agreeing with them in the plural, וַיְמַהֲרוּ הָעָם וַיַּעֲבֹרוּ *and the people hasted and passed over* Josh. 4:10, צֹאן אֹבְדוֹת *lost sheep* Jer. 50:6, כָּל־הָעֵדָה כֻּלָּם קְדֹשִׁים *all the congregation, all of them are holy* Num. 16:3.

a. When a predicate consists of more than one verb or adjective, the first sometimes agrees with it formally in the singular and the rest logically in the plural, וַתִּשָּׂא כָּל־הָעֵדָה וַיִּתְּנוּ אֶת־קוֹלָם *and all the congregation lifted up and uttered their voice* Num. 14:1; וַיַּאֲמֵן הָעָם וַיִּשְׁמְעוּ *and the people believed and they heard* Ex. 4:31.

b. The noun אֶרֶץ *land, earth,* which is properly a feminine singular, may, when it is put for its inhabitants, be construed with the masculine plural, 2 Sam. 15:23, Ps. 66:4. Names of nations borrowed from those of their progenitors, as Israel, Edom, Amalek, may be strictly construed in the masculine singular, Ex. 17:11, Am. 1:11, or as a collective in the masculine plural, Hos. 8:2, Ob. ver. 6, 2 Sam. 10:17, or again in the feminine singular, whether this arises from a prominent reference to the land or from the frequent personification of a people as a maiden, 2 Sam. 10:11, Jer. 13:19, 49:17; so עַם *people* in the following examples, חָטָאת עַמִּי *thy people has done wrong* Ex. 5:16, הָעָם יוֹשֶׁבֶת *the people dwelling* Judg. 18:7. Different constructions may be united in the same passage, Jer. 48:15, Hos. 14:1.

3. Nouns, which are plural in form but singular in signification, commonly have verbs, adjectives, and pronouns agreeing with them in the singular, בָּרָא אֱלֹהִים *God created* Gen. 1:1, בְּעָלָיו יוּמָת *its owner shall be put to death* Ex. 21:29, אֲדֹנִים קָשֶׁה *a hard master* Isa. 19:4, תִּתְחַדֵּשׁ נְעוּרָיְכִי *thy youth is renewed* Ps. 103:5.

a. When the word אֱלֹהִים refers to false deities, the sense is plural and it is construed accordingly, אֵלֶּה אֱלֹהֶיךָ *these are thy gods* Ex. 32:4, 8, כֹּה־יַעֲשׂוּן אֱלֹהִים *so may the gods do* 1 Kin. 19:2; but where it refers to the true God, it is with few exceptions construed in the singular. Yet see Gen. 20:13, 35:7, Ex. 22:8, Josh. 24:19, 1 Sam. 17:26, 2 Sam. 7:23. The exceptional construction in these and similar passages may have arisen from the attention being directed to the Supreme Being in general, and to the fulness or variety of his manifestations without specific reference to the divine unity, and may, besides, involve an allusion to the personal distinction in the Godhead. See Alexander on Ps. 11:7 and 58:12.

4. Plural names of inanimate or irrational objects of either gender are occasionally joined with the feminine singular, בַּהֲמוֹת שָׂדֶה תַּעֲרוֹג אֵלֶיךָ *the beasts of the field pant for thee* Joel 1:20, תִּשְׁטֹף סְפִיחֶיהָ *its floods wash away* Job 14:19, חֲבָלִים אֲחָזַתָּה *pangs have taken her* Jer. 49:24, תַּנִּים רִבְצָהּ *wild beasts, their lair* Isa. 35:7.

a. In objects devoid of personality the individual is of small account, and may be easily sunk in the mass. A *pluralis inhumanus* may consequently be regarded as equivalent to a collective, the proper form of which is the feminine singular, § 198, and words belonging to it may be dealt with accordingly. The same principle prevails in the construction of neuter plurals in Greek, τὰ ζῶα τρέχει.

5. Masculine verbs, adjectives, and pronouns are sometimes used when females are spoken of from a neglect to note the gender, if no stress is laid upon it, וַיְהַלְלוּהָ *and they* (queens and concubines) *praised her* Cant. 6:9; *the Lord deal kindly* עִמָּכֶם *with you* (Ruth and Orpah) *as* עֲשִׂיתֶם *ye have dealt* Ruth 1:8; מֵתִי *my dead* (Sarah) Gen. 23:4; אַתְּ שָׁדוּד *thou art destroyed* Jer. 4:30; this last passage may, however, be rendered *thou, it is destroyed, what wilt thou do?*

6. Singular predicates and pronouns are sometimes employed in a distributive sense of plural subjects, מְבָרֲכֶיךָ בָרוּךְ *they that bless thee shall each be blessed* Num. 24:9; מְחַלְלֶיהָ מוֹת יוּמָת *they who profane it shall every one be put to death* Ex. 31:14; צִדְקַת צַדִּיקִים יָסִירוּ מִמֶּנּוּ *they take away the righteousness of the righteous from each of them* Isa. 5:23.

§ 276. 1. When the subject consists of two or more words connected by the conjunction *and*, the predicate, if it precedes its subject, may be put in the masculine singular as its primary form, וְיָצָא מֵהֶם תּוֹדָה וְקוֹל *and from them shall proceed thanksgiving and a voice* Jer. 30:19, or it may be put in the plural, referring to them all, וַיַּעֲשׂוּ מֹשֶׁה וְאַהֲרֹן

and Moses and Aaron did so Ex. 7:20, or it may agree with the nearest word, וַתְּדַבֵּר מִרְיָם וְאַהֲרֹן *and Miriam and Aaron spake* Num. 12:1; לֹא יָדַעְתָּ אַתָּה וַאֲבֹתֶיךָ *thou and thy fathers have not known* Deut. 13:7.

2. If the predicate follows a compound subject it is commonly put in the plural, though it may agree with the principal word to which the others are subordinate, אֲנִי וְנַעֲרֹתַי אָצוּם *I with my maidens will fast* prop. *and my maidens* Est. 4:16, עַבְדֵי דָוִד וְיוֹאָב בָּא *the servants of David and Joab came* 2 Sam. 3:22.

3. If a predicate refers equally to two words of different genders, it will be put in the masculine in preference to the feminine, אַבְרָהָם וְשָׂרָה זְקֵנִים *Abraham and Sarah were old* Gen. 18:11; if they are of different persons, the predicate will be put in the second in preference to the third, and in the first in preference to either of the others, אֲנִי וִיהוֹנָתָן בְּנִי נִהְיֶה *I and Jonathan my son will be* 1 Sam. 14:40, אַתָּה וְאַהֲרֹן אָחִיךָ וְדִבַּרְתֶּם *thou and Aaron thy brother and ye shall speak* Num. 20:8.

§ 277. If two or more nouns are united in the construct state the predicate ordinarily agrees with the first as the leading word in such combinations: it may, however, agree with the second, if that is the more important, or the predicate might with propriety be referred directly to it, שַׁדְמוֹת חֶשְׁבּוֹן אֻמְלָל *the fields of Heshbon languish* Isa. 16:8, נִמְצְאוּ דַּם נַפְשׁוֹת אֶבְיוֹנִים *is found the blood of the souls of the poor* Jer. 2:34.

a. The predicate agrees generally though not invariably with the second noun when the first is כֹּל, or an abstract expressing a quality of that which follows, וַיִּהְיוּ כָּל־יְמֵי־שֵׁת *and all the days of Seth were* Gen. 5:8, וַתֵּצֶאןָ כָּל־הַנָּשִׁים *and all the women went out* Ex. 15:20, מִבְחַר שָׁלִשָׁיו טֻבְּעוּ *the choice of his captains were drowned* ver. 4.

§ 278. Nouns in the dual have verbs, adjectives, and pronouns, agreeing with them in the plural, עֵינֵי לֵאָה רַכּוֹת *the eyes of Leah were tender* Gen. 29:17.

§ 279. The abrupt changes of the person from the third

to the first or second, and *vice versâ*, which are especially frequent with the prophets and psalmists, Isa. 1:29, Ps. 81:17, are due to the boldness and vividness of their conceptions, in virtue of which they often pass in the course of the same sentence from speaking of God to speaking in his name, and from describing men to directly addressing them.

a. The occasional combination of the pronoun of the first person with a verb in the third is to be explained by an ellipsis, הִנְנִי יִסַּד *behold I* (am he who) *has laid* Isa. 28:16, הִנְנִי יוֹסִף *behold I* (am he who) *will add* 29:14, 38:5.

Repetition of Words.

§ 280. The repetition of nouns may denote

1. Distribution, שָׁנָה שָׁנָה *year by year* Deut. 14:22, בַּבֹּקֶר בַּבֹּקֶר *in the morning, in the morning* i. e. *every morning* 2 Sam. 13:4, אִישׁ־אֶחָד אִישׁ־אֶחָד לַשֵּׁבֶט *one man for each tribe* Josh. 3:12; so with numeral adjectives, § 252. 4, שִׁבְעָה שִׁבְעָה *by sevens* Gen. 7:2, and adverbs, מְעַט מְעַט *little by little* Ex. 23:30.

2. Plurality, דֹּר־וָדֹר *generation and generation* i. e. *many generations* Deut. 32:7, צַו לָצָו צַו לָצָו קַו לָקָו קַו לָקָו *precept upon precept, precept upon precept, line upon line, line upon line* Isa. 28:10, 13, בֶּאֱרֹת בֶּאֱרֹת *pits on pits* Gen. 14:10; or with the implication of diversity, אֶבֶן וָאָבֶן *a weight and a weight* i. e. *weights of two sorts* Deut. 25:13, לֵב וָלֵב *a double heart* Ps. 12:3.

3. Emphasis or intensity, צֶדֶק צֶדֶק *justice, justice* i. e. *nothing but justice* Deut. 16:20, עָמֹק עָמֹק *exceeding deep* Eccl. 7:24; so with adverbs, מְאֹד מְאֹד *mightily, mightily* Gen. 7:19, and even a conjunction, יַעַן וּבְיַעַן *because even because*.

a. Sometimes the second word is put in a different gender from the first, מַשְׁעֵן וּמַשְׁעֵנָה *all kinds of support* Isa. 3:1, comp. Jer. 48:19, or a different number, חֲמוֹר חֲמֹרָתָיִם *a heap, two heaps* Judg. 15:16, שֵׁפִי Eccl. 2:8. Or a cognate word may be employed, שְׁמָמָה וּמְשַׁמָּה *waste and desolate* Ezek. 6:14, שַׁבַּת שַׁבָּתוֹן Lev. 23:3.

b. Instances occur of triple repetition, קָדוֹשׁ קָדוֹשׁ קָדוֹשׁ *holy, holy, holy,* Isa. 6:3, אֶרֶץ אֶרֶץ אֶרֶץ *O earth, earth, earth,* Jer. 22:29, Jer. 7:4, Ezek. 21:32, Ex. 25:35.

§ 281. A separate pronoun may be added to a pronominal suffix for the sake of emphasis, מוּתִי אָנִי *my dying, mine* 2 Sam. 19:1, אַתָּה יוֹדוּךָ *thee, thee shall they praise* Gen. 49:8, or to a noun to which it refers, לְשֵׁת גַּם־הוּא *to Seth, to him also* Gen. 4:26.

§ 282. In verbs the absolute infinitive is joined with the finite forms to add emphasis or intensity to the idea, הֲמָלֹךְ תִּמְלֹךְ *shalt thou actually reign over us?* Gen. 37:8, מוֹת תָּמוּת *thou shalt surely die* Gen. 2:17. This combination sometimes expresses continuance or repetition, particularly when two infinitives are connected together and both follow the finite verb, וַיֵּצֵא יָצוֹא וָשׁוֹב *and it went out going out and returning* i. e. *it kept going to and fro* Gen. 8:7, הָלְכוּ הָלוֹךְ וְגָעוֹ *they went on lowing as they went* 1 Sam. 6:12, וָאֲדַבֵּר אֲלֵיכֶם הַשְׁכֵּם וְדַבֵּר *and I spake to you rising up early and speaking* Jer. 7:13.

a. The infinitive is mostly of the same species with the finite verb to which it is added, although this is not always the case. Thus, the Kal, on account of its greater simplicity of form, may be joined with a derivative species. e. g. Niphal סָקוֹל יִסָּקֵל Ex. 19:13, Piel וַיְדַבְּרָה בָּרוֹךְ Josh. 24:10, Pual שָׂרֹף טֹרַף Gen. 37:33, Hiphil עָרוּם יַעְרִים 1 Sam. 23:22, Hophal מוֹת יוּמָת Ex. 19:12, Hithpael מוֹט הִתְמוֹטְטָה Isa. 24:19; or one derivative species with another of like signification, הִפָּדֵה לֹא נִפְדָּתָה Lev. 19:20, הָחְתֵּל לֹא חֻתָּלְתְּ Ezek. 16:4. Occasionally the infinitive is borrowed from a cognate verb, אָסֹף אָסֵף Zeph. 1:2 (אָסֹף and סוּף), אָדוֹשׁ דְּרוּשֵׁהוּ Isa. 28:28 (אָדוֹשׁ and דּוּשׁ).

b. The construct infinitive is very rarely used in such combinations instead of the absolute, חַבֹּל חָבַלְנוּ Neh. 1:7, הָיוֹ־אֶהְיֶה Ps. 50:21; once it is added in a varied form to a preceding construct infinitive, בְּהִגָּלוֹת נִגְלֹה 2 Sam. 6:20. The finite verb is repeated, יָשׁוֹב יְשֻׁבֵנִי 2 Sam. 15:8 K'thibh. A verbal noun takes the place of the infinitive, קְרֹא תָבוֹא Hab. 3:9.

c. When two verbs are connected together to express continuous action, a participle is sometimes substituted for the absolute infinitive in the case of one or both, הוֹלֵךְ הָלוֹךְ וּבֹכֶה ... כֹּלֹה וּבוֹכֶה 2 Sam. 15:30, דָּוִד עֹלֶה וּבוֹכֶה Jer. 41:6; an adjective may even take the place of the second, וַיֵּלֶךְ הָלוֹךְ וְגָדֵל Gen. 26:13, וַתֵּלֶךְ הָלוֹךְ וְקָשָׁה Judg. 4:24; the finite verb is omitted in מָרְדֳּכַי הֹלֵךְ וְגָדוֹל Est. 9:4, the substantive verb takes its place, הָיָה הָלוֹךְ וְחָסוֹר Gen. 8:5, וַיֵּלֶךְ יְהוֹשָׁפָט הָלוֹךְ וְגָדֵל 2 Chron. 17:12. The second verb may also be put in one of the finite tenses, הֹלְכִים הָלוֹךְ וְתָקְעוּ Josh. 6:13, הֹלֵךְ הָלוֹךְ וַיִּקְלֵל... 2 Sam. 16:13, and in fact other constructions, begun with a participle or infinitive, are not infrequently continued in the preterite or future, Job 12:21.

Interrogative Sentences.

§ 283. 1. A direct question is indicated by the interrogative particle הֲ, הֲתֵלְכִי *wilt thou go?* Gen. 24:58, הֲתַחַת אֱלֹהִים אָנִי *am I in the place of God?* Gen. 50:19; an indirect question by הֲ or אִם *if, to know* הֲיִשְׁכֶם אֹהֲבִים *whether you love* Deut. 13:4, *inquire* אִם־אֶחְיֶה *whether I shall recover* prop. *if I shall* 2 Kin. 1:2.

a. The particle הֲ is in Job 4:2 separated from the proper interrogative clause.

2. In a disjunctive question the first member is commonly introduced by הֲ and the second by אִם or וְאִם, הַכְּתֹנֶת בִּנְךָ הִוא אִם־לֹא *is this thy son's coat or not?* Gen. 37:32; הַחֵפֶץ *is it any pleasure to the Almighty that thou art righteous* וְאִם־בֶּצַע *or is it gain to him,* etc., Job 22:3.

a. The second member is more rarely introduced by אוֹ *or, who knoweth* הֶחָכָם יִהְיֶה אוֹ סָכָל *whether he shall be a wise man or a fool* Eccl. 2:19, or by הֲ repeated הֶחָזָק הוּא הֲרָפֶה *whether they be strong or weak* Num. 13:18, הַלְהוֹרִישֵׁנוּ קְרָאתֶם לָנוּ הֲלֹא *have ye called us to impoverish us or not?* Judg. 14:15. The construction of the second clause is interrupted and resumed again in Gen. 17:17.

b. If a question stand in a disjunctive relation to something previously expressed or implied, it may begin with אִם, הַפְכְּכֶם אִם־כְּחֹמֶר הַיֹּצֵר *your perversion! or is the potter to be reckoned as the clay?* Isa. 29:16, אִם מֵאֵת אֲדֹנִי *or is this thing from my lord?* 1 Kin. 1:27.

§ 284. A question may also be asked by means of the interrogative pronouns or interrogative adverbs. Or it may, without any particle of interrogation, be indicated simply by the tone of voice in which it is uttered, שָׁלֹם בֹּאֶךָ *thy coming is peaceful?* 1 Sam. 16:4.

Relative Pronoun.

§ 285. 1. From simple we pass to compound sentences. These are made up of distinct clauses united for the most part by the relative pronoun or by conjunctions. As the relative invariably occupies the first place in its own clause, and as the Hebrew admits of no inflections to represent case, some special device was necessary to indicate its relation to the following words. Accordingly, when the relative אֲשֶׁר is governed by a verb, noun, or preposition, this is shown by appending an appropriate pronominal suffix to the governing word, אֲשֶׁר שְׁלָחוֹ *whom he has sent* 2 Kin. 19:4; *the ground* אֲשֶׁר אֲרָרָהּ *which he has cursed* Gen. 5:29; אֲשֶׁר זַרְעוֹ *whose seed* Gen. 1:11; *houses of clay* אֲשֶׁר בֶּעָפָר יְסוֹדָם *whose foundation is in the dust* Job 4:19; *the place* אֲשֶׁר ... עָלָיו *upon which* Ex. 3:5; *thou* אֲשֶׁר בְּחַרְתִּיךָ *whom I have chosen* Isa. 41:8.

a. When the relative is the object of a verb the suffix is frequently omitted, the sense being sufficiently plain without it, אֲשֶׁר־בָּרָאתִי *whom I have created* Gen. 6:7.

2. When the relative אֲשֶׁר is preceded by אֶת the sign of the definite object, or by a preposition, these pertain not to the relative but to its antecedent, which is in this case embraced with it as in the English compound relative *what* = *that which*, וַיְצַו אֶת־אֲשֶׁר עַל־בֵּיתוֹ *and he commanded him who was over his house* Gen. 44:1; *to make thee understand* אֵת אֲשֶׁר־יִקְרֶה *what shall befall* Dan. 10:14.

a. The only exception is עִם אֲשֶׁר *with whom* Gen. 31:32. Gesenius finds another in בַּאֲשֶׁר Isa. 47:12, but see Alexander *in loc.*

3. The relative is frequently omitted, not only as in English, when it is the object of its clause, בְּשַׁחַת עָשׂוּ *into the pit* (which) *they have made* Ps. 9:16, but also when it is the subject, *and he forsook God* עָשָׂהוּ (who) *made him* Deut. 32:15, and even when it would stand for the compound

relative and include its antecedent, בְּיַד־תִּשְׁלָח *by the hand of* (him whom) *thou wilt send* Ex. 4:13, (so doth) שְׁאוֹל חָטָאוּ *the grave* (those who) *have sinned* Job 24:19.

§ 286. The demonstrative זֶה or זוּ is frequently used in poetry with the force of a relative, and it then, like the English *that*, suffers no change for gender or number, מָקוֹם זֶה יָסַדְתָּ *the place that thou hast founded* Ps. 104:8, מְזִמּוֹת זוּ חָשָׁבוּ *devices, which they have contrived* Ps. 10:2.

CONJUNCTIONS.

§ 287. The Hebrew sedulously avoids all involution of sentences. Consequently, instead of linking its clauses together into a complex whole by conjunctions of various power expressing their precise relation of dependence and subordination, it prefers, where this is possible, to connect them by means of the simple conjunction וְ *and*, leaving the exact nature of the connection intended to be inferred from the meanings of the clauses themselves.

1. The conjunction וְ may accordingly be employed not only where we would use *and*, but before an adversative clause, *of every tree thou mayest eat* וּמֵעֵץ *but of the tree of the knowledge*, etc., Gen. 2:16, 17, or one expressing a reason, *give us help from trouble* וְשָׁוְא *for vain is the help of man* Ps. 60:13, an inference, *I have no pleasure in the death of him that dieth* וְהָשִׁיבוּ *wherefore turn* Ezek. 18:32, design, זֹאת עֲשׂוּ וִחְיוּ *do this and live* i. e. in order that you may live, Gen. 42:18, a comparison, *man is born unto trouble* וּבְנֵי רֶשֶׁף *and* (i. e. as) *the sparks fly upward* Job 5:7, or a co-existing act or condition, *Noah was six hundred years old* וְהַמַּבּוּל *and* (i. e. when) *the flood was upon the earth* Gen. 7:6.

2. It serves to introduce the apodosis or second member

of a conditional sentence, *if God will be with me and keep me* וְהָיָה יְהֹוָה *then shall Jehovah be my God* Gen. 28:20, 21.

3. It may also connect a statement of time or a noun placed absolutely, with the clause to which it relates, בַּיּוֹם הַשְּׁלִישִׁי וַיִּשָּׂא אַבְרָהָם אֶת־עֵינָיו *on the third day Abraham lifted up his eyes* Gen. 22:4; תִּקְוָתְךָ וְתֹם דְּרָכֶיךָ *thy hope*, (is it not) *the integrity of thy ways?* Job 4:6. Both these uses, which are wholly foreign from our idiom, are combined in 2 Sam. 15:34, *thy father's servant* וַאֲנִי *I have been so hitherto, but now* וַאֲנִי *I will be thy servant.*

a. For the meanings and usage of other conjunctions see the lexicon.

GRAMMATICAL ANALYSIS.

GENESIS, CHAPTER I.

VERSE 1.

בְּרֵאשִׁית composed of the inseparable preposition בְּ, §231. 1, with Daghesh-lene, §21. 1, and the feminine derivative noun רֵאשִׁית, §198. a. (4), without the article, §248, comp. ἐν ἀρχῇ John 1:1, Ger. *anfangs*, Eng. *at first;* position of the accent, §32. 1.

בָּרָא, לֹא verb, §162. 2, the preterite denoting past time absolutely, §262. 1, lack of formal agreement with its subject, §275. 3, order of words, §270. a, position of accent, §32. 2.

אֱלֹהִים a monosyllabic noun of class I., §183, plural, §199, of majesty, §201. 2, without the article, §246. 1.

אֵת sign of the definite object, §270.

הַשָּׁמַיִם the article, §229. 1, §245. 4, and noun of the second form of class I., §185. 2. d, only used in the plural, §201. 1, §203. 5. c.

וְאֵת the conjunction וְ, §234, and אֵת.

הָאָרֶץ׃ the article, §229. 3, and Segholate noun of class I., §183; Seghol changed to Kamets by, §229. 4. b, or §65 (1).

This verse is divided by the accents into two clauses, §36. 1; Athnahh is preceded by Munahh and Tiphhha, §38. 2; Silluk by Merka and Tiphhha, and Tiphhha again by Merka, §38. 1.

VERSE 2.

הָיְתָה, לֹה verb הָיָה, §169.1, with Methegh, §45.2, Kamets distinguished from Kamets-Hhatuph, §19.2.

בֹּהוּ, תֹּהוּ Segholate nouns of class I. from לֹה roots, §184. *b*, abstracts used instead of adjectives, §254.6. *a*, assonance or paronomasia. Double accent, §30.1.

עַל־פְּנֵי Makkeph, §43, פָּנֶה noun of class I., form 2, §185. 2. *d*, only used in the plural, §201.1, §209.1; here in the construct state, §214.2, §216.1, with its possessive sense, §254.1.

תְהוֹם noun of class III from ע root §190. *b*, article omitted as if from a proper noun, §246.1, or by a kind of poetic brevity, §247, *the face of ocean.*

מְרַחֶפֶת Piel participle of the Ayin Guttural verb רָחַף, §116.4, §121.1, feminine, §205, as the predicate without the article, §259.2, although its subject is definite, §246.3; the participle expresses continuous action, §266.1, belonging to the period before spoken of, §266.3.

הַמָּיִם׃ noun used only in the plural, §201.1, §203.5. *c;* vowel changed by the pause accent, §65.1.

This verse consists of two clauses, §36.1; the clause of Athnahh is subdivided by Zakeph Katon and R'bhia, §36.2; Zakeph Katon is preceded by Pashta, and Pashta by Merka, §38.4, Athnahh by Munahh and Tiphhha, §38.2. The clause of Silluk is subdivided by Zakeph Katon; this is preceded by Munahh, §38.4, and Silluk by Merka and Tiphhha, §38.1.

VERSE 3.

וַיֹּאמֶר Kal future of Pe Aleph verb אָמַר, §110.3, with Vav Conversive, §99.1, §265, which removes the accent to the penult and changes the vowel of the ultimate, §99.3. *a*, §111.2. *a.*

GENESIS, CHAPTER I.

יְהִי apocopated future of לה verb הָיָה, § 171. 1, § 177. 1, with a jussive sense, § 264.

וַיְהִי־ future with Vav Conversive; Daghesh-forte omitted, § 99. 3, Methegh, § 45. 2.

VERSE 4.

וַיַּרְא Kal future of לה verb רָאָה with Vav Conversive, § 171. 1, § 172. 4.

טוֹב the predicate adjective without the article, § 259. 2.

וַיַּבְדֵּל Hiphil future of בָּדַל with Vav Conversive, § 99. 3.

וּבֵין Vav Conjunctive, § 234, with the preposition בֵּין, § 237. 1.

VERSE 5.

וַיִּקְרָא from the לא verb קָרָא, § 162. 2.

אֱלֹהִים ׀ P'sik, § 38. 1. a.

לָאוֹר preposition ל with the vowel of the article, § 231. 5.

יוֹם noun, whose plural is יָמִים, § 207. 1. f.

קָרָא the preterite, used rather than the future with Vav Conversive, because the verb does not begin the clause, § 265, the accent removed to the penult, § 35. 1.

לַיְלָה paragogic ה ׇ, § 61. 6, § 219. 2, with the noun לַיִל, a Segholate of class I. from an עי root, § 184. b, having a pause accent, § 65. 1.

אֶחָד׃ numeral, § 223. 1, agreement and position, § 250. 1.

VERSE 6.

רָקִיעַ noun of class I. form 2, § 185. 1.

בְּתוֹךְ preposition ב, § 231. 1, with the construct of תָּוֶךְ, § 216. 1. d, in a partitive sense, § 254. 2.

מַבְדִּיל Hiphil participle of בָּדַל, § 84. 5, denoting continuous action, § 266. 1, and referred by the tense of the accompanying substantive verb to the future, § 266. 3. a.

VERSE 7.

וַיַּעַשׂ פ guttural and לה verb עָשָׂה with Vav Conversive, § 109. 3, § 171. 1, § 172. 4.

מִתַּחַת composed of the prepositions מִן and תַּחַת, § 237. 2 (1).

מֵעַל composed of the prepositions מִן and עַל.

VERSE 8.

שָׁמָיִם with pause accent, § 65 (1).

עֶרֶב, בֹּקֶר class I. Segholates, § 183.

שֵׁנִי: ordinal number, § 227. 1, agreement with noun and position, § 252. 1.

VERSE 9.

יִקָּווּ Niphal future of לה verb קָוָה, § 169. 1, with an imperative sense, § 263. 1.

מָקוֹם noun of class III. from an ע״ו root, § 190. b.

תֵּרָאֶה Niphal future of רָאָה, § 109. 4, § 168.

VERSE 10.

וּלְמִקְוֵה conjunction ו, § 234, preposition ל, § 231. 1, and noun of class III. from לה root, § 190. b, in the construct state, § 215. 2, followed by the material of which it consists, § 254. 4.

יַמִּים plural, § 207. 2, of יָם, a noun of class I. from an ע״ע root, § 186. 2. c.

VERSE 11.

תַּדְשֵׁא apocopated Hiphil future of דָּשָׁא, §97. 2, §264, governing its cognate noun דֶּשֶׁא, §271. 3. Methegh by §45. 2.

מַזְרִיעַ the participle expresses what is constant and habitual, §266. 1.

עֵץ collective noun, §201. 1, probably abridged from a ל"ה root, class I. form 2, §185. 2. *d*, in the construct, §215. 1, with the following word, which denotes its quality, §254. 6.

פְּרִי noun from ל"ה root class I. form 1, §184. *b*.

עֹשֶׂה Kal participle of ל"ה verb, §168; the accent is not Y'thibh but Mahpakh, as is shown by its standing before Pashta in the subdivision of Zakeph Katon, §30. 2, §38. 4, shifted to the penult by, §35. 1, followed by Daghesh-forte conjunctive in the first letter of the next word, §24. *a*.

לְמִינוֹ preposition ל, §231. 1, noun מִין from an ע"י root class I, §186. 2. *b*, and pronominal suffix, §220. 1.

אֲשֶׁר זַרְעוֹ־בוֹ oblique case of the relative pronoun, §74, §285. 1; the preposition בּ with a pronominal suffix, §233.

VERSE 12.

וַתּוֹצֵא Hiphil future of י"פ and ל"א verb, §144. 1, §162, with Vav Conversive, the accent remaining on the ultimate, §147. 5, §166. 4.

לְמִינֵהוּ suffix of third person, §220. 1. *b*, singular in distributive sense referring to the preceding collective, §275. 6.

VERSE 13.

שְׁלִישִׁי׃ ordinal number, §227. 1, §252. 1.

VERSE 14.

יְהִי lack of agreement with subject, §275.1.

מְאֹרֹת masculine noun in the plural, §200.c, class III. from an עו root, §190.b.

לְהַבְדִּיל the construct form of the infinitive used with prepositions, §267.b.

וְהָיוּ preterite with Vav Conversive, §100.1, §265, in the plural because following the noun, §275.1.b.

VERSE 15.

לְהָאִיר Hiphil infinitive construct of עו verb, §153.1.

VERSE 16.

שְׁנֵי cardinal number, §223.1, joined with noun, §250.2 (2), without the article, §251.4.

הַגְּדֹלִים qualifying adjective with the article after the noun, §249.1.

הַגָּדֹל ... הַקָּטֹן class I. form 2, §185.1, emphatic use of the positive degree, §260.2 (2).

מֶמְשֶׁלֶת noun of class III., §190, in the construct state, §214.1.b, the following noun denoting the object, §254.9.

הַכּוֹכָבִים: noun of class II. from an עע root, §187.1.e.

VERSE 17.

וַיִּתֵּן from פנ verb נָתַן, §129.1.

אֹתָם sign of the definite object with a pronominal suffix, §238.2.

VERSE 18.

וְלִמְשֹׁל ... וּלְהַבְדִּיל construct infinitive with the preposition, §267.b; Methegh with וּ, §45.2.a.

GENESIS CHAPTER I.

VERSE 20.

יְעוֹפֵף Piel future of עוּף verb, §154. 2.

VERSE 21.

הַתַּנִּינִם plural of תַּנִּין, §199; the Hhirik of the ultimate is long, §19. 1.

הָרֹמֶשֶׂת Kal feminine participle, §205, with the article, §249. 1.

אֲשֶׁר the object of the verb שָׁרְצוּ though without the appropriate pronominal suffix, §285. 1. a.

לְמִינֵהֶם plural noun with plural suffix, §220. 2. b.

VERSE 22.

וַיְבָרֶךְ Piel future of ע Guttural verb, §116. 4, §121. 1, with Vav conversive, §99. 3. a, no Daghesh-lene in ב since the preceding Sh'va is vocal, §25.

לֵאמֹר the preposition with Tsere, §231. 3. a, so as to say i. e. *in saying.*

פְּרוּ, רְבוּ Kal imperatives of פָּרָה, רָבָה, §169. 1.

יִרֶב Kal apocopated future, §171. 1, Hhirik short though accented, §19. 1.

VERSE 24.

וְחַיְתוֹ- construct of חַיָּה, §214. 1, with ו paragogic, §218. Methegh, §45. 2, Daghesh-forte omitted, §25.

VERSE 26.

נַעֲשֶׂה Kal future of עָשָׂה, §109. 1, §168, in the plural number, §275. 3. a.

בְּצַלְמֵנוּ preposition, §231. 1, Segholate noun, class I., §183, and pronominal suffix, §221. 5.

וַיִּרְדּוּ from רָדָה, § 169. 1.

בִּדְגַת preposition, § 231. 2, construct of the collective noun דָּגָה, § 198, § 214. 1, § 216. 1; no Daghesh-lene in ג, § 22. a (5).

VERSE 27.

זָכָר וּנְקֵבָה predicates, § 273. 4, and consequently indefinite.

אֹתָם: pronoun, referring to both genders put in the masculine, § 276. 3.

VERSE 28.

וְכִבְשֻׁהָ conjunction ו, § 234, imperative Kal of כָּבַשׁ, § 84. 4, and pronominal suffix, § 101. Kibbuts is long, § 19. 1.

VERSE 29.

נָתַתִּי from נָתַן, § 130. 1, preterite in the sense of the present, § 262. 1. b.

יִהְיֶה singular, referring formally to the nearest collective subject, § 276. 1, or taken distributively, § 275. 6.

VERSE 30.

אֶת, אֶת־כָּל־יֶרֶק before כָּל without the article, § 270. c.

VERSE 31.

מְאֹד position of adverb, § 274. 1.

יוֹם הַשִּׁשִּׁי: article omitted before the noun, § 249. 1. c.

INDEX I.

SUBJECTS TREATED FULLY OR INCIDENTALLY.

The numbers in this and the following Indexes refer to the Sections of the Grammar.

Abbreviations 9. 1.
Absolute infinitive. *See* Infinitive absolute.
Abstract nouns, feminine 198, plural 201. 1. *a, c.*
Accents 28, use in cantillation 28. *b,* forms and classes 29, meaning of names 29. *b,* like forms distinguished 30, position of 32–35, aid in distinguishing words 34, change of position 35, effect of Vav conversive 33. 4, 99. 3, 100. 2, in place of Methegh 39. 3. *b,* 45. 5, give stability to vowels 60. 1. *a,* vowel changes produced by 64.
Accents, consecution of in prose 36–39, poetic 31, consecution of 40–42.
Accents pause 37. 2. *a,* position of 35. 2.
Accentuation double 39. 4. *a,* 42. *a.*
Addition of letters 50. 3.
Adjectives in place of participles of neuter verbs 90, 185. 1. *a,* formation of 185. 2, expressing permanent or variable qualities 185. 2. *a,* intensity 187. 1, 189, defects 187. 1. *b,* diminutives of color 188, declension of 217, qualifying nouns 249. 1, qualifying nouns in the construct 256, predicate 259. 2, comparison of 260, emphatic use with verbs 282. *c.*
Adjectives numeral 223–227, 250–252.
Adverbial idea expressed by a verb 269. *a.*
Adverbial expressions 274.
Adverbs 235, with suffixes 236, as the subject 242. *c,* numeral 252. 4, position of 274.
Affixes 33.
Agreement neglected 275–279.
Aleph, sound of 3. 4, used as a vowel-letter 11. 1, in a few verbal forms 120. 2, 122. 2, 156. 3, once in 3 f. s. suffix 220. 2. *b,* otiant 16. 1, with Mappik 26, with Daghesh forte (?) 121. 1, substituted for He in Chaldee 51. 3, in Niphal infinitive 91. *b,* in Hiphil 94. *a, b,* in Hithpael 96. *a,* in feminine ending of verbs 86. *b,* and nouns 196. *d,* for Vav in fem. plur. of nouns 199, prosthesis of 53. 1. *a,* 183. *c,* omitted 53. 2, 3, 57. 2 (2) *a,* 111. 2. *b, c,* 151. 2, 164. 2, quiescent 57. 2, after prefixed prepositions 231. 3. *a, b,* after Vav Conjunctive 234. *c,* prefers diphthongal vowels 60. 1. *a,* 110. 3, 111. 2, previous vowel rarely short if Daghesh forte omitted 60. 4. *a,* 121. 1, 229. 3, added to 3 pl. preterite 86 *b,* prefixed in the formation of nouns 189.
Alphabet 2, order of 6, Lepsius' theory 6. *a.*
Animals, names of 177. *c.*
Apocopated future 97. 2, 264, not in passive species 97. 2. *b,* in Ayin Guttural verbs 119. 1, Lamedh Guttural 126. 1, Ayin Vav and Ayin Yodh 153. 5, 157. 3, 158. 2, 160. 3, Lamedh He 171. 1, 172. 4, 173. 3, 174. 4, 175. 3, 176. 3.
Apocopated imperative 98. 2, 171. 1.
Apposition of nouns 253.
Arabic letters 3. 1. *a,* currently read without vowels 10. *a,* syllables 18. 2. *c,* Teshdid 23. 3. *b,* accent 33. 4. *a,* Elif prosthetic 53. 1. *a,* conjugations 83. *c* (1), comparative or superlative 189. *a,* nouns of unity 198. *b,* plural ending 199. *c,* dual 202, article 229. 1. *a,* conjunction with the accusative 271. 4. *b.*
Article definite 229, use of 245, with verbs, etc. 245. 5. *b,* with proper nouns 246. 1. *a,* before nouns with suffixes 246. 2. *a,* before nouns in the construct 246. 3. *a,* when omitted 247, 249. 1. *b, c,* 249. 2. *b, c.*
Article indefinite 229. 1. *b,* 248. *a.*
Aspirates 3. 1, 7. 2, receive Daghesh lene 21, their original sound 21. *b,* affected

by concurrence of consonants or doubling 54. 1.
Athnahh divides verse 36. 1, train of 38. 2.
Augment, Greek and Sanskrit 99. 1. *a*.
Ayin, sound of 3. 4, Chaldee substitutes for Tsadhe 51. 3, elided 53. 3. *a*, 128, previous vowel sometimes short when Daghesh omitted 60. 4. *a*.
Ayin doubled verbs, origin of term 76. 3, their peculiarities 133–137, paradigm 138, remarks 139–142.
Ayin Guttural verbs 116, paradigm 117, remarks 118–122.
Ayin Vav and Ayin Yodh verbs, origin of term 76. 3, their peculiarities 152–154, paradigm 155, remarks 156–161.
Biliteral roots 68. *b*.
Bohemian accent 33. 4. *a*.
Cardinal numbers 223–266, with dual ending 223. 1. *a*, position and agreement 250, 251, with suffixes 250. 2 (2) *a*, 251. 4. *a*, with the article 251. 4.
Chaldee syllables 18. 2. *c*, words modified from Hebrew 51. 3, dual 202.
Changes of person 279.
Cities names of, feminine 197. *d*.
Collectives with feminine ending 198, construed with the plural 275. 2.
Commutation of letters 50. 1, Aleph for He 86. *b*, 91. *b*, 94. *a*, 96. *a*, 196. *d*, He for Aleph 189. *b*, Aleph for Yodh 56. 4, or Vav 56. 4. *a*, 199, Vav for Aleph 57. 2 (2) *a*, 111. 2. *b*, *d*, Yodh for Vav 56. 2, Teth for Tav 54. 4, 82. 5.
Comparison, how expressed 260.
Compound numbers 224, 225. 2, with nouns 251. 3, with the article 251. 4. *a*.
Compound predicate 275. 1. *b*, 275. 2. *a*.
Compound sentences 285. 1.
Compound species 83. *c* (2).
Compound subject 244. 1, 276.
Conjugations 76. 1.
Conjunctions 239, 287.
Consecution of accents in prose 36–39, in poetry, 40–42.
Consonant changes, 53–56.
Consonants changed to vowels 57, vowel changes occasioned by contiguous consonants 60, by concurrent consonants, 61.
Construct infinitive. *See* Infinitive construct.
Construct state of nouns 212–216, relations denoted by 254, resolved by preposition Lamedh 257.
Constructio praegnans 272. 3.
Contraction of two similar letters 61. 3, 134. 1.
Contracted verbs 107.
Copula 258. 2, 3.
Countries names of, feminine 197. *d*.
Daghesh meaning of word 21. 2. *a*.

Daghesh-forte 23, distinguished from Daghesh-lene 23. 2, from Shurek 23. 3, different kinds of 24, conjunctive, instances of 24. *a*, 75. 1, separative 24. *b*, 190. *a*, 216. 2. *a*, 221. 5. *a*, 230. 2. *a*, emphatic 24. *c*, 86. *a*, 149. 1, omission of 25, resolved by the insertion of a liquid 54. 3, 221. 6. *b*, or Yodh 141. 1, or by prolonging the previous vowel, 59. *a*, never in gutturals 60. 4, 108, rarely in Resh 23. 1, 60. 4. *a*, omitted from Hithpael 96. *a*, in suffixes of verbs 104. *a*, 105. *b*.
Daghesh lene 21, 22, omitted from Kal imperative 89 (f. s. and m. pl.), from guttural forms 109. 3. *a*, from construct plural of nouns 216. 2. *a*, after prefixes 101. 2. *b*.
Daleth assimilated to the feminine ending Tav 54. 2, 148. 2, 205. *b*.
Day of the month 252. 2. *b*.
Declension of nouns, adjectives and participles 217.
Demonstrative pronouns 73, qualifying nouns 249. 2, qualifying nouns in the construct 256, predicate 259. 2, used for relative 286.
Dental letters 7. 1.
Dialects, effect upon words 51. 3.
Diphthongal vowels 15.
Distributive numbers 252. 4.
Distributive sense expressed by repetition 252. 4, 280. 1.
Division erroneous, of words 43. *b*.
Divisions of Grammar 1.
Dual, ending of 202, signification of 203, superadded to the plural 203. 5. *b*, nouns with suffixes 221. 4, joined with the plural 278.
Emphasis expressed by repetition 280–282.
English accent 33. 4. *a*.
Excess, how denoted 260. 2 (2) *b*.
Feminine endings 196, how related 55. 2. *c*, 196. *b*, compared with Indo-European endings 196. *e*, used to form abstracts, collectives, official designations 198, and nouns of unity 198. *b*, appended to infinitive. *See* Infinitive construct.
Feminine nouns without fem. ending in the singular 197. *a*, with masc. ending in plural 200. *b*, with two plural forms 200. *c*, with suffixes 221. 2.
Feminine sign of, duplicated 88 (3 f.), 167. 3, 169. 1. *a* (?), neglected 88 (2 f. s, 3 f. pl.), 197. *a*.
Final forms of letters 4, in middle of words 4. *a*.
Flexibility various, of different languages 69. *b*.
Formative syllables differ from prefixes and suffixes 33, 69. *c*, 101. 2. *b*, 123. 4.
Fractional numbers 227. 3, 252. 3.

INDEX I. 325

Future, formation of 84. 3, its personal endings and prefixes 85. 1. *a* (2) with suffixes 105, uses of 263, shortened form. *See* Apocopated future.
Galilean pronunciation 51. 4. *a*.
Grammar, function and divisions of 1.
Grammatical subject 244. 2.
Grave suffixes 72, 221. 1.
Greek alphabet 5. *a*, 6. *b*, 7. 2. *a*, accent 33. 4. *a*, augment 99. 1. *a*, feminine and neuter 196. *c*, numerals 223. 2. *a*, construction of neuter plurals 275. 4. *a*.
Guttural letters 7. 1, their peculiarities 60, 108, attract or preserve vowels 60. 3. *c*.
Guttural verbs 107.
He and Hheth 3. 3.
He as a vowel letter 11. 1, 57. 2 (2) *b*, with Mappik 26, prosthesis of 53. 1. *a*, rejection of 53. 2, 3, 85. 2. *a* (1), 95. *b*, 211. *a*, 229. 5, 231. 5, preceding vowel often short when Daghesh omitted 60. 4. *a*, 121. 1, 229. 3, added to 2 m. s. and 2 f. pl. preterite 86. *b*, to 2 m. s. suffix 104. *b*, 220. 1. *b*, to 2 f. s. suffix 220. 2. *c*, to 2 and 3 f. pl. suffix 104. *g*, 220. 1. *b*, 220. 2. *c*, for 3. m. s. suffix 104. *d*, 220. 1. *b*, omitted from f. pl. future 88 and imperative 89, omitted after prefixes 85. 2. *a* (1), 91. *b*, 94. *b*, 95. *b*, 113. 2, 229. 5, retained in exceptional cases 95. *c*, 142. 3, 150. 2, 231. 5. *a*, for Aleph 165. 1, prefixed in the formation of nouns 189. *b*.
He directive 219. 1.
He interrogative 230.
He paragogic, effect on accent 33. 1, with Methegh 33. 1. *a*, examples of 61. 6. *a*, 219. 2, distinguished from feminine ending 196. *c*, added to preterite 93. *c*, to future. *See* Paragogic future.
Hhateph Seghol in 1 Sing. future Piel 92. *c*.
Hheth, preceding vowel mostly short, when Daghesh omitted 60. 4. *a*, 121. 1, 229. 3.
Hhirik, quantity of 14, 19. 1, between concurring consonants 61. 1, 85. 2. *a*, 216. 2, 231. 2, 234, in Segholates 61. 2, 184. *b*, never in the ultimate of Kal active participles 90, in 1 sing. Niphal future 91. *c*, 149. 2, in Piel before suffixes 104. *h*, in penult of Piel infinitive 92. *d*, in Hiphil infinitive 94. *b*, rejected from Hiphil future 94. *c*, and participle 94. *e*, in the inflected preterite of Kal, Hiphil 119. 2, and Hithpael 96. *b*, retained in Hiphil before suffixes 104. *h*, in the ultimate of nouns 207. 1. *c*, 209. 2.
Hholem, stability of 60. 1. *a* (4), in inflected verbs Ayin doubled 61. 3, 136. 2, 141. 2, and Ayin Vav and Ayin Yodh 153. 4, 159. 1, 160. 2, shortened to Kamets Hhatuph in Kal infinitive construct 87, future 88, and imperative 89, once retained in Kal future before Makkeph 88, in intensive species 92. *b*, rejected from Kal future before suffixes 105. *d*, in the ultimate of nouns 207. 1. *c*, *d*, 207. 2. *c*, 215. 1. *c*, 209. 2, in the penult 210. *d*, 216. 1. *c*.
Hiphil, signification of 79, relation to Piel 80. 2. *a* (1), formation of 82. 4, origin of prefixed He 82. 5. *b* (2), nouns derived from 187. 2. *a*, 189.
Hithpael, signification of 80, relation to Niphal 80. 2. *a* (2), formation of 82. 5, origin of prefixed syllable 82. 5. *b* (1), verbs having two forms of 122. 2. 141.
Hophal, signification of 79. 3, formation of 82. 4, origin of prefixed He 82. 5. *b* (2), no imperative 84, except in two instances 95. *d*, in Ayin doubled verbs 140. 6, in Pe Yodh verbs 150. 5, in Ayin Vav verbs 160. 5, in Lamedh Aleph verbs 167. 2, in Lamedh He verbs 175. 5.
Imperative, formation of 84. 4, its personal endings 85. 1. *a* (3), Kal with suffixes 101, 3. 106. *b*, paragogic 98. 1, 111. 3. *a*, 125. 1, 132. 1, 148. 3, 157. 2, apocopated 98. 2, 171. 2, twice in Hophal 95. *d*.
Imperfect verbs classified 107.
Impersonal subject 243. 2, construction of passive and neuter verbs 271. 4. *a*, 275. 1. *c*.
Inanimate objects, names of 198. *c*, in plural 203. 5. *a*, plural with feminine singular 275. 4.
Indefinite subject 243. 2, article 229. 1. *b*, 248. *a*
Indo-European roots 69. *a*, pronouns 71. *b*, feminine and neuter 196. *c*, dual 202. *a*, numerals 223. 2. *a*, conception of time 261.
Infinitive, a verbal noun 267, as the subject 242. *b*, 267. *a*, does not admit article 245. 5. *b*, with prepositions 242. *b*, 267. *b*, governed by verbs or nouns 267. *b*, *c*, construction changed to preterite or future 282. *c*.
Infinitive absolute, formation of 84. 1, with feminine ending 160. 4, for preterite or future 268. 1, for imperative 268. 2, emphatic use of 282.
Infinitive construct, formation of 84. 2, in Kal usually without Vav 87, with feminine ending in perfect verbs 87, in Pe Guttural 111. 3. *a*, in Ayin Guttural 119. 3, in Lamedh Guttural 125. 2, in Pe Nun 131. 4, in Ayin doubled 139. 2, in Pe Yodh 148, in Piel 92. *d*, in Hophal 150. 5, in Hiphil 128, in Lamedh Aleph verbs 166. 2, in Lamedh He 168, with suffixes 101. 3, 106. *a*, following

noun or suffix denote subject or object 102. 3, 254. 9. *b*, emphatic use of 282. *b*.
Inseparable prepositions 231–233.
Intensity expressed by repetition 280. 3, 282.
Interjections 240.
Interrogative and indefinite pronouns 75, trace of neuter in 196. *a*.
Interrogative sentences 283, 284.
Intransitive verbs construed transitively 271.
Irrational objects, plural, with feminine singular 275. 4.
Jews modern, use Rabbinical letter 2, their pronunciation of Ayin 3. 4, use abbreviations 9. 1.
Kal, meaning of term 76. 2, formation in perfect verbs 82. 1, remarks upon 86–90.
Kamets and Kamets-Hhatuph distinguished 19. 2.
Kamets in the ultimate of nouns 207. 1. *b*, 207. 2. *b*, 215. 1, in the penult 210, 216. 1.
Kamets-Hhatuph in Kal infin. constr. before Makkeph 87, before suffixes 106, in future 88, in imperative 89, 106, in passive species 82. 5. *b* (3), 93. *a*, 95. *a*.
Kaph and Koph 3. 2.
Kaph initial rejected 53. 2. *a*, assimilation of 54. 2. *a*.
Karne Phara 38. 10.
Kibbuts, quantity of 19. 1, in passive species 82. 5. *b* (3), 93. *a*, 95. *a*, in Hithpael 96. *a*.
K'ri and K'thibh 46–48, number of 46. *a*.
Kushoi 21. 2. *a*.
Labial letters 7. 1.
Lamedh initial rejected 53. 2. *a*, 132. 2, medial rejected 53. 3. *b*, 88 (1 c.), assimilated to following consonant 54. 2, 132. 2, appended in formation of nouns 193. 2. *c*.
Lamedh Aleph verbs 162, paradigm 163, remarks 164–167.
Lamedh Guttural verbs 123, paradigm 124, remarks 125–128.
Lamedh He verbs, origin of term 76. 3, their peculiarities 168, 169, paradigm 170, shortened future and imperative 171, remarks 172–177.
Latin alphabet 6. *b*, 7. 2. *a*, accent 33. 4. *a*, feminine and neuter 196. 2, numerals 223. 2. *a*.
Lazian accent 33. 4. *a*.
Letters, sounds of 3, double forms of 4, of unusual size or position 4. *a*, names of 5, order of 6, classification of 7, numerical use of 9. 2, commutation of 50. 1, transposition of 50. 2, addition of 50. 3.
Lettish accent 33. 4. *a*.
Light suffixes 72, 221. 2–4.

Linguals 7. 1, substituted for sibilants in Chaldee 51. 3.
Liquids 7. 2.
Logical subject, 244. 2.
Makkeph 43.
Manner 274. 2. *e*.
Mappik 26, omitted from 3 f. s. suffix 104. *e*, 220. 1. *b*.
Masculine for feminine, suffixes 104 *g*, 220. 1. *b*, future 88 (3 f. pl.), 105. *e*, predicate and pronouns 275. 1. *a*, 275. 5.
Masculine nouns with suffixes 221. 3, with fem. ending in plural 200. *a*, with two endings in plural 200. *c*.
Matres lectionis 11. 1.
Measure 274. 2. *c*.
Medial letters for finals 4. *a*.
Medium strength, letters of 7. 2.
Mem dropped from Pual participle 53. 2. *a*, 93. *e*, final rejected 55. 2, 214. 2, appended to 3 m. pl. future (?) 88, prefixed in formation of nouns 193. 2. *c*, omitted from plural ending (?) 199. *b*.
Methegh 44, 45, aid in distinguishing doubtful vowels 19, 45. 2. *a*, with He paragogic 33. 1. *a*, in place of an accent shifted in position 35. 1, or removed by Makkeph 43, 44. *a*, 64. 1. *a*, after He interrogative 230. 2. *a*, its place supplied by an accent 39. 3. *b*, 45. 5.
Modern Hebrew read without vowel points 10. *a*.
Monosyllabic nouns 183.
Mountains, names of, masculine 197. *d*.
Multiliteral nouns 195.
Mutes 7. 2, a p-mute missing (?) 7. 2. *a*.
Names of letters 5, their antiquity 5. *a*, their origin and signification 5. *b*.
Nations, names of 197. *d*, 275. 2. *b*.
Neuter gender, trace of 196. *a*.
Neuter verbs rarely have participles 90, with suffixes 102. 2.
Niphal, signification of 77, relation to Hithpael 80. 2. *a* (2), its formation 82. 2, origin of the prefixed Nun 82. 5. *b* (1), participle from a noun 91. *e*, from an adverb 80. 2. *b*, nouns derived from 187. 2. *a*.
Nouns, formation of 181, Class I 182–186, Class II 187, 188, Class III 189–192, Class IV 193, 194, multiliterals 195, from imperfect roots 184. *b*, 185. 2. *d*, 186. 2. *c*, 187. 1. *d*, *e*, 187. 2. *b*, *c*, 190. *b*, plural from quiescent roots 207. 1. *f*, 208. 3. *c*, with suffixes 221. 5. *a*.
Nouns, gender and number of 196–211, construct state of 212–216, declension of 217, with suffixes 220, 221, paradigm 222.
Nouns, feminine, without fem. ending 197. *a*, with masc. ending in plural 200. *b*, masculine with fem. ending in plural

200. *a*, with either ending 200. *c*, of doubtful gender 197. *b*, 200. *c*, having but one number 201. 1, definite without the article 246, used for adjectives 254. 6. *a*, in construct before adjectives 250. 1. *a*, 254. 6. *b*, in construct before prepositions 255. 1, in construct before a clause 255. 2, placed absolutely 271. 4. *b*, 274. 2, repetition of 280.
Nouns, primitive 181. *a*, derivative 181. *b*, of unity 198 *b*.
Number, relations of 274. 2. *d*.
Numeral adjectives 223-227, 250-252, adverbs 252. 4.
Numerical use of letters 9. 2.
Nun, rejected 53. 2. *a*, *b*, 55. 2, from verbs 129. 2, 131. 3, 4, from nouns 184. *b*, 194. 2. *b*, assimilated to a following consonant 54. 2, in verbs 129. 1, 131. 2, 132. 1, in nouns 184. *b*, 190. *a*, 205. *b*, to initial Mem (?) 55. 1, 88 (m. pl.), inserted in lieu of reduplication 54. 3, 221. 6. *b*, epenthetic 56. 1, 101. 2, 105. *b*, added to 3 pl. preterite 86. *b*, to future 88 (2 f. s., m. pl.), before suffixes 105. *c*, in Niphal absolute infinitive 91. *b*, 131. 5, 166. 3, 173, 2, in Niphal imperative (?) 91. *d*, appended in formation of nouns 193, in masc. plur. ending 199. *a*.
Object, definite, sign of 238. 2, 270, of transitive verbs 270, of intransitive verbs 271, indirect 272, multiple 273.
Occupations 186. 2. *a*, 187. 1. *a*.
Office, names of 198. *a* (2).
Official designations 198.
Ordinal numbers 227, 252.
Orthographic symbols 1-49, changes 50-66.
Orthography, various 11. 1. *b*, 51. 4. *a*.
Palatal letters 7. 1.
Paradigm, see Verbs paradigms of, and Nouns.
Paragogic, future 97. 1, 264, not in passive species 97. 2. *b*, in Lamedh He verbs 172. 3, imperative 98, 1.
Paragogic letters, effect on accent 33. 1, instances of 61. 6. *a*, 218, 219.
Participles, formation of 84. 5, of neuter verbs 90, with personal inflections 90, declined 217, qualifying nouns 249. 1, qualifying nouns in the construct 256, in the construct before nouns and infinitives 254. 9. *b*, signification of 266, emphatic use of 282. *c*, construction changed to preterite or future 282. *c*.
Particles prefixed 228-234, separate 235-240.
Parts of speech 70.
Passive species with suffixes 102. 2, of doubly transitive verbs 273. 5.
Pattahh preferred by gutturals 60. 1, 108, changed to Seghol 63. 1, assimilated to Seghol 61. 1. *b*, 63. 2, to Kamets or Tsere 63. 2, in Segholates 61. 2, with pause accents 65, in Kal constr. infin. 87, in f. pl. future Niphal 91. *c*, and Piel 92. *e*, in preterite and imperative Piel 92. *c*, in Hithpael 96. *b*, in the ultimate of nouns 207. 2. *a*.
Pattahh furtive 17, 60. 2, 109. 2, 114 (?), 123.
Pausal forms with inferior accents 65. *b*.
Pause accents 37. 2. *a*, position of 35. 2, occasion vowel changes 65, with the preterite 86. *a*, with the future 88, with the imperative 89 (f. s. and m. pl.), with 2 m. s. suffix 104. *b*, 220. 1. *b*, with Pe Guttural verbs 119, 121. 3, with Lamedh Guttural 126. 1.
Pazer, clause divided by 36. 2, train of 38. 7.
Pe Aleph verbs 110. 3.
Pe Guttural verbs, origin of term, 76. 3, their peculiarities 108, 109, paradigm 110, remarks 111-115.
Pe Nun verbs, origin of term 76. 3, their peculiarities 129, paradigm 130, remarks 131, 132.
Perfect verbs 81-85, paradigm of 85. 2, remarks 86-96, with suffixes 101, 102, paradigm 103, remarks 104-106.
Periods of human life 201. 1. *b*.
Persian construct state 61. 6. *a*.
Personal endings and prefixes of verbs 85. 1. *a*, before suffixes 101. 1, more closely attached than suffixes or prefixed prepositions 101. 2. *b*.
Personal pronouns 71, not expressed in the subject 243. 1.
Pe Yodh verbs, origin of term 76. 3, peculiarities 143-145, paradigm 146, remarks 147-151.
Piel, signification of 78, relation to Hiphil 80. 2. *a* (1), formation of 82. 3, with the active vowels 82. 5. *b* (3), unusual forms of 92. *a*, *b*, verbs with two forms of 122. 2, 141. 4, nouns derived from 187. 2. *a*.
Pilel, Pilpel, Poel not distinct species from Piel 83. *c* (1).
Place where 274. 2. *b*.
Plural endings 199.
Plural for singular in verbs (?) 88 (3 f. pl.), of majesty 201. 2, 275. 3.
Pluralis inhumanus 275. 4. *a*.
Plurality expressed by repetition 280. 2.
Points extraordinary 4. *a*.
Points Masoretic 10, accuracy of 49.
Polish accent 33. 4. *a*.
Predicate 258, compound 275. 1. *b*, 275. 2. *a*, agreement with nouns in the construct relation 277.
Prefixed particles 228-234, two constituting a word 228. 2. *a*.

Prepositions inseparable 231–233, separate 237, with suffixes 238.
Preterite, personal endings of 85. 1. *a* (1), with suffixes 101. 1, 104, Kal before suffixes 101. 3, uses of 262.
Pretonic vowels 64. 2, in Kal preterite 82. 1, not rejected from Niphal 91. *b*, 106. *a*.
Primary preferred to a secondary form 275. 1.
Pronominal roots 68, the basis of adverbs, prepositions and conjunctions 235. 1. *a*.
Pronominal suffixes 72. *See* Suffixes.
Pronouns, personal 71, 243. 1, repetition of 281, demonstrative 73, 249. 2, 256, 259. 2, relative 74, 285, interrogative and indefinite 75, 196. *a*, 284.
Proper nouns with the article 246. 1. *a*, in loose apposition 253. 2. *b*.
Pual, signification of 78. 3, formation of 82. 3, with the passive vowels 82. 5. *b* (3), no imperative 84, in perfect verbs 93, Ayin Guttural verbs 121. 1, Ayin doubled verbs 142. 1, Ayin Vav verbs 161. 4, Lamedh Aleph verbs 167. 1, Lamedh He verbs 174. 6.
Pure vowels 15.
Quadriliteral roots 68. *a*, verbs 180, nouns 195. 1, Segholates plural of 208. 3. *a*.
Question, direct and indirect 283. 1, disjunctive 283. 2.
Quiescent letters 11. 1, their two uses distinguished 13, softened to vowels 57. 2.
Quiescent verbs 107, 143.
Quinqueliteral roots 68. *a*, nouns 195. 2.
Radical letters 7. 3.
Raphe 27.
R'bhi*a*, clause divided by 36. 2, train of 38. 6.
Reduplication of second radical in verbs 82. 3, in nouns 187, of third radical in verbs 92. *a*, 115, 122. 1, 154. 2, 161. 3, 174. 1, 176. 1, in nouns 187. 1. *d*, 187. 2. *c*, of two radicals in verbs 92. *a*, 115, 122. 1, 137, 141. 2, 154. 3, 161. 2, in nouns 187. 1. *c*, 187. 2. *b*, 188, of a short word 132. 1, 233. *a*.
Relative pronoun 74, 285.
Repetition of nouns 280, pronouns 281, verbs 282.
Resh, sound of 3. 3, assimilated to a following consonant 54. 2, inserted in lieu of reduplication 54. 3, preference for Pattahh 60. 1. *a*, with Pattahh furtive (?) 60. 2. *a*, 114, with simple or compound Sh'va 60. 3. *a*, 120. 3, with Daghesh-forte 23. 1, 60. 4. *a*, previous vowel lengthened on the omission of Daghesh, 60. 4. *a*, as the first radical of verbs 114, as the second radical 118. 1, 120. 3, as the third radical 125. 3, 126. 2, 127. 2.
Rivers, names of, masculine 197. *d*.

Roots of words 67, 68.
Rukhokh 21. 2. *a*.
Samaritan Pentateuch, its negligent orthography, 51. 4. *a*, 99. 1. *a*, and variant forms 156. 2.
Samekh, Shin and Sin 3. 1, 3. 1. *a*.
Sanskrit laws of euphony 21. 2. *b*, 53. 1. *a*, accent 33. 4. *a*, augment 99. 1. *a*, feminine and neuter 196. *c*, numerals 223. 2. *a*.
Scriptio plena, defectiva 14.
Seasons, names of 185. 2. *a*.
Seghol inserted between concurring consonants 61. 2, 171. 1, in Ayin doubled verbs 61. 3, 136. 2, 141. 2, in Ayin Vav verbs 153. 4, 157. 3, 160. 3, final rejected 66. 1 (1), 171. 1, with pause accents 65, in Kal active participle 90, in Niphal 91. *a*, *b*, in Piel 92. *c*, *d*, 126. 2, before suffixes 104. *h*, in Hiphil 94. *a*, *b*, in Hithpael 96. *b*, in the ultimate of nouns 208, 209. 1, 215. 2, in the penult of feminine nouns 207. 1. *e*.
Segholate forms from triliteral monosyllables or final syllables 61. 1. *b*, 183, 184. *a*, in feminine 205, construct 214. 1. *b*.
Segholate nouns 183, signification of 184, their feminine 208. 2, plural 208. 3, dual 208. 4, construct 216. 2, with He paragogic 219. 1, with suffixes 221. 5.
Segholta, verse divided by 36. 1, train of 38. 3.
Sentence, elements of 241. 2, subject of 242, predicate of 258. 1.
Separate particles 235–240.
Septuagint, equivalents for Ayin 3. 4, mode of writing Hebrew words 49. 2, 3.
Servile letters 7. 3, anagrams of 7. 3. *a*.
Shalsheleth, when used 38. 9.
Shin, Sin, and Samekh 3. 1, 3. 1. *a*.
Shurek, quantity of 14. 19. 1, in the ultimate of Segholates 61. 2, in the penult of Segholates 61. 4. *a*, 205. *e*, in Kal future of perfect verbs 88, before suffixes 105. *d*, in Kal active participle 90, in the ultimate of nouns 207. 2. *d*, 209. 3.
Sh'va 16, silent and vocal 16. 2, 20. 1, simple and compound 16. 3.
Sh'va compound, with gutturals 16. 3, 60. 3, 108, with Resh 60. 3. *a*, 120. 3, with strong letters 16. 3. *b*, before gutturals 120. 2, 127. 3, in construct plural of nouns 216. 2. *a*, after He interrogative 230. 2. *a*, after Vav Conjunctive 234. *a*, which is selected 60. 3. *b*, 109. 3, 112, changed to a short vowel 60. 3. *c*, with pause accent to a long vowel 65.
Sh'va simple with gutturals 60. 3. *a*, in Pe Guttural verbs 112. 2, 5, in Lamedh Guttural verbs 123. 4, 127. 1, changed to Seghol by pause accent 65.
Sibilants 7. 2.

INDEX I.

Silluk, position of 36. 1, train of 38. 1.
Singular predicate or pronoun with plural subject 275. 1. *a*, 275. 6.
Sounds of the letters 3.
Species of verbs 76–80, mutually supplementary 80. 2. *a* (3), what number in use in different verbs 80. 2. *a* (4), formation of 82, with double forms in distinct senses 83. *c* (1), 122. 2, 141. 4, compound 83. *c* (2).
Strong letters 7. 2.
Subject 242, omitted 243, indefinite 243. 2, impersonal 243. 3, compound 244. 1, 276, grammatical and logical 244. 2.
Suffixes, pronominal 72, of verbs 101. 2, of nouns 220. 3, relation denoted by 254, more loosely attached than affixes 101. 2. *b*, with neuter verbs and passive species 102. 2, with infinitives and participles 102. 3, with cardinal numbers 223. 1. *a*, 250. 2 (2) *a*, omitted 247. *b*, with nouns in the construct 256.
Superlative degree 260.
Syllables 18, intermediate 20. 2, mutations in, a source of vowel changes 59.
Syriac currently read without vowels 10. *a*, aspirates 21. *a*, doubling of letters 23. 3. *b*, words modified from Hebrew 51. 3, dual 20. 2.
Systema morarum 18. *b*.
Tav and Teth 3. 2.
Tav unites with Tav of personal affixes 86. *b* (2 m.), or feminine ending 54. 1, 205. *b*, prefixed in anomalous verbal forms 94. *a*, 115, 161. 5, in the formation of nouns 190, 192. 2, in Hithpael assimilated 54. 2, 54. 4. *a*, 82. 5, 131. 6, transposed 54. 4, 82. 5.
Tav of feminine ending rejected 55. 2. *c*, 196. *b*, origin of 196. *c*, added to suffix 86. *b*, 166. 1, 169. 1, 172. 1, in nouns 196. *b*, 205.
Tenses, primary 84, 262–264, secondary 99, 265, past and future not promiscuously used 263. 5. *a*.
Time, conception of 261.
Time, when and how long 274. 2. *a*.
T'lisha Gh'dhola, clause divided by 36. 2, train of 38. 8.
Transitive construction of intransitive verbs 271.
Transposition of letters 50. 2, 54. 4, 82. 5.
Tsere rejected from the ultimate of verbs 66. 1 (1), 171. 2, in Kal preterite 86. *a*, 164. 1, in fem. plur. future Niphal 91. *e*, and Piel 92. *e*, in Piel inf. abs. 92. *d*, in Hiphil 94. *b*, *e*, in Hophal inf. abs. 95. *c*, with Aleph in place of Sh'va 60. 3. *c*, 92. *c*, 112. 1, 184. *b*, as union vowel with the preterite 104. *a*, in the ultimate of verbs before suffixes 104. *h*, of Lamedh Guttural verbs 126. 1, of Lamedh Aleph verbs 164. 5, in the ultimate of nouns 207, 215. 1, in the penult of nouns 210, 216. 1.

Vav rejected after vowelless consonants 53. 3. *a*, 184. *b*, initial changed to Yodh 56. 2, 144. 1, rarely reduplicated 56. 3, in verbs 154. 1, 161. 1, or nouns 187. 2. *c*, softened or rejected 57. 2, 152, 184. *b*, 186. 2. *c*, 190. *b*, 207. 1. *f*, 208. 3. *c*, 211. *a*, 216. 1. *d*, preceding a vowelless consonant 61. 1. *a*, 234, paragogic 61. 6. *a*, 218, omitted from 3. pl. preterite 86. *b*, in Kal infinitive 87, in Kal future 88, in Kal imperative 89, in Kal passive participle 90, in Pual 93. *b*, added to 3. m. pl. suffix 104. *f*.
Vav in K'thibh, where K'ri has Kamets-Hhatuph 13. *a*, 88, 105. *d*, 215. 1. *c*, Pattahh 125. 1, or Hhateph-Kamets 13. *a*, 214. 2. *b*, 89 (f. s.).
Vav Conjunctive 234, 287.
Vav Conversive of the future 33. 4, 99, with Ayin Guttural verbs 119. 1, Lamedh Guttural 126. 1, Ayin doubled 140. 1. 5, Pe Yodh 147. 5, 150. 3, 150. 2 (p. 182), Ayin Vav and Ayin Yodh 153. 5, 157. 3, 158. 2, 160. 3, Lamedh Aleph 166. 4, Lamedh He 171. 1, 172. 4, 173. 3, 174. 4, 175. 3, 176. 3, time denoted by 265. *a*.
Vav Conversive of the preterite 33. 4, 99, with Pe Guttural verbs 112. 3, time denoted by 265. *b*.
Verbs, their species 76–80, occurring in all the species 80. 2. *a* (4), denominatives 80. 2. *b*, perfect 81–100, with suffixes 101–106, imperfect 107–177, doubly imperfect 178, defective 179, quadriliteral 180, syntax of 261–269, coördinated 269, object of 270–272, with more than one object 273, passive, object of 273. 5, repetition of 282.
Verbs, paradigms of, perfect 85. 2, with suffixes 103, Pe Guttural 110, Ayin Guttural 117, Lamedh Guttural 124, Pe Nun 130, Ayin doubled 138, Pe Yodh 146, Ayin Vav and Ayin Yodh 155, Lamedh Aleph 163, Lamedh He 170.
Verbs, personal endings and prefixes of 85. 1. *a*, 85. 2. *a*, suffixes of 101–106.
Verbs, middle *ē* and *ō* 82. 1. *a*, have Pattahh in Kal future 84. 3. *a* (1), inflected 86. *a*, before suffixes 104. *h*.
Verbs with Pattahh in Kal future 84. 3. *a*, 111. 1, 116. 1, 123. 1, 140. 1, 144. 2, with Tsere in Kal future 84. 3. *b*, 130, 144. 2, 147, 172. 3.
Vowel changes 58–66, significant 58. 1, euphonic 58. 2, causes of 59, due to mutations of syllables 59, to contiguous gutturals 60, to concurrent consonants 61, to concurring vowels 63, to the accent 64, to pause accents 65, to the

shortening or lengthening of words 66, of short vowels in mixed penult 58. 2, 210. *c*, 216. 2. *b*.

Vowel letters 7. 2, use of 11. 1, distinguished from their consonantal use 13.

Vowels 10–17, Masoretic signs for 12, different modes of dividing them 12. *a*, meanings of their names 12. *b*, mutual relations of their notation by letters and by points 13, 14, mutable and immutable 14, 58. 2, pure and diphthongal 15, ambiguity of certain signs 19, 20, *o* and *u* more stable than *i* and *e* 60. 1. *a*, inserted between concurrent consonants 61. 1, 2, *ē* and *ō* preferred before concurrent consonants 61. 4, *ī* and *ū* before doubled letters 61. 5, paragogic 61. 6, 218, 219, concurring 62, proximity of, a source of changes 63, pretonic 64. 2, rejected or shortened 66. 1, 2, of union before suffixes 101. 2, twice *e* with preterite 104. *a*, sometimes *a* with future 105. *a*, final of verbs before suffixes 104. *k*, *l*, vowel *a* retained in ultimate before suffixes 105. *d*, 118. 3, 164. 5.

Weak letters 7. 2, effect of upon syllables 18. 2. *c*.

Words not divided in writing 8, ambiguity when unpointed 10. *a*, sources of change in 51, three stages in the formation of 67, changes in formation and inflection 69.

Written symbols of two sorts 2.

Yodh as a vowel letter 11. 1, in Kal active participle 90, in Niphal future 113. 1, before suffix 105. *a*, 220. 1. *b*, initial rejected 53. 2. *a*, *b*, 144. 3, 148, 150. 1, 184. *b*, 188. *b*, medial rejected 53. 3. *a*, *b*, 150. 3, 168, 169, softened or rejected 57. 2, 152, 184. *b*, 186. 2. *c*, 190. *b*, 207. 1. *f*, 208. 3. *c*, 211. *a*, 216. 1. *d*, changed to Aleph 56. 4, paragogic 61. 6. *a*, 218, added to 2 f. s. preterite 86. *b*, to 2 f. s. suffix 104. *c*, 220. 1. *b*, 220. 2. *c*, omitted from 1 sing. preterite 86. *b*, from Hiphil 94, in Lamedh He verbs 169, 172. 1, prefixed in formation of nouns 190, 192. 1, appended in formation of nouns 194, quiescent after prefixed prepositions 231. 3. *b*, after Vav Conjunctive 234. *c*.

Zakeph Gadhol, clause divided by 36. 2, when used 38. 5.

Zakeph Katon, clause divided by 36. 2, train of 38. 4.

INDEX II.

TEXTS OF SCRIPTURE EXPLAINED OR REFERRED TO.

GENESIS.

1: 1... § 21. 1, 36. 1, 242, 245. 4, 262. 1, 270. a, 275. 3
2... 21. 1, 258. 3
4... 270. b
5... 31. 1
6, 7... 245. 1
7... 36. 1, 203. 5. c
9... 250. 1
11... 45. 2, 254. 6, 285. 1
12... 220. 1. b
14... 275. 1. b
16... 245. 2, 254. 9
18... 45. 2. a
22... 33. 1. a
24... 198. a (4), 218
24, 26... 38. 1. a
29... 270. c
31... 249. 1. c, 274. 1
2: 1... 244. 1
2... 262. 1
3... 249. 1. c
4... 4. a, 259. 2. 267. d
5... 258. 3. b
6... 263. 4
7... 147. 5, 273. 3
9... 245. 5. b
10... 248
11... 245. 3
12... 16. 3, b, 234. a, 250. 2. a
14... 258. 2
16, 17... 287. 1
17... 106. a, 282
18... 242. b
19... 147. 5
23... 16. 3. b, 24. a, 127. 3
25... 263. 5. a
3: 2, 3... 263. 1
5... 106. a
6... 258. 1
13... 262. 1
15... 30. 2
16... 53. 3. a
22... 21. 1, 177. 2
4: 3... 231. 3. a
4... 220. 2. b
12... 267. d
13... 260. 2 (2) b
14... 245. 3, b, 262. 1. b
16... 147. 5

4: 17... § 35. 1
18... 275. 1. c
23... 88 (f. pl.), 89 (f. pl.), 98. 2, 127. 1
26... 281
5: 5... 177. 2, 251. 2. a
8... 277. a
17... 38. 1. a
18... 225. 2
29... 39. 4. a, 285. 1
6: 3... 74. a, 139. 2, 157. 3, 158. 2
7... 285. 1. a
9... 96. b
13... 262. 2
17... 266. 2
18... 100. 2. a (1)
19... 45. 2. a, 229. 3. a
22... 273. 2
7: 1... 262. 1, 273. 4
2... 252. 4, 280. 1
4... 251. 2
6... 287. 1
9... 252. 4
13... 200. e, 246. 3, 249. 2, 251. 1. a
19... 280. 3
23... 173. 3
8: 5... 282. c
7... 282
10... 269. a
12... 149. 2
17... 150. 1
18... 147. 5
9: 14... 139. 1
20... 258. 3. a
24... 147. 5, 270. c
10: 5... 220. 2. b
19... 56. 4, 126. 2
21... 256. a
25... 250. 2 (2)
26... 229. 1. a
11: 1... 223. 1. a
6, 7... 141. 1
7... 56. a
9... 57. 1
16... 251. 2
30... 56. 2
31... 22. b
12: 2... 263. 1
4... 10. a
5... 254. 1 bis
7... 262. 1. b
8... 19. 1, 220. 1. b

12: 12... § 243. 3
20... 43
13: 2... 245. 5. d
4... 4. a
6... 275. 1. a
9... 119. 1, 180. a
14: 2... 71. a (3)
4... 252. 2
6... 221. 6. b
8... 203. 5. c
9... 250. 2 (1)
10... 63. 1. a, 219. 1. b, 280. 2
19... 10. a
15: 1... 246. 3, 249. 2, 274. 1
2... 47, 253. 2. b
3... 262. 1. b
11... 229. 3
12... 245. 4
17... 275. 1. c
18... 254. 3
18–21... 270. b
22... 245. 5. a
16: 5... 4. a, 254. 9. a
11... 90 (2 f. s.)
13, 15... 43. a
30... 60. 3. b (2)
17: 4... 65. a
4, 5... 215. 1. e
5... 271. 4. a
5, 6... 205
8... 30. 2, 254. 5
11... 273. 5
12... 254. 6. a
17... 24. b, 230. 2. a, 254. 6. a, 283. 2. a
19... 90 (f. s.)
20... 205. b
18: 1... 262. 1. a, 274. 2. b
6... 253. 2
11... 276. 3
20... 254. 9. a
21... 24. b, 39. 3. b, 230. 2. a
28, 29... 251. 4
19: 1, 4... 266. 3
9... 131. 3
11... 207. 1. a, 245. 5
12... 38. 1. a
14... 24. a
19... 86. b (2m.), 105. a, 105. d
30... 251. 4

19: 33... § 240. 2. b
33, 35... 106. a
35... 38. 1. a
20: 5... 71. a (3)
6... 164. 2
9... 22. b, 75. 1, 263. 1
11... 254. 9
13... 275. 3. a
18... 127. 1
21: 6... 60. 2, a, 120. 2
8... 65. a
14... 214. 1. b
16... 119. 1, 174. 1
17... 39. 3. b
28, 29... 220, 1. b
22: 1... 262. 1, 265, 270. b
3... 265
4... 287. 3
5... 244. 1
8... 44
14... 126. 2
23: 1... 251. 2, 3
4... 275. 5
6... 165. 3
10... 254. 9. b
11... 125. 1
11, 13... 262. 1. b
16... 36. 1
19... 246. 3
24: 1... 119. 1
8... 249. 2. b
14... 39. 4
15... 39. 3. a
20... 245. 3
22... 251. 2. c, 254. 4
23... 158. 3
30... 36. 1
33... 111. 2. b
35... 245. 5. d
42... 21. 1
42, 48, 65... 39. 4
48... 131. 1
58... 263. 1
65... 73. 2. a, 176. 3, 245. 3. a
67... 246. 3. a, 256. d
25: 5... 43
8... 38. 1. a
12... 254. 1
27... 229. 4. b
31... 98. 1. a, 125. 1
34... 65. a
26: 3... 262. 1. b

332 INDEX II.

26: 4....§ 30, 2, 246. 3
    6....30. 1
    8....245. 3
    13....282. c
    15, 18....104. g
    22....156. 4
    28....36. 1
    29....60. 3, a
27: 1....88 (f. pl.)
    4....263. 1. b
    0....119. 1
    12....141. 6
    16....36. 2
    19....105. b
    23....270. b
    25....263. 1
    26....131. 3
    27....120. 3
    29....177. 1
    33....263. 1, b, 200. 2. a
    36....252. 4
    38....16. 3, b, 230. 2. a
    42....271. 4. a
    44....223. 1. a
28: 2, 5, 6, 7....33. 1. a
    9....39. 4
    12....55. 1
    20, 21....287. 2
29: 2....263. 4
    3....139. 1
    5....22. a, 230. 2. a
    6....34
    8....139. 1
    9....34, 257
    10....10. a
    17....278
    20....223. 1. a
    23....10. a
    32....105. a, 118. 3
    35....245. 3. b
30: 1....34
    5....127. 1
    6....104. a
    7....252. 1
    15....245. 3. b
    16....249. 2. b
    19....215. 1. b
    27....131. 3
    31....43
    32....44. a
    33....24. a
    36....45. 2, 88 (f. pl.) bis, 216. 2. a
    39....60. 3, b (2)
31: 4....45. 2. a
    6....71. a (2)
    9....220. 1. b
    13....10. 2. a, 246. 3. a
    27....126. 1
    30....86. b (2 m.), 91. b
    32....104. i, 285. 2. a
    36....75. 1
    39....61. 6, a
32: 1....270. c
    5....111. 2. b
    10....250. 2 (3)
    20....61. 1. c, 88 (pl.), 55. 2. a
    22....45. 3
    23....249. 2. b
33: 5....220. 1. b
    6....88 (f. pl.)
    11....43, 106. 1, 270. b
34: 17....100. 2. a (1)
    21....258. 2

34: 30....§ 254. 5
    31....230. 2
35: 7....275. 3. a
    15....270. b
    18....34
    22....39. 4. a
    26....275. 1. c
    29....22. b
37: 2....249. 1. b
    8....282
    9....271. 3
    12....257
    14....10. a
    19....73. 2. a, 254. 6. a
    20....104. i
    22....60. 3. b (2)
    32....24. b, 283. 2
    33....105. a, 282. a
38: 9....131. 4
    11....274. 2. b
    25....71. a (3)
39: 4....119. 1
    7, 12....98. 1
    11....231. 5. a
    12....22. b
    14....119. 1
    14, 17....92. d
    20....255. 2
40: 15....93. d, 150. 4
    16....251. 1
    20....150. 5
41: 8....119. 1
    11....99. 3
    12....257. 2
    19....254. 3
    21....220. 1. b
    33....35. 2
    35....249. 2
    40....260. 2 (2) a
    43....94. b
    51....92. c
42: 7....262. 2. a
    11....71. a (1)
    13....38. 1. a
    18....287. 1
    21....30. 4
    25, 35....216. 2. a
    36....220. 1. b
43: 7....45. 1
    8....125. 1
    14....65. a, 82. 1. a (3), 249. 1. b
    26....26
    29....141. 3
44: 1....285. 2
    4....114, 271. 2, 272. 2
    17....30. 2
    18....263. 1. a
    40....271. 4
45: 22....251. 2. c
    25....45. 3
    28....45, 5, a
46: 2....38. 1. a
    3....148. 2
    22, 27....275. 1. c
    28....22. b
47: 24....275. 1. c
48: 20....270. c
    22....223. 1. a
49: 3....65. a
    5....216. 1. b
    8....281
    10....24. b
    11....53. 2. a, 61. 6, a, 218, 220. 1. b, 221. 5. b
    12....215. 1. a, 259. 2. b
    17....216. 2. a

49: 19....§ 140. 1
    23....139. 1
50: 9....248
    10....271. 3
    17....273. 3. a
    19....283. 1
    23....22. a
    26....147. 5

EXODUS.

1: 1....§ 21. 1
    7....273. 5
    10....88 (3f. pl.)
    10....177. 2
2: 3....24. b, 104. e
    4....53. 3. b, 148. 2, 150. 3 (p. 182)
    7....230. 3
    9....150. 2, 151. 1, 161. 5
    10....104. k
    17....104. g, 105. a
    20....60. 3. c, 98. 2, 164. 3
    23....51. 2
3: 1....260. 3. a
    2....53. 2. a
    4....39. 1. a
    5....131. 3, 285. 1
    8....248
    13....75. 1
4: 2....24. a, 75. 1
    10....254. 6. a
    11....158. 2
    13....255, 2, 285. 3
    23....126. 1
    29....112. 3
    31....275. 2. a
5: 5....86. b (2m.)
    7....151. 2
    8....39. 1. a
    16....106. 1, 275. 2. b
6: 14....255. 3
    16....251. 3
    29....10. a
7: 10....262. 1
    11....53. 2. a
    20....276. 1
    22....53. 2. a
    26....205. b
8: 1....131. 3
    17....258. 3. b
    23....100. 2. a (1)
9: 3....10. a, 177. 1
    15....119. 1
    18....27, 104. c
    25....126. 2
    29....88 (pl.)
10: 1....249. 2. b
    3....173. 2
    8....271. 4. a
    24....150. 5
    11....249. 2. b
12: 7....45. 2
    16....256. c
    21....80 (f. s. & m. pl.)
    39....141. 6
    49....275. 1. c
13: 1....24. a
    2....92. c
    9....254. 7
    10....220. 1. b
    22....263. 4
14: 4....22. b, 91. c
    14....119. 1
    17....22. b, 91. c
15: 1....22. b, 263. 5

15: 2....§ 56. 1, 105. b, 131. 1, 247. b
    4....277. a
    5....61. 6, 104. f
    6....60. 3. a, 61. 6. a
    9....104. f
    10....11. 1. b, 61. 6, 139. 1
    11, 13....22. b
    14, 15....263. 5. a
    16....22. b, 61. 6. a
    17....24. b, 190. a
    20....277. a
    21....22. b
    26....112. 3
16: 5....38. 1. a
    7, 8....71. a (1)
    14....180. a
    15....30. 3. b
    23....38. 1. a, 112. 1
    27....242. a
17: 1....207. d
    8, 10....110. 1
    11....275. 2. b
18: 8....104. i
    10....215. 1. b
    11....262. 2
    21, 25....225. 1. a
    26....88
19: 5....44. a
    9....215. 1. a
    12....282. a
    13....149. 2, 282. a
    21, 24....111. 1
20: 2-17....39. 4. a
    4....27, 243. 2
    5....111. 3. a
    8....268. 2
    10....249. 1. c
    11....43
    13....27
21: 7....98. 1. a
    9....275. 3
    11....215. 1. c
    19....92. d
    22....19. 2. a, 39. 3. b
    28....270. c
    30....55. 1
    35....19. 2. a, 39. 3. b
    36....92. d
22: 2....216. 1. b
    3....106. 3
    4....220. 1. b
    8....43, 275. 3. a
    26....220. 1. b
23: 11....254. 2
    14....252. 4
    26....207. 1. a
    30....260. 1
    31....104. f
24: 4....246. 3
25: 31....11. 1. b, 113. 1
    35....260. 3. b
26: 2....250. 1
    23....216. 2. a
    24....53. 3. a
    33....100. 2. a (1), 100. 2. a (2), 229. 4. b
27: 21....247. a
28: 1....119. 1
    2....254. 6. a
    7....275. 1. c
    40....207. 1. a
29: 3....248. a
    9....273. 3
    20....38. 4. a
    30....105. a

INDEX II. 333

29: 35....§ 65, *a*
    37....229, 4. *b*
30: 18....109, 3
    23....215, 1. *c*
    34....38, 1. *a*
31: 13....104. *h*
    14....275. 6
32: 1....75. 1, 119. 1,
        249. 2. *a*
    4, 8....275. 3. *a*
    19....220. 2, *b*
    25....104. *d*, 156. 2
33: 3....63. 1. *b*, 174. 4
    13....220. 2, *b*
    20....105. *a*
    24....111. 3, *a*
36: 3....38. 1. *a*
    28....216. 2. *a*
38: 27....250. 2 (2)
39: 30....105. *d*
40: 3....166. 4

LEVITICUS.

2: 15....§ 71. *a* (3)
4: 13....60. 3. *a*
    23, 28....150. 5
5: 21....61. 4, *a*,
        205. *c*
    22....119. 1
    24....220. 2. *a*
6: 14....114
    15....95. *a*
7: 38....216. 1. *a*
8: 3....119. 1
9: 7....98, 1. *a*
10: 4....39, 4. *a*
    11....273, 2
    12....39, 3. *b*
    16....271. 4. *a*
    19....230. 2. *b*
11: 7....126. 1
    9....270. *c*
    18....229. 4. *b*
    32....38. 1. *a*, 254. 4
    39....71. *a* (3)
    42....4. *a*
    43....104. 2
    44....96, *b*, 242
13: 3....258. 3. *a*
    4....27, 57. 2 (2)
        b, 220. 1. *b*
    10, 21....71. *a* (3)
    51, 52....139. 3
    55, 56....96, *a*
14: 8....126. 1
    13....175. 2
    35....242. *a*
    38....274. 2. *a*
    42....156. 2
    43....92. *d*, 94. *b*
15: 24....87
    29....100. 2. *a* (2)
    32....87
16: 4....104. *h*
    8....11. 1. *a*, 183.*a*
    31....71. *a* (3)
18: 4....263. 1
    7 ff....172. 3
    28....156. 4
19: 20....175. 5, 282. *a*
20: 3....256
    7....96, *b*
21: 1....96, *a*
    4....140. 4
    5....97. 1. *a*
    9....71. *a* (3),
        140. 3
23: 3....280. 3. *a*
    13....220. 1. *b*

23: 17....§ 26
    18....216. 2. *a*
    22....106. *a*
    30....112. 3
    39....22, *a*
24: 5....100. 2. *a* (1)
    22....250. 1, *a*
    23....273. 3
25: 5....216. 2. *a*
    21....172. 1
    46....39. 3. *b*
26: 9....100. 2. *a* (1)
        bis.
    15....141. 3
    18....92. *d*
    25....132. 1
    33....92. *e*
    34....172. 1
    34, 35....65. *a*
    34, 43....140. 6
27: 7....251. 2. *a*
    8....112. 3
    23....246. 2. *a*

NUMBERS.

1: 10....§ 13. *b*
    47....96. *a*
2: 33....96, *a*
3: 26....271. 4. *b*
    40....55. 1
4: 23....22, *a*
5: 13, 14....71. *a* (3)
    22....131. 2
6: 23....120. 3
8: 7....121. 3
    24....22. *a*
9: 6....275. 1. *b*
    7....249. 2
    14....275. 1. *c*
    20....253. 2
10: 23....45, 5
    29....21. 1
    35....4. *a*
11: 4....57. 2 (2) *a*,
        229. 3. *a*
    5....263. 4
    11....164. 2
    15....71. *a* (2)
    16....111. 3, *a*
    20....196, *d*
    25....111. 2. *c*
12: 1....276. 1
    4....250. 2 (2) *a*
13: 18....283. 2. *a*
    32....156. 4
14: 1....275. 2. *a*
    2....202. 1
15: 6....252. 3
    21....39. 3, *b*
    28....27, 250. 1. *b*
    29....275. 1. *c*
16: 3....275. 2
17: 3, 4....104. *g*
    10....140. 4
    28....125. 2
20: 3....125, 2
    5....104. *l*
    8....276. 3
    14....104. *i*
    21....131. 4
21: 5....104. *l*
    30....105. *a*, 140. 5
    33, 35....44. *a*
22: 6....269. *b*
    8....274. 2. *a*
    11....19. 2, 141. 1,
        267. *b*
    25....119. 1
    29....202. 1

22: 33....§ 105. *a*
    37....141. 1
23: 7....19. 2, 119. 3,
        141. 1, 263. 5
    13....141. 3
    18....61. 6. *a*
    19....121. 3
    24....160. 5
    25....139. 1, 2
    27....104. *j*
24: 3....61. 6. *a*
    4....260
    7....19. 2. *b*, 131. 6
    9....275. 6
    11....127. 2
    15....61. 6, *a*
    17....161. 2
    21....158. 3
    22....35. 1
25: 13....24. *a*
26: 30....246. 3. *b*
    62....96. *a*
28: 4....249. 1. *b*
    6....254. 6. *b*
    8....104, *d*
    26....39. 3. *b*
29: 15....251, 1
30: 11....274. 2. *b*
31: 2....131. 3
    12....45. 5. *a*
32: 5....271. 4, *a*
    7....113. 1
    21....254. 9. *b*
    33....71. *a* (1), 246.
        1. *a*
    42....27
33: 30....111. 2, *d*
34: 5....61. 6, *a*
    6, 7, 9....24. *a*
    18....101. 1
    28....57. 2 (2) *b*
35: 4....251. 2. *a*
    19....125. 2
    20....105, *d*

DEUTERONOMY.

1: 2....§ 38. 1. *a*
    14....250, 2
    15....225. 1, *a*
    19....271. 2
    22....99. 3. *a*
    28....38. 1. *a*
    35....38. 1. *a*, 249. 1
    38....273. 1
    44....245. 5, *d*
    45....112. 3
2: 9....60. 4. *a*
    12....203. 5. *a*
    24....131. 3
    35....139. 1
3: 4....250. 2 (1)
    13....246. 1. *a*
    17....216. 2. *a*
    26....21. 1, 151. 2
4: 10....119. 1
    11....99. 3. *a*
    26....44. *b*, 91. *b*
    30....265. *b*
    33....35. 1
    41....219. 1. *b*,
        256. *c*
5: 6-21....39. 4. *a*
    8....27
    9....111. 3, *a*
    14....249. 1. *c*
    17....27
    24....71. *a* (2)
6: 4....4. *a*
    25....45. 1

7: 2....§ 119. 1
    5....126. 1
    10....92. *c*
    13....104. *h*
    15....105. *a*
    17....254. 9, *b*
    23....273. 2
    24....94. *b*, 112. 3
8: 3....86. *b* (3 pl.)
    9....207. 2. *a*
    16....55. 2. *a*, 86.
        b (3 pl.)
9: 3....112, 3
    6....38. 4. *a*, 249. 2
    14....98. 2
    25....251. 4
    26....119. 1
10: 15....119. 3
    17....30. 2
11: 12....247. *a*
    14....270. *b*
    18....249. 2. *b*
    22....87. 88 (pl.)
12: 6....270. *b*
    10....274. 2. *e*
    31....45. 5
13: 3....111. 3. *a*
    4....283. 1
    5....65. *b*
    7....276. 1
    14....254. 6. *a*
14: 5....57. 2 (3) *a*
    7....196. *c*
    17....229. 4. *b*
    22....280. 1
15: 16....119. 1
    18....126. 1
16: 1....22. *b*
    3....30, 2
    20....280. 3
17: 2, 3....265. *a*
18: 2....275. 1. *c*
19: 6....114
    15....43
20: 2....19. 2, 119. 3
    7....119. 1
21: 7....13. *b*, 86. *b*
        (3 pl.)
    8....83, *c*, (2)
    11....214. 1. *b*
22: 7....126. 1
    24....255. 2
23: 5....253. 2. *b*
    11....24. *b*
24: 3....104. *h*
    4....96, *a*
25: 4....158. 3
    7....60. 3. *a*
    13....250. 2
26: 2....39. 4
    5....254. 6. *b*
    12....94. *b*, 113. 2
27: 4....106. *a*
    7....24. *a*
28: 24....104. *b*
    45....104. *b*
    48....94. *b*
    52....126. 1
    57....164. 2
    58....249. 1
    59....165. 1, 2, 226.
        2. *a*
    66....177. 3
29: 11....106. *a*
30: 3....92. *c*
        3, 4....104. *h*
    11....166. 1, 205. *c*
    20....39. 4, 67
31: 28....22. *b*
    29....166. 1
32: 1....245. 2

32: 6....§ 228. 2. *a*
7....104. *h*, 280. 2
8....11. 1. *b*, 94. *b*
10....63. *c*, 105. *b*
13....13. *u*
15....285. 3
18....172. 4
21....111. 2. *b*
22....147. 4
26....104. *f*, 172. 3
28....215. 1. *b*
29....262. 1
32....24. *b*, 57. 2 (2) *a*
34....90 (pass.)
36....35. 1, 86. *b*
37....172. 1
37, 38....220. 2. *c*
41....141. 2
33: 16....61. 6. *a*, 88 (3 f.), 167. 3
21....177. 3

JOSHUA.

1: 1....§ 265. *a*
8....36. 2
14....256
16....263. 1
2: 8....88 (pl.)
14....249. 2. *b*
16....157. 1, 164. 2
17, 18, 20....104. *k*
18....112. 3
20....249, 2. *b*
3: 3....246. 3
9....131. 3
11....246. 3. *a*
12....280. 1
13....246. 3
14....253. 2. *a*
4: 4....251. 4. *a*
5....255. 3
6....88 (pl.)
8....104. *g*
10....275. 1
13....45. 5. *a*
23....127. 2
24....262. 1
6: 5....125. 2
7....46
13....282. *c*
17....166. 1
7: 7....60. 3, *b* (2), 94. *b*, 112. 2
9....172. 3
21....246. 2. *a*
8: 11....246. 3. *a*
19....271. 2
22....272. 2
24....22. *b*
33....246. 2. *a*
9: 4....101. 1
6....119. 4
8....262. 2. *a*
12....161. 1, 249. 2. *a*
13....126. 1
24....93. *c*, 172. 3
10: 11....38. 4. *a*, 39. 1. *a*
20....22. 8
24....86. *b* (3 pl.), 245. 5. *b*
26....56. 4
29....272. 2
30....21. 1
31, 38....272. 2
11: 8....21. 1
14....94. *b*

12: 21....§ 55. 2. *a*
13: 13....196. *b*
23....247. *a*
14: 8....62. 2, 175. 1
15: 36....203. 5. *b*
38....22. *a*
56....22. *a*
17: 1....30. 2
18: 12, 14....86. *b* (3 pl.)
20....88
19: 43....61. 6. *a*
50....172. 4
51....39. 1. *a*
21: 10....227. 1. *a*
22: 5....87
12....45. 5
16....119. 3
17....271. 4. *a*
25....148. 1
27....44. *b*
23: 7, 12....249. 2. *a*
24: 10....92. *d*, 282. *a*
15....88 (pl.)
19....275. 3. *a*

JUDGES.

1: 1....§ 265. *a*
15....273. 3. *a*
2: 7....256
3: 15....246. 3. *b*
24....140. 5
25....157. 1
27....272. 2. *b*
30....274. 2. *a*
4: 10....164. 2, 262. 2
20....104. *a*, 127. 2
21....11. 1. *a*, 156. 3
22....266
23....126. 1
24....282. *c*
5: 5....86. *a*, 141. 1, 249. 2. *a*
7....24. *c*, 74, 74. *a*
8....92. *d*, 121. 1
12....45. 2. *a*
13....148. 3
15....199. *c*, 207. 2. *a*
26....88 (3 f. pl.), 105. *b*
28....60. 3, *b* (2), 121. 2
31....263. 1
6: 9....99. 3. *b*
11....246. 3. *b*
14....249. 2. *b*
15....250. 2 (2) *a*
17....74, 74. *a*
20....73. 2. *a*
25....249. 1. *c*
31....230. 3. *a*
34....119. 1
36....258. 3. *b*
7: 6....22. *a*
12....74. *a*
19....208. 1
8: 1....160. 2
2....25
10....224. *a*
11....229. 4. *b*
19....111. 3. *b*
26....74. *a*
9: 2....230. 2. *a*
8....93. 1. *a*
9....53. 2. *b*, 63. 1. *a*, 95. *b*
10....89 (f. s. & m. pl.)

9: 11....§ 53. 2. *b*, 95. *b*
12....89 (f. s. & m. pl.)
13....95. *b*
14....89
24....220. 1. *b*
25....174. 5
29....164. 5, 172. 3
35....274. 2. *b*
38....91. *b*
48....75. 1
53....140. 5
10: 2....60. 3. *b* (1)
4....207. 1. *f*
9....243. 3
14....119. 4
11: 1....254. 6
18....90. 3. *a*
25....91. *b*, 119. 1
37....98. 2
40....250. 2 (2), 263. 4
12: 4....272. 2
5....230. 3. *a*
6....3. 1. *a*
13: 2....248. *a*
3....16. 1
5, 7....90 (2 f. s.)
6....119. 2
8....93. *b*, 245. 5. *b*, 266. 3
12....275. 1. *a*
23....273. 1
14: 1....61. 6. *a*
6....245. 5. *d*
11....251. 2. *b*
15....283. 2. *a*
18....61. 6. *a*
15: 16....280. 3. *a*
16: 5....130. 1. *b*
13....112. 3
14....246. 3. *a*
16....27
25....51. 2
26....150. 1
27....271. 1
28....22. *b*, 27, 223. 1. *a*
17: 2....71. *a*. 2
18: 7....94. *a*, 275. 2. *b*
29....93. *b*
30....4. *a*
19: 5....19. 2. *a*, 89
11....150. 1 (2)
22....82. 5. *a*
20: 13....46
15, 17....96. *a*
25....224. *a*
31....131. 2
32....24. *b*
39....131. 5
43....24. *b*
44....271. 4. *b*
21: 9....66. *a*
21....39. 3. *b*
22....158. 3
25....258. 3. *b*

RUTH.

1: 8....§ 275. 5
9....89 (f. pl.)
11....45. 4
13....25, 71. *a* (3), 88 (f. pl.), 91. *c*
10....104. *g*
20....60. 3. *c*, 196. *d*

2: 8....§ 88, 88 (2 f.), 127. 1
9....88 (pl.), 165. 3
14....150. 3
16....139. 2
3: 3....86. *b* (2 f.)
4....16. 1, 53. 2. *a*, 88 (2 f.), 106. *a*
12....258. 3. *b*
13....119. 3
15....60. 3. *b* (2), 120. 1, 164. 2, 251. 2. *c*
20....220. 1. *b*
4: 1....147. 5
15....104. *c*, *i*

1 SAMUEL.

1: 1....§ 265. *a*
3....219. 1. *a*
4....245. 3. *b*
6....24. *b*, 104. *l*
8....263. 2
9....104. *d*, 172. 4, 254. 1
14....88 (2 f.)
17....53. 2. *a*
20....110. 2
24....104. *f*
28....119. 2
2: 5....24. *c*
10....110. 1
13....203. 5. *a*
22....88 (pl.)
27....91. *b*
3: 2....258. 3. *a*
4....263. 1. *b*
7....263. 1. *b*
8....254. 9. *b*
19....263. 4
4: 8....266. 2. *a*
12....266. 3
14....75. 1
19....148. 2
6: 10....104. *g*, 165. 3
12....88 (3 f. pl.), 147. 4, 282
14....246. 3. *b*
15....119. 1
7: 8....119. 1
8: 19....24. *a*
9: 0....270. *c*
9....243. 2. *a*, 245. 3
24....245. 5. *b*
10: 1-8....100. 1
4....251. 2. *c*
5....266. 3
6....165. 3, 273. 3. *a*
13....165. 3
19....250. 2 (2) *a*
24....24. *b*
12: 3....38. 1. *a*
7....91. *c*
13....119. 2
24....94. *a*
13: 5....230. 2 (1)
8....149. 2
19....86. *b* (3 pl.)
21....19. 2. *b*, 65. *a*
14: 1....73. 2. *a*
22....94. *c*
24....111. 2. *d*
29....249. 2. *c*
32....157. 3, 172. 4
33....57. 2 (3) *a*, 104. 3

INDEX II.

14: 36....§ 141, 1
   40....276, 3
15: 1....125, 2
   5....111. 2. c
   6....151. 2
   9....91. e
   19....157. 3, 172. 4
   30....100. 2. a (1)
16: 4....284
   12....214. 2, b
   15....221. 2. a
   18....246. 3. b, 254.
       6. a, 257, 2
   23....245, 3. a
17: 12....249. 2. c, 253.
       2. b
   25....24. b, 104, h
   26....73. 2. a, 275,
       3. a
   34....245. 5. d, 265.
       b, 271. 4. b
   35....14. a, 112. 3,
       205. b
   42....172. 4
   47....150. 2
   55....245. 2, 249.
       2. a
   56....249. 2. a
18: 1....105. a
   6....158. 3
   7....250. 2 (2) a
   9....156. 1
   17....119. 1
   20....243. 2
   22....220. 2. b
   28....104. i
   29....148. 1, 151. 2
19: 10....249. 2. b
   13, 16....201. 2
   17....104. k
   21....260. a
   22....249. 1. c
20: 6....119. 1
   13....271. 4. a
   21....39. 4
   28....119. 1
   31....254. 6. a
   38....199. b
   42....250. 2 (2) a
21: 2....219. 1, b
   3....92. b, 221. 3. a
   7....44
   12....44. a
   14....66. 1 (1), 105.
       a, 174. 4
   15....126. 1
22: 2....165. 2
23: 11....94. d
   22....282. a
24: 14....245. 5. a
   17....260. 1
   19....71. a (2)
25: 7....94. a
   8....164. 2
   14....157. 3
   18....172. 5, 209.
       3. a
   33....165. 3
   34....88 (3 f.), 167.
       3
   43....250. 2 (2) a
26: 16....271. 4. b
   22....246. 3. a
27: 12....119. 1
28: 7....214. 1. b
   8....89 (f. s. & m.
       pl.)
   10....24. b
   14....60. 3. b (2)
   15....63. 1. c, 97.
       1. b, 164. 5

28. 24....§ 111. 2. b
30: 1....14. a
31: 2....94. c

2 SAMUEL.

1: 4....§ 242. c
   6....91. b, 166. 3
   9....256. c
   10....99. 3. b, 106. a
   15....131. 3
   21....255, 1
   26....166. 1
2: 19....13. b
   27....65. a
   32....274. 2. b
3: 2....257. 1
   8....165. 3
   22....276. 2
4: 6....71. a (3)
5: 2....164. 2
6: 1....151. 2
   3....249. 1. b
   5....16. 3. b
   13....282. c
   16....253, 1
   20....282. b
   23....56. 2
7: 10....114
8: 18....199. b
10: 3....253. 2
   11, 17....275. 2. b
11: 1....11. 1. b
   24....177. 3
   25....245, 5, 271.
       1. e
12: 1, 4....156. 3
   4....249. 1. c
   14....02. d
13: 4....280. 1
   31....254. 10
   32....158. 3
   39....253. 1
14: 2, 3....16. 1
   7....38. 4. a, 158. 3
   10....104. k
   19....57. 2 (1),
       180. a
   30....149. 1, 150. 4
15: 8....282. b
   12....125. 2
   23....275. 2. b
   30....282. c
   32....273. b
   34....287. 3
   37....215. 1. e
16: 1....250. 2 (1)
   16....215. 1. e
17: 9....243. 2. a
   10....140. 4
   12....71. a (1)
   22....223. 1. a
   23....113. 1, 275.
       3. a
18: 3....113. 2
   18....270. b
19: 1....281
   14....111. 2. b
   18....224. a
   19....113. 2
20: 1....257. 2
   4....119. 1
   5....111. 2. d
   9....111. 2. b
   21....95. a
   22....166. 2.
   6....60. 3. a, 127.
       2
   9....160. 5, 223. 1.
       a, 250. 2 (2) a

21: 11....§ 271. 4. a
   12....177. 3
22: 7....142. 2
   24....45. 1
   33....160. 1
   37, 40....238. 1. b
   40....53. 3. a. 111.
       2. c
   41....53. 2. b, 132.
       1
   43....118. 3, 141. 3
   44....199. b
   48....228. 1. b
23: 1....160. 5
   6....33, 3, 140. 6,
       221. b
   8....199. b
   27....24. b
24: 12....208. 2
   13....253. 2

1 KINGS.

1: 6....§ 243. 1
   14....259. 2. a
   15....54. 1, 205. b
   21....87
   27....283, 2. b
2: 24....105. a
   31....254. 6. b
3: 3....126. 1
   7....267. b
   15....147. 4
4: 5....150. 4, 215.
5: 3....253. 2. a
   10....254. 8
   11....260. 2 (2) a
   20....119. 1
   25....53. 2. a
6: 16....10. a
   19....132. 1
   21....207. 1. c
   38....251. 4. a
7: 12....249. 1. c
   14....132. 1, 253. 1
   37....220. 1. b
   44....251. 4. a
8: 1....119. 1
   48....66. b (1 c.)
9: 11....165. 2
10: 3....112. 3
   9....254. 8
   12....275. 1. b
   15....254. 3
11: 1....210. d
   3....275. 1. a
   13....16. 1
   22....24. a
   25....271. 4. b
   30....57. 2 (2) a
12: 10....221. 5. a
   12....164. 2
   32....257. 3
13: 7....234. a
   12....75. 2
   20....60. 3. b (2)
14: 2....71. a
   3....60. 2. a, 127. 1
   6....273. 5
   24....246. 3. a
   26....257. 3
15: 16....60. 3. a
   23....271. 4
   29....94. b
   33....257. 3, 4
16: 10....252. 2
   16....247. a
   17....172. 4, 175. 3
   25....172. 4

16: 26....§ 254. 9. a
   29....252. 2. a
17: 3....100. 1
   14....177. 3
   21....43
18: 1....252. 1
   12....100. 2. a (1)
   13....104. e
   30....131. 3
   32....273. 3
   42....175. 3
   43....254. 9. a,
       274. 2 d
   44....104. b
19: 2....275. 3. a
   4....274. 2. c
   7....38. 1. a
   10....02. d
   11....275. 1. c
   15....66. 2 (2) b,
       219. 1
   19....251. 4. a
   20....98, 1. a
20: 9....39. 4
   13....229. 1. b
   27....96. a, 161. 4
   35....172. 3
   39....91. b
21: 1....45. 1
   8....46
   29....164. 2
22: 12....126. 1
   23....249, 2. b
   25....165. 1
   27....253. 2. a,
       270. c
   35....147. 4
   54....119, 1

2 KINGS.

1: 2....§ 249, 2. c,
       283. 1
   6....36, 2, 39, 4
   7....75, 1
   10....172. 4
   10, 14....250, 2
       (2) a
   16....39. 4
2: 1....16, 3, b
   10....93. c
   11....16. 3, b
   16....208, 3. c
   21....165, 2
   22....165, 3
   24....251, 2. b
3: 4....253, 2. a
   23....119, 1
   25....65, b, 111. 1
   27....263, 1
4: 7....220. 1. b
   16, 23....71. a, 2
   24....131. 1
   25....73, 2. a
   32....95, a
5: 1....39, 1. a
   3....112. 3
   6....104. j
   7....254. 9. b
   9....257
   18....46, 176, 1
6: 5....271. 4. b
   8....230, 2. a
   10....252. 4
   11....74. a
   18....98. 2, 207.
       1. a
   19....88 (pl.)
   22....230. 3
   23....172. 4

6:32....§ 24. b
7:12....165. 1
  13....246. 3. a
8: 1....71. a (2)
  8....249. 2. c
  12....126. 1
  13....75. 1
  21....11. 1. b, 90
9:17....196. b
  25....220. 1. b
  37....172. 1
10:14....118. 3
  30....39. 4
11: 4....199. b
  13....199. a
12: 1....252. 2. b
  8....216. 1. a
  0....60. 3. c, 132. 2
  10....230. 1. a
13: 6....164. 2
  14....263. 1
15: 1....252. 2. a
  10....19. 2
  16....246. 2. a
16: 7....156. 2
  17....253. 2
17:13....39. 4. a
  36....39. 4
18:23....119. 1
  30....126. 1, 271.
     4. a
19: 4....285. 1
  23....254. 2. a
  25....175. 2
  29....131. 3
22:19....106. a
23: 1....251. 2. b
  17....73. 2. a, 246.
     3. a
25:17....251. 2. b
  29....177. 3

1 CHRONICLES.

2:13....§ 57. 2 (1)
  16....13. b
3: 5....149. 1
4:10....100. 2. a (1)
5:20....74. a
12: 1....14. a
  2....150. 1, 180. a
  14....260. 2 (2)
  20....14. a
13: 3....104. l
  12....51. 2
15:24....94. e, 180. a
  27....180. a, 246.
     3. a
17: 4....266. 3. a
20: 2....254. 5
  8....73. a, 149. 1
21:13....259. 2
22:14....250. 2 (3)
23: 6....59. a
24: 3....59. a, 113. 1
  28....275. 1. c
25:10....251. 4. a
26:28....245. 5. b
27:15....251. 4. a
28: 1....36. 1
  5....249. 1. a
29:17....245. 5. b
  18....125. 1

2 CHRONICLES.

1: 4....§ 245. 5. b
  10....164. b
2: 7....14. a, 254. 3

3: 3....§ 247. a
5: 2....119. 1
  12....180. a
6:42....98, 1
7: 6....94. e
8:16....246. 3. a
  18....13. a
10: 7....231. 5. a
  10....19. 2
15: 8....246. 3. a
16: 7. 8....119. 1
  12....177. 3
17:11....62. 2. b, 209.
     2. d
  12....282. c
  13....275. 1. c
18:22....249. 2. b
  23....38. 4. a
19: 2....112. 5. c
20: 7....105. a
  35....96, a
21:17....125. 1, 200.
     2 (2)
22: 5....53. 2. a
  11....39. 1. a
23:19....242
24:18....249. 2. b
25: 4....254. 7
26:15....148. 1, 177. 3
  17....251. 2. b
  20....119. 3
  21....198. a. 4
28:23....94. e
29:31....65. b
  36....245. 5. b
31: 7....148. 1
  14....219. 1. a
32:15....256. c
  30....150. 2 (p.
     182)
33:19....190. c
34: 4....126. 1
  5....220. 1. b
  6....43. b
35:13....57. 1

EZRA.

3:11....§ 95. c, 150. 5
7:25....39. 4
8:18....26
  23....99. 3
  25....98. 1. a, 207.
     1. b, 245. 5. b
  26....98. 1. a
  29....246. 3. a
  31....90. 3
10:14....245. 5. b
  16....122. 2, 141. 1
  17....245. 5. b

NEHEMIAH.

1: 4....§ 125. 2
  7....282. b
2: 4....111. 2. e
  7....111. 2. b
  12....39. 4
  13....4. a, 164. 5
3:13....53. 2. b, 62. 1
  20....94. a
  33....274. 1
  34....210. c
4: 7....216. 2. a
5: 8....255. 1
  14....65. a
  10....112. 3
6: 6....177. 1
  8....57. 2 (3) a,
     164. 3.

6:11....§ 233. a
7:34....251. 3
8: 2....166. 4
  5....106. a, 125. 2
9: 5....161. 4
  6....71. a (2)
  18....63. 1. a
  19....249. 1
  26....63. 1. a
  28....249. 1. a
  32....271. 4. a
  35....249. 1. c
10:39....94. b, 113. 2
11:17....150. 2
12:44....99. 3. b
13:13....111. 2. d
  16....11. 1. a
  23....210. d

ESTHER.

2: 8....§ 126. 1
  9....207. 2. d
4: 3....150. 5
  4....161. 2
  14....127. 1
  16....276. 2
7: 5....82. 1. a (1)
8: 6....269
  15....256
9: 4....282. c
  27....86. b (3 pl.)

JOB.

1: 3....§ 250. 2 (2),
     260. 2. (1)
  5....263. 4, 274.
     2. d
  6....245. 3. b
  7....45. 1
  10....71. a (2)
  11....45, 4, 131. 3
  14....220. 1. b, 258.
     3
  21....164. 2
2: 3....36. 1. a
  5....45. 4
  7....46
  10....248. a
3: 3....263. 5
  8....267. b
  11....263. 5
  13....263. 1
  25....168. a, 172. 3
4: 2....283. 1. a
  4....200. e
  6....287. 3
  19....285. 1
5: 7....93. b, 287. 1
  8....263. 1
  10....61. 6. a
  18....165, 3
6: 2....263. 1
  16....96. b
  22....60. 3. b (2),
     119. 4
  26....126. 1
7: 3....243. 2. b
  5....119. 1, 139. 3
  14....104. j, 105. b
  18....105. b
8: 8....57. 2 (2) a,
     227. 1. a
  21....165. 1
9: 2....22. h
  6....88 (pl.)
  15....92. b

9:13....§ 24. b, 105. a,
     190. a.
  30....121. 1
  34....105. b
10:12....19. 2
  22....61. 6, a
11: 3....94. a
  12....139, 3
  15....150. 5
  17....97. 1. a, 260.
     2 (2) c
12:14....111. 1
  21....282. c
13: 9....24. c
  15....83. b
  21....119. 1
  27....204. a
14: 1....254. 9. b
  19....112. 3, 275. 4
15: 7....227. 1. a
  11....260. 2 (2) b
  18....121. 2
  22....172. 5
16: 5....104. h
  11....147. 3
  12....161. 2
  13....126. 1, 216.
     1. b
  16....60. 3. b (2)
  19....10. 2
17: 2....24. b
  3....126. 1
  10....215. 1. c
  16....88 (3 f. pl.)
18: 2....54. 3
  4....91. b, 230. 2
19: 2....105. c
  3....94. c, 252. 4
  7....113. 1
  15....105. e
  16....45. 4
  17....139. 2
  23....88 (pl.), 141.
     1
  29....74, 74. a
20: 4....158. 3
  8....139. 3
  17....255. 3. a
  24....112. 5. c
  26....60. 3. c, 93. a,
     111. 2. e
  28....140. 2
21: 5....140. 5
  13....24. c
  18....104. i
  24....88 (pl.)
22: 3....283. 2
  20....220. 1. b
  21....88 (3.f.), 94
     d, 167. 3
23: 3....269. b
  9....34
  11....79. 3. a
  17....86 b (2 m.)
24:14....83. b
  19....265, 3
  21....150. 2
  24....139. 1
  25....264. a
  33....220. 2. c
25: 3....220. 1. b
26: 9....180. a
  11....161. 4
27: 3....256. c
  4....92. e
  12....271. 3
  33....220. 2. c
28:12....245. 5
29: 3....139. 2
  6....53. 3. b
  14....105. d

INDEX II.

29 : 21....§ 24. *c*
30 : 8....24. *b*
    26....99. 3. *b*
31 : 5....157. 3
    15....61. 3, 105. *b*, 161. 3.
    18....273. 3. *a*
    22....27
    24....60. 1. *a*
32 : 2....269. *b*
    10....125, 1
    11....53. 2. *a*, 111. 2. *c*
    18....164. 2
33 : 5....111. 3. *a*
    9....71. *a* (1)
    13....158. 1
    21....26, 121. 1
    25....180. *a*
    27....158. 2
    30....159. 2
34 : 5....65. *a*
    13....61. 6. *a*
    18....112. 1
    22....91. *b*
    25....216. 1. *a*
35 : 11....53. 3. *a*, 111. 2. *c*
37 : 6....177. 1
    12....61. 6. *a*
    24....104. *h*
38 : 1....4. *a*
    12....86, *b* (2 m.)
    24....60. 4. *a*, 113. 1
    35....230. 2. *a*
39 : 2....104. *g*
    3....161. 2
    4....112. 5. *c*
    24....165. 2
40 : 2....268. 1. *a*
    21, 22....208. 3. *a*
    22....221. 6. *b*
41 : 1....160. 5
    2....105. *b*
    17....131. 4, 164. 2
    25....172. 5
    26....43, 44. *a*
42 : 2....86. *b* (1 c.)
    13....223. 1. *a*

PSALMS.

1 : 1....§ 245. 2
2 : 2....247
    3....45. 4, 97. 1
    7....71. *a* (2)
    12....35. 1, 271. 4
3 : 2....141. 1
    3....61. 6. *a*
    8....273. 2
4 : 3....111. 2. *c*
    7....3. 1, *a*, 131. 3, 165. 1
5 : 9....31. *b*, 150. 1
    11....42
    12....112. 5. *c*, 254. 9. *b*
    13....31. *b*
6 : 3....42
    4....71. *a*. 2
7 : 6....31. *b*, 60. 2. *a*, 114
    10....263. 1. *a*
    17....254. 9. *a*
8 : 2....132. 1
    3....94. *b*
    5....199. *e*
9 : 14....141. 1
    15....220. 2. *a*
    16....285. 3

9 : 17....§ 140. 1
    18....219. 1. *a*
    19....126. 1
10 : 2....31. *a*, 286
    5....31. *b*
    8, 10....209. 1. *a*
    12....131. 3
    13, 14....31. *b*
11 : 1....257. 1
    7....220. 2. *c*, 275. 3. *a*
12 : 3....280. 2
    4....119. 1
    8....73. 1, 249. 2. *b*
13 : 4....271. 3
    5....104. *h*
16 : 5....19. 2. *a*, 90, 151. 3
17 : 3....139. 2
    9....263. 5. *a*
18 : 6....104. *l*
    10....147. 5
    15....82. 1. *a* (3)
    21....21. 1
    27....142. 2
    41....132. 1
19 : 6....249. 1
    8....254. 9. *b*
    14....11. 1. *b*
20 : 4....63. 1. *c*, 97. 1. *a*, *b*
    9....243. 1
22 : 2....104. *j*
    9....42
    10....157. 1
    17....156. 3, 199. *b*
    22....272. 3
    32....266. 3
23 : 6....148. 2, 267 *d*
24 : 14....131. 3
25 : ....6, 7. 2. *a*
    : 27....71. *a*. 2
26 : 2....98. 1. *a*
    4....112. 3
27 : 10....112. 3
    13....4. *u*
28 : 7....150. 2
29 : 9....111. 1
30 : 4....13. *a*
    8....221. 6. *b*
    13....105. *b*
31 : 10....31. *a*
    14....31. *b*
    24....119. 4
32 : 1....165. 3
    10....249. 1. *a*
33 : 5....266. 1
34 : ....6, 7. 2. *a*
35 : 8....105. *a*
    10....19. 2. *a*, 22, *b*, 215. 1. *c*
    19....102. 3
    25....127. 2
36 : 13....121. 1
37 : 6
    9....91. *b*
    15....24. *b*
    23....161. 4
38 : 3....131. 1
    11....92. *a*
    21....19. 2. *a*
39 : 2....97. 1
    5....75. 1
    14....35. 2, 175. 4
40 : 19....71. *a* (2)
41 : 5....119. 3, 164. 5
    9....220. 1. *b*
    10....111. 2. *b*
44 : 5....258. 2
    18, 21....127. 2
    27....61. 6. *a*

45 : 3....§ 92. *a*
    9....199. *b*
    10....14, *a*, 24. *b*
47 : 5....43. *a*
    10....112. 5. *c*
49 : 9....55. 1
50 : 21....112. 3, 282. 5
    23....105. *b*
51 : 6....263. 1
    7....121. 2
    6....220. 1. *b*
55 : 10....92. *c*
    16....164. 2
    18....274. 2. *a*
    19, 22....19. 2. *a*
    22....141. 1
57 : 2....172. 1, 275. 1. *a*
    9....247. *b*
58 : 2....88 (pl.)
    4....156. 2
    7....131. 3
    8....129. 3
    9....24. *b*, 214. 1. *b*
    12....275. 3. *a*
60 : 2....43. *a*
    4....165. 1
    5....253. 2. *a*
    13....287. 1
61 : 1....196. *b*
62 : 4....93. *a*, bis
    10....260. 2 (2) *c*
    12....252. 4
63 : 2....275. 1. *c*
    4....105. *c*
    8....61. 6. *a*
64 : 7....54. 3
65 : 7....112. 5. *c*
    10....104. *h*, 105. *b*
66 : 4....275. 2. *b*
    12....114
68 : 3....91. *b*, 131. 2, 5, 140. 4
    5....111. 3. *a*
    8....119. 3
    18....21. 1
    21....231. 3. *a*
69 : 10....22. *a*, 104. *i*, 216. 2. *a*
    19....98. 1. *a*
    24....119. 1
70 : 6....71. *a*. 2
71 : 6....157. 1
    7....256. *b*
    12....158. 2
    23....88. (f. pl.)
72 : 15....105. *b*
    17....159. 3, 247
    20....93, *a*
73 : 2....172. 1
    10....254. 6. *b*
    16....99. 3. *b*
    27....86, *b* (2 m.)
74 : 4....220. 2. *a*
    5....19. 2. *a*
    8....105. *a*
    10....119. 1
    17....11. 1. *b*
    19....196, *b*
75 : 11....161. 4
76 : 3....203. 5. *c*
    4....22. *a*, 126. 2, 216. 2. *a*
    6....96. *a*
77 : 2....112. 3
    4....172. 3
    10....139. 2
    18....92. *b*
    20....24. *b*
78 : 9....255. 3. *a*

78 : 63....§ 93. *b*
    65....141. 5*
80 : 3....61. 6. *a*
    5, 8....253. 2. *b*
    6....112. 3
    11....93. *a*
    14....4. *a*, 180. *a*
    15....253. 2. *h*
    16....4. *a*, 139. 2
    19....157. 3
    20....253. 2. *b*
81 : 3....45. 5. *a*
    11....119. 1, 246. 2. *b*
    17....279
84 : 2....200. *e*
86 : 2....19. 2, 126. 1
88 : 17....24. *b*, 92. *a*
89 : 2....216. 2. *a*
    8....111. 3. *b*
    9....253. 2. *b*
    10....131. 4
    40....272. 3
    44....104. *j*
    45....24. *b*, 86. *b* (2 m.)
    51....249. 1. *a*
    52....24. *b*, 216. 2. *a*
90 : 2....263. 1. *b*
    10....22. *a*
91 : 6....140. 1
    12....105. *c*
92 : 2....242. 6
    16....61. 6. *a*
93 : 1....126. 2
    5....174. 1
94 : 1, ...94. *d*
    9....126. 1
    17....61. 6. *a*
    19....141. 6
    20....93. *a*, 111. 2. *e*
101 : 5....92. *b*, 93. *a*
102 : 5....14. *a*
    14....139. 2
    16....266. 3
103 : 3, 4....220. 2. *c*
    4....104. *c*, 246. 2. *b*
    5....275. 3
    7....263. 5
    13....119. 1, 262. 3
104 : 8....286
    18....249. 1. *c*
    26....119. 1
    28....88 (pl.)
    29....111. 2. *b*, 151. 2
105 : 15....264
    28....99. 3
106 : 25....114
    47....126. 1
107 : 20....109. *d*
    27....126. 1
109 : 13....173. 3
    23....112. 5. *c*
110 : 4....61. 6. *a*
111 : 6
112 : 6
113 : 5-9....61. 6. *a*
    6....218
114 : 8....61. 6. *a*
115 : 17....242
116 : 6....141. 2, 150. 2
    12....220. 2. *c*
    15....61. 6. *a*
    19....220. 1. *b*
118 : 10....105. *a*
    11....139. 1
    18....92. *d*, 104. *c*

118: 23....§ 166. 1
119: 6
  18....98. 2
  22....139. 2
  43....60. 4. a
  47....141. 6
  71....126. 1
  101....105. 2
  117....172. 3
  129....104. i
  133....97. 2
  137....275. 1. a
  139....24. b
  155....275. 1. a
122-124: ....74. a
122: 4....274. 2. e
123: 1....61. 6. a
  4....246. 3. a
124: 4....61. 6. a
125: 3....61. 6. a
  5....79. 3. a
127: 2....196. d, 254. 9. b
129: ....74. a
  3....243. 2. a
  86....114
132: 1....174. 6
  6....127. 2
  12....65. a, 220. 2. a
133: 1....24. a
134-137: ....74. a
134: 2....220. 2. b, 273. 2
135: 7....94. e, 165. 2
137: 6....104. c
138: 6....147. 2
139: 1....104. j, 147. 5
  2....158, 1
  5....220. 1. b
  8....53. 3. b, 88 (1. c), 161. 2
  19....83. b
  20....57. 2 (3) a, 86. b (3 pl.), 164. 3
140: 10....172. 3
  13....86. b (1 c.)
141: 3....24. b, 98. 1. a
  5....111. 1, 164. 2
  8....60. 4. a
143: 3....165. 2
  6....272. 2. b
144: ....74 a
  2....199. b
145: 6
  8....215. 1. c
  10....104. b
147: 1....92. d
148: 5....112. 5. c

PROVERBS.

1: 10....§ 111. 2. b, 177. 3
  20....97. 1. a
  22....31. b, 60. 3. c, 111. 2. e
  28....105. c
2: 11....104. b
3: 3....125. 1
  12....43. a
  17....256. 1
4: 6....118. 3
  13....24. b, 105. b
  16....88
  25....150. 1
5: 22....105. c
6: 3....49

6: 11....§ 11. 1. a
  21....104. g
  27....118. 4
7: 13....141. 1
  14....53. 2. a
8: 3....31. a, 97. 1. a
  11....260. 1
  13....166. 2
  15....88
  17....53. 2. a, 111. 2. b
  25....263. 1. b
  27, 29....141. 3
10: 3....111. 1
  4....11. 1. a, 156. 3
  11....249. 1
11: 7....208. 3. c
  25....150. 5
12: 25....197. b
13: 23....156. 3
14: 3....105. d
  10....60. 4. a, 110. 1
  34....263. 3
15: 1....24. a, 60. 4. a
  9....112. 5. c
16: 4....246. 2. a
17: 4....111. 2. c, 140. 5
  10....131. 1
  14....120. 1, 131. 3
  26....342
18: 5....267 d
19: 7....19. 2. a, 215. 1. c
  13....216. 1. d
  19....215. 1. c
  24....51. 1
  25....94. d
20: 16....111. 3. a
21: 8....56. 2
  13....254. 9. a
  15....207. a
  22....63. 1. a
22: 11....215. 1. c
  21....253. 2
  24....60. 4. a
23: 1....158. 3
  12....243. 2
  24....158. 2, 3
  27....207. 1. c
24: 2....92. e
  7....156. 3
  14....97. 1. b, 148. 3
  17....91 b, 231. 5. a
  23....94. b
  31....93. a, 207. 2. d, 271. 1
25: 6....126. 2
  7....60. 3. b (1)
  9....174. 4
  11....10. a
  17....127. 2
  19....90
26: 7....141. 1
  18....141. 6
  21....141. 6
27: 10....215. 1. c
  15....63. c (2)
  17....140. 1
  25....24. b, 216. 2. a
28: 6. 18....203. 3.
  21....94. b
29: 6....140. 1
30: 4....65. b
  6....22. b, 66. 1 (2) a, 151. 2
  8....11. 1. a
  9....65. a
  17....14. a, 24. b, 57. 2 (3) a

30: 25....§ 200. e
  31....229. 1. a
31: 3....199. a
  10-31....6
  12....104. i
  31....247. a

ECCLESIASTES.

1: 4....§ 266. 1
  9....256. c
  15....161. 4
  17....3. 1. a
  18....00
2: 5....207. 1. a
  7....275. 1. c
  8....280. 3. a
  13....57. 2 (3) a, 231. 3. b
  15....260. 2 (2) a
  19....230. 4, 283. 2. a
  22....74, 177. 1
3: 2, 4....267. b
  17....245. 5. a
  18....74, 139. 2
4: 2....268. 1. a
  9....251. 4
  12....105. a
  14....53. 2. a, 111. 2. c
5: 5....113. 2
  7....38. 1. a, 201. 2
  8....112. 5. c
7: 16....82. 5. a
  22....71. a (2)
  24....280. 3
  25....273. 4
  26....91. b, 165. 2
8: 1....177. 3
  9....268. 1
  12....165. 2
9: 1....139. 2, 216. 1. a
  12....59. a, 93. e
  18....165. 2
10: 5....164. 3
  10....121. 2
  17....220. 2. c
11: 3....177. 1
  6....75. 2
12: 1....201. 2
  4....87
  5....11. 1. a, 122. 2, 140. 5
  6....140. 1, 2
  11....19. 2. b, 65. a

SONG OF SOLOMON.

1: 6....§ 105. e, 141. 1, 207. 1. a
  7....45. 5. a, 74, 209. 1. a
  8....24. b, 260. 2 (2)
  10....174. 1
2: 5....254. 7
  10....221. 2. b
  15....60. 3. b (2), 119. 4
3: 1....45. 5. a
  11....148. 3, 164. 3
4: 1....254. 4
  2....220. 1. b
  5....216. 1. c
  9....104. k
5: 2....57. 2 (3) a, 60. 4. a

5: 3....§ 105. d
  9....104. k
  12....57. 2 (3) a
6: 5....45. 5. a
  6....220. 1. b
  9....105. e, 275. 5
  11....141. 1
7: 3....221. 6. b
  4....216. 1. c
  8....210. e
  13....141. 1
8: 2....199. b
  5....104. i
  6....22. a, 216. 2. a

ISAIAH.

1: 3....§ 262. 3
  5....256. c
  6....60. 2. a, 156. 2
  9....262. 1
  11....271. 1
  15....104. h, 119. 1
  16....54. 4. a, 82. 5. a
  17....165. 2. c, 267. c
  18....245. 5. d
  21....33. 1, 61. 6. a, 218
  22....245. 5
  24....245. 4
  29....279
  31....60. 3. b (2)
2: 2....265. b
  4....207. 1. a
  20....43. b, 207. 1. a, 256
3: 1....280. 3. a
  9....273. 3. a
  15....24. a, 75. 1
  16....172. 5, 209. 3. a
  24....53. 3. a
4: 4....202. 1
5: 10....22. a, 216. 2. a
  19....97. 1, 97. 1. a
  20....10. a
  23....275. 6
  28....24. b
6: 1....205. a
  2....203. 5. a
  5....254. 10
  9....56. 3. a, 175. 4
  12....119. 1
  13....92. d
7: 2....157. 1
  4....91. 1
  11....119. 3, 126. 1
  14....166. 1
  15....267. c
  19....156. 4
  25....274. 2. e
8: 2....22. b
  11....104. a
  17....100. 2. a (1)
  23....61. 6. a
9: 3....24. b. 221. 5. a
  4....142. 1
  6....4. a
  12....246. 2. b
  17....45. 2
10: 1....207. 2. a, 247. b
  9....22. b
  10....260. 2 (2) c
  12....255. 3
  13....11. 1. b, 57. 2 (3) a, 92. b, 174. 1, 231. 3. b

INDEX II. 339

10 : 14....§ 245. 5. d	28 : 10....§ 280. 2	44 : 8....§ 14 7. 3	64 : 6....§ 94. d
16....147. 4	12....86. b (3 pl.)	13....19. 2, 60. 3. b	10....139. 1
17....221. 5. b	13....280. 2	(2), 120. 1	65 : 20....165. 2, 248
27....24 b	16....150. 5, 279. a	16....141. 2	24....263. 1, b
34....19. 1, 45. 2	21....249. 1. a	17....13. a	66 : 12....142. 1
11 : 2....100. 2. a (2),	27....113. 1	18....156. 2	13....45. 5
156. 4	28....282. a	21....102. 2	20....39. 1. a
8....141. 6	29 : 1....131. 2	27....111. 3. a	
15....60. 3. a	7....165. 3	45 17....139. 2	JEREMIAH.
13 : 8....65. b	9....141. 6	11....118. 3	
16....91. c	14....90, 279. a	47 1....269. b	1 : 6....§ 105. d
18....92. e	16....283. 2. b	2....88 (f. s. & m.	11....266. 2
20....53. 3. a, 111.	21....86. b (3 pl.)	pl.), 111. 3. a	2 : 11....11. 1. b, 230. 3
2. c	22....156. 1	5....269. b	12....111. 3. a
14 : 6....114	30 : 2....157. 1	10....102. 3, 104. c	19....105. e
11....150. 5	5....157. 3	12....285. 2. a	21....220. 1. b, 249.
19....95. a	11....79. 3. a, 232 a	13....220. 2. a	1. b
23....57. 2 (2) a,	12....19. 2, 119. 3	14....104. i	24....105. c
94. b, 161. 2	18....106. a, 119. 1,	48 : 7....104. g	27....104. k
31....119. 4	139. 2	8....87	34....277
15 : 5....142. 2, 161. 2	19....104. b, 106. a,	11....39. 1. a	36....111. 2. b
16 : 8....277	141. 3	49 : 8....207. 1. a	3 : 3....267. b
9....168. a, 174. 4	21....180. a, 258. 1	18....65. b	5....86. b (2 f.),
10....86. b (2 in.),	23....273. 3	26....112. 3, 273. 1	131. 2
161. 4	28....160. 4	51 : 14....126. 1	6....172. 3
17 : 8....229. 3. a	20....96. b	15....126. 1	7....249. 1. a
11....156. 2, 161. 2	31 : 4....22. a, 43	20....57. 2 (3) a	8....60. 3. b (2),
14....139. 2	32 : 1....88	21....255. 2	207. 1. a
18 : 2....139. 3	11....275. 1. a	52 : 5....96. a, b, 122.	10....249. 1. a
4....98. 1. a	33 : 1....24. b, 87, 131.	2, 131. 6, 150. 2	11....207. 1. a
5....65. a	2, 141. 3, 258. 3. a	7....174. 1	22....177. 3
19 : 3....141. 1	6....255. 2	11....140. 4	4 : 3....158. 2
4....275. 3	7....24. a	14....60. 3. b (2)	7....24. b, 221. 5. a
6....24. c, 94. a,	9....82. 1. a (1)	53 : 2....111. 1	13....141. 1
180. a	10....82. 5. a	3....94. e	19....86. b (2 f.)
9....199. c	12....24. c, 149. 1	4....254. 9. b, 262. 4	30....71. a (2),
17....11. 1. a, 196. d	15....271. 2	5....60. 2. a, 142. 1	275. 5
21....92. c	21....56. 1	10....175. 1	31....156. 1
20 4....199 c	31 4....140. 2, 245.	11....207. 1. a	5 : 6....141. 1
21 : 3....207. 1. a	5. d	54 : 1....207. 1. a	7....75. 2, 125. 1
9....262. 4	6....96. a	5....201. 2	13....245. 5. b
12....112. 1, 172. 1,	11....21. 1, 229. 4. b	6....104. c	22....56. 1, 105. b, c
177. 3, 247	17....104. i	9....125. 2	26....139. 2
14....111. 2. c	35 : 1....55. 1, 68 (pl.),	12....22. b	6 : 27....185. 2. c
22 : 1....254. 6	158. 2	55 : 5....104. b	7 : 4....280. 3. b
5....161. 2	7....275. 4	11....273. 3	10....65. a
10....25	36 : 8....35. 1, 246. 3. a	56 : 3....105. a, 245.	13....282
11....221. 7. a	9....250. 1. a	5. b	27....104. b
17....161. 2	15....271. 4. a	12....164. 5	29....141. 1
19....45. 3, 111. 1	37 : 23....270. c	57 : 5....140. 2	8 : 11....165. 3
21....221. 3. a	32....254. 9. a	6....24. b	22....220. 2
24....254. 6. b	38 : 5....90, 279. a	8....68 (2 f.)	9 : 2....94. c
23 : 9....254. 2	14....19. 2	13....119. 3	17....118. 4
11....54. 3, 94. b,	16....256. c	58 : 3....24. b, 131. 2	19....220. 1. b
221. 6. b	40 : 1....263. 2	216. 2. a	10 : 5....57. 2 (3) a, 86.
13....249. 2. a	7....22. b, 35. 1	9....125. 2	b (3 pl.), 164. 3
17, 18....220. 1. b	12....215. 1. c	10....216. 1. b	12....88
18....113. 1	17....260. 2 (2) c	59 : 3....83. c. (2),	17....89 (f. s. & m.
24 : 2....165. 2, 246.	21....263. 2	122. 2	pl.)
2. a	24....92. b	5....112. 3, 156. 4,	11 : 15....220. 1. b
3....140. 3, 4	30....147. 4	196. d	12 : 5....94. a
19....139. 2, 282. a	31....245. 5	10....189	9....229. 3
20....82. 1. a (1)	41 : 7....90, 270. b	12....127. 2	10....121. 2
25 : 1....104. h	8....285. 1	13....92. b, d, 174. 1	17....92. d
6....209. 1. a	14....254. 3	16....104. i	13 : 5....127. 1
10....159. 2	23....97. 2. a, 172. 3	17....172. 4	7....147. 2
11....119. 1	24....260. 2 (2) c	60 : 1....157. 2	13....36. 1
26 : 5....105. a, b	42 : 4....140. 1	4....88 (f. pl.)	19....172. 1, 275.
11....254. 9. a	5....126. 1, 221.	7....105. c	2. b
16....66. b (3 pl.)	7. b	9....104. c	21....60. 3. b (1),
19....221. 2. b	6....97. 2. a	10....105. c	86. h (2 f.)
20....172. 3	11....156. 1	61 : 1....43. b	25....60. 2. a
27 : 3....105. d	22....65. a	62 : 2....105. d	15 : 3....119. 1
4....127. 3	24....267. c	3....16. 1	10....93 (pl.), 104.
8....24. a	43 : 5....105. b	63 : 3....94. a, 119. 1	k
11....88 (3 f. pl.)	8....94. d	16....105. a	15....106. b
12....223. 1. a	9....91. d	19....86. a	17....112. 5. c
28 : 3....88 (3 f. pl.),	23....112. 3	64 : 2....86. a	16 : 16....158. 1, 249.
91. c	44 : 2....105. b, 193.	5....132. 3	L a
6....60. 3. a	2. b	6....161. 3	

17 : 3....§ 221. 6. *b*
     4....80. *b* (2 m.),
     112. 3
     17....172. 3
     18....94. *d*
18 : 23....46, 172. 3,
     175. 3
19 : 11....165. 1
20 : 9....22. *b*
21 : 3....88 (pl.)
     4....30. 4
     13....131. 1
22 : 3....185. 2. *c*
     6....13. *b*
     14....161. 4, 199. *c*
     15....94. *a*
     20....234. *a*
     23....61. 6. *a*, 86.
     b (2 f.) 90 (2 f.
     s.), 140. 2
     24....105. *b*
     26....104. *i*
     29....280. 3. *b*
23 : 13....131. 6
     23....254. 6. *b*
     29....161. 2
     37....104. *b*
     39....177. 3
24 : 2....91. *c*
25 : 3....94. *b*
     16....96. *a*
     26....246. 3. *a*
     34....161. 5
     36....57. 2 (3) *a*,
     234. *c*
26 : 9....165. 3
     21....44. *b*
27 : 3....249. 1. *c*
     18....156. 2
     20....13. *a*
28 : 16....245. 3. *b*
29 : 8....94. *e*, 112. 5. *c*
     23....229. 1. *a*
     25....220. 1. *b*
     27....24. *b*
30 : 10....139. 3
     19....276. 1
31 : 12....87, 119. 3
     18....273. 4
     21....249. 2. *b*
     32....112. 3
     33....16. 3. *b*, 105. *d*
     38....46
32 : 4....91. *b*, 131. 5
     9....98. 1. *a*
     12....246. 3. *a*
     14....249. 1. *c*
     33....92. *d*
     35....104. 2
     37....10. *a*
     44....268. 1
33 : 8....13. *a*
     24....45. 1
     26....11. 1. *b*
34 : 1....44. *a*
     36 : 16....272. 3
     23....251. 1
37 : 12....113. 2
     14....266
     16....209. 3. *a*
38 : 9....270. 1
     12....56. 4
     14....249. 1. *c*
39 : 18....92. *d*
40 : 1....57. 2 (2) *a*
     3....249. 1. *c*
41 : 6....282. *c*
42 : 2....175. 2
     6....46, 71. *a* (1)
     10....53. 2. *b*, 148. 2

44 : 18....§ 271. 1
     19....104. *e*
     23....166. 1
     25....160. 4
46 : 7, 8....122. 2
     8....96. *a*, 111. 2. *d*
     11....86. *b* (2. f.)
     20....43. *b*
48 : 11....159. 1
     19....280. 3. *a*
     32....246. 3. *a*
49 : 3....54. 4. *a*, 82.
     5. *a*
     8....95. *d*
     10....165. 1, 262. 4
     11....88 (3 f. pl.),
     98. 1
     15, 17....275. 2. *b*
     18....45. 4
     20....140. 5
     24....104. *i*, 275. 4
     28....141. 1
     37....86. *b* (2 m.),
     112. 3, 5. *c*, 139. 3
50 : 3....156. 2
     5....71. *a* (3),
     91. *d*
     6....275. 2
     11....196. *d*
     20....165. 2
     23....91. *a*
     27....111. 3. *a*
     34....04. *b*, 114,
     158. 3
     44....105. *b*
51 : 3....46
     9....165. 2, 3
     13....90 (2 f. s.)
     30....24. *c*
     33....04. *b*
     34....165. 2
     50....151. 1
     58....24. *c*, 140. 1
52 : 13....254. 6. *b*

LAMENTATIONS.

1 : ....§ 6
1 : 1....33. 1, 61. 6. *a*,
     218
     4....149. 1, 199. *a*
     8....141. 3
     12....142. 1
     16....207. 1. *a*, 209.
     1. *a*, 271. 1
     17....272. 2. *b*
     20....60. 3. *b* (2),
     92. *a*
2 : 6
2 : 8....126. 1
     11....92. *a*, 113. 1,
     2, 115
     15, 16....74. *a*
3 : 6
3 : 12....196. *d*
     14....199. *b*
     22....54. 3, 216.
     2. *a*
     33....150. 2 (p. 182)
     42....71. *a* (1)
     45....267. *c*
     48....147. 2
     53....53. 3. *a*, 150.
     2 (p. 182)
     58....158. 1
4 : 6
4 : 1....96. *b*, 177. 3
     3....43. *b*
     9....39. 3. *b*, 45. 5. *a*

4 : 14....§ 83. *c*. 2, 122,
     2
     17....236. 2
5 : 5....160. 5

EZEKIEL.

1 : 4....§ 53. 2. *a*
     6....203. 5. *a*
     11....220. 2. *c*
     14....179. 1. *a*, 208.
     1. *a*
2 : 10....53. 2. *a*, 53. 3. *a*
3 : 7....254. 10
     15....139. 3
     20....88 (f. pl.)
4 : 3....54. 1
     9....199. *a*
     12....157. 3
5 : 12....220. 1. *b*
     13....121. 3, 131. 6
     16....119. 1
6 : 3....208. 3. *c*
     6....147. 4
     8....173. 2
     9....24. *c*
     11....98. 2
     14....280. 3. *a*
     16....118. 4
7 : 17....203. 5. *a*
     24....141. 1, 216.
     2. *a*
     25....196. *c*
     27....118. 4
8 : 2....66. 2 (2) *a*
     3....165. 3
     6....75. 1, 119. 3
     16....90. (2 m. pl.),
     176. 1
9 : 2....249. 1. *c*
     8....120. 2
     10....254. 9. *b*
10 : 17....157. 1
13 : 2....207. 1. *b*, 255.
     1
     8....199. *c*
     11....71. *a* (2)
     17....220. 1. *b*
     19....157. 3
     20....24. *b*, 71. *a*
     (2), 220. 2. *c*
14 : 3....53. 1. *a*, 91.
     b, *c*, 119. 1
     8....141. 3
15 : 5....104. *i*
16 : 4....60. 4. *a*, 93.
     a, 95. *c*. 121. 1,
     126. 1, 127. 1,
     150. 5, 221. 6. *b*,
     282. *a*
     5....87, 95. *a*, 111.
     3. *a*, 150. 5
     8, 10....99. 3. *b*
     22....86. *b* (2 f.)
     27....256. *b*
     28....127. 1
     31....173. 2
     33....60. 3. *b* (2),
     120. 1
     34....14. *a*, 10. *b*
     36....91. *b*
     50....128
     52....92. *d*, 220. 2. *a*
     53....220. 1. *b*
     57....150. 3
     59....86. *b* (1 c.)
17 : 5....132. 2
     9....166. 2, 191. 4,
     216. 2. *a*

17 : 15....§ 65. *b*
     23....88 (f. pl.)
18 : 26....221. 5. *b*
     32....287. 1
19 : 2....196. *d*
20 : 9....140. 4
     16....271. 4. *b*
     21....65. *b*
     27....119. 3
     36....91. *c*
     37....53. 2. *a*
21 : 15....24 *c*, 177. 1
     15, 16....93. *a*
     18....121. 1
     19....219. 1. *a*
     21....180. *a*
     26, 28....87
     29....91. *b*, 106. *a*
     31....04. *b*, 196. *c*
     32....280. 3. *b*
     33....111. 2. *c*
     34....87
22 : 20....131. 2
23 : 5....111. 1
     16, 20....97. 1. *a*
     19....175. 3
     42....21. 1
     48....83. *c* (2), 150.
     3 (p. 182)
     49....165. 2, 220.
     1. *b*
24 : 10....197. *b*
     11....140. 1
     12....172. 1
     26....128, 189. *b*
25 : 6....57. 2 (3) *a*,
     106. *a*, 125. 2
     13....219. 1. *b*
     15....57. 2 (3) *a*
26 : 2....140. 2
     9....19. 2. *c*, 221.
     5. *a*
     15....113. 1, 2
     18....112. 5. *c*
     21....234. *a*
27 : 3....90 (2. f. s.)
     8....156. 3
     9....24. *c*, 216. 1. *a*
     12....22. *a*
     15....13. *a*
     19....93. *b*
     23....54. 2
     26....156. 3
     30....96. *b*
     31....11. 1. *a*, 106. *d*
     0....230. 4
     13....19. 2. *b*, 161. 4
     14....71. *a* (2)
     15....61. 6. *a*, 104. *b*
     16....53. 2. *a*, 111.
     2. *c*, 165. 3
     17....168 *a*, 172. 2
     18....104. *i*, 184. *b*,
     216. 1. *d*
     23....92. *a*
     24....139. 3
     24, 26....156. 3
29 : 3....102. 1. *a*
     15....166. 5
     18....95. *a*
30 : 16....254. 6. *b*
     25....112. 3
31 : 3....140. 5
     5....11. 1. *a*, 86. *b*
     8....11. 1 *a*, 100
     15....93. *c*
32 : 16....88 (f. pl.)
     18....11. 1. *b*
     19....95. *a*, *d*

INDEX II. 341

32: 20....§ 69 (f. s. & m. pl.)
32....95. *a*
33: 12....166. 2
13....221. 5. *b*
30....53. 2. *b*, 223. 1. *a* bis
34: 12....249. 1. *b*
17....71. *a* (2)
31....71. *a* (2)
35: 6....105. *d*
8....216. 1. *d*
9....147. 2
11....220. 2. *a*
12....63. 1. *a*
36: 3....139. 2, 141. 1
5....220. 1. *b*
8....221. 5. *c*
11....161. 5
13....71. *a* (2)
28....71. *a* (1)
35....73. 2. *a*
37: 7....88 (2 f. pl.)
9....131. 3
10....131. 6
17....119. 1, 223. 1. *a*
38: 8....161. 4
23....96. *b*
39: 26....165. 3
27....249. 1. *b*
40: 4....65. *b*
16....220. 2. *c*
22....250. 2 (3)
43....19. 2. *b*
41: 7....141. 1
9, 11....160. 5
15....220. 2. *c*
22....274. 2. *c*
25....19. 2. *a*
42: 5....45. 1, 57. 2 (2) *a*, 111. 2. *b*
43: 13....197. *b*
18....113. 1
20....104. *j*
24....100. 2. *a* (2)
27....177. 3
45: 16....246. 3. *a*
46: 17....86. *b*
22....95. *e*
47: 7....102. 3. *a*
8....164. 3
11....11. 1. *a*, 199
15....246. 3. *a*
48: 10....39. 4. *a*
16....46
18....220. 1. *b*

DANIEL.

1: 8....§ 119. 1
13....172. 3
17....250. 2 (2) *a*, 251. 4. *a*
2: 1....99. 3. *a*, 119. 1
3: 3....22. *b*
25....94. *e*
5: 9....203. 5. *c*
11....22. *b*
8: 1....245. 5. *b*
11....95. *a*
13....98. 1. *a*, 247, 249. 1. *b*
16....73. 2. *a*
22....88 (3. f. pl.)
9: 2....158. 1
19....119. 3, 125. 1
25....97. 2, 225. 2

10: 14....§177. 3, 285. 2
17....51. 2
11: 6....11. 1. *b*
12....19. 2. *a*
14....131. 6
30....11. 1, *b*
31....249. 1. *b*
34....91. *b*
35....94. *b*
36....82. 5. *a*
40....126. 1
44....196. *d*
12: 13....199. *a*

ΠΟΣΕΔ.

1: 2....§ 255. 2
6....269
2: 14....104. *g*
16....221. 7. *a*
3: 2....24. *b*
4: 2....267. *a*
6....11. 1. *a*, 104. *b*
13....118. 4
18....43. *b*, 92. *a*, 122. 1, 149. 3
5: 2....119. 3
8....272. 2. *b*
11....269
6: 2....172. 3
4....269
9....174. 3
7: 4....106. *a*, 111. 3. *a*, 158. 3
6....22. *a*
12....150. 1
8: 2....60. 3. *a*, 275. 2. *b*
3....105. *a*
6....275. 2. *b*
12....88
9: 2....119. 1
4....208. 3. *c*
10....119. 3
10: 10....105. *d*
11....61. 6, *a*
12....158. 2
13....61. 6, *a*
14....11. 1. *a*, 156. 3
11: 3....94. *a*, 115, 132. 2
4....57. 2 (2) *a*, 111. 2. *d*
7....177. 3
7, 8....56. 4
12: 1....104. *l*, 201. 2
4....274. 2. *b*
5....105. *b*
13: 3....92. *b*
14....19 2, 221. 5. *a*, 275. 2. *b*
15....177. 3
14: 1....88 (3. f. pl.), 209. 1. *a*
3....256 *c*

JOEL.

1: 2....§ 230. 4
8....254. 9. *b*
17....24. *b*, 190. *a*
20....275. 4
2: 5....60, 3. *b* (1)
3: 3....263. 5. *a*
4: 11....91. *d*, 131. 1
18....271. 1

AMOS.

1: 11....§ 104. *e*, 275. 2. *b*
13....125. 2
2: 4....119. 3
3: 11....86. *a*, 140. 2
15....156. 4
4: 2....165. 2
3....86. *b* (2 pl.)
5: 11....92. *b*, 161. 3
15....139. 3
21, 25....24. *b*
6: 2....54. 2, 253. 2. *b*
10....243. 1
7: 1....199. *c*
8: 4....94. *b*, 231. 5. *a*
8....53. 2. *a*, 53. 3. *a*, 128
9: 1....125. 1
8....94. *b*

OBADIAH.

ver. 4....§ 158. 3
9....183. *a*
11....45. 2, 106. *a*
13....105. *b*
16....156. 4

JONAH.

1: 5....§ 114
2: 1....125. 2
10....61. 6. *a*
3: 3....254. 5
4: 11....22. *b*

MICAH.

1: 7....§ 92. *c*
9....275. 1. *a*
10....53. 3. *a*, 96. *b*
15....164. 2
16....89 (f. s. & m. pl.)
2: 3....274. 2. *e*
4....141. 2
6....275. 1. *a*
7....229. 4. *a*
8....88 (pl.)
12....92. *d*, 246. 2. *a*
3: 12....199. *a*, 245. 4
4: 6....151. 2
8....111. 2. *b*
10....158. 2
10, 13....157. 2
5: 2....262. 1
6: 10....57. 2 (1)
13....139. 3
7: 4....260. 2 (2), 260. 2 (2) *c*
10....35. 2

NAHUM.

1: 3....§ 13. *a*, 215. 1. *c*
4....150. 2 (p. 182)
12....140. 2
13....220. 1. *b*
2: 4....220. 2. *c*

2: 9....§ 69 (f. s. & m. pl.) 220. 1. *a*
14....220. 2. *c*
3: 5....114
7....93. *a*
8....147. 4
11....112. 3
17....24. *b*, 142. 1, 199. *c*

HABAKKUK.

1: 8....§ 100. 2. *a* (2) bis
10....197. *b*, 265. *a*
11....73. 1, 249. 2. *a*
12....104. *j*
13....126. 1
15....112. 2
16....197. *b*
2: 1, 2....265. *a*
7....161. 2
17....104. *g*, 141. 3
19....254. 6, *b*
3: 6....99. 3. *a*
8....256. *b*
9....282, *b*
10....220. 2. *c*
16....140. 1
19....47

ZEPHANIAH.

1: 2....§ 282. *a*
17....100. 2. *a* (1)
2: 4....126. 2
9....220. 1. *c*
14....229, 4. *b*
15....30. 4. *a*
3: 9....274. 2. *e*
11....125. 2
14....89 (f. s. & m. pl.), 111. 3. *a*
18....149. 1
19....198, 246. 3. *a*

HAGGAI.

1: 4....§ 230. 3, 249. 1. *b*

ZECHARIAH.

1: 9....§ 75. 1
17....157. 3
2: 8....73. 2. *a*
3: 1....106. *a*
7....94. *e*, 151. 1
9....203. 5. *a*
4: 5....258. 2
7....246. 3. *a*, 249. 1. *c*
10....156. 2
12....24. *b*
5: 4....156. 4
11....160. 5
6: 7....96. *b*
7: 1....252. 2, *b*
3....199. *e*
5....102. 2, 104. *b*, 252. 2. *b*, 273. 3. *a*

7 : 9....§ 89 (f. s. & m. pl.)
    14....45. 5, 60. 3. c, 92. e
8 : 2....271. 3
    14, 15....139. 1
    17....111. 2. e
9 : 5....35. 2
10 : 6....151. 3
11 : 4....254. 6

11 : 5....§ 57. 2 (3) a, 111. 2. c, 234. c
    7....223. 1. a
    8....119. 1
    10....140. 5
    17....61. 6. a
12 : 11....55. 2. a
13 : 4....166. 2
14 : 2....45. 2, 91. c
    5....199. c
    10....156. 3

MALACHI.

1 : 6....§ 263. 3
    7....106. a, 127. 2
    11....95. a
    13....24. a, 75. 1
    14....54. 1, 205. b
2 : 14....86. b (2 m.)
3 : 9....140. 2

3 : 19....§ 119. 1
    20....156. 2

MATTHEW.

26 : 73....§ 51. 4. a

ROMANS.

3 : 20....§ 256. o

INDEX III.

HEBREW WORDS ADDUCED OR REMARKED UPON.

Words preceded by Vav Conjunctive or Vav Conversive will be found in their proper place irrespective of these prefixes. A few abbreviations are employed, which are mostly of such a nature as to explain themselves as *v.* verb, *n.* noun, *pron.* pronoun, *adj.* adjective, *adv.* adverb, *int.* interjection, *inf.* infinitive, *imp.* imperative, *pret.* preterite. The numbers refer to the sections of the Grammar.

אֲאַמִּצְכֶם 104. *h*
אָב 68. *b*, 200. *a*, 215. 1. *e*, 220. 1. *c*
אָבַד 78. 2, 110. 3
אֹבַד 215. 1. *b*
אַבֵּד 92. *d*
אַבֵּד 92. *c*
אֲבֵדָה 216. 1. *b*
אֲבַדּוֹן 193. 2
וָאֹבְדָה 53. 2. *a*, 111. 2. *c*
אַבְדָן 22. *a*, 193. 2
אֲבַדְתָּם 112. 1
אָבָה 110. 3
אָבוּא 86. *b* (3 pl.)
אָבוֹי 240. 1
אֵבוּס 60. 3. *c*, 216. 1. *b*
אֲבוּסִים 112. 1

אֲבוֹתֵיהֶם 220. 2. *a*
אֲבוֹתָם 220. 2. *a*
אֲבַטִּחִים 53. 1. *a*
אָבִי (בּוֹא) 164. 2
אָבִי 61. 6. *a*
אָבִיב 185. 2. *a*
אֲבֵידָה 111. 2. *d*
אֲבִי הָעֶזְרִי 246. 3. *b*
אֲבִיּוֹן 193. 1
אֲבִיכֶם 220. 1. *b*
אָבַל 84. 3. *a* (2)
אָבֵל 185. 2. *b*, 215. 1. *b*
אָבֵל (pr. n.) 215. 1. *b*
אֲבָלִי 216. 1. *b*
אֶבֶן 197. *b*, 200. *b*
אֶבֶן 183. *b*
אַבְנֵט 183. *c*
אַבְנְטִים 207. 1. *a*

אַבְנְטָה 221. 3. *a*
אָבְרֵךְ 94. *b*
אַגְדָּלְתִּי: 94. *a*, 119. 1
וָאַגֵּד 99. 3
וָאַגִּיד 99. 3
אֲגַם 207. 2. *a*
אֲגַן 200. *a*
אֲגַפִּים 53. 1. *a*
וָאֶגְרֹשׁ 99. 3. *b*
אִגֶּרֶת 207. 1. *c*, 211
וָאֲדַבֵּר 99. 3
וָאֲדַבְּרָה 99. 3
אֱדוֹם 60. 3. *b* (1), 197. *d*
אָדוֹן 231. 3. *a*
אדירים 11. 1. *b*
אָדָם 112. 5. *a*
אָדֹם 185. 2. *b*, 207. 2. *c*
אֲדָמְדָּם 188

אֲדַמְדֶּמֶת 207. 1. e	נַאֲרִי 99. 3. a	אוֹר (n.) 197. b
אֲדַמְדֶּמֶת 205	אֹהֶל 61. 2. a, 184. b, 208. 3. b	אוֹרְחוֹ 220. 1. b
אֲדָמָה 201. 1		אוֹרִי 157. 2
אַדְמִי 60. 3. b (1)	אָהֱלֹה 220. 1. b	אִירַשׁ 149. 2
אֲדֹנִי 199. c, 201. 2, 231. 3. a	אָהֳלוֹת 200. c	אִוָּשֵׁעַ 149. 2
וַאדֹנִי 234. c	אָהֳלֵי 216. 2. b	אוֹת 197. b, 200. a
וַאדֹנָי 234. c	אֹהָלִים 60. 3. c	אִוָּתֵר 149. 2
אֲדֹנֵי בָם 21. 1	אֳהָלִים 200. c	אוֹתֹתָם 220. 2. a
אֵלוֹנִים 201. 2	אֲהָמְיָה 172. 3	אָז 235. 1
אֶדְקַם, אֶדְקֵם 141. 3	אוֹ 239. 1, 283. 2. a	אֵזוֹר 60. 3. c, 184. b, 216. 1. b
אֶדֶר 112. 5. a	אוֹב 200. a	
אֲדַרְכֹּנִים 53. 1. a	אוֹדֶךָ 105. b	אָזִין 53. 2. a, 111. 2. c
אדרם 11. 1. b	אִוָּדַע 149. 2	אַזְכָּרָה 189
אֶדְרשׁ 91. c	אוּרִי 240. 1	אֶזְכְּרָכִי 104. c
אֶדְרשׁ 53.1.a, 91.b, 119.1	אוֹיֵב 180. 2	אָזְלַת 86. b
אָהַב 82. 1. a (2), 110. 3, 112. 5. c	אֱוִיל 194. 2	אָזְלַת יָד 35. 1
	אֱוִילִי 194. 2	אֹזֶן 197. a, 217, 221. 5
אָהַב: 119. 1	אוֹכִיל 57. 2 (2) a, 111. 2. d	אָזְנַח 189
אָהֵב 53. 2. a, 111. 2. 5	אִגֵּד 149. 2	אָזְנֵי 221. 4
אַחֲבָה 87, 119. 3	אוּלָם 207. 2. b, 215. 1. a	אָזְנַיִם 203. 1
אֲהָבָה 118. 3		אָזְנֵינוּ 221. 4
אֱהָבוּ 119. 4	אוֹמַר 111. 2. b	אָזְנְכֶם 220. 1. b
אֲהָבוּ הֲבוּ 43. b, 92. a, 122. 1	אָוֶן 63. 2. a	אֲזִקִּים 53. 1. a
	אוֹן 186. 2. c	אָזַר 112. 5. c
אֹהֲבִים 201. 1	אוּרִיּוֹת 13. a	אֶזְרָח 60. 3. b (1), 92. e
אֲהַבְךָ 101. 3. a, 104. h, 119. 1	אוּרִים 208. 3. c	
	אִגֵּסֶר 149. 2	אֶזְרֹעַ 53. 1. a, 183. c
אֹהַבְכֶם 221. 3. a	אִוָּעֵד 56. 3	אָח (n.) 68. b, 197. a, 207. 2. b, 215. 1. e, 220. 1. e
אָהַבְתָּם 119. 3	אוֹפָן 207. 2. a	
אֲהַבְתִּחֻהוּ 104. i	אוֹצָר 200. a, 216. 1	
אֲהַבְתִּי 61. 6. a	אוֹצְרָה 111. 2. d	אָח (int.) 240. 1
אֲהַבְתָּךְ 104. c	אוֹר (v.) 82. 1. a (3), 156. 2	אֶחָד 223. 1, 248. a, 250. 1.
אָהָה 240. 1		אֲחָדִים 223. 1. a

INDEX III.   345

אַחְוָה 189
אָחוּז 90 pass.
אָחוֹת 205. c, 209. 3
אָחַז 34, 110. 3, 118. 2
אֶחָז 34, 172. 4
אָחֻז, אָחֻז 112. 1
אֲחֻזַּת 60. 3. b(2), 119. 4
אֲחֻזָּתִי 60. 3. b (2), 120. 1
אַחְזֵק 97. 2. a
אֲחִזָּתָה 104. i
אֲחִי 61. 6. a
אֲהִיוֹתָךְ 220. 2. a
אַחִים 60. 1. a
אֹהֶל 140. 3
אַחַר 237. 1, 238. 1
אַחֵר 210. c
אַחֵר 60. 4, 111. 2. b
אֲחֵרוּ 60. 3. b(2), 121. 2
אַחֲרוֹן 193. 1
אַחֲרֵי 238. 1. a
אַחֲרִית 198. a (4)
וָאֶחְשְׁבָה 99. 3. b
אֲחַשְׁדַּרְפָּן 195. 2
אֲחַשְׁתְּרָן 195. 2
אַחַת 54. 2, 205. b, 223. 1. a
אֶחָת 223. 1. a
אַט 175. 3
אִטּוּן 216. 1. b
אָטֵם 112. 5. a
אֲטֶר 112. 5. a, 125. 3
אִי 61. 6, 236
אִי (n.) 184. b
אִי (int.) 240. 1

אָיֹב 156. 1
אַיֵּה 61. 6
וָאֲנִיחָה 99. 3. b
אֵי זֶה 75. 2
אֵירְ 51. 2
אַיִל 208. 3. c
אֵיל 183. b
אַיָּלוּת 60. 3. b (1)
אֵי לָזֹאת 75. 2
אֲיָלִילָה 150. 2
אֵילְכוּ 151. 1
אֵילָם 200. c
אָיֹם 207. 2. c
אֵימָה 200. c
אֵימָתָה 61. 6. a
אַיִן 236, 258. 3. b
אוֹסִירֵם 150. 1
אִישׁ 207. 2, 243. 2. a
אִישׁוֹן 193. 2. a
אַשְׁרֵי 57. 2 (1)
אִיתָם 11. 1. b
אִירָם 140. 1
אֵיתָן 189, 210. c
אַךְ (adv.) 235. 2 (2)
וָאַךְ (v.) 175. 3
אַבְגָּדָה 91. c
וְאָבֶה 175. 3
אַכְזָב 189
אַכְזָר 189
אַכְזָרִי 194. 2
אַכְזָרִיּוּת 198. a (4)
וָאֶכְחַד 119. 1
אָכֹל 110. 3
אָכֹל, אֶכֹל 112. 1

(לֹה) וַיֹּאכַל 174. 4
אֹכַל 111. 2. b
רָאֹכַל 99. 3. a
אָכְלָה 104. d
(לֹה) אֶכְלָה 63. 1. b, 174. 4
אָכְלָה 106. a
אֲכַלְכֶם 106. a
אֲכָלַתְהוּ 104. i
אֲכָלַתְהוּ 104. i
אֲכַלְתִּי 65. a
אֲכַלְתָּה 104. i
אֲכָלָם 112. 1
אֲכָלַתְנִי 104. i
וַאֲכַסֶּה 99. 3. b
וָאֲכַסֵּךְ 99. 3. b
אִפֹּה 140. 3
אִכָּר 187. 1. a
אִקְרָה 24. b
אַבֹּת 140. 1
אַכְתַּבְנָה 16. 3. b, 105. d
אֶכְתּוֹב־ 88
אַל 235. 1, 264
אֵל (pron.) 58. 1, 73. 1
אֵל (n.) 186. 2. c
אֶל־ 237. 1, 238. 1
אֶלְגָּבִישׁ 229. 1. a
אַלְגּוּמִּים 14. a, 51. 4
אָלָה 216. 1. a
אֵלָה 200. b
אֵלֶּה 58. 1, 61. 6, 73. 1
וֵאלֹהֵי 234. c
אלהים 11. 1. b
אֱלֹהִים 201. 2, 231. 3. a

INDEX III.

אֱלֹהֵימוֹ 220. 2. c
וַאֲלֹהֵינוּ 234. c
אֱלוֹהַּ 11. 1. b
אֱלוֹת (v.) 172. 2
אֵלַי 238. 1. a
אֱלֵיהֶמָּה 220. 2. c
אֱלִיל 184
וָאֵלֵךְ 99. 3
אֵלְכָה אֱלֹכָה 45. 5. a
אַלְלַי 20. 2, 240. 1
אִלֵּם 187. 1. b
אִלְּמִים 51. 4
אַלְמָה 200. c
אַלְמוֹדָד 229. 1. a
אֶל־מוּל 237. 2 (1)
אַלְמָן 193. 1
אַלְמָנוּת 108. a (4), 109. d, 200. b
אֶל־עֵבֶר 237. 2 (2)
אַלָּה 84. 3. a (2), 112. 5. a
אָלְקֶה 226
אַלְפִּי 250. 2 (2) a
אַלְפֵיכֶם 250. 2. (2) a
אֲלָפִים 203. 4, 226
אַלְקוּם 229. 1. a
אֱלָתִי 221. 2. b
אֵם 68. b, 107. a
אִם 239. 1, 283
אֲמַאסְאָד 11. 1. a
אֲמָאסָאךְ 104. b
אָמָה 53. 3. b, 211. a
אַמָּה 198. c
אֻמָּה 200. c

אָמוֹן 184. b
אֱמוּנָה 60. 3. b (1), 201. 1. a
אֱמוּנִים 201. 1. a
אֲמִילָם 105. a
וָאֲמַלְּטָה 99. 3
אֻמְלַל 187. 1. d
אָמְלַל 92. a, 115
אֲמַלֵּל אֲנִי 42
אֲמֵלָלִים 210. c
אָמְנָם 235. 2 (1)
אֻמְנָם 235. 2 (1)
אָמֵץ 79. 2, 84. 3. a (2)
אֹמֶץ 112. 1
אָמַר 110. 3, 125. 3
אָמַר 65
אָמְרִי 86. b (3 pl.)
אָמַר 208. 3
אֱמֹר 60. 3. b (1), 112. 1
אֱמָר־ 60. 3. b (1)
אִמְרָה 208. 3
אֲמָרָה 60. 3. b (1)
אֲמַרְכֶם 106. a, 127. 2
אֲמָרְתְּ 127. 2
וָאֲמַרְתָּ 33. 4
אֲמִשְׁךָ 157. 3
אֱמֶת 60 3. b (1), 205. b
אֲמִתּוֹ 60. 3. b (1), 221. 2. a
וָאֲמֹתְתֵהוּ 99. 3. b
אֲנָחָה 101. 3. a
אָנָה רָאֲנָה 63. 1. c
אָנוּ 71. a (1)
אָנוּ 46

אֲנַחְנוּ 131. 1
אֱנוֹשׁ 184
אֲנִי 197. b
אֲנִי 71
אֲנִי 65, 71. a (1)
אֲנִי 65. b
אֲנִיָּה 108. b
אָנֹכִי 71
אָנֵן 141. 3 (p. 175)
אָנָה 84. 3. a (2)
אָנָק 112. 1
אֲנָק 50. 1
אֲנָשִׁים 207. 2. e
אָסִיף 185. 2. a
אָסְלָיָהוּ 125. 1
וְאַסְפְּרֵם 60. 3. c, 92. e
אָסַף 110. 3, 112. 5. c, 115, 151. 2
אֱסֹף 112. 1
אֲסֻפָּה 111. 3. a, 112. 1
אֲסֵפָה 151. 2
אֲסַפִּי 80 (f. s.)
אֲסֻפָּה 151. 2
אֲסַפְסֻף 188
אֲסָפְתוֹ 104. j
אָסֵף 53. 3. b, 88 (1 c.)
אָסַר 112. 5. b
אֲסֹר 60. 3. c
אָסֹר 60. 3. c
אַחֲרֵי 61. 6. a
אֶחְרֶם 105. d
וָאָעִיד, רָאֲעֵד 160. 3
רָאֲעַל 172. 4, 175. 3
וָאֲעַן 172. 4

INDEX III. 347

אֶעֱנֶה 113. 1	אֲקִים 56. 3	אֶרֶז 216. 1. e
וָאעֲנֶה 57. 2 (2) a	וָאָקָם 99. 3. a	אַרְמוֹן 200. a
וַאַעַשׂ 172. 4	וָאֶקְרָאָה 63. 1. c, 97. 1.	אֲרַמִּי 194. 1
וָאֶעֱשֶׂה 172. 4	b, 164. 5	אֲרָמִית 235. 3 (3)
וָאעְשֹׁר 57. 2 (3) a,	וָאֵרָא 99. 3. a, 172. 4	אַרְמְנָתוּ 56. 1, 105. b
111. 2. c, 234. c	וָאֶרְאָה 172. 4	אַרְמְנוֹת 216. 1. c
אַף (n.) 184. b, 207. 2	אֶרְאֶלָם 24. a	אַרְנֶבֶת 197. c
אַף (conj.) 239. 1	וָאֶרְבָּה 175. 3	אֶרֶץ 51. 3, 63. 2. a,
אפאיהם 104. f., 172. 3	אָרְבָּם 22. a	197. b
אָפַד 112. 5. a	אַרְבָּעָה 207. 2. a, 214.	אֶרֶץ 65
אָפָה 110. 3	1. b, 223. 1	אַרְצָה 61. 6. a, 219. 1
אֵפוֹ 112. 1	אַרְבָּעִים 225. 1	אַרְצָה גֹּשֶׁן 22. b
אַפַּיִם 203. 1	אַרְבַּעְתַּיִם 223. 1	אַרְצָה כְּנַעַן 22. b
וְאָפִיתָ 100. 2. a (1)	אַרְבַּעְתָּם 250. 2 (2) a	אָרַר 141. 1 (p. 175)
אַךְ כִּי 239. 2 (1)	אַרְגָּז 51. 4	אֲרַשׂ 119. 1
אֲפֵלָה 198. a (2), 216.	אַרְגָּמָן 51. 4, 195. 2	אִשְׁמָאִילָה 180. a
1. b	אָרָה־ 141. 1	אֵשׁ 197. b, 201. 1
וָאֶאֱסֹף 172. 4	אָרְחֲלִי 19. 2	אֵשׁ 57. 2 (1)
אֶפֶס 235. 3 (1)	אַרְיֵה 208. 3. b	אֶשְׁאָלָה 101. 3. a
אֶפְעֶה 127. 3	אֲרוֹמָם 82. 5. a	וָאֵשֵׁב 99. 3. a
וָאֵפַת 173. 3	אֲרוֹמִמְךָ 104. h	אַשְׁדּוֹדִית 210. d
אִצָּה 164. 5	אָרוֹן 197. b	אֲשֵׁדִית 216. 2. a
אֶצְבַּע 183. c, 107. a	אָרוּר 139. 2	אִשָּׁה 200. b, c, 207. 2
אֶצְבָּעוֹת 207. 2. a	וְאָרוּתִי 141. 2	אַשּׁוּר 197. a
וָאֵצוּ 174. 4	אֹרַח 197. b, 200. a,	אֶשְׁחָקֵם 118. 3
אֱצוּרָה 105. d	208. 3. b	אֲשִׁישָׁה 200 c
אֵצֶל 237. 1	אֹרַח 198	אַשְׁפִּים 94. b
אֹצָר 50. 3	אֹרְחָה 198	אֶשְׁכֹּל 200. a, 210. e
אֲצָרָה 101. 3. a	אֹרְחֹתָיו 60. 3. c	אֶשְׁכְּלוֹת 216. 1. c
אֲצָרְנָה 105. d	אֲרִי 200. c. 208. 3. d	אֶשְׁכְּלוֹת 216. 1. c
אֲקַבְּצֵן 105. b	אֲרָיֶךָ 56. 3. a, 168. a,	אֶשְׁלַח 60. 2. a
וָאָקוּם 99. 3. a	174. 4	אֶשְׁלַח 60. 2. a
אֲקוֹמֵם 56. 3	אָרַךְ 79. 2, 118. 1	אֶשָּׁלֵחַ: 60. 2. a
וְאָקִים 99. 3. a	אָרֹךְ 185. 2. b, 207. 2. c	אֶשָּׁלֵחָה 126. 1
		וְאַשְׁלִיךְ 99. 3

וְאַשְׁלִיכָה 99. 3	אֵת, אֶת 71. a (2)	בְּאִי 216. 1. a
אָשָׁם 82. 1. a (2), 112. 5. a	אֵת 71. a (2)	בְּאָסְפְּכֶם 22. a
	אָתָא 177. 3	בְּאֵר 121. 1
וְאַשְׁמִיד 99. 3	אתה 11. 1. a	בְּאֵר 60. 3. c, 197. a
אָשְׁמָן 189	אַתָּה 71	בְּאֹשׁ 60. 3. c
וְאַשְׁמָעָה 98. 1. a	אַתָּה, אָתָּה 71. a (2)	וּבָאת, וּבֵאתְ 16. 1
אָשְׁמְרָה 97. 1	אָחוֹן 197. a, c	וּבָאתָ, וּבָאתִי 100. 2. a (1)
אֶשְׁנָב 183. c, 221. 6. a	אֶתְחַבָּר 96. a	
אֶשְׁעָה 172. 3	אֹתִי 71. a (2)	בְּכֹל 57. 1, 187. 1. e
אֶשְׁפֹּט 91. c	אִתִּי 61. 5	בִּבְלִי 237. 2 (4)
אִשָּׁפֵת 207. 2. c	אָחִיו 112. 1, 172. 1	בְּנַד 84. 3. a (3)
אֶשְׁקָה 98. 1. a	אַתִּיקִיךָ 220. 2. c	בֹּגֵד 90
וְאַשְׁקֶה 175. 3	אֹתָךְ 65. a	בֶּגֶד 22. a, 197. b, 200. c, 221. 5. a
אֶשְׁקוֹטָה 98. 1. a	אֹתְכָה 65. a	
וְאֶשְׁקוֹלָה 98. 1. a	אֶתְמוֹל 53. 1. a, 183. c	בֶּגֶד 87
וְאֶשְׁקְלָה 98. 1. a	אֵתָן 210. c	בֶּגְדָה 207. 1. a
אֲשֶׁר 74, 285	אֶתֵּן, אֶתֶּן 71. a (2)	בִּגְדְתָה 86. b (2·m.)
אֲשֶׁר (conj.) 239. 1	אַתָּנָה, אַתֵּנָה 71. a (2)	בָּגוֹד 87, 210. a
אֲשֵׁרָה 200. c	אָתָנוּ 177. 3	בִּגְלַל 237. 2 (2)
אַשְׁרָיו 221. 5. d	אֶתְנַן 207. 2. b	בְּדָבָר 61. 1
אַשְׁרֶיךָ 220. 2. c	אֶתְנַנָּה 220. 1. b, 221. 6	בָּדָל 80. 2. a (3)
אַשְׁרֶיךָ 221. 5. d	אֶתְקְנֵךְ 105. b	בְּהִבָּרְאָם 4. a
אֵשֶׁת 205, 214. 1. b		בֹּהוּ 57. 2 (4), 184. b
וְאֶשְׁתְּ 172. 4	בְּ 231. 1, 233, 267. b, 272. 2. b	בְּהִיוֹת 177. 1
אֶשְׁתּוֹלְלוּ 96. a		בַּהֲכִין 245. 5. b
אֶשְׁתַּעֲשַׁע 141. 6	בֹּא 157. 2	בִּהְפֶּצְלָם 91. b
אֵת (n.) 207. 2. e	בָּאָה 34	בָּהַל 121. 1
אֵת, אֹת 58. 2. a, 238. 2, 270	בָּאָה 34	בְּהֵמָה 216. 2
	וּבָאָה 156. 4	בְּהֵמוֹת 201. 2
אֶת־ 43. a	בְּאָהֳלִים 229. 4. b	בְּהֵן 61. 2. a, 184. a, 197. a, 208. 3. b
אֵת 43. a	בְּאֵר 156. 2	
אֵת (prep.) 237. 1, 238. 2	בֹּאִי (pret.) 156. 2	בְּהָרֵג 113. 1, 2
	וּבֹאִי 156. 4	בְּהֹשָׁמָּה 140. 6
אֶת־ 61. 5	בָּאזְקִים 57. 2 (2) a	בּוֹא 79. 1, 157. 1

INDEX III.

בֹּאֲנָה 104. g
בֹּגֵד 90
בִּדְאָם 57. 2 (3) a, 164. 3
בִּכְיָה 209. 1. a
בִּיל 53. 2. a, 184. b
בִּיסִים 156. 2
בֹּקֶר 186. 2. a
בִּיר 139. 2
בּוֹר 200. a
בִּירְאֵיָה 201. 2
בּוֹשׁ 82. 1. a (3), 156. 2, 157. 1, 2.
בּוֹשִׂים 156. 2
בִּישַׁסְכֶּם 92. b, 101. 3
בַּז (n.) 207. 2. a
בַּז (from בִּיז) 156. 2
בֹּז 139. 2
בְּזַאוּ 139. 3
בַּדּוּי 141. 2
בָּזַז 141. 1 (p. 175)
בְּזָזְנִי 139. 1
בָּחוּן 185. 2. c
בָּחוּר 210. a
בַּחוּרִים 60. 3. c
בְּחֶטְאָה 27
בָּחִיר 185. 2
בָּחַן 50. 1
בֹּחַן 121. 1
בָּחַר 50. 1
בָּחַר בְּתֵיהֶם 43. b
בְּחִרִי 19. 2
בְּחָרִים 201. 1. b
בְּטוּחַ 90. pass.

בֶּטַח 184. b
בֹּטֵחַ 126. 1
בִּטָּחוֹן 103. 2
בֶּטֶן 197. a
בְּטָנִים 208. 3. a
בְּטָרֶם 239. 2 (3), 263. 1. b
בְּעִי (for בִּי) 53. 3. a, 240. 2
בְּיָד 237. 2 (2)
בְּיָד 16. 2. a
בִּיהוּדָה 57. 2 (2)
בִּין 158. 2, 3
בֵּין 237. 1, 238. 1
וּבְרֵיעוֹ 4. a
בִּינָתִי 158. 1
בְּיַעֲקֹב 16. 2. u
בֵּיצִים 200. b
בִּיקְרוֹתָיו 14. a, 24. b
בַּיִת 61. 2, 63. 2. a, 197. b, 208. 3. c
בֵּית 57. 2 (5), 62. 1, 216. 1. d
בֵּית־הַלַּחְמִי 246. 3. b
בֵּית־הַשִּׁמְשִׁי 246. 3. b
בֵּיתָה 63
בַּךְ 65. a
בָּכָה 184. b
בְּכוֹ 172. 2
בָּכוֹ (for בַּעֲבוֹ?) 53. 3. a
בְּכֹר 50. 1
בִּכּוּר 50. 1
בְּכִי 184. b

בְּבִטְּלוֹ 91. b, 231. 5. a
בִּכְתוֹב 22. a, 101. 2. b
בַּל 53. 3. a
בַּלָּהָה 198. a (3)
בְּלוֹאֵי 56. 4
בֵּלְטְשַׁאצַּר 18. 2. c
בְּלִימָה 195. 3
בְּלִיַּעַל 195. 3
בָּלַל 141. 3 (p. 175)
בֶּלַע, בָּלַע 126. 1
בִּלְעֲדֵי 237. 2 (4)
בְּלַעֲנוּהוּ 127. 2
בִּלְתִּי 61. 6. a, 237. 1
בִּמְאֹד 235. 3 (1)
בַּמָּה 231. 4. a
בְּמוֹ 233. a
בָּמֳתֵי 13. a, 214. 2. b
בָּמֳעַי 45. 4
בַּמַּעֲנֶה 45. 3
בְּמַקְהֵלוֹת 16. 2. a
בְּמָתַי 19. 2, 216. 1. c
בֵּן 51. 3, 185. 2. d, 215. 1. b
בֶּן־הַיְמִינִי 246. 3. b
בָּנָה עִיר 35. 1
בְּנוֹ (from בּוֹא) 104. 2
בָּנוּ 34
בָּנוּ 34
בְּנוֹ (suf.) 221. 3. a
בְּנוֹ (parag.) 61. 6. a
בָּנוֹת 207. 1. a.
בְּנוֹתֶיךָ (r.) 173. 2
בְּנוֹתֵיכֶם 220. 1. b
בְּנֵי 61. 6. a, 218

בָּנִים 207. 1. a	בּרָאָה 164. 4	גָּאֹה גָּאָה 22. b
בָּנִית 80. b (1 c.)	בָּרָד 185. 2. b	גֵּאָה 185. 2. d
בִּנְה 221. 3. a	בָּרוּךְ 92. d	גְּאוּלִים 201. 1. a
בִּנְסֹעַ 4. a	בְּרוֹשׁ 51. 1	גֵּאָיוֹת 208. 3. c
בִּנְפֹּל 22. a, 101. 2. b	בְּרוֹת 51. 1	גָּאַל 117
בִּנְתָּהּ 132. 1, 158. 1	בַּרְזֶל 193. 2. c	גָּאַל 116. 4
בְּסָאסְאָה 24. a	בָּרַח 50. 1	גְּאֻלָּה 201. 1. a
בִּסְעָרָה, בַּסְּעָרָה 16. 3. b	בָּרִיחַ 210. a	גְּאֻלָּה 119. 3
בַּעֲבוּר 237. 2 (2)	בְּרִיעִי 194. 2. a	גְּאַלְכֶם 221. 3. a
בְּעַד 237. 1	בָּרֵךְ 80. 2. a (1), 80. 2. a (2), 120. 3	גַּב 200. c
בָּעֶצֶם, בְּעֶצֶם 113. 1. 2	בָּרַךְ, בֵּרַךְ 119. 1	גֵּבָה 143. a
בְּעָיוּ 172. 1	בֶּרֶךְ 197. a	גְּבַהּ 215. 1. c
בַּעַיִם 60. 3. a	בְּרָכָה 16. 2. a	גְּבֹהַּ 185. 2. b
בְּעָלִים 201. 2	בְּרָכָה 216. 1. b	גֹּבַהּ 184. b
בַּעַר 121. 1	בֵּרְכוֹ 60. 3. a, 120. 3	גבהא 11. 1. a
בֹּעֲרָה 196. c	בִּרְכֵי 22. a, 216. 2. a	גְּבֵהָא 86. b
בַּעֲשֹׂר 113. 2	בִּרְכֵיהֶם 22. a	גְּבֹהָה 125. 2
בַּעְשָׂא 60. 3. a	בִּרְכַּיִם 208. 4	גְּבִהַת 60. 3. a
בָּעֵת 121. 1	בָּרָם 139. 2	גְּבוֹהִים 201. 2
בְּצֹאת 199	בָּרְקַת 19. 2. b, 196. b	גְּבוּל 184
בצאתו 11. 1. a	בָּרַר 141. 1 (p. 175)	גְּבוּרוֹת 201. 1. c
בָּצִיר 185. 2. a	בְּשֻׁגָּם 74. a, 139. 2	גְּבַחַת 198. a (3)
בֶּצַע 42. a	בִּשּׁוּבֵנִי 102. 3. a	גְּבִיעַ 50. 1
בְּצָעָם 125. 1	בָּשַׁל 80. 2. a (1)	גִּבּוֹר 187. 1, 215. 1
בָּצֵק 82. 1. a (2)	בִשְׂמְכָה 220. 1. b	גְּבוֹרֶיהָ 220. 2. c
בַּצֹּרֶת 207. 1. d	בִּשְׁקָתוֹת 45. 2	גְּבִר 199. c
בָּקַע 80. 2. a (4)	בַּת 205. b	גְּבִיר 184
בְּקָעָם 125. 2	בִּתּוֹ 221. 2. a	גָּבַל 50. 1
בָּקַק 141. 3 (p. 175)	בְּתָחְבֻּכֵי 220. 1. b	גבלת 11. 1. b
בָּקַר 197. c, 201. 1	בְּתוּלִים 201. 1. b	גַּבֵּן 187. 1. b
בֹּקֶר 50. 1, 208. 3. b	בִּתִּי 58. 2	גַּבְּנֻן 207. 2. c
בַּר 186. 2. c	בָּתִּים 208. 3. c	גַּבְנֻנִּים 187. 2. c
בָּרָא 78. 1	בִּתְכֶם 221. 6	גִּבְעֹל 193. 2. c
בָּרָא 166. 3		גָּבַר 82. 1. a (2)

INDEX III.

גְּבַר 183. b, 184. a
גֶּבֶר 184. a
גַּבְרִיאֵל 61. 6. a
גְּבֶרֶת 205
גַּג 200. a
גָּד 141. 3 (p. 175)
גָּדוֹל 58. 1, 185. 2. b, 210, 217
גְּדוֹל־ 215. 1. c
וּגְדָול־כֹּחַ 13. a
גְּדִי 208. 3. d
גְּדִיָּה 209. 2. b
גְּדָיַי 216. 1. a
גָּדֵל 82. 1. a (2)
גָּדַל (v.) 58. 1
גָּדֵל (adj.) 185. 2. b
גָּדֹל 58. 1, 184
גְּדָל־ 215. 1. c
גִּדֵּל, גַּדֵּל 92. c
גֶּדַע 126. 1
גָּדֵר 197. b, 216. 1. e, 217
גְּדֵרֹת 217
גְּדֵרוֹתָיו 221. 2. b
גְּדֵרֹתַיִם 203. 5. b
גֵּו 50. 3, 68. b
גֵּוִי 157. 1
גֵּוִי 221. 3. a
גּוּר 220. 1. c
גּוּרֵהֶם 220. 2 b
גְּיוֹתַיחֻנָּה 220. 2. c
גֵּוָה 221. 3. a
גּוֹל 158. 3
גּוֹלֵל 141. 4

גּוּפָץ 186. 2. b
גְּוַע 125. 2, 156. 1
גּוּר (v.) 179. 2. a
גּוֹרָל 200. a
גַּז 139. 2
גִּזְבָּר 195. 1
גִּזָּה 68. b
גָּזַז 50. 3, 68. b
גָּזַז 139. 2
גָּזִי 141. 1
גָּזִית 50. 3
גָּזַל 50. 3, 68. b
גָּזֵל 216. 1. e
גָּזַר 50. 1, 3, 68. b, 84. 3. a (3), 125. 3
גֹּחַ 158. 3
גָּחוֹן 4. a
גֵּחִי 157. 1
גֵּחִי 157. 2, 158. 2
גֶּחָלִים 216. 2. b
גַּחֶלֶת 200. b, 210. e
גַּיְא 183. b, 197. b, 208. 3. c
גַּיְא 216. 1. d
גִּיחַ 158. 2, 3
גִּיל 158. 2, 3
גַּל (לֹה) 98. 2, 174. 5
גַּל, גַּל (עֵץ) 139. 2
גִּלְגַּל 187. 1. e, 207. 2. a
גִּלְגָּל 187. 1. e
גַּלְגַּל 141. 4
גַּלְגֹּלֶת 187. 1. e, 207. 1. d, 217
גלה 11. 1. a

גָּלָה 57. 2 (5), 80. 2. a (4), 143. a, 170
גָּלוּת 216. 1. a
גָּלַח 126. 1
גְּלִילָה 196. c
גְּלִילִים 16. 2. a
גָּלִיתִי, גָּלִיתִי 174. 2
גַּלֻּלוּ 139. 1
גַּלְמוּד 195. 1
גָּלְתָה 61. 6
גָּמָל 197. c, 207. 2. b
גְּמַלָּה 101. 3. a
גְּמָלַתְהוּ 104. i
גְּמָלַתִּי 104. i
גַּן 197. b, 217
גָּנַב 77. 1
גַּנָּב 187. 1. a
גַּנָּב 93. d
גְּנֵבָה 216. 1. b
גְּנַבְתִּי 104. i
גְּנַבְתִּי 65. a
גְּנַבְתִּי 61. 6. a
גְּנָבְתָם 104. i
גַּנָּה 217
גָּנֹון 139. 2
גְּנָזִים 50. 1
גַּע 131. 3
גָּעֹו 172. 2
גְּעָר־ 125. 2
גַּעַת 131. 4
גֶּפֶן 197. b. 200. b
גָּרַר 207. 2. a
גָּרַד 50. 3, 68. b
גֵּרָזֶן 193. 2. b

INDEX III.

גֹּרֶן 197. b, 200. a, 208. 3. b
גׇּרְנָה 219. 1
גְּרָנוֹת 216. 2
גָּרַר 141. 3 (p. 175)
גְּרֻשִׂנִי 194. 1
גְּרָשָׁתְּמוֹ 104. f.
גֵּשׁ־, גַּשׁ 131. 3
גָּשׁוּ, גֹּשׁוּ 131. 3
גַּשׁ 65. b
גֶּשֶׁשׁ 141. 1 (p. 175)
גֶּשֶׁת 131. 4
גִּשְׁתּוֹ 131. 4
גַּת 207. 2. a

דַּאֲבָה 87, 119. 3
דָּאַג 11. 1. a
דֹּאַג 51. 4
דְּבוֹרָה 198. b, 200. b
דְּבֵלָה 200. b, 214. 1. b
דָּבַק 82. 1. a (2)
דָּבְקָה 87
דבר 10. a
דָּבָר 210
דָּבַר 80. 2. a (2)
דַּבֶּר־ 92. d
דִּבֶּר, דָּבַר 92. c, 126. 2
דִּבֶּרוּ 65
דִּבְרֵי 61. 1, 216. 2
דִּבֶּרְתָּ 65. a
וְדִבַּרְתָּ 100. 2. a (1)
דִּבַּרְתִּי 86. b (2 f.)
דִּבַּרְתִּי 61. 6. a
דְּבַשׁ 183. b

דִּבְשִׁי 221. 5. c
דָּג 185. 2. d, 198, 217
דָּגָה 198, 217
דָּגְקָה 219. 1. b
דּוּד 207. 1. f.
הוּדָאִי 216. 1. a
הוּדָאִים 56. 4, 207. 2. a
הוּדִי 194. 2. b
הוֹרֵג 51. 4
דָּוִיד 11. 1. b
דֹּם 139. 2
דּוֹר 200. c
הוֹרוֹתִינוּ 44. b
דוּשׁ 158. 3
דּוֹשִׁי 157. 2
דֹּחִי 121. 1
דַּי 215. 1. d
דַּיָּג 187. 1. a
דִּיגִים 158. 1
דִּיוֹ 184. b
דִּין 158. 2, 3
דַּיָּן 187. 1. a
דִּישֹׁו 158. 3
דְּכָא 165. 2
דְּכָאוּ 107. 1
דַּל 207. 2. a
דָּלָה 50. 1
דַּלּוּתִי 141. 2
דַּלְיוּ 141. 1
דָּלְיוּ 19. 2. b
דָּלִיּוֹת 209. 2. a
דָּלִית 210. a
דֶּלֶת 107. b, 199. d, 211
דַּלְתוֹת 216. 2. a

דַּלְתַי 216. 2
דְּלָתַיִם 203. 2, 208. 4
דֹּם 139. 2
דָּמִי 57. 2 (4)
דְּמָכָם 58. 2, 221. 1. a
דָּמַם 141. 3 (p. 175)
דַּמֶּשֶׂק 51. 2
הִמְשַׁק 195. 1
דָּנִי 194. 1
דָנֵּנִי 104. a
דַּע 148. 3
דַּע 148. 2
דֵּעָה 53. 2. a, 148. 2
דֵּעָה, דְּעָה 97. 1. b, 148. 3
דֵּעוּ 16. 2. a
הָעִי־אָפוֹ 45. 4
דְּעָךְ 50. 1
דַּעַת 148. 2
דַּעְתִּי 148. 2
הָרְבָּן 19. 2. b, 65. a, 200. a
הָרְבָנוֹת 19. 2. b, 65. a
דָּרוֹם 193. 2. c
הָרִישׁ 122. 2, 141. 1
דֶּרֶךְ 197. b, 200. b
דֶּרֶךְ, דֶּרֶךְ 65. a
דְּרָכִים 203. 3, 208. 4
דִּרְכָּה 220. 2. b
דַּרְמֶשֶׂק 51. 2, 54. 3
הְרַשְׁנָהוּ 104. l
דָּשָׁא 196. d
דֶּשֶׁא 18. 2. c
דָּשֵׁן (v.) 82. 1. a (2)
דָּשֵׁן (adj.) 185. 2
דָּת 200. b

INDEX III.

הָ, הָ, הָ 229, 245
הָ, הָ, הָ 230, 283
הָאָבַדְתִּ 112. 3
וְהָאֲבַדְתִּ 112. 3
הֶאֱבַדְתִּי 60. 3. b (1)
וְהַאֲבַדְתִּי 60. 3. b (1)
הָאָדָם 246. 1. a
הָאֳהָלִי 246. 2. a
הָאָזִין 80. 2. b, 112. 3
וְהַאֲזִין 112. 3
הַאֲזֵנָה 88 (pl. f.)
הַאֲזִינֵהוּ 94. a, 180. a
וְהַאֲזַנְתָּ 112. 3
הָאָח 240. 1
הַאֲחַיְכֶם 60. 3. c
הָאֶעֱזָרִי 246. 3. b
הָאִישׁ 230. 3. a
וְהַאֲכַלְתִּי 112. 3
הֶאֱכַלְתָּם 112. 3
הָאֱלֹהִים 246. 1. a
הַאֵלֵךְ 60. 3. c
הָאָמוּר 229. 4. a
הָאָמֹר 112. 1
הַאֲנֶה 126. 1
הָאֲסַפְסֻף 57. 2 (2) a, 229. 3. a
הָאֶפְרָתִי 230. 3. a
הָאָרֶץ 63. 2. b, 229. 4. b
הָאַתֶּם 230. 3. a
הַב 148. 3
הֹבְאִישׁ 151. 3
הַבְאֵשׁ 119. 1
הֵבֵאת 106. 1, 107. 2
וַהֲבֵאתָ 100. 2. a (1)

הֲבֵאתָה 107. 2
הֲבֵאתוֹ 104. k
הֲבֵאתָם 160. 2
וְהִבְדִּילָה 100. 2. a (2)
הַבְדֵּל 94. b
הָבָה 148. 3, 240. 2
הַבְהָבִים 188. b
הַבוּ 148. 3
הַבּוֹז 140. 4
חָבוֹק 140. 4
הַבֵּט־ 94. d
הָבִי (from בּוֹא) 164. 2
הָבִיא (imp.) 94. d
וְהָבִיאָה 100. 2. a (2)
הֲבִיאֹתָם 160. 2
הֵבִישׁ 179. 2. a
הֹבִישׁוּ 150. 2
הֲבִישׁוֹת 160. 2
הַבַּיְתָה 219. 1
הָבֵל 84. 3. a (2), 112. 5. a
הֶבֶל 210. 1. e
הַבְלֵהִי 111. 3. a
הַבָּנוֹת 173. 2
הַבַּעַל 240. 1. a
הָבְרוּ 140. 5
הֻבְרָאֲךָ 104. b
הִבָּרְאָה 164. 4
הַבְרוּ 140. 4, 141. 1
הַבְּרָכָה 16. 3. b, 230. 2. a
הַבָּתִּים 45. 2
הִגְבִּיהַּ 126. 1
הַגֵּר 94. d
הַגֵּד 95. c

הַגְדֵּל 94. a
הָגָה 112. 5. a
הֵגָה 18. 2. c, 184. b
הָגוּ 172. 2
הֹגוּ 92. b, 174. 1, 3
הַגּוּת 210. 1. a
הִגְלָה, הָגְלָה 175. 1
הִגָּלוֹת 173. 2
הִגְלִיתָ 175. 1.
הִגְלֵיתִי 175. 1
הָגְלָת 172. 1
הִגַּעַתְּ 127. 1
הִדְבַּק 82. 5
הִדְבְּרוּ 246. 2. a
הֻדַּשׁ 159. 2
הֲדָמְנִי 141. 3
חֲדָס 207. 2. a
הַדַּעַת 245. 5. b
הָדָף 112. 5. a
הָדַק 140. 5
הֵדַק (pret.) 140. 5
הָדֵק (inf.) 140. 5
הֲדָקוֹת 141. 2
הָדָר 112. 5. a, 125. 3
הִדְרִיכָה (inf.) 94. b
הֲדַשְׁנָה 96. a
הָה 240. 1
הֶהָלְכִיא 245. 5. b
הִתְקַדִּישׁ 245. 5. b
הָהָר 63. 2. b, 229. 4. b
הִתְהָרָה 219. 1
הַהֲרוֹתֶיהָ 246. 2. a
הֶהָרִים 63. 1. a, 229. 4
הוּא 177. 1

INDEX III.

הוּא 47, 71. a (3)	הוּקַם 153. 1	הַחׇכְמָה 229. 4. a
הוּא 58. 1, 71, 73. 3, 258. 2	הוּקֲעֲנוּם 60. 3. a, 127. 2	הָחֵל 140. 5
	הוּרַד 57. 2. (2)	הָחֵל 140. 4
הִיא 30. 2	הוֹרַדְתֵּנוּ 104. k	הֵחֵלּוֹ 140. 4
הוּבָא 167. 2	הוֹשֵׁב 66. 1 (2) b	הֶחֱלִי 175. 1
הוּבְאוּ 167. 2	הוֹשְׁבוֹתִים 151. 3	הַחִלֹּתִי 141. 2
הוֹבִישׁ 179. 2. a	הוֹשִׁיב 57. 2 (5)	הַחֲמָנִים 229. 3. a
הָרוּבִנִים 13. a, 208. 3. a	הוֹשִׁיבִי 61. 6. a	הֶחֱצִיוֹ 246. 2. a
הוֹדַע 150. 5	הוֹשַׁע 126. 1	הָחֳרָב 119. 1
הֲוָה 57. 2 (5) a, 177. 1	הוּשַׁר 150. 1	הַחֲרֵם 119. 1
הֹוֶה 177. 1	הַזְּבָחִים 24. b	הֶחֱרַמְתִּי 60. 3. b (1)
הוּחֲדָה 140. 6	הָזִיל 160. 1	וְהַחֲרַמְתִּי 60. 3. b (1)
הוּחַל 140. 6	הִזְלִיחָה 141. 3	וְהָחֳרַשְׁתִּי 112. 3
הוֹי 240. 1	הִזִּפּוּ 54. 2, 4. a, 82. 5. a	הָחָתַל 95. c
הוֹידַע 229. 1. a	הִזְכִּרְכֶם 91. b, 106. a	הַחְתַּת 141. 2
הוֹיָה 177. 1	הֳזֵנֵיתָ 175. 1	וְהַחֲמַתִּי 86. b (2 m.), 112. 3, 139. 3
הוֹכַח (inf.) 126. 1	הַזְעֵק 119. 1	
הוֹכִיחַ (imp.) 94. d	הִזְּרוֹתֵיכֶם 173. 2	הַט 175. 4
הוּלֶּדֶת 150. 5	הָחְבָּאוּ 167. 2	וְהֵטַבְתִּי 161. 5
הוֹלִיךְ 151. 1	הֶחְבֵּאתָה 166. 1	הַטֵּה 175. 4
הוֹלַל 141. 4	הַחְבָה 165. 1	הַטֳהַר 82. 5
הוּקָלוּ 93. b	הֶחָג 63. 1. a, 229. 4	הַשְׁהֵרוּ 63. 1. a, 121. 3
הוֹלֵלוֹת 198. a (4)	הֶחְדַּלְתִּי 53. 2. b, 63. 1. a, 95. b	הַטּוֹנַח 159. 2
הוֹלֵם 90		הֲטִילֵנִי 160. 2
הוּנַח 160. 5	הַחֳדָשִׁים 63. 1. a, 229. 4	הֲשִׁיתוֹתִי 175. 1
הוּסַד 95. c, 150. 5	הַחֲזִיקִי (inf.) 112. 3	הַשַּׁמְאָה 96. a, 166. 5
הֻזְסְדָה 27, 104. e	הֶחֱזַקְתִּי 112. 3	הִי 53. 2. a, 184. b
הוֹפִיעַ (imp.) 94. d	וְהֶחֱזַקְתִּי 112. 3	הִיא 71. a (3)
הוּצָא 150. 1	וְהַחֲזַקְתִּי 112. 3	הַיְדַעְתֶּם 230. 2. a
הוּצְאָה 167. 2	הַחְתִּי 164. 2	היה 11. 1. a
הוּצֵאתָ 16. 1	הֶחְתִּי 164. 2	הָיָה 50. 1, 77. 3, 112. 5. a, 152. 2. a, 156. 1, 177. 1, 258. 2
הוֹצִיא (imp.?) 94. d	הֳחַי 229. 3. a	
הוֹצִיתִיהָ 149. 1, 150. 4	הַחֱיִיתָם 111. 3. b	
הוּצַק 57. 2. (5)	הֶחָכָם 63. 1. a, 229. 4	הָיָה 86. b (3 pl.)

INDEX III. 355

הָיֵה (imp.) 112. 1, 177. 1
הֱיֵה (inf.) 177. 1
וְהָיָה 61. 1. a, 234. b
וְהָיוּ 61. 1. a, 234. b
וְהָיוּ 46
הַיּוֹלָד֔ 245. 5. b
הַיּוֹם 245. 3. b
הָיוֹת 112. 1, 177. 1
הֵיטֵב 235. 3 (2)
הֵיטִיב 145. 2
הֵיטִיב 230. 2. b
וְהָיִית, וְהָיִיתִי 16. 1
הֱיִיתֶם 60. 3. b (1), 112. 1
וִהְיִיתֶם 112. 2, 234. b
הֵיךְ 51. 2
הֵיכָל 189. b, 197. b, 200. c, 210. c, 216. 1. b
הֵילִיכִי 151. 1
הֵילֵל 57. 2 (5)
הֵילֵל 186. 2
הֵימִיר 11. 1. b
הֵימִשִׁי 150. 1
הֵיצֵא 150. 1
הִיצְלַח 65. b
הַיַּרְדֵּן 246. 1. a
הַיָּשָׁר 150. 1
הֵית 172. 1
הַיַּחַד 246. 3. a
הַךְ 98. 2, 175. 4
הַכְבֵּר 94. b
הַכְבֵּשׂ 96. a
הַכֵּה 175. 4

הָכוֹן 159. 2
הָכִיל (ע׳) 160. 4
הָכִיל (הֶאֱכִיל) 111. 2. c
הָכִינוֹ 160. 2
הֲכִינוּ 160. 2
הֲכִינוּנוּ 160. 2
הֲכִינוֹת 160. 2
הַכְפֵּר 246. 1. a
הַכְלִמוֹ 95. a
הֶכְלַמְנוּם 94. a
הַכֻּנּוּ 160. 2
הַכְצַעֲקָתָהּ 24. b, 230. 2. a
הָכֵר 112. 5. a
הַכֵּר 94. b
הַכַּרְמֶל 246. 1. a
הַכְּתֹנֶת 94. b
הִלְאַת 172. 1, 175. 1
הַלְּבָן 24. b, 230. 2. a
הַלְּבָנוֹן 246. 1. a
הַלְבֵּשׁ 94. b
הָלְדָה 150. 5
הֲלֹא 139. 2
הֲלוֹא־זֶה 44. a
הַלָּז 58. 1, 73. 2
הַלָּזֶה 58. 1, 73. 2
הַלָּזוּ 58. 1, 73. 2
הִלָּחֵם 119. 1
הִלָּחֵם 91. b
הַיֶּלֶד 150. 2
הַלַּיְלָה 245. 3. b
הָלַךְ 84. 3. a (3), 112. 5. c, 115, 151. 1, 179. 2. a

חַלָּךְ 151. 1
הִלְכוּ 151. 1
הָלְכוּא 86. b (3 pl.)
וְהָלַכְנוּ׃ 100. 2. a (1)
וְהָלַכְתָּ 100. 2. a (1)
הֹלֶכֶת 205
הִלֵּל 137, 141. 4
הִלֵּל 137
הַלְלוּ 20. 2, 45. 2
הַלְלוּיָהּ 130. 1
הָלַם 111. 1
הֵמָּ 4. a
הֵמָּה, הֵם 61. 6
הָמוֹן 197. b
הַמּוֹל 159. 2. bis
הַמּוֹלוּ 159. 2
חֲמוֹרָאִים 177. 3
הֵמִין 150. 2
הֵמִית 160. 4
וַהֲמִיתִיו 14. a
הֲמִיתָהּ 160. 2
הַמִּשְׁפָּחוֹ 246. 2. b
הָמְכוּ 140. 6, 141. 1
הָמְלַח 126. 1
הָמְלַח 80. 2. b
הַמְלַחַת 127. 1
הָמְלַךְ 95. a
הַמַּמְלָכוֹת 246. 3. a
הַמְנַשֶּׁה 246. 1. a
הֶמֶס 140. 4
הַמַּסּוּ 140. 5
הֲמָסִירוּ 62. 2, 175. 1
הַמֹּעֵד׃ 119. 1
הַמְעַטְרְכִי 104. c, 246. 2. b

INDEX III.

הַשְׁעָלָה 246. 2. b	הֲנִיפְכֶם 160. 4	הֵעִידֹתִ 160. 2
הֻפְצָא 160. 3	הֵנִיקִי 150. 2	הַעִידֹתִי 60. 3. c
הִמְצִיתָהּ 165. 3	הִנָּמְצְאוּ 245. 5. b	הַעִידֹתִי 44. b
הַמַּצְפֶּה 246. 1. a	הָנֵפָה 160. 4	הָעִיט, הַעִיט 229. 3
הֵמֵר 140. 5	הֻנַּפְתָּ 160. 2	הַעִירוֹתִי 160. 2
הֵמַר 140. 5	הֲנִצּוּ 141. 1	הַעַל (v.) 175. 4
הַמָּרוֹתָם 24. b	הֻנְקָה 173. 2	הֶעֱלָה, הָעֱלָה 112. 2
הַמְשֵׁל 45. 2, 230. 2	הֲנִתִיךְ 131. 2	הֹעֲלָה 60. 3. b (2), 112. 2
הַמְשֵׁל 94. b	הֻנְתָן 91. b, 131. 5	הֶעֱלָה 63. 1. a
הֻמָת 160. 4	הֻנְתְּקוּ 131. 2	הֶעֱלִיתָ 245. 5. b
הֱמִתוּ, הֱמִתוּ 160. 5	הַס 240. 1	הֶעֱלִיתִנוּ 104. l
הֵמַתִּי 160. 2	הָסֵב 140. 5	הַעֲלֹתוֹ 173. 2
הֲמִתָּם 160. 2	הֵסֵב 61.4, 135. 3, 140. 5	הָעָם 63. 2. b, 229. 4. b
הֵן (pron.) 71. a (3)	הֲסִבּוּ 61. 4. a, 140. 5	הֶעֱמִיד 60. 3. b (2)
הֵן (adv.) 236	הֲסִבִּי 61. 4	הַעֲמִיד 94. b
הֻנְבְּאוּ 54. 2	הֻסַבַּת 61. 5, 136. 2	וְהֶעֱמִידוֹ 112. 3
הִנָּבְאתוֹ 166. 2	(הָאֲסוּרִים) הָסוּרִים 53. 2. a, 111. 2. c	הַעֲצָבָה 104. e
הִנַּבֵּאתִי 131. 6	הֲסִירָה 160. 2	וְהֶעֱרִיךְ 112. 3
הֻנַּדְלוּ 91. b, 131. 5	הֲסִירְךָ 160. 4	הֶעָרִים 229. 4
הִנֵּה 236, 240. 2	הֵסִית, הֵסִית 160. 1	הָעָרְפָּה 246. 2. a
הִנֵּה (pron.) 71. a (3)	הָסֵךְ 140. 5	הַעֲשֹׂתוֹ 173. 2
הִנֵּה (adv.) 235. 3 (4)	הֻסַּכֵּן 94. b	הַעֲשֹׂתוֹ 113. 1
הִנְחֵנִי 131. 1	הֻסְכַּן 94. d	הֵעֵת 18. 2. c
הֶעְתַּר 246. 1. a	הִסְתַּבֵּל 82. 5	הַפְגְלוֹת 187. 2. a
הִנָּחָה 189. b	הִסְתּוֹלֵל 141. 5	הִפְדָה 175. 1
הִנְחַל 94. b	הִסְתֵּר 91. b	הָפְדָה 175. 4
הִנְחַמְתִּי 63. 1. a, 121. 3, 131. 6	הָעֲבַרְתָּ 63. 3. b (2)	הֻפַח 140. 5
הִנְחַת 131. 1	הֶעֱבַדְתִּיהָ 112. 3	הֻפַח 80. 2. b
הֻנַּחְתִּי 160. 2	וְהֶעֱבַדְתִּיהָ 112. 3	וַהֲפִיצוֹתִי 160. 2
הֵנִיחַ, הֵנִיחַ 83. c (1), 160. 1	הַעֲבִיר (inf. abs.) 94. b	הָפִיר 140. 5
הִנִּיחָה 160. 5	הֶעֱבַרְתָּ 112. 2	הֻפַּךְ 112. 5. b
הֱנִיחוֹתִי 160. 2	הַעֲדֹתָה 160. 2	הֻפְכִּי 61. 6
	הַעֲנֹת 141. 1	הַפְּכְפַךְ 188
		הִפָּלֵא 166. 3

INDEX III.

הִפְלָא 165. 2
הִפְנוּ 95. d
הִפְעַם 245. 3. b
הִפְקֵד (inf. abs.) 91. b
הִפְקֵד 93. a, 95. a
הִפֵר 220. 4. b
הִפֵר 140. 5
הֵפֵר: 65. a, 140. 5
הֻפַר 140. 5
הִפְרָד 119. 1
וְהִפְרֵיתִי 100. 2. a (1)
הִפְרְכֶם 141. 3
הִפְרָם 141. 3
הַפְרָתָה 141. 2
הִפְתַּח 126. 1
הִצְטַדָּק 82. 5
הִצְטַיֵּד 80. 2. b
הִצְטַיַּדְנוּ 161. 1
הִצְטַיְּרוּ 161. 1
הַצִּיג 145. 2
הַצִּיקָה 160. 2
הַצָּלָה 189. b
הַצְלַח 126. 1
הִצְמָתָה 86. b (2 m.)
הִצְפִּינוּ 24. b
הָצַר 140. 5
הֻצַר 140. 5
וְהִצַּרֹתִי 100. 2. a (1), 141. 2
הַקְאַת 220. 4. b
הֵקֵאתוֹ 160. 2
הִקְדִּישׁ 94. b
הִקְדֵּשׁ 94. b
הַקֳּדָשִׁים 229. 4. b

הַקְהֵל 119. 1
הַקְהֵל־ 119. 1
הַקְטִיר 94. b
הָקִים 160. 4
הֻקַם 160. 4
הֵקִים 57. 2 (5), 59, 153. 1
הֲקִימוֹת 66. 2 (2) c
הָקֵל 140. 5
הֻקַל 140. 5
הָקֵם 160. 4
הָקֵם, הָקֵם 160. 5
הֻקַמְנוּ 66. 2 (2) c
הֲקִמֹתוֹ 104. j
הֻקְצוֹת 94. b, 175. 2
הַקְרֵב 119. 1
הַקְשִׁיבָה 98. 1
הַר 207. 2. a
הַרְאָה, הֶרְאָה 114, 175. 1
הֵרָאֹה 173. 2
הֵרָאוֹת 173. 2
וְהִרְאִיתִי 114
הִרְאִיתִיךָ 175.
הִרְאִיתָם 24. b
הַרְבֵּה, חָרֵב 175. 4
הַרְבֵּה 175. 2
הַרְבֵּה, הַרְבֶּה 175. 2, 235. 3 (2)
וְהִרְבֵּית 100. 2. a (1)
וְהִרְבֵּיתִי 100. 2. a (1)
הִרְגִּיז (inf.) 94. b, 114
הִרְגִּיעַ (inf.) 114
הִרְדִּיפָתִי 24. b

הָרָה 63. 1. a, 219. 1. b
הָרוֹ 172. 2
הֹרוּ 92. b, 174. 1, 3
הֹרוֹנֵךְ 53. 3. a
הַרְחֵב־ 119. 1
הַרְחֵק, הַרְחִק 119. 1
הָרִי 199. c
הָרִיּוֹת 209. 1. a
הָרִים 59
הֲרִימוֹת 160. 2
הָרִימִי 160. 4
הֲרִימְכֶם 160. 4
הָרִיעוּ 160. 2
הֲרִיעֹתֶם 160. 2
וְהִרִיתִי 16. 1
הָרֵךְ 140. 5
חֶרְפַּת 114
הֵרַמּוּ 140. 4
הָרָמִים (הָאֲרָמִים) 53 2. a
הָרֵמֹת 160. 2
הָרֵס 111. 1
הָרֵעַ, הָרַע 140. 5
הָרַע 140. 5
הָרֵעִי 160. 2
הַרְעָמָה 24. b
הֲרֵעֹתֶם 160. 2
הָרֹף 66. 1 (1), 98. 2, 175. 4
הִרְפֵּה 175. 4
הִרְפָּה 165. 1
הִרְצָת 172. 1
הֲרָרִי 221. 6. b
הָרָרִי 221. 6. b

הָרָרִים 207. 2. a	הָשָּׁמֵד 94. b	הִשְׁתַּפֵּךְ 82. 5
הָרְרָם 221. 6. b	הִשָּׁמֵד (inf. abs.) 91. b	הִתְאַוֵּיתִי 176. 2
הַשָּׁאָן 246. 1. a	הִשָּׁמְרָה (inf.) 94. b	הִתְאַנֵּף 126. 2
הַשְׂכֵּיל, הַשְׂכֵּל 94. b	הִשָּׁמְרָה 104. b	הִתְבּוֹנֵן 158. 4
הַשְׂמִילִי 180. a	הָשַׁמָּה 140. 6	הִתְבַּקֵּשִׁי 126. 1
הִשְׁתָּרֵג 82. 5	הָשַׁמּוּ 140. 5	וְהִתְגַּדִּלְתִּי 96. b
הַשֵּׁא 166. 3	הֻשַּׁמּוּ׃ 140. 5	הִתְגַּלָּח 126. 1
הִשְׁאַלְתִּיהוּ 119. 2	הָשַׁמּוֹתִיהוּ 141. 3	הִתְגֹּעֲשׁוּ 96. a
הָשֵׁב׃ 65. a	הַשְׁמֵם 139. 3	הִתְגָּר 170. 4
הָשֵׁב 160. 4	הַשְׁמַע 126. 1	הִתְגָּרִית 176. 2
הִשְׁבַּעְתָּנוּ׃ 104. k	הַשְׁמָעִית 128, 189. b	הִתְהַלֵּךְ 96. b
הִשְׁבַּתִּי 86. b (2. m.)	הַשְׁמֵעַ עָם 35. 1	הִתְהַלָּךְ 96. b
וַהֲשִׁבֹתִי 100. 2. a (1)	הַשְׁמֵר 64. 1, 91. b	וְהִתְהַלַּכְתִּי 100. 2. a (1)
והשבתים 10. a	הַשָּׁנָה 245. 3. b	הִתְהַלֵּל 137
הָשַׁח 140. 5	הַשְּׁנַיִם עָשָׂר 251. 4. a	הִתְוַדָּה 150. 3 (p. 182)
הָשִׁיב 160. 4	(עֲ״וּ) הָשַׁע 140. 5	הִתְוַדַּע 150. 3 (p. 182)
הֲשִׁיבוּ 60. 3. b (2)	(לה״) הָשַׁע 35. 2, 175. 4	הִתּוּךְ 187. 2. a
הָשִׁיבוּ 60. 3. b (2)	הָשְׁפוֹת (הָאַשְׁפוֹת) 53.	הִתְוַכַּח 150. 3 (p. 182)
וַהֲשִׁיבוֹתִי 33. 4	2. b, 62. 1	הַתּוֹעֵבֹת 246. 3. a
הֲשִׁיבָה 101. 3. a	הַשְׁפֵּיל (inf. abs.) 94. b	הַחָז׃ 65. a
הֲשִׁיבֹתָם 100. 2	הַשְׁפֵּךְ 91. b	הִתְחוֹלֵל 161. 2
הַשְׁכֵּב 94. b	הַשְׁקָה 50. 1, 179. 2. a	הִתְחַזֵּק 96. b
הֲשָׁכֵב 95. a	הַשְׁקֵט 94. d	הִתְחֵל 176. 4
הָשְׁכְּבָה 95. a, d	הִשְׁתַּבֵּחַ 126. 1	הִתְיַהֵד 80. 2. b
הַשָּׁכִים, הַשְׁכֵּם 94. b	הִשְׁתּוֹנֵן 141. 5	הַתְיוּ 111. 2. c, 172. 1
הִשְׁלִיג 80. 2. b	הִשְׁתַּחֲוָה 168. a	הִתְיַחְשׂוּ 60. 3. a
הִשְׁלִיךְ 94. b	הִשְׁתַּחֲוִית 176. 2	הֶתְיְמָה 141. 3
וְהִשְׁלִיכוּ 100. 2. a (2)	הִשְׁתַּחֲוָיתִי 176. 1	הִתְיַצֵּב 50. 1, 179. 2. a
הַשְׁלֵךְ (inf.) 94. b	הִשְׁתַּחֲוֵיתִי 176. 2	הִתְכַּבֵּד 96. b
הַשְׁלֵךְ (imp.) 94. d	וְהִשְׁתַּחֲוֵיתִי 100. 2. a (1)	הָתֵל 115
הָשְׁלַךְ 95. a	הִשְׁתַּחֲוִיתֶם 176. 2	הָתֵלִּים 142. 3
הָשְׁלַכְתְּ 95. a	הִשְׁתַּחֲוֹת 176. 1	הֻתַּם 140. 5
הָשְׁלַכְתְּנָה 86. b (2 pl.)	הִשְׁתַּחֲוֵיתִי 176. 2	הִתְמֹדֵד 141. 5
הָשְׁלְמָה 95. a	הִשְׁתַּעֲשַׁע 141. 6	הִתְמַהְמַהּ 141. 6

INDEX III.

הֵתַמּוּ׃ 140. 5
הִתַּמָּם 82. 5
הִתְמַרְמַר 141. 5
הִתְנַבּוֹת 165. 3.
הִתְנַבִּיתָ 165. 3
הִתְעוֹלֵל 141. 5
הִתְעַלֵּל 141. 5
הִתְעַנִּית 176. 2
הִתְעָרֵב 119. 1
הִתְפַּלְּשִׁי׃ 96. b
הִתְפָּקְדוּ 59. a, 96. a
הָתְפָּקְדוּ 96. a
הִתְקַדֵּשׁ 96. b
הִתְקַדֶּשׁ־ 96. b
הִתְקַדְּשׁוּ 96. b
וְהִתְקַדִּשְׁתִּי 96. b
הִתְקַדִּשְׁתָּם 61. 4. a, 96. b
הִתְקַלְקַל 137
הִתְקַצַּה 96. b
הִתְרוֹנֵן 141. 5
הִתְרַחַצְתִּי 121. 1
הִתְרַפִּית 176. 2
הִתְשׁוֹטַטְנָה 54. 4. a, 82. 5. a
הָתְשַׁלַּח 45. 2, 230. 2. a
הָתָת 141. 3 (p. 175)

וְ 100. 1, 234, 287
וָ־ 99. 1
וָ 56. 2
וָד 56. 2
וָלֵד 56. 2
וָלֶד 56. 2

זְאֵב 183. b, 197. c
זְאֵבֵי 216. 1. b
זֹאת 11. 1. a
זֹאת 39. 4. a
זָבַח 50. 1
זָבַח 200. c
זִבְחוֹ 125. 2
זְבָחֵימוֹ 220. 2. c
רְזָבַחְנוּ 100. 2. a (1)
זְבֻלוּן 193. 2. a
זֵד 186. 2. c
זֶה 73. 1, 235. 3 (4), 249. 2. a
זֶּה 39. 4. a
זוּ, זֹה 11. 1. b
זוּ, זֹה 73. 1
זָהָב 50, 1, 51. 3, 201. 1
וּזְהָב 16. 3. b, 61. 1. a, 234. a
זוּ 73. 1
זָר 53. 3. a
זוּ גָּאַלְתָּ 22. b
זָוִיֹּת 209. 2. a
זָוִית 210. a
זוּלַת 237. 1
זוּלָתִי 61. 6. a
זוּנָה 14. a, 93. b
זֵרְחָה 156. 4, 196. d
זִידוֹן 193. 2. a
זִידוֹנִים 210. c
זַיִת 208. 3. c
זַכּוּ 141. 1
זָכוּר 90. pass.
זָכְרָה 98. 1

זִכְרוֹן 25
זִכָּרוֹן 200. c, 210, 210. b, 217
זְכָרַי 106. b
זָכַרְתִּי 86. b (2 f.)
זַלְעַף 68. a
זַלְעָפָה 210. e
זְמוֹרָה 200. b
זָמִיר 185. 2. a
זָמַמְתִּי 139. 1
זְמָן 207. 2. b
זַמְּרָה 92. d
זִמְרָת 196. b
זַמֹּתִי 139. 2
זִמַתְכֶנָה 220. 1. b
זַן 207. 2. a
זָנָב 200. a
זָנוּת 200. b
זָעַף 51. 1
זַעַם 84. 3. a (3), 118. 2
זְעֵמָה 119. 3
זְעֵפוּ 119. 3
זָעַק 51. 1
זְעֹק 119. 1
זַעֲקִי 60. 1. a, 119. 4
זַעֲקִי 119. 4
זָעַקְתָּ 119. 3
זָקֵן 197. b
זָקֵן (v.) 79. 2, 82. 1. a (1)
זָקֵן (adj.) 90, 215. 1
זְקֵנִים 201. 1. b
זָקַק 141. 1 (p. 175)
זָרָא 196. d

זָרוּ, זֵרוּ 156. 2
זְרוֹעַ 183. c, 197. a, 200. c
זַרְזִיר 187. 1. e
זָרְמוּ 92. b
זֶרַע 60. 3. c, 216. 1. e
זֶרַע 216. 1. e
זָרַק 80. 2. a (3)

חָבָא 112. 5. a
חֻבְּאוּ 167. 1
חֲבֵרָה, חַבּוּרָה 60. 2. a
חָבַט 112. 5. a
חֲבִי 172. 3
חֶבֶל 50. 1, 112. 5. b
חֹבֵל 186. 2. a
חֶבְלֵי 61. 1
הִתְבַּלְהָתָ 104. i
חִבֵּק 187. 2
חָבַר 112. 5. a
חֲבַרְבֻּרוֹת 188
חָבַשׁ 84. 3. a (3), 112. 5. b
חָג 186. 2. c
חָגָא 11. 1. a
חַגָּא 196. d
חָגַר 112. 5. a
חַד 53. 2. b, 223. 1. a
וְחִדּוּ 100. 2. a (2)
חָדַל 82. 1. a (2), 112. 5. a
חָדְלוּ 24. c
חֶדֶר 216. 1. e
חֹדֶשׁ 208. 3. b

חֳדָשִׁים 60. 3. b (2)
חוֹזַי 199. c
חוּחַ 207. 1. f
חוּפָּה 14. a
חִיל 158. 2
חוֹלֵל 161. 4
חוֹלֵל 141. 4
חוֹנֵן 141. 4
חוּץ 200. a
חוּקוֹ 59. a, 141. 3
חֻקִּי 14. a
חִוֵּר 125. 3
חוֹרָי 104. 2. b
חוֹרָי 199. c
חוֹרֵשׁ 186. 2. a
חוּשָׁה 158. 2
חוֹתָם 186. 2
חָזָה 200. a
חִזָּיוֹן 200. a, 210. b, 216. 2. b
חָזַק 84. 3. a (2), 110. 2, 112. 5. b
חָזַק 185. 2. b
חָזֵק 185. 2. b
חֲזַק 92. c
חִזְקִי 61. 1
חִזְקִיָּה, חֲזַקְיָהוּ 57. 2 (2) 5
חָח 207. 2. b
חָטָא 183. b, 208. 3
חֹטֵא 165. 2
חֲטָאָה 220. 1. b
חַטָּאָה 198. a (3)
חַטָּאֵי 60. 3. c, 216. 1. a

חֹטְאִים 57. 2 (3) a, 164. 3
חַטָּאת 166. 1
חַטָּאת 198. a (3), 205, 217
חַטָּאת 57. 2 (3) a
חֶטְאָתוֹ 166. 2
חַטֹּאתָם 220. 2. a
חָטֹב 50. 1, 112. 5. a
חִטָּה 200. b
חֹטֶר 164. 2
חִטִּין 199. a
חַי (v.) 177. 2
חַי (n.) 215. 1. d
חַיָּב 161. 1
חָיָה 50. 1, 112. 5. a, 152. 2. a, 177. 2
חָיָה: 177. 2
וְחָיָה 234. b
חַיָּה 201. 1. a
וְחִיוּ 234. b
הַחֲיֻכִי: 220. 2. c
חַיִּים 201. 1, 201. 1. a
וְחִיִיתֶם 234. b
חַיִל 158. 2
חַיִל 208. 3. c
חִישָׁה 158. 2
חַיַּת 196. b
חַיָּתוֹ 61. 6, 218
חִכִּי 174. 3
חֲבֵרֵנוּ 172. 3
וְחִכִּיתִי 100. 2. a (1)
חַכְלִילִי 187. 2. c
חַכְלִלוּת 198. a (4)

INDEX III.

חָכָם 80. 1, 84. 3. a (2), 112. 5. a
הָכְמוֹת 193. a. 4
חַכְמֵי 216. 2
חָל 174. 5
חָלָב 215. 1. a
חֶלְבְּנָה 220. 2. b
חָלָה 80. 2. a (4), 112. 5. b
חִלָּה 80. 1
חֲלוֹם 200. a
חַלּוֹן 197. b, 200. c
הַלּוֹיִ 194. 2. b, 199. c
חֶלְחָלָה 187. 1. c, 198. a (3)
חָלַט 112. 5. a
חֲלִי 208. 3. d
חֲלִי 65
חֲלִילָה 219. 1. a, 240. 2
הלכאים 209. 1. a
הלכה 209. 1. a
חָלָל 141. 4
חָלַם 112. 5. c
חַלָּמִישׁ 195. 1
חָלַף 80. 2. a (1), 112. 5. c
חָלַץ 92. d
חֵלֶק 112. 5. b
חֶלְקָה 51. 3
חַלְקֵי 24. b, 216. 2. a
חֲלַקְלַק 188
חֲלַקּוֹת 104. i
חָלַשׁ 84. 3. a (3)
חַלָּשׁ 187. 1

חֶמְאָ 196. d
חָמַד 111. 1, 112. 5. a
חֶמָה (חֶמְאָה) 53. 3. b
חֵמָה 184. b, 216. 1
חָמוֹץ 185. 2. c
חֲמוֹר 197. c
חָמוֹת 205. c
הַמּוֹתַי 141. 2
חֲמִישִׁי 59. a, 227. 1
חָמָל 112. 5. a
חֶמְלָה 87, 111. 3. a
חָמָס 84. 3. a (3), 141. 1 (p. 175), 170. 2. a
חָמַס 112. 5. a
חֹמֶץ 82. 1. a (2), 112. 5. a
חֹמֶץ 184
חָמְצָתוֹ 106. a, 111. 3. a
חֲמֹר 112. 5. a
חֲמַרְמָרוּ, חֳמַרְמָרוּ 60. 3. b (2)
חֳמַרְמָרוּ 92. a, 115
חמש 46
חָמֵשׁ 205, 215. 1. b
חֹמֶשׁ 227. 3
חֲמִשָּׁה 223. 1
חֲמִשֵּׁי 59. a, 227. 1
חֲמִשִּׁיהֶם 250. 2 (2) a
חֲמִשִּׁיר 250. 2 (2) a
חֲמִשִּׁיָה 250. 2 (2) a
חֲמִשִּׁים 225. 1
חֲמִשְׁתָּיו 220. 2. a
חֲמֵשֶׁת עָשֹׂר 224. a
חָמַת 214. 1. b

הֹמֹתַיִם 203. 5. b
חֵן 186. 2. c
חָנוֹן 139. 2
חִנּוּן 187. 1
חָנוּת 139. 2
חָנִיּוֹת, חֲנָיוֹת 209. 3. a
חָנִית 199. d, 200. c
חָנָךְ 112. 5. a
חֹנֶךְ 220. 1. b
חִנָּם 235. 2 (1)
הֶחְנַמָּל 195. 1
חָנַן 80. 1, 84. 3. a (3)
חִנֵּן 141. 4
חֲנֻפָה 139. 2
חֲנֻפֵי 61. 5
חֲנָנְכֶם 106. a, 139. 2
חָנָנִי 141. 1
חָנַס 82. 1. a (2)
חָנַק 50. 1
חַסְדֵי, חַסְדֵי 216. 2. a
חָסָה 112. 5. b
חָסָיו, חֲסָיָה 109. 1, 172. 1
חָסַל 112. 5. a
חָסַם 112. 5. a
חָסֵר 82. 1. a (2), 112. 5. a
חָפָה 112. 5. a
חָפַז 112. 5. a
חָפֵץ (v.) 82. 1. a (1), 84. 3. a (1), 112. 5. a
חָפֵץ (adj.) 185. 2. b
חָפְצָה׃ 80. a
חָפְרִי 216. 1. b

INDEX III.

חָפַר 82. 1 a (2), 112. 5. a	חָרַג 112. 5. a	חַשְׁמַל 53. 2. a
	חַרְגֹּל 193. 2. c	חַשְׁמַלָה 66. 2 (2) b
חָפֵר 82. 1. a (2), 112. 5. a	חָרַד 112. 5. c, 118. 1	חַת 139. 2, 207. 2. a
	חָרֵד 185. 2. b	חִתָּה 112. 5. a
חַפַרְפֵּרוֹת 188	חָרוּל 207. 2. d	חֲתַחַת 187. 1. e, 207. 2. a
חָפַשׂ 112. 5. a	חָרוּץ 210. a	הִתִּיר 209. 2
חִפֵּשׂ 80. 1	חַרְחֻר 187. 2. b	חָתַךְ 112. 5. a
חפשׂות 198. a (4)	חַרְטֹם 193. 2. c, 207. 2. c	חָתַל 112. 5. a
חָפְשִׁי 209. 2	חָרִישׁ 185. 2. a	חָתַם 112. 5. a
חָפְשִׁית 198. a (4)	חַרְמָשׂ 195. 1	חָתַף 112. 5. a
חָצַב 50. 1, 82. 1. a (1), 84. 3. a (1), 112. 5. a	חַרְסָה 61. 6. a	חָתַר 50. 1, 112. 5. a
	חֹרֶף 118. 1	חָתַת 112. 5. c, 141. 1 (p. 175)
חצי 199. b	חֲרָפוֹת 22. a, 216. 2, 2. a	
חָצִי 65, 227. 3	חָרַץ 118. 1	חִתַּתָּנִי 104. j
חָצָץ 141. 1 (p. 175)	חַרְצֹב 207. 2. c	
חֲצֹצְרָה 188. a	חָרַר 141. 2 (p. 175)	טֵאטֵאתִיהָ 57. 2. a (2), 161. 2
חָצֵר 50. 3, 197. b, 200. c	חָרָשׁ 187. 1. a, 210. a, 216. 1. a	טֶבַח 50. 1
חֹק 207. 2, 207. 2. a, 215. 1. c, 217	חָרַשׁ 50. 1, 80. 2. a (2), 84. 3. a (3), 118. 1	טָבָה 187. 1. a
חַק 61. 5	חֶרֶשׁ 187. 1. b, 210. c	טָבַעַת 207. 1. e
חִקָּה 217	חָרָשֵׁי 216. 1. a	טָהוֹר 185. 2. b
חִקּוֹ 59. a	חָרַת 50. 1	טְהָר־ 215. 1. c
חִקִּי 61. 5	חֲשׂוּפַי 194. 2. b, 199. c	טָהַר 50. 1, 82. 1. a (1)
חֻקַּק 141. 5	חָשָׂה 112. 5. b	טוּב 186. 2. c
חֻקָּק 141. 5	חָשֹׂךְ 112. 5. b	טוֹב (v.) 82. 1. a (3), 156. 2, 179. 2. a
חִקְקֵי 20. 2, 207. 2. a	חַשְׂפֵּי 80 (f. s.), 111. 3. a	טוֹב (adj.) 186. 2. c, 235. 3 (3)
חָקַר 50. 1, 112. 5. a	חָשַׂב 112. 5. b	
חֲקַרְתָּנִי 104. j	חֶשְׁבּוֹן 200. a	טוֹטָפוֹת 57. 1, 187. 1. e
חָרֵב 118. 1	חָשָׁה 112. 5. c	טָח, טַח 156. 2
חָרֵב 197. a	חָשַׁךְ 84. 3. a (2), 112. 5. b	טְלָאִים 209. 1. a
חָרְבוּ, חָרְבִי 111. 3. a		טַלְטֵלָה 187. 1. e
חֳרָבוֹת 216. 2. a	חֲשֵׁכָה 200. b, 201. 1. a	טָלַל 141. 1 (p. 175)
חַרְבוֹתָם 220. 2. a	חֲשֻׁכִים 201. 1. a	טָמֵא 82. 1. a (1)
חַרְבִּי 111. 3. a		

INDEX III. 363

טָמְאָה 87, 166. 2	יַאַסְפוּ 112. 3	וַיִּבְנֶה 172. 4
טַמֵּאֲכֶם 164. 4	יַאַסְפֵנִי 112. 3	יִבְקָעוּהָ 125. 1
טָמֵאת 164. 1	יַאַסְרוּם, יָאֱסֹר 60. 1. a	וַיְבַקְשׁוּ 20. 2
טָמֵן 50. 1, 77. 2	וַיַּאַסְרוּם 104. g	יְבָרַךְ 60. 4
טַעַם 131. 4	וַיַּאֲצֵל 111. 2. b	וַיְבָרֶךְ 99. 3. a
טַף 201. 1	יָאַצֵר 113. 1	וַיְבָרְכֵהוּ 60. 3. a
טָפוֹךְ 139. 2	יָאֹר 159. 3	יְבָרֲכוּהָ 104. b
טֶפַח 200. a	יָאֳרֵגוּ 112. 3	יְבָרְכֶנְהוּ 105. b
טָרִי 185. 2. d	יְאָשׁוּרוּהָ 105. e	יָבֵשׁ (v.) 82. 1. a (1), 146, 147. 1
טֶרֶם 263. 1. b	וַיֵּאָת 61. 2. a, 172. 4	
טָרַף 84. 3. a (3), 118. 1	יֵאָתוּ 159. 3	יְבֵשׁ 147. 1
טַרְפֵּי 216. 2. a	יֶאֱתָיוּ 172. 1	יָבֵשׁ 148. 1
	וְיֶאֱתָיֵנִי 172. 3	וַיְיַבְּשֵׁהוּ 150. 2 (p. 182)
יֹאבַד, יֹאבֵד 111. 2. a	יָבֹא 60. 1. a	יְבֹשֶׁת 148. 1
יְאַבֵּד 16. 2. a	וַיְבֹא 10. a	יִגְבַּהּ 60. 1
וַיֶּאֱהָבוּ 105. a	וַיָּבֵא 160. 3, 166. 4	יִגְבּוֹל־ 88
יְאֵהָבַנִי 105. a, 118. 3	יָבָב 141. 1 (p. 175)	יַגְבִּיהַּ 60. 2
וַיֹּאחֶז, יֹאחַז 111. 2. a	יַבְדִּילֵנִי 105. a	יָגֵד 140. 1
יֹאחֲזוּהוּ 60. 3. b (1)	וַיַּבְדֵּל 66. 1 (2) b	יַגְדֶּךָ 104. h
יֹאחֲזוּךְ 60. 3 b (1)	וַיָּבוֹ 164. 2	וַיִּגֶּה 150. 2 (p. 182)
יָאִיץ 158. 2	יָבוֹא 157. 3	יָגוֹל 158. 2
יֹאכַל 57. 2 (2) a, 60. 1. a	יְבוֹנְנֵהוּ 158. 4	וַיָּגַז 140. 1
וַיֹּאכַל 99. 3. a	יְבוּסִי 194. 1	יִגְילוּן 158. 2
יֹאכֵל 111. 2. d, 175. 3	יֵבוֹשׁ 157. 3	יְגִיעַי 216. 1. b
יֶאֱמַץ 111. 2. a	יָבֶז 172. 4	יָגֵל, רָגֵל 158. 2
יֹאמַר, רַאמֵר 126. 2	יָבוֹז 141. 1	וַיָּגֶל (עֵר) 158. 2
וַיֹּאמֶר 111. 2. a	יַבְטַח 126. 1	וַיָּגֶל (עֹץ) 140. 5
יֹאמְרוּ 46	וַיָּבִיא, וַיָּבֵא 160. 3, 166. 4	יָגֵל 172. 4
וַיֹּאמֶר לֹא 24. a		וַיָּגֶל 90. 3. a
יְאָנֶה 111. 2. a	וַיְבִיאוּ 26	וַיִּגַּל 99. 3. a
יֶאֱנַק 111. 2. a	וַיֵּבְךְ 61. 4, 172. 4	וַיָּגֶל 175. 3
יֶאֱסֹף 111. 2. a, 112. 3	יִבְכָּיוּן 172. 1	יִגַל 140. 3
וַיַּאַסְפוּ, וַיֶּאֶסֹף 99. 3. a	יָבֶן 158. 2	יִגְלָה 57. 2 (5)
וַיֵּאָסֶף 151. 2	יָבֵן 172. 4	יִגְמָא 165. 2

INDEX III.

וַיִּגְמֹל 65. a
יָגֵן 140. 5
יָגַע 147. 1
יִגְעוּ, יָגְעוּ 147. 4
יָגְעַתְּ 60. 2
יָגֹר (v.) 82. 1. a (3), 179. 2. a
יָגֹר (adj.) 90
וַיָּגָר 157. 3
יָגֹר 140. 1
וַיְגָרֶשׁ 99. 3. a
וַיְגָרְשׁוּם 104. g
יָגְרָתָּ 86. a
יָד 197. a, 215. 1, 217, 222
וַיֵּדְא 172. 4
יַדְבֵּק 97. 2
וַיַּדְבֵּק 94. c
וַיְדַבֵּר 99. 3
יָדֹד 139. 3
יָדוּ 148. 3
וַיָּדוּ 53. 3. a, 150. 2 (p. 182)
יְהוּד 139. 3
יָדוֹן 157. 3, 158. 2
יְדוֹת 203. 5. a
יְדֵי 216. 1
יָדַי 199. c
יְדֵיהוּ 220. 2. c
יְדֵיהֶם 220. 1. b
יָדַיִם 203. 5. a
יָדִין 157. 3
יִדְכֶּא 167. 7
יִדְכְּאוּ 54. 2
יָדְכָה 220. 1. a

יָדְכֶם 58. 2, 63. 2. a, 221. 1. a
יָדְכֶם 220. 2. b
יָדַל 140. 3
יִדֹּם 140. 1
יִדְּמוּ 141. 1
יָדַע 80. 2. a (4), 147. 2
וַיֵּדַע 147. 5
יָדְעוּן 55. 2. a, 86. b (3 pl.)
יְדָעָנוּ 60. 3. a
יְדָעָנוּהָ 60. 3. a
יִדְּעֹנִים 127. 2
יָדַעְתָּ 86. b (1 c.)
יְדַעְתָּהּ 86. b (2 m.)
יְדַעְתִּין 104. g
יְדַעְתָּם 60. 3. a
וַיִּדַּק 140. 5
ידרך 46
וַיַּדְרִכוּ 94. c
יִדַּשְּׁנָה 63. 1. c, 97. 1. a, b
יָתֵב 179. 2. a
יֶהְגֶּה 60. 3. a
יְהָדֹת 111. 1
יֶהְדְּפֵנוּ 105. d
יְהִיא 177. 1
יְהוּדָה 197. d
יְהוּדָה 150. 2
יְהוּדִי 194. 2. a
יְהוּדִית 235. 3 (3)
יהוה 47
וַיֶּהֱוָה 234. c
יַהְוִיקִים 195. 3
יְהוֹיָקִים 44. b

יְהוֹשִׁיעַ 150. 2
יְחִי 57. 2 (4), 177. 1
יְהִי 177. 1
וַיְהִי 45. 2, 61. 1. a, 177. 1
יהיח 11. 1. a
יִהְיֶה 19. 1, 60. 3. a, 112. 2, 177. 1
וַיְהִי כְכַלּוֹת 22. b
יְהֵילִילוּ 150. 2
יָהֵל 140. 5
וְיָאֱהַל, יַהֵל 53. 3. a, 111. 2. c
יַהֲלֹךְ 151. 1
יְהַלְלוּהָ 105. e
יַהֲלֹם (n.) 190. a
יְהַלְמֵנִי 111. 1
וַיֵּהָם 140. 1
יֵהֹם 140. 3
וַיַּהַס 80. 2. b
יַהֲרוֹס 111. 1
יֶהֶרְסוּ, יַהַרְסוּ 111. 1
יֶהְרְסָה 111. 1
יִתְחַל 142. 3
יְהֶחֱלוּ 142. 3
יוֹאַר 140. 6
יוּבָא 167. 2
יוּבְאוּ 167. 2
יוּבַל 197. b
יוֹדַעְתִּי 92. b
יוּלַק 140. 6
יִיּוֹחָר 111. 2. d
יוּכְלוּ 57. 2. (2) a, 111. 2. b

יוּלַד 93. b	יִזְרְעֶאל 57. 2 (3) a	יָחֵם 147. 2, 179. 2. a
יוֹלֵדָה 207. 1. a	יְחָבֵט 113. 1	יְחֵם 140. 1
יוֹם 200. c, d, 207. 1. f	יְחָבְרָה 93. a	יֶחֱמוּ 60. 3. b (2)
יוֹמָיִם 203. 3	יָחֲבֹשׁ 60. 3. a, 65. a	יֶחֱמוּ 140. 1
יוֹמָם 235. 2 (1)	יְחֻבָּשׁ 65. a	יֶחֱמָיוּן 172. 1
יוֹנֵן 215. 1. b	יַחְבְּשׁוּ 60. 3. a	יַחְמְטָה 88 (3 f. pl.)
יוֹנָה 197. c, 200. b	יַחַד (ע') 140. 1	יְחַמְצֵנִי 121. 2
יוֹנֵק 217	יַחַד (פ') 147. 2	וַיָּחָן, יָחֹן 140. 1
יוֹנֶקֶת 207. 1. c, 217, 221. 5	יַחַד (ע') 140. 5	יָחֵן 61. 2
	יַחְדָּו 100. 2, 172. 4	וַיִּחַן 60. 1. a, 172. 4
יוּשָׁב 140. 6	יַחְדֵּו 235. 3 (1)	יָחֹן 140. 6
יוֹסְפָה 90	יֶחְדַּל 63. 1. b	יַחֲנֶה 172. 4
יוֹעֲדֻנִי 105. b	יֶחְדְּלוּ, יַחְדְּלוּ 63. 1. b	יַחֲנוּ 60. 1. a
יוּעַם 140. 6	יֶחְדְּלוּן 64. 2, 88 (m. pl.)	וַיַּחֲנוּן 99. 3. a
וַיּוֹצֵא, וַיּוֹצֵא 166. 4	יָחוֹם, יָחוּם 157. 3	יָחְנֶה 61. 1, 141. 3
יוֹצֵר 186. 2. a	יֶחֱוָרוּ 156. 1	יָחֳנַן 139. 3
יוּקָשִׁים (מְיֻקָּשִׁים) 59. a, 93. e	יֶחֱזָיוּן 172. 1	וַיַּחֲנַק 113. 1
	יָחֳזְקוּ 61. 1	יַחֲשִׂיוּן 169. 1, 172. 1
וַיֹּאוֹר 175. 3	יֶחְטָא 63. 1. b	יֶחְסֹן 113. 1
יוֹרָא 150. 5	וַיַּחֲטִיא 166. 4	וַיְחִיִּק 25
וַיּוֹשֵׁב 99. 3. a, 150. 3	וַיְהִי, יְהִי 177. 2	יַחְפֵּץ, יַחֲפֹץ 65. a
יוּשַׁד 140. 6	יְחִי 65	יַחְפְּרוּ, יַחְפֹּרוּ 111. 1
יוֹשִׁיבִינִי 105. a	יִחְיֶה 177. 2	וַיַּחַץ, יֶחֱצָה 172. 4
יוֹשְׁכָן 105. a	יְחַיֵּינוּ 172. 3	יֶחֱזָק: 141. 1
יוֹשָׁפָט 53. 3. a	יְחִישָׁה 97. 1	יַחַר 147. 1
יוּשַׁת 158. 4	יְחִיתַן 104. g, 141. 3	וַיִּחַר 175. 3
וַיַּז 175. 3	יָחֵל, יַחֵל 140. 5	יָחַר 140. 3
וַיַּז, וַיֵּז 172. 4	וַיִּחַלָא 177. 3	יְחַר 172. 4
יָזַח 140. 3	יַחְלוּ 141. 1	וַיְחַר 60. 1. a
יָזֻמוּ 141. 1	(וַיַּחַלוּ) וְיַחֲלוּ 24. c	יֶחֱרֶה 172. 4
וַיִּזֶן 175. 3	יַחֲלֹק 60. 4. a, 113. 1	יַחֲרֹף 119. 1
וַיִּזְעַק 119. 1	יְחַלֵּקֵם 59. a	וַיֶּחֱרַף 99. 3. a
וַיִּצַּר 157. 3	וַיְחַלְּקֵם 113. 1	יֶחְשָׂה 111. 1
וַיִּיצֶר 172. 4	יָחַלְתִּי 60. 4. a	וַיַּחֲשֵׂךְ 99. 3

INDEX III.

יַחַת (פֶּן) 131. 1 | יְכַחֵשׁ 119. 1 | יְלַבְּשֵׁנִי 105. d
יַחַת (עַשׁ) 140. 1 | יְכִינוּ 160. 3 | יֶלֶד 56. 2, 80. 2. a (4), 147. 2
יְחַתּוּ, יֵחַתּוּ; 24. c | וַיַּכִירָהּ 105. a |
וַיֵּט 175. 3 | יַכִּירֶנּוּ 105. a | יְלָדוּן 64. 2
יַט 172. 4 | יָכֹל 80. 2. a (3), 82. 1. a (3) | 22. a יַלְדוּת
יְטַב 150. 1, 179. 2. a | | יְלָדַי 216. 2. a
יְטַל, יָטֵל: 160. 5 | יֻכַל 172. 4 | יֻלַּדְתְּ 90 (2 f.)
יְפֵמָא 54. 2, 96. a, 166. 5 | וַיָּכֹל 174. 4 | יְלָדַתּוּ 104. i
יָטְרוּ, יִכְרֶה 65. a | יִכְלֶה 165. 3 | יְלָדַתְהָ, יְלָדַתְהָּ: 104. i
יִירַבְשׁ 144. 2 | יָכְלוּ 86. a | יְלָדַתְנוּ 104. k
יֵדַע: 147. 2 | יִכְלְיוּן 172. 1 | יְלָדַתְנִי 104. k, 150. 1 (p. 182)
וַיִּגְחַל 149. 1 | יִכְלַת 148. 1 |
יִיטַב 147. 4 | וְיָכָלְתָּ 86. a, 100. 2 | יָלּוֹבוּ 159. 3
וַיִּיטַב 147. 5 | יָכֹלְתִּי 86. a | יִלְהֶם 119. 1
וַיִּיטַב 150. 3 | יְכָלְתִּיו 86. a, 104. h | וַיִּלָּחֵם 99. 3. a, 119. 1
יֵיטִיב 145. 2, 150. 2 | וַיִּכָּנַע 126. 1 | יָלִיד 160. 1
יְיטִיב 150. 2 | וַיְכַס 174. 4 | יָלִין, יָלִין 160. 1
יְיֵלִיל 150. 2 | יְכַסְיֻמוּ: 61. 6, 104. f, 172. 1 | יֵלֵךְ 151. 1
וַיִּיף 172. 4 | | וַיֵּלֶךְ 65. a
וַיִּיצֶר 147. 4, 5 | יְכַסְיֻמוֹ 172. 3 | יָלַד 91. b
יִיקַץ 63. 2. c, 147. 4 | וַיַּכְעֵס 119. 1 | וַיִּלָּכֵד 99. 3. a
וַיִּיקַץ, וַיִּקֶץ 147. 5 | וַיִּכְרֶה 172. 4 | יִלְבְּדוּ 105. c
יִיקַר, יִיקַר 147. 4 | יְכָרְסְמֶנָּה 180. a | יָלַל 139. 3, 150. 1
וַיִּירָשׁ 147. 5 | יָכְרֵת 119. 1 | יְלֵל 183. b
וַיִּרְשֻׁם 147. 5 | יְבָרַתוּן 91. b | וְיִלְלַת 57. 2 (3) a, 234. c
יְירֻשִׁירוּ 150. 1 | יכשולו 88 | וַיֵּלֶךְ 158. 2
וַיִּישַׁן 147. 5 | יָפֵת 140. 6 | יַלְקוּט 192. 1
וַיִּישַׁר 147. 4 | יִכְתָּב, יִכְתּוֹב 88, 101. 2. b | יַלְקְטִין 88. (m. pl.)
וַיִּישְׁרֵם 150. 2 (p. 182) | | יָם 207. 2, 215. 1. a
וַיַּךְ 175. 3 | וַיִּכָּתֵב 99. 3. a | וַיִּמָּאֵס 119, 1
יְכַבְּדָנְנִי 105. b | יָכְתְּבוּן 88 (m. pl.) | יְמָאֵס 139. 3
יִכּוֹן 159. 3 | יָכְתוּ 140. 5, 141. 1 | וַיָּמָד 140. 1
יְכִינְיָה 13. a | יִלְבַּב 139. 3 | יָמַד 140. 3
יְכוּפֻּנוּ 61. 3, 105. b, 161. 3 | יִלְבַּשׁ 105. a | וַיְמוֹדֵד 99. 3. a

INDEX III.

יִמּוֹט 159. 3	יִנְאַץ 57. 2 (3) a (?),	יָסַךְ 147. 1
יִמּוֹל 159. 3	122. 2, 140. 5	יָסֻךְ 140. 5
יִמַּח 60. 1. a	וַיִּנָּקָה 99. 3. a	יָסַךְ 140. 6
וַיִּמַּח 173. 3	יָנָח 147. 1	יְסֻכִּים 157. 3
יְמֵי הִיא 220. 1. a	יָנוּחַ 60. 2	יַסְעֵר 92. b
יָמִים 53. 3. a	יָגוֹן 159. 3	יָסַף 80. 2. a (3), 151. 2
יָמִימָה 219. 1. a	יָנוֹעַ 159. 3	וַיֹּסֶף 151. 2
יָמִין 197. b, 199. a	וַיִּנַח 157. 3	וַיִּסָּפֵר 99. 3
יְמִישׁוּן 160. 3	וַיָּנַח 160. 3	יָסַר 147. 3
יְמִיתַם 160. 3	יִנְטוֹר 131. 2	יָסֹר 92. d
יִמָּךְ 140. 3	יְנִי 164. 2	וַיִּסֹּר 60. 1. a
וַיִּמַּל 157. 3	יָנִין 159. 3	יַסְרָה 92. d
יִמַּל 140. 1	וַיְנִיפֵהוּ 160. 3	יִסְּרַנִּי 104. a
יְמַלֵּא 165. 1	וַיִּנַע 157. 3	יִסְּרַנִּי 104. a
יִמְלָךְ־, יִמְלָךְ 88	וַיִּנְגָּה 160. 3	יַעֲבָרְנְהוּ 56. 1, 105. b
וַיִּמְלֹךְ 99. 3. a	יָנַק 147. 1, 150. 1	יַעֲבָרְנְהוּ 105. c
יִמְלְכוּ 88	יִנְקֹב־ 131. 2	יַעַבְרוּ 56. 1
יָמָן 150. 1	יִנְקֹפוּ׃ 131. 2	יָעַד 56. 2, 147. 1
יָמַס 140. 3	יִנְצֹרוּ׃ 131. 2	יְעֹדַד 161. 1
יִמְעַל 60. 1. a	יִנָּשׂוּא 57. 2 (3) a, 86. b	יָעוֹר 159. 3
וַיִּמְעַץ 172. 4	(3 pl.), 164. 3	יְעִירֶנּוּ 105. b
יִמְצָאֵהוּ 60. 3. c	יָסֹב 61. 3, 64. 2, 135. 2,	יָעֹז 140. 1
יִמְצָאוּנָה 105. c	140. 1	יַעֲזֹב־ 64. 1
יִמְצָאָה 164. 5	וַיָּסָב 64. 1, 99. 3. a	יַעְזְרֵךְ 105. b
יִמְצָאֻנוּ 105. b	יָסַב 140. 5	(ע׳) וַיַּעַט 157. 3
יִמְצָאֻנִי 105. c	יָסֹב 135. 2, 140. 1	(לֹה) וַיַּעַט 172. 4
יָמַר 150. 1	יְסֻבֵּי 136. 1	וַיַּעַט 157. 3
יָמַר 135. 2, 140. 1	יְסַבִּי 61. 3	וַיַּעֲלָה, וַיַּעַל (א.) 172. 4
יָמֵשׁ 140. 5	יִסְבָּהוּ 141. 3	וַיַּעֲלָה, וַיַּעַל (Pi.) 175. 3
יָמֹת 157. 3	יְסַבְּנִי 61. 5, 141. 3	יַעֲלָה 207. 1. a
וַיָּמָת 65, 157. 3	יִסְגּוֹד־לוֹ 13. a	וַיַּעֲלוּ 45. 3
וַיִּמַּת 157. 3	יְסֹד 148. 1	יַעֲלִפוּ 161. 2
וַיָּמָת 160. 3	יְסֹדֵי 148. 1	יַעֲמֹד 60. 3. b (1)
יִנְאַץ 11. 1. a	יָסוּר (n.) 102. 1	יַעֲמָד 60. 3. b (2)

INDEX III.

יַעֲמְדוּ 109. 3. a	וַיִּפֶּר, יְפֶר 140. 5	יָצֵר־ (עֵ׳) 140. 5
יַעֲמְדוּ 112. 4	וַיֶּפֶר 175. 3	יְצֹר 140. 1
יַעֲמֹדְנָה 88 (2 f. pl.)	יַפְרִיא 177. 3	וַיֶּצֶר 147. 5
יַעַן 100. b, 237. 1, 267. b	יִפְשֹׁט 65. a	יְצֹר 147. 4
	יִפְשְׁטוּ 65. a	יִצְרְהוּ 105. b
יַעַן אֲשֶׁר 239. 2. (2)	יַפְתְּ 175. 3	יָצַת 147. 3, 150. 4
וַיַּעֲנֶה, וַיַּעַן 172. 4	וַיִּפְתְּ 172. 4	יִצַּת 144. 2
יַעֲנֶה 207. 1. a	יִפְתַּח 192. 1	יִצִּתוּ 24. c, 149. 1
יַעֲנוּכָה 104. b	יָפְתִי 221. 2. b	יָצָתִי 164. 2
יְעַטְּרוּ׃ 142. 2, 161. 2	יָצָא 147. 2	וַיִּקַּע 166. 4
יָעֵף (v.) 82. 1. a (2), 147. 1	וַיֵּצֵא 147. 5	יִקְּבֶנּוּ 105. d
	יֹצֵא 164. 3	וַיִּקְבַּע 99. 3
יָעֵף (adj.) 185. 2. b	לֵצֵאת 164. 2	יְקַבְּצָה 104. h
וַיִּיעַף 157. 3	יָצַג 150. 4	וַיִּקָּבֵר 99. 3. a
וַיָּעָף 157. 3	יָצֻג 145. 3, 150. 5	יֵקַד 144. 2, 147. 4
יָעַץ 77. 2, 147. 1, 179. 2. a	יִצֹּהַר 192. 1	יְקֹד 140. 1
	וַיְרֻצּוּ 66. 1 (1), 174. 4	יֹקְדוּ 141. 1
יָעֲצְרְכָה 104. b	יִצְרֻחוּ׃ 156. 1	יְקָדְעָם 22. a
יעקוב 11. 1. b	וַיָּצִים 157. 3	יַקְהִיל, יַקְהֵל 119. 1
יַעַר 200. c	יִצְחָק 192. 1	וַיַּקְהֵל 119. 1
וַיַּעֲשֶׂה, וַיַּעַשׂ 172. 4	יִצְחָק 120. 2	יְקֵהַת 24. b
יְעָשְׂרֻפוּ 104. h	יַצִּיעַ 145. 2	יָקוּם 190. b, 192. 1
יָפָה 147. 1	יָצִיץ 158. 2	יָקוּם 153. 2
יָפֶה 185. 2. d, 209. 1, 210	יָצַע 150. 4	יְקוּמוּן 157. 3
יְפֵה־פִיָּה 43. 5, 188	יִצַּע 150. 5	יְקוֹמֵם 161. 1
יָפַח (v.) 160. 3	יָצָה 172. 4	יָקוֹשׁ, יָקוּשׁ 185. 2. c
יָפֵחַ (adj.) 215. 1. b	וַיִּצָּה 25	יָקַח 54. 2, 132. 2
יְפֵיפִיתָ 92. a	יָצַק 150. 4	יָקַח 132. 2
יֹפַל 101. 2. b	יִצֹּק 148. 3	יָקְטֹל 51. 3
יְפַלַּח 126. 1	יָצֹק 144. 2, 147. 4	יָקִים 153. 1
וַיִּפֶן 172. 4	וַיִּצֶּק 147. 4	יָקִים 161. 1
יָפֵץ 160. 3	יִצְקוּ 148. 3	יֵקַל 64. 2
יְפַצְפְּצֵנִי 161. 2	יָצַר 50. 3, 84. 3. a (3), 147. 2	לָקַם, יָקָם 157. 3
יִפְצַע 101. 2		וַיָּקָם 99. 3. a, 157. 3

INDEX III.

יָרוֹק 185. 2. b
יְרוּשָׁלֵם, יְרוּשָׁלַיִם 47, 203. 5. c
יְרוֹת 148. 1
וַיָּרַח, יָרַח 160. 3
יִרְצֶנִי 147. 3
יְרֻשָּׁשׁוּ 88. (3. f. pl.)
יָרִיב (n.) 190. b, 192. 1
יָרִיב (v.) 153. 2
יָרִיד 158. 2
יָרֵךְ 197. a, 216. 1. e
יָרֵךְ 140. 1
יַרְכָה 198. c, 207. 1. a
יַרְכָתַיִם 22. a, 203. 5. a
יַרְמוּ 140. 3
יָרַע 140. 1
יָרַע 140. 5
וַיָּרַע (ע"ע) 140. 5
וַיָּרַע (ע"ו) 160. 3
יָרַע (ע"ע) 34
רַע (ל"ה) 34, 172. 4
יַרְעֵם 119. 1
יִרְעַץ 161. 4
וַיֶּרֶף 172. 4
יָרַק 170. 2. a
יָרָק 185. 2
יָרֹק 140. 1
יֵרָקוֹן 193. 2
יְרַקְרַק 186, 207. 2. a
יָרַשׁ 82. 1. a (2), 147. 1
יְרֻשָׁה 148. 3
יְרֻשָׁתָה 150. 1 (p. 182)
יְרֻשָׁתָם 61. 4. a, 150. 1 (p. 182)

יִרְאוּ 19. 1, 147. 1
יִרְאוּ 19. 1, 147. 1
וַיֵּרְאוּ 177. 3
יִרְאֻהוּ 104. h
יִרְאֵנִי 105. a
יָרֵאתְ 104. 1
יָרָב 158. 2
(וַיָּאֶרָב) וַיָּרֶב 111. 2. c
יָרֵב 61. 2, 172. 4
יְרֵב 63. 2. a
וַיֶּרֶב 175. 3
יִרְבִּין 172. 1
יִרְגַּז 114
וַיִּרְגְּנוּ 114
יָרַד 148. 3
יָרֵד 175. 3
יָרַד 79. 1, 147. 2
וַיָּרֶד 140. 5
וַיֵּרֶד 172. 4
וַיֹּרֶד 147. 5
וַיּוֹרִדֵם 114
יְרֻדֹּה 114
יָרֹד 60. 2. a, 114
יִרְדְּפוּ 105. a
יִרְדְּפֶה 105. d
יָרַדְתִּי 86. b (2 f.)
יָרָה 147. 1
יָרֹה 148. 3
יָרֹא 148. 1, 177. 3
יְרִיּוֹן 172. 1
יָרוֹם 19. 2. a
יָרוֹן 140. 1
יְרוֹפֵף 161. 4
יָרוּץ (ע"ע) 140. 1

וַיָּקָם 99. 3. a, 160. 3
וַיָּקֶן 172. 4
יָקַע 147. 2, 179. 2. a
יָקַע 179. 2. a
וַיִּקַּע 157. 3
יָקַץ 147. 4
יַקְצָפוּן 88 (m. pl.)
יִקָּצְרוּן 64. 2, 88 (m. pl.)
יָקַר 147. 4
וַיִּיקַר 172. 4
וַיּוֹקַר 173. 3
יִקְרָאֻנִי 105. c
יִקְרָה 177. 3
יִקְרְחָה 97. 1. a
יָקְרוּ 24. b
יָקֹשׁ 82. 1. a (3)
וַיִּקֹשׁ 172. 4
וַיִּקֶשׁ 99. 3
יִקָּשׁוּן 86. b (3 pl.)
יְקֻתְאֵל 22. a
יְרָא 148. 3
יְרֵא 148. 1
יָרֵא (v.) 82.1.a(1), 147. 1
יָרֵא (adj.) 215. 2. c
וַיַּרְא (ק.) 60. 1. a, 61. 2. a, 114, 172. 4
וַיַּרְא (Hi.) 175. 3
יֵרֶא 61. 2. a, 172. 4
וַיֵּרֶא 173. 3
יִרְאָה 87, 148. 1, 166. 2
יִרְאָה 114
וַיִּרְאֶה 172. 4
יִרְאֶה־לּוֹ 19. 1
יִרְאוּ 104. 3

24

INDEX III.

יִשָּׂאוּנְךָ 105. c	יָשַׁבְתִּי 90 (2 f.)	יְשָׁפוּטוּ 88
יִשְׂבְּעוּן 88 (m. pl.)	יִשְׂדְּדֵם 141. 1	יַשְׁפִּילָה 105. a
יִשְׂבָּעָה 127. 2	יָשֻׁד 140. 1	יַשְׁפִּילֶנָּה 105. b
יַשְׂבִּעֵנִי 105. a	יְשׁוֹמֵם 82. 5. a	וַיִּשָּׁאֶךְ 99. 3. a
יָשׂוּם 158. 2	יָשׂוֹן 148. 1	וישק 10. a
יֵשֵׂט 172. 4	יְשׁוּעָתָה 61. 6. a	וַיִּשַּׁק 175. 3
יְשִׂימָם 105. a, 158. 2	יְשׁוּפֵנִי 157. 3	וַיִּשָּׁקָהוּ 4. a
יָשֵׂם 147. 1	יָשֹׁחַ 140. 1	יָשֹׁר 158. 2
יָשֵׂם 158. 2	יִשַּׁח 140. 3	יְשָׁרוּן 193. 2. a
וַיָּשֶׂם 64. 1, 158. 2	יִשְׂחָטוּם 118. 3	יְשָׁרְנָה 88 (3 f. pl.), 147. 4
יִשְׂרָאֵלִי 194. 1	יְשַׂחֲרֻנְנִי 105. c	
יְשָׂשׂוּם 55. 1, 88 (m. pl.), 158. 2	יָשַׁי 164. 2	וַיְשָׁרֵת 99. 3. a, 119. 1
	וַיְשִׁיבֵם 160. 3	יְשָׁרְתוּנְךָ 105. c
יִשָּׂשכָר 47	יָשִׂים 140. 5	יָשַׁת 66. 1 (2) b, 158. 2
יְשׂתָּעֵר 54. 4	יִשְׂכְּבֻן 88 (m. pl.)	וַיָּשֶׁת 66. 1 (1), 172. 4
יֵשׁ 236, 258. 3. b	יִשְׁכַּח 126. 1	יִשְׁתּוֹמֵם 82. 5. a
יִשְׁאָלוּן 88 (m. pl.)	יֵשֵׁל 172. 4	וַיִּשְׁתַּחוּ 57. 2 (4), 176. 1
יָשֹׁב 146, 147. 2	יְשָׁלוּהָ 141. 3	וַיִּשְׁתַּחֲווּ 176. 1
יָשֹׁב 66. 1 (2) b, 153. 5, 157. 3	יִשְׁלָיוּ 172. 1	יִשְׁתָּיוּן 172. 1
	יְשַׁלֶּם־ 92. c	יִשְׁתַּמֵּר 54. 4
יָשַׁב־ 157. 3	יֵשֹׁם 140. 1	יֵתֵא 111. 2. b
וַיֵּשֶׁב 153. 5, 157. 3	יִשָּׁמַע 60. 1. a	וַיֵּתַא 177. 3
וַיֹּשֶׁב 157. 3	יִשְׁמָעֵאל 57. 2 (3) a	וַיֵּתָאוּ 176. 3
וַיֵּשֶׁב, יָשַׁב 153.5, 160.3	יָשֵׁן 147. 1	יִתְאָרְחוּ 60. 3. b (2)
יֶשֶׁב 63. 2. c, 84. 3. b, 144. 2	יִשְׂנָא 177. 3	יִתְאָרְחוּ 19. 2, 60. 3. b (2), 120. 1
	וְשִׂנֵּא 177. 3	
וַיֵּשֶׁב׃ 147. 5	יִשְׁנוּ 19. 1, 147. 1	יִתְגָּאֲלוּ׃, יִתְגָּאָל 119. 1
וַיָּשַׁב 99. 3. a	יְשֵׁנוּ 19. 1, 147. 1	יִתְגַּדָּל 96. b
וַיָּשָׁב 172. 4	וַיְשָׂא 105. a	וַיִּתְגַּל 176. 3
יְשַׂבְּחוּנְךָ 105. c	יִשְׁנֵי 216. 1. b	יִתְנַגֵּב 96. b
יֻשְׁבִּי 61. 6. a	יָשַׁע, רֶשַׁע 65. a, 201. 1	יִתְגָּעֲשׁוּ 96. a, 122. 2
וְיִשָּׁבְתָּ 33. 4	וַיְשַׁע 172. 4	יִתְגֹּעֲשׁוּ 96. a, 122. 2
יָשַׁבְתִּי 61. 6. a (?), 90 (2 f.)	יְשַׁעְשֵׁעוּ 141. 6	יָתֵד 197. b
	יָשְׁפָה 19. 2. b	יִתְחַדְתָיוּ 221. 2. b

INDEX III.

וַיִּתְוּ‎ 66. 1 (1), 174. 4
יִתְחַשָּׂא‎ 166. 5
וַיִּתְחָל‎ 176. 3
יָתִיר‎ 100. 1
וַיִּתְחַפֵּשׂ‎ 176. 3
יִתְלַכָּדוּ׃‎ 96. b
יִתֹּם‎ 140. 5
יִתֹּם‎ 140. 1
יִתְּמוּ‎ 141. 1
יִתַּמּוּ׃‎ 140. 1
יִתְמַלָּאוּן׃‎ 106. 5
יִתְמַלְטוּ‎ 96. b
יִתֵּן‎ 54. 2, 84. 3. b
יִתְנַגַּח‎ 126. 1
יִתְנַחֵם‎ 121. 3
יִתְנַשֵּׂא‎ 106. 5
וַיִּתַּע‎ 175. 3
יִתְעַל‎ 176. 3
יִתְעַלַּם־‎ 96. b
יִתְעָרַב‎ 119. 1
יִתְפַּלְּצוּן׃‎ 88.(m.pl.),96.b
יִתְפַּלָּשׁוּ׃‎ 96. b
יִתְפָּקַד‎ 96. a
יִתְקַדֵּשׁוּ‎ 96. b
יִתְקַלָּס‎ 96. b
יִתְקָעֵ׃‎ 126. 1
יִתְקְפוּ‎ 105. a
וַיִּתֶר‎ (עֹ"ר) 160. 1
יִתְרוֹמֵם‎ 82. 5. a

כְּ‎ 231. 1, 242. a, 267. b
כְּאֵב‎ 183. b
כַּאבִּיר‎ 57. 2 (3) a, 231. 3. b
כְּאוֹר‎ (כִּיאוֹר) 53. 2. a
כְּאֲרִי‎ 156. 3, 199. b
כַּאֲשֶׁר‎ 239. 2 (2)
כָּבֵד‎ (v.) 82. 1. a (1), 85. 2
כָּבֵד‎ (adj.) 216. 1. e, 217
כְּבֵדָת‎ 198. a (4)
כָּבוֹד‎ 185. 2, 197. b
כְּבוֹשׁ‎ 87
כָּבַס‎ 82. 5. a
כִּבֵּס, כִּבֶּס‎ 92. c
כֻּבְּסָה, כֻּבַּס‎ 51. 2, 197. c
כָּבַשׁ‎ 87
כַּגְּבִרְתָּהּ‎ 240. 2. a
כַּד‎ 197. b, 200. b
כֹּח‎ 235. 3 (4)
כָּתָה‎ 121. 1
כְּהַיּוֹם‎ 231. 5. a
כֹּהֵן‎ 186. 2. a
כֹּהֵן‎ 80. 2. b
כְּהֵנָּה‎ 198. a (2)
כּוֹבֵס‎ 186. 2. a
כּוֹבַע‎ 50. 1, 216. 1. e
כּוֹכָבִים‎ 207. 2. a
כוח‎ 11. 1. b
כּוֹכָב‎ 57. 1, 187. 1. e
כּוּן‎ 82. 5. a
כּוֹנַן‎ 59
כּוֹנָנוּ׃‎ 161. 4
כּוֹס‎ 184. b, 197. a
כְּזֶכֶר‎ 22. a
כְּחַד‎ 116. 4
כְּחַדוּ‎ 121. 2
כְּחָשׁ‎ 119. 1

כִּי‎ (n.) 53. 3. a, 184. b
כִּי‎ (conj.) 239. 1
כִּי אִם‎ 239. 2 (1)
כִּידֹד‎ 187. 1. c
כִּידֹר‎ 187. 1. c
כִּיּוֹם‎ 16. 2. a
כִּיּוֹר‎ 200. c
כִּילַי‎ 184. b, 194. 2. b
כִּילָה‎ 186. 2, 210. c
כִּי עֵינַיִם‎ 43. b
כִּיתְרוֹן‎ 57. 2 (3) a, 231. 3. b
כִּכָּר‎ 187. 1. e, 197. a, 200. c, d, 207. 1. b
כְּכָרַיִם‎ 203. 3
כֹּל‎ kål 215. 1. c
כֹּל‎ köl 19. 2. a, 215. 1. c
בֹּל‎ 277. a
כָּלָא‎ 179. 1. a
כָּלָא‎ 184. a
כִּלָּא‎ 220. 1. b
כִּלְאַיִם‎ 203. 4
כִּלְאֲתִי‎ 165. 2
כָּלֶב‎ 197. c
כַּלָה‎ 179. 1. a
כַּלָה‎ 174. 3 bis.
כַּלָּהֶם‎ 33. 3, 220. 1. b
כְּלָתְהָ‎ 220. 1. b
כָּלוּ‎ 165. 3
כָּלוּ‎ 93. a
כְּלוּ‎ 220. 1. b
כְּלוּלֹת‎ 201. 1. b
כָּלוּת‎ 174. 3
כְּלִי‎ 61. 2, 184. b

כְּלִיא 184. a	כָּסוּ 93. a	כָּפַת 60. 4. a, 61. 5
כְּלָיָה 221. 5. c	כסואתה 220. 1. b	93. a, 121. 1
כֵּלִים 208. 3. d	כָּסַל 51. 1, 84. 3. a (2)	כְּרָתִי 119. 4
כְּלִיתַי, כִּלְיֹתַי 174. 2	בִּסְמוֹ 61. 6	כְּרֵתִי 199. b
כִּלְיֹתֶיהָ 174. 2	כָּסְמָת 200. b	כְּשִׂפָּה, כָּשָׁב 51. 2
כִּלְיֹתִים 174. 2	כָּסַף 80. 2. a (3)	כְּשָׂדִים 107. d
בִּלְבֵּל 154. 3, 161. 2	בַּסְפִּי 216. 2. a	כָּשֵׁר 82. 1. a (1)
כְּלֻבְלוּ 161. 4	כָּסָת 199. d	כְּשָׁרוֹן 193. 2
כָּלָם 220. 1. b	כְּסָתוֹת הַיְכָנָה 24. b, 220. 2. c	כָּתַב 183. b, 215. 1. a
כָּלָנָה 220. 1. b		כָּתָב 77. 1, 78. 1
כִּלְתָנִי 165. 3	כָּעַס 121. 1	כָּתוֹת 139. 2
כַּמָּה 231. 4. a	בַּעֲסָתָה 104. i	כְּתֹנֶת 216. 2. b
כְּמַהְפֵּכַת 45. 4	כַּף 197. a, 217	כְּתֹנֶת 207. 1. d
כְּמוֹ 233. a	כָּפָה 198. c	כָּתֵף 197. a, 216. 1. e
כָּמֵס 90 (pass.)	כְּפִי 237. 2 (2)	כֶּתֶף 61. 1. b
כִּמְרִיר 187. 2. c	כַּפֵּימוֹ 220. 2. c	כְּתֵפוֹת 203. 5. a
כֵּן (n.) 221. 6. a	בַּפְּכָה: 220. 1. b	כֶּתֶר 50. 1
כֵּן (adv.) 43. a, 235. 3 (4)	כְּפָלַיִם 203. 4	כָּתַת 141. 1 (p. 175)
כַּנָּה 139. 2	כָּפַר 82. 5. a	
וְכַנָּה 4. a	כֹּפֶר 208. 3. b	לְ 231. 1, 233, 242. b,
כַּנֶּה 54. 2	כְּפָר 80. 2, 92. c, 126. 2	267. b, 272. 2. a
כִּנּוֹר 200. c	כְּפָרִים 187. 2	לֹא 11. 1. a, b
כְּנוֹת 211. a	כְּפַרְתָּהוּ: 104. j	לֹא 51. 4. a, 235. 1
כַּנְלוֹחָה 24. b, 131. 2	כָּרִי 199. b	לַאדֹנֵינוּ, לַאדֹנֵי, לָאָדוֹן
כְּנֵס 50. 1, 2	כְּרִיתוּת 199. d	57. 2 (2) a
כְּבַעַן 208. 3. a	כֶּרֶם 50. 3, 197. b	לַאדֹנָיו, לַאדֹנָי, לַאדֹנִי
כָּנָף 197. a, 210, 217	כֶּרֶם 183. b	57. 2 (2) a
כְּנָפוֹת 203. 5. a	כֹּרֶם 186. 2. a	לְאֻמִּים 14. a
כְּנָפַיִם 203. 1	כַּרְמֶל 50. 3, 193. 2. c,	לָאוֹר 159. 2
כִּנְפָּל 22. a	221. 6. a	לָאט 11. 1. a
כִּנָּרוֹת 45. 2	כַּרְסֵם 68. a	לָאט 156. 3
כְּנָת 198	כָּרַר 141. 2 (p. 175)	וּלְאָלָה 39. 4. a
כִּסֵּא 51. 3, 200. a	כְּרֵשׂוֹ 221. 5. c	לֵאלֹהִים, לֵאלֹהוּ 57. 2
כִּסְאָה 221. 3. a	כְּרָת־ 119. 1	(2) a

INDEX III. 373

לֶאֱלוֹהַּ 57. 2. (2) a
לְאֹם 207. 2. c
לֵאמֹר 57. 2 (2) a, 111. 2. c, 231. 3. a
לֹא תִּרְצָח 27
לֵב 61. 3, 186. 2. c, 197. b, 215. 1
לְבָאִם 208. 3. d
לְבַב 141. 1 (p. 175)
לֵבָב 61. 3, 200. c, 216. 1, 217, 221. 1, 3, 222
וּלְבָב 61. 1. a
לְבַבְתִּנִי 104. k
לְבַד 235. 3 (1), 237. 2 (2)
לְבַדְּהֶן 220. 1. b
לְבָדְנָה 220. 1. b
לָבוּשׁ 90 (pass.)
לָבִיא 106. d, 209. 2. b
לִבְלֹעַ 125. 2
לָבָן 80. 2. b
לָכֵן 207. 1. b, 215. 1. a
לִבְנֵה 200. b
לִבְעֵר, קֵיוֹן 35. 1
לָבַשׁ 82. 1. a (1)
לְבַשׁ 90 (pass.)
לְבֻשָׁם 104. h
(לְהָבַת) לַבַּת 53. 2. a
לְגוֹיִ 125. 2
לָגֶשֶׁת 231. 4. a
לָדָה 148. 2
לֶרֶת 148. 2
לְדָתִי 148. 2
לְדִתְהֶן 104. g

לָהּ 27
לַהֲבַת, לְהָבָה 63. 1. a, 214. 1. b, 216. 2. b
לָהּ 141. 2 (p. 175)
לָהֵט 119. 1
לִהְיוֹת 112. 2, 177. 1
לְהֻעָם 231. 5. a
לְהִפָּקֵד 91. b
לְהַשְׁמִיל 180. a
לְהַשְׁבִּית 94. b
לְהַשְׁמִיד 94. b
לוֹ 11. 1. b
לוֹ 51. 4. a
לוֹ 239. 1
לוּחַ 200. a
לָוִי 194. 2. a, 210
לוּלֵא 4. a
לִלְאוֹת, see לֻלָּאוֹת
לוּלֵי 194. 2. b
לוּלֵי 239. 2 (3)
לוּלִים 187. 1. e
לוּן 158. 3
לַח 207. 2. a
לַחֲטִיא 113. 2
לְחַיִּים 208. 4
לְחָיַי 216. 1. a
לֶחֱלִי 61. 1
לַחֲלִיק 113. 2
לֶחֶם 77. 2
לָחֶם 92. d, 121. 1
לָהֶם 60. 1. a, 61. 2. a, 184. b, 197. b
לַחְטָם 130. 2
לַחֲנָה 63. 1. b

לַחְפֹּר 61. 1
לַחְפֹּר פֵּרוֹת 43. b
לְחַרְחַר 141. 6
לַחְשׂוֹת 175. 2
לֶחָתִים 203. 5. b
לָהֶם 53. 2. a
לַיהוָה, לַיהֹוָה 231. 3. a
לַיִל 184. b, 200. a, 208. 3. c
לַיְלָה 61. 6
לִין 158. 2, 3
לִיסֹד 148. 1
לִיקְהַת־ 14. a, 24. b
57. 2 (3) a
לָךְ 65. a
לְךָ, לָךְ 151. 1
לֵכָה 151. 1, 240. 2
לִכְרֹל־ 13. a
לָכֵן 239. 2 (3)
לָכֶן, לָכֵנָה 151. 1
לֶכֶת 61. 2, 151. 1
לֶכֶת 151. 1
לִכְתוֹב 22. a
לִכְתִּי 151. 1
לֻלָּאֹת 187. 1. e, 207. 2. a
לַלְּבֵן 94. b
לָמַד 78. 2, 84. 3. a (2)
לָמַד 92. d
לָמַד־ 92. c
לְמַדְתִּי 86. b (2 f.)
לָמָה, לָמָּה 231. 4. a
לָמוֹ 233. a
לַמִּזְרָחָה 219. 1. a
לְמַטָּה 219. 1. a

INDEX III.

לְמִינֵהוּ 220. 1. b	לָקַחַת 64.2, 127.1, 132.2	מַאֲכֶלֶת 191. 5. a, 207. 1. e
לְמִן 237. 2 (1)	לָקַק 141. 1 (p. 175)	
לַמְנַצֵּחַ 45. 2	לִקְרַאת 57. 2 (3) a, 237. 2 (3)	מָאֵן 60. 4
לְמַעְלָה 219. 1. a		מְאָסְכֶם 19. 2, 119. 3
לְמַעַן 237. 2 (2), 267. b	לְרֹא 148. 1	מְאָסָם 119. 3
לְמַעַן אֲשֶׁר 230. 2 (2)	לָרֹב 231. 4. a	מְאַסְתִּיו 33. 2
לְמַעֲנֵהוּ 246. 2. a	לָרֶדֶת 231. 4. a	מְאַסְתִּים 33. 2
לְסָרְבָה 4. a	לְרַחֲמָכֶם 119. 1	מַאֲפַלְיָה 195. 3
לְנֶגֶד 237. 2 (1)	לָרִיב 231. 4. a	מֵאֵת 237. 2 (1)
וְלָנָה 156. 4	לָשֵׂאת 131. 4	מָאתַיִם 203. 4, 226
לָנִים 156. 2	לִשְׂחֹק 119. 1	מִבְטָח 207. 2. b
לְנֹכַח 237. 2 (1)	לִשְׁאוֹלָה 219. 1. a	מִבְטָחוֹ 63. 1. a
לִנְפֹּל 131. 2	לַשְּׁבִית 94. b, 231. 5. a	מִבְטָחִי 60. 1. a
לִנְפֹּל 22. a	לָשׁוֹן 197. b	מֵבִי 164. 2
לַעֲבִיר 113. 2	לְשִׁכָּה 51. 4	מִבַּלְעֲדַי 237. 2 (4)
וְלָעֻ 156. 4	לְשַׁלַּח, לִשְׁלֹחַ 60. 2. a	מִבָּעִתֶךָ 119. 1, 221. 2. a
לְעוֹלָם 16. 2. a	לַשְׁמֵד 94. b	
לְעֻמַּת 237. 2 (2)	לַת 54. 2, 148. 2	מִבְצִיר 25
לַעֲנוֹת 173. 2	לָתֵת 231. 4. a	מִבְצָר 197. b, 200. c, 207. 1. b
לַעֲשֵׂר 94. b, 113. 2	לָתֵת לָהּ 35. 1	
לְפֻדָה 22. a		מַנְבִּיתִי 61. 6
לְפִי 237. 2 (2)	מֵ, מָ see מִן	מִגְדּוֹ, מִגְדּוֹן 55. 2. a
לְפָנַי 194. 2	מְאֹד 235. 3 (1)	מִגְדָּל 200. c
לְפָנַי 237. 2 (2), 267. b	מְאָדָם 93. a	מְגוֹלָלָה 142. 1
לֵץ 156. 2	מֵאָה 207. 1. f, 226	מָגוֹר 207. 1. c
לְצָבָא, לִצְבָא 22. a	מְאִיל 93. b	מָגֵן 190. b, 207. 2, 210. a, 215. 1. b, 216. 1. a
לְצִחֲק 119. 1	מַאֲוַי 207. 2. a	
לִקְחִי, לָקְחֵי 132. 2	מְאִימָה 195. 3	מַגַּעַת 205
לָקַח 132. 2	מָאוֹר 190. b, 191. 5. a, 200. c	מַגֵּפָה 216. 1. b
(מִלְקַח) לֶקַח 53. 2. a, 93. c		מִגְרָשׁ 207. 1. b
	מֹאזְנַיִם 203. 2	מֵנָשׁ 61. 5
לָקְחָה 16. 3. b, 127. 3	מֵאַחֲרֵי 237. 2 (1)	מַד 207. 2. a
וְלָקַחְנוּ 100. 2. a (1)	מַאֲכָל 190. a, 191. 5, 197. b	מָדְבָּק 95. 2
לָקַחַת 60. 2. a, 127. 1		מִדְבָּרָה 219. 1

INDEX III.

מִזְמוֹר 191. 5
מַזְמֵרוֹת 207. 1. a
מְחַעְזְנֶיךָ 161. 2
מִזְרָחָה 219. 1. b
מִזְרָק 200. c
מַחָאָה 164. 4
מַחֲבַת 54. 1, 205. b
מְחוֹלָל 142. 1
מָחֵל 140. 5
מַחֲלָיִם 190. b
מַחֲלָמִים 94. e
מַחֲלֹקֶת 207. 1. d
מַחֲלֹת 190. a
מַחֲנֶה 197. b, 200. c, 209. 1
מְחָרֲחֵהוּ 220. 1. b
מְחַנֵּק 190. a
מַחְסְפָּס 180. a
מַחְצְצְרִים 180. a
מַחְצְרִים 94. e
מַחְצְרְרִים 180. a
מֶחְקָר 190. a
מָחֳרָת 19. 2. b, 196. b
מַחְשָׁבוֹת, מַחֲשָׁבוֹת 60. 3. a, 216. 2. a
מַחְשָׁק 207. 2. b
מַטְבֵּחַ 191. 4
מַטֶּה 197. b, 200. c
מֹטֵהוּ 220. 1. b
מְטַהֲרוֹ, מִטְהֲרוֹ 24. b
מְטַחֲוֵי 168. a, 174. 1
מְטֻלָּאוֹת 167. 1
מְטַלְטְלָה 161. 2
מְטֻמָּאָה 167. 1

מוֹסָד 200. c
מוּסָד 150. 5
מוּסָר 190. b
מוֹסָר 200. c
מוֹעֵד 190. b
מוֹעָדָה 90
מוֹעֵצוֹת 207. 1. a
מוּפָז 140. 6
מוֹצָא 191. 5. a
מוֹצָא (פִּי) 94. e, 165. 2
מוֹצָא (לֹא) 165. 2
מוֹצָאֵי 60. 3. c, 216. 1. a
מוּצָאת 167. 2
מוּצֶקֶת 150. 4
מוֹרַג 207. 2. a
מוֹרִיגִים, מוֹרִגִּים 59. a
מוֹרָשֵׁי 216. 1. a
מוֹשָׁב 191. 3, 5. a, 200. c, 215. 1
מוֹשִׁיבִי 61. 6. a
מָוֶת 61. 2, 183. b, 208. 3. c, 217
מוֹת 57. 2 (5)
מָוְתָה 61. 6. a
מוֹתַר 221. 5. a
מִזְבֵּחַ 60. 2. a, 190. a, 191. 3, 197. b, 200. a, 215. 1. b
מְזֻבַּח 126. 1
מִזְבְּחוֹתֵיהֶם 220. 1. b
מִזְבְּחֹתָם 220. 2. a
מֶזֶה 24. a, 75. 1
מֵזִין 53. 2. a, 111. 2. c
מַזְלֵג 207. 1. a, 210. e

מִדְבָּרָה (2) 66. 2 b, 219. 1
מִדַד 141. 5
מָדְוֶ 184. b
מַדְוֶנָה 190. b, 191. 4
מָדוֹן 190. b, 207. 1. f
מַדּוּעַ 235. 2 (3)
מִדְיָן 190. b
מִדְיָנֵי 216. 1. d
מִדְכָּא 167. 1
מִדָּן 190. b
מַדָּע 190. b
מֹדַעְתָּנוּ 220. 1. b
מָה, מֶה, מַה 75. 1, 196. a
מָהֵדָה 141. 2 (p. 175)
מְהוּמָה 198. a (3)
מָהִירוּת 177. 1
מֵהֲלֹאֶה לְ 237. 2 (4)
מַהֲלְכִים 94. e, 151. 1
מָהֶם 75. 1
מֶה עָשִׂית 63. 1. a
מַהְפֵּכָה 191. 4, 198. a (3), 207. 1. a, 216. 1. b
מִהְקְצָעוֹת 95. e
מָחָר 60. 4. a, 235. 3 (2)
מַהֲתַלּוֹת 142. 3
מוֹאָב 197. d
מוֹאָבִית 205
מוּבָא 167. 2
מוֹט 157. 1
מוֹל, מוּל 237. 1
מוֹלָל 141. 4

INDEX III.

מַטְמֹנֵי 216. 1. c	מָלֵא 82. 1. a (1)	מֶלֶךְ 63. 2. a, 217. 221. 5, 222
מַטָּע 190. a	מָלֵא (v.) 77. 3, 82. 1. a (1)	
מַטָּעַי 60. 3. c, 216. 1. a		מֶלֶךְ 65. a
מָטָר 200. a	מָלֵא (adj.) 90	מֶלֶךְ־בָּבֶל 44. a
מִצְרָא 196. d	מִלֵּא 166. 2	מלכה 11. 1. a
מִי 75. 1, 196. a	מִלָּא 165. 2	מַלְכָּה 211, 217, 222
מִידָו 220. 2. b	מְלֵאָה 201. 1. a	מֶלֶךְ־הַבָּשָׁן 44. a
מִיּוֹרְדֵי־ 13. a	מְלֹאות 166. 2	מלכו 11. 1. a
מִיכָה, מִיכָיָהוּ 57. 2 (2) b	מַלְאוּת 166. 2	מַלְכּוֹ 66. 2 (2) a
	מְלֵאִים 201. 1. a	מָלְכוֹ 61. 1
מַיִם 201. 1, 203. 5. c	מְלָאכָה 57. 2 (3) a, 214. 1. b	מַלְכוּת 22. a, 209. 3, 217
מֵימֵי 57. 2 (2)		מַלְכוּת 64. 2
מְיָמִינִים 150. 1	מלאכים 11. 1. b	מלכי 11. 1. a
מֵינִיקוֹת 11. 1. a	מַלְאֲכֵהֶ׃ 220. 2. c	מַלְכֵי 61. 1, 216. 2, 2. a
מֵינֶקֶת 61. 4, 207. 1. e	מְלֹאת 166. 2	מָלְכִי 89 (f. s.)
מֵיצַר 4. a	מְלַאתִי 33. 1, 61. 6. a, 218	מַלְכִיוֹת 62. 2
מִיצֶקֶת 150. 4		מְלָכִים 64. 2
מִישׁוֹר 190. b	מִלְּבַד 237. 2 (2)	מְלָכִין 199. a
מִישְׁנֵי 57. 2 (2)	מִלְּבְהֶן 220. 1. b	מַלְכִּי־צֶדֶק 61. 6. a, 195. 3, 218. a
מֵישָׁר 190. b, 101. 4	מַלְבֵּן 191. 3	
מֵישָׁרִים 210. c	מִלָּה 200. b, e	מַלְכֶּם 75. 1
מַכְאוֹב 200. c	מְלֹא 165. 3	מִלַּל 141. 4
מִבֹּל 260. 2 (1)	מְלוּכָה 198. a (2)	מַלְמַד 101. 2
מַכְלֻם, מַכְלִים 94. a	מְלוּכָה 98. 1. a	מִלְמַעְלָה 235. 2 (3)
מַכְלֵת 53. 2. a	מָלוֹן 207. 1. c	מִלְּמָטָּה 53. 3. a, 111. 2. c
מֶכֶס 190. b	מלושני 92. b	מִלְּפְנֵי 237. 2 (2)
מָכַר 77. 2, 80. 2	מֶלַח 187. 1. a	מַלְקוֹחַ 191. 5
מִכְרַבֵּל 54. 3, 180. a	מַלָּחַי 216. 1. a	מַלְקוֹשׁ 190. a
מִכְרָה 216. 1. b	מָלַט 92. d	מַלְקֹחַיִם 190. a, 203. 2
מִכְרָה 98. 1. a, 125. 1	מִמַּלַּט־, מִלַּט 80. 1, 92. c	מִלְשְׁנִי 93. a
מַכְרֵי 216. 1. a	מִלִּין, מִלִּים 199. a	מָלָתִי 104. 2
מִכְשָׁלִים 95. a	מֵלִיץ 217	מַלְתָּעוֹת 51. 4
מִכַּשֵּׁפָה 207. 1. a	מְלִיצָה 217	מֵמְאִיר 139. 3
מַכְתָּם 220. 2. a	מֶלֶךְ־ 89	מַמְּגֻרוֹת 24. b, 190. a

INDEX III. 377

מְמָחִים 209. 1. a
מִמְּכָר 191. 5. a
מְמֻלָּאִים 167. 1
מְמְלָכָה 191. 5. a, 211, 214. 1. b
מַמְלֶכֶת 61. 1. b
וּמִמַּעֲמָדָהּ 45. 3
מֵמֵר 190. b
מַמְרוֹרִים 24. b, 190. a
מִמְשָׁץ 93. e
מֶמְשָׁלָה 198. a (3), 214. 1. b, 221. 2. a
מָן 174. 5
מִן 232, 233, 242. a, 260. 1, 207. b
מְנִ 4. a
מוֹצֵאץ 96. a, b, 122. 2, 131. 6
מִנַּד, מִנֵּד 140. 6
מָנוֹחַ 207. 1. c
מָנוֹס 207. 1. c
מִנְזָרַיִךְ 24. b
מָנֹחַ 160. 5
מִנִּי 61. 6. a, 199. b, 232. a
מֶנִּי 232. a
מְנָקָה 127. 2
מְנַקִּיוֹת 209. 2. a
מִנַּשֶּׁה 4. a
מְסָת 196. b, 211. a
מְנָת־ 19. 2. a
מַס 54. 2. a, 207. 2. a
מֵסַב 140. 5
מִסָּה 54. 2. a

מֵסִיךְ 140. 5
מְסָךְ 190. b, 216. 1. a
מַסֵּכָה 216. 1. b
מִסְכֵּן 190. a
מִסְכָּן 93. e
מִסְכְּנוֹת 50. 2
מְסֻלָּאִים 167. 1
מַסְמֵר 200. c
מְסֹס 139. 2
מִסְפֵּד 190. a, 191. 4, 215. 1. b
מִסֹּרֶת 53. 2. a
מִסְתָּר 94. e
מִסְתַּתֵּר 54. 4
מַעְבָּדָי 216. 1. a
מַעֲשֵׂה 207. מַעְבְּרוֹת, מַעְבָּרוֹת 1. b
מֵעֲבָר לְ 237. 2 (2)
מַעֲדָן 200. c
מֵעָה 210
מָעוֹד 190. b, 210. a, 216. 1. a
מָעוֹן 207. 1. c
מְעִיתָ 161. 4
מַעְזְנֶיהָ 54. 3, 221. 6. b
מַעְזְרִים 94. e
מְעַט 60. 3. c, 183. b, 207. 2. a
מָעַט 78. 1, 121. 1
מְעֵירָם 221. 2. b
מֵעַיִם 201. 1
מֵעָיָן 200. c
מֵעָיְנוֹ 61. 6. a
מֵעִיר 158. 3

מַעֲכָה 196. b
מַעֲבָתַי 194. 2. a
מַעַל 190. b
מָעַל 84. 3. a (3), 118. 2
מֵעַל 237. 2 (1)
מֹעַל 190. b
מַעֲלָה 190. b
מַעֲלָם 119. 3
מֵעַם 237. 2 (1)
מַעַן 190. b
מַעֲנֵה־דַּךְ 60. 4. a
מְעָרָה 216. 1. a
מַעֲרָכוֹת 216. 2. a
מַעַרְכֵי 216. 2. a
מְעָרָת 60. 3. c
מַעֲשֶׂה 209. 1
מַעְצוֹר 200. a, 215. 1
מָפָל 191. 1
מִפְּנֵי 237. 2 (2)
מִפְקָדִים 95. a
מֵפֵר 140. 5
מִפְתָּח 191. 2, 215. 1. b
מִפְתָּחָיו 221. 7. a
מֵץ 156. 2
מצא 11. 1. b
מָצָא 57. 2 (2), 103
מֹצַאֲכֶם 61. 1. c, 104. 4
מִצְאָן 89 (f. pl.)
מֹצָאת 57. 2 (2), 205
מְצָאתָם 104. i
מְצָאתִהוּ 104. i
מַצְבְּתָם 220. 2. a
מִצַּד 190. b, 200. a
מִצְנָה 190. b

מָצוֹר 207. 1. c	מָרָא 196. d	מְרֵרָה 216. 1. b
מִצְחָה 198. c	מַרְאָה 217	מִדַּת 60. 4. a
מֵצַל 140. 5	מַרְאָה 217	מְרָחַיִם 203. 5
מַצָּע 190. b	מַרְאָה 220. 1. b	מַשֹּׂאוֹת 166. 2, 191. 4
מִצְעָר 191. 5	מַרְאֵהוּ 220. 1. b	מִשְׁגָּב 221. 6. a
מָצָק 150. 5	מְרַאֲשׁוֹת 201. 1	מַשּׂוֹר 190. a, 191. 2
מֵצַר 190. b, 210	מְרַאֲשֹׁתַי 214. 2. b	מַשְׂכִּיל 191. 1
מִצְרִי 194. 1	מַרְבָּע 80. 2. b	מַשְׂמְאִילִים 180. a
מִצְרַיִם 197. d	מַרְבֵּץ 191. 3, 215. 1. b	מַשּׁוֹת 164. 2
מִצְרַיִם 207. 2. a	מַרְדּוּת 22. a	מְשֻׁאָרֶת 3. 1. a
מָצְתִי 164. 2	מָרְדְּכֶם 119. 3	מַשְׁבֵּר 215. 1. b
מַק 186. 2. c	מִרְדָּף 114	מִשְׁגֶּה 191. 4
מְקֻדָּשׁ 191. 5. a	מָרָה 34, 141. 1	מְשׁוֹבֶבֶת 161. 4
מִקְדָּשׁ 24. b, 190. a	מָרָה 34	מְשָׂחֲךָ (inf.) 125. 2
מִקְדָּשֵׁי 216. 2. a	מַקָּה 61. 5	מַשְׁחַת 215. 1. b
מִקְדָּשְׁכֶם 104. h, 221. 3. a	מָרוֹ 172. 2	מָשְׁחַת 54. 1, 205. b
מָקוֹם 197. b, 200. a, 216. 1	מְרִיחִים 161. 4	מֵשִׁיב 210
מַקְטִיל 217. a	מְרוֹמָם 161. 4	מְשִׁיתִהוּ 104. k
מְקֻטָּר 95. a	מֵרוֹץ 190. b	מִשְׁכָּב 200. c
מְקִימִי 61. 6. a	מַרְזֵחַ 215. 1. b	מִשְׁכָּב 95. a
מַקֵּל 200. a, 215. 1. b	מֶרְחָק 191. 5, 207. 2. b, 210. e	מָשְׁכוּ, מִשְׂכּוּ 89 (m. pl.)
מַקֶּלְכֶם 221. 3. a	מֹרְטָה 24. c, 93. e	מְשֻׁכָּלָה 207. 1. a
מְקַלְלוֹנִי 90 (3 pl.)	מְרִירוּת 198. a (4)	מִשְׂכְּמָה 27.
מִקְנֶה 165. 3	מֹרֶךְ 190. b	מִשְׁכָּן 200. c, e
מִקְנֶה 221. 7	מֶרְכָּב 190. a	מַשְׂכֻּנִי 66. 2 (2) c
מִקְנֻנְתִּי 90 (2 f.)	מֶרְכָּבָה 58. 2. a, 210. e, 214. 1. b, 216. 2. b	מִשְׁלָה 95. a
מִקְצֹעַ 216. 2. a	מֶרְכֶּבֶת 114	מַשְׁמִים 139. 3
מִקְרָאֵי 167. 1	מֵרָע 140. 5	מַשְׁמַנִּים 191. 5
מִקְרָאֵי 216. 1. a	מִרְעֶה 190. b	מִשְׁמַעְתָּם 60. 3. a
מִקְרֶה 24. b	מֵרֵעֵהוּ 220. 1. b	מִשְׁמָר 217
מִקְרֶה 95. a	מַרְעִית 190. b	מִשְׁמֶרֶת 214. 1, 217
מְקַרְקֵר 161. 2	מָרַר 141. 5	מַשְׁעֵנָה 207. 1. a
		מִשְׁפָּחָה 214. 1. b
		מִשְׁפַּחַת 61. 1. b

INDEX III. 379

מִשְׁפַּחְתּוֹ 60. 3. a	סָתְחָנַיִם 208. 4	נְבוּכַדְרֶאצַּר 51. 4
מִשְׁפָּטִי 92. b	מְחַטֵּעַ 141. 6	נָבוֹן 158. 4
מַשְׂכִּילִי 61. 6. a, 218	מָתַק 79. 2, 84. 3. a (2)	נְבוֹנָה 141. 1
מָשָׁק 190. b	מִתְרוֹגֵן 141. 5*	נָבוֹהּ 140. 2
מִשְׁקָד 80. 2. b, 93. e	מַתָּת 54. 2, 205. f	נְבִיתָ 165. 3
מַשְׁקוֹף 190. a		נָבֹכּוּ 150. 1
מֵשָׁרִים 210. c	נא 46	נְבָכִים 159. 3
מְשָׁרֵת 54. 1, 205. b	נָא 240. 2, 263. 1. a	נָבֵל 82. 1. a (1), 84. 3.
מָשׁשׁ 141. 1 (p. 175)	נֹאד 200. a	a (1)
מִשְׁתַּגֵּעַ 126. 1	נְאַדְרִי 60. 3. a, 61. 6. a	וַיִּנָּבֵל 132. 3
מִשְׁתַּחֲוִיתֶם 90 (2 m.), 176. 1	נָאוָה 108. a, 174. 1	נבל 90
מִשְׁתֵּי 22. b, 223. 1. a	נָאוָה 57. 2 (2) a, 187. 1. d	נְבֵלָה (עץ) 141. 1
מְשָׁתִּים 22. b	נָאווּ 174. 1	נֵבֶל צִיץ 35. 1
מֵת 57. 2 (5), 82. 1. a (1), 153. 1, 156. 2 bis	נָאוֹר 159. 1	נִבְלָתוֹ 221. 2. b
מַת 54. 1	נְאוֹת 56. 4	נִבְלָתִי 221. 2. b
מְתֻדַּפְּקִים 82. 5. a	נֶאֱחָז 111. 2. d	נִבְלָחָה 221. 2. b
מֵתָה 34	נְאֻם 90 (pass.)	נְבֻנוֹתִי 158. 4
מֵתָה 34	נָאַף 121. 1	נָבַע 50. 1
מַתָּה 86. b (2 m.)	נָאֲפָה 60. 3. b (2)	נִבְקָה 141. 1
מָתוֹק 185. 2. b, 207. 1. c	נַאֲפוּפִים 187. 2. c	וַתִּבָּקְשָׁה 99. 3
מְתִיקָה 66. 2 (2) c	נָאַץ 82. 5. a, 121. 1	נָבַר 140. 2
מְתוּשֶׁלַח 218. a	נִאֵץ 60. 4. a, 92. d	נִגְאָלוּ 83. c (2), 122. 2
מִתְחָרָה 94. a	נָאצוֹת 63. 1. a	נִגְבָּה 219. 1
מִתַּחַת 237. 2 (1)	נָאֲצוֹתֶיךָ 63. 1. a	נֶגֶד 237. 1
מְתִים 201. 1, 207. 2. a	נָאַר 121. 1	וַיֻּגַּד־ 99. 3
מִתְכַּבֵּד 96. b	מְאָרִים 140. 2	נֶגְדַּע 91. a
מַתְלָאָה 24. a, 75. 1	נָאֱשַׁאר 120. 2	נֹגַהּ 184. a, 197. a, 208. 3. b
מְתַלַּהְלַהּ 141. 6	נָבָא 50. 1, 82. 5. a	נְגוֹהַת 184. a, 198. a. 2
מִתְלַע 80. 2. b	כִּבָּא 207. 1. b	נָגוֹהוּ 140. 2
מַתְלְעוֹת 51. 4	נֹבֶה 219. 1. b	נָגוֹף 131. 5
מְתֹם 190. b	וְנִבְהָלוּ 65. b	נְגִינַת 196. b
מָתָן 215. 1. a	נְבוּאָה 108. a (2)	נִגְלָה 91. b, 173. 2
	נְבוּכַדְנֶאצַּר 51. 4	נָגֹלּוּ 140. 2

INDEX III.

נִגְלוֹת 173. 2	נוּעַ, בוּעַ 157. 1	נָחֲנוּ 53. 2. a, 71. a (1)
נִגְלֵינוּ 173. 1	נוֹקֵשׁ 149. 1	נְחַנְתִּי 140. 2, 141. 2
נִגְלֵית 173. 1	נוֹשְׁבָה 13. b	נָחָר 140. 2
נָגֹעַ 131. 4	נָזִיד 158. 4	נִחַר 135. 2, 140. 2
נְגֹעֲנוּ 60. 3. a	נָזֹל 82. 1. a (3), 84. 3. a (1)	נֶחֱרוּ 141. 1
נֹגְעַת 207. 1. e		נְחֹשֶׁת 197. b, 205, 211
נְגָרוֹת 140. 2	נִזְלוּ 86. a, 141. 1	נְחָשְׁתָּן 193. 1
נָגַשׁ 80. 2. a (3), 84. 3. a (2), 130. 1	נָזֹלוּ 86. a	נֵחַת 131. 1
	נֹחַ 60. 2	(עֵץ) נַחַת 140. 2
נֵד (v.) 156. 2	נֶחְבָּא 63. 1. b	(אֹז) נְחַתוּ 131. 1
נָדַד 84. 3. a (3), 141. 3 (p. 175)	נַחְבֵּאתָ 63. 1. b	נָטָה 79. 3. a
	נֶחְבָּה 165. 1	נְטֵה 131. 3
נָדוּ 156. 2	נֶחְבְּתָם 164. 2	נְטוּרוֹת 172. 5, 209. 3. a
נָדוֹשׁ 57. 2 (5)	רְנָחָה 100. 2.a (2), 156. 4	נְטוֹשׁ 131. 3
נִדְמָה 173. 2	רְנָחוּ 156. 4	נָטוּי 172. 1
נָדַר 84. 3. a (3), 125. 3	נְחוּמִים 187. 2. a	נְטוּיֵ 172. 1
נֵהַג 131. 1	נָחוּשׁ 185. 2	נִטְמָא 207. 1. b
נְהִיָה 112. 2	נְחִישָׁה 205	נִטְמֵינוּ 173. 1
נָהֵל 121. 1	נָחַל 80. 1	נְטָמַתֶם 164. 2, 173. 1
נַהֲלָאָה 80. 2. b	נַחַל 60. 3. a	נֶטַע 60. 3. c, 184. a
נַהֲלֵל 187. 2. c	נְחֹל 131. 1	נָטֹעַ 131. 4
נָחַם 118. 2	נְחֹל 140. 2	נֶטַע 184. a, 216. 1. e
נֶהְפַּךְ 60. 3. a	נַחֲלָה 60. 3. a, 61. 6. a	נֹטַע 126. 1
נָהָר 200. c, 207. 1. b	נַחֲלָה 60. 3. a	נְטֻעוּ 131. 3
נַהֲרַיִם 203. 3,	נַחֲלוּ 141. 1	נָטַר 51. 1
נוּגוֹת 149. 1	וַתְּחַלְּמָה 99. 3	נֹטְרָה 207. 1. a
נוּגֵי 149. 1	נֶחֱלָץ 113. 1	נִי 53. 3. a
נוֹדָד 142. 1	נַחֲלַת 196. b	נִידָה 59. a
נָוָה 156. 1	נַחֲלָת 141. 2	נִיחֹחַ 187. 2. c
נוּחַ, נוֹחַ 157. 1	נָחָם 77. 2	נִינָם 105. a
נוֹטֵרִיהֶם 221. 7. a	נָחָם 60. 4. a, 131. 1	נִיצוֹץ 187. 1. c
נוּפְדוּ 149. 1	נֶחְמָדֵהוּ 111. 1	נִירוּ 158. 2
נִוַּסְּרוּ 83. c (2), 150. 3 (p. 182)	נֶחְמִים 140. 2	נִירָם 105. a
	נֵרַח 135. 2	נִכְאוּ 24. b

נִכְבָּד 207. 2. b	נִתְקָה 45. 4, 97. 1	נֹעַר 184. b
נָכָה 210	נָס 174. 5	נַעֲרָה 58. 1
נָכוֹן 159. 3	נָסַב 135. 2, 140. 2	נָּאָרֶץ 111. 3. b
נְכוֹנָה 159. 1	נִסְבְּאָה 164. 5	וַתַּעֲשֶׂה 172. 3
נְכוֹנָה 159. 1	נְסִבָּה 141. 1	נִפוּגֹתִי 159. 1
נֹכַח 237. 1	נְסָבָּה 140. 2	נָפוֹעַ 150. 1
נֹכַחַת: 127. 1	נָסָה 3. 1. a, 131. 3, 165. 1	נְפוֹצוֹתָם 159. 1
נֶכֶס 50. 2		נְפוֹצִים 159. 3
נְכַסּוּ 91. b	נָסוֹג (K. fut.) 157. 3	נִפְלָאוֹת 235. 3 (3)
נִכְסַפְתָּה 86. b (2 m.)	נָסוֹג (Ni.) 159. 1	נִפְלֵאת 166. 1
נָכַר 83. c (2)	נְסוּגִים 159. 3	נִפְלֵאת 166. 1, 205. c
נֵכָר 216. 1. b	נסוגתי 11. 1. a	נִפְלָאתָה 166. 1
נָכְרִי 194. 2	נְסוּגֹתִי 66. 2 (2) c, 159. 1	נָפְלוּ 106. a
נִלְבָּב 80. 2. b		נִפְלִינוּ 173. 1
נָלוּוּ 91. d	נָסַח 50. 1	נִפְלֵיתִי 173. 1
נָלוֹז 159. 3	נֶסֶךְ 184	נִפְעַל 92. a
נִלְחָם 91. b, 119. 1	נסכה 220. 1. b	וַפֶּן 61. 4
נִלְקַח 132. 2	נִסְפַּר 216. 2. a	נָפַץ 179. 2. a
נִמְבְזָה 91. c	נָסַס 141. 3 (p. 175)	נֶפֶשׁ 50. 2, 102. 1, 197. b, 200. c
נָמוֹג 159. 1	וַנִּסְעָה 99. 3	
נָמוֹג 159. 1	וַנִּסְפֵּר 99. 3	נְפְתִּילִים 187. 2. a
נְמוֹטוּ 159. 1	נֶעֱבְדָם 111. 3. a	נֵץ 217
נִמּוֹל 159. 1	מְעוֹר 159. 1	נָצַב 50. 1, 179. 2. a
נְמוֹלִים 159. 3	נְעִירָיךְ 62. 2	נִצָּה 217
נְמֵלָה 200. b, e	נְעִירִים 201. 1. b	וַנְּצֻמָּה 99. 3
נִמְלוּ 159. 1	נַעַל 197. a, 200. c	נֵצַח 61. 2
נִמְלַלְתָּם 141. 2	נְעָלִים 203. 2, 208. 4	בְּצֶדֶק 54. 4, 96. b
נֶמֶס ,נָמֵס 140. 2	נְעָלָם 60. 3. a, 112. 3	נִצְלָנוּ 65. a
נִמְצָא 207. 1. b, 209. 3. b	נַעֲלָמִים נַעֲלָמָה 112. 3	נִצְמַתִּי 86. b (2 m.)
	נָעֵם 82. 1. a (2)	נָצַר 50. 3, 51. 1
נִמְצָאתִי 60. 1. a	נָעֳמָדָה 32. 3. a	נֵצֶר 131. 3
נִמְקֹתָם 141. 2	נַעֲצוּץ 187. 2. c	נִצְרָה 24. b, 98. 1. a
נָמֵרוּ (ע׳) 159. 1	נַעַר 121. 1	נְצֻרָה 24. b, 106. b
נָמֵר 185. 2	נַעַר 58. 1, 184. b	נִצְרָתַם 104. i

נִצַּת 149. 1
נָקְבָה 131. 3
נִקְבְּצוּ 91. d
נָקֹד 185. 2. b
נָקָה 174. 3
נָקוֹטוּ 24. c
נִקְטָל 217
נָקֹטוּ 150. 1
נָקִי, נָקִיא 185. 2. d, 209. 2
נְקִיָּת 173. 1
נְקִיתִי 173. 1
נָקַל, נְקַל 140. 2
נְקַלֹּתִי 141. 2
נָקָם 217
נָקָם 131. 3
נִקְמָה 217
נָקַע 179. 2. a
נִקְרָא 91. b, 166. 3
נֵר 43. a, 200. a
נרא 97. 2. a
נֵרְדְּ 183. b
וַנֵּרֶד 99. 3, 147. 5
נִרְפָּאוּ 164. 3
נָרֹץ 140. 2
נָשָׂא 82. 5. a
נְשָׂא 131. 3
נְשָׂא 131. 4
נַשֵּׂא (Pi.) 165. 2
נְשָׂאוֹ 164. 4
נְשָׂאָה 164. 4
נָשׂוּא 165. 3
נָשׂוּא 57. 2 (3) a, 86. b (3 pl.), 164. 3

נָשׂוּי 165. 3
נָשָׂא 177. 3
נְשָׂא 165. 2
נִשְׂאַל 119. 1
וַיֵּשֶׁב 150. 3
נִשְׁבֶּרֶת 205
נִשְׁדָּאוּ 141. 2
נְשִׂיכִי 220. 1. b
נָשִׁים 207. 2. e
וְנָשִׁים 140. 5
נָשַׁךְ 84. 3. a (3)
נִשְׁכָּה 51. 4
נָשָׁל 84. 3. a (2)
נִשְׁלַח 124. a
נַשְׁלִיכָה 97. 1
נָשַׁמָּה 141. 1
נָשַׁמָּה 141. 1
נַשֵּׁנִי 92. c
נָשֹׁב 50. 2
נשקה 53. 3. a, 128
נָשָׁתָה 24. c
נִשְׁתָּוָה 83. c (2)
נִשְׁתָּעָה 172. 3
נתון 11. 1. b
כתונם 11. 1. b
נָתַךְ 50. 1, 80. 2. a (3), 84. 3. a (2)
נָתַן 130. 1, 132. 1
נְתָן 131. 4
נְתָן־ 130. 1. b
נְתָנוּ 24. c
כתנים 11. 1. b
נְתָנָה 101. 3. a
נָתַץ 50. 1

נָתַץ 131. 3
נְתַקְנוּהוּ 24. b
נָתַר 125. 3
נָתַשׁ 50. 1
נְתָתֶם 132. 1

סְאָה 200. b, 207. 1. f
סָאתַיִם 203. 3
סָבַב, סֹב 134. 1, 139. 2
סָבַב 138
סְבַב 141. 4
סְבָבֻנִי, סַבּוּנִי 104. l, 139. 1
סַבּוּנִי 139. 1
סַבּוֹתִי 61. 3
סביב 11. 1. b
סָבִיב 235. 3 (1)
סֹבִיב 90
סָבֹךְ 10. 2. a
סָבְכוֹ 24. b, 221. 5. a
סָבְכֵי 19. 1, 45. 2
סַבָּל 187. 1. a
סָבְלוֹ 24. b, 221. 5. a
סַבֶּלֶת 3. 1. a
סְנֹר 51. 1
סַגְרִיר 187. 2. c
סוֹבֵב 137, 141. 4
סוֹד 184. b
סוֹחֵר 186. 2. a
סוּס 58. 1
סוּסָה 58. 1
סוּסִי 62. 2
סוּסֵי 66. 1 (2) b
סוּסָיו 62. 2

INDEX III.

סוֹפֵר 186. 2. a
סוּר 3. 1. a
סוּחָה 53. 2. a, 220. 1. b
סָחַב 119. 1
סְחַרְחַר 92. a, 122. 1
סִיר 197. b, 200. c, d
סָכַךְ 51. 1, 141. 2 (p. 175)
סָכַל 3. 1. a, 51. 1, 80. 2. a (1)
סִכְסֵךְ 138
סָכַר 3. 1. a, 51. 1
סְלָחָה 125. 1
סַלְסֵל 141. 5
סַלְסִלּוֹת 187. 1. e, 207. 2. a
סָלַק 84. 3. a (2)
סָלָם 55. 1, 193. 2. c
סֹלֶת 197. b
סְמָדַר 195. 1
סְמָכְתָּהוּ 104. i
סְנֶה 183. b, 184. b
סַנְוֵרִים 207. 1. a
סַנְסִנִּים 207. 2. a
סְנַפִּיר 195. 1
סָעַד 19. 2. a, 89
וּסְעָדָה 234. a
סְעוּ 131. 3
סֹעַר, סַעַר 122. 2
סְעָרָה 51. 1
סַף 200. c, 207. 2. a
סָפָה 3. 1. a
וְסָפוּ 156. 4
סָפַן 50. 1
סָפַק 141. 3 (p. 175)
סֵפֶר 61. 4

סָרִיס 210. a
סָרִיסֵי, סָרִיסֵי 60. 3. c
סְרָעַפָּה 68. a
סְתָו 184. b
סְתֻמִּים 104. g
סָתַר 217
סִתְרָה 217
סִתְרוֹ 66. 2 (2) a

עָב 197. b, 200. c, 215. 1. a
עָב (ōbh?) 10. 2. a
עָבַד 112. 5. c
עֶבֶד 65
עֲבֹדָה 111. 3. a
עָבְדוֹ 220. 2. b
עָבְדוּ 65
וַיַּעַבְדוּ 61. 1. a
עֲבָדַי 216. 1. a
עֲבָדַי 61. 1
עֲבַדְיָהוּ 195. 3
עֲבָדְךָ 220. 1. b
עֲבֹדַת 22. a
עָבַר 112. 5. b
עִבְרִי 194. 1, 209. 2, 217
עִבְרִיָּה 62. 2
עִבְרִיּוֹת 62. 2
עִבְרִיִּים, עִבְרִים 62. 2
עִבְרִית 217
עָבְרָה 106. a
עֶבְרָכֶם 106. a, 127. 2
עָבֹת 200. c
עֵנָב 112. 5. a
עֵנָב 186. 2. b

עֵגֶל 185. 2. b
עֵגֶל 197. c
עֶגְלָה 197. c
עַד 237. 1, 238. 1, 267. b
עַד 65. a
(וְעַד), עַד 46
עַד 43. a
עֵדָה 112. 5. a
עֵדָה 184. b
עֵדוּת 209. 3
עֲדִי 238. 1. a
עַד כִּי 239. 2 (2)
עָדַף 112. 5. a
עָדַר 112. 5. a
עֶדְרִי 220. 2. a
עוֹגָב 186. 2. b
עוֹד 295. 3 (1), 236
עֻזַּד 161. 1
עוֹז (v.) 157. 1
עִיֵּן 156. 1
עָרֵל, עֲרֵל 184. b, 216. 1. d
עֵיל 161. 1
עוֹלָה 51. 1, 208. 3. c
עוֹלוֹ 221. 5. b
עוֹלָל 142. 1
עוֹלֵל 141. 5
עוֹלָם וָעֶד 63. 1. c
עוֹלָתָה 61. 6. a
עוֹן 156. 1
עָוֹן 200. c
עוֹנֵן 141. 4
עוֹפִים 187. 1. e
עוֹף 201. 1

INDEX III.

עוּץ 179. 2. a
עוּר 200. a
עִוֵּר (v.) 57. 2 (5) a, 161. 1
עִוֵּר (adj.) 187. 1. b
עִוָּרוֹן 193. 2
עֲוֶרֶת 198. a (3), 201. 1
עִוֵּת 161. 1
עַז, עֹז 65. a
עֵז 200. b, 207. 2
עֲזָאזֵל 11. 1. a, 168. a
עֲזוּבָה 98. 1
עַזְבוֹנָיִךְ 22. a
עֹזְבֵי 61. 6. a
עֲזוּבָה 111. 3. a
עֲזַבְתָּנִי 104. j
עֱזוּז 60. 3. b (1), 184
עָזוּז, עִזּוּז 221. 6
עַזָּה 61. 5
עָזַר 112. 5. b
עֵזֶר 184
עֶזְרָת 196. b
עֶזְרָתָה 61. 6. a
עָטָה 112. 5. b
עֲטִיָּה 209. 1. a
עֲטַלֵּף 195. 1
עֲטוּפִים 207. 1. a
עָטַר 50. 1, 112. 5. b
עֲטָרָה 214. 1. b
עִי 53. 3. a
עַיִט 201. 1
עִיִּין 199. a
עַיִן 184. b, 197. a, 208. 3. c bis, 217

עֵינוֹת 203. 5. a
עֵינוֹת 216. 1. d
עֵינֵי 221. 5. b
עֵינֵיהוּ 220. 2. c
עֵיפָה 156. 1
עַיִר 208. 3. c
עִיר 197. a, 200. b, 207. 1. f
עִירָה 220. 1. b, 221. 5. b
עֵירֹם 207. 2. c
עַיִשׁ 197. a
עַכְבִּישׁ 195. 1
עָכָן, עָכָר 51. 4
עָכַר 112. 5. a
עַל 237. 1, 238. 1, 267. b
עֹל 186. 2. c
עַלְוָה 51. 1
עֲלוּמִים 201. 1. b
עָלַז 112. 5. c
עָלֵז 185. 2. b
עָלְזוּ 111. 3. a
עָלְזִי 89 (f. s.), 111. 3. a
עָלֵי 238. 1. a
עֲלִי 3. 4
עֶלְיוֹן 193. 1
עֲלִילִיָּה 198. a (4)
עַל־כֵּן 239. 2 (3)
עָלַם 112. 5. b
עַל־יַעֲקֹב 237. 2 (2)
עַלְפֶּה 93. c
עַל־פִּי 237. 2 (2)
עָלַץ 112. 5. c
עִלְתָה 61. 6. a
עִם 197. b, 207. 2. a

עַם 237. 1
עָמַד 110. 1
עָמֹד 60. 3. b (1)
עָמְדוּ 65, 89 (m. pl.)
עִמְדוּ 60. 1. a
עָמְדִי 111. 3. a
עֲמָדָה 45. 2, 106. a
עַמּוֹנִית 209. 2, 210. d
עַמִּי 199. b
עַמִּי 214. 2
עַמָּה 65. a
עֲמָלָל 3. 4
עֲמָמִים 207. 2. a
עָמֹק 185. 2. b, 207. 1. c, 217
עֵמֶק 184
עֹמֶר 208. 3. b
עֲמֹרָה 3. 4
עֶבְרִי 24. b, 216. 2. a
עֲנָה 174. 3
עָנָו 185. 2. d
עֲנָוֹת 60. 3. b (1)
עַזּוּתוֹ 174. 6
עָנִי 185. 2. d
עָנְךָ 104. b
עָנָן 198, 217
עִנָּן 141. 4
עֲנָנָה 198, 217
עֲנָנִי 139. 1
עֲנַפְכֶם 221. 5. c
עָנָק 50. 1
עֲנֹתִי 24. b
עֲסוּתֶם 141. 2
עֲפָאִים 208. 3. d

INDEX III.

עָפָל 112. 5. a
עָפָר 200. a
עָפָר 208. 3. b
עֳפָרִים 60. 3. b (2)
עֻפְתָה 61. 6. a
עֵץ 43. a, 185. 2 d, 198, 217
עִצָּבוֹן 193. 2
עַצְבֵיכֶם 24. b, 216. 2. a
עֵצָה 184. b (פ׳), 217
עֲצָה 198
עֲצַלְתַּיִם 203. 5
עֶצֶם 80. 2. a (1), 82. 1. a (2)
עֶצֶם 197. b, 200. c
עֹצֶם 217
עָצְמָה 217
עָצַר 50. 3, 112. 5. b
עַצְרֹתֵיכֶם 24. b
עֶצְתְךָ 220. 2. a
עָקֵב 112. 5. b
עָקֵב 200. c, d, 215. 1. b
עֵקֶב אֲשֶׁר 239. 2 (2)
עִקְּבוֹת 24. b, 216. 2. a
עִקְּבוֹתֶיהָ 24. b
עַקְבֵי 24. b, 216. 2. a
עָקֹד 185. 2. b
עֲקַלְקַל 188
עַקְרָב 195. 1, 207. 2. b
עָקֵשׁ 112. 5. a
עִקֵּשׁ 187. 1. b
עֵר 156. 2
עָרַב 118. 1
עֲרָב 197. b

עֲרָבוֹת, עַרְבוֹת 45. 5. a
עַרְבִי 22. a
עַרְבִיאִים 62. 2. b, 209. 2. a
עַרְבַּיִם 208. 4
עָרוּךְ 60. 3. b (1)
עָרוֹעֵר 187. 1. e
עָרַי 216. 1. a
עָרִיץ 210. a
עֲרָכָה 111. 3. a
עֲרֵמָה 200. c, 216. 1. b
עַרְעָר 187. 1. e
עָרַךְ 80. 2. b
עָרְפֶּל 193. 2. c
עֶרֶשׂ 197. a
עָשָׂב 200. a
עֲשָׂבוֹת 24. b, 216. 2. a
עָשֹׂה 172. 2
עָשֹׂה 62. 2. c
עֲשָׂהאֵל, עֲשָׂהאֵל 13. b
עָשׂוֹ (pret.) 62. 2. c
עָשׂוֹ (part.) 172. 5
עָשׂוֹ 172. 2
עָשׂוֹ 172. 2
עָשׂוֹ 62. 2. c
עָשׂוֹת 172. 5, 209. 3. a
עֲשִׂיָה 221. 7. a
עֲשׂוּךְ 201. 2
עֲשִׂירִי 227. 1
עֲשִׂיתָ 86. b (1 c.)
עֲשִׂיתָנִי 102. 1. a
עֲשָׂה 62. 2. c
עָשָׂר 224
עָשָׂר 80. 2. b, 112. 5. a

עֲשָׂרָה 214. 1. b, 223. 1
עֲשָׂרָה 196. d, 224
עִשָּׂרוֹן 210. b, 227. 3
עֶשְׂרִים 208. 3. a, 225. 1
עֲשָׂרֹת 225. 1. a
עָשׂוֹחַ 172. 1
עָשׁוֹק 185. 2. c
עָשֵׁן 84. 3. a (2), 112. 5. b
עָשָׁן 216. 1. e
עֲשֻׁקָה־לִי 17. 2
עָשַׁר 79. 2, 112. 5. b, 125. 3
עֵשֶׁת 197. a
עַשְׁתֵּי 224. a
עַשְׁתֹּרֶת 207. 1. d
עֵת 43. a, 197. b, 200. c, 207. 2, 215. 1. b
עִתֵּד 80. 2
עַתָּה 219. 1. a
עִתִּי 194. 2
עָתַם 112. 5. a
עָתַק 84. 3. a (2), 112. 5. a
עָתַר 112. 5. a, 125. 3

פֹּא 11. 1. b
פָּארוּר 189. 2. c
פֵּאָרְךָ 104. c
פֵּאָרְךָ 104. b
פִּגְעוֹ 125. 2
פְּדַהאֵל 57. 2 (2) b
פְּדַהצוּר 13. b
פִּדְיוֹם 55. 1, 193. 2. c

פּדְיוֹן 193. 2. c	פְּלִילָה 198. a (2)	פְּקַח 187. 1
פַּדֶּנָה אֲרָם 33. 1. a, 219. 1. b	פְּלִילִיָּה 198. a (4)	פְּקַח־קוֹחַ 43. b, 188
	פָּלַל 141. 1 (p. 175)	פַּר 197. c
פֹּה 11. 1. b	פַּלְמֹנִי 68. a, 75. 3	פָּרָא 18. 2. c, 61. 2. a, 209. 3. b
פֶּה 185. 2. d, 209. 1. a, 215. 2. b, 220. 1. c	פְּלֹנִי אַלְמֹנִי 75. 3	
	פִּלַּשְׂתִּי 194. 1	פְּראֹת 11. 1. a
פֹּה 235. 3 (4)	פָּלַתִּי 199. b	פֹּראֹת 199
פּוּ 11. 1. b	פֵּן 239. 1	פִּרְבָּר 207. 1. b
פּוּץ 179. 2. a	פָּנָה 143. a	פַּרְדֵּסִים 207. 1. a
פּוּר 139. 1	פָּנַי: 39. 4. a	פָּרָה 197. c
פּוֹרֵר 141. 4	פָּנִים 197. b, 201. 1	פַּרְוָרִים 207. 1. b
פָּזַז 141. 1 (p. 175)	פָּנֵימוֹ 220. 2. c	פַּרְזוֹן 193. 2
פָּחַד 78. 1	פְּנִימִי 194. 2	פְּרָזִי 194. 2
פַּחַד 184. b	וּפָלִיתִי 100. 2. a (1)	פָּרַח 50. 1, 79. 2
פָּחָה 198, 211. a	פֶּסַח 187. 1. b	פִּרְחָח 187. 1. d
פְּחִי 131. 3	פֶּסֶל 208. 3. b	פְּרִי 57. 2 (4), 184. b, 221. 5. c
פַּחַת 131. 4	פָּעַל 76. 2, 83. b, 84. 3. a (3), 118. 2	
פָּטַר 125. 3		פֹּרִיָּה 62. 2. c, 209. 1. a
פִּי 61. 6. a	פֹּעַל 60. 1. a, 61. 2, 4, 208. 3	פָּרִיר 62. 2. b
פֵּיָה 198. c		פָּרִיץ 210. a
פֵּרוּ, פִּרחוּ 62. 2	פֹּעֲלוֹ 60. 3. b (2), 221. 5. a	פָּרֹכֶת 216. 1. a
פִּילֶגֶשׁ 59. a, 195. 1, 107. a, 200. b	פָּעֲלוּ 221. 5. a	פַּרְסָה 200. c
	פָּעֳלִי 60. 3. b (2)	פָּרַע 200. a
פִּילַגְשֵׁחוּ 220. 1. b	פְּעֻלָּה 61. 1	פַּרְעה 11. 1. a
פֶּלֶא 18. 2. c	פָּעֳלְכֶם 19. 2	פַּרְעֹה 104. d
פֶּלַג 92. c	פַּעַם 60. 1, 63. 2. a, 197. b, 200. c, d	פַּרְפַּר 141. 4
פֶּלֶג 92. c		פָּרַץ 50. 2
פִּלֶּגֶשׁ 59. a, 195. 1, 107. a, 200. b, 208. 3. a	פָּצַר 50. 2, 125. 3	פֶּרֶץ 200. c
	פָּקַד 80. 2. a (4)	פָּרַק 50. 1
	פְּקֹד 89	פָּרַשׂ 210. a, 216. 1. a
פְּלֵטִים 66. 2 (2) c	פְּקָדוּ 86. a	פָּרַשׁ 50. 3
פָּלִיט 207. 1. c	פָּקְדֻנִי 106. b	פֶּרֶשׁ 119. 1
פְּלֵיטָה 198	פְּקוּדִים 187. 2	פַּרְשֵׁז 50. 3, 68. a, 180. a
פְּלִיטֵי 216. 1. b		פָּרְשְׁכֶם 104. h, 119. 1

INDEX III.

פָּרַח 196. *b*, 209. 1. *a*
וּפָשׂוּ 100. 2. *a* (2)
פָּשַׁט 80. 2. *a* (1), 84. 3. *a* (3)
פָּשְׂתָה 200. *b*
פְּשָׁתָם 156. 1
פַּת 197. *a*, 200. *b*, 207. 2. *a*
פִּתְאֹם 235. 2 (1)
פִּתְגָּם 215. 1. *a*
פָּתוֹת 139. 2
פֶּתַח 80. 1
פִּתְחוֹ 106. *a*, 125. 2
פֶּתִי 208. 3. *d*
פְּתַלְתֹּל 188

צֵא 148. 3
צֵאָה (n.) 216. 1. *b*
צֵאָה: (v.) 148. 3, 164. 5
צְאִינָה 148. 3, 164. 3
צֶאֱלִים 208. 3. *a*
צֹאן 201. 1
צַאֲצָאַי 216. 1. *a*
צֶאֱצָאִים 188. *a*
צֵאת 148. 2
צֵאתִי 148. 2
צֵאתְךָ 30. 2
צָבָא 200. *a*, 215. 2. *c*
צְבָאִים 56. 4
צְבוֹאִים 56. 4
צְבִי 208. 3. *d*
צְבִיָּה 209. 2. *b*
צִבְיָה 165. 3
צַד 207. 2. *a*

צַדִּיק 187. 1
צָדַק 84. 3. *a* (2)
צֶדֶק 184, 198. *a* (2)
צֶדֶק 65. *a*
צָדַק 80. 1
צְדָקָה 198. *a* (2), 216. 2
צִדְקָתִי 65. *a*
צִדְקָתֵךְ 92. *d*
צָהֹב 50. 1
צֹהַר 197. *a*
צָהֳרַיִם 19. 2, 203. 5, 208. 4
צַו 174. 5
צַוָּאר 11. 1. *a*
צַוָּאר 200. *c*, 215. 1, 216. 1. *d*
צַוָּה 174. 5
צָוָה 57. 2 (2)
צִוִּיתִי 11. 1. *a*
צִוִּיתָם, צִוִּיתִים 11. 1. *a*
צוֹק 207. 1. *c*
צוּר (v.) 50. 3
צוּר (n.) 51. 3
צָחַק 51. 2
צָחֹק 92. *d*
צָהַר 50. 1
צָחֹר 185. 2. *b*
צִי 209. 2
צַיָּד 208. 3. *c*
צַיִד 187. 1. *a*
צֵידָנִי 210. *d*
צִנֹּק 187. 1. *c*
צִיקְלַג 14. *a*
צֵל 207. 2. *a*

צָלַח 82. 1. *a* (2)
צְלָחוֹת 57. 1
צַלַּחַת 57. 1, 210. *e*
צָלְלוּ 139. 1
צִלְלוֹ 20. 2, 221. 6. *b*
צְלָלִים 209. 2. *a*
צַלְמָוֶת 195. 3
צֶלַע 197. *a*, 200. *c*, 216. 1. *e*
צְלָעָה 198
צִלְצָל 187. 1. *e*, 207. 2. *a*, 216. 2
צֶלְצְלִים 16. 3. *b*
צָמֵא (v.) 82. 1. *a* (1)
צָמֵא (adj.) 185. 2. *b*
צִמְאִי 22. *a*, 216. 2. *a*
צָמַח 80. 2. *a* (1)
צָמַת 165. 3
צָמַתִּי 164. 2
צָמַתְנִי 102. 2, 104. *l*
צִמְתָּתִינִי 24. *b*, 92. *a*
צִמַּתַתְנִי 24. *b*
צָנִיף, צָנוֹף 185. 2
צִנְתָּר 200. *a*
צְעָדָה 119. 3
צָעַק 51. 2, 121. 1
צָפוּי (part.) 172. 5
צָפוֹן 197. *b*
צְפוֹנָה 219. 1
צְפוֹנִי 194. 2
צִפּוֹר 197. *c*, 200. *a*, 207. 1. *d*
צָפַן 50. 1
צָפְנַת 132. 1

צָפַף 141. 2 (p. 175)
צָפַרְדֵּעַ 68. a, 195. 2
צִפֹּרֶן 193. 2. b, 208. 3. a
צַק 148. 3
צִקּוּן 86. b (3 pl.)
צֶקֶת 148. 2
צָרָה 216. 1. a
צָרוּפָה 98. 1. a
צְרוֹר 200. a
צָרַר 50. 3, 141. 3 (p. 175)

קָאָה 156. 4
קָאם 11. 1. a
קָאם 156. 3
קָאַת 196. b
קֹב 139. 2
קָבָה 184. b
קָבַד־ 19. 2, 141. 1
קַבֹּח 104. d
קָבֹל 86. b (3 pl.)
קַבְּלוֹ, קַבְּלוּ 19. 2. c, 221. 5. a
קְבָל־עָם 19. 2
קָבְנוֹ 141. 3
קָבֵץ 92. d
קֻבְצָה 92. c
קֻבְצָה 92. c, 101. 3. a, 104. h
קָבַר 78. 1
קֶבֶר 200. c
קִבְתוֹ 104. j
קָדוֹשׁ 185. 2. b
קְדוֹשִׁים 201. 2

קֶדֶם 65. a
קָדְקֹד 187. 1. e
קָדַשׁ 80. 2. a (1), 82. 1. a (2)
קֹדֶשׁ 208. 3. b
קַדָּשׁ־ 92. c
קָדֵשׁ 92. c
קְדָשִׁים 19. 2
קֵהָה 121. 1
קֹהֶלֶת 197. d
קִהֲתִי 194. 1
קוֹבַע 50. 1
קוּדשׁ 11. 1. b
קֵהֶה, קֵוָה 174. 3
קְוִיתִי, קִוִּיתִי 174. 2
קוֹל 200. a
קוּם 153. 2, 155
קוּמָה, קִימָה 157. 2
קוּמִי 34
קִימִי 34
קוֹמִים 156. 2
קוּמֵם 83. c (1)
קוֹמְמִיּוּת 198. a (4)
קוּץ 179. 2. a
קוֹצוֹת 57. 2 (3) a
קַר־תֹחַ 21. 1
קַח 132. 2
קַח 53. 2. a, 132. 2
קְחִי 132. 2
קְחָם 132. 2
קְחַת־ 60. 3. c, 132. 2
קַחַת 132. 2
קַחְתִּי 132. 2
קְטָבָה 19. 2, 221. 5. a

קָטוּל 217
קָטַל 51. 3, 83, 83. b, 85. 2, 103
קֹטֶל 183. a
קֹטֶל 217
קָטֹן 185. 2, 207. 2. b, 217
קָטֹן (adj.) 185. 2
קָטֹן (v.) 82. 1. a (3), 84. 3. a (1)
קָטְנִי 19. 2, 221. 5. a
קָטַר 80. 2. a (1)
קִיטוֹר 187. 1. c
קָיָם 83. c (1), 154. 1, 161. 1
קִימוֹשׁ 59. a, 187. 1. c
קִימָנוּ 220. 1. b
קִיקָלוֹן 187. 1. e
קִיר 200. a
קַלּוּ 141. 1
וְקַלּוּ 100. 2. a (2)
קָלוֹת 214. 2
קַלּוֹת 141. 2
קָלַל 84. 3. a (2)
קַלֵּל 141. 4
קִלְלַת 20. 2
קְלָסָה 198. a (3)
קִלְקֵל 141. 4
קַלְקַל 187. 1. e
קָם 57. 2 (5), 153. 1, 185. 2. a
קָמוֹשׁ 59. a, 187. 1. c
קָמִים 156. 2
קָמֵל, קָמַל 82. 1. a (1)

INDEX III.

קָמְלוּ 24. c
קְמָנָה 61. 4, 66. 2 (2), 157. 2
קֹמֶץ 208. 3. b
קָמִיתָ 59
קֵן 215. 1. b
קִנֵּא 92. d, 166. 3
קִנְאָתוֹ 166. 2
קָנֶה 200. c
קָנֹה 172. 2
קָנוֹ 172. 2
קִנְיָנְךָ 215. 1. c
קִנֵּן 141. 1 (p. 175)
קִנֵּן 80. 2. b
קִנְצֵי 54. 3
קְסוּמֵי 89 (f. s.)
קֶסֶם 84. 3. a (3)
קְסָם־ 87
קֶסֶס 141. 3 (p. 175)
קְפָדָה 106. c
קֶצֶב 50. 1
קָצָה 18. 2. c
קְצֵהוּ 220. 1. b
קָצוּר 184. b
קָצִיר 185. 2. a
קִצֵּץ 141. 1 (p. 175)
קָצַר 50. 1, 2, 84. 3. a (3), 125. 3
קִצְרָכֶם 106. a
קָצַת 196. b, 211. a
קָרָא 179. 1. a
קְרָא 166. 2
קְרָא 167. 1
קְרָאוֹת 166. 2

קְרָאֲךָ 104. c
קָרָא לַיְלָה 35. 1
קָרְאָן 60. 3. c, 98. 2, 164. 3
קְרָאת 166. 1
קְרָאת 166. 2
קָרַב 77. 3, 78. 2, 82. 1. a (2), 118. 1
קָרַב (imp.) 119. 1
קָרֵב 185. 2. b
קֶרֶב 200. a
קְרָב־ 19. 2. a
קָרְבָה 98. 1. a
קָרְבוּ 39. 4. a
קָרְבְכֶם 19. 2, 119. 3
קָרְבָּן 19. 2. b, 193. 2
קָרְבָּנִי 216. 1. a
קָרְדֹּם 200. c
קָרָה 179. 1. a
קָרוֹב 185. 2. b
קָרַח 187. 1. b
קָרְחָא 11. 1. a
קָרְחָא 196. d
קָרְחִי 89 (f. s.)
קָרַם 118. 1
קֶרֶן 197. a
קַרְנוֹת 203. 5. a
קַרְנֵי 214. 2
קַרְנָיו, קַרְנָיו 221. 4
קְרָנַיִם, קְרָנַיִם 203. 1, 208. 4
קַרְסֹל 193. 2. c
קָרַץ 50. 2
קַרְקַע 187. 1. e

קַרְקַר 161. 2
קַשְׂקַשׂוֹת 207. 1. e
קָשֵׁב 79. 2, 84. 3. a (2)
קָשָׁה 210
קָשׁוֹת 216. 1. d
קֹשֶׁט 61. 4, 183. b
קָשַׁר 80. 2. a (2)
קֶשֶׁר 80. 1
קָשְׁרָם 125. 1
קַשָּׁשׁ 141. 3 (p. 175)
קֶשֶׁת 197. b, 109. d
קַשָּׁת 187. 1. a
קַשְׁתוֹתָם 24. b
קָשָׁתוֹת 216. 2. a

רָאָה 77. 2, 79. 1, 80. 1, 114
רְאֵה 172. 2
רְאִי 172. 2
רְאִי 26, 121. 1
רְאוּבֵנִי 57. 2 (3) a
רַאֲוָה 172. 2
רְאוֹת 172. 2
רֳאִי 60. 3. b (2)
רְאָיוֹת 207. 2. d
רִאשׁוֹן 227. 1. a
רָאמָה 156. 3
רָאמוֹת 11. 1. a
רָאמוֹת 156. 3
רֹאֲנִי 102. 3
רֹאשׁ 11. 1. a bis
רֹאשׁ 156. 3
רֹאשׁ 61. 2. a, 207. 1. f
רִאשׁוֹן 11. 1. b

רִאשׁוֹן 193. 1, 227. 1	רַגְלִי 194. 2	רַחֲמִים 201. 1, 208. 3. *a*
רִאשׁוֹנָה 235. 3 (3)	רְגָלִים 203. 5. *a*	רָחַץ 80. 2. *a* (3)
רָאשִׁים 57. 2 (3) *a*	רֹגֵעַ 126. 1	רִחְצָה 119. 3
רֵאשִׁית 198. *a* (4)	(יָרַד) רַד 53. 2. *b*, 150.	רָחֵק 185. 2. *b*
(עֵ") רַב 153. 1	1 (p. 182)	רָחַק 119. 1
(עַ") רֹב ,רָב 82. 1. *a* (3)	(עֹ") רַד 139. 2	רָחֲקָה 119. 3
רַב 217	רָדָה, רַד 148. 3	רָטָב 84. 3. *a* (2)
(עֵ") רֹב 158. 3	רָדָה (inf.) 148. 2	רְטָפַשׁ 68. *a*, 180. *a*
רֹב (n.) 186. 2. *c*	רָדַף 78. 1	רִי 184. *b*
רָבַב 141. 1 (p. 175), 179. 2. *a*	רְדֹף 114	רִיב (v.) 153. 2, 155, 158. 2, 3
רִבְבֹתָיו 250. 2 (2) *a*	רְדָפוּנִי 114	רִיב (n.) 186. 2. *c*
רָבָה 179. 2. *a*	רָדְפִי 19. 2. *a*	רִיבוֹתָ 158. 1
רַבָּה 235. 3 (3)	רֶדֶת 148. 2	רֵיק 186. 2. *c*
רַבָּה 172. 3, 174. 5	רְדִפְתִּי 148. 2	רֵיקָם 235. 2 (1)
(עֵ") רָבוּ 156. 4	רְהָבָם 22. *a*	רֵישׁ 186. 2. *c*
רַבּוּ 141. 1	רוֹב 158. 3	רִישׁוֹן 57. 2 (2) *a*, 227. 1. *a*
רֻבּוּ 139. 1	רוּחַ 57. 2 (5) *a*, 156. 1	
רְבוֹ, רִבּוֹא 197. *a*, 209. 3, 226	רֵוַח 184. *b*	רַךְ 50. 1, 186. 2. *c*
רִבּוֹת 60. 3. *a*	רוּחַ 197. *b*	רָכַב 84. 3. *a* (2)
רִבּוֹתַיִם 203. 4, 226	רִוַּח 161. 1	רַבּוּ 141. 1
רַבִּים 249. 1. *a*	רוֹכֵל 186. 2. *a*	רְכָךְ 141. 1 (p. 175)
רְבִיעִי 227. 1	רוּם 80. 2. *a* (4)	רָכַל 50. 1
רְבִיעִית 227. 3	רוֹמָם 157. 1	רְכֻלָּה 198. *a* (2)
רֹבַע, רֶבַע 227. 3	רוּץ 179. 1. *a*	רֹמוּ 139. 1
רְבֵעִים 207. 1. *a*	רוֹצֵץ 141. 4	רְמוֹנִי 199. *b*
רָבַץ 84. 3. *a* (2)	רֹאשׁ 57. 2 (2) *a*	רָמַח 208. 3. *b*
רִבְתָ 158. 1	רְחוֹב, רְחֹב 197. *b*, 200. *a*	רְמִיתֵנִי 104. *k*
רַבַּת 235. 3 (3)	רַחוּם 187. 1	רָוִי, רָבוּ 141. 1
רַבְּתִי 33. 1, 61. 6. *a*, 218	רָחוֹק 185. 2. *b*	רָנַן 139. 3
רָגַז 84. 3. *a* (2)	רָחָל 197. *c*, 200. *b*	רֻנַּן 141. 5
רָגַל 50. 1	רָחַם 118. 2	רֵעַ 60. 2, 215. 1. *e*
רֶגֶל 197. *a*, 217	רִחַם 119. 1	רָעֵב (v.) 82. 1. *a* (2)
	רֻחַם 61. 2. *a*, 197. *b*	רָעֵב (adj.) 185. 2. *b*
	רָחָמָה 196. *c*	

INDEX III. 391

רֹעָה 139. 2	רִשְׁפֵּי, רְשָׁפַי 22. a, 216. 2. a	שָׂחַק 51. 2
רֹעָה 186. 2. a, 215. e		שָׂטָן, שׂטֵם 51. 4
רֵעֵהוּ 220. 1. b	רֹשֵׁשׁ 141. 5	שִׂטְנוֹ 106. a
וְרֵעִי 141. 1	רֹשָׁשׁ 141. 5	שִׂיא 184. b
רֵעִי 221. 3. a	רֶשֶׁת (v.) 148. 2	שִׂיחֵהוּ 221. 7. a
רֵעֶה 221. 3. a	רֶשֶׁת (n.) 184. b	שִׂיוֹ 221. 7. a
רְעַל 114	רִשְׁתָּה 148. 2	שִׂיחַ 158. 2, 3
רַעֲנַן 122. 1	רָתוֹק 200. a, 207. 1. c	שִׂים 158. 2, 3 bis
רַעֲנָן 187. 1. d, 207. 2. b	רֹתֵם 197. b, 208. 3. b	שִׂימָה 158. 3
רָעַע 141. 3 (p. 175)		שִׂישׂוֹ 158. 2
רְעָתְכִי 220. 1. b	שָׂא 131. 3	שָׂכַב 51. 1
רֹפֵא 186. 2. a	שָׂאוּ, שְׂאוּ 16. 2. a, 45. 5. a	שָׂכַל 3. 1. a, 79. 2
רֻפָּא 92. d, 166. 3		שְׂכֻלוֹת 3. 1. a, 51. 4. a
רְפָאָה 164. 5	שְׂאוֹר 3. 1. a	שָׂכַר 3. 1. a
רְפָאֻנִי 105. 2	שְׂאֵת 16. 2. a, 61. 2. a, 131. 4	שָׂלָו 184. b, 207. 1. b
רְפֻאֹתַי 165. 2		שָׂמוּ 156. 4
רְפַד 84. 3. a (2)	שֵׂאת 61. 2. a	שָׂמֵחַ 82. 1. a (2)
רְפֵה 165. 1	שָׂבַע 82. 1. a (2)	שְׂמֵחִי, שְׂמֵחַי 216. 1. b
רְצָאתִי 177. 3	שָׂבֵעַ 185. 2. b	שַׂמְּתוֹ 104. j
רָצוֹא 179. 1. a	שְׂבָעַתְּ׃ 127. 1	שֹׂנֵא 82. 1. a (1)
רָצִין 199. a	שָׂבַר 3. 1. a	שִׂנְאָה 87, 166. 2
רָצֵץ 141. 4	שָׂדַד 141. 1 (p. 175)	שְׂנֵאָה 104. h
רַק 50. 1	שָׂדֶה 185. 2. d, 200. c, 210, 215. 2, 221. 7	שֹׂנְאַי 102. 3
רָקַב 84. 3. a (2)		שִׂנְאָה 60. 1, 164. 4
רֹקַח 186. 2. a	שָׂדְחוּ 220. 1. b	שְׂנֵאת 166. 2
רֹקֵם 186. 2. a	שָׂדַי 185. 2. d	שְׂנֵאתִי 104. 1
רֹקַע 126. 1	שֶׂה 201. 1, 215. 2	שְׂנֵאָחֶיךָ 220. 2. a
רַקָּה 106. a, 125. 2	שָׂהֲדִי 19. 2	שָׂעַר 3. 1. a, 121. 1
רָקַק 179. 2. a	שׂוֹא 131. 4	שֵׂעָר 207. 1. b
רָשׁ (פ״י) 186. 2. c	שׂוּחַ 158. 3	שְׂעָרָה 51. 1
רָשׁ, רֵשׁ (פ״י) 148. 3	שׂוּם 158. 3	שְׂעֹרָה 198. b
רֶשַׁע 198. a	שׂוּמָה 158. 3	שְׂעֹרָה 200. b
רִשְׁעָה 198. a (1)	שׂוּר 3. 1. a, 179. 2. a	וּשְׂעֹרָה 27, 57. 2 (2) b, 220. 1. b
רִשְׂעָתַיִם 203. 5	שָׂחוּ 184. b	

שָׂפָה 3. 1. a, 199. d, 217, 221. 2. 4	שֵׂאסִיךָ 139. 3	שֶׁבֶר, שְׁבָרִים 126. 2
שׂפֶן 50. 1	שְׂאָר 183. b	שַׁבָּת 84. 3. a (3), 86. b
שִׂפְתֵי 216. 2. a	שְׂאֵרִית 198. a (4)	שַׁבָּת 148. 2
שִׂפְתוֹתֵיהֶם 221. 1	שָׁב 53. 2. a, 144. 3, 148. 3	שַׁבָּת 144. 3, 148. 2
שִׂפְתָיהֶם 221. 1	שָׁבָה, שָׁב־ 148. 3	שַׁבָּת 197. b, 221. 6. a
שַׂר 207. 2. a	שֹׁב 157. 1	שַׁבָּתוֹן 193. 2. a
שָׂרָה 179. 2. a	שׁוּבוּ 11. 1. a	שַׁבְּתִּי, שָׁבַתִּי 148. 2
שָׂרַי 190. c	שָׂבוּ 34	שֵׁגָל 197. a
שְׂרָעַפִּים 68. a	שָׂבוּ 34	שֵׂגֶר 216. 1. e
שְׂרָפָתַם 104. i	שָׁבוּ 39. 4. a	שַׂד 207. 2. a
שׂרֵק 185. 2. b	שָׁבוּעַ 200. c, 210. a	שֹׁדוֹד 139. 2
שָׂרַר 141. 1 (p. 175)	שָׁבוּת 198. a (4)	שֻׁדַּד 141. 4
שָׂרִיתִי 61. 6. a	שְׁבוּתְחָן 220. 1. b	שָׁדְדָה 93. a
שֵׂת 131. 4	שְׁבָט 51. 2, 197. b	שָׁדְדוּ 141. 1
שְׂתָם 90 (pass.)	שִׁבְעִי 216. 2	שָׁדוֹד 139. 2
	שִׁבִּי 221. 5. c	שַׂדַּי 199. c.
שֶׁ 53. 2. a, 74	שְׁבִיעִי 227. 1	שֵׂהֶם 45. 5. a
שְׁאָהֲבָה 45. 5. a	שְׁבִית 198. a (4)	שָׁוְא 61. 2. a
שְׁאוֹל 197. b	שַׁבְלוּל 24. b	שׁוּב 157. 1
שָׁאַט 57. 2 (3) a	שַׁבְּלִי 24. b	שׁוּב (יָשׂוּב?) 53. 2. b, 148. 2
שָׂאטִים 156. 3	שִׁבֹּלֶת 3. 1. a, 200. b, 207. 1. d	שׁוּבְכָתֶךָ 104. c
שְׂאֶטְךָ 57. 2 (3) a	שֻׁבְנָה 157. 2	שׁוּבָה, שׁוּבָה 157. 2
שָׁאַל 78. 1, 121. 1	שֶׁבַע 216. 1. e	שׁוּבוּ 11. 1. a
שָׁאֲלוּ, שָׁאֵל 119. 2	שִׁבְעָה 223. 1	שׁוּדַּד 141. 4
שָׁאֲלָה 119. 3	שִׁבְעִים 208. 3. a, 225. 1	שׁוֹמֵמָה 207. 1. a
שְׁאֵלוּנוּ 110. 2	שִׁבְעַיִם 203. 3	שֹׁמְרִים 199. a
שְׁאֵלוּנִי 118. 3	שְׁבַעְנָה 223. 1. a	שׁוּרִי 194. 2. a
שָׁאֲלָה 119. 2	שִׁבְעֹתֵיכֶם 221. 2. b	שֶׁוַע 161. 1
שָׁאֲלָה 104. a	שִׁבְעָתַיִם 203. 4, 223. 1. a	שׁוּעָל 186. 2
שְׁאֵלְתִּיו 119. 2	שִׁבְעָתָם 223. 1. a, 250. 2 (2) a	שׁוֹעֵר 186. 2. a
שְׁאֵלְתָּם 119. 2	שָׁבַר 3. 1. a	שׁוֹפֵט 186. 2. a
שָׁאָן 122. 1		שׁוֹפָר 200. a
שַׁאֲנָן 187. 1. d, 207. 2. b		שׁוּק 207. 1. f.

INDEX III.

שׂוֹק 197. a
שׁוּר 3. 1. a
שׁוּר (v.) 158. 3
שׁוֹר (n.) 197. c, 201. 1, 207. 1. f.
שׁוֹשַׁתִּי 92. b, 174. 1
שׁוֹשָׁן 207. 2. b
שְׁחָדוּ 60. 3. b (2), 119. 4
שָׂחָה 141. 1
שַׁחוּ 60. 4. a, 141. 1
שַׂחֲוָה 119. 3
שְׁחִית 190. d
שָׁחֹר 185. 2. b
שְׁחַרְחֹר 188
שָׁחַת 78. 2
שִׁחֲתוּ 121. 2
שַׂחָתְכֶם 119. 1
שִׂטָּה 200. b
שְׁטִים 156. 3
שִׂיחוֹר 187. 1. c
שִׁילֹנִי, שִׁילֹנִי 55. 2. a
שִׁיר 158. 2, 3
שִׁירָה 220. 1. b
שִׁית 158. 2, 3
שִׁיתוֹ 221. 5. b
שַׁךְ 139. 2
שָׁכַב 84. 3. a (2)
שָׁכֹב 87
שָׁכַב 87
שִׁכְבַת 98. 1
שִׁכְבָה 106. a
שִׁכְבוֹ 106. a
שַׁכּוֹל 184
שָׁכוּן 90 (pass.)

שָׂכוּן 87
שָׁכַח 80. 2, 82. 1. a (2)
שְׁכֵחֵי 216. 1. b
שְׁכַחְתָּנוּ 127. 2
שְׁכַחֲנוּךָ 127. 2
שָׁכַחְתְּ 60. 2. a, 127. 1
שָׂכַל 3. 1. a
שֵׂכֶל 82. 1. a (3), 84. 3. a (1), 85. 2
שְׂכַלְתִּי 65. a, 82. 1. a (3)
שִׁכַּלְתִּי 65. a
שְׁכֶם 183. b
שֶׁכֶם 65
שִׂכְמִי 221. 5. c
שָׁכַן 82. 1. a (2), 84. 3. a (1)
שָׁכֹן 87
שָׁכֵן 90 (pass.)
שְׁכֵנִי 61. 6. a
שָׁכַנְתְּ 132. 1
שֹׁכַנְתִּי 90 (2 f.)
שָׂכָר 3. 1. a, 125. 3
שֵׂכָר 185. 2
שֶׁל־ 131. 3
שֶׁל 130. 2
שַׁלְאֲנָן 68. a
שַׁלְהֶבֶתְיָה 195. 3
שָׁלוּ 185. 2. d
שְׁלִי 184. b
שָׁלוּ בָהּ 21. 1
שְׁלוּחִים 187. 2
שְׁלוּם 187. 2
שָׁלַוְתִּי 168. a
שָׁלַח 80. 2. a (1), 124

שָׁלַח 60. 1
שִׁלַּח 125. 2
שָׁלַח 126. 1
שָׁלַח 126. 1
שִׁלְחָה 125. 1
שֹׁלַחַה 221. 3. a
שַׁלְּחָה 126. 1
שִׁלְחָן 200. a
שְׁלַח־נָא 45. 4
שָׁלַחְתִּי 123. 5. a
שָׁלַו 84. 3. a (2)
שְׁלִי 54. 2
שָׁלִישׁ 210. a
שְׁלִישִׁי 199. b
שְׁלִישִׁי 227. 1
שְׁלִישִׁית 227. 3
שְׁלִישִׁתָה 219. 1. a
שַׁלֶּכֶת 92. d
שָׁלַל 141. 3 (p. 175)
שָׁלֵם 84. 3. a (2)
שָׁלֵם 92. d
שָׁלֵם 92. c
שָׁלֵם 93. a
שָׁלֵמוּ 92. c
שַׁלְוִי 104. 2. a
שְׁלָשׁ־ 215. 1. c
שָׁלֹשׁ 51. 3
שְׁלשָׁה 220. 1. b
שְׁלֹשָׁה 223. 1
שְׁלֹשִׁים 225. 1
שְׁלֹשִׁים 207. 1. a
שִׁלְשׁוֹם 235. 2 (1)
שִׁלְשֹׁתֶיךָ 220. 1. b
שִׁלְשְׁתָּכֶם 250. 2 (2) a

INDEX III.

שִׁלַּשְׁתָּם 250. 2 (2) *a*
שֶׁלָּתֶךָ 53. 2. *a*
שֵׁם 235. 1
שֵׁם 43. *a*, 200. *a*, 215. 1. *b*
שָׁמַד 80. 2. *a* (3)
שָׁמָּה 219. 1. *a*
שְׁמוֹ 221. 3. *a*
שָׁמוֹת 64. 2
שֵׁמוֹת 139. 2
שְׁמַטְתָּה 86. *b* (2 m.)
שְׁמִי 66. 2 (2) *c*
שָׁמַיִם 10. *a*
שָׁמַיִם 201. 1, 203. 5. *c*
שְׁמַיְמָה 219. 1
שְׁמִינִי 227. 1
שָׁמֵם 82. 1. *a* (2), 84. 3. *a* (1), 141. 3 (p. 175)
שֹׁמֵם 90
שָׁמֵן 79. 2, 84. 3. *a* (2)
שְׁמֹנָה 223. 1
שְׁמֹנִים 225. 1
שִׂמְלֹת עָשׂוּר 224. *a*
שָׁמַע 80. 2. *a* (1), 82. 1. *a* (2)
שְׁמַע 60. 1. *a*
שָׁמֵעַ 65. *b*
שָׁמֵעַ 184. *b*
שֹׁמֵעַ 60. 1. *a*
שֹׁמֵעַ 60. 1
שָׁמְעָה 125. 1
שִׁמְעָה 98. 1, 125. 1
שָׁמְעִי 125. 2
שָׁמְעָה 106. *a*

שָׁמְעֲכֶם 125. 2
שָׁמַעַן 89 (f. pl.), 98. 2, 127. 1
שְׁמַעֲנָה 127. 2
שָׁמְעֵנִי 125. 1
שְׁמַעְתְּ 127. 1
שֹׁמַעַת 205
שָׁמְעָתוֹ 106. *a*
שָׁמַר 77. 2
שֹׁמֵר 186. 2. *a*
שָׁמְרָה־ 125. 1
שְׁמִירָה 19. 2
שָׁמְרָה 104. *e*
שֶׁמֶשׁ 197. *b*
שֵׁן 197. *a*, 217
שְׁנָא 196. *d*
שְׂנֵא 177. 3
שָׁנָה 200. *c*, *d*, 211, 216. 1
שְׁנוֹתַי 141. 2
שֵׁנִי 227. 1
שְׁנַיִם 203. 4, 223. 1
שְׁנֵים הֶעָשׂוֹר 251. 4. *a*
שְׁנֵינוּ 250. 2 (2) *a*
שֵׁנִית 235. 3 (3)
שָׁנָן 141. 1 (p. 175)
שֵׁנָּן 141. 5
שִׁנַּת 196. 5
שִׁנְתַיִם 203. 3
שֹׁסֵעַ 126. 1
שֶׁעֲטְנֵז 195. 2
שֹׁעַל 208. 3. *b*
שַׁעֲלִי 216. 2
שֶׁעַע 141. 2 (p. 175)
שַׁעַר 197. *b*

שָׂעֹרָה; שְׂעֹרָה 60. 3. *a*
שַׁעֲרוּר 3. 1. *a*
שַׂעֲרוּרָה 187. 2. *c*
שְׁעָשֵׁעַ 60. 3. *b* (2), 141. 6
שַׁעֲשֻׁעִים 187. 2. *b*
שָׁפוֹךְ 89
שִׁפְחָה 214. 1
שְׁפֹטוּ 89 (m. pl.)
שָׁפַךְ 80. 2. *a* (2)
שְׁפֹךְ 89
שְׁפָכָה 13. *b*, 86. *b* (3 pl.)
שִׁפְכָה 22. *a*
שָׁפָל 82. 1. *a* (1)
שָׁפָל 87
שִׁפְלָה 196. *c*
שָׁפָן 207. 2. *b*
שִׁפְעַת 196. *b*
שַׁפְרִיר 187. 2. *c*
שְׂפָתוֹת 203. 5. *a*
שְׂפָתַיִם 203. 5. *a*
וּשְׁקָה 131. 3
שָׁקוּ 209. 3
שִׁקּוּץ 187. 2
שִׁקְמוֹת, שִׁקְמִים 208. 3. *a*
שָׁקַק 141. 2 (p. 175)
שֹׁקֶת 199. *d*
שִׁקֻּתוֹת 216. 2, 216. 2. *a*
שָׁרֹאשִׁי 60. 4. *a*
שַׁרְבִיט 22. *a*, 51. 2, 68. *a*
שָׁרֵךְ 60. 4. *a*, 221. 6. *b*
שָׂרְרֵךְ 221. 6. *b*
שֹׁרֶשׁ 208. 3. *b*
שֵׁרֵשׁ; שֹׁרֶשׁ 83. *c* (1), 92. *b*, 122. 2

INDEX III.   395

שָׂרְשָׁה 187. 1. e	תַּאַרְגִי 112. 3	תְּבָרְכוּ 120. 3
שָׂרָשִׁים 19. 2	תְּאָרוֹ, תֹּאֲרוֹ 60. 3. b (2)	תְּבָרְכֵנִי 105. b
שֵׁשׁ 43. a	תָּאׇרְנָה 157. 3	וַתִּגְבְּהֶינָה 128
שָׂשָׂה 223. 1	תְּאַשּׁוּר 190	וַתִּגְדַּל 99. 3
שִׂשִּׂי 227. 1	תֵּאָתֶה 111. 2. b	תְּגַנְּדְעוּן 126. 1
שִׂשִּׂים 225. 1	תֹּבֵא 111. 2. b, 177. 3	וַתַּנַח 158. 2
שֵׁת 200. a	תְּבֹאֶינָה 157. 3	תּוֹגְיוֹן 172. 1
שָׁתָה 50. 1, 179. 2. a	תָּבֹאן 88 (f. pl.)	תִּגַּל: 174. 4
שְׁתוֹ 172. 2	תָּבֹאנָה 157. 3	תִּגַּל 66. 1 (1), 173. 3
שָׁתוֹת, שָׁתוֹת 172. 2	תָּבֹאתִי 88 (3 f.), 167. 3	תִּגְלֶה 172. 3
שְׁתִי 209. 2. b	תִּבְהַלְנָה 118. 4	וַתִּגְלֶה 173. 3
שְׁתִיָּה 209. 2. b	תְּבוֹאָה 97. 1. a	תִּגְלָה 158. 2
שְׁתִיתֶן 250. 2 (2) a	תבואתה 220. 1. b	תַּגְמוּלוֹהִי 220. 2. c
שְׁתַּיִם 22. b, 223. 1. a	תְּבוֹאָתָה 88 (3 f.), 167. 3	וַתִּגָּשְׁן 88 (f. pl.)
	תְּבוֹאָחָה 88 (3 f.), 167. 3	תִּדְבָּקִין 88 (2 f.)
תָּאַב 51. 1	תִּבּוֹז 140. 3	תִּדְבָּקֵנִי 105. a, d
תֶּאֱבַל 111. 2. a	תָּבוּן 192. 2	וַתְּדַבֵּר 99. 3
וְלֹאאָבְדוּ דָּרֶךְ 35. 1	תָּבוֹק 140. 3	תִּדְבְּרוּן 55. 2. a, 88 (m. pl.)
תֹּאבֵדוּן 64. 2	תִּבְחֲנֵוּ 105. b	
תֶּאֱגֹר 111. 2. a	תִּבְטָחוּ 88 (3 f. pl.)	תִּדְבְּרוּן 88 (m. pl.)
תֶּאֱהָבוּ 60. 3. c, 111. 2. e	תָּבִיאוּ 26	תְּדַבְּרֶינָה 92. e
תְּאוֹ 57. 2 (3) a, 184. b	תָּבִישׁוּ 160. 3	תֻּדַּד 139. 3
תְּאוֹמֵי 216. 1. c	וַתִּתְבְּכֶה 172. 4	תִּדְהָר 192. 2
תֶּאָחֵז 111. 2. a	תִּבְכֵּינָה 172. 3	תִּדְכְּאוּנֵנִי 105. c
תְּאַכְּלֵהוּ 60. 3. c (?), 93. a, 111. 2. e	תֵּבֵל 190. b, 107. a	תִּדְלֶה 172. 3
	תֵּבֵל 190. b	תִּדְמָיוּן 172. 1
תֵּאָכַלְנָה 91. c	תְּבַלֵּל 190	וַתֵּדַע: 147. 5
תֵּאָלֶה 111. 2. a	וַתָּבֶן 158. 2	תִּדְשָׁא 45. 2
תְּאָמֵי 216. 1. c	תַּבְעִיוּן 172. 1	תֹּהוּ 61. 2
תֵּאָמַנָה: 88 (f. pl.)	תַּבְעֵנָה 126. 1	תֹּהוּ 30. 1
תֹּאמְרָן 88 (m. pl.)	תְּבַעֲתַנִי 105. b	תְּהוֹם 190. b, 107. b, 200. a
תְּאֵנָה 200. b, 216. 1. b	תִּבְקַע: 126. 1	
תֹּאסְפוּן 151. 2	תְּבַקְשׁוּן 88 (m. pl.)	תִּהְיֶה 172. 3
תַּאַסְפִי 112. 3	וּתְבַקְשִׁי 234. a	תְּהִיֶין 88 (f. pl.)

INDEX III.

תְּחִינָה, תְּחִנָּה 11. 1. *a*	יַתְזְרֵנִי 53. 3. *a*, 111. 2. *c*	תֵּיעָשֶׂה 113. 1
תְּהִימֶנָּה 160. 3	וַתַּחְבֹּא 166. 4	תִּיקַד 147. 4
תַּהְכְּרוּ 94. *c*	תַּחְפֻּלוֹת 201. 1	תִּירֹשׁ 190. *b*
תָּהֵל 140. 5	תַּחְבֹּל 60. 3. *a*	תַּיִשׁ 208. 3. *c*
תְּהִלָּה 190. *b*	תַּחַז 172. 4	תישבנה 147. 2
תְּהֲלַךְ 19. 1, 60. 3. *b* (2), 112. 2, 151. 1	וַתַּחַז 111. 2. *b*	תִּישָׁמְנָה 147. 4
	תְּחֱזֶה 172. 4	תְכַבְּדֻךָ 101. 3. *a*
תְּהִלָּתִיָּה 220. 2. *a*	תֶּחֱזִי 16. 2. *a*	וַתְּכַהּ 172. 4
וַתַּהַר 172. 4	תְּחִילִין 158. 2	וַתִּכְהֶיןָ 88 (f. pl.)
תַּהְרְגֶנָה 118. 4	וַתָּחַל 158. 2	וַתִּבָּחֵר 119. 1
וַתַּהְרִין 172. 3	תָּחֵל 140. 3	תֵּכַל 172. 4
תַּהְתֵּלּוּ 24. *c*, 142. 3	תְּחִלָּה 190. *b*	תִּכְלָה 177. 3
תָו 185. 2. *d*	תַּחֲלוּאֵיכֶם: 220. 2. *c*	תִּבֶּן 50. 1
תוֹא 57. 2 (3) *a*	תְּחֻלֶּינָה 141. 2	תִּבְסֶה 54. 2
תוּגָה 190. *b*	תַּחְמֹס 190. *a*	תַּכְרִיךְ 192. 2
תּוֹךְ 63. 2. *a*, 184. *b*	וַתַּחְמְרָה 104. *c*	תִּכְרָת־ 88 (2 f.)
תּוֹךְ 216. 1. *d*	תַּחֲנוֹת 190. *b*	וַתֵּלֶא 172. 4
תּוֹכֵחָה 220. 1. *b*	תַּחֲנֻתִי 220. 2. *a*	תְּלָאָה 190. *b*, 198. *a* (3)
תּוֹכַחַת 105. *e*	וַתַּחְפֹּם 60. 1. *a*, 157. 3	תְּלָאִים 177. 3
תּוֹמִיךְ 90, 151. 3	תַּחַץ 173. 3	וַתֵּלֶד 147. 5
תּוֹסָף 22. *b*, 151. 2	וַתַּחֵשׁ 157. 2	תֵּלַדְנָה 147. 2
תּוֹסֶף 151. 2	תְּחָשְׁבֵנִי 105. *e*	תָּלָה 50. 1
תּוֹעֵבָה 207. 1. *a*	תַּחַת 237. 1, 238. 1	תְּלוּאִים 56. 4, 177. 3
תּוֹר 217	תַּחַת (פֶּן) 131. 1	וַתִּלָּחֵץ 119. 1
תּוֹרָה 217	תַּחְתַּי 194. 2	תִּלְכְּדוֹ 105. *a*
תּוֹרִישֵׁמוֹ 104. *f*	תַּחְתֵּיהֶם 238. 1. *b*	תֵּלְכוּ 65. *b*
תּוֹשָׁב 190. *b*, 192. 2	תַּחַת כִּי 239. 2 (2)	תֵּלַכְנָה 61. 4. *a*, 151. 1
תּוֹשְׁבֵי 216. 1. *a*	תַּחְתָּם 238. 1. *b*	תִּלְמָדוּ 88
תְּזוּרָה 157. 3	תַּחְתַּנִי 238. 1. *b*	תַּלְמִיד 192. 2
תִּזְכְּרֵן 88 (f. pl.)	תֵּיטְבִי 147. 4	תֵּלֵן, תָּלַד 158. 2
תִּזְכְּרֶנָּה 61. 4. *a*	תִּיכוֹן 193. 1	תָּם 186. 2. *c*, 207. 2
תַּזְלִי 111. 2. *b*	תֵּימָן 190. *b*, 197. *b*	תֹּם (v.) 139. 2
תַּזְנוּת 190. *b*, 199. *d*	וַתִּינַק 150. 3	תֹּם (n.) 186. 2. *c*
וַתִּזְנִי (3 f.) 172. 3	תיעשה 11. 1. *b*	תָּמָה 143. *a*

INDEX III.

תְּמַהֲרֶנָה 118. 4	תִּנְחַת 131. 1	תַּעַר 197. *b*
וַתְּמוּגֵנִי 161. 3	וַתַּנִּיקֵהוּ 150. 2, 161. 5	תְּעָר 60. 4. *a*
תְּמוּשֵׁינָה 157. 3	תִּנְצְרֶכָה 104. *b*	וַתָּעַר 174. 4
תְּמוֹל 183. *c*	תִּנָּשֵׂא 131. 6	תֵּעֹשׁ 173. 3
תְּמִיתוּן 157. 3	תְּנַשֵּׁנִי 102. 2	תַּעֲשֶׂה 172. 3
תְּמִיתֶנָה 157. 3	תְּסַבֵּינָה 61. 3, 136. 2, 141. 2	תַּעֲשֶׂה־לָּךְ 27
תֵּמַת 175. 3		תַּעֲשִׂין 55. 2. *a*, 88. 2. *f*
תָּמַחִי (2 m.) 172.3,175.3	תָּסֶךְ 140. 5	תַּעֲשַׂרְנָה 105. *b*
תַּמִּים 53. 3. *a*	תֹּסַף 111. 2. *b*, 151. 2	תִּפְאָרֶת 192. 2. *a*
תְּמַלְאֵמוֹ 104. *f*	תָּעַב 51. 1, 121. 1	וַתִּפְתֵּהוּ 111. 2. *b*
וַתַּמְלִיכוּ 99. 3	תָּעֵב 60. 4. *a*	תַּפּוּחַ 192. 2
תָּמַם 84. 3. *a* (3), 141. 1 (p. 175)	תַּעַבְדוּן 88 (m. pl.)	תְּזֹצוֹתֵיכֶם 161. 5
	תַּעָבְדֵם 19. 2, 111. 3. *a*	תְּפוּצֶינָה 157. 3
תִּמְנִי 54. 3, 141. 2	תַּעֲבוּרִי 88	תְּפוּצֶתָה, תְּפוּצֶנָה 157.3
תִּמְנָחָה 61. 6. *a*	וַתַּעֲגַב 111. 1	תִּפְלָה 190. *b*
וַתָּמֶס 175. 3	וַתַּעְגְּבָה 97. 1. *a*	וַתֵּפֶן 172. 4
תִּמְעַל 60. 1. *a*	תַּעֲגֶנָה 25, 88 (f. pl.), 91. *c*	וַתֹּפַע 150. 3
תִּמְצָאֶינָה 165. 2	תְּעֻנֶּה, תְּעֻנֶּה 157. 3	וַתִּפְעֵם 99. 3. *a*, 119. 1
תִּמְצָאָן 60. 1. *a*	וַתַּעַר 172. 4	תָּפַח 141. 3 (p. 175)
תִּמְקְנָה 141. 2	תָּעָה 51. 3	תִּפְקְדֵנוּ 105. *b*
וַתָּמֶר 175. 3	תְּעוּדָה 198. *a* (3)	תֵּפַר 140. 5
תַּמֹּר 140. 5	וַתָּעָז 140. 1	תַּפְשִׂטוּן 88 (m. pl.)
תֹּמְרוּ 111. 2. *b*	תֵּעָזֵב 91. *b*	תַּצְאנָה 147. 2
תַּמְרוּר 192. 2	תֵּעָזֻב 60. 4	תְּצוֹרְדְנָה 161. 3
תַּמְרוּרִים 187. 2. *c*	(עֵי) וַתַּעַט 157. 3	תִּצְלֵינָה 141. 2
תֹּמֶשׁ 157. 3	תְּעָלָה 216. 1. *a*	תִּצְלָנָה 141. 2
תֵּן 53. 2. *a*	וַתַּעֲלוּ 140. 5	תִּקְבְּנוּ 139. 1
תִּנָּאֲפְנָה׃ 118. 4	וַתַּעֲלֵינָה 172. 3	תִּקְוָה 190. *b*, 198. *a* (3)
תִּנָּגְשׂוּ׃ 131. 2	תְּעָלַת 60. 3. *c*	תִּקְטֹרְנָה 88 (f. pl.), 161. 3
תֹּנֹד 157. 3	וַתַּעֲמַדְנָה 99. 3. *a*	תְּקִימֶנָּה 160. 3
תִּנְהֹק 131. 2	תַּעֲנוּג 192. 2, 200. *c*	תֵּקַל 140. 1
תִּנֶה 132. 1	תַּעֲנֶינָה, תַּעֲנֶינָה 172. 3	תַּקֵּן 50. 1
תָּנוּר 192. 2	תֹּעַע 141. 2 (p. 175)	תֹּקְעֵי 46
וַתָּנַח 60. 1. *a*	תְּעֻפָה 97. 1. *a*	תָּקֹץ 157. 3
תִּנְחֻמֹת 205. *c*	תֶּעְקַר׃ 126. 2	וַתִּקְרָא 166. 4

תִּקְרֶאןָ 88 (3 f. pl.)	תִּשֶּׂאןָ 164. 2	תִּשְׁתַּפְּרִין 88 (2 f.)
תִּקְרְבוּ 88 (3 f. pl.)	תִּשְׂגְּבֶנִּי 161. 2	תִּשְׁתַּע 176. 3
וַתִּקְרְבוּן 99. 3. a	תְּשׂוּמֶת 61. 4. a, 205. c	תִּשְׁתַּפְּכֶנָה, תִּשְׁתַּפֵּכְנָה 96. b
וַתָּקָשׁ 174. 4	תִּשְׂכַּל 97. 2	
תְּקַתֵּר: 95. a	תַּשְׂמְאִילוּ 180. a	תַּת 131. 4
תֵּרֶא 35. 2	תִּשָּׂנֵה 164. 2	תַּת־ 61. 5
וַתֵּרֶא 172. 4	תִּשָּׂבְנָה 157. 3	תִּתְבַּלַּע: 126. 1
תִּרְאָה 172. 3	תִּשָּׁבְנָה 61. 4, 160. 3	תִּתְבֵּר 142. 2
תִּרְאַנִי 105. e	תִּשְׁבְּרֶנָה 88 (3 f. pl.)	תִּתְגָּר 60. 4. a, 176. 3
וַתֵּרֶב 172. 4	תִּשְׁבֹּת, תִּשְׁבַּת 65. a	תַּתָּה (נָתַתָּה) 53. 2. b, 132. 1
וַתִּרְבֶּה 175. 3	תִּשְׂבִּיעֶנָה 157. 3	
תַּרְבִּית 190. b	תְּשׁוֹמֵם 54. 2	תִּתְהַדָּר 126. 2
תִּרְגַּלְתִּי 94. a, 115	תְּשׁוּעָה 190. b, 192. 2. a, 198. a (3)	תִּתְהַלַּכְנָה 96. b
תֵּרַד 147. 2		תִּתְחֹלָחַל 161. 2
תַּרְדֵּמָה 102. 2. a, 216. 1. b	תִּשְׁחֲדִי 60. 3. b (2), 120. 1	תִּתְחָר 176. 3
תֵּרַדְנָה 88 (3 f. pl.), 147. 2	תַּשְׁחֵת 119. 1	תִּתְחָרֶה 94. a
תִּרְהוּ 147. 3	תָּשִׁי 172. 4	תִּתִּי 61. 5, 131. 4
תֵּרוּ 156. 4	תִּשִׁיעִי 227. 1	וַתִּתְכַּס: 176. 3
תְּרוּמָה 100. b	תְּשֻׁכַּבְנָה 91. c	תִּתֹּם 140. 1
תְּרוּמָמְנָה 161. 4	תִּשְׁכַּנָּה 88. (f. pl.)	תִּתְמוֹגַגְנָה 161. 3
תֵּרוֹץ 140. 3	תִּשְׁלַחְנָה 88 (3 f. pl.), 105. b	תִּתְּמֵם: 142. 2
תְּרַשְׁנָה 92. e		תִּתֵּן 132. 1
תַּרְמִית 192. 2. a	תִּשְׁלַט־ 97. 2	וַתִּתְּנָה 105. a
תַּרְמֵסְנָה 88 (3 f. pl.), 91. c	תִּשְׁלְכִי 95. a	תִּתְנַשֵּׂא 166. 5
תֹּרֶן 190. b	תֵּשַׁם 147. 4	תִּתָּע 172. 4
תָּרֹנָּה 97. 1. a	תִּשְׁמוּרֵם 105. d	תִּתְעַל: 142. 2
תִּרְגֶּנָה 88 (f. pl.)	תִּשְׁמֹרוּ 65. b	תִּתְפַּלָּא 166. 5
תָּרַע (v.) 140. 5	תִּשְׁמְרוּן 88 (m. pl.)	וַתִּתְפָּשֵׂב 99. 3. a, 119. 1
תֶּרֶף 175. 3	תֵּשַׁע 216. 1. e	תִּתְפַּתָּל: 96. b
תְּרָפִים 201. 2	תֵּשַׁע 60. 3. c	תִּתְצַב 53. 3. b, 150. 3 (p. 182)
תִּרְפֶּינָה 165. 3	תֵּשְׁעָה 223. 1	
וַתָּרָץ 140. 5	תִּשְׁעִים 208. 3. a, 225. 1	תִּתְצוּ 25
וַתָּרָץ 172. 4	תְּשַׁעֲשָׁע: 142. 1	וַתֹּתַר: 150. 3
תִּרְצָחוּ, תִּרְצָחוּ 93. a	וַתַּשַׁר 158. 2	תִּתְרַע 60. 4. a, 176. 3
תִּשֶּׂאןָ 165. 2	תִּשְׂרָפְנָה 118. 4	תִּתְשׁוֹטַטְנָה 161. 3

INDEX IV.

HEBREW GRAMMATICAL TERMS.

אֲהַוִי 13	כשתיל אב המון 7. 3. a	נִמְצָא 71. c
אוֹתִיּוֹת 2	כְּתִיב 46	נִסְמָךְ 212
אֵיתָן מֹשֶׁה וְכָלֵב 7. 3	כְּתִיב וְלֹא קְרִי 46	נִסְתָּר 71. c
אֱמֶת 31	לְנַרְמֵהּ 29. b	נָע 16. 2
אֲנִי שלמה כותב 7. 3. a	לְשׁוֹן יָחִיד 199	נְקֵבָה 196
בֶּגֶד כְּפַת 21. 1	לְשׁוֹן רַבִּים 199	נְקוּדִים 2
בֵּינוֹנִי 85. 1. a	לְשׁוֹן שְׁנַיִם 199	סוֹף פָּסוּק 36. 1
בִּנְיָנִים 76. 1	מַאֲרִיךְ 45. 4. a	סָמוּךְ 212
גַּבְרָא 45. 4. a	מְדַבֵּר 71. c	עֲבָדִים 28
דָּגֵשׁ חָזָק 23. 1	מוּכְרָת 212	עָבַר 85. 1 a
דָּגֵשׁ קַל 21. 1	מִלִּים 70. a	עָתִיד 85. 1. a
הֵא הַיְדִיעָה 229. 1	מְלָכִים 28	פֹּעֲלִים 70. a
הֵא הַשְּׁאֵלָה 230. 1	מַלְעֵיל 32	צִוּוּי 85. 1. a
הֶאֱמַנְתִּיו 7. 3	מִלְרַע 32	קְרִי 46
וְגוֹמֵר 0. 1, 243. 2. a*	מָסוֹרָה 10. 46	קְרִי וְלֹא כְּתִיב 46
וָו הֲפוּךְ 99. 1	מַפִּיק 26	רָפֶה 27
זָכָר 196	מָקוֹר 85. 1. a	שַׁאל חיך מכחבי 7. 3. a
חָטְפָה 16. 3. a	מַקֵּף 43	שְׁוָא, שְׁבָא 16. 1
חִירוּק 45. 4. a	משה כתב אלינו 7. 3. a	שלומי אך תבנה 7. 3. a
טַעַם 28	מֶתֶג 44	שֵׁמוֹת 70. a
טַרְחָא 29. b	נְגִינוֹת 28. b	שְׁמוֹת הַמִּסְפָּר 223. 1
כְּבֵדִים 76. 2	נָח 16. 2	שמלאכתו בינה 7. 3. a
כִּנּוּיִים 71. c		תְּנוּעוֹת 12

Names of the letters § 2, their signification § 5. b
Names of the vowels § 12, their signification § 12. b
Names of the accents § 29, their signification § 29. b
Names of the verbal species § 76. 1, 2.
Designations of imperfect verbs § 76. 3.

POSTSCRIPT

The folded leaf which follows contains a general view of the inflections of the various kinds of verbs, perfect and imperfect, the rules for the changes to which nouns are liable, the personal pronouns in their separate and suffixed forms, and the different vowels assumed by the inseparable prefixes and the interrogative מה. It is designed to be taken out of the book and mounted upon pasteboard. The student will thus have the most material parts of the grammar brought together and exhibited to his eye upon a single page.

Two sections of the grammar have been inadvertently numbered 141 and two 150. To prevent embarrassment from this cause in the use of the indexes, the page is almost always added when the second of the duplicate sections is intended.

www.ingramcontent.com/pod-product-compliance
Lightning Source LLC
Chambersburg PA
CBHW022113290426
44112CB00008B/655